On the Properties of Things

On the Properties of Things

John Trevisa's translation of
*Bartholomæus Anglicus
De Proprietatibus Rerum*

A CRITICAL TEXT

Volume III

CLARENDON PRESS · OXFORD
1988

Oxford University Press, Walton Street, Oxford OX2 6DP

Oxford New York Toronto
Delhi Bombay Calcutta Madras Karachi
Petaling Jaya Singapore Hong Kong Tokyo
Nairobi Dar es Salaam Cape Town
Melbourne Auckland
and associated companies in Beirut Berlin Ibadan Nicosia

Oxford is a trade mark of Oxford University Press

Published in the United States
by Oxford University Press, New York

© Oxford University Press 1988

British Library Cataloguing in Publication Data

Bartholomaeus Anglicus
[De proprietatibus rerum. English] On the
properties of things: John Trevisa's translation of Bartholomaeus Anglicus De proprietatibus rerum: a critical text. Vol. 3
1. Encyclopedias and dictionaries
2. Encyclopedias and dictionaries, Middle English
I. [De proprietatibus rerum. English]
II. Title III. Trevisa, John
039'.71 AE2
ISBN 0—19—818530—8

Library of Congress Cataloging in Publication Data
Bartholomaeus, Anglicus, 13th cent.
On the properties of things.
Includes index.
1. Encyclopedias and dictionaries—Early works to
1600. 2. Civilization, Medieval—Sources. 3. Science,
Medieval—History—Sources. I. Trevisa, John, d. 1402. II. Title.
AE2.B3 1975 032 75—328632
ISBN 0—10—818530—8 (v. 3)

Set by Joshua Associates Ltd.
Printed in Great Britain
at the University Press, Oxford
by David Stanford
Printer to the University

CONTENTS

GABRIEL M. LIEGEY

Professor Liegey died on 17 September 1978 while this volume was in its early stages. He joined the editorial team at a memorable party at his house on Christmas Day 1968 and, having edited Book III and being, in his own phrase, 'a classicist gone wrong', he willingly agreed to read the editorial drafts of the English text against the Latin manuscript used as the initial reference. This reading was of immense assistance. His judgement on textual and other matters that occurred along the way was always shrewd and our discussion of them always lively and a source of strength. 'An Oxford man', he would say, gleefully pointing out some scribal or editorial distortion, 'could never have written *that*.' Later, though in failing health, he insisted on undertaking the revision and commentary of Book XVIII originally entrusted to one of his students, for the completion of the edition was near to his heart. We hope that our efforts here without him would have earned his approval, and dedicate them, in affection and gratitude, to his memory.

INTRODUCTION

1

TREVISA'S COPY-TEXT

The search for the Latin manuscript which Trevisa used for his translation has three possible lines of inquiry: first, the known locations of
extant or reported manuscripts during the period of translation,
c. 1394–8; secondly, a collation of the Latin description of menstruation in Book IV chapter 8, which Trevisa left untranslated, with the
corresponding passage in extant Latin manuscripts; thirdly, a comparison of readings in his translation which depend upon variant
readings in Latin manuscripts with the relevant *variae lectiones*.

The location of known manuscripts c. *1394–8*

Trevisa rented a room in Quenehalle, Oxford from 1394 to 1396, and it
is a reasonable assumption that he worked there on the translation of
De Proprietatibus Rerum at that time before returning to Berkeley to
write out his fair copy, completed on 6 February 1398/9. Quenehalle
acquired a copy of *De Proprietatibus Rerum* (now lost) at the bequest of
Simon Bredon (d. 1372),[1] and perhaps Trevisa used it. However, other
colleges at Oxford possessed copies at that time. One of these
survives, MS. Bodley 769, which was deposited in the university chest
in 1390 as a caution against a loan by fifteen named men, presumably
fellows of an academic community.[2] On the evidence of textual

[1] F. M. Powicke, *The Medieval Books of Merton College* (1931), p. 84. Five of Bredon's
manuscripts survive, each with his mark. It is unlikely that Bredon made this bequest in
response to Trevisa's expressed interest; Merton already had two copies of the book,
and Trevisa's translation, twenty-seven years after Bredon's death, was undertaken at
Sir Thomas Berkeley's direction.

[2] *Bodleian Library Record*, ix (1974), 156–65. To that record may be added: Ralph Higden, who based part of his *Polychronicon* I on *De Proprietatibus Rerum* XV, the so-called
Geographia universalis in MS. Arundel 123 being merely that; Henry Knighton the
chronicler, who gave a *summa* of the work to St. Mary's, Leicester; the author of *Dives
and Pauper*, who cites Bartholomaeus XII. 9 and 30, XVI. 28; Sir John Meritt of Wilts.,
whose arms occur in Gonville and Caius MS. 280; the author of the *Prick of Conscience*,
who cites Bartholomaeus at lines 966, 7581; Thomas Brinton, bishop of Rochester
(1373–89), who cites Bartholomaeus in his sermons; the compiler of the bestiary in
C.U.L. MS. Gg.6.5, who partly takes his material from Book XVIII; William Elphin-
stone (d. 1514), bishop of Aberdeen, who owned a copy (perhaps MS. Ashmole 1474).

comparison (recorded in the Textual Commentary below) it was not the copy-text used by Trevisa. It has, however, a general textual affinity with that text, and it would presumably have been available to him if he consulted more than one manuscript.

Outside the university other libraries known to have had extant copies of *De Proprietatibus Rerum* at this time were those of Llanthony Secunda (now Lambeth Palace MS. 137) and of the Benedictine houses at Bury (now Hunterian Museum MS. U.i.13) and Canterbury (now C.C.C.O. MS. 249). None of these manuscripts was, on the evidence of textual comparison, used by Trevisa. The location of other extant manuscripts of *De Proprietatibus Rerum* known to have been in England before 1398 and arguably accessible to Trevisa *c.* 1394–8 is unknown.[3]

The text of Book IV chapter 8

The untranslated description of menstruation, which comprises the latter half of the chapter, is not very long.[4] Collation shows minor variations among the Latin manuscripts and between them and the Trevisa manuscripts and only one noteworthy difference between the common Latin text and Trevisa's text as it is extant, the reference to *Constantinus super Rufus* 155/17. This reference to the *Viaticum* VI. 9 (where he cites Ruphus of Ephesus) is different from the reading *Ruffus* of the examined Latin manuscripts (cf. O *Const. Rufus*, R *Rufus*); presumably he or a scribe expanded an ambiguous reading or conflated two readings (for the suggestion that the archetype of the English text read *Constantinus siue Rufus* see the Textual Commentary at 155/17). Other differences between the common Latin text and Trevisa's text (e.g., the loss of *animalium* after *corporalia* 154/22 and of *propter* 154/26 and of the adverbial clause 154/29 with subsequent corruption of the following phrase *a.l. autem anno in antea*) may all have originated within the English scribal tradition. Like the previous line of investigation, therefore, a detailed comparison of the texts of Book IV. 8 fails to yield any useful information (apart from the *Constantinus super Rufus* reading) about Trevisa's Latin copy-text

---

[3] *Bodleian Library Record*, loc. cit. See further p. 9 below.
[4] A similar but very short reference to sperm in Book V. 48 (p. 263) is also left untranslated, *ne forte spermatis explanando originem, progressum, vel finem, videar carnalibus occasionem cogitandi carnalia exhibere*. Six lines of verse, with translation by Trevisa, are quoted in Book XV. 14: see A. B. Scott, 'Some poems attributed to Richard of Cluny', *Medieval Learning and Literature. Essays presented to R. W. Hunt* (1976), pp. 181–99. Neither clause nor verse shows noteworthy variant readings.

except, negatively, that it was not one of the Latin manuscripts written in England which are extant.

Variant readings in the Anglo-Latin manuscripts

The Latin manuscripts of *De Proprietatibus Rerum* written in England do not form a homogeneous scribal tradition. There are specific reasons for this complexity, which is now intensified by the undoubted loss of many Anglo-Latin manuscripts. First, all extant Anglo-Latin manuscripts apparently derive from copies made for the schools of Paris, where the major dissemination of the work in the thirteenth century took place.[5] Several of these Paris-derived manuscripts were imported into England before and after 1300 at different times;[6] and the Anglo-Latin manuscripts thus have several archetypes, not one.

Secondly, though none of the extant Anglo-Latin manuscripts is a *pecia* copy, their Parisian archetypes were certainly affected by the *pecia* system.[7] Thus, the copies of *De Proprietatibus Rerum* imported into England may well have been of mixed scribal traditions. These traditions were exceptionally extensive. Well over one hundred manuscripts of the work are extant, which suggests that the number of copies made must have exceeded one thousand.

Thirdly, once the Paris-derived manuscripts were imported into England and began to be copied there, their derivatives were subject to the normal accidents of time, such as loss of leaves and quires, scribal omissions and illegibilities and editing. When copyists noticed such accidents in their exemplars, they were liable in traditional manner to have recourse for their repair to the nearest copy of the text. Thus, one Anglo-Latin manuscript derivative of one imported archetype was always liable to be conflated in small places, and sometimes in large, with a derivative of another archetype.

Fourthly, in a large and much-copied text like *De Proprietatibus Rerum* the scope for identical scribal error (especially through a misreading of abbreviated forms) and for identical loss of text (especially through eyeskip) in two or more unrelated manuscripts was enormous. Such coincidental textual distortions exist in sufficient numbers in the Anglo-Latin manuscripts to make the task of textual analysis hazardous.

[5] *Scriptorium*, xxvii (1974), 100–2.
[6] *Bodleian Library Record*, loc. cit.
[7] G. Pollard, 'The *pecia* system in the medieval university', *Medieval Scribes, Manuscripts, and Libraries. Essays presented to N. R. Ker* (1978), pp. 145–61. The system had begun on the Continent by 1228, and in Oxford it had apparently ended by 1347.

These four factors effectively prevent the establishing of any firm picture, for example by stemma, of the interrelationships of the Latin manuscripts written in England. The most that one can do, on the evidence of textual collation, is to suggest some groupings.[8]

Three manuscripts (PRW) have texts predating 1333 and may be separated from direct affiliation with the other Anglo-Latin manuscripts, although the manuscript O may be partly based on R or a close affiliate (now lost). These three early manuscripts are apparently copied from distinct scribal traditions imported into England from the Continent.[9]

With one exception (the fragmentary X3)[10] all other Anglo-Latin manuscripts were written after 1350. Three subgroups may be discerned. The manuscripts I and K form one subgroup, sharing numerous *variae lectiones* and each having numerous unique readings and omissions which argue independent descent from a common ancestor. The manuscripts JLOTV and the fragmentary X (Books I–VI only) form a second subgroup, with J, L, and V being close affiliates. The manuscript O, written after 1400, shares a number of readings with R as well as a predominant relationship with this subgroup. A third subgroup, the manuscripts MNQSUY and the fragmentary X2 (books VIII–IX only) and X3 (Books XVI–XIX only), are more loosely associated, more by their divergence from the textual patterns of the other two subgroups (IK and JLOTVX) than by their own homogeneity. MNQ individually show signs of consistent conflation. S appears to change its character at the end of Book IV.

These groupings are too simplified, within the complexities of the Latin scribal traditions, to determine the precise point of origin of Trevisa's lost copy-text. Yet comparison of the *variae lectiones* which lie behind many of his peculiar translations with the corresponding readings in the examined Latin manuscripts suggests that Trevisa's primary copy-text was affiliated to the subgroup JLOTVX. The

---

[8] In addition to the collations for each book made for the Textual Commentary, a detailed textual analysis of the Latin manuscripts for Book V was made by Mr. Hanna; for Book XI by Mr. Lawler, who also supervised work on the Latin text of Book X by Mrs. S. Clinton (Northwestern Ph.D., 1982: D.A.I. 8225899); the first five folios of each book by Mr. Seymour. The sigla of manuscripts cited here are given on pp. 36–7 below.

[9] P was copied after 1350 from an exemplar dated 1296. See J. Long, 'A note on the dating of MS. Ashmole 1512', *Manuscripta* xviii (1974), 113–14; O. Pächt and J. J. Alexander, *Illuminated MSS in the Bodleian Library, Oxford* (1972), no. 741.

[10] This manuscript, MS. Ashmole 1474, apparently copied directly from an MS. of continental provenance, has been extensively altered by reference to an MS. of Anglo-Latin origins.

validity of this suggestion may be gauged by a table of selected readings where the first column gives Trevisa's text, the second the relevant Latin corruption with the relevant sigla, and the third the palmary reading of all other examined manuscripts.

44/5	o	LQVX o	oo
47/8	al	MNX omnium	nominum
57/17	discretus	LOTVX discretus	disertus
73/28	dei vidi	KMOT dei uidi	diuidi
77/18	kyngdoms	IJLOPQVWX regnum	regimen
86/29	puttiþ forþ	JLTV abicit	allicit
93/26	vncerteyn	JORSTVWX incertum	insertum
93/28	litil þing	LTVX paruum (O *blank*)	peruium
95/4	worchinge	IKR operacionem	comparacionem
98/31	logica	STX logica	logistica (V log^ica)
186/15	reulers	JLNRSV regimina	tegmina
267/30	rounde	IKOU rotundi	reconditi
312/9	childehode[1]	L infancia	infamia
351/1	compleccioun	JLMNPQRTVW compleccione	opilatione
375/7	quyttir	IK saniem	sanguinem
416/20	matiere	IKNOW materiam	naturam
417/13	to þe sight	LOS uissibiliter	(in)sensibiliter
420/28	kynde	JKLPR naturam	materiam
427/36	oynementis	OR unguentis	apozimatibus
444/11	kynde	LQV naturam	materiam
445/23	charite	JLMOPRTVW caritatis	claritatis
449/16	kynde	JLMNRTUVW naturam	materiam
507/3	i-oned	IJLOTVX unitur	innititur
518/4	and no mo	JLMORV non plura	uel plura
522/10	cicle	IJLNPUVX ciclus	circulus
553/36	oþir	IJLNRTV aut	autem
560/7	amendiþ	ILOTVW emendat	emundat
633/34	hungir	JKLMNOPQRSTVW fame	sanie
706/16	Israel	IJLMNOQTV israel	superius
711/34	eendeles many	JLT innumerabiles	immeabiles
716/19	myrthe	IJLOTV iocunditate	rotunditate
719/32	toures	JLORTUV arcium	arborum
737/1	treen	NPR arboribus	ardoribus
764/5	welles	OPW fontibus	faucibus (V fraucibus)
832/35	matier	JLO materiam	naturam
836/29	place	JLOPRSUV locum	lacum

In these readings no exact correspondence is discernible between any one Latin manuscript or group and Trevisa's translation, but there appears a tendency for the JLOTVX subgroup to emerge as an affiliate of Trevisa's copy-text, often with JLV and O (sometimes in association with R) as the most common correspondent among the complete manuscripts. This tendency is supported by a similar comparison of exotic names (even though the English manuscripts are themselves not always in exact accord), as these examples illustrate:

602/20 echydes: JLNPQ ethedes   MOY achates   T achades   SVW echedes   I ethates   U Echites   R achites

613/27 kaliroyz: JLNV Kaliroiz   O caliroz   T Kamin   M Kaliroim R kalinus   P Kaliron   Q kalibis   S kaliroz   W kalycoyz   Y kalicoir

623/2 Ennucus: JLQV ennicus   OR ouidius   T emuc'   M m'r   N mic' P eonuc'   S comitus   W comicus   IU emilius   Y cerpodus

676/24 antiphidia: JLMTV antiphidia   O anchidia   KN antiphilia R āphibilia   P accipida   QW antiphda   S amphibia   U antiphudua

691/18 danesca: JPSV danesca   LW danesta   O da/uesta   T danastena MN uesta (N *from* dauesta),   R honesta   IKUY dea uesta Q deauesta

697/1 Ceraurei: JLMOQRS ceraurei   T seraurei   I ceraunii   K Cerauni N cerauneii   P eburuei   R cecaurei   U cerarari   V Cerarures   W senuriai

701/19 Thodolamor: JLV thodaloamor   O todoloamor   T cadaloamor I codoloamor   K Codorlaomor   MNU chodorlaomor (N *altered*) R Chocolaomor   P Ochoda loamor   S touloamor   Y thodarlamor W totaloamor

707/9 Aurilibanus: JLOTV Aurilibanus   PRSUW Libanus   IKMQY antilibanus

712/26 Hiercora: JLMOQV hierora   T Ierara   IK gerera   R iheriora N ierrora   P iberora   Y ierora   W hierroea

727/30 Iupiter: OR Iouis   JLV cus   KMQUY chus   IPW thus   N nun S rus

When one allows for the possibility of misreadings by Trevisa himself (e.g. 395/7 *saniem*, 765/5 *fontibus*) and undetected corruption of exotic names in the English scribal tradition, such sampling appears almost conclusive. However, the evidence recorded in the Textual Commentary shows more complex patterns, which prevent a firm conclusion. In particular, one must note these reservations:

(1) all the Latin scribal corruptions noted above could have occurred in Trevisa's copy-text independently of the JLOTVX subgroup and its lost affiliates;

(2) the copy-text itself could have been a conflation, like MNQ;

(3) Trevisa, like all scholars working under pressure in imperfect conditions, was probably (though not, in the absence of his copy-text, demonstrably) liable to omit and misread words and phrases;

(4) Trevisa, when faced with an uncertain abbreviation or form, gave two possible alternatives in translation, thus making the reading before him less certainly recoverable. Over forty such doublets of ambiguity are recorded in the Textual Commentary. While some may have been inherited from the Latin copy-text, their number strongly suggests a deliberate attempt by Trevisa to be faithful to his author's meaning despite graphic ambiguity;

(5) he avoided in translation some of the Latin scribal corruptions which occur in the JLOTVX subgroup and elsewhere—

206/20	chinne	JLOPRW merito/mento (N *corrected*)
556/31	meuablenesse	IOQRTY nobilitatis/mobilitatis
588/17	dryeþ	IORSTUY rarefacit/arefacit
599/12	wildirnesse	IJLOPSTVW solicitudinem/solitudinem
832/17	mouth	JLMSV ere/ori
854/18	malicolik	JLOTV multiplice/melancholice (R multe)

In some cases, perhaps, he misread an already corrupted word, so unconsciously restoring the correct sense. All that may be said, therefore, on this analysis is that:

(1) the copy-text itself is not extant;

(2) the hypothesis (adopted as a working position at the beginning of this edition) that this lost text belonged to the Anglo-Latin traditions, rather than to traditions imported directly from the Continent, is supported by the evidence of the *variae lectiones* set down in the Textual Commentary and sampled above;

(3) the lost copy-text was more closely affiliated to the JLOTVX subgroup (known to have been represented in Oxford in 1390–98) than to any other Anglo-Latin manuscript or group, the manuscripts J, L, V, and X having the closest agreements to that copy-text.

Since this linking is tentative, it is necessary to consider two further possibilities: first, that Trevisa revised his translation by reference to another Latin manuscript which differed from his copy-text in important particulars; secondly, that more than one manuscript lies behind a conflated translation. The first possibility is inherently improbable.[11] Trevisa worked on the translation between 1394 and

---

[11] Cf. S. L. Fristedt, *The Wycliffe Bible*, Parts II and III (Stockholm, 1967–73), who argues for textual revision of the 'Trevisa' sections of the early English bible; see *Review of English Studies* 27 (1976), 334–5. The marginal and interlinear corrections made by a later hand in the English manuscript MS. Harley 614 (perhaps by Dr. John Dee) are wholly different.

1398, and died in 1402. Like all his other translations, this one shows no signs of his revision, and it would have indeed been strange if, having once completed such a labour and presented it to Thomas, lord Berkeley, he had immediately begun to revise it.

The second possibility, that Trevisa's text depends upon more than one manuscript, has apparent textual support in the phrase *zuger oþer actata secundum alium librum* 978/27, which is clearly a doublet of conflation, though whether Trevisa or a scribe was the conflator here is unclear. Subsequent comparable doublets of exotic names occur without the qualification *secundum alium librum* at 983/20 *ysopon oþer esapon*, 1023/7 *opium oþer opion*, 1058/28 *Ophir uel Effir*, 1227/23 *locidas and ilqwyde*. The relevant Latin readings are instructive (K lacks leaves):

I *zuccarra*   MO *zucara*   U *zuccara*   X *zukaro* over erasure   PR *accara*
J *actaca*   L *actata*   S *arcla*   TW *aceto*   Q *ata* after erasure

I *esapon*   the rest *ysopon*

I *opion*   the rest *opium* (L om. clause   P om.   M *suopium*   U *obpium*)

IM *Ophir*   JLQRVWX *effir*   NOTSU *offir*   P *ofir*

I *ictides*   JLOQVW *locidas*   R *licida*   S *locidalus*   U *locidamie*   M *ictidas*
P *lucidam*

A pattern emerges. At these five places at least Trevisa's text reflects the conflation of an I-type manuscript with an L-type manuscript.

Scattered throughout the text are other occasional readings which reflect a Latin variant found in I or its affiliate K (often in association with other manuscripts). These examples are typical:

Book V. 163/9 special: IK speciali (specie)   163/29 oþir suche: IK similia (consimilia)   183/6 worchinge: K operacionis (apercionis) 266/19 body: I corporis (carnis)   267/30 rounde: IKOU rotundi (reconditi)   278/27 30°: KL xxx° (xix)

Book XI. 568/24 eyry þingis: I aerea (aera)   577/4 purifieþ: INSUY purificant (putrificant)   581/9–10 a maner of broune coloure: IU iacinctiuum (lactatiuum)   587/14 strenge: I uigore (rigore)   593/15 stones: IR lapidum (lampadum)

Book XIX. 1269/25 matiere: IQ materiam (naturam)   1288/18 bright: I lucidus (uiridis)   1294/33 þere: IM vbi (vnde)   1336/35 of openynge: INPTX aperitiua (asperitiua)   1348/28 wanne: INOT liuida (humida)   1349/17 beres: IV ursi (nisi)   1368/1 many: IPQRUX plures (om.)   1382/10 *semis*: I semis   OPQUW semitu (semita) 1387/22 gronynge: IPQRU clamores (clangores)   1393/18 sixe: IPQU vi (vii) 1394/10 ei3tene: I xviii (xix)

Such readings are too random and too liable to the possibility of co-incidental origins to give much support to a theory of consistent conflation. Even if some of the doublets of ambiguity listed in the Textual Commentary are interpreted as doublets of conflation, the bulk of the Latin variant readings gives evidence that marches the other way. Since Trevisa is unlikely to have made only sporadic conflation, the conflator is likely to have been a copyist. And though he may have been a scribe of the English text, it is more probable that he was a Latin scribe; among the Anglo-Latin manuscripts conflation is evident, O offering an exact parallel (primarily an L-type text with many R-type readings) to such a hypothesis for Trevisa's copy-text. Within present knowledge, therefore, one may tentatively conclude that Trevisa worked from a single Latin manuscript, no longer extant, primarily of an L-type text which had been sporadically conflated with an I-type manuscript.

---

[3] (See p. 2 above.) Two other copies arguably available to Trevisa were owned by Master Nicholaus Brydport (bequeathed by William Davy, rector of Kingsland, Hereford, d. 1383) and John Trevenant, bishop of Hereford (d. 1404), 2nd fol. beg. *siue localis*.

2

THE ENGLISH MANUSCRIPTS

During the hundred years or so between its completion in 1398/9 and its first printing by De Worde *c.* 1495 Trevisa's translation of *De Proprietatibus Rerum* seems not to have achieved a wide circulation. In the fifteenth century copies of the Latin text were widely diffused throughout England, and the reputation of Bartholomaeus as 'the master of properties' was well established among the religious and the learned.[1] And in educated and courtly circles, where there was a growing demand for vernacular books, Corbichon's French translation made in 1372 was beginning to establish itself; among the books of Sir John Fastolf listed in 1450 is *lez propretez dez choses*, and in 1482 an illuminated copy of this version (now MSS. Royal 15 E ii and iii) was made at Bruges for Edward IV.[2]

If the market for Trevisa's translation was thus limited, it was further curtailed by its size and expense. The surviving copies, with one exception all products of the fine book trade, suggest that it was almost always a bibliophile's book, beyond the reach of all but the most affluent. Significantly, the two people known to have owned the book in the fifteenth century, in addition to Sir Thomas Berkeley,[3] were both bibliophiles, Sir Thomas Chaworth and Richard Beauchamp, bishop of Salisbury. And when De Worde printed the work *c.* 1495, he had to obtain through the good offices of Robert Thorney, mercer, the Chaworth copy (now MS. Plimpton 263) which cannot easily be lifted by one man for his base text, although he also made use of another manuscript. It was certainly not a book available to jobbing scribes who partly created the demand they satisfied, and though it may have had a certain attraction for English physicians (as the epitome in MS. Sloane 983 shows) these were often their own scribes and accustomed to read Latin. The only example of a 'cheap' copy, in every way an exceptional though still handsome

---

[1] *Bodleian Library Record*, ix (1974), 156–65. *Archiv* 137 (1985), 121–8.

[2] *Scriptorium*, xxvii (1974), 100–2, H. S. Bennett, *The Pastons and their England* (2nd edn. 1932), p. 111. *Historical Manuscripts Commission*, viii. 268.

[3] His arms and motto *in domino confido* are in MS. Bodley 953, Rolle's commentary on the psalter. His daughter Elizabeth (d. 1423) was a patron of Walton, Trevisa's successor as family chaplain; her husband, Richard Earl of Warwick (d. 1439), owned after his marriage a copy of Trevisa's *Polychronicon* (now MS. Additional 24194).

manuscript, is C.U.L. MS. Ii.v.41, possibly made by a university teacher for his own use.

There is confirmation, if of a negative kind, of the limited circulation of the work in manuscript in fifteenth-century English wills, where it is not mentioned once, although books of much less monetary value (such as *Prick of Conscience*, the *Plowman*, *Mandeville's Travels*) and copies of the Latin text are frequently listed.[4] Indeed, apart from one occurrence in a fifteenth-century list of books,[5] the work is not recorded in contemporary documents until 1482 when Caxton referred to it in his preface to his edition of Trevisa's translation of the *Polychronicon*:

one Treuisa vycarye of barkley which atte request of one Sir thomas lord barkley translated this sayd book the byble & bartylmew de proprietatibus rerū out of Latyn in to englyssh.

This reference, however, suggests that the work was known, at least by repute, to those likely to be interested in it.[6]

More positively, the textual evidence of the extant manuscripts suggests that the work did not develop an extensive scribal tradition, compared for example with the three English books cited earlier. None of these manuscripts lies at a great remove from the lost holograph, three of them were written within thirty years of the holograph, and only one (Bristol City Library MS. 9) was written after 1460. Perhaps not more than forty manuscripts of Trevisa's translation were written before its printing by De Worde *c.* 1495; a pointer to such an estimate being the comparative states of textual corruption in the manuscripts written at the beginning of the extant tradition (MS. Additional 27944, probably *c.* 1410) and at the end (Bristol City Library MS. 9, after 1475).

The extant manuscripts themselves descend from their lost common ancestor, which was not Trevisa's fair copy, in two subgroups of two and six manuscripts respectively. The larger subgroup contains at least three manuscripts which were produced by the fine book trade in London or Westminster, perhaps more. The smaller subgroup (MSS. e Musaeo 16 and Harley 4789) was possibly provincial in origin.

---

[4] R. M. Wilson, *The Lost Literature of Medieval England* (1952); J. A. Burrow, 'The audience of Piers Plowman', *Anglia*, lxxv (1957), 373–84; M. C. Seymour, 'The English manuscripts of *Mandeville's Travels*', *Trans. Edinburgh Bibl. Soc.* iv (1966), 174. *Bodleian Library Record*, loc. cit.

[5] R. A. B. Mynors, *A catalogue of the manuscripts of Balliol College library* (1963), pp. 339–40. The citation is not certainly of the English version.

[6] *Bodleian Library Record*, loc. cit. and p. 1 fn. 2 above.

This lost common ancestor was perhaps the copy, or a close derivative, professionally made for Sir Thomas Berkeley, a bibliophile, from Trevisa's own fair copy. On the one hand, it is unlikely that Trevisa's own copy was of high professional standard; on the other, a professional scribe, unused to Trevisa's thoroughgoing dialect forms, could have introduced all the errors common to the extant manuscripts. The time between Trevisa's stated date of completion, 6 February 1398/9, and the estimated date of writing of MS. Additional 27944, the earliest extant copy, *c.* 1410 suggests that the errors of the common ancestor developed very early in the scribal tradition.

BRITISH LIBRARY MS. ADDITIONAL 27944

ff. i + 335. Parchment. 420 × 295 mm. Double-columned frame, each column 300 × 85 mm. and containing 48 lines. Eighteenth-century brown leather binding, with tooled and gilt bordering on the outer top cover, not listed by W. H. J. Weale, *Early Stamped Book-bindings in the British Museum* (1922) or J. B. Oldham, *English Blind-stamped Bindings* (1952).

Collation: 2 + 1⁸ (wants 1, 2) 2–48⁸, 43⁶ (wants 4). Catchwords, no signatures.

Contents: f. 2ʳ tabula for *De Proprietatibus Rerum*, alphabetically by book; f. 8ʳᵃ Trevisa's introductory verse, followed by his translation of *De Proprietatibus Rerum*; ff. 331–5 blank, apart from scribbles.

Scribes: before 1420 and probably *c.* 1410. Standardized southwestern dialect with southern admixtures, copied *verbatim* from its exemplar in London or Westminster.

1st scribe: ff. 8–151ᵛᵇ (i.e., to end of quire 19 and of Book XII) *anglicana formata*: headed *a*, ascenders of *b*, *h*, *l* hooked and of *d* looped, open *e*, short *r*, kidney-shaped final *s*.

2nd scribe: ff. 152ʳᵃ–196ʳᵇ (i.e., ends on leaf 5 of quire 25 medially in column and chapter as noted at 831/6 above) *cursiva formata*: headed *a*, ascenders of *b*, *d*, *h*, *l*, *w* (but not *v*) looped, open *e*, closed-tailed *g*, short *r*, final *s* delta-shaped. The scribe copied one column of his exemplar twice; see 653/15 ll. above.

3rd scribe: ff. 2–7ᵛ, 196ʳᵇ–335ᵛᵇ *anglicana formata*: described and illustrated by A. I. Doyle and M. B. Parkes, 'The production of copies of the *Canterbury Tales* and the *Confessio Amantis* in the early fifteenth century', in *Medieval Scribes, Manuscripts, and Libraries. Essays presented to N. R. Ker* (1978), pp. 163–210, who record nine other manuscripts partly by this scribe. See J. J. Smith (Ph.D. Glasgow, 1985).

Punctuation: 1st scribe uses *littera notabilior* after paraph marks and ends sentences with point and, more often, with solidus. 2nd scribe uses *littera notabilior* after paraph marks and lightly points the end of clauses (but not before a paraph). 3rd scribe uses *littera notabilior* before paraph marks and very lightly points sentences.

Decoration: executed before 1420 in a metropolitan *atelier* and of high quality. On f. 8 a heavily styled vinet with three vertical bars. The four outer bars form a gilded frame, with inner edging of mauve, blue, green, with white tracery, and the centre of each bar is a coloured panel with acanthus scroll. The inner vertical bar is of the same style without the coloured edging. The centre-pieces at the upper (now largely trimmed away), outer, and lower margins are intricate leaf knots on gold ground from which issue leaf sprays with gilded dots. The corner pieces are less elaborate roundels maintaining the border motif within leaf clusters. The bar at the inner margin has a leaf and trumpet-like flower extension. Incorporated with it is an illuminated initial *F* (27 × 27 mm.) depicting a black-gowned religious before a reading desk. The miniature is clearly drawn and coloured.

Demi-vinets incorporate illuminated initials at the beginning of each book, having outer bars of gold, edged with blue and mauve with white line, and leaf and gold sprays which issue into the margins from trumpet-like flowers at terminal points. Smaller initials, alternately gilt on magenta ground and blue on red ground, with simple penwork in adjacent margins, begin each chapter.

History: given by William Radcliffe of Staunforde, possibly after 23 December 1542, to John Cooke, doctor of laws, whose monogram appears on ff. 174, 327; Cook was admitted to Lincoln's Inn 16 February 1519/20. Examined by John Stow (d. 1605) who wrote a marginal note on the first page of the tabula.

Inscribed in 1658, with some English verses, by Julius Glanvill of Lincoln's Inn; Julius was the fourth son of Sir John Glanvill, who contributed commendatory verse to William Browne's *Britannia's Pastorals* in 1616, and may have owned the manuscript in the belief that Bartholomaeus, traditionally surnamed Glanville, was an ancestor.

Owned in 1814 by Mr. Elliston of Stratford Place, and then by the Revd. Thomas Corser, at whose sale in 1868 it passed to the British Museum. On the flyleaf in a nineteenth-century hand occur '2571' and '52"10"o', perhaps the lot number and purchase price of an earlier sale. Corser lot 189 was sold to Boone for £91.

On ff. 186, 228, 255, 327 respectively occur these names in fifteenth-century hands: *William* (cropped), *Cheste* (cropped), *Robart* (erased).

Printed notices: *Catalogue of Additions to Manuscripts in the British Museum* (1854–75), p. 383. E. Brydges and J. Haslewood, *The British Bibliographer*, iv (1814) part XIII, pp. 107–8. Sotheby S. C. 28 July 1868, lot 189. A. J. Perry, *Dialogus . . . by John Trevisa*, *E.E.T.S.* o.s. 167 (1925), pp. lxxxviii–ix.

BRISTOL CITY LIBRARY MS. 9

ff. 137. Parchment, with many leaves excised or mutilated by the excision of initial chapter decoration, and with some fading. 400 × 280 mm. Double-columned, each column 315 × 90 mm. and containing 58 lines. Modern brown leather binding.

Collation: undetermined, perhaps in eights. No catchwords. At top right *recto* are remnants (generally trimmed away) of three series of signatures, the second series perhaps ending at f. 82 (i.e., the end of Book XIII). These leaves are textually consecutive, a solidus marking the loss of one or more leaves and Roman numerals indicating the component books: V ff. 2–8/9–11/ VI ff. 12–23/ VII ff. 24–46/ VIII ff. 47–50/ IX ff. 51–7/ X ff. 58–60/ XI ff. 61–6/ XII ff. 67–73/74/75/ XIII ff. 76/ 77/78–82/ XIV entirely missing XV ff. 83–5/86/87–90/ 90–2/ XVI f. 93 inner column only XVII ff. 94/95–125/ XVIII ff. 126–37

Contents:

f. 1ra Trevisa's translation of *De Proprietatibus Rerum*. Begins imperfectly, *beest may not lyue* (237/14). Ends imperfectly, *and piccheth his hornes into the tree* (1152/4). Much matter lost through excisions and loss of initial and final quires.

Scribe: After 1475 and possibly before *c.* 1495 (De Worde's edition). Perhaps Surrey. The vocabulary has been modernized, cf. the similar modernization by De Worde. *fere-textura*, the first word or line of each chapter being in a display script, and the first letter after each decorated initial being doubled: headless *a*, ascenders of *b*, *h*, *l* vertical and of *d* oblique, open *e*, open-tailed *g* with horizontal flourish, short *r*, delta-shaped final *s*, dotted *y*.

Punctuation: the first word or line, sometimes two or three lines, of each chapter is display script. *Littera notabilior* begins each sentence and most proper names. Paraph marks. Final point generally ends each sentence.

Decoration: last quarter of fifteenth century, of fine quality. Each chapter begins with a large gilded initial on blue or magenta ground with white tracery and foliate work in the adjacent margin (spray with gilded studs and leaves supporting blue and green leaves). Many such initials have been excised, and all leaves on which new books began (probably finely and ornately illuminated demi-vinets) have also been excised.

History: the sad relic of a once handsome folio, this manuscript was copied from an exemplar which had lost a quire towards its end (corresponding to the matter in Book XVIII. 27–67) on the evidence of the lacuna which occurs in mid-column of f. 100rb.

Inscribed on f. 117 after 1592 by a friend of 'Master Thomas Androwe dwellinge in the medle temple'. Thomas Andrewe, third son of Robert Andrewe of Harlston, Northants. was admitted to the Middle Temple 5 February 1592/3. Since the friend was apparently from Northants. also, this location of association may be significant for the earlier history of the manuscript.

Owned by Tobie Matthew, fellow and canon and dean of Christ Church, vice-chancellor of Oxford, who married Frances Barlow, widow of Matthew Parker junior, the son of Archbishop Parker, the collector of manuscripts. Matthew probably included this manuscript in his donation of books to his native Bristol in 1615 when the Library was founded; D. Mathew, Sir Tobie Mathew (1950), pp. 16–19.

Printed notices: E. Bernard, *Catalogi librorum manuscriptorum Angliae et Hiberniae* (1697), ii. 40, item 1, listed as 'Bateman upon Bartol. Imper. fol.' N. Matthews, *Early Printed Books and Manuscripts in the City Reference Library* (1899), p. 69, plates 14 and 15 being reduced facsimiles of parts of ff. 58 and 122. N. R. Ker, *Medieval Manuscripts in British Libraries*, ii (1977), 204.

BODLEIAN LIBRARY MS. E MUSAEO 16

ff. i + 310 + i. Parchment, early leaves holed and torn. 405 × 270 mm. Double-columned frame, each column 305 × 85 mm. and containing 46–51 lines. Early eighteenth-century brown leather binding.

Collation: 1 (last leaf of a quire, with stub of conjoint leaf) + 1^{10}, 2^{8}, 3–4^{12}, 5^{12} (wants 11), 6^{12}, 7^{12} (4 and 9 crossed, i.e., ff. 70 and 75), 8^{12} (wants 5–8), 9^{12}, 10^{12} (wants 6), 11–13^{12}, 14^{12} (wants 2), 15–17^{12}, 18^{10}

(wants 8), 19^{12}, 20^{12} (wants 10), 21^{12}, 22^{12} (wants 9), 23^{12}, $24-25^8$, 26^8 (wants 1), $27-29^8$, 30^8 (wants 4, 5, 7, 8).

Catchwords: ff. 31, 43, 54, 66, 78, 86, 98, 109, 121, 133, 145, 156, 168, 180, 192, 201, 213, 224, 236, 247, 259, 267, 275, 282, 290, 298, 306.

Signatures: first series in brown ink (ai, bii, ciii, diiii, ev for each quire) are later than the second series in red ink (a, b, c, etc.) which begin at f. 237 (i.e., quire 22) and are contemporary with the scribe. Many signatures cropped.

Contents: f. 1ra Trevisa's translation of *De Proprietatibus Rerum*. Begins imperfectly, *a litel hurting* (166/27). Ends imperfectly, *contynuall and discrete* (1355/3). Probably thirty-five leaves of text lost before f. 1, and at least twelve leaves of text lost elsewhere (i.e., after ff. 82, 103, 146); but no text is lost through excisions after ff. 53, 199, 222, 244.

Scribe: second quarter of fifteenth century. Standardized south-western midland dialect, perhaps written in Oxford. *Cursiva formata*: headed *a*, ascenders of *n*, *h*, *l* looped and of *d* oblique, open *e*, open-tailed *g*, kidney-shaped final *s*, dotted *y*.

Punctuation: *littera notabilior* begins each sentence and most names. Paraph marks. Final point ends most sentences and some clauses.

Decoration: large gilded initial and ornate foliate and gilt-studded vinets mark the beginning of each book. As an example, on f. 33 the outer bar is gilded, the inner bar alternately blue and mauve with white central line; the illuminated initial *F* in the lower left corner is of mauve and blue (with orange) with white tracery on a gilded ground; from the bars issue gilt-studded sprays, green oval leaves, and larger leaves in blue, green, and mauve; from the centre of the bottom bar a large blue leaf produces a strawberry-type fruit. Similar vinets occur on ff. 47^v, 74^v, 90, 100^v, 112, 126, 137^v, 169^v, 204^v, 290^v.

Smaller gilded initials, on tinted blue and magenta ground with white tracery, with foliate and gilt-studded work in the adjacent margins, mark the beginning of each chapter. Similar initials in this gilded style occur in one manuscript of Trevisa's translation of the *Polychronicon* (St. John's College, Cambridge MS. H 1). The solidity of the style suggests an early date, *c.* 1425 rather than *c.* 1450.

History: owned by Sir William Dethick, Garter herald (d. 1612), for the dispersal of whose books see A. R. Wagner, *The Records and Collections of the College of Arms* (1952), p. 11. On f. 141 is recorded the birth of 'my daughter Marye', 2 January 1651. Purchased by the Library in 1723 from Nathaniel Crynes, fellow of St. John's College, Oxford.

Printed notices: F. Madan, *Summary Catalogue of Western Manuscripts* vi. 329, no. 27, 667. Pächt and Alexander, *Illuminated MSS in the Bodleian Library, Oxford* (1972), no. 918.

CAMBRIDGE UNIVERSITY LIBRARY MS. Ii.v.41

ff. i + 343. Paper, with one vellum leaf added at the front. 290 × 215 mm. Double-columned frame, measuring 240 × 165 mm. and containing 53–5 lines. Bound *c.* 1700, perhaps for Bishop Moore, with a copy of Jordanus, *Arsmetrica demonstrativa* (24 ff., parchment, fourteenth-century English hand).

Watermarks: imperfectly visible, perhaps quires 1–5 *chien*; quires 6, 9, 10, 42–4 *balance*; quires 7, 8, 11, 27, 28 *fleur* (cf. Briquet 6391); quires 13–22 *corne*; quires 23–6, 38 *fleche* (cf. Briquet 793); quires 39–40 *double crescent* (cf. Briquet 5367).

Collation: 1 + 1–4⁸, 5¹⁰ (wants 1), 6–7⁸, 8¹² (wants 12), 9–36⁸, 37⁶ (wants 6), 38–40⁸, 41², 42–3⁸, 44⁴ (wants 4). Many guard strips used to strengthen sewing.

Catchwords: on final verso leaf of each quire throughout except quire 8.

Signatures: many cropped. 1st series (ai, aii, aiii, aiiii) begins f. 10, 2nd series (Ai, Aii, Aiii, Aiiii) f. 182.

Contents:

f. 1 title-page, in a seventeenth-century hand.

f. 1ᵛ blank.

f. 2ʳᵃ tabula for *De Proprietatibus Rerum*, alphabetically by book.

f. 9ʳᵇ–9ᵛ blank, apart from pen trial 'whanne Aprill with his'.

f. 10ʳᵃ Trevisa's introductory verse, printed by R. H. Robbins, *Secular Lyrics of the XIVth and XVth Centuries* (1952), pp. 94–5, followed by the translation of *De Proprietatibus Rerum*.

Scribes: before 1450. South-east midland dialect, modernized. 1st scribe ff. 2–324ᵛ, 336ᵛᵃ–343: *cursiva formata* on f. 10, headed *a*, ascenders of *b*, *h* vertical and fractured and of *d* obliquely curved and of *l* looped and fractured, open *e*, *g* with horizontal tag, short *r*, kidney-shaped final *s*. Thereafter, an increasingly cursive script, ascenders of *b*, *h*, *l* looped, closed *e*, long *r*, delta-shaped final *s*. The scribe has regularly rephrased and 'corrected' his copy. This scribe also wrote Durham Cathedral MS. A.iv.22 ff. 1–97, a commentary on the *Pater Noster*. On f. 324vb (the second leaf of the separate bifolium) over the scribe's text of Book XIX. 63 *de lacte* (i.e., 1324/15 to 1327/1) has been pasted a sixteenth-century copy of the corresponding matter from De Worde's edition *c.* 1495, immediately before two stubs of excised leaves and the stint of a new scribe.

2nd scribe ff. 325–333va, i.e., quire 42, plus 6¼ columns: *cursiva formata*, headless *a*, ascenders of *b*, *h*, *k*, *l*, *v* looped, closed *e*, looped *g* with long tag, delta-shaped final *s*.

3rd scribe ff. 333va–336rb: *cursiva formata*, headed *a*, otherwise similar in feature to Hand 2.

Punctuation: (1st scribe) *littera notabilior* generally after paraph marks. *Virgula*, solidus, and point mark end of phrases and clauses, the *virgula* being the most emphatic, and solidus and point used in uncertain variation.

Decoration: none.

History: owned by Bishop Moore of Ely (d. 1714), whose library (in which it was item 477) was presented to the university by George I in 1715.

Printed notices: E. Bernard, *Catalogi librorum manuscriptorum Angliae at Hiberniae* (1697), ii. 402, item 477. *Catalogue of the MSS. . . . of the University of Cambridge* (1856–67), iii. 494. *Neuphilologische Mitteilungen*, lxxvi (1975), 227–8.

BRITISH LIBRARY MS. HARLEY 4789

ff. v + 286 + iv. Parchment. 410 × 290 mm. Double-columned frame, each column measuring 290 × 90 mm. and containing 51–2 lines. Harleian binding.

Collation: 1 (wants 5), 2, 3 (wants 7), 4 (wants 5, 6), 5 (wants 3), 6–8, 9 (wants 8), 10–15, 16 (wants 1), 17, 18 (wants 3, 4), 19–20, 21 (wants 5), 22 (wants 7), 23 (wants 3–6), 24–26, 27 (wants 3), 28–30, 31 (wants 1). Catchwords, signatures. All quires of 8 folios.

Contents:

f. 1 Trevisa's translation of *De Proprietatibus Rerum*. Ends imperfectly, *moderat drienesse and of moderat hete cometh* (1310/8). Elsewhere, 17 missing leave affect the text thus: after f. 4 matter lost from book II. 2–4; after f. 21, IV. 3–4; after f. 26, V. 1–3; after f. 30, V. 13–16; after f. 66 VII. 11–15; after f. 114, X. 10–XI. 2; after f. 131, XII. 24–XIII. 2; after f. 115,

XV. 44–53; after f. 164, no matter lost; after f. 167, XV. 152–XVI. 6; after f. 195 XVII. 48–53; after f. 224, XVII. 48–53; after f. 259, XVII. 171–176; after f. 286, most of XIX. 46.

Scribe: before 1430. South-west midland dialect. *Cursiva formata*: headed *a*, ascenders of *d*, *l* looped and of *b*, *h* hooked, open *e*, *g* with final horizontal flourish, short *r*, kidney-shaped final *s*, tail of *y* with cursive flourish.

Punctuation: *littera notabilior* generally after paraph marks and occasionally elsewhere to begin sentences and proper names. Occasional point ends sentence. Single solidus at interlinear division of word.

Decoration: the beginning of each book is marked by a large gilded initial with associated foliate work (spray with gilded studs and green tinted leaves) running the length of the adjacent margin. On f. 1 the initial (37 × 28 mm.) includes a tinted drawing of a now faded gowned figure reading, much cruder than that of MS. Additional 27944 f. 8 but apparently deriving from the same pictorial tradition. Two leaves which presumably contained similarly gilded initials and foliate work are excised after ff. 114, 131. Initials at the beginning of each chapter are alternately gilded on magenta ground and blue on red ground. Within each chapter occur smaller initials of the same alternating types.

History: on f. 164 occurs a Latin inscription 'by me your said frende Edwarde Coke' in a seventeenth-century hand; perhaps that of Edward Coke, made baronet in 1641 and eldest son of Clement (d. 1629), the sixth son of Sir Edward Coke, Attorney-General (d. 1634). Old Harleian library marks (135.C.18 and 2.IV.F), cf. MS. Harley 614 purchased in 1706, suggest that the manuscript came to Harley after that date. There is no reference to either volume in Wanley's diary 1717–26.

Printed notices: *Catalogue of the Harleian Manuscripts* (1808–12), ii. 205. Perry, *Dialogus*, p. lxxxviii.

COLUMBIA UNIVERSITY MS. PLIMPTON 263

ff. i + 390. Vellum. 550 × 390 mm., many outer margins being extensively repaired. Double-columned frame, each column measuring 365 × 115 mm. and containing 43 lines, the final item containing 56 lines. Rebound in 1969.

Collation: 1–48⁸, 49⁶. Catchwords, some signatures.

Contents:

f. 1 tabula for *De Proprietatibus Rerum*, alphabetically for the whole work.

f. 8–8ᵛ blank.

f. 9 Trevisa's introductory verse, printed by G. A. Plimpton, *The Education of Chaucer* (1935), pp. 34–5, followed by his translation of *De Proprietatibus Rerum*.

f. 379 *The abbey of the holy ghost*, without associated charter.

f. 386 *The meeds of the mass*, prose version.

f. 389 blank.

Scribes: 1st scribe ff. 1–386: before 1459, perhaps *c.* 1440. Standardized south-east midland dialect. Probably written in London or Westminster. *Fere-textura*: headed *a*, ascenders of *b*, *h*, *k*, *l* hooked and of *d* looped and oblique, open *e*, *g* has horizontal terminal flourish, short *r*, delta-shaped final *s*, descender of *y* has almost horizontal terminal flourish.

The scribe initially made many mistakes, mainly by eyeskip. Almost all these errors were detected by him or a supervisor and, where necessary, the surrounding text erased and the fuller text inserted in a smaller hand. This process has happened to the whole of f. 32, the palimpsests now have a distinctive yellow appearance, cf. the clear rich vellum of the unscraped pages. In addition, a number of small marginal and interlinear corrections with associated caret marking in the margins, not derived from the scribe's exemplar, are possibly connected with De Worde (in view of the known history of the manuscript).

2nd scribe (ff. 386–8): after 1450. South-east midland dialect. *Cursiva formata*: headed *a*, ascenders of *b*, *d*, *h*, *l* looped and of *d* also oblique, open *e*, open-tailed *g*, short *r*, delta-shaped *s*.

Punctuation: *littera notabilior* begins each sentence and most proper names. Paraph marks. Final point ends each sentence. *Virgula* marks end of clause in complex sentence. Occasionally solidus marks end of phrase.

Decoration: on f. 9 a vinet has four outer borders of gold bar, and the inner borders of blue and mauve bar with white hairline and occasional russet leaves. The hairline is conceived as a branch or stem and frequently becomes or sprouts leaves. Some of these leaves curl around the whole bar, around which curl three acanthus leaf scrolls separated by individual leaf growths. The centre pillar is a double-gold bar with minor blue and mauve bar. The corners of the vinet are large floriate growths of blue, mauve, and gold. The inner margin bar incorporates a large illuminated F, blue on gold ground with foliate designs within open spaces, and a smaller and simpler C, gold on blue pen ground. In the lower margin the arms of Chaworth are incorporated into the vinet and possibly added later by another illuminator. From the major bars comparatively simple, large clusters of daisy leaves and pears extend into the margin. The outer bar has an intricate branched knot at its centre (blue and mauve on gold) from which ascend and descend, parallel to the major bar, heavily leafed branches which taper to sprays like those in the lower margin.

Demi-vinets, in the style of the vinet, mark the beginning of each book. Champs are simple red-pen design supported by the red-pen ground of the large initials in blue ink which begin each chapter. On f. 379 in the outer margin of the demi-vinet are seven spaced examples of one gothic-styled design (alternately dark and gold) which may be a cryptogram.

History: written for Sir Thomas Chaworth (d. 1459, great-great-grandson of Sir Geoffrey Luttrell) of Wilverton, Notts. who succeeded his father in 1398. The family name is inscribed by the first scribe on f. 379. In his will dated 16 January 1458/9 and proved 27 March 1458/9 (printed in *Testamenta Eboracensia*, Surtees Society xxx. 220) Sir Thomas Chaworth bequeathed 'vnto my cosyn Richard Willughby squyer an Englisse boke called Grace de Dieu', i.e., the English translation of *Pèlerinage de l'âme*, also so described in the wills of Sir Thomas Cumberworth (1450) and John Clerk (1451). No mention is made of the Trevisa manuscript, which passed to Richard Willoughby, Chaworth's principal executor and *cosyn* 'friend' at an early date, probably in 1459. Chaworth also owned a copy of Trevisa's *Polychronicon*, bequeathed to Robert Clifton, husband of Maud Willoughby: J. M. Manly and E. Rickert, *The Text of the Canterbury Tales* (1940), i. 609–10.

The manuscript was used, with another, by De Worde as the base-text of his *editio princeps* of *De Proprietatibus Rerum* printed *c.* 1495 and was obtained for his use through the good offices of Roger Thorney, mercer (d. 1515).

The manuscript remained in the Willoughby family (a family pedigree is in MS. Harley 381 ff. 176–82) until its sale in 1925 to Quaritch, who sold it to G. A. Plimpton, who presented it to Columbia University in 1935.

Printed notices: *Report on the Manuscripts of Lord Middleton*, H.M.C. (1911), p. 240. Christie, Manson, and Woods, *Sale Catalogue* (15–18 June 1925), p. 51, lot 371, with facsimiles. R. W. Mitchner, 'Wynkyn de Worde's use of the Plimpton manuscript of *De Proprietatibus Rerum*', *The Library*, v (June 1951), 7–17. B. M. Frick, 'Columbia's giant encyclopaedia Plimpton Manuscript no. 263', *Columbia Library Columns*, ii (1953), 8–15. S. de Ricci and W. S. Wilson, *Census of Medieval and Renaissance Manuscripts in the United States and Canada* (1935–40), ii. 1801.

PIERPONT MORGAN LIBRARY MS. M 875

ff. i + 338. Parchment. 430 × 300 mm. Double-columned frame, each column measuring 305 × 35 mm. and containing 43 lines. Seventeenth-century brown leather binding with one clasp and the remnant of another, and with the Tollemache armorial stamp embossed in gold.

Collation: undetermined because of the tight binding. Apparently the first and last quires (ff. 1–6, 333–8) and one other are of six, and the remainder are of eight. No leaves containing text are missing. The bifolia of the penultimate quire (ff. 325–32, or ff. 324–31 in the unrevised pencilled pagination which doubles f. 313) are wrongly bound; their order should be 328/327/326/325/332/331/330/329. No catchwords, a few signatures.

Contents:
f. i blank.
f. 1 tabula for *De Proprietatibus Rerum*, alphabetically by book.
f. 7 blank.
f. 8 Trevisa's introductory verse, followed by his translation of *De Proprietatibus Rerum*.
f. 338 blank.

Scribe: before 1430. South-east midland dialect. Probably written in London or Westminster. *Cursiva formata*: ascenders of *b*, *h*, *l* looped and of *d* oblique, open *e*, short *r*, kidney-shaped final *s*.

Punctuation: *littera notabilior* begins each sentence and some (not all) proper names. Paraph marks. Point generally ends sentence and line and sometimes clause and phrase.

Decoration: sumptuously prepared by a first-class illuminator, possibly more than one, and probably in London. A vinet occurs on f. 7. The top and bottom borders consist of a double gold bar, separated by blue and pink strip with white central hairline, around which curl acanthus sprays, with green-tinted leaves in blue and pink. From these bars hairline pen-drawn sprays, with green-tinted leaves interspersed with gold dots and trefoils, issue into margins and space dividing written columns, and encircle larger blue and pink and occasionally green flowers in blossom. The bottom border has a large flower piece protruding into the centure of the lower margin. The side borders have outer gold and inner blue and pink bars.

The inner border has intricate interlace of acanthus leaf scroll on gold ground at the centre of the page. The outer border has a large illuminated *W* on gold ground, within the middle and innermost of the four of which, alternately pink and blue, are curling leaves in blue and red, and blue and green. The red is also found in the centre piece of the bottom border and the corner pieces.

From the outer border pink branches lead into sprays. The corner pieces are intricate knots interlacing each border and developing additional growths, using all the colours and gold of the vinet. Demivinets in the style of the vinet mark the beginning of each book. Champs, pen-drawn with green leaves and gold dots, grow into the margin from the illuminated initial which begins each chapter. These initials are gold, alternately on pink and blue ground, tricked out with white hairlines.

History: owned by Richard Beauchamp while bishop of Salisbury (1450–81), whose signature 'R. B. Sarum Eps.' occurs on ff. 6, 337, and whose will (dated 16 October 1481, proved 8 February 1482) is P.R.O. MS. Logge f. 31–31ᵛ; his father, Sir William Beauchamp (d. 1457), speaker of the House of Commons in 1416, was a book-collector, according to W. C. Hazlitt, 'A Roll of Book Collectors 1316–1898' in B. Quaritch, *Contributions towards a Dictionary of English Book-collectors*, Part XII (1898), p. 5. The signature 'Thomas Cave', probably of the sixteenth century, occurs below the words *Difficilia quae pulchra* on f. 337. Owned by Sir Lionel Tollemache (d. 1668), who married Elizabeth, daughter of William Murray, First Earl of Dysart (d. 1653), in whose family the manuscript remained until its private sale to Mr. E. J. Beinecke, who gave it to the Pierpont Morgan Library.

Printed Notices: *First Report of the Royal Commission on Historical Manuscripts* (1874), appendix p. 60. C. Rondell, *Ham House* (1904), ii. 129. F. B. Adams, *Seventh Annual Report* (Pierpont Morgan Library publication, 1957), pp. 17–19. C. U. Faye and W. H. Bond, *Supplement to the*

Census of Medieval and Renaissance Manuscripts in the United States and Canada (1962), p. 367. Perry, *Dialogus*, p. lxxxvii.

BRITISH LIBRARY MS. HARLEY 614

ff. ii + 242 + iii. Parchment. 415 × 230 mm. Double-columned frame, each column measuring 320 × 95 mm. and containing 54 lines. Harleian binding.

Collation: 4 + 1, 2 (wants 1), 3–39, 30 (wants 8). Catchwords, signatures.

Contents:
f. 1 tabula for *De Proprietatibus Rerum* in three columns.
f. 4 Trevisa's introductory verse, printed by H. N. MacCracken, *The Nation*, lxxxvii (1908), 92 and A. J. Perry, *Dialogus*, p. cxxix.
f. 5 Trevisa's translation of *De Proprietatibus Rerum*. One leaf missing after f. 12, containing matter from Book III. 2–9, viz. *þe kynde of a spirit Austin* [f. 13] *sireþ what is needful* (i.e., 91/15–97/23).

Scribe: before 1430. Standardized central midland dialect, with some southern relict forms. *Cursiva formata*: headless *a*, ascenders of *b*, *h*, *l*, *k* hooked and occasionally faintly looped, distinctive tadpole-shaped *d*, open *e*, open-tailed *g*, short *r*, kidney-shaped final *s*, descenders of *þ* and of *y* oblique.

Punctuation: *littera notabilior* begins each sentence. Paraph marks. *Virgula* and final point at the end of sentence. Solidus marks off some clauses and phrases.

Decoration: a large gilded initial *P* on quartered ground (blue and mauve, tricked with white) with small gold-studded marginal sprays begins f. 1. A demi-vinet, having its vertical stem and outer bar gilded and its inner bar blue and mauve with white centre line, occurs on f. 5. The centre-piece and ends of this bar have simply developed interlace (in blue and mauve) on gold ground in a design of leaf and bud; from which issue (as horizontal bars of the demi-vinet) two gold-studded sprays, the upper bar having trumpet buds, and the lower unfurled buds. The colours are now badly faded. The draughtsmanship is of inferior quality.

Joined to this demi-vinet, at the upper left, is an illuminated initial *F* (30 × 21 mm.) depicting St. Christopher and the Christ child. The miniature is well-drawn and coloured. A gilded initial *W* (on blue and mauve, with white tracery) with marginal sprays occurs independently in the second column.

Thereafter, no other decoration except chapter initials (in blue on a square carmine ground) with elementary vertical tracery in adjacent margins occurs. The beginnings of books are not marked by specific decoration.

History: on f. 242 is inscribed in a late fifteenth-century or early sixteenth-century hand *nouerint uniuersi per presentes me Thomam mannoke*; a Thomas Mannoke, of the Essex and Suffolk family, of approximately the right date is recorded in *The Visitations of Essex*, Harley Society xiii (1878), 72.

Acquired, perhaps after 1583, by P. Saunders (whose signature occurs on f. 1) for Dr. John Dee (d. 1608), who perhaps made the marginal and interlinear corrections, apparently after reference to a printed edition, and bought at the sale of his library in 1626 for fifteen shillings by Sir Simonds D'Ewes; see M. R. James, 'Lists of manuscripts formerly owned by Dr. John Dee', *Supplement to the Transactions of the Bibliographical Society*, vol. i (1921), and J. O. Halliwell, *The Private Diary of Dr. John Dee*, Camden Society xix (1842), where items 31 and 90 are *De Proprietatibus Rerum* manuscripts (now C.C.C.O. MS. 249 and MS. Harley 614).

The manuscript is not certainly recorded by Bernard among D'Ewes' books purchased for £450 in 1705 by Wanley acting for Harley, but cf. items 9933 and 9937 in his catalogue ii. 386.

Printed Notices: *Catalogue of the Harleian MSS.* (1808–12), i. 390. A. G. Watson, *The Library of Sir Simonds D'Ewes* (1966), p. 140. Perry, *Dialogus*, p. lxxxviii.

BRITISH LIBRARY MS. SLOANE 983

ff. i + 113 + Paper. 210 × 140 mm., much frayed and repaired. Frame 160 × 110 mm., containing 24–32 long lines. Modern binding.

Watermark: *raisin*, cf. Briquet 13006.

Collation: unknown, each leaf being mounted separately. One leaf lost after f. 3. No leaves lost between ff. 81 and 103. No catchwords, no signatures.

Contents:

f. 1 miscellaneous medical entries. Begins imperfectly, *of a sponefull at evyn another at morn.*

f. 37 John of Bourdeux, *Treatise against the plague.*

f. 40 medical items, in Latin.

f. 45 *Precyous medycens of surgury.*

f. 36 miscellaneous medical items, some in sixteenth-century hands on leaves previously left blank.

f. 81 *abstractus Bartholomei Anglici*, Book VII, printed in *Anglia*, lxxxvii (1969), 1–25.

f. 95 ibid., Book XVII, printed in *Anglia*, xci (1973), 18–34.

f. 103 medical items.

f. 108 more medical items, in later hands.

Scribe: about 1450. Probably a medical practitioner, abridging his material. *Cursiva*: headed *a*, ascenders of *b*, *d*, *h*. *l* looped, closed *e*, final *s* delta-shaped. *Decoration*: none.

History: much worn, but no marks of ownership before Sir Hans Sloane (d. 1753) whose pressmarks B 618 (altered to 983) and VII D occur on the flyleaf. A reference by E. Bernard, *Catalogi librorum manuscriptorum Angliae*, p. 336, item 9403 'Barth. *De medicina* in English' in Bishop Moore's library is not to this manuscript.

Printed notices: S. Ayscough, *Catalogue of the Manuscripts . . . of Sir Hans Sloane* (1782), i. 61. M. C. Seymour, 'The English Abstract of *De Proprietatibus Rerum*', *Anglia*, lxxxvii (1969), 3–4.

BRITISH LIBRARY MS. ADDITIONAL 45680 (Part N, ff. 48–9)

Two leaves, forming a bifolium (1 and 10 of a quire of 10). Parchment. 345 × 222 mm., trimmed. Double-columned frame, each column measuring 290 × 90 mm. and containing 42–5 long lines.

Collation: no signatures, catchwords at end of the final column.

Contents:

f. 48 begins, *3if he be at large*. Ends, *It is saide þat* (i.e., 617/31–621/28).
f. 49 begins, *Paradise and passeþ aboute*. Ends, *holde in bondes* (i.e. 655/9–658/27). Printed in *Neuphilologische Mitteilungen*, lxxviii (1977), 47–56.

Scribe: after 1450. *Cursiva libraria*: headless *a*, open-tailed *g* with horizontal flourish and curve, short *r*.

Printed notices: *Catalogue of Additions to Manuscripts in the British Museum* (1936–45), p. 219. K. Bitterling, *Neuphil. M.* loc. cit.

PROFESSOR TAKAMIYA, KEIO UNIVERSITY

Two leaves lacking top 7–8 lines (Books V. 1–2, XVIII. 62–5), described in Quaritch S.C. 1036 (1984), p. 91, lot 121, with facsimile of f. 2ʳ (beg. *beth betre*, ends *indignacyoun*, i.e. 1212/15–3/22).

THE AFFILIATION OF THE MANUSCRIPTS

The lost common ancestor[1]

The eight extant manuscripts contain errors in common that could not, on comparison with the Latin text, have been made by Trevisa in translation. These errors are marked by asterisk in the critical apparatus below the text.[2] One example from each book (giving the scribal reading, the emendation, the Latin equivalent) illustrates the evidence:

47/5 primatiue   priuatiue   priuatiue   59/10 warnynge   seruynge
ministerium   106/30 brayn   brawn   lacertos   130/8 folewiþ
file   lima   180/14 middel   milde   pie   293/17 nede   elde
senio   342/23 venemes   vneuenes   inequalitate   442/7 belle
balle   spere   518/18 risinge   reson   rationem   553/23 fulliche   vnliche   disparata   599/21 certeyn   cleyn   mansuete
655/25 londe   Atlonde   Atlante   701/23 oppressinge   ouerpassinge
enormitate   739/24 ryuer   Ryne   Renum   868/8 of þe   ofte
sepe   887/6 bestes   herbes   plantis   1116/21 fleissh   flees
uellere   1274/1 togidre   to gendre   generacionem

These errors clearly occurred in the lost common ancestor of the extant manuscripts, which may have been the professional copy of the translation (or a very close affiliate) made from Trevisa's holograph for Sir Thomas Berkeley.

The manuscripts D and E (MSS. Harley 4789 and e Musaeo 16)

Throughout the translation two manuscripts, D and E (the latter beginning imperfectly at Book V. 1), demonstrate their independent descent from the lost common ancestor by having errors unique to themselves and by avoiding errors common to the six other manuscripts. First, a list of representative unique errors in DE (with better readings of other manuscripts and the Latin equivalents):

262/19 be   appere   apparent   263/5 ofte   of whiche   utriusque
263/28 reneyeþ   lesiþ   spoliat   345/27 herte   heer   capillorum

[1] Individual statements of affiliation, mentioned in vol. i, p. xiv, being in close agreement with each other, are here compressed into one statement because of costs.

[2] The asterisk also marks common omissions and errors of roman numerals which, in editorial judgement, occurred in the common ancestor.

471/23 worst   first   primum   501/19 phisicians   philosophris
philosophi   553/10 here   þerfore   ideo   572/26 bowiþ
blowiþ   inflatiuus   573/24 esterne   norþesterne   septentrionem
667/18 animalibus   elementis   elementis   846/30 spekeþ   speweþ
vomentibus   868/28 chaunge   staunche   constringendi

Secondly, a list of representative readings of DE (with inferior readings of other manuscripts and the Latin equivalents):

48/5 supposito   supposet   supposito   67/19 berne   verne (*va.*
vudum, cuntrei)   horreum   98/16 eien   eren   occulos   146/
26 reuleynge   releuynge   regitiua   262/9 wounde   wombe   uul-
neris   333/27 reule   releue   regi   355/8 asse   ele   asininum
458/12 pultinge   puttinge   inpulsu   525/26 cleuith   clensith   fin-
dit   561/18 quykeþ   quakeþ   excitat   569/4 erþe   eyr   terra
610/25 hugenes   hy3nes   magnitudinem   668/17 fenne   þenne
lutem   692/6 wyntir   watir   hyeme   767/27 ilonde   londe
insule   878/20 swet   wel   aromatica   903/6 setteþ   sitteþ
adheret   1124/32 wralle   wrappe   torqueri   1312/30 mater
water   materiam

These readings, supported by a mass of similar examples and by comparable and extensive evidence of scribal omissions in DE avoided by the other manuscripts and *vice versa*, put beyond doubt the relationship of DE and the other manuscripts as two independent subgroups of their common ancestor.

None the less, there are numerous readings which D and E, sometimes singly, sometimes together, share with one or more manuscripts of the larger subgroup. Such identical readings may be broadly interpreted in three ways: partial survival of original textual reading; coincidental errors and omissions; and coincidental scribal alterations or 'corrections' of a corrupt form inherited from the common ancestor. These examples are typical:

Book I: 45/26 *nocio*] DF nacio   45/31 gost] CDF *add* þe sone spireþ þe
holy gost   47/20 neutre] DH neutro   49/7 habilite] DFGH *add*
þerto abilite

Book II: 60/12 godliche] AD goodliche   66/6 brennyþ] AD brennynge
86/35–6 lioun . . . rugiens] AD *om.*

Book III: 90/6 bodiles] CD bodiliche   90/15 bestissche] DFG beistes
92/15 foure] CD fourþe   96/21 as] DG *om.*   103/17 comyn] CD
comyng   104/2–3 what is . . . row3e, and] DG *om.*   112/17 light]
ACDFG sight   123/23 veynes] DH veynes of

Book VII: 346/19 we 3eueþ] EFG weueþ   347/3 touchiþ] AD touchinge

348/15–16 and[2] ... brayn] DG *om.*
2 noseþrilles] ABEFGH *add* oþir
385/11 veynes] ACDFG reynes
421/28 abideþ] ABCEFGH beþ traries

367/11 oiles] AE oile 368/
374/5 þe longen[2]] DFH *om.*
417/9 crabbe] ABEFGH *add* be
437/31 contries] ABCEFGH con- traries

Book X: 552/15 in] ADFGH de
555/27 as] ABCEFGH and as ABCEFGH *om.*

552/24 cause] ABCDFGH causid
557/8 fro] BE of 560/23 lye] ABCEFGH *om.*

Book XI: 571/13 contray] DEFG contrarie
573/18 eyry] ADE erþy 579/5 þe[1]] ABCEFGH to
ACEFGH and to 583/16 eyry] DH erþy
BDH pluralite 584/34 *imbuendo*] CD imbendo
EG sotelliche 585/9 beriþ] AE betiþ

573/14 as] ADE and
579/6 into]
584/32 *pluralitate*]
585/4 softliche]

Book XIII: 655/5 special] DH *om.*
667/26 stone] BCDFH stone of
30 swoloweþ] DH swolweþ ham

657/9 her] ABCEFGH hert
680/18 þanne] CD *om.* 681/
682/16 freseþ] BD fresscheþ

There is no pattern of readings in any of the eight manuscripts which militates against their division into these two independent subgroups or which supports a theory of conflation.

Neither D nor E, which has a high incidence of error, is copied from the other, as these representative examples from Book XI testify:

unique errors in D: *omits* 570/18–19 wiþ ... eyre 570/21 and puttiþ
582/9 dome 585/15 as we ofte seen þat aftir strong hete 586/
3 and slidrynesse 586/5 corrumpiþ and 586/8 tarieþ and
570/35 stryueþ] destroyeþ 571/2 souþest] souþwest 571/
28 percyþ] peryscheþ 573/9 tronglynge] stronglynge 578/
5 ly3tnesse] hy3tenesse 585/17 a3eines] a reyne

unique errors in E (p. 582 only): *omits* 3 faire 12 of heuene 12–
13 but alwey toforne 26 þe neþir partye 28 is 29 so þe
33 gendringe of 34 þerfore 14–15 is in þe souþ] in þe souþ is
16 in þe souþ, as Beda seiþ] as Beda seiþ in þe souþ 20–1 þe raynbowe
is not seyne] *repeats*

The manuscripts AFG (MSS. Additional 27944, Plimpton 263, Morgan 875)

Of the six manuscripts which stand apart from DE in their scribal descent AFG form a closely affiliated cluster, having in common a very large number of generally minor errors and omissions. These common errors and omissions, noted in the critical apparatus below the text, may be illustrated here by examples from Books II and VI:

61/1 influens] influes　　　　61/29 wiþout] wiþ　　　　65/9 to] *omit*
66/7 he] ho　　69/19 beth] hath　　71/2 ʒit] ʒif　　83/2 he] ho
84/5 *Euanuit*] euenauuit　　295/11 whice] white　　299/32 lullinges]
lullinge　　　303/10 fedinge] ledinge　　304/28 songes] songe
319/21 drede] dede　　321/9 fonging] fongiþ　　326/8 y-oned] ʒeued
334/15 sikernes] in sikernes

Each of these three manuscripts has a number of unique errors and
omissions which preclude the possibility of its being copied from
either of the other two. Those of A are recorded in the critical apparatus below the text. These examples from Books VII and XI are representative of unique errors and omissions in F and G:

unique errors in F: 343/3 þe¹] *om.*　　348/11 of] of þe　　353/33 þerof]
þerfore　　357/13 bynemynge] bi meving　　362/7 lepwink] wype
363/20 nouʒt] *om.*　　365/17–18 liþ naked ... blynde] *om.*　　368/
12 breþinge] brenynge　　378/5 þe herte] it　　379/13 of¹] of þre
þinges of　　384/26 hete] heteþ　　388/13 nouʒt kynde] vnkinde
392/30 of³] of kinde　　394/32 wiþ hote¹] withoute　　402/5 hasty]
hasteli　　409/6–7 Somtyme þey beþ somdel istoppid] *om.*　　413/
6 þese] þose　　422/5 Skabbe] scabbes　　429/11 by þe lengþe of þe
spere] *om.*　　567/6 clere] clere clere and　　567/35 by] *om.*
569/28 is] *om.*　　570/17 of drye] of drye of　　572/33 is] *om.*
573/19 And] þat　　573/25 est] *om.*　　574/6 also] *om.*　　574/
7 moche] *om.*　　574/20 is] *om.*　　574/22 vnbindiþ] vnbideþ
575/22 grete] *om.*　　582/7 dryenge] durynge　　584/11 and] *om.*
587/25 is] his　　588/5 and sprediþ itsilf vpon þerþe] *om.*　　591/1–
2 smytynge togedres and of here] *om.*　　591/5 hem] men　　594/
16 þan] þat

unique errors in G: 345/14 rootis] rotills　　346/1 humours] humoure
346/32 redynes] remedies　　347/4 menþ] meueþ　　348/17 drede-
ful] grete　　348/19 angwissch] anguischis　　567/27 bemes] benes
568/14 vndirstondenge] vndirstonde　　568/31 in] *om.*　　571/
5 þanne] þat þanne　　574/20 menynge] mene　　575/17 felynge]
felynges　　575/24 out of] *om.*　　577/23, 24 contrey, contreye] con-
treis　　579/5 of hete] *repeats*　　579/27 þe ilke] þat　　580/
25 and somme to schappe and fyguracioun þerof] *om.*　　580/28 dewy]
dewli　　581/9 of²] *om.*　　585/22 restreyneþ] restreyned　　586/
8 and tarieþ] *repeats*　　586/9 rennynge flux] *om.*

The three scribes of A have each produced a copy which, while not
free from error, is generally accurate; their most common fault is
omission by eyeskip, and the most extensive example of this eyeskip-
ping is, paradoxically, retrospective, the repetition of one column in

Book XIII. 3 (p. 653 above). The scribe of F produced a copy which originally was marred by numerous omissions, later corrected by him by scraping and smaller writing; these original omissions could have been inherited from his examplar and corrected by conflation, for which there is no other evidence, however. The scribe of G produced a generally accurate copy.

Within the cluster AFG there are some persistent very minor agreements in error between A and F which suggest that these two manuscripts may derive from an ancestor immediately independent of G. There are also random very minor agreements in error between A and G on the one hand, and F and G on the other; numerically, both the AG and FG agreements are less than the AF agreements, approximately in the proportion 1 : 3. The AF agreements, recorded in the critical apparatus below the text, may be represented by these examples from Books I–III:

44/10 to gadre] togedre	48/29 God is] god*us*	62/11 not] none
88/25 synneþ] synweþ	88/30 hi han ybrou3t] hi3 brou3t	107/
1 for] fro;	112/33 afferrde] as ferre	124/27 þis] þus

The stemma in Vol. I, p. xiv, gives these AF agreements the weight of evidence; if they are occasional independent errors, perhaps due in part to an unclear or ambiguous exemplar and scribally altered in G, AFG each derives independently from their common ancestor.

The manuscript H (MS. Harley 614)

H avoids the errors and omissions characteristic of DE, includes all the errors and omissions characteristic of ABCFGH, and avoids all those more closely characteristic of AFG, while sharing all errors and omissions common to all manuscripts. Its affiliation to these other manuscripts is thus clear; it belongs to the larger subgroup ABCFGH but derives from their common ancester at a point antecedent to that which produces the ancester of AFG.

H is comparatively free from omissions by eyeskip, though they occur; e.g. in Book X it uniquely omits:

559/2 for he byschyneþ   561/13–14 and vnwryeþ þingis   561/
26–7 Leye fondiþ to meve vpwarde and drawiþ fro þe neþire partyes
565/16–17 and 3if it is coolde it quenchiþ and distroyeþ fire þat is reke
þerinne.

It has a number of unique readings. Some of these are copying errors; in particular, confusion between abbreviated *and* and *in*, omission and insertion of definite and demonstrative articles, and singular and plural forms. Others are attempts to make sense of a bad reading. Others are substitutions of words, generally with a more modern currency. The most important of its unique readings are, however, those few which avoid errors present in all other manuscripts. Some of these unique readings are due to marginal and interlinear corrections which have, confusingly, two sources: the scribe or a contemporary corrector, and another (perhaps Dr. John Dee who owned the manuscript *c.* 1583–1608 and also a manuscript of the Latin text) who referred to the Latin text. In this first list of such corrections in Book II an asterisk marks those which almost certainly derive from a Latin reference.

60/14* aftir (of *added above line*)   ACDFG aftir   ex   86/28 witt (h *and*
e *added above line*)   A wt CFG wit D wy3t   pondere   88/17* in duwe
tyme (successioun *above line*)   ACDFG in dewe tyme   successiue
88/30 hand (*added above line*)   G haue ADCF *om.*   intulerint   89/
10* venemes parfite (pestifer *above line*)   ADFG venemes parfite C parfite
pestifere   89/26* We (Whoo *in margin*)   AFG We   C but who so D
Who   si quis.

A second list gives other corrections in Book II which are supported by readings in other manuscripts:

62/21 [by] aungeles   64/24 [for] þey   85/1 [wiþ] him   85/
9 mowe [not]   89/6 [at] þe laste

These are probably ordinary scribal corrections.

    The marginal and interlinear corrections, which occur mainly in the early books but sporadically throughout the manuscript, may be disregarded in establishing the affiliation of the extant manuscripts (though not necessarily in establishing the text) since their sources lie elsewhere. More important are those unique readings which H preserves as an integral part of his copy. These are all minor and may be the result of intelligent correction or happy misreading, as these examples illustrate (manuscripts defective where their sigla are lacking).

80/12 her office   A þee   CDFG þe   ipsius honus   84/12 bi nede
ACDFG bineþe   necessitate   278/34 body   ABCDEFG bodyes
corporis   475/29 moste   ACDFG in ofte   maxime   499/
29 he   ACDEFG hem   *cf.* uidentur   501/22 he   ACDEFG *om.*
cf. nouit   570/23 discryed   ABCDEFG distroyed   descriptum
653/15 swiftliche   ACDEFG softliche   velox

No important or substantial corrections to the common text can be made by reference to H alone, though its evidence for minor correction (e.g. in the words cited above) and for supporting more widely based emendation is invaluable. This is especially true where H shares a common reading with D (with or without E) and with A. Such readings almost invariably preserve the text of the lost common ancestor and so are the basis of many emendations recorded in the critical apparatus. H also shares a number of readings with B and C (discussed below) and occasionally and separately with F and G; these FH and GH agreements are apparently random coincidences and are all trivial.

The manuscripts B and C (MSS. Bristol City 9 and C.U.L. Ii.V.41)

B lacks almost half of its original text, Books I–IV, XIV, XVI and many lost leaves and portions of leaves elsewhere. It was written after 1475; its vocabulary has been modernized, and verbs in conditional clauses have been put into the subjunctive; it has frequent omissions by eye-skip (though its largest omission, pp. 925–58, is due to the loss of a quire in its exemplar) and frequent unique errors. Despite its defects it is clear that B, avoiding readings and omissions characteristic of DE and sharing readings and omissions characteristic of ACFGH, belongs to the larger subgroup. Since it also avoids the readings and omissions more closely characteristic of AFG, B must derive from the common ancestor of the larger subgroup at a point antecedent to the immediate ancestor of AFG.

A similar situation obtains with C which, exceptionally, rephrases and reorders its text. In addition, it modernizes the language and makes frequent and spirited correction whenever its exemplar offered difficult or nonsensical readings; sometimes these corrections are intelligent guesses which restore Bartholomaeus' sense (though not necessarily Trevisa's text), sometimes they miss their mark completely. C also introduces its own copying errors and omissions.

The question thus arises whether B and C, separately or together, are closely affiliated to H (like them, not derived from the immediate ancestor of AFG, though sharing a number of their characteristic readings and omissions). Since B, C, and to a less extent H each shows signs of modernizing and correction, there may have been a tradition associated with them that Trevisa's work was an archaic and difficult text that needed such treatment in its copying; by contrast, the scribal tradition behind AFG seems to have been a policy of conservative *literatim* copying.

However, the evidence for such affiliation is neither clear-cut nor extensive. There are faint indications of a common derivation, e.g.:

255/23 istreitid] BCH strecched   262/9 is] B be CH ben   278/
27 be sone] BCH soone be   346/34 his] BCH *om.*   349/
20 smered] BCH anoynted.

There are equally faint indications of a link between B and H, e.g.:

264/28 iput] BH hadde   269/3 *grece*] BH grewe   281/4 hete] BH
helth   587/25 swiþe] BH suche

and of a link between C and H, e.g.:

261/34 voys] CH þe vois (*cf.* D a voyce)   262/9 is] CH ben   262/
12 and[1]] CH *om.*   345/29 nytes] CH *add* &   346/22 fomentz] CH
fomentis &   348/14 to] CH into   349/12 nyce] CH *om.*

Since all such variant readings may be coincidental and without significance even in their aggregate, selected columns of transcription of all manuscripts (with abbreviations expanded) were put into a computer programmed first to disclose patterns of identity in word-order and identity of forms and patterns of dissimilarity in single words and phrases and sentences; secondly, to count variant readings and record reciprocal patterns (e.g. of 100 variants in B, 60 recur in C; and of 100 variants in C, 60 recur in B).[3]

The results of this computer analysis, as far as BCH are concerned, are not uniform but not inconsistent. Thus, Book XI shows no clear grouping of BCH or BH or CH, and Books VIII and XVI show some grouping of CH. However, overall the analysis sharply distinguishes the groups DE, AFG, and BCH, and suggests that BC share a common ancestor posterior to the ancestor of BCH. Given the often fragmentary state of B and the highly idiosyncratic language of C, that affiliation lies within the degrees of probability.

The validity of the stemma

While the conclusions about the affiliation of all medieval manuscripts of one work are necessarily tentative in the absence of all their exemplars, the stemma in Vol. I p. xiv appears reasonable. Two qualifications need to be made, however. First, the relationship

[3] Cf. W. N. Francis, 'Graphemic analysis of late Middle English manuscripts', *Speculum*, xxxiii (1962), 32–47; H. M. Logan, 'The computer and Middle English dialectology', *Canadian Journal of Linguistics*, 13 (1967), 37–49.

between A and F may not be as close as it there appears. Secondly, the affiliation of B and C, expressed there by broken lines to mark editorial uncertainty at that time, may now be more closely linked to H and less closely to the common ancestor of AFG.

TEXTUAL COMMENTARY

This commentary has nineteen sections, one for each book, and each section has two parts. The first part contains *corrigenda et addenda* to the printed text, the second part contains an analysis of the English text in relation to the extant Latin manuscripts of *De Proprietatibus Rerum* written in England.

The *corrigenda et addenda* record the correction of errors of transcription and printing, some newly emended readings with their footnotes, and the restoration of material (largely footnotes, occasionally folio references) which under pressure of space had to be suppressed during proofing. Since the text of a critical edition can never be static, such corrections were always envisaged, but they have been substantially augmented by four mishaps: the need to reconstruct Book XII in its entirety from transcription two months before the text was due to go to press; the need to remake Books IV and IX during proof under pressures of timetable and spacing which precluded the necessary total revision; the need to rework Book XVIII due to the theft from the U.S. mail of the corrected First Proofs and the return of the uncorrected Revises at a very late date. These unscheduled revisions, amounting to almost one third of the printed text, so exercised the time and energies of the General Editors that the planned final co-ordination of the text had to be severely compressed to meet the printing timetable, the typescripts of Books VIII and XIX which were delivered late could be only cursorily examined, and the corrections to all books had to be restricted to absorb the cost of resetting the two deficient books within the printing budget. In all books corrections made at the Revise stage could not be proofed.

The second part of each section of this commentary records the ways in which Trevisa's translation has been affected by scribal error and omission in his Latin copy-text and in the subsequent English scribal tradition. Incidentally it comments on his translation habits and his English usage. The Latin manuscripts of *De Proprietatibus Rerum* of English provenance (all of the second half of the fourteenth century unless otherwise dated) are cited by these sigla, the English manuscripts being cited by the sigla A to H adopted in volumes I and II:

I   Hunterian Museum MS. U.i.13 (before 1379)
J   Hereford Cathedral MS. 154

K Corpus Christi College, Oxford MS. 249 (Books I. 6–IX. 7, XII. 33–XVI. 64 only)

L Bodleian Library MS. Bodley 749 (before 1390)

M Magdalen College, Oxford MS. 137

N Magdalen College, Oxford MS. 197

O Balliol College MS. 294 (early 15c.)

P Bodleian Library MS. Ashmole 1512 (copy of an exemplar dated 1296 of Continental provenance)

Q Lambeth Library MS. 137 (before 1361)

R Trinity College, Cambridge MS. 1512 (before 1333)

S Peterhouse MS. 67

T Gonville and Caius College MS. 280

U Lincoln Cathedral MS. 154 (perhaps before 1375)

V Cambridge University Library MS. Ii.2.21

W Wellcome Historical Medical Library MS. 115 (late 13c.)

X British Library MS. Additional 24011 (Prologue to Book VI only)

X2 British Library MS. Sloane 3539 (Books VIII. 13–XI. 34 only)

X3 Bodleian Library MS. Ashmole 1474 (Books XVI–XIX only) (before 1351; later corrected by reference to another MS. or print of non-English provenance)

Y Trinity College, Dublin MS. 224 (not certainly of English provenance and used sparingly in this Commentary)

The three incomplete manuscripts designated X for editorial convenience have no connection with each other. The sigla S and W refer in this second part to manuscripts and not to the printed editions which have those sigla in the critical apparatus below the text. The manuscripts O and T were most kindly deposited in the Bodleian Library by their librarians during preparation of this commentary.

The siglum Z denotes the hypothetical copy-text used by Trevisa. It comprehends two possibilities: first, that he may have consulted more than one Latin manuscript; secondly, that such hypothetical readings may sometimes be misreadings or eyeskips made by Trevisa himself. There is no conclusive evidence for either possibility. The first, on a comparative judgement after collation of the manuscripts listed above, seems unlikely. The second, in view of the comparatively minor state of scribal degeneration found in the individual extant Anglo-Latin manuscripts, seems likely, especially in cases where an abbreviated Latin word has been falsely read and where the Latin syntax has been misconstrued. The hypothesis of Z is generally not invoked where the relevant *varia lectio* is extant. The commentary refers to the printed text as amended by the *corrigenda et addenda*.

BA denotes Bartholomaeus Anglicus, and JT John Trevisa. ME. denotes Middle English, and the asterisk after the head-word or words indicates that an addition has been made to the sense of the Latin text during or after translation; many such additions were probably made by Trevisa himself, but the evidence for positive identification is lacking. The cited Latin forms are generally from L.

In addition to the standard works on the English language reference has been made to M. F. Wakelin, *Language and History in Cornwall* (Leicester, 1975); cf. his 'Medieval Written English at Bodmin', in *So meny people longages and tonges*, ed. M. Benskin and M. L. Samuels (Edinburgh 1981), pp. 237–49. The most detailed linguistic study of Trevisa manuscripts to be printed so far is B. Pfeffer, *Die Sprache des 'Polychronicons' John Trevisa's in der Hs. Cotton Tiberius D vii* (Bonn 1912), which serves as a base for A. J. Perry, *Dialogus*, E.E.T.S. o.s. 167 (1925), pp. cxxxiii–clvi and reflects a S.W. Glos. dialect.

The method of linguistic analysis adopted for this edition depends upon establishing dates and affiliations of the ME. manuscripts and then retracing the scribal changes of forms of individual words where the evidence permits. This process is made easier by a knowledge of the sense of the original words (as determined by the reconstructed readings of the lost Latin copy-text); of Trevisa's translation habits in linguistically comparable environments in other texts (in editions of the *Polychronicon* and of two minor texts and in the unique manuscript of the *Regiment*, MS. Digby 233); and of the wider linguistic evidence of these other Trevisa texts. Such procedures reveal something of Trevisa's spelling habits, which reflect at an exact date (1394–8) the language of a man born *c.* 1340 at Trevisa, Cornwall and living at Berkeley.

The traces of this language are only imperfectly preserved in the printed text, more frequently in the earlier pages of each of the three scribes than elsewhere. An awareness of them, as of Trevisa's translation habits, is an aid to reading. The particular features listed below are not, of course, intended as description of Trevisa's language but form a consistent and observable underlay of the scribal forms of the printed manuscript which elucidates many cruces.[1]

---

[1] The presence or absence of such linguistic underlays in the early Wycliffite bible will confirm or refute the claim of Trevisa's hand therein, advanced by D. C. Fowler, *The Bible in early English literature* (1976), pp. 155–9. A description of Trevisa's language will appear in the edition (in progress) of his minor works.

Phonology

(*a*) voicing of initial *f-*: e.g., *uuyre* 'fire', *uyle* 'file', *uul* 'full'. The last word is generally written by scribes as *ful* or *wel* in free variation; *wel* 'full' often occurs in collocations equivalent to superlative adjective or adverb.

(*b*) spirantization of *d* to *th* and subsequent raising to *t*: e.g., *þewe* 'due', *flecchit* 'flinches'.

(*c*) elision of unstressed vowel of the definite article: e.g., *þelementis*, *þeffect.*

(*d*) retention of OE. *y* as *u*: e.g., *put* 'pit', *hulle* 'hill'. When the vowel was long, its length was indicated by following *i/y*: e.g., *uuyre* 'fire'. Such marking of length was not confined to *u*: e.g., *moyste* 'most', *saide* 'sad', *myistik* 'mysterious', *dinyuynge* 'denying'.

(*e*) retention of doubled medial consonant in Class III weak verbs: e.g., *sigge* 'say', *wiþsigginge* 'gainsaying', *habbeþ* 'have' (alongside *libbeþ* 'live' in Class IV).

Morphology

(*a*) noun inflexions in *-us*: e.g., *manus* 'man's', *nedus* 'needs', *menus* 'men's'. The absence of inflexion in plural forms of words of romance origin ending in a sibilant (e.g., *caas*, *place*, *vers*, *vois*) extends to nouns with the suffix *-nes* (e.g., *sicknes*), cf. historical pl. *hors*; all such forms may, to the confusion of scribes, be singular or plural. An occasional noun suffix *-uþ* appears in *dryuþ* 'dryness'.

(*b*) adjectival and adverbial suffix *-lich*(*e*).

(*c*) personal pronouns: *ic* 'I', *a* 'he', *heo* 'she', *hi* 'they'. Such forms often confused scribes, *a* becoming *an* or *and*, *heo he*, *hi he*. The indefinite pronoun *me* was often misread as *men*. The form *he* 'she' was not used by Trevisa.

(*d*) prepositions: *o* 'of' before consonants.

(*e*) conjunctions: *a* 'and', *or* 'or' (not *oþir*), *of* 'if', *þei3* 'though', *seþ* 'since'.

(*f*) present participle suffix *-eng.*

(*g*) past participle prefix *y-.*

(*h*) 3rd present indicative pl. *-uþ.*

(*i*) the verb *ben* 'to be' has a present tense *am*, *be*, *buþ*. The scribal form *is* is sometimes written *his.*

Dialect

Specific dialect words are few: e.g. *þikke* 'this', generally altered to *þilke* and frequently confused with *þikke* 'thick'; *moste* 'moist', often confused with *moyste* 'most' (see above, phonology (*d*)); *licpot* 'the long finger'; *litwat* 'a small amount'. Some dubious scribal forms (e.g. *crullynge* and *rogelynge* alongside *grollynge* 'rumbling in the bowels') may be dialectal.

In addition to an understanding of Trevisa's language, an awareness of his practices as a translator is an aid to reading. He himself set down the principles of his method in a dialogue between Lord and Clerk prefaced to his translation of Higden's *Polychronicon* in 1367, and amplified them in an accompanying letter:

for to make þis translacion cleer and pleyn to be knowe and vnderstonde, in som place Y schal sette word for word and actyffe for actyffe and passiue for passiue arewe ryȝt as a stondeþ withoute changyng of þe ordre of wordes. Bot yn som place Y woll change þe rewe and þe ordre of wordes and sette þe actyffe for þe passiffe and aȝenward. And yn som place Y woll sette a reson for a word to telle what hyt meneþ. Bote for al such chaungyng þe menyng schal stonde and noȝt be ychanged. Bot some wordes and names of contrayes, of londes, of cites, of waters, or ryuers, of mounteyns and hulles, of persones, and of places most be yset and stonde for hemsylf in here oune kuynde.[2]

These principles inform his translation of *De Proprietatibus Rerum*.[3] Where the matter is short and simple, as in the brief descriptions of mountains, countries, and precious stones in Books XIV–XVI, he generally translates literally. Where the matter is more complex, as in the medical Books V and VII, he generally translates more freely, sometimes blurring the edge of meaning, occasionally mistaking the sense.

Some of his more common practices are:

(*a*) doublets (in almost every sentence and unrecorded in the Textual Commentary) where two ME. words render one Latin word. Occasional triplets, perhaps doublets expanded by scribes, occur.

(*b*) doublets of ambiguity where two translations are given for one graphically ambiguous Latin word.

---

[2] British Library MS. Stowe 65, f. 2ᵛ. See R. A. Waldron in *Medieval English Studies...George Kane*, ed. E. D. Kennedy *et al.* (1987).
[3] T. Lawler, 'On the properties of John Trevisa's major translations', *Viator*, xiv (1983), 267–88.

(c) contraction of two Latin near-synonyms (nouns, adjectives, adverbs, verbs) into one ME. word or phrase (generally not recorded).

(d) occasional suppression of phrases of clarification, often introduced by *scilicet* or *id est*, and of phrases too garbled to be translated.

(e) glossing of Latin technical words which are retained in the translation with the gloss or sometimes with a more general explanation.

(f) reversal of word-order in pairs of Latin nouns, adjectives, verbs, and sometimes in subject and object (generally not recorded).

(g) alteration of voice, mood, and tense, with frequent simplification (and sometimes distortion) of sense, and often with the addition of words and phrases to expand the sense.

(h) reduction of degree in comparative and superlative adjectives and adverbs.

(i) levelling of conjunctions (e.g. *and* may translate *et*, *etiam*, *autem*, *vel*, *sed*), with occasional suppression of associated adverbs, often with disturbance of the logical sequence.

(j) use of linguistic formulae to translate unformulaic Latin.

Since none of these practices is consistently applied, and each is liable to scribal confusion, most critically in the practice (f) above, the distinction between Trevisa's translation and scribal distortions is often blurred. In noting the discrepancies in sense between the printed ME. text and its Anglo-Latin putative source, the commentators have deliberately erred on the side of caution, recording many additions, omissions, and variations which most probably originated with Trevisa. None the less, at the end of the day they remain sharply aware that the dense scatter of scribal confusions has prevented their recovery of the precise Latin copy-text and the precise English translation. They therefore offer their printed text and commentary in the hope that, with the appearance of other editions of Trevisa's work now in progress, they promote a more informed awareness of the problems and so a correction of all those particulars wherein their work is deficient.

At a late stage the cost of things compelled a substantial reduction in the scope of the Commentary. Three areas of omission require comment. First, all Latin variant readings which do not illuminate the translation have been omitted from the cited Latin readings; they will appear as apparatus to a planned edition of the Latin text. Secondly, collations of the ME. manuscripts (severally available in dissertations) have been lost. Thirdly, the source material has been withheld to form the basis of a separate study of Batholomaeus and his book.

BIBLIOGRAPHY

(*a*) *Editions*

c. 1495   *Bartholomeus de proprietatibus rerum* (Wynkyn De Worde, Westminster).

1535   *Bertholomevs De Proprietatibus Rerum* (Thomas Berthelet, London).

1582   *Batman vppon Bertholome His Booke De Proprietatibus Rerum* (Thomas East, London). Reproduced in facsimile with introduction by J. Schäfer (Hildesheim, 1976).

1893   R. Steele, *Medieval Lore from Bartholomaeus Anglicus* (London).

1976   *On the Properties of Things* (Clarendon Press, Oxford): reviewed *T.L.S.* (1976), 615; *R.E.S.* 28 (1977), 203–4; *Archiv*, 214 (1977), 138–41; *N. & Q.* 222 (1977), 463–4; *Anglia*, 98 (1980), 492–9.

(*b*) *Theses*

ANDREW, M. R., 'A Critical Edition of the Seventh Book . . .' (York, 1972).

BLECHNER, M. H., 'An Edition of Book IV . . .' (Princeton, 1971).

BOYAR, G. E. SE, 'An Introduction . . . an Edition . . . of the First Three Books . . .' (Yale, 1917).

BROCKHURST, E. J., 'The Life and Works of Stephen Batman' (London, 1947).

— 'Bartholomaeus Anglicus, *De Proprietatibus Rerum* I–IV' (London, 1952).

CLINTON, S. M. M., 'The Latin Manuscript Tradition in England . . . Book Ten' (Northwestern, 1982).

FARLEY, P. P., 'Book XIII *De Aqua* . . .' (Fordham, 1974).

FISCHER, N. A. H., 'Animal Illustrations . . .' (Leeds, 1967).

GAUMER, M. C., 'An Edition of the Plimpton MS.' (Washington, 1969).

HAMILTON, R. J., 'A Commentary on Books 10 and 11 . . .' (Northwestern, 1982).

HARDER, B. D., 'The Medieval Lapidary . . . A Critical Edition . . . of Book XVI . . .' (Toronto, 1974).

HUTCHISON, A. M., 'An Edition of Book VI . . .' (Toronto, 1974).

LIDAKA, J. G., 'Book XIX . . . A Critical Edition of the Latin Text in England' (Northern Illinois, 1987).

18 81 n. Insula] insula

44 5 *oo*] *o and delete fn.*

46 30 þessencia] *fn.* A þessenca

47 16 nocional] *fn.* A nocial

48 10 þe] *fn.* A De

49 10 þe] the

50 32 n. p/] p/

51 7 and²] *read* and [aȝenward and] *and fn.* A *om.*   LS e contra

52 34 a is] *fn.* *ACDFGH and *cf.* LS est

55 33 alle] *add* [f. 11ᵛᵃ]

The English MSS. ACDG give the Tabula in the printed form, F gives it alphabetically for the whole book, H omits it. BE lack the relevant leaves. The English MSS. ACDFGH for the Prohemium and Book I are complete. BE lack the text. De Worde's edition gives an abridged paraphrase of Book I, based on F. The Latin MSS. IJLMNOPQRUVWXY are complete for Book I. KST lack the initial leaf.

44 5 *o*: LQVX *o*   cf. the better *oo* (the graph for *omega*)

45 12–15 *for to* . . . *þe sone*: an expanded paraphrase of *non tamen aliud*
24 *þe bettir*: *apercius*
31–2 *and þat he hath*: *et quod filius spiritum sanctum spirat hoc habet* (X *hoc habet* only, omitting all else)

47 8 *al*: MNX *omnium* cf. the better *nominum*
17 *þe trinite*: *ista tria predicta in diuinis*   Z *ista predicta iii. diuinis*. The translation recurs at 552/24
24 *if*: ACFGH *of*. The first of many occurrences of *of* in this sense which (though always emended here) may be dialectal
30 *participles fals*: *participiis personalibus uel nocionalibus* (S *accidentalibus*) *reddunt propositiones falsas*

49 10 *swiche*: adds *Que autem connotant* (S *conuocant*) *effectum in actu predicatur de deo ex tempore unde deus incepit esse miserator quando incepit miseri*, which is translated in lines 18–20. This misordering is perhaps related to the appearance of *God and þerwith* sommewhat in line 10 (cf. *God and þerwith* in line 20) where BA reads *sed ea que connotant*
24 *at ones*: adds *pluraliter et non singulariter* (Q *pluraliter* only), which is partly visible at the end of the next sentence in *þe plurel noumbre*, where BA concludes *sed dicitur sunt similes*

51 1–5 *Innascibilis* . . . sone*   14–15 *Pater* . . . *procedens**
22 3°: 1°
24 *begynnynge wiþoute beginnynge*: JKLMNOQSTV *sine principio principium*, cf. the better *sine fine ex principio*

29 *innumerabil*: JM *inuer^{lc}*   KOST *inuertible*   L *immersi^{lc}*   N *in'abile*   P *interminabile*   Q *innu'sabile*   X holed perhaps *inua'iale*

53 5 *spere*: adds *quia non habet principium neque finem sed prout consideratur ut deducens res inesse et eas limitans et finiens sic dicitur esse centrum quia sicut centrum finit lineas*

54 1 *perpetuel*: adds *ad omnia perpetranda*. Unless Z read *perpetuanda*, JT mistranslated, perhaps misled by a suprascript *ra* (as in L)
   7 *þat is*: JKLOQST *id est deus enim*   cf. the better *id est qui est deus deus enim*

55 3–4 *to him þat is to him . . . prayeres*: *quia apud ipsum propiciacionem fore et deprecacionis suscepcionem asserere non timemus*. JT perhaps wrote *for to him þat is to hym ny3 a wol be vmble and vonge and graunte prayeres*

56 12–13 *haueþ . . . menynge*: *sunt ad figuratiuum intellectum mistice referenda*

57 5 *lyueth*: adds *ueritas quia nec fallit nec fallitur*
   16–17 *toward eucrasis dedes*: ACDFGH *to withdrawe eutraes* (CDFG *eutrases* H *eutracis*) *dedes*   cf. *in discreta et in moderata actuum hominum ordinacione* 'in the discreet and moderate ordering of the deeds of men'. The emendation supposes that JT rendered a simple phrase by a more sophisticated phraseology against his normal habits of translation, after the corruption in Z of *discreta*; but possibly MS. *eutraes* depends on a garbled *discrete* properly translated by JT
   17 *discretus*: LOTVX *discretus*   cf. the better *disertus* 'fitly persuasive and elegant' (as in Isidore VII. 3. 20)

BOOK II

75 35 ierarchie] *fn.* A ierarch/chie

76 9 will] wille

28 vnsey] vn*s*ey *and fn.* *ACFGH vnfey   D vsen   LS inuisibilem

77 5 confermeþ] conformeþ *and fn.* ACH confermeþ   G comforteþ   LS conformantes

18 *pertinet*] *pertinet uniuersalis*

78 26 þe] the

79 17 which] whiche

80 13 v°] 5°

83 29 neþer] ne*þ*er

84 30 veer] v*oo*r *and fn.* *ACG veer   D feer   F weer   H veei   LS semitam
5 n. euenauuit] euenauut

88 13 eueriche] *Ench. and fn.* *AFGH eueriche   C euery   D eu'   L ench
S *om.*

27n 5°] 50

The English MSS. ACFGH are complete. D lacks 61/7–65/26. BE lack the whole book. De Worde's edition is based on F. The Latin MSS. IJLMNOPRTUVWXY are complete. K ends imperfectly at 88/11. Q lacks 67/23–77/1. S begins imperfectly at 59/22 and ends imperfectly at 88/14. Collations from the English MSS. CDFH are given by E. J. Brockhurst, 'Bartholomaeus Anglicus, *De Proprietatibus Rerum*' (Ph.D. London 1952).

59 9–10 *and is . . . englisch**   22 *for he may not deye**
24 *spiritualis: intellectualis*
26–8 *þat is . . . þinges**   29–30 *þat may . . . wisdom**

60 3 *þat nediþ . . . konnynge**   4–5 *þat beþ . . . inwit**
6 *commento:* LWX *comm^o* (as ADFGH)   JKOPQ *commentator*   IMSU *comm̄*
N *comētu*   R *cȯm*   T *comtū*
17–27 *As if . . . þat oþir**
18, 20, 24 *incongrue . . . conger . . . conger:* 'incorrect . . . correct . . . by logical deduction'

62 28–9 *wel-schape blesside schap of þe godhede: beneformate dei formitatis*   cf. CGH *wel* (C adds *blessid*) *schap of þe godhede.* JT perhaps wrote *wel schape godhede*

64 11 *and tunges**
28 *grace:* U *gracie*   cf. the better *gracie . . . semina* 'seeds of grace'.
33–4 *Ierarchie; for . . . contagioun: ierarchie nam describuntur pennati et alati quia ab contagione terrena penitus alieni* 'for they are described as feathered and winged because they are completely removed from earthly contagion'

66 29–30 *and somtyme*... *vertu*: *quandoque uarii propter uarium usum suscepte potestatis nam in uario extremi coloris uniuntur* 'they are sometimes painted in various colours according to the different use of the power they have for in a variety the outermost colours are united'

68 8, 9 *Epiphia*... *Epiphia*: ILNOPT *epiphia*... *epiphia*   cf. the better *epiphania*, a variant of BA's *yperphania* 'highest'. Similar distortions occur at 75/36, 78/26, 79/6
    9 *resultacio distributa*: 'a distributed result', i.e., a term in Logic. *þe balaunce of doom* is distributed to Thrones, *inwit and vndirstondinge* to Cherubim, *þe brennenge of hote loue* to Seraphim

69 7–8 *be knowinge, to*: *ut eos adducant* 'that they may lead them to'. Perhaps JT wrote *beledinge to*
    9 *induccioun*... *percepcioun*: *in induccionem per cognicionem in communicacionem per percepcionem* 'to induction by conversion, and to illumination by knowledge, and to communication by perception'. Perhaps JT wrote *communicacioun*, and not *cognicioun* (MS. *commencoun*)

71 1 *ful trewe*: *diuinissima* (W *dignissima*)   Z *uerissima*
    4 *inempned*: *cognominacio seraphin proprietatis et officii discrecionem et uariam gracie participacionem manifestat in angelis seraphin nuncupatis* 'that the name seraphin shows in the angels called seraphin a separation of property and office and differing participation of grace'

73 28 *dei uidi*: KMOT *dei uidi*   JLSVWX *diuidi*   I *Diuidēdi*   R *didi*   U *dei*. The reference is to *contemplatrices* (as in Pseudo-Dionysius, *De celestia hierarchia* vii)
    31 *dacionis racionis*: JLMRSTVWX *dacionis*   IKNOU *donacionis*   P *donacionis uel dacionis*. A doublet of ambiguity, *dacionis uel racionis*

74 18 *þey buth*... *knowinge*: *dicuntur etiam diuino alimento domestico atque uiuifica unitate diuine refectionis repleti quia in hoc quod replentur lumine cognicionis reficiuntur dulcedine dilectionis*

75 36 *epophonia*: I *epiph'ia*   KOP *yperphania*   LNRWX *epophonia* (N *yperphonia* in margin)   M *theophania*   S *epiphania*   T *epoph'ina*   cf. the better *epiphania* 'middle'. Cf. 68/8 n. above
    36 *diuina*... *of him*: *diuina illuminacio sui participes* 'divine illumination partaking of itself'

36–76 1 *reuerens in grees hiʒtinge*: *interscalari reuerentia insigniens* 'distinguishing with reverence according to the degrees'
    6 *Romanos*: MS. *Iohñ* may have been JT's reading. Cf. IJLPRSTW *Iohn* alongside the better *Romanos*. Another possible correction of a biblical reference in D occurs at 86/10

77 18 n. *pertinet uniuersalis*: *al* is probably a relic of *uniuersalis*. A conjunction has been lost before *ledinge*
    18 *kyngdoms*: IJLOPQWX *regnum*   cf. the better *regimen*. The whole clause was probably corrupt in Z, cf. BA's *ad principatus pertinet uniuersalis ducatus et regimen ductiuum ad dei similitudinem* 'to the order of princes universal leadership belongs and government leading to the likeness of God'
    20–1 *and teche*... *prelate*: *doceant ipsum reuereri in seipso et proximo specialiter in prelato* 'to be reverent in himself and to reverence his neighbour and especially a prelate'

78 26 *epiphonia*: ITX *epiphonia*   LRW *ephiōia*   N *ephiphia* (corrected)   S *epyphania*   cf. the better *ypophania*. Cf. 68/8n. above

30, 33–4 *as he may take discreet*: *pro capacitate discreta* 'in a separate capacity'

79 4–6 *and þis was iseye . . . stede** *

6 *epi*: ILRSTWX *epi*   cf. the better *ypo*

24 *in þat þat þese angeles*: *quasi diceret in hoc quod isti angeli uirtutes sunt uocati deiformes et deo similes dinoscuntur* 'as if he would say that because these angels are called virtues they are distinguished as being in the form of God and like God'

81 28–9 *and is . . . frensche* *

82 18 *penaunce*: M *penitencie*   I *pc̅c̅i*   P omits   R *pñe*   U *pnie*   cf. the better *patrie* (as in 1 Kings 19)

26, 27, 34 *24°*, *24°*, *60°*: these three corruptions of the better *63* are present in all examined Latin MSS.

83 13–14 *An instant . . . schal be* *

17–32 *Treuisa . . . imaad*: a JT addition

36 *Alle þis þinges*: UW *hec omnia*   IJKLMNOPQRSTVX om. phrase

85 11 *þe clere presence of God*: *penitencia* (as in Damascenus, *De orthodoxa fidei* 2.4)   Z *dei presencia*

24 *ruens*: *ruens*, cf. the better *fluens* (as in Isidore VIII. 11. 18), occurs in all examined Latin MSS.

86 10 *Isidre*: R *ysid*   T *ysi*   cf. P *dyo* and the better *Io'* (i.e., Jerome, on Isaiah 16: 6). D *Ierom is* may be a scribal correction, cf. note to 76/6 above; if it reflects JT's text, *is* is the source of error

13 *Isidorus*: L *ysid' id'*   T *ys*   PR *ibidem*   cf. the better *idem* (i.e. Jerome)

22 *a destroyere*: *id est exterminator in latine*

29 *puttiþ forþ*: JLT *abicit*   cf. the better *allicit* 'entices to'

36 *Petri*: IMNPT *petri*   cf. the better *i. petri*

87 5 *sine*: *sine* or *siue* (I *seu*), cf. BA's *sent.*, i.e. the *Sententiae* of Peter Lombard (as in St. Augustine's commentary on Genesis 1: 26 and 30, viz. book 3 chapters 9–10)

14 *iprisond*: LWX *recursus*   JQ *recrusus*   S *intrusus*   cf. the better *retrusus*   Z *inclusus*

29 *tonge*: adds *conuicio* 'to abuse'

31 *and setteþ at nouȝt*: *ut adnichilat*

34–5 *þerfore tofore him . . . assayle*: *contra quem animus debet esse tantum paratus ad resistendum quantum ille est paratus ad inpugnandum*

88 17 *of kynde*: the preposition may be a scribal intrusion, cf. *quod enim posset per se facere natura* 'for what thing nature may do'

89 4–5 *libro 3° capitulo 13°*: *libro xxii*. (JL *xiii*.   OQI *xii*.   P 17) *primo*. JT's text is not recoverable, but D *li. xiii. i.* (alongside C *xxii. book xiii. c°*   FH *xxii. xiii. cap°* AG as printed) agrees with JL and so suggests emendation. The reference is to the *Moralia* 33.3

8 *41°*: R only reads the better *40*

8 *Fugiat*: *fugiat*   cf. the better MNO *stringit*

17 *beþenke*: adds *tunc superbie ceruicem altius erigeret* 'then he shall in his pride raise up his neck higher'

20 *dome*: adds *misterio*

BOOK III

91 27 substaunce partener of resoun] substaunce, partener of reson,
28 some] som

92 28 angels] angels,
30 *24°*] *26° and fn.* *ACDFGHW 24°   LS xxvi

93 8 *5° supra*] *supra [dicto] and fn.* *ACDFGW 5 supra   LS supradicto

94 14 is, and] is. And

95 1 iclipid] iclepid
1 haþ] and haþ *and delete fn.*
19 bodililes] bodiles *and fn.* A bodililes
27 þinges] þingis

96 7 desireþ] desireth
29 cercle] cer[c]le *and fn.* A cerle

97 20 *Iohannis*] *Iohann [ic] i and fn.* *ACDFGW Iohannis   LS Iohannicus
15 n. *reverse square bracket*

98 24 wosen; from wosen] wosen *and fn.* *ACDFGHW wosen from wosen   *cf.* LS
neruos arterias et musculos

99 10 estimatiue] estima[t]iue *and fn.* A estimaiue
24 þe vertu of lif] 'þe vertu of lif'
26 place] a place

104 7 *delete comma*

106 8 repliynge] repli[t]ynge *and fn.* A repliynge
30 n. brnaw] brawn

109 1 imene] imeue
12 philosoir] philosofir
29 þere rehersiþ] *y*rehersiþ *and fn.* *ACDFGH þere rehersiþ   W reherseth
cf. LS sicut habetur

110 34 vppoun] vppon

111 4 piram … and] piram 'a scheld oþir a toppe' of þis liȝt, and of *and fn.*
*ACDFGHW piram a scheld oþir a toppe of liȝt and of þis liȝt (D *om. phrase*)
and   *cf.* LS piramis scilicet ipsius lucis et omnium istorum piramidum

112 34 toschift] tosch*en*t *and fn.* *ACDFGHW toschift   LS consumitur

116 14 keruynge] keruynge,

117 10 doynge and makynge] 'doynge and makynge'

120 2 ihurt somtyme,] ihurt, somtyme
2 oþir] o*tt*ir *and fn.* *ACDFGH oþir   LS superiores

121 29 n. sinewes] sinewis

127 18 blo men lond] 'blo men lond'

The English MSS. ACDFG are complete. H lacks 91/15–97/23. BE lack the whole book. De Worde's edition is based on F until the last chapter at 126/13 when it follows a lost D-type manuscript. Collations from the English MSS. CDFH are given by E. J. Brockhurst, op. cit. The Latin MSS. JLMNOPQRTUWX are complete. I lacks 112/21–118/27. K begins at 93/11. S begins at 91/27; the preceding folio and the last folio (from 127/7) are torn from top to bottom.

90 6 *bodiles: penitus incorporea*
  6 *substaunce*: adds *scilicet*
  7 *angelis*: adds *quantum ad hoc spectat opusculum*
  14 *liknes*: adds *in potentia*
  19 *angels*: *cum substantia angelica*
  24 *arered vp*: adds *ab humo*

91 3 *man*: adds *scilicet* (IJLRT om.)
  4 *man³*: adds *scilicet ab anima*
  6 *First*: adds *igitur* (I om.)
  6–7 *disposicioun*: *diffinicionem*
  10 *þe propirte*: *eius proprietas*
  20 *soule*: *racionalis anime*. Also at 96/32
  28–9 *some propirte*: *spiritus proprietas*

92 17 *maner*: adds *anima est omnium similitudo ex quo patet quod anima ex sui natura ad suscipiendum in se omnium rerum similitudines est apta nata ut dicitur in libro de anima et spiritu*

93 26 *vncerteyn*: JORSTWX *incertum*   cf. the better *insertum*
  28 *sich a litil þing*: LTVX *paruum*   cf. the better *peruium*
  33 *of þe soule*: *de substancis anime*

94 22–3 *while he . . . inne*: *eo quod uiuit et corpus cui infunditur animat et uiuificat*
  24 *spiritual and kynde*: *spiritualem animalem et naturalem*
  29–30 *Also . . . mynde*: *dicitur etiam anima mens quia tanquam caput eminet uel quia meminit* 'also the soul is called mind because the head is pre-eminent or because it remembers'. *haþ* is a scribal form of *hat* 'is called'. The translation of the subordinate clause may have been affected by scribal error
  By þe soule man is: *vnde et homo secundum mentem dicitur* 'and so because of the mind man is called'

95 1 *sciencia*: so all examined MSS., cf. the better *sentencia* (as in Isidore XI. 1. 13). The error arose from a misreading of the abbreviated *scīa*, perhaps in BA's copy of Isidore
  2 *IIº*: *xi* (R *x*)
  2 *14º*: STWX *x et iiii*   MNOPR *iii*   cf. the better *primo*
  4 *The soule is on in substauns*: *anima uero plures habet potencias cum sit in substancia una*
  4 *worchinge*: IKR *operacionem*   cf. the better *comparacionem*
  18–19 *materles and bodiles þinges*: *non materiales sed intelligibiles* (KOU *intellectuales*). *bodiles* may be the second part of a double translation of *non materiales* or the result of a variant *incorporeales*

96 2 *and of euel*: *fuga contrarii scilicet mali*

97 27 *passinge: passiua*   OP *passitua*   I *passibilia*   N om. Perhaps JT wrote *passiua*

34 *vegitatiua*: R *uegetatiua*   cf. the better *vegetabili*

98 30 *I*: IJLTWI *i*   U C   KMNOPQRS om.

31 *logica*: STX *logica*   cf. the better *logistica* (I *logicata*)

31 *þe vertu estimatiue*: *racio sensibilis seu estimatiua uirtus*. Cf. 98/34, 99/10

100 1 *ioyned*: D *y Inned*   cf. *moti*. Unless JT pictured a chain of motions, he probably wrote *imoued*

103 5 *Of þe propirtees*: *postquam diximus de proprietatibus*. Z lacked the initial words, which clouds BA's syntax

20 *plaunte*: adds *operatione nature facta*

105 12 *blast, breþ, and onde*: *flatus siue hanelitus*

107 13 *vertues vitales and spirituales*: *spirituali siue uitali uirtute*. The errors of number and conjunction may be due to an ME. scribe; only one virtue has been discussed

24 *demeþ*: adds *et diffinit*

110 2 *schap*: the original figure does not survive in any ME. or examined Latin MS. but IK leave blank space

5 *iknowe*: L adds *uerte folio*, SW add nothing, MQR add the following passage after *lyne* in 4, IJKNOPTUX add the passage here: *axis uisualis est radius iste siue linea que intelligitur duci a medio uisus ad punctum rei uise directe ad oppositum in medio uisus ut patet in hac figura* (K leaves blank, NQ insert different figures) *c. et d.* (MNOP *a. enim et b.*, JQR *a. et b.*, TUX *c. et b.*) *sunt axes quando uidens directe intuetur punctum c. quando uero intuetur punctum d. tunc ille due linee exeuntes ab dicuntur axes quia exeunt inmediate ab oculi medio ad rem uisam*

7 *iseye*: adds *vnde et aer non uidetur eo quod est in fine dyaphonitatis et non habet densitatem*

8 *þat is . . . si3t**

14 *liknes of þe þing þat is iseye*: *quantitate uisibili*. Either *liknes* is an error for *þiknes* or Z *uniformitate*, cf. 456/34

27 *ten and ix.*: LTUWX *x. et ix.*   cf. NPR *xix.* and IKMO *x. et xi.*

32 *comeþ out*: adds *quia corrumperetur*

34-5 *þing in himself*: *rei uise*   Z *rei in se*

111 4 *piram*: *tercia piramis scilicet ipsius lucis*. The preceding tautology *nedus it nediþ*, cf. *necessaria*, may be due to a ME. scribe

7 *þese*: has *tres*

19 *Constantinus*: MSS. *he*. The emendation may be unjustified either because the abbreviation of the name was too cryptic to be identified or because (as in X) it was omitted in Z

35 *liflichnesse*: adds *unde a uiuacitate uisus nomen accepit ut dicit Ysidorus*

36 *wittis*: adds *et ideo secundum situm aliis* (IK *ceteris*) *est superior*

112 4 *esy*: *faciliori* (T *subtilior*) cf. 382/31

5 *of þe more noble þinges*: LPW *nobiliorum*   cf. the better *nobiliorem*

113 9 *þinges*: adds *ad minus*

18 *circulernes*: MSS. *clernes*. If Z *claritate*, cf. the better *circularitate*, the emendation is unjustified

114 3 *and some schap and liknes of soun: formam alicuius soni referens et immediate* 'bringing a form of some sound and at once'
12 *aier: sonum aeris*

115 11–12 *naturalis vel animalis:* PRSWX *naturalem*   cf. the better *animalem* (as at lines 7, 26, 33). A doublet of ambiguity
24 *smellid:* CDFGHW add *þe which liknes þe aier haþ of þe same þing þat shal be ismellyd* and C then omits the next sentence. The omission of this sentence in A may be scribal, cf. *in ipsis carunculis incorporetur*
30–1 *smale pappis: illas duas carunculas*

119 1 *seide:* adds *composicio primarum qualitatum*
18–22 *he is . . . doynge:* the examined Latin MSS. transpose these two sentences, and their reordering here may be due to an ME. scribe
30 *gropinge:* adds *ut dicit philosophus*

120 7 *passe: libere per membrum transire*
8 *complexioun: mala cerebri complexione*

121 8 *demeþ:* UX *iudicat*   cf. the better *dicit*

122 10 *hymsilf:* adds *a corde*
13 *meuynge:* NOPQRUWX *motu*   cf. the better *ortu*
26 *but:* NOPQR *nihilominus*   cf. the better *nihilominus tamen*

123 5 *soþely:* adds *ut dicit Augustinus eiusdem*
17 *seiþ:* adds *ut plane ostendit*

124 22 *and nediþ to be keled: ex nimio calore qui indiget infrigidacione*

125 24 *fingres:* adds *et subito recedit*

126 23 *more strong:* adds *et uiuacior*

127 7 *coold: temperancium frigiditatis et caliditatis*
15 *þe puls: uirtutem et pulsum*
21 *wintir: tempore uernali*   Z *iemali*, similar in abbreviation to *uernali*. Cf. 519/28
36 *opir þat he is be kinde ismyte of:* D *opir wyse þan kynde wille awake a man*, which seems a scribal attempt at better sense, cf. *natura discutitur*. JT perhaps wrote *opir he is be kinde ismyte or*, mistaking the nominative *natura* for the ablative

BOOK IV

129 7 propertees] propretees
19 þereof] þerof
23 principal] pri[n]cipal *and fn.* A pᶦcipal

130 12 ioynynge] onynge *and fn.* *ACDFGHW Ioynynge   LS coherentiam

131 18 briȝt] *l*iȝt *and fn.* *ACDFGHW briȝt   LS alleuiatur
25 moistfulle] mo*r s*[ot]*i*lle *and fn.* AFG moist fulle   C moist   D most sotill
H moost fulle   LS subtiliores
26 sadfast] sad, fast,

132 18 comeþ] *read* com[mun]eþ *and fn.* *ACDFGHW comeþ   LS communicatiua
22 worchiþ] *dra*wiþ *and fn.* *ACDFGHW worchiþ   LS attractiua
29 sauores] sauoures
36 ripe¹] *add* [raþir] *and fn.* *ACDFGHW *om.*   LS celerius

133 18 from] fro
7 n. eiry] eiery

134 5 n. Than] Thā

135 5 and n. c*r*esinge] censinge
10, 11 litil] *fn.* ACFGH a litil … ACFG a litil
15 þe] *d*e[we] *and fn.* *ACDFGHW þe   LS debita
20 new] newe

136 15 folwinge] folewinge

137 20 30ʳᵇ] 30ᵛᵇ

138 19 and moist] a*s* [in] moist[ure] *and fn.* *ACDFGHW and moist   LS ut pote in humiditate
32 partie] partise

139 6 parties] partise
11 smothe] mo[i]*st and fn.* *ACDFGHW smothe   *cf.* LS humectant
23 superfluyte] s[u]perfluyte *and fn.* A sperfluyte
4 n. *add* DW *add þe* moysture

140 12 þe] *d*e[we] *and fn.* *ACDFGHW þe   LS debitam
25 passif] *add* [f. 31ᵛᵃ]
27-8, 35 moisture] *fn.* A moist/ture Also at 141/22, 148/33
29 lost] *fn.* ACDFGHW *om.* L *om. phrase* S deperditorum
31 beþ bredde beþ] *fn.* AFG bredde beþ beþ   CDH bredde beþ   W bred bothe

142 9 causalle] casualle *and fn.* ACFGHW causalle   LS casuales
16 somtyme] *fn.* A sōmty/me

143 7 beþ] beþ kindeliche *and prefix Latin in fn.* naturaliter (S *adds* generaliter)
22 to sad] tos[ch]ad *and fn.* ACFG to sad   W be schad   *cf.* LS circumfusione
22 hete] he *and* fn. *ACFGHW hete   *cf.* LS replendo

33 worchip] worchiþ Also at 144/1
9n. *delete all before Latin and read* an] A *om.* CFGH for W of is]
ACFGHW i
28n. vne/þis] v̄ne/þis

144 25 eueles] diuers eueles *and expand fn.* LS diuersas . . . infirmitates
4n. *delete*

145 1 *particula*] *fn.* A picul1
2 *temporum*] *fn.* A tempor'

146 12 malicious] *fn.* A maliciōus
16 tongue] tonge
20 kynde] hete *and alter fn. cf.* LS uirtus corporis

147 19 *epedimarum*] *fn.* A epidi'mar'

148 3 þe] *d*e[we] *and fn.* *ACDFGH þe W *om.* LS debita
5, 19 humours] *fn.* A humou's
8 suche] such
13–14n. *alter Latin to* L obtinetur S obuietur

149 13 *sanguinis*] *sangu*[*in*]*is and fn.* A sā/guis D *om. rubric*
22 waineþ] wanieþ

150 3 lustiliche] liȝtliche *and fn.* *ACDFGH lustiliche LS facile
30 a mannes] *delete and fn.* *nyȝe] ACDFGHW *add* a mannes LS prope
35 case] *fn.* *ACDFGHW cause LS forsan

151 8 beþ] of þe body beþ *and prefix to Latin in fn.* corporis
8 it is] is þat *and fn.* is þat] AC it is FGH is LS accidit
14 siuere] smere

152 35 serueþ] ser*u*eþ *and fn.* ACFGHW se/meþ LS deseruit

153 1 shortliche] schortliche
6 ouer] *v*ter *and fn.* ACFGH ou' LS superficie
9 Wiþ] *read* [Medlid] wiþ *and fn.* *ACDFGHW wiþ LS admixtus
4n. LS] L iuuentus S

154 2 ischet] ise[n]t *and fn.* *ACDFGHW ischet LS transfunditur
3 apunlich] openlich
9 houndis] hounde
12 *menstruales*] *menstrualis*
22 corporalia] *read* corpora [animalium] *and fn.* *ACFGHW corporalia D
corporalium LS corpora animalium

155 14 et] *read* et[iam] *and fn.* *ACDFGHW et LS etiam
21 exiendum] exeundum *and fn.* ACFGH exiendū LS exeundum

156 25 body] *read* b[l]od *and fn.* *ACDFH body G þe body *cf.* LS eius scilicet
(S frigore) sanguinis
25 with . . . and] and . . . with *and fn.* *ACDFGHW with . . . and *cf.* LS et
liquiditate fleumatis
28 lustiliche] liȝtliche *and fn.* *ACDFGHW lustiliche LS facilius

157 15 short] schort

158 10 bitwenne] bitwene

159 11 hard] h*ery and fn.* *ACDFGHW hard   *cf.* LS hispidi et hirsuti
    21 smoke] smoke prickinge and bitynge þe synewes in þe stomak *and add to fn.*
pungente neruos stomachi et mortificante (S mordicante)
    25–6 changeinge] *read* [s]*tr*angeinge *and fn.* *ACDFGHW changeinge   LS
alienacio
    28 chalaungiþ] chaungiþ *and delete fn.*

160 23 þe¹] *read* þ*i*[k] *and fn.* ACFGHW þe   *cf.* LS ypostasis
    24 residewe] reside*ns and fn.* ACFGHW residewe   LS residencie
    28 trobly] turbly

161 1 greueþ] reueþ *and fn.* *ACDFGHW greueþ   LS penetrat
    26 whanne] *fn.* A wha^anne
    32 *mania*] *fn.* A Inania
    8n. *delete ampersand and insert*   *om.*

The English MSS. ACFGH are complete. D lacks 140/20–144/22. BE lack the
whole book. De Worde's edition is based throughout Book IV on a lost manuscript
similar to D. Collations for CDFH are given by E. J. Brockhurst, op. cit., and by
M. H. Blechner (Ph.D. Princeton, 1971). The Latin MSS. IJKLMNOPQR
STUVWXY are complete.

129 7–9 *To trete . . . maad**: the addition translates the rubric of the book
    27 *haue maistrie*: ab . . . *preualentia et dominio*

130 8 *þan*: sic. JT perhaps wrote *þus*
    11 *þan*: quibus dissolutis
    15 *cause*: adds *generationis tocius . . . Est autem duplex caliditas caliditas solaris siue celestis scilicet generans*
    19 *an*: MSS. *as* The emendation may be unjustified, cf. KLMOST *sicut* alongside JNPQRUW *si*
    25 *þe²*: sua
    26 *harde*: adds *compaccionis*

131 8 *lesiþ*: minoratur. Perhaps JT wrote *lessiþ*
    16 *mosture*: adds *resoluta*
    18–19 *a sotile and liȝt substaunce of aier*: spiritum scilicet substantiam leuem et aeream
    20 *ben*: incomparibiliter sunt
    34 *ȝeueþ it a liknes*: K *immitantium*   cf. the better *immutantium* (JLST *mutancium*)

132 2 *in þe body or in þe herte*: in corpore. A doublet of ambiguity, *in corpore uel in corde*
    6 *and of hem is gode colour*: ex quorum presencia fiebat coloracio. *gode* may be a scribal error for *made*
    7 *colour is ilost, þanne discolour is igendrid*: color discolor generat
    13 *couenabliche*: competens   Z *conueniens*
    22 *bringiþ*: deductiua (KN *reductiua*)
    25, 26, 27 *makeþ*: inuenitur, which governs the whole sentence
    28 *destroieþ*: corumptiua   Z *consumptiua*

34 *in þe watir*: Q only *aqua*

35 *defieþ and sepiþ rawe þingis, and ripiþ grene þinges*: *crudorum et indigestorum maturatiua.* Z *crudorum et digestiua maturatiua*

133 3 *smale bestis and wormes*: J *numerabilibus*   N *metal^cis*   OT *m'ialibus*   P *m'iabilibus*   Q *metallis*   cf. the better *mineralibus* (K *minerabilibus*, LRS *minerialibus*) Z *uerminalibus*

8–9 *þat buþ ihud*: *de potencia*

10 *rene and cloudes*: *plurimarum passionum ut puta nubium*   Z *pluuiarum et nubium*

15 *som into*: adds *quas diuersimode tandem dissoluit et dissolutas nunc*

22 *maistrie*: adds *naturaliter*

29 *for good digestioun**

134 14 *and bene iryue nere togidres**

15–16 *make a þing boistous*: *fit . . . coniunctiua*

19 *falliþ of*: *dilabitur et . . . dispertitur*

21 *and falleþ into þe brest**

31 *þing*: adds *accidentaliter*

33–**135** 1 *wringe out . . . heuy*: *ex uirtute compremente facta euacuacione spirituum sit frigiditas naturaliter grauatiua*

13 *drawe*: *exalent*

19 *salues and medicynes*: *nimis*   Z *medicinis*

31 *falliþ*: *deficiunt omnino.* JT perhaps wrote *failiþ*

31 *if*: *sic*   Z *si*

136 7 *and¹*: adds *dum interius detinentur*

13 *mater*: LOPRW *naturam*   cf. the better *materiam*. Cf. 832/35

24 *londes*: adds *ex dominio frigiditatis*

33 *nedeliche*: adds *simpliciter*

137 12 *effecte*: adds *principalis*

17 *þing*: adds *interminabiliter*

18 *to lette þe fleting and schedinge**

22 *seiþ*: adds *expresse*

23–4 *Ieremiam*: adds *v.*

28 *þerof*: adds *prout patet ad sensum sue fluxibilitatis repercussiua est in parte uel totaliter in extremitatibus consumptiua est itaque siccitas humiditati contraria tam in effectu quam in natura accidentaliter tamen potest esse aliquando humectacionis inductiua*

29 *excitid*: *excitat et intendit . . . qui excitatus*

34 *so*: adds *per constriccionem*

138 3 *irrassula**

15 *hote ayer*: *calidi*

23 *þing þat is vnliche þerto*: *superfluorum autem sibi dissimilium*

25–6 *and so*: *qua consumpta*   cf. 130/11

27 *destroyeþ . . . neissche*: *consumendo humiditatem in* (J om.) *materia efficit ipsam duram*. The translation, accurate in sense, is unusually compressed.

28 *þing*: adds *ut in aeream substantiam siue aqueam*

139 2 *falleþ*: *cedentem* (J *cadentem*) *redigitur*

17 *heuy*: *diminucione*

20 *partees bendiþ aboute*: *ducit circumferencie partes ad medium et fit parcium circumflexio equaliter*

140 15–16 *makeþ þe body lene and lowe*: JLPTW *excecat*   N *attenuat*   U *siccat*   cf. the better *extenuat*
27 *sodeynly*: JN *subita* (N corrected)   cf. the better *subdita*
37 *itself*: *in suis uisceribus*

141 4 *humour*: adds *quam inuenit in terra sibi similem*
7 *þat oþir dele*: *illam* (W *alia*) *humiditatem*
22–3 *þat beþ vndir þe mone**
24 *and*: adds *induccio*

142 2–3 *to slake* . . . *tofalle*: *adiuuante siccitatis mitigatione et partium terre separabilium unione*
10 *and euel iboundid of oþir þingis*: *male in se terminabilis sed tamen sistitur termino alieno*
13–14 *and schulde* . . . *bounde*: *quod eius fluxibilitatem per reductionem partium ad centrum terminaret*
14 *as*: *unde*. JT perhaps wrote *an so*. The whole clause may be corrupt, cf. *unde uidemus fluctus maris arene siccitate in maris littoribus a suo fluxu compesci* 'therefore we see that the flux of the sea is restrained from its flowing by the dryness of sand on the shores of the sea'. Z perhaps omitted *fluctus maris*, cf. 137/20–2
15–16 *turneþ it somtyme inward*: *in se quodammodo reuocari*   Z *in se quandoque reuertere*
16 *neissche*: adds *partes enim materie duras et compactas per sui subtraccionem et diffusionem relaxat et rarificat et remollit*
18 *bocchis*: the emendation of MS. *bunchis* may be unjustified, cf. 1309/29
28 *by kynde*: *substantialiter*   Z *naturaliter*

143 13 *kyndeliche and more apt*: *aptiores*
15 *hete*: *ignee uirtutis*
32 *ikept*: adds *in esse*

144 4 *destroyed*: adds *uel corumpta*
12 *worchinge*: *suas peragere actiones*
13 *binymeþ*: adds *subito*
36 *and chaungiþ*: *aut corumpunt alterant et immutant ut patet*

145 3–4 *þat* . . . *þat*[1]*
6 *complexioun*: adds *aeris que deberet congruere tempori in oppositam commutatur sicut quando complexio*
20 *whanne*: *ubi*. JT perhaps wrote *wher*
23 *salt*: adds *mordificando intestina*
29 *aier*[2]: *humiditatis*
32 *coolde*: adds *aere*

146 15–17 *ryueþ* . . . *faille*: *linguam rationis interpretem titubando contrahit et peruertit*
20 *kynde*: MSS. *he þat*. The emendation, revised to *hete* in the *corrigenda*, is speculative. Perhaps JT wrote *herte*, cf. 153/5
21 *ouersett*: adds *regere et erigere satagit et intendit*. The ME. syntax suggests that JT completed the main clause

25 *comeþ*, **147** 1 *iseye*: adds *sepius*
25 *qualitees*: adds *per digestionem in animalis corpore generata*

148 7–8 *renneþ, lykeþ, and droppiþ*: *subiacet fluxui*
13 *somdel*: adds *per consequens*
14 *nedful*: adds *ut corpus animale in uigore ipsis mediantibus incolume conseruaretur*
16 *place*: adds *primo*
33 *drieþ*: adds *et subtiliantem*

149 27 *16° capitulo 3°*: JLMNQRSUW *x. cap. ii°*   O *xvi. cap. i*   T *x. c.*   cf. the
better KP *xi. cap. primo* (as in Isidore XI. 1. 122)

150 20 *capitulo**

151 7 *is*: *se profundat*. Other translations of *fundere* verbs by *ben* occur at 194/3,
207/29
17 *scabbis*: JLM *insaniem*   R *sanguinem*   cf. the better *saniem*.

152 3 *capitulo*: *et*
17 *kepe*: adds *diligenter*
22–4 *þe craft . . . body**

153 4 *complexioun*: *perfecte complexionis*
5 *herte*: *uigoris cordis*
13 *idroppid*: adds *calidus*
23 *for it is ihid**
27 *enutrichie*: *enutrichie*. BA wrote *emitrithie* 'semi-tertian fever', as at 872/15
29 *iknowe*: adds *iudicio*
31 *ivoyded*: adds *beneficio*
35 *membres*: adds *quandoque ydropysim*

154 4 *voyde*: adds *cicius*
4 *blood*: adds *nec mirum si sanguis sit corruptus*
29 *quinquagesimum*: adds *quia in iuuenculis meatus sunt angusti et uirtus debilis a quin-
quagesimo*

155 17 *Constantinus super Rufus*: O *Const. Rufus*   R *Const.*   cf. the better *Ruffus* (S
Ruffius   W *Russus*). Perhaps JT wrote *siue* instead of *super*, subsequently
corrupted by scribal confusion of the abbreviations *sĩ* and *s̄r*.

156 29 *ioyntes*: adds *membrorum*
31 *þat my3te falle*: *insuper inducta*

157 15 *He*: *statura*
20 *of fleume*: *temporis . . . fleumatis*

158 2 *of þise humours*: *huiusmodi membrorum*
14 *lesse hoot and more noyeful*: *nimis calida et nociua*
20 *and oþir suche of lekes kinde*: *alleis nasturciis et huiusmodi*
21 *strengþe*: Q *uigorem*   cf. the better *uirorem*
28 *it*: *color* (R *calor*) *eius*
36 *of pestilence*: *pessimas*   Z *pestilencias*

159 4 *brede, and þickenesse*: Q *latitudinis*   cf. the better *altitudinis*
4–6 *brediþ . . . Venus*: *generatiuus . . . effectiuus . . . excitatiuus . . . prouocatiuus*

21 *spewinge*: adds *cum siti*

160 3 *somwhat sournes*: *ponticitatem existit uicinius acetositati*

6–7 *membres*: adds *iuuat etiam sanguinem*

11 *make*[3]: *excitet . . . et cooperetur ad*

16 *donward opir inwarde*: *interius*. A doublet of ambiguity, *interius uel inferius*

20 *gleymynesse*: MSS. *glaymnesse*, though otherwise unrecorded, may be right

26 *by*: adds *nimiam*

161 5 *By brennynge*: *ex admixtione igitur incinerati per adustionem nimiam*

162 13 *armes*: adds *et se percuciunt*

27 *ƿurouȝ diuers schappis*: O *transformem*   cf. the better *triformem*   Z *transformas*

NOTE: this difficult book was initially edited by a graduate student who left the team in 1971. The General Editor improvidently did not discover the high incidence of error until First Proof, when he remade the whole book within the constraints of the printed page and passed to the Commentator those emendations which could not be accommodated on proofs.

BOOK V

165 21 Constantyn] Constantinus

172 25 *Trenos*] *Trenum*

176 Aristotel] Aristoteles Also at 183/5, 19, 28, 33; 184/4; 187/17, 30; 192/8; 197/20, 29; 203/17; 218/12; 225/34; 226/16; 236/6; 249/10; 278/19.

180 27 and n. *albugineus*] *albugine*[*u*]*s*

181 9 *cornua*] *cornea and fn.* ACEFGH cornua   LS cornea

182 18 þridde] *read* [ferþe] *and fn.* *ACDEFGHW þridde   LS iiii°
21-2 and n. next to] next*e*

183 17 nere] *add comma*

185 2n. *add after* as (*in repetition* A ȝ)

187 28 womm*a*n] womm*a*n[isch] *and add to fn.* DEFG womman

190 14n. delete and insert *De*] A *reads* D
16 and n. soun] so*un*

193 31 *Cantica*] *Canticum and fn.* *ACEFGHW cantica   LS canticum

194 15 wourste] *fn.* A wo^r ste

195 3-4 berd, berde] berde, berd

199 28-9 interpretacioun] temptacioun *and delete fn.*
14n. As] as

202 10 Isidir] Isidorus. Also at 248/18; Ysidir at 235/27.

205 16 and n. *s*ore] *read s*o[u]re

207 25 *amphorismorum*] *Amphorismos*

209 3 twistid] twis*l*id *and fn.* *ACDEFGHW twistid   LS bifurcari

213 14 witnes] witnes[eþ] *and fn.* A witnes
15 goodnesse of] *delete and fn.* *ACDFGHW goodnesse of   LS *lack words*

218 4n. suche] *add solidus*

219 12 of] *read* [þat] *and fn.* *ACDFGHW of   E *om. phrase*   LS ne

230 9-10 strong to bere] *fn.* *ACFGHW to bere/ strong   D to ber and strong
E stronge ber and
1 n. *add asterisk*

234 12 *commento*] *fn.* A cō/mcto

239 8 schulde] *fn.* A schlde/
28n. *delete and read* fro þe laste, and breþ] ACDEFGHW ȝ at þe (DE *om.*) laste
(D lest) breþ *cf.* LS distinguitur medium et ultimum et hanelitus

243 24 infectiþ *add* [ham þat comeþ nyȝe to ham. Suche breþe infectiþ] *and fn.*
ABCDFGHW *om.*   LS aeris uicini corruptiuus unde talium flatus solet esse
appropinquancium corruptiuus et infectiuus inficit

244 3 and] *om. and fn.* *ABCDEFGHW and   *cf.* LS ut

254 19 oynes] loynes

257 2 and n. id*e*yed] idr[u]yed *and alter fn. to* LS colatur

260 12 *Ezekiel*] *Ezekielis*
    19 priuey] priuey-

263 5 *add marginal line number*

264 1 folweþ] fal*l*eþ *and fn.* *ABDEFGH folweþ   C folewiþ þe   W flowyth
LS s̄olet accidere

266 17 us] vs

267 27 n. whāne] whānne

268 2 and holou3] *delete and fn.* *ABCDEFGHW *add* and holou3

275 18 veynes] Ven*u*s *and fn.* *ACDEFGHW veynes   LS uenereo

284 6 scarsete] scarsite
    32 n. parfite resoun] pfite resoū
The English MSS. ACFGH are complete. B begins imperfectly at 237/14 and
lacks 272/26–277/1. D lacks 165/31–175/3 and 193/14–198/6. E begins imperfectly
at 166/27. De Worde's edition is based on a lost manuscript similar to D except for
chapters 38–48 (224/25–261/13) where it follows F (ff. 67ᵛ–70ᵛ). The Latin MSS.
IJKLMNOQRSTUVWXY are complete. P ends imperfectly at 279/16, and two
bifolia (at 252/6 and 279/16) are reversed in binding.

163 1–4 *DE . . . MENCIONEM*: so I, PKW om., cf. *de partibus humani corporis*   S
corpore hominis et singulis eis partibus   U *huius corporis* only
    5–6 *it falliþ: restat*
    9 *special*: IK *speciali*   W *aˊialē*   and cf. the better *specie*. Cf. 164/18
    19–20 *compouned of þinges of craft and of office*: *compositorum siue officialium*
    20–2 *For . . . symple*: *nam consimilia membra dicuntur et simplicia quorum partes eiusdem
nature sunt cum toto*
    22 *And so blood is a symple membre**
    25–7 *for þe semple . . . icompowned*: *ut puto ea componencia principia componens enim
composito prius etiam organica siue officialia membra dicuntur ex consimilibus generata et
statuta*
    28 *þe membres and þe lymes serueþ to*: *que ad complecionem*
    29 *oþir suche*: IK *similia*   cf. *consimilia*
    30 *worchinge*: adds *compleretur* (JLW *completur*)

164 3 *þey mowen*: *per eos possint*
    12 *spiritis of lif*: D *spiritual*   F *of spirit*   GH *spirit of*   cf. *uitalis spiritus*. JT
perhaps wrote *spiritual lif*, as at 242/31
    12 *to*: *et*. JT perhaps wrote *an to*
    17–18 *þingis in kynde*: *speciei*
    27 *suche*: adds *instrumenta cibabilia*

165 4 *in*: *cum*
    8 *tendirnes*: *teneritudines*. BA probably wrote *testudines* 'arched parts'
    9–10 *principal welle of a best*: *tocius uite animalis . . . principium*

12 *herte*: adds *et fumosus calor superfluus ab ipso remouetur cuius defensiua interius sunt*
17 *principal*: adds (except U) *quia aliorum membrorum inferiorum sunt principia*
17–18 *rootes and*: O *radicalia et*   P *radicabilia*   cf. *radicalia*
21 *omiomerata*: P *omiom̄ta*   cf. *omiomerea*
21 *symple*: adds *et hoc ab omi quod est vnum et meros quod est pars quia . . . sunt*
22 *partye*: adds *uisibilis carnis est caro et quelibet*
25 *influens of vertue*: I *influencie uirtutis*   cf. the better *influencie et uirtutis*
29 *here werkes and**
31 *myddel and mene*: *media uero utriusque*
31 *couplep and onep*: *impendunt* (L *impedunt*   R *impendent*) *copulam et cooperacionem*

166 1 *opir*: JLOTVX *aliorum*   cf. the better *altiorem*
4 *parfite worchinge*: *complecionem sue accionis*
6 *clene*: KNW *inturbate* cf. the better *inperturbate*
17 *swagip*: adds *superueniens*
18 *moche del of pe ache perof*: *eius . . . sensibilitatem*
22 *hed*: adds *superius*
22 *sotillicher*: LRW *nobiliores*   cf. *nobilioris*   Z *subtiliores*
23 *soorer*: AFW *soore* may reflect an earlier comparative *sorre*
27 *pan in pe opir*: C *opere lymes*   H *opere membris*   cf. *quia in eo spiritus sensibilis amplius dominatur*

167 14 *opir minished*: ACEFGH *om.*   cf. *diminuta*, translated elsewhere as *binome*, *wipdrawe* 166/18 and 20. But if Z read *nimis* (*modica*), cf. *to litil*, the emendation is unjustified
16–17 *of kynde opir of matere*: *nature*   cf. the better KSUW *materie*. A doublet of ambiguity, *nature uel materie*

168 2 *he sendip no3t furper*: *ad alia membra quantum est de se ulterius non diffundunt*
11 *heed*: adds *uel cordis*
29 *presentip pe persone*: *personam gerit* 'the head takes on the character'

169 9–10 *pat growip peron**
20 *of wax*: IK *terre*   cf. *terrei*   Z *cerei*
21 *stickes opir spoones*: *ligna*. A doublet of ambiguity, *ligna uel ligule*
31 *ben¹*: *coniunguntur*. JT perhaps wrote *ben i-ioyned*

170 5 *balled hedes and bare tofore pe pate*: *allopicia*   Z *occipite*   cf. 289/19
5 *byhinde on pe nol*: *decaluatis*   Z *caluaria*
8 *pe skolle*: *per interpositionem cranei*
16 *compaccioun*: N *compaccione*   QW *comparatione*   cf. the better *composicione*
33 *pe opun fumositees and boystous filpe*: *grossiora*. BA adds *ne caput lederetur*

171 16 *and hedeache**
22 *opirwise distempred*: *alterius distemperancie* (IJKLSUZ *om.* phrase). BA adds *et immutacione siue qualicumque uulneracione*
24 *in pe stomak*: *nam ex* (M *om.*) *stomacho*
27 *and bredip*: *et sic pungendo . . . inferunt et includunt*
32 *pe wyn*: *nimio* (Q *minio*)   Z *uino*

172 18–19 *lokinge dounward**

22, 25–6 *as a grym fissche*: *beluinam* ... *beluinum*   Z *belluam* ... *belluam*   cf. 681/27

173 12 *changed and likned*: *imitaretur*. A doublet of ambiguity, *mutaretur uel imitaretur*

32–3 *þat somwhat* ... *þe eseloker*: *parum ut* ... *facilius* 'lest ... too easily'

174 18–19 *but departid perfram*: *immo pocius suspenditur*   Z *separatur*

175 4 *þe brayn*: *medulla cerebri*

11–12 *þe spirit*: *ipsum spiritum* 'that spirit', i.e. of feeling

15–16 *and comeþ þerof, and chaungiþ**

19–21 *as þe blood* ... *kynde*: *sicut nec sanguis nec alie superfluitates animales et non est in corporibus animalium nisi ad saluandam naturam*

32 *beest*: adds *scilicet cordi*

176 21 *þinges*: adds *unde propter uelocitatem sigillacionis formarum rerum est*

26–7 *superfluite*: PS *fluxitas*   cf. the better *fluxibilitas*   Z *fluitas*

177 2 *to þe brayne*: *capiti*   Z *cerebro*, unless JT wrote *brayne pan*. Cf. 181/21 n. below

2 *coolde*: *humida*   Z *frigida*

4 *noyeþ*: *adest*   Z *obest*

8 *superfluytees*: adds *sensus siquidem habent tales satis claros et a superfluitatibus mundos*

24 *in*: *et in*   P *et hanc in*   JLOQS *in Tegni et in*

29 *neutra*: ACFGH *vertex*   LW *neutra*   OR *uertex*   cf. the better *neutraliter* (as in Isidore XI. 1. 27). Presumably JT wrote *neutra*, as in D, and the scribe of the common ancestor of ACFGH altered this to *vertex* (as in line 30), an error which also occurred in OR

33 *isette afore*: *contra capucium*   Z *contra captum* or *positum*

178 6–7 *al þe dome of mynde**

9 *and*[1]: *et* 'also'. JT misunderstood the word order

25 *sedeurina*: perhaps JT wrote *secundina* or *secundaria*, as at 180/17 and 181/4

25 *serotica*: here and at 180/19 perhaps JT wrote *scerotica*, as at 181/16 and 18

31 *first*: *peruius* (I *purus*   O *paruus*   P *pius*)   Z *primus*

32 *haue and fonge*: *immutaretur* (K *immutetur*   NPR *mutaretur*)   Z *immitteretur* cf. 173/12

179 2 *to be of*: *ad* ... *duceretur* (Q *uerteretur*). JT perhaps wrote *to be led to*

4 *in eueryche side*: *elisa in sua latera*

17 *white*: adds (except U) *est a parte interiori albugineus uero a parte anteriori*

27 *and is*: *que respectu ipsius* 'which with regard to the crystalline lens (are)'

180 15 *fedinge**

17 *þe secounde kertil*: *tunica secundaria*. Perhaps JT wrote *þe kertil secundaria*, as at 181/4

181 1 *sponge*: adds *et uillosa*. Perhaps as a result of this passage JT generally translates the word as a synonym of *porosus*, *ventriculosus* (cf. 190/9 and 11, 237/31 and 33), rather than 'rough, hairy'

2 *to purge*: adds *et spiritum circumstantibus aliis ministraret*

4 *of þe heed**

21 *brayne*: *craneo*   Z *cerebro*, unless JT wrote *brayne pan*. Cf. 177/2 n. above.

28 *ben*: adds *per modum crucis*
29 *a point*: *termino siue puncto contactus*

182 2–3 *come þe þridde touche*: *conueniunt in termino contactus* Z *inuenit tertius* (or *iii.*) *contactus*

183 1 *of wille*: *affecionum mutabilitatem*
4 *apprehencioun*: adds *mentis . . . et in apprehensis debitam fixionem*
5 *Aristotel*: adds *libro xii°* (NW *xxii* P *xi*)
6–7 *worchinge . . . worchiþ*: *apercionis* (K *operacionis* N *apericionis*) *fuerit . . . apercio* (N *apericio* P *apperet*) Z *operacionis . . . operacio*
8 *sikenes*: *compaccionem* Z *passionem*
26 *heuyere*: *difficiliorem*

184 4 *heuy*: *grauioris*
10 *þe dayliȝt passiþ, and þere*: *nondum recedente* (L *excedente*) Z *diem excedente*
10 *he*: i.e. the *vertu of seeinge*
27 *And*: K *aut* P *enim* cf. the better *autem*
31 *tokene of despeire of lif*: *desperatio*

185 9 *leest . . . moost*: *maxima sicut et minima comprehendit*
14 *in a topwise oþir a schildewyse**
15 *þe scharpe ende . . . þe brode ende*: *conus . . . basis*
16 *siȝt*: adds *quere ibi*
19 *vtmest*: *extremis*. JT perhaps wrote *vttirmest*
20 *is heuy and faint*: *contristatur*
34 *in a corner*: *tamquam in cono angulariter* Z *in angulo*

186 3 *myddel*: *cono* Z *medio*
6 *sonnest*: LW only *citissime* (L expuncted), a Latin scribal intrusion from line 8
11 *þe propirtes and**
15 *reulers*: JLNRSV *regimina* cf. the better *tegmina* (IU *tegimina*)
16 *reulen*: RW *regant* cf. the better *tegant*
27 *þe more esiliche*: *quietius*. JT perhaps wrote *þe more softliche*, copied as *eþeliche*, cf. 209/28 n. below
31 *icroked*: adds *in extremitatibus*

187 11 *kouere and kepe*: *ad custodiam*
24–5 *to þe iȝen**: in the context the reference should be to *yȝeliddes* (as in line 24)

188 2 *hard*: adds *et obtusum*

189 1 *tokene*: adds *scilicet signum iusticie et salutis ut signaculum*
7 *a slogard þat drawiþ*: *ponderosum declinantem* Z *desidiosum declinantem*. At 176/31 *slogard and slouȝ* translates *piger*
10 *colera*: ACFGH *hete* cf. *colere* (O *caloris*). JT perhaps wrote *calor 'hete'* or, more likely, the scribe of the common ancestor of ACFGH misread *colera* and translated it as *hete*
25–6 *sondry tymes*: *interuallis temporum*
29 *meuynge*: *sensum et motum*. This frequent pairing is regularly reduced by JT

190 12 *trappinge*: *eliquacionem* Z *laqueacionem*

191 8 *wormeliche malschaue*: IK *ueruca uel uernea*　JLQU *uernea*　cf. the better *ueruca* 'wart'　Z *uermea eruca* 'wormlike caterpillar'
36 *a man*: *racionali animali*. Cf. 281/20

192 1 *hierep*: *uocum et sonorum differencias comprehendit*

193 11–12 *by snytinge place and clensinge perof*: *per sua emunctoria*. JT regularly (e.g. 170/34, 209/29) translates *emungere* and derivatives by *snite*, but cf. 134/19 *emunctories* (possibly a scribal anglicization of JT's *emunctoria*) and the definition there
17–18 *pe act and dede of smellinge*: *opus propositum*
23 *hereof*: *breuiter ex predictis*

194 3 *liknes and colour*: *colorem . . . et ruborem*
3 *is*: *infunditur*
7 *scharpe nose and holow eiʒen*: the syntax follows BA, *ibi nares acuti oculi concaui et cetera*
16 *ham pat hap*: *in pacientibus*. Cf. 134/20–1

195 11–13 *But . . . browys**
16 *fleischi brayne*: I *craneo*　PQRW *carneo cerebro*　cf. the better *craneo cerebri*
24 *hote*: *candida*　Z *calida*
25 *and*: adds *composicionem*
26–7 *moste . . . in pe chekes*: the apparently tautological *moste* depends upon BA, *maxillis* (K *maxille*) *maxime* (S *maxille etiam*　KR om.)
30 *and temperat*: *et ipsius temperamentum*
32 *exces and superfluyte*: *discursum et excessum*　Z *excessum*

196 9 *helpip and seruep*: *est . . . ad maxillarum adiutorium et famulatum*

197 12 *of heer*: *pilorum barbe*
15 *wipdrawynge*: *interceptionem*. At 197/18 *withdrawyng* translates *diminucio*; 199/26 *to putte of* translates *interceptiua*
32 *and workinge**: perhaps Z *operacionis* by dittography from the later *apercionis*. Cf. 183/6–7 n. above

198 17 *cancre*: *casum*　Z *cancrum*

199 5–6 *to norische and to forkutte*: IJMOW *nutriendum* (P *trahendum*　KSU om.) *et intercidendum* (S *inmittendum*　NQR om.). BA reads *immitendum et intercidendum* 'to admit and to shut off'.
22 *felinge*: *sensus tactus scilicet* (IKNP om.). JT construed *tactus* as dependent on *sensus*, i.e. 'sense of touch', rather than in apposition to it
28–9 *in propir temptacioun*: MS. reading restored in the *corrigenda*. RW *in temptatione*　Q *interpretacione* altered from *in temptacione*　M *intemptatiue*　P *intemperacione*　cf. the better *interpretacione*

200 2 *tep*: adds *quadrupli atque pares*. Cf. 202/14–18
25, 26 *dore*: *hostium . . . hostio*, which clarify the etymology
25 *spotil and breep*: P *sputis*　cf. the better *sputum* (MQR *spiritum*). A doublet of ambiguity, *sputum uel spiritum*

201 15 *perinne*: *in ipsius concauitate*
22 *comep*: adds *crebram*

24 *of þe beest*: JLNO *animalis cerebro*   cf. the better *et animalis cerebro* '(the spirit *vitalis* in the heart) and the spirit *animalis* in the brain'. Cf. 268/29 n. below
28 *office*: *officium*   JLS *olfactum*   cf. the better N *orificium*

202 25 *necke of a mayde*: *collum puelle* (P *columpne uel collum puelle*). BA read *columpnelle* 'small columns' (*colomellos* in Isidore XI. 1. 52)

203 4 *pares*: adds *et hii sunt quattuor*
5–6 *houndisshe*: *collaterales seu canini*
6 *neþer*: adds *se mutuo collidentes*
12 *þe*: I *dui et*   J *uel*   K *vero et incidentes tres*   LMNOR *et*   P *etiam*   Q *duo* S .*q.*   U *ii. ac* (interlined)   W om.
22 *as he seiþ*: *quos dicit habere proprium quod*

204 3–4 *fiȝttes and maunes, here and feþeres*: *culmos prominentes* 'tusks', cf. 1193/21. Z *crines plumas*. JT intended 'manes, hair', since *fiȝttes* is 'fitches' (see *O.E.D.* s.v. *sb.*[2])
8 *aside*: *a locis suis*
14 *moo*: adds *quam in prima creacione*

205 14 *perschiþ*: adds *corrodendo*
21 *for*: adds *subtraccionem*

206 1 *vse and office*: MPS *usum*   cf. the better *risum*
1 *and*[3]: *ad*
4 *couenabliche**
5 *þe voys of word and of spekinge*: *articulate . . . uocis* 'the voice distinctly'
20 *to þe chinne*: JLOPRW *merito*   cf. the better *mento*
21 *sotil*: *sensibiles*   Z *subtiles*

207 24 *semen*: *iudicentur*   Z *uidentur*
33 '*ly*' for '*y*': *l* (IK *i*   NPW *li*) *pro r* (KS *ri*   NPW *n*   O *x*)
34 '*c*' for '*t*': *c* (JLMORU *s*) *pro t* (JLMO *c*   S *te*)
36 *Ratelinge men ben most itake*: *trauli a diarria* (IKQ *duaria*   P *driaria*   JL om. phrase) *maxime capiuntur longa*

208 17 *bloody*: adds *et porosa*
22 *iclosid*: adds *dentibus et labiis quasi*
23 *schiepe*: *uaria*   Z *ouiaria*
32 *ȝif he hongiþ*: *apparet semper*

209 28 *epi*[*liche*]*r*: Perhaps JT wrote *epir* 'easier', cf. *esyliche* in lines 27 and 31
29–30 *ben imaad drye*: *inuiscantur*

210 4 *imellid wiþ**
14 *quyttir*: adds *superfluitate*
24 *passiþ*: *fiat*

211 2 *wastinge*: *resolucionem uel dissolucionem*
12 *vois*: adds *secundum Constantinum*
31 *voys*[2]: *strepitum*. JT perhaps wrote *noys*

212 10 *þe tyme of*: *sepius*. JT perhaps wrote *ofte tyme*
16 *of turturs*: IK *cocturnicis*   MS *conturnitum*   cf. the better *coturnicum* 'of quails' Z *turturum*. At 249/8 *watircrowes* translates *coturnices*

213 32 *sicut*: MNPRW *sicut*   cf. the better *sic*

214 22 *ayer*: *ventus*

24 *voyce*: *guttur*. Perhaps an ME. scribal confusion

34 *grustles*: *glande* 'of a granular material'

215 4 *weye*: *cataracta*. The translation is influenced by the phrase in lines 2–3

10 *bondes and obstacles*: *uuulam* (JLOPRSTUW *vincula*) *pro obstaculo* 'the uvula for a hindrance'. *Z vincula et obstacula*

11 *falle nou3t inne, no þir entre*: *ualeant subintrare*. Perhaps JT gave *ualeant* a purely phonetic translation, i.e., his dialectal form *valle* 'fall'

14 *þat tonge of þe þrote*: *radicitus* 'with the roots'. JT perhaps wrote *of þe rote*

28 *breeþ*: adds *perficiendum*

216 9 *strecchiþ*: QS *augmentat*   cf. the better *angustat*

11–12 *of corrupcioun in body*: JLO *corrupcione*   cf. the better *corpore*. A doublet of ambiguity, *corrupcione uel corpore*

13 *blood*: adds *sentitur gustus*

14 *þan þe forehed akeþ and haþ grete angwissche*: *dolor est frontis angustia nimia* 'the pain is overgreat narrowness of the forehead'

24 *and þat wiþ compressinge*: *ex compressione enim*

217 18 *marou3 comeþ to þe riggebon*: *cerebrum* (JLNOPQRW om.) *ad medullam spine dirigitur* Z *medulla ad spinam dirigitur*

19 *vi*: JOR *ui*   LW *in ui*   P *a ui uel via*   cf. the better *uia*

25 *it*: *et etiam sensitiue et receptam* 'and also (influence of the virtue of) feeling and (it sends) the virtue that is received'. Cf. 189/29

218 19 *streccheable*: IK *debile*   JLMOPQRTW *delectabile*   NSU *plicabile*   cf. the better *declinabile* Z *dilatabile* or *pliabile*

23 *and he breþe nou3t*: *tale uero quod non hanelat*. Properly the antecedent of *tale* is *collum*, not *animal* as in JT's translation

25–6 *elys . . . hemself**

31 *humeri*: adds *quasi armi*

32–3 *oure schuldres hatte humery and haþ armes*: *nos humeros illi uero armos habere dicuntur*. Z lacked *illi*, causing JT to miss the force of *dicuntur*

219 15 *withoute*: IJKLMO only add *interius uero concaua*

20 *bones*: JLMO only add *uitalium*

30 *smere*: adds *oleo oliue*

33 *igreued*: adds *ex causa intrinseca*

220 3–4 *brawne and grete strengþe*: *thori lacercorum sunt et insigne* (IK add *musculorum*) *robur existit hii thori dicuntur musculi*

8 *ibore*: adds *conchathenatur autem brachium cum armo superiori et connectitur neruis fortissimis*

16 *fleischy*: adds *minus* (N *parum*   JPR the better *nimis*)

17 *of boones and synewis*: JLMO *ossium et neruos*   P *osseam*   cf. the better *osseam* (R om.   W *ossium*) *et neruosam*

20 *holde*: U *stringendum*   cf. *constringendum*

24 *fatnes*: adds *medullarum*

221 22 *purpos*: JLW *propositum*   M *proportionem*   cf. the better *proprium*

26–8 *Also . . . armes*: reverses the order of these sentences, adding finally *ut dicitur in Pronosticis*

222 8–9 *suffringe þe riȝt hond*: *sine dextra siue*   Z *sinens dextram*
17 *sikerliche*: *sensibilis*
18 *hond*: *uola* (KPQSU *sola*) *manus*
29 *þerof*: adds *concauitate quinque ossium subintrante*

223 7 *vndirstondinge*: *intelligenti*, modifying *homini*   Z *intelligenta*, modifying *instrumenta*
23 *is nouȝt . . . hond**
26 *mouþ*: adds *reddit etiam per nasum ori suo potum*

224 5–6 *olde . . . defecte*: *decrepitis et squalidis*
7 *ouercome wiþ age, trauaile, and desese*: IK *in fame conflictis*   J *in confractibus* LOPRU *in confectibus* (PU *contractis*   R *conflictis*)   Q *confictis* altered   cf. the better *in confractis*
14 *bladdres swellinges*: *vesice turgentes*. The final *-s* in *swellinges* is probably scribal
16 *in þe vttir side*: *intus superficialiter* (I *superficiali*)
18 *chynes*: adds *et pruritus*
33–4 *and þe lyme falleþ out of his place**

225 15 *discenter*: *decenter*
18–19 *he haþ most vertue and myȝt*: *uirtute plus polleat et preualeat* (L *preualet*   Q om.) *potestate*
24 *colirium aboute þe yȝe*: *circa coliria*   cf. the better MQ *trita coliria* 'common eye-salves'
24–5 *colirium is a chief medicyne for þe yȝe**
33 *strenger*: *lacius*

226 2 *lengþe*: adds *graciles*
16 *8°*: *vii°*
35 *growinge and²**: perhaps to make the balance of the two members more explicit

227 2 *fyngres*: adds *ut dicit Constantinus generantur ex quibusdam fumositatibus a corde resolutis usque ad digitorum extremitates circumfusis*
9 *þan*: adds *carne autem et*
10 *and clere playnes*: *et ideo habet in se quoddam corneam luciditatem et planiciem*
28 *fiȝtiþ*: see *O.E.D.* s.v. *fetch*. LPU *portant*   NR *pariunt*   W *parcant*   cf. *potant*
29 *schort*: *curuum*   Z *curtum*, but *schorte* in line 30 translates *breue*
35 *of doynge**

228 2 *feet*: adds *atque armant animalium uero pedes*
9 *yre*: W *ferra*   cf. the better *serra* 'a saw'. Cf. 850/20–1
12 *ihidde*: adds *secundum Ysidorum*
18 *swerd*: adds *pharetram* 'quiver'
22 *kepen*: *custodiuntur*, which clarifies the etymology
31 *seuene*: R *septena*   cf. the better *septena et septena*
35 *þerof and of þe herte*: MOQ *sui et cordis*   cf. the better *sui cordis*

229 26 *vndir þe smale ribbes*: *ex* (IKU *in*   Q om.) *ypoconderis . . . sub costis*

28 *strif*: *distensione* 'stretching'. Z *dissensione*

30 *is ihaled and irent*: *lateralia*　Z *lacerari*

230 10 *suffre and to dure*: *ad paciendum durabilis*

12 *vpriȝt*: adds *in terga*

12 *may a man doo and not oþir beestis*: *solus homo potest*

15 *betinge and beringe*: *terrendo. beringe* may be a corrupted repetition of *betinge*. BA adds *quia uariis flagellis teritur*

24 *causes*: adds *fuit necessarium*

26 *kele*: adds *est locata*

27 *inner parties*: *uiscerum*

29 *in eueriche partye*: *hinc et inde* 'from different directions'

31 *greues*: *intrinseca lesione*

31-2 *þe rigge*. . . *þat þe beest*: *ex multis autem ossibus compositum est animal ut* (IKN *ut animal*). Perhaps confused by the inversion, JT has added *þe rigge* as subject of the clause.

231 12 *hurtynge*: adds *scilicet inferentis lesionem*

18 *stoppinge*: *horripilacionem* 'bristling of hair'. Z *opilacionem*

21 *pappis and tetis*: *papas et pulpas*. Cf. 232/9. If the ME. is a doublet for *papas*, Z om. *et pulpas* 'and the fleshy parts'.

25-6 *to kepe*. . . *membres*: *ut intra posita* (JLRW *positas*) *custodiat et cor ac pulmonem cum aliis membris spiritualibus protegat et defendat*

232 2-4 *to kepe*. . . *oþer partye*: *ut flatus pectoris in una parte casu aliquo amitteretur in altera parte concauitatis ad uite animalis custodiam seruaretur*

17 *makinge*: *compago*

26-7 *wiþdrawinge*: *raucitas*

29 *breeþ*: adds *et animal aliquociens suffocatur*

233 7 *oþur suche*: NPQR *sues*　cf. the better *oues*　Z *similes*

8-9 *many*. . . *þan*: *plures*. . . *quam* 'more . . . than'

9 *houndes*: adds *et in porcis*

15 *pray*: *predictam causam* (KPQRSU om.). Z *predam*

19 *clawis*: adds (except JLRU) *accipiter est armatus*

34 *substaunce*: adds *glandulosa*

234 1 *melk*: adds *per caloris cordis decoccionem*. . . *facilius*

11 *tyme*: adds *si uero sinistra femina aborciabitur*

23 *a coppe*: *siciam* (IMUW *sciciam*　P *u'ciam*) *maiorem id est uentosam* 'a large gourd-shaped cupping glass'. Cf. 234/25

25 *by suche cuppinge and drawinge*: *per attractionem uentosarum*

31 *disposid*: adds *ideo enim non diminuitur lac*

235 17 *to defye it*: IJKLMO only add *immutatiuum* (L *immitatiuum*) *dealbatiuum*

23 *herte*: adds *a pneuma greco*

23 *spirit*: *pneuma id est spiritus*

236 2 *colde**　　34 *ibroke**　　35 *kynde**

2 *and to tempre*: *ut post*. . . *temperaret*

237 7 *of þe soule*: *animate*　Z *anime*

11–12 *makeþ it more sotile*: *immutat* (L *immitat*)   Z *inuitiat* or *inmaciat* unless JT, having translated *alterat* by *chaungiþ* in the previous clause, here rephrases

13 *to helpe*: *ad supplementum* 'to fill up'

17 *couenabliche**

21 *lettiþ*: IJKLMOQW only add *in corde* (LW *cor*)

28 *of þe body*: IKMU *corporis*   cf. *cor*

238 3 *ischape as a toppe*: *ut in forma pineum uel pireum scilicet ut tendens in acutum*

27 *anoþir wey*: *arteria maior*   Z *altera uia* or *alter meatus*

32 *holouȝnes*: adds *dextram*

239 2 *ben ipiȝt*: adds *et solidantur*

3 *tweye*: *quedam*

9 *ibred*: IJLMOS only add *uel regeretur*

30–1 *cite*... *herte*: *ex genere uenarum et situs cordis est conueniens*

240 25 *herte*: adds *in generacione* 'in the development (of the embryo)'

30 *and crodded and so deþ foleweþ**

241 9 *herte*: adds *et cordis meatus corumpente*

22 *body*: RSU *trunci*   LMOQ *cruri*   cf. the better *cruci*

22 *tree²**   32 *somdel**

36 *kynde*: *uitalem* (Q altered from *naturalem*)   Z *naturalem*

242 8 *wel disposid*: JT translated *bene*... *se habencia* twice

12–13 *eueryche place and side of þe body*: *omnes dimensiones*

13 *is*: *sequitur*

31 *þe spiritual lif*: *uitalis spiritus et animalis* 'the vital spirit and the spirit of feeling'. Z *uite spiritualis*

32 *of breeþ**

243 1 *into þe spiritual lif*: *uitalis spiritus* 'of the vital spirit'. Z *uite spiritualis*. Cf. 242/31

13 *longen*: adds *substancie dominante*. JT regularly ignores *substancia* in such contexts

17 *hoot*: adds *et* (OR om.) *sitis* (IJKLPS *siccus*)

29 *is þe dore*: *grece os dicitur eo quod sit ostium*

244 2 *digestioun*: adds *caro enim calida et humida ex quibus qualitatibus maxime uiget digestio*

16 *sotilnes of felinge*: *sensibilitatis* (L *subtilitatis*   S *sensibilitatem*). A doublet of ambiguity, *subtilitatis uel sensibilitatis*.

17–18 *in one place with þe lyuour*: *epate*. A doublet of ambiguity, *parte uel epate*. Cf. 216/11–12

22 *woos, ius, and humour**

245 5 *of mete and of drinke**

7–8 *of yuel mete and yuel drinke and of þe*: *cibi* (LW om.)

24 *likynge of fleische*: *concupiscencie*. Cf. 263/13, 18, 20

28 *offrid*: adds *et succensis*

30 *membre*: adds *calidum*

35 *men*: adds *in quantitate et parcium multitudine quia in hominibus*

246 5–6 *þe partyes*: v. *partes*

9 *is imaad*: *celebrata*

247 6 *what for*: *propter quod* 'on that account'
    12 *tendre skynnes*: *pelliculas* 'small skins'

248 5 *is more or lasse*: *intenditur . . . et remittitur* 'is spread out . . . and slackened'
    16 *a caas of a þinne felle*: O *felli*ˢᵘˢ   P *folium follis*   R *fellis*   S *folliolus*   W *felli*
cf. the better *folliculus* 'a small sack'. Cf. 247/12

249 31 *appeireþ*: *immutat* (L *immitat*)   Z *iniuriat*

250 23 *3if þese ben*: the tautology is probably scribal
    25 *schap*: adds *naturaliter*

251 1 *drawe*: adds *et remissionem*
    7 *quantite and qualite*: *quantitate*. A doublet of ambiguity, *quantitate uel qualitate*
    7–8 *þat he drawiþ and fongiþ*: JT has confused the word-order, *contrahat* (*lesionem*)
being the main verb, cf. *he be not esiliche ihurt*
    24 *The bowellis . . . þe guttis*: *uiscera . . . inferiora intestina*
    26 *and ben ibounde togedres*: *quod quodam*. JT has supplied a verb based on the sub-
sequent *nexu* (cf. *bounde*) for clarity
    28 *þe instrumentis*: adds *necessaria sunt*
    29–30 *ben . . . herte*: *locis uitalibus circa precordialia . . . sunt* (IJKMQ *sunt in*   L *sicut
in*) *interioribus circumfusa*

252 10 *noþing*: adds *de acceptis*
    11–12 *Take . . . distingwed**
    14 *somwhat*: *corpulencia* cf. *litwhat*
    21 *yleoum*: adds (except Q) *et hoc a dextra in sinistram tendit et dicitur yleon*
    27 *þat gut*: adds *uiarum*
    30 *into feedinge**: AH *into foodinge*. JT perhaps wrote *an þe drinke* as part of his
translation of *cibum*, cf. 245/7–8

253 4–5 *icloþid . . . oþir iwrappid*: *ad minus inuoluta*. A doublet of ambiguity, *inuestita
uel inuoluta*
    32 *gnawinge**

254 1 *of¹*: cf. *et neruos*
    1 *bittir and soore*: *dolor grauis*. JT perhaps wrote *a bittir soore*
    12 *humour semynal*: *obsceni humores*
    13 *into*: *in* (*renibus*). JT perhaps wrote *in*
    14 *resolued*: *rursus a renibus* (OPRSU *rursus* only)
    21 *humour*: *sanguinem*. Cf. 254/26
    22–3 *And . . . vryne**
    26 *wattry moysture and blood*: *aquositatem sanguinis*

255 7 *þe lyuour*: *concauitate epatis*
    7–8 *dieþ and coloureþ*: *collatiui*   Z *coloratiui*, unless JT wrote *druyneþ and coleþ*
'drain and strain', cf. 256/36, or *druyeþ and coleþ*
    22 *smal*: adds *necessario*
    30–1 *takynge and fonginge*: *capacitate* cf. 244/3–4

256 2 *ikept*: Q *seruantur*   cf. the better *separantur*
    3 *gisarne oþir mawe*: *iecore*. A doublet of ambiguity, *secure uel iecore*
    14–15 *þat purginge and clensinge þat is vrine*: *ipsius*

34 *reynes*: adds *recipit*
35–6 *þe reynes*: *renum regionem*

257 9–10 *scabbes smale and grete*: *scabiem serpiginem* (I *serpetiginem*   L *secundum piginem*   W *piginem*) *et impetiginem*. JT glosses the Latin
10 *þe sore*: *patiens*. The translation recurs at 369/18
20 *counseile*: IJKLO add *exterius*   MW *inde*   R *idem*   QSU *indicium*
21 *þe state*: IJKLO only *qualitatem*
23 *dyuers regiouns*: *sedimen siue subsistenciam . . . certificamur*. JT's reduction of the technical vocabulary of medieval uroscopy is general. *regioun* is generally used to translate technical terms; exceptionally at 257/27 and 34 it translates *regio*
24–5 *þat regioun þat is*: *illa residencia*
28 *demen of*: adds *media regione corporis id est*
35 *reed*: IK *igninouius*   JLQRW *ignous*   MN *ignosus*   OS *igneus*   U *ignominus*

258 15 *defaute of digestioun*: *indigestionem*
16 *bygynnynge*: *imperfectam inchoacionem*
24 *coloures*: adds *et . . . eorum causas*
29 *of þre maner of wombes*: *inter se differunt*. W omits chapters 46–7

259 10 *fonginge*: adds *liberiorem*
10 *conteynynge*: *collocacionem*
21 *hap*: *contrahit aliquando et incurrit*
23 *bene*: adds *cordi et aliis*
29 *iholpe*: *soluit* 'removed' Z *sanauit*

260 7 *in his modir wombe**
19 *fongiþ fedinge*: *alitur* (JLNORU *alitus*   MQ *alicus*   S *alicuius*)   Z *alimentum*
23 *xiᵒ*: K *ixᵒ* cf. the better JQU *xl.*
30 *childe*: NQR *umbilico*   S *eo*   cf. *embrione*

261 11 *out of mankynde*: *a uiri natura*. JT perhaps wrote *out of man of kynde*
14 *synewe and strengþe*: JLNORUW *neruus*   cf. the better *numerus*
15 *tweyne reynes*: *duobus*. An ME. expansion, following the *varia lectio* in line 14

262 12 *and brok and bausines**
16 *stones*: adds *eis dentibus*
25 *þe cause and mater*: *materiale principium* 'the material cause'. JT perhaps wrote *cause material*, as at 263/1
28–9 *to multeplie beestis of his owne kynde*: *ad conseruacionem speciei et multiplicacionem sui*
31 *were ilost*: MN *amitteretur*   K *demitteretur*   RW *emitteretur*   cf. the better *omitteretur* 'should be neglected'
34 *beest*: *indiuiduum*

263 6 *schap and commyxioun of þat mater*: *commixtio uel creatio* (L *ulceratio* for phrase) *embrionis*. *schap* may be a scribal intrusion from line 4
7 *matere*: *principium*
12 *frute*: adds *generacionis*
14 *matere*: adds *dignum* 'it is proper'

28 *lesiþ*: *spoliat* 'deprives himself of', cf. DE *reneyeþ*

34 *Of monþes*: *propter menstrualem fluxum et refluxum*

264 13 *is³*: *conseruatur*

21-2 *þat haþ boþe sexus, male and female**

23-4 *hatte fetus in latyn. þe childe**

265 10 *in lengþe and brede**　　　13 *in widnes**　　　13 *axiþ more place**

16 *to moche foreward*: *plus debito*

34 *hymself*: adds *mouendo*

266 11 *wiþ*: adds *pauore et*

19 *body*: I *corporis*　cf. *carnis*

19 *þeruppon*: adds *in natibus itaque fertur truncus corporis*

22 *þe ioyntes of þe þyes*: *coxarum* (JLO *crurarum*　NS *crurium*) *et femorum*

23 *coldenes*: adds *neruorum et*

267 4 *þei3**

17 *couered and iwardid*: MOQRSUW *munita*　N *uestita*　P *iniuncta*　IK *mixta et munita*　JL *immixta uel munita* (J adds *uel munita* in margin). A doublet of ambiguity, already present in Z

21 *þe ouer parties and þe neþire*: *extrema*

24 *kneen*: adds *secundum Ysidorum*

26 *and*: adds *cognata sunt*

26 *iuges*: I *iudiciis* (S adds *et matrix*)　cf. the better *indicibus* 'disclosers'.

30 *rounde*: IKOU *rotundi*　S *rotondici*　W *recondi*　cf. the better *reconditi* 'hidden, deeply set.'

268 1 *18°*: *viii*

3 *ipi3t*: P *mergerentur*　cf. the better *iungerentur*

7 *meouynge¹*: *motum gressibilem* (JL *grossibilem*　I *ingressibilem*　O *grossiorem*)

19 *þerto*: *cum superioribus* (PRU om.) *et inferioribus* (OQ om.)

20 *of goynge and of meouynge*: *gressibilis motus et*

23 *openliche*: O *aperte superiori*　cf. the better *a* (R om.) *parte . . . superiori*

29 *þe vertue of þe beest*: MNPQUW *uirtus uitalis animals*　R *uitalis animalis uirtutis* cf. the better *spiritus uitalis et animalis* 'the vital spirit and the spirit of feeling'. Cf. 201/24, 242/31, 243/1

269 3 *grece*: adds *quod est indeclinabile*

3-4 *on þe grounde*: IJKPSU *solo fixi*　LO *fixi*　M *infixi*　QRW *philofixi*　N *philoflexi*　Z *solo*

5 *body*: *pondus . . . corporis*

7 *cheynes oþir ancle bone*: *manicularum*. The number of bones follows BA, but is the figure for both feet combined, not one foot

10-11 *to defende synewys, strengis, and veynes fram hardnes of þe boones*: *ut ossa a terrarum* (INPRU *et arteriarum*　JKMSW *arteriarum*) *duricia tuerentur* (JLOS *seruentur*　K *tueantur*　NP *tenerentur*　U *tueretur*　W om.)

12 *þe playn*: *pes acuto*. Cf. 271/18

14 *to holde**

15 *þe more movynge li3tliche*: *motum . . . leuiorem*

22 *hondes*: adds *pedes autem posteriores necessarii sunt ut portent pondus animalium et fuit hoc necessarium ut essent quattuor pedes in quadrupedibus*

23 *erþe*: adds *et etiam ad terram mouetur toto brutali appetitu*

24 *vpholderes*: adds *erigi*

27 *large*: IJLMOSU only add *et temperancior*

28 *meue*: *erigi*. JT perhaps wrote *rere*, cf. *moue* in the next clause

31-2 *and on fete*: *incuruati* Z *et crura*

34 *þis chaungiþ ȝet in ȝouþe, for ȝet in**

35 *is more þan*: *attenuatur*

35 *partye*[2]: adds (except W) *vnde paulatim sursum erigitur dispositio autem quadru-pedum est e conuerso quia*

36 *ouer*: *inferior*. Perhaps JT wrote *neþer*

270 5 *bestis*: adds *in parte anteriori*

7 *olifaunt*: adds *in sedendo*

10 *hindir*: L only *posterioris*

15 *dromodarye*: *arabicus* (L *ambitus*) *scilicet* (IJO om.) *dromedarius*

24 *it be*: *gestauerit*. JT perhaps wrote *heo bere*

25 *sche moueþ ferst þe left foot*: *e conuerso*

29 *of*[1]: *et*

35 *4*[°]: *xiii*[°]

271 13 *to getynge*: adds *et curui unguis ad uictus*

29 *calcaneus in latyn*: *a calcando*

29-30 *ben knit, piȝt, and prented*: *terre* (JNRW *certe* L *trice*) . . . *imprimuntur*

30 *round*: IJKLMO only add *disposicione ut dicit Constantinus et aliquantulum oblongus rotundus*

272 3 *Constantinus*: adds *libro ii° capitulo x*

5 *itretid*: adds *proprietatibus*

8-10 *As we . . . boones**

29 *Meny*: adds *in specie*

273 1 *þerfore*: *ubi* (N *ut* LW om.) Z *unde*

1 *to make*: *compegit* 'joins' Z *componit*

4 *euene iliche in quantyte and**

13-14 *falle neþir parte atwynne*: *se iungerentur* 'join together' Z *se iugarentur*

19 *51°*: *ii*

20 *Libro 2° capitulo*: IJKPU *libro* N om. LOQ *enim libro* MR *uero libro ii* (R om.) *et* (R om.) SW *ii. capitulo*. The numeral is a misreading of an abbreviated *enim* or *uero* (basically two minims with suspension sign)

21 *þe bones þerof*: *natura ei*

35 *oþir*: adds *et similiter piscium*

274 3 *at þe fire**

4-5 *may be hewen, coruen, or thwiten*: NRUW *concenduntur* OS *contenduntur* P *conceduntur* cf. the better *contunduntur* 'are broken to pieces'. Z *conciduntur*

8 *harde*: adds *spissa et*

13 *ben*: adds (except L) *naturaliter*

18 *felle*: adds *quasi utriusque fulcimenta*

18-19 *and þay beþ ibounden togedre wiþ ioyntes, wiþ synowys and strenges*: *nerui . . . iunctura temperamentum recipiencia* 'the nerves, sinews, and joints are bound together'

30 *of complexioun*: *et replecione*   Z *complexionis*

275 4 *medulla*: adds *secundum Ysidorum*

7 *holouȝnes*: adds *ossium*

7 *humours*: *humoris nutribilis*

15 *felinge*: *substanciam*   Z *sensibilitatem*

16 *sotilte*: adds *et liquida unctuositate*

24–5 *it wexiþ and wanyeþ*: *crescente luna crescit et decrescente decrescit*

29–30 *in þe fulle of þe mone*: *tunc*

276 4 *som men seyn*: *fingitur* 'he is formed'   Z *fertur*

7 *brekynge out*: *conglutinat* 'it cements together'   Z *contagiones*

21–2 *þat þay be nouȝt igreued*: *ne in suis iuncturis* . . . *exasperentur*

23 *14⁰*: *xiii*

27 *moueþ*: *mouetur*   Z *mouet*

277 24 *gretter and more softer*: *molliores et maiores* conclude the previous sentence

29 *fro þe brayne**, *in kynde**

30 *byhynde þe firste*: *a posteriori parte priorum*   Z *posterior primo*

278 7 *of þese comeþ þre*: *horum trium* (M *tres*) *iterum exeunt*

10 *ȝet herewiþ*: *adhuc preter ista paria*

12 *partyes*: *lacertos*   Z *partes*

16–17 *bene ispredde and todeled and ifastned*: *defenduntur et* . . . *diuiduntur* Z *defundun-tur* . . . *defiguntur*

18 *body*: adds *et membrorum*

19 *12⁰*: *x*

20 *bones*: adds (except MP) *et* (IKQU *est*   S *etiam*)

21 *brede*: adds *et ipse extenditur extensione multa*

27 *30⁰*: KL *xxx⁰*   N *ix⁰*   cf. the better *xix*

29 *he is²**   *also**   30 *in lengþe**

279 9 *burgiþ*: AFGH *bringiþ* (BC *springe*   DE *purgen*). JT's form may have been *burgniþ*, cf. *incipiunt*

15 *lyuour*: adds *nature*

16 *of hem*: *ad se*. JT perhaps wrote *to hem*

32 *spirit*: Q *spiritum*   KW *spiritum* (W *se*) *seipsam*   cf. *seipsam*

280 5 *liȝtliche and sone**

8 *pulsatif*: *pulsatilis*   Z *pulsatiua*

13 *to* . . . *and to*: *et* . . . *ad*. Perhaps ME. scribal alterations

18 *vpward and donward*: *antrorsum et retrorsum*   Z *sursum et deorsum*

281 25 *whanne it was i-oned to Goddes sone*: *ex assumpcione a uerbo*

31 *and hatte*: *ut*

31–2 *kernelly, and þis fleisch*: *pars glandosa sola caro*

33 *bones*: *coxarum* . . . *ossium*

282 12 *þe partye*: *alia* . . . *pars*

14 *socoureþ*: adds *loca*

34 *of*: Perhaps JT wrote *oþ* or *o*

283 5 *þe verrey and pure fleisch*: *pars* . . . *corporis carnosa*

25 *and turne**
32 *colde*: adds (except IK) *naturaliter*

284 2 *to kepe and saue*: cf. I om. JNUW *iungeretur* K *defenderentur* LOS *mergeretur* M *tuerent* Q *munirentur* R *mungerentur* Z *defenderentur* or *munirentur*
2 *wiþ*: adds *calore et*
9 *xvi°*: *xiii*
11 *in place and stede**
12 *hete*: adds *naturalis*
21 *to helpe*: *augeatur* Z *iuuetur*, unless JT wrote *eche*
21 *hete*[1]: adds *et sic pinguedo congelata dissoluitur*
26 *sore of**
28 *hete*: NQSW add *uitalis* M *naturalis* IJKO *uirilis* RU *uisibilis* L *naturalis uirilis*
29 *ande makeþ neische felle and skynne*: in BA this clause follows *þerof* in line 27
32 *parfite*: *complementi* 'the completion'

285 13 *Pinguedo*: adds *autem secundum substanciam*
17 *vbis*: adds *id est communiter pinguedo de omnibus dicitur*, perhaps replaced by the ME. gloss on the verse
28 *þat is seyde*: *autem* (LR om. OW *aut* S adds *dicitur*) *diminutiue*

286 8 *wiþ gropinge**
12 *body*: *ut cicius ad tactum immutaretur* (I *mutaretur* L *immitaretur*)
15 *it is iput out*: *expurgantur* Z *expelluntur* cf. *puttynge out* 286/13 for *expulsionem*
20 *se þerþurgh*: *peruia* 'passible (by)' Z *peruisibilis*
33 *nauel*: *prepucio*

287 2 *schap and colour*: *species*
5 *withinne and somtyme wiþoute*: *extrinseca*
7 *Herwiþ þey waxiþ**
28–9 *þe aier . . . smoke*: *aer exeuntem et non se diuidentem*
32–3 *in alle bodyes of beestes**

288 7 *of kynde** 16 *and liȝt** 22 *colour**
12 *ipinchid*: *obuoluuntur* Z *inuoluuntur*
19 *and more stif*: *plusquam prius* Z *plus rigidus*
20 *humours*: adds *item ibidem dicitur cum castratur homo non crescunt in eo ulterius pili et hoc propter paucitatem humoris*
25 *water*: *aer* Z *aqua*
30 *The heeres of þe heed hatte capilli*: *capilli dicuntur quasi capitis pili*. The translation avoids the etymological repetition
32 *cesaries*: adds *a cedendo*

289 22–3 *for þe heer of hem falliþ happilicche*: *paciuntur pilorum casum casualem pilorum fluxum paciuntur*
36 *lengþe*: *maturitatem*

290 18 *and defaute**
20 *polle*: *occipite* Z *capite* unless JT wrote *nolle*
28–9 *þat it may not passe and be iwastid*: *euaporare non permittit*

BOOK VI

293 5 of²] and *and delete fn.*
  5 welþe] wel*l*e *and fn.* *ACDEFGHW welþe   LS principium

295 31 gristles] grustles

296 24 meuep] meueþ
  29 *Sep*] *Sex and fn.* *ABCDFGH Sep   E sepcie   LS sex

297 33 nexte] n*ynt[h]e and fn.* *ACDEFGHW ix   LS nonum

298 5 Of] *read* [For] of *and fn.*   *ABCDEFGHW of   LS ex . . . enim
  8 Al] al *and delete stop*

302 2 age] *add comma*

303 25 strecchiþ] tecchiþ *and fn.* *ABCDEFGHW strecchiþ   LS instruit

304 6 douȝtir] doutir
  25 schoueþ] sch*ew*eþ *and fn.* *A schouueþ   BCH putteþ   DE schewith   FG shyueþ   LS masticat

306 19 and¹] *add* [actiue] *and fn.* *ABCDEFGHW *om.*   LS actiue
  19 of schapinge and werchinge] *enclose within inverted commas*

309 21 ipinchid, and iwrolled] ipinchid and iwrolled,

313 10 *change colon to semi-colon*

314 6 and] a *and fn.* AFGH and   C þat   *cf.* LS recognoscit

316 6 folewiþ] *add colon*
  20 for] *read* [þer]for *and fn.* *ABCDEFGHW for   LS ideo

317 19 Also] als *and delete preceding stop and fn.* *ABCFGH also   D so   E and so   LS ut
  19 Gregor, and . . . iknowe,] Gregor. And . . . iknowe
  20 riȝtwisnesse. For] riȝtwisnesse: for

319 25 lawes and] lawes. And

320 18 ouerdronk] w*y*[n] d*ro*nk *and alter fn.*
  24 þanne] *delete and fn.* *ABCDEFGHW þanne   LS *lack word*

322 12–14, 15–16 þat is . . . degre] *enclose each phrase within round brackets*
  18 qualitiees] qualitees

323 19 sleþe] slepe

325 12 drynk] þat drynk

326 12 also.] *repunctuate to begin next sentence*

328 20 n. *seu ignea . . . pars uinea*] *delete*

331 2 *delete first comma*

332 13 fnlliche] fulliche
  28 iseide] iseie *and fn.* *ABCFGHW seid   DE *om.*   *cf.* LS patet

335 24 matere, as] matere *of and fn.* *ABFGHW as   C as of   DE *om. phrase*   *cf.*
LS humiditatis

336 21–2 þinges, as . . . *Cipionis.* Sweuen] þinges. As . . . Cipionis, sweuen

339 9 vrnnyng] vrnuyng

In Book VI barred final *h* has been expanded as *he*; the forms affected are *kynde-liche* 291/6, *barnische* 292/4, *neische* 292/6, *parfitliche* 296/15, *schortliche* 297/22, *open-liche* 298/23, etc. The English manuscripts ACDEFGH are complete. B begins imperfectly at 294/18. Until chapter 14 De Worde's edition is based on a lost manuscript similar to D; thereafter it is based on F. Collated readings from the English manuscripts are given by A. M. Hutchison, 'An edition of Book VI . . .' (Ph.D. Toronto, 1974): *D.A.I.* 38.10.6017A. All Latin manuscripts are complete.

291 5 *of sexus*: *secundum sexus distinctionem.* Cf. 320/20
    17 *wiþouten teeþ*: *dencium plantatiua*, translated *þat bradiþ teeþ* at line 21
    26, 28, 30 *anoþir childehode . . . þe age of fourtene . . . þe age of a yonge stripelinge**: prob-ably JT's glosses of *puericia, pubertate, adolescentia*

292 6 *growe*: adds *et ideo crescunt*
    18–20 *for to clepe . . . age*: *in hac etate est declinacio a iuuentute in senectutem* (as in Isidore XI. 2. 6)

293 3 *of fleischelich likinge*: *impetum* (cf. BA's *impetum ire*). *of* may be adverbial 'off' or the remnant of an earlier *rese of*
    35 *iburied*: adds *quasi seorsum pulsus*

294 7 *soule*: *mentem*
    18 *childe*: adds *itaque*
    22 *mater²*: *humor*

295 7 *kynde hete*: *caloris*
    7 *smale*: *tenuissima*
    9 *of þe childe**: perhaps JT reads *ē* as *eius*, not *est*
    14 *matir*: adds *ergo*

296 13 *as it were melk*: *adhuc . . . lacti*
    24 *meueþ*: adds *plus*
    31–4 *The menynge . . . ischape**

297 1 *And*: *ex quo patet quod*
    20 *foure score*: M *lxxx*   T *lxx*   cf. the better *nonaginta*. Adds *masculus uero ix. mensium formatur in xl. diebus et in lxxx. completur*
    24 *ther, fore*: *ut patet ibi et huiusmodi assignatur ibidem ratio quia*

298 2 *childe*: adds *igitur*, cf. 294/18, also a new chapter
    9 *ones²*: adds *enim*. Also after *mele* 314/28, *reste* 315/25, *cetera* 318/30, *charite* 330/ 13, *parties²* 332/4, *men* 332/35, *spiritis* 332/36, *reste* 340/35
    13 *when . . . meueþ*: *ad ipsius rupturam mouetur*, i.e. 'when the child moves the skin breaks'
    26 *32°*: P *xi*   cf. the better *xxii.*

299 2 *ben*: *debent esse*
    2 *þan þe lymes of females**

2 *Also*: O only *enim*

6 *And*: *et ideo*

15 *norische*: *gerule seu nutricis*

15 *be in stede and supplie and fulfulle*: *suppleat*

19 *childes*[1]: *pueri uel infantis*

20–1 *into humours, fleisch, and blood**

21 *And*: *unde*. Perhaps JT wrote *an so*. Also at 312/8, 323/20

32 *lullinges and opir cradil songis*: *cantus*

33 *childe*[1]: adds *ex uocis dulcedine*

300 4, 5 *and, and*[1]: *et per consequens*

7–8 *pe secounde . . . fourtene*: *etatis puerilis*

19–20 *pat is . . . schare**: cf. line 27

23 *witty to lerne caroles*: *animo dociles*

23–4 *wipoute . . . busines*: *sine cura et solicitudine et tutam uitam ducentes*

27 *or pe nepir berd springe**: cf. lines 19–20

301 10 *and*[2]: KL *enim*   MNPT *a*   O *et a*

24 *slepe*: *dormiunt uel dormitant*

26–7 *kyken . . . hondis*: *recalcitrant*, translated *kykep* at 313/27

35 *moist*: adds *et tenelle*

37 *affeccioun*: adds *quoad exteriorem compositionem moribus disciplinate in sermonibus caute et tacite*

302 13 *smale*: *magis angustum*

17 *Esy*: adds *uox tenuis sermo uolubilis et facilis*

18 *hede*: adds *ad iracundiam pronus tenax odii*

18 *enuyous*: adds *laboris impatiens*, translated *mowen not wip trauaile* at 303/20–1

22 *ben*: *reputantur*

303 19 *hauep*: *sepius patiuntur*

304 9 *in pis same book*: *supra in eodem libro capitulo proximo*   cf. lines 33–4

305 4 *with pe lasse woo and sorwe*: *facilius . . . et infantulus partus tempore periculum non incurrat*

6 *and helpip . . . wise**

306 14 *pat is . . . female**   cf. 598/3

26–7 *gret . . . stronge*: *maiori . . . forcioribus*. Perhaps JT wrote *gretter . . . strenger*, but his translation of comparatives varied according to context; e.g. in the next two sentences all the adjectives, comparative in Latin, are translated as simple, while at 307/16–18 the Latin comparatives are translated grammatically.

32 *blood*: *spirituum et sanguinis*

307 6 *6°*: *v*

23 *Aristotel*: adds *libro iiii*

27 *3°*: LM *iiii*. cf. the better *iii*

308 13 *many 3iftis and meche good and catelle*: *multa*

21 *scharp*: *ardenti*   Z *acuto*, unless the translation is contextual

34 *amys*: adds *et custodiam circa eam adhibet et apponit*

36 *entringe*: adds *trucinat atque pensat*

309 4–5 *stoute and gay*: *curiosam*   Z *gloriosam*   cf. 318/12 *ioye and stoutnes*
   7 *matere*: adds *superius posita*
  12 *meyne*: adds *quantum ad extraneos*
  24 *in*: *ex*
  28 *and*[3]: adds *naturaliter*

310 23–4 *reward an mede*: *remuneratio specialis*

311 9 *þe childe*: *sua effigies in filio*
  13 *is wel iloued*: LMT *diligitur*   cf. the better *dirigitur*
  21 *For*: *sed propter*
  30 *tofore*: *infra*. The reference is properly to chapter 16.

312 2 *seruise of office*: *officiis*
  3 *children*: adds *mancipantur*
  9 *childehode*[1,2]: *infamia . . . infamie* (L *infancia . . . infamie*)   Z *infancia . . . infancia*
  10–11 *straungeres, aliens*: *barbaris*
  17 *ancilla*: adds *Quere ibi*

313 1–3 *Talentum . . . folweþ**: JT's addition. The last clause notes the return to
BA's text
  7 *coueitous*: *cupidus lucri auidus*
  14 *þey beþ*: *cum sit* 'when he is'
  23 *an yuel speker*: *item maledicus*
  27 *delicatliche bilad*: *delicatus et deliciose nutritus*
  29 *And*: *et iterum*, which introduces another biblical quotation

314 4 *as who seiþ*: *quasi diceret*, an idiomatic translation
  5 *for he is*: *item cum sit*, introducing a new sentence
  13 *gileful*: MS. *gleful* is perhaps right, cf. *M.E.D.* sub *gle* 1.c. and *O.E.D.* s.v. *glee*
v.
  25 *seruysable*: adds *ad quolibet obsequium*

315 5–6 *þing þat is bitake him*: *commisso scilicet negocio*
  9 *and he takeþ more hede*: *plus enim intendit bonus seruus*
  12–13 *mna . . . valewe**
  15 *curious*: *multum curiosus*
  20 *þerfore*: *ubi*   Z *unde*
  32 *A trewe seruaunt*: *item seruus fidelis*

316 4 *worthiliche*: adds *Abner* (L *adner*) *et*
  8 *wiþ his hond, and**
  17 *costelew*: *onerosus*   cf. *sumptuosam* 309/4
  24 *A seruaunt*: *item seruus*
  27 *clennes . . . seruise*: *mundiciam seruientis . . . exhibitionem seruitutis*

317 3 *apayed*: adds *unde*
  17 *he*: JT may have written *hit* or even *heo*, cf. *hirsilf* l. 18 and *potestas . . . opponit*
  19 *Also*: *ut*. Perhaps JT wrote *as* or *als*
  32 *Whanne*: *cum inquit* (P *cum*)

318 1 *not*: properly modifies *ouer men*, cf. *non hominibus sed bestis*
  10 *may drede þe punyschinge*: *peccare metuant*

11–12 *And . . . þat**
19 *herte, of fleische*: *corde*. A doublet of ambiguity, *corde uel carne*
24–5 *beþ isette . . . of opir*: *inueniuntur*
26 *kynde*: adds *nobiliter*

319 2 *sesiþ*: *sedat   Z cedat*
11 *Propter munera*: if JT left untranslated part (as he thought) of this quotation of Micah 3: 9, his practice elsewhere may have been to leave all biblical quotations in Latin (cf. the mixed translations at 319/21, 320/1) unless the initial words only were left untranslated
18 *opir meyne*: *aliena*. Perhaps JT wrote *opir menus* i.e. other men's
30 *and colour**: perhaps JT's expansion of *occasiones*

320 13 *al þat is idoo to him*: *omnia que fiunt debita fore*
20 *sexus*: *sexus discretionem*   cf. 291/5
23 *þanne²*: *tertio*   cf. 321/9
32 *þeyr*: MS. *þis þing*   cf. *aere*. If Z had *eo re* instead of the better *aere*, the emendation is unjustified

321 8 *þerof*: adds *unde*
28 *to men þat trauaileþ*: properly begins the next sentence
28 *þat mete*: *omnis cibus*. Perhaps JT wrote *al mete*
29–30 *þanne is*: *laborantibus tamen est conueniens*

322 3 *also*: *enim*
12–13 *þat is . . . moisture**   15–16 *þat is . . . moist**
19 *some mete is sotille**: probably a scribal attraction from the next line

323 4 *replecioun*: adds *Vnde*

324 7 *3eue is nedeful*: *dandus est necessarius*. Perhaps JT wrote *is nedeful to 3eue*. At line 29 *schal be 3eue* translates *sunt dande*
27 *For Ypocras seiþ þat*: *sicut dicit Ypocras*, properly modifying the previous sentence
35 *In wintir*: *quoniam igitur in yeme*
38 *champiouns and hard trauailing men*: *athletis*

325 6 *hungur*: *sterilitatem siue famem*. The phrase recurs at 586/10
7 *For so*: *ut*
9 *sikernesse*: *saturitatem   Z securitatem* 'safety'
17 *withoute help of moisture of drink**
23–4 *þe maner and þe weye*: *uiam*. JT probably wrote *þe mater and þe weye*. A doublet of ambiguity, *materiam uel uiam*
31 *coolde*: adds *huiusmodi autem ut dicit Constantinus*

326 7–9 *for in wyntir . . . coolde*: *propter hoc enim quod libere exponitur uentis septentrionalibus ex motu uentorum subtiliatur est in yeme calide nature et frigide nature in estate frigus enim septentrionale fugat calorem ad interiora foncium sibi obiectorum qui coadunatus frigiditati obuiat et resistit*
13–14 *welles and mounteynes*: *montibus*. A doublet of ambiguity, *fontibis uel montibus*
33 *olde**

327 2 *Auycenne*: adds *testificati sunt* (KLO om.)
12 *is erþy and worst*: *ceteris sunt illaudabiliores   Z terrea et illaudabilior*

25 *humours*: *humorem*

29 *inneremore*: adds *de sulphure*. The reference is to Book XVI. 94

328 2–3 *He . . . litil**

20 *fiery*: *uinea*   Z *ignea*

27 *with his portynans*: *et sue pertinentie* 'and parts belonging to it'. Z *sua pertinentia*, which JT possibly rendered *with his pertinens*. BA continues *nocencia alia sunt acerba et diuretica alio uero amara ceteris minus calida*

29 *and³*: *quia*

31 *wakeþ*: JT perhaps wrote *makeþ* (as in CH), cf. *commotiuum*

31 *norischinge*: adds *ceteris*

329 11 *3if*: *si uero*

13 *deþ*: adds *erit potius*

23 *Mete*: *Cibus itaque*

28 *Children*: *filie domine*

34 *forþ*: adds *sibi inuicem fercula apposita*

330 20 *siker*: adds *in locis enim spatiosis amenis et securis solent nobiles facere festa sua*

23 *lord of þe hous*: *facies hospitis*

331 1 *cornemuse*: *chorum*

5 *lampis*: adds *et candele*. JT probably wrote *beþ itende*, cf. *accenduntur*

12 *al be ese and nou3t to hastilyche*: *morose* 'in a delayed manner'

13 *seuenscore . . . and ten*: *100 et 50*

23 *of felinge and of meuynge*: *animalium*, perhaps scribally confused with *sensibilia et motiua* 'of felinge' in the next line. The ME. phrase translates *animales et sensibiles* at 332/26, 333/35

29 *to þe soule*; *so*: *anime passio sicut enim*

30–1 *an þat . . . þat is*: *quod autem dicit . . . dicit*. Perhaps JT wrote *a seiþ þat . . . a seiþ þat*

332 1 *þis*: *alio*

1 *likinge*: *mulcebris*

3 *clepiþ*: *reuocans*

7 *parties*: *sensuum particularium*, correctly translated in the next clause

9 *stoppid*: *ligato et opilato*

16 *and*: LMOT *et*   cf. the better *ut*

21 *whanne*: *et ibi*   Z *ubi*

26 *vertues*: *uirtus*

333 2–3 *And in þat manere slepte Ezechias**

7 *Also*: *sicut*. JT perhaps wrote *als*

15 *if*: *quia si*

21 *herte*: *animus*

23 *and**: probably due to loss of text in the next phrase

23–4 *kynde hete*: *calor naturalis debilis per somnum fit maior humorum resolutio quam intrans calor naturalis*

31 *schortly*: adds *ex predictis*

34 *vertues*: *motus*   Z *uirtus*

334 1 *good turnynge and changinge*: *bonam crisim denunciat*. Perhaps JT wrote *turnyþ to a good change*
   2 *suspecte*: adds *merito*
   12 *þat*[1]: *enim*
   14 *swetnes*[2]: adds *quam sequitur quis*
   20 *of worchinge*: *efficiens*   cf. IRS *effigies*
   27 *and þat**
   32 *soule*: *multe anime*
   33 *þe liknes and þe schap*: *formas et similitudines*

335 30 *stikeþ and prickeþ*: *pungens*   Z *pingens*
   34 *in wakinge**

336 2 *dryeþ þe yȝen*: JT has mistaken the syntax, the verb properly belonging to the previous clause and the noun to the next, cf. *corpus attenuant et dessiccant oculos palpebras nimis*
   4 *þe stomake and**
   8 *kynde*: adds *ut dicit Constantinus*
   13 *and*: adds *maxime*
   15 *iourney*: J *diem*   cf. the better *dietam*
   16 *praye*: *orantibus*. JT perhaps wrote *prayynge*
   21 *also**
   23 *body*: adds *aliquando*
   25 *in þe soule*: *ad animam . . . in ipsa mente*

337 2–3 *and nouȝt . . . sweuenes*: *item idem ibidem in somnis rerum et corporum uidemus*
   4 *for*: adds *solam*
   5 *wakinge*: adds *itaque*
   8 *clere and playne*: *tranquilla*   Z *transparentes*. In the next line *opun and playne* translates *nuda*
   23 *Whenne sweuenes*: *sed quando huiusmodi*
   24–5 *wiþ help of goddis grace*: *quando diuinitus per graciam est adiutus*
   33 *witt*: *sexui*   cf. Q *sensu*, which was presumably JT's reading

338 1–2 *lacke and defaute of mete and drinke**
   5 *and*[1]: *semper uidetur*
   13 *liknes and changing*: *immutatione*. A doublet of ambiguity, *immitatione uel immutatione*

339 7 *sadde*: *eis soliditatem tribuit*
   8 *traueile*: adds *inequale*   cf. line 16
   9 *vrnuyng*: the addition of this word from DE is tentative, cf. *itinerare*. JT nowhere else in this work certainly uses the *vrn* form
   11 *suche*: adds *hec autem uaria exercitia corpus uariant*, perhaps partly reflected in the following line *Some of þese diuers traueilles* where BA has *quoddam* only
   13 *erthe is*: *fornace . . . cum sit* 'hearth . . . when it is'
   16 *Som particuler trauaile*: *exercitium uero particulare* 'but travail is particular'
   17 *traueile*: adds *igitur*
   18 *qualite*: adds *tempus locus quantitas ut non sit nimis intensa uel nimis remissa in qualitate*
   22 *wiþ suche superfluytees*: I *superfluitantes*   cf. the better *superueniens*

28 *suche a place*: *talis quantum est*
30 *somtyme*: *unde quidam*   Z *quondam*
34 *chastisinge*: *fuga*

340 1 *lore*: *disciplina*
2 *modir*: *nutricis*   Z *matricis* or *matris*
7–8 *good busines of traueile*: *pii laboris exercitium*. In line 9 *busines and traueile* translates *labori*
23–4 *what lackeþ . . . durable*: i.e. a quotation of an unidentified verse, *Quod caret alterna requie durabile non est*

341 6 *vicious*: *hec similiter uiciosa*
9 *and*[1]: adds *recreat*

BOOK VII

343 15 n. onlich] onelich

344 2 n. continual] continuale

350 21 iholpe] holpe

354 31 seruyse] seruysis

355 10 and n. þe] þe fallyng

359 12 oþir] *read* oᴜir *and fn.* *ABCDEFGH oþir   LS superiorem

361 5 mataratifes] materatifes

364 9 wastinge] *fn.* wast/tinge
        14 grete and] *fn.* a grete/te   *and delete fn. 14*

366 1 vniȝed] ᴏn-iȝed *and fn.* ABCEFG vniȝed   LS luscus

375 15 from] fro

378 31 comfortatiues] confortatiues

379 7 strong] stra ng *and fn.* *ABCDEFGHW strong   LS extraneus

383 20 semeþ] sounᴇþ *and fn.* *ABCDEFGHW semeþ   LS sonat

391 32 n. oripulcacione] oripulacione

399 7 gleymy] glemy

403 29 outpassinge] outepassinge

412 17 humours] humors

415 22 principal] pri[n]cipal *and fn.* A pricipal

422 27 upwarde] vpwarde

424 12 *elephancia*] el[e]phancia *and fn.* A elphancia

426 15 reþeren] roþeren

427 8 manes] mannes

429 29 of¹] *delete and fn.* *ABCDEFGHW of   *cf.* LS combustio

430 4 laste] laᵴte *and fn.* A laſte

438 31 redeliche] redeliche

The English MSS. ACEFGH are complete. B begins imperfectly at 344/6 and lacks 439/4–443/27. D lacks 356/13–360/12. The abstract in British Library MS. Sloane 983, ff. 81–94ᵛ belongs to the ABCFGH (rather than the DE) manuscript tradition: see *Anglia* lxxxvii (1969), 1–25. Throughout Book VII De Worde's edition is based on F. The Latin MSS. JKLMNOQRSTUW are complete. I lacks 378/20–410/18, P lacks 406/19–419/18 and 431/35–end. X is wholly lacking. Collations of the ME. MSS. are given by M. Andrew (Ph.D. York 1972).

342 4–5 *þe tretys . . . þinges: de illorum proprietatibus*
        5–6 *comfortiþ . . . saueþ: perficiunt et custodiunt*

6–7 *þat . . . aȝens kynde*: *que contra naturam sibi accidunt eiusque naturam destruunt et corrumpunt*   Z om. *eiusque . . . corrumpunt*

7–8 *cause of sikenes, sikenes*: the ME. is potentially confusing (DE omit *sikenes²*), but cf. *causa morbi ipse morbus*

9–12 *as of . . . continuauns*: *sicut est mala complexio nimia replecio uel inanicio uirtutis defectio qualitatum alteracio et continuitatis dissolutio*

13–14 *Iohannicius . . . noyed*: *morbus autem secundum Iohannicium est res ex quo accidit oppilationi corporis lesionis nocumentum*

15–16 *þat comeþ and is ibrouȝt*: *introductam*

17 *cephatica*: *cephatica*   cf. the better IKMN *cephalica*

20 *is in suche state*: *tale existit*

22 *falleþ*: *incidit necessario*

23–6 *For . . . hond*: the ME. appears to lack a verb after *humours* line 23, cf. *ex distemperantia et inequalitate humorum accidit morbus consimilis ut est febris ydropisis et huius modi ex mala uero dispositione membrorum incipit* (R om.) *morbus dissimilis* (KNRU *difficilis*   IMQS *officialis*) *ut in oculo obtalmia uel in manu arthetica*. Possibly Z lacked *accidit* (cf. the lack of *incipit* in R). On JT's translation of technical terms, cf. notes to 257/23 above, 369/13–14, 373/15–16 below

30 *and oþir siche**

30 *vnliche*: JKLMNOTUW *officialis*   IPRS *officialia*   Z *dissimilis*   cf. the variants *dissimilis, officialis, difficilis* at 342/23–6

343 3 *effectis and doinge*: *effectibus*. Possibly JT wrote *effectis* 'doinge', but at 353/9 *doynge* translates *effectu*. Cf. 344/8n. below

5 *makeþ þerof generallich mynde*: *exprimuntur*

5–6 *þerfore . . . proces*: JT's translation is awkward, cf. *et ideo de ordine prosequendi non est hic curandum*

12–14 *and . . . stomak*: *uel ex causa priuata uel ex remota ex priuata que aliunde quam ex capite non uenit aut causa remota ut a stomacho*

16–17 *of⁴ . . . melencolia*: BA assumes a better informed readership, cf. *utpote sanguinis fleumaticis et cetera*

17–18 *comeþ and gooþ*: *sit interpolatus modo ueniens modo recedens*. BA glosses the technical term *interpolatus*, for which JT's ME. has no equivalent, cf. 370/5–6, 33

22 *þe hed . . . heuy*: *calorem patitur in capite grauitatem in fronte*

23 *sege and sete*: *sedes*, translated *place* in 343/27 and 344/2

28 *þe mouþ is bittir*: *amaritudo sentitur in ore*

30 *erþy colour and hiew*: *liuida quasi terrei coloris*.

33–4 *with . . . gronynge*: *cum tussi et graui spiritus retractione et querela*

344 3–4 *in þre . . . foure*: *in quattuor partes*

5–6 *þe nolle of þe heed*: *occipitio*

7 *many oþir*: *aliis modis*

8 *scharpnes and doinge*: *acumine*. A doublet of ambiguity, *acumine uel actione*

12 *an ache and an yuel*: *dolorem*. Cf. 375/16n. below

12–14 *þat phisicians . . . greuous*: *quem physici ut dicit Constantinus uocant emigraneam et hic dolor secundem Constantinus molestissimus est*. JT avoids the awkward repetition of *Constantinus*.

17 *of . . . ventosite*: *ex fumo colerico et calido cum uentositate*

18 *picchinge and prickerge*: *puncturam*. Also at 397/24

*23 as . . . honycombe**

24 vicious and gleymy: uiscoso. JT normally translates *uicio* as *vicious*, and *uiscoso* as *gleymy*, cf. 346/18 and 24, and 366/32 n. below. Perhaps a doublet of ambiguity, *uicioso uel uiscoso*

25 and brediþ . . . whelkes: et ulcerante

26–7 wiþ . . . ofte: pueris familiarem passionem

28–345 /1 for . . . faste: quia ad modum tinee superiorem cutis capitis corrodit substantiam et quasi inseparabiliter tenet eam

15, 17 icured and ihelid, ihelid and isaued: sanari, sanatur

18–19 but . . . þeraftir: quin semper post in capite uestigium relinquatur

23 is disesid: JT translates *patitur* thus in 344/26

32–346 /2 3if . . . humours: si accidit dolor ex humoris uicio sicut uel alteriusmodi humoris repletione

*2 in . . . hatte**

3 couenable: debitis et congruis

7–8 to . . . body: ut pori aperiantur et fumi facilius euaporent. JT paraphrases BA's technical term

9–10 þe hed: fronte, which JT normally translates *forehed*, but cf. 369/21 n. below

11 legges: tibias, also at 413/5 and 424/35, is more precise

17–18 fondiþ . . . aslepe: sompnum prouocamus   cf. 349/17–18

*19 a sponful**

30–1 3if . . . medicine: fortioribus si uis uti medicinis

347 *8–10 somtyme . . . holdinge: quandoque ex abundantia humorum per incontinentiam affluentium*

12 þristynge and wringinge out: comprimente uel exprimente. Cf. 347/7 *þristinge and wringinge* for *constringentis* and 347/23 *outþurstinge and wringinge* for *constringens*

23–4 3if . . . tokenes: IJKMOST *frigiditas constringens his cognoscitur signis* LNPQRUW om. sentence

31 beste . . . contrarye: ualent in contrarium

34 seþinge: decoctionem et subfumigationem

348 *6–7 Here . . . frenesie: furorem uocat frenesim*

13 by . . . pipes: per uenas neruos et arterias

15 to þe brayn: a corpore ad cerebrum

22–3 haueþ . . . colera: colere cooperantur

27–8 and þanne . . . isaued: et parafrenesis tunc curatur

349 *10 lest . . . woodnes: ne insania irritetur*

10–11 Al . . . scilence: silentium circumstantinus indicatur

26–7 of þe furþir . . . infeccioun: anterioris cellule capitis cum priuatione imaginationis sicut melancholia est infeccio   PT om. Without the emendation the sense is lost, but only a medical expert would be aware of this

350 *13–14 lotieþ . . . hidelis: in latebris latitant*

23–4 anoþir letter seiþ stupore: alia littera stupore 'in another verse (of scripture) *stupore*' or perhaps 'in another word *stupore*'. If *littera* means 'word', BA could still be referring to Deuteronomy 28: 28 (*Percutiat te Dominus amentia et caecitate ac furore mentis*), *stupore* 350/24 then being a misreading of *furore*. JT understands BA to be referring to another verse, possibly 2 Corinthians 4: 4 or Ephesians 4: 18

28 *30°: xxx* cf. the better KQ *xix* The reference is to Genesis 19: 11
31–2 *weyes of þe spiritis: uias spiritum in cerebro*

351 1 *compleccioun: compleccione* cf. the better KOS *opilatione*
3 *comelinge*: the only recorded occurrence of the word and perhaps a scribal creation. *comelinge and stonynge* translates *rigor*, which is translated *beueringe* at 387/
11 and 24, and *grillinge and beueringe* at 391/11 and 392/15
8 *a maner slepy slombirnes: sompniculositas*
18 *þristinge: oppressio*
20 *he raueþ and spekeþ vanite: loquitur aliena*
24 *þere ... disputesoun: loquentium et disputantium assit garulitas*
34 *it ... deeþ: mortale est*

352 4–5 *for ... aboute: qua omnia subito uidentur uolencia et tenebrosa*
5–6 *to ... imedled: nimia humorum habundantia cum uentositate mixta*. The function of *ny3*, normally JT's word for *uicina*, is not clear
14–16 *If ... wyne: horum remedium est medicina purgatiua et flebotomia si aliud non impediat pedes infirmi in aqua sunt ponendi a uino abstineant*
20 *Wakynge ... slepe: vigila est insompnietas*
31 *melk*: adds *perfundantur*
34 *et cetera*: i.e. Mark 9: 18. MQR add the reference

353 9 *doynge: effectu* cf. 343/3 n. above
10–11 *poure ... spiritis*: an awkward translation of *a regimine spiritum depauperantur*
16–17 *wiþ ... meuynge: cum priuatione rationis et diminutione sensus et motus*
22–3 *þe mouþ ... aside: obtorquetur os*
34 *certeyn: determinata* cf. JLQRW *deteriata* S *deteriate*

354 5 *stomak*: adds *non in concauitate sed in neruis eius et arteriis ipsius stomachi*
8–9 *þey ... cathalempcia*: IQ *cathalemptici* K *catilemptici* JOR *cathalentici* M *cathalemtisi* S *cathalentisi* U *cathalempsi* cf. LNPW *cathelentica* T *cathalencia*
9 *feliþ and knowiþ: presentiunt*. The doublet defines the meaning precisely: *feliþ* 354/10 translates *sentiunt*; *presentiunt* is also translated *beþ war* 354/18
35–6 *as ... axith: secundum humoris peccantis exigentiam*

355 3 *ibore and idronke: portatam et potatam* cf. NR *potatam* PQ *portatam* S *pertatam* U om. Apparently a doublet of ambiguity already present in Z
5–6 *þat is ... euel**
22 *corica: corica* NOR *colica* I *torica* K *thorica* S *coruza* T *coria* cf. the better QU *coriza*

356 10 *þat makeþ it stynte**
16 *meuynge of wood herte*: *agitationem furiose mentis*
17 *Constantinus ... rucciacio*: IKMQU *iectitatio* (as in Constantinus) cf. JLNOPRSTW *rectitatio*
19 *synewis: neruis spondilium* 'sinews of the vertebrae'
29–30 *owen wei3t*: AF *o wei3t* could be an apocopate form

357 1 *rennynge and hardinge: coagulans et constipans*
2–3 *þurle ... þerby: penetrare*
16–17 *þat beþ sore acolde: infrigidatorum*

18 *vttir*: U *extrinseca* cf. the better *intrinseca*

22 *and . . . sore**

358 8 *and wel ifedde, and gorels*: *ingurgitatis*

9 *schedinge*: *infusione* cf. OR *inflatione*

13–14 *if . . . yuel*: *febris superueniens soluit egritudinem*

21–2 *wiþdrawinge*: *diminutione*

359 1 *þe palesie comeþ of*: *est* (P *ex*) *simthoma*

16–17 *is . . . iholpe*: *penitus incurabilis est*

20–1 *medicyne þat neisschiþ and laxiþ*: *mollicatiuis et relaxatiuis*

21–2 *medycynes þat dryen and harden*: *desiccatiuis et constrictiuis*

360 3–4 *fleischlich . . . Venus*: *uenera uoluptate*

22 *and . . . hiჳe*: *capite alto dormiat*

29–30 *He . . . watir*: *balneis aque dulcis temperatis* (T *temperatiue*) *utatur* Z probably lacked *temperatis*

361 7 *hote*: adds *et dolor fortis*

12–13 *makeþ . . . hem*: *palpebras ingrossans et inuertens* (OR *inuectens*)

14 *as . . . fleissche*: *quasi carneas crudas facit*

23–4 *and . . . posteme*: *ex quo fit obtalmia dolor scilicet et apostema*

33 *depe*: *in profundum*

34–5 *þe kertil of þe yჳe þat hatte**

362 4–4 *philosophres*: *physici* cf. 554/9, 644/30

14, 15 *veynes, veynes*: *uenis* 'veins', *uenulas* 'small veins'

21 *experimentis and assaies*: *experimenta*

29 *defaute . . . in*: *incontinentiam*

34 *wanne*: *subalbidi uel liuidi* cf. 387/9–10 n. below

35 *comeþ*: adds *ex percussione et*

363 3 *confortinge*: *fomentum* Z *conformitiuum*

14–15 *and . . . wemmes*: *ex cataractis ex panno ex macula*

22 *defaute, defaute*: *uicio, defectus*

32 *membres and lymes*: *organorum*

364 3 *synewis*: adds *si enim fuerit*

16 *iჳe²*: adds *tunc enim non est pupilla spiritui uisibili peruia et ideo compactio est cecitatis in oculo inductiua*

23 *as it were*: IJMQSW *quasi* KLORUT om. NP om. phrase

365 13 *heuyþ it vpwarde*: *eleuat et suspendit*

13–14 *He . . . graspinge*: *undique palpitando et contretando manus dirigit*

17 *liþ*: *iacet uel sedet*

22–3 *betiþ and smytiþ and greueþ*: *uerberat et percutit et offendit*

36 *fikelinge and flateringe*: *blandiciis*

366 21–2 *dissoluyth and todeleþ*: *dissoluente*

22 *reueþ and constrayneþ*: *constringente*

31 *and also . . . þerof*: *et sanie effluente*

32 *and clemy*: *inuiscatis* cf. 344/24 n. above

34 *is sette in þe sonne*: *soli exponatur*

367 3 *wiþoute*... *betokeneþ*: *sine manifesta causa signum est*
4 *ere*: *capite*. Perhaps JT wrote *hede*
6 *Seche*... *toforehande*: *alias autem aurium passiones*
7 *is moche þing seide*: *sunt multa inserta*
9 *þe helpe is wiþ*: *insistendum est*, translated *men schal worche ferst wiþ* 367/14
11 *eren*: adds *non enim actu frigida debent auribus instillari*
15 *ripinge*: adds *deinde mundificatiuis*
20–1 *be*... *þerto*: *ibi fuerint*
27–8 *opir drawe*... *cuppe*: *et extrahatur*. JT's instructions on this topic are always far longer than BA's: cf. notes to 373/34 and 434/1 below
36 *at þis tyme**

368 2 *growinge of noseþrilles*: *ex naribus excrescens*
4 *he þat haþ þis yuel*: *poliposo*
8 *renneþ and comeþ*: *fluunt*
18 *and þis*... *place*: *que locum ulcerant et excoriant*
28 *and ido into þe noseþrilles*: *si naribus sint iniecte*
30 *ferst wiþ*: *precentibus* 'preceeding', translated *þat goþe tofore* 373/1
35–6 *in males onliche*: *in masculis*

369 4 *in þe lift noseþrille*: IK *per narem sinistram*   cf. the better *per partem sinistram*
6–7 *and somtyme nouȝt profitable**
9 *nouȝt good*: IK *non bonus*   S *nam non bonus*   cf. the better *nam bonus*
13–14 *Wheþir*... *euel*: *siue autem fuerit fluxus creticus siue sinthomaticus*. JT paraphrases the technical terms, cf. notes to 257/23, 342/23–6 above
15 *changinge of þe euel*: *crisis*
18–19 *þere þe sore is*: *pacienti*
21 *front*: *fronti*. See 346/9–10n. above

370 3 *be hidde*: *palliari*
4 *and*... *steuines*: *interpolationem non accipiens*   cf. 343/17–18n. above
5–6 *is*... *maner**
7 *or*: ABCDEFGH *by* may have originated from the scribe's reading *none* as 'noon'. See 724/9n. below
21–2 *somtyme²*... *whanne*: JT avoids the repetition in *quandoque uitio cerebri ex uitio cerebri quandoque*
22 *rewmatik*: *reumatizantes*

371 4–5 *lockinge, waging and meuynge*: *relaxationis et motus*
10 *dikkinge and þurlinge*: *tenebratione* 'boring'
14–15 *ipurgid*... *clensinges*: *debita purgatione purgentur*
29 *oþir of somme humour*: *uel humor*
30 *swelliþ*: adds *et sermo impeditur*

372 5 *imaginacion in mynde and resoun*: *imaginatione memorie et ratione*
12 *and¹*... *voys*: *dum enim ex siccitate exasperatur arteria asperitate sequitur inequalitas et ex inequalitate raucedo et uocis impedimentum*
14 *and¹*... *hoosnes*: *sequitur utrumque predictorum*
18 *into*: adds *tracheam arteriam*
19 *worchiþ þe same lettes*: *predicta operatur*
25–6 *þat*... *drye*: *ex frigiditate fistulas pulmonis*

36 *in þe cause*: *in causa*. JT does not usually translate *in*, cf. 347/28

373 4 *colde*: *calidis*   cf. the better NQ *frigidos*. The variant readings reflect scribal confusion between *frā* (*frigida*) and *cdā* (*calida*). The error recurs at 379/26, 383/16, and 393/13. Cf. a similar confusion between *siccitas* and *frigiditas* at 405/10, and between *humore* and *humiditate* at 400/16

15–16 *bitwixe ... drinke*: *inter tracheam arteriam et ysophygum*. BA's technical vocabulary is clearer than JT's, cf. 342/23–6n. above

19 *scharpe*: *acutissima*, cf. *harde* for *grauissime* at 388/24. The loss of the superlative may be due to JT. However, elsewhere he does translate it, using a variety of constructions: *þe more perilous* 395/25 for *periculosius*, and *þe more hardere* 418/1 for *difficilius*; *wel greuous* 399/6 for *grauissimus*, and *wel yuel* 388/22–3 for *pessimis*; *ful gret* 408/15 and 408/30 for *pessimas* and *grauissimus*. Cf. 382/31 n. below on the treatment of comparatives

33 *lettinge ... tonge*: *sanguinis extractio in quantitate multa incidantur etiam uene sub lingua*

34 *garsinge and coppinge or horninge*: *scarificationes cum uentosis*. Cf. notes to 367/27–8 and 434/1

374 2 *of breþinge*: *inspirandi et respirandi*

2 *asma*: adds *uel dipsma*

22 *emoptoicis*: *emptoicis*   (K *emothoycis*   M *emothoicis*   P *emoptortis*   T *semptricis*)   cf. the better INQRUW *emoptoicis*

24–5 *and*[1] *... longen*: *et hoc contingit in causis reumaticis et pleureticis et peripleumonicis*

375 1 *iclepid*: *indicari*   Z *diceri*

6 *bolnynge*: *subtumida*   cf. *bolnynge and swellinge* for *inflatio* at 405/14 and 33

7 *quyttir*: IK *saniem*   cf. the better *sanguinem*

8 *superfluite*: *multitudinem*

14 *mouþ*: adds *a cerebro*

16 *trauaile and ache*: *dolore*, which JT usually translates *ache*, as at 343/14 and 17. But cf. 344/12n. above

376 5 *flux*: adds *et cetera*

8–9 *And ... boccis*: *qui dum ulceratur*

11 *perfore ... and litil*: *quare paulatim calor intenditur*

19–20 *for ... closeþ*: *dilatat enim et aperit*

22 *while it is so vnstedefast*: *dum ita circinat*

28 *holownes of*: *concauitas secundum*

29 *fallinge*: *fluxus*

32 *Siche ... diet*: *talis est nutriendus dieta*

35–6 *be war ... flux*: *cauendum est ne nimis soluatur quia si fluxus accidit*

377 8–9 *þe firste**

15 *hat*: *fit*

23 *opene ne meue*: *dilatari*

23–4 *and simpliche meouynge*: *exiliter tantum moueri*

29 *sendiþ*: *mandatur*

378 8 *sleuþe*: *pinguedo*   (MQ *pigrido*   NS *pigredo*   OW *pingredo*)   cf. the better U *pigritia*

22–3 *And . . . modir*: adds *nimis repleti*
26–7 *þat . . . aȝen*: *reparatiua et resumptiua*
32 *whiche*: adds *cum aliis confortatiuis*

379 14 *more bodiliche þinges*: *solidis corporibus*. At 379/18 *solidis* is translated *sad*
15 *membres*: *ipsis membris*. Cf. 382/18–19 n. below
19 *likneþ*: *aptauit*
26 *colde*[1]: the emendation, based on JKLMNOPRST *frigida*, may not be justi-
fied, cf. QW *calida*   U *calido*   and 373/4 n. above
34–**380**/1 *þat . . . effimeron*: *effimera ab effimeron*
10–11 *betinge, meovinge, and stiringe*: *conculcatione*
15 *companye and onynge*: *colligantium*
18 *trauaile*: adds *precedente*
20 *tendiþ of and waxiþ strong*: *intenditur*. A doublet of ambiguity, *incenditur uel
intenditur*
22–3 *and is perilous*: *multum tamen periculosa est*
24 *And þis feuere comeþ*: *accidit autem*
25 *þe clift bitwene þe buttockes*: *inguine*
28 *fer*: *multum distans*
29 *vrine . . . clere*: *aliquantulum intensa*
32 *þis feuere is sone iholpe*: *hec de facili febris curatur*
35 *The . . . membres*: *ethica febris est que ledit solida membra*

381 14 *sorowe*: *tristitia ira*
16 *kynde*: *innaturalis*
21 *scarste*: *ablatione*, translated *benemynge* at 381/25
34 *etik*: adds *siue habitualis*

382 5 *wanne*: JLMOPRSTUW add *et*
18–19 *of þe maner of membres*: *ipsorum membrorum*
31 *esy*: *facilior*. The loss of the comparative may be due to JT, cf. 112/4. *fortiora*
translates *strong* at 396/20 (perhaps earlier *strenge*), *periculosior* translates *strengere*
at 399/21. Cf. 373/19 n. above
38 *telliþ*: *assignat*

383 4 *hit is excitid*: *saltem calor interius sopitus excitatur*
6 *a lymeston þat is ibrent*: *calcem viuam*
16 *hete*: the emendation based on *calor* may be unjustified. See 373/4 n. above
16 *If þey beþ vnhelid and naked*: *detecti*

384 5–7 *and*[1] *. . . humours*[1]: *ex calore extraneo et innaturali quocunque casu superueniente
quedam fit humorum perturbatio*
14–15 *and meoueþ and betiþ hitsilf*: *in se conculcatur*. See 389/21–2 n. below
34 *for . . . vnkynde*: *cum talis calor sit innaturalis*

385 1–2 *þat . . . rotidnesse*: *que omnia interiori corruptione uel putredini cooperantur*. Z
probably lacked *omnia interiori*
4 *comeþ*: *petit*
11 *conteyned*: adds *intra uasa scilicet*
16 *or discontinual*: *siue sint discontinue et interpolate*
20–1 *in dede*: *in effectu*   cf. 343/3 n. above

21 *þe secounde*: *secundo significatio est quod*
22 *wiþoute*: *intra*   cf. the better U *extra*
25 *þridde*: adds *significatio*
29 *i-ordeined*: adds *ad interiora*

386 6 *þe feuire*: *ipse febres*
9 *axes*: *paroxismos*. JT uses *accesse* to translate *accessio* at 386/6 and 21, and *afflixio* at 388/3
15–16 *and somme cotidiane comeþ*: *ut cotidiana aliqua est*
20–1 *and euery day axesse*: *singulis diebus accessio renouatur*
24 *turne*: *terminetur*. Perhaps JT wrote *terme nouȝt in*
28 *ȝelouȝe*: *uitellina*. See 387/9–10n. below

387 6–7 *þe forsaide* . . . *hiȝe*: *predicta signa non sunt ita intensa*
9, 10 *ȝelouȝe*, *ȝelouȝ*: *crocea, citrina uel uitellina*. JT had difficulty with BA's distinctions between the different shades and qualities of yellow. JT's *ȝelouȝ* usually translates *croceus*, as at 393/13, 397/17, and 407/6, but also *citrinus* 382/5, *citrinus uel uitellina* here, *uitellina* 386/28, and *croceus et citrinum* 425/7. His one attempt to specify a shade of yellow is *somdele ȝelouȝe* for *citrina uel subcitrina* at 388/19–20. Elsewhere JT's translation of colour words ranges from the effectiveness of 343/30 to the vagueness of 362/34
12 *wiþ hote*: *lento calore*
18, 20, 21 *double*: *composita* in 18 and 20, *dupliciter* in 21. JT regularly uses *double* to translate both *duplex* and *compositus*
29–30 *as* . . . *vneuennes*: *secundum etatem secundum temporis et nature qualitatem*. An abbreviated *n^c qualitatem* (as in JLMNOQR) probably led to Z *inequalitatem*

388 1 *by raþer and raþer comynge*: *per anticipationem*
3 *accesse*: *afflixionis*. See 386/9n. above
15 *wiþ grillinge and risinge of here*: *horripilatione*
19–20 *somdele ȝelouȝe*: *citrina uel subcitrina*. See 387/9–10n. above
24 *harde*: *grauissime*. See 373/19n. above
26 *iointis*: *coxarum*. See 412/36–7n. below

389 21–2, 22 *is ouersett, þat beþ imeued and ibete*: *conculcatur, conculcate*. Cf. 384/14–15n. above
27 *brenneþ and tendiþ*: *urit et incendit*
28 *veines*: adds *putrescit*

390 3–4 *bollinge outward*: *eminentia*. Probably JT wrote *bolninge*. Cf. 404/24n. below
17–18 *þat is toforehand isode*: *prima cocta et huiusmodi*
22 *helefulliche*: adds *sudore quandoque*
27 *it is*: *et*
32 *wiþoute warnynge, with beueringe or grillinge*: *sine typo* 'without intermittent fever'; *wiþ grillinge and wiþ beueringe* at 391/10–11 translates *rigore*

391 7 *But* . . . *continual*: *sed illud non summum summus est cotidiane continue*
11 *beueringe*: adds *precedente*
21 *tokenes*: *pronunciationes*. Elsewhere (e.g. 347/24, 351/32) *token* translates *signum*
34 *þat comeþ*: *surgens*

392 10 *arisiþ and stondiþ*: *subito eleuantur*

19–20 *fastidium . . . seiþ*: *fastidium bolismus uomitus et huiusmodi fastidium est immutatio appetitus ut dicit Constantinus*

393 13 *coold*: MSS *hote* for *frigidos*. See 373/4n. above

31 *Hete schal be comfortid*: *calidis confortetur*

394 3–4 *and haþ . . . humour*: *dominante aut existente cum humore*

10 *neþir membres*: *membrorum*

11 *certeyne veynes þat hatte*: *uenas*

16 *euel*: adds *scilicet quod*

22 *hery*: *lanuginem* 'woolly'

395 4 *and whan . . . reuelen*: *quibus contractis*

28 *sodeinliche*: *improuiso*

396 1 oþir . . . sikenes: *aut ui sinthomatis*

4–5 *and puttiþ . . . spuynge*: *fit eorum per uomitum expulsio*

9 *aboue forþ*: *per uomitum*, elsewhere translated *by spuynge* (e.g. at 396/22)

9 *is*: *fit ex*

397 8 *sich*: adds *et hec de uomitu dicta sufficiant*

21 *cause*: KSU *causa*   cf. the better *culpa*

22 *raueþ*: *alleuiatur* 'is relieved'. Z *alienatur*   cf. 351/20n. above

25–6 *of þe mouþe of þe stomake*: *orificii*. JT normally uses this translation for *os stomachi*

31 *it is curable*: *curetur*

398 2 *ventositees of þe wombe*: *uentositas*

12 *diaria*: this rubric (in ABCDEFGH) is misleading (*diaria* is discussed in chapter 51). KLMOPTW omit rubric, U is unclear after *de dolore*, JR *de dolore et tortura uenis*, NQS *de dolore ventris*

17 *fumositees*: adds *interclusa*

20 *bowellis*: adds *aliquando ex lumbricorum multitudine uiscera interius corrodente*

21–2 *þat . . . bowels*: *compassionem intestinis inducente*

399 25–7 *medicyne . . . posteme*: *medicina mediocriter refrigeratiua ratione febris mitigatiua ratione doloris maturatiua et mundificatiua ratione apostematis*

28–9 *bocchy, nou3t wel ihelyd*: *ulcerosus*

32–3 *scharpe at þe endis*: *acuti*

400 16 *moisture*: *humore*   cf. the better U *humiditate*. See 373/4n. above

19 *ache and turmentis and gnawinge*: *corruptione*. Cf. 1038/27n. below

401 10 *þat gut is þe bomme**: *bomme* normally denotes the external buttocks, and *þat gut is in þe bomme* would read less awkwardly

12 *haþ seuen maner causes*: *est septiformis*

12 *Constantinus*: *idem*

34 *nou3t passinge*: *lentus*, translated *slaw* at 408/33

402 2 *turment*: adds *sequitur*

23–4 *as . . . hatte*: *ut in*

25 *beþ þre diuers fluxis*: *inter se differunt*   Z *in ter* for *inter*

35–6 *hem . . . of*: *detruncatis*

403 21 *þat þe defaute is inne*: *peccans*. Cf. 412/26

31–2 *so*... *ende*: *sic emittitur*

404 1 *by doynge of kynde*: *sensu nature*

3 *as*... *dissenteria*: *sicut supradicta*

8–9 *þanne*... *dissenteria*: *potius dissinteriam induceret*

12 *wiþ blowen bolles*: *et ampulas*

13 *þat diaria*: *in diaria apparent*. Possibly JT wrote *þat comeþ in diaria*

22 *superfluite*: *superfluitates*

24–**405** /14 In this passage *inflatio* is given four different ME. equivalents: *swellinge* 404/33, *blowinge and swellinge* 404/24, *bollinge ande swellinge* 404/30, *bolnynge and swellinge* 405/14. *blowinge* and *bollinge* are probably scribal distortions of the better *bolnynge*. Cf. 245/13, 375/6, 870/10

405 10 *drynesse*: *frigiditas*   Z *siccitas*   see 373/4 n.

24 *wombe*: *uentrem et sifac*

25 *as a flaket oþir a botel*: *sicut uter aschis enim uter dicitur*

31–2 *for*... *tymbir*: *quia ad modum tympani sonat uenter*

406 8 *Twey þe firste maner*: *due prime spes*

8–9, 9–10 *confermed and irotid*: *confirmationem*

20 *Iawndis*: *hictericia siue aurigo*

24 *hatte somtyme*: *uocatur*

26 *ibrend*: *adusta*, left untranslated at 402/32

407 10–11 *for*... *lasse*: *omnia superiora sunt magis tincta et inferiora minus*. Z perhaps reversed *superiora* and *inferiora*

17 *bodiþ, bodeþ and tokeneþ*: *pretendit, signat*

18 *for licnesse*: *sui multitudinem*   Z *similitudinem*

32 *partye*: *partes*

408 10 *heuynesse, heuynes*: *grauedo, ponderositas*

24 *þe euel þat hatte**

28 *swellinge*: here, as at 414/3, 4, this translates *tumor(e)*. Cf. the use of *swellinge* to translate *inflatio* 412/9 and 14–15, and *tuberositas* 424/23

409 2–3 *of stones*: *lapidis uel arenularum*

4–5 *disauauntagis*: adds *scilicet*   .

8–9 *þe weyes beþ alle istoppid*: *ex toto*

10 *bladder*: adds *coagulatis*

14 *þicke*: *magis grossa*

18 *in*[1]... *side*: *coxe dextre partis si in dextro rene sit causa sinistre uero si in sinistro*

410 4 *grete superfluite*: *multa fit emissio superfluitatis*

9 *dronkelew bollers*: *bibulis ebriosis*

19–20 *wise*... *and redy*: *prudens*, also translated *good* 435/13, *wise* 436/11. Cf. the treatment of *cautus* 420/33 n. below

21 *moiste*: *nimis humida*

31 *De hernia*: the rubric is editorial, but cf. R *de hernia siue siphat*

411 2–6 *And*... *genytrace**

6–7 *it*... *hernia*: *contingit siphat*

15 *crienge*: adds *et huiusmodi*

412 14 *disposicioun*: *habitudine*

26–7 *and* . . . *blood*: *subtrahi debet sanguis et minui*

36–7, 38 *of þe hanche, of þe ioyntes and of þe haunche*: *coxe siue hanche, hanche*. JT translates *coxarum* as *iointis* at 388/26, 408/11

413 1 *colera*: *colera rubea*

3, 12 *cause*: J *causa*　cf. the better *ratio*

14–15 *and þe* . . . *destroye*: *et materia magis est compacta*

22 *replecioun*: *plenitudine*. JT normally uses *replecioun* to translate *repletio*, as at 342/10 and 346/1

414 4–5 *haueþ but litil fleische*: *spoliati sunt et denudati a carne*

10 *droppiþ doun*: *reumatizant*

415 3 *lest þe mater wexe hard*: *ne forte materia indurescat*

10 *seiþ*: adds *contingit autem membrum apostemari aliquando ex causa exteriori ut dicit Constantinus*

11–12 *of brekynge* . . . *busschinge*: *fractura et concussione*

13–14 *and puttiþ* . . . *oþir*: *quia mutuo se conculcantes*

416 1 *þe ordur of settynge of membres*: *suppositio*

3 *of*[1]: *ad*

5 *longen*: adds *et sic de aliis*

9 *and rotiþ*: *ebulliunt et plutrefiunt*

16 *colour*: JMQTUW *colore*　cf. the better *calore*

20 *matiere*: IKNOW *materiam*　cf. the better *naturam*

23 *þat* . . . *spekinge**

28–9 *superfluyte* . . . *wose*: *superfluitatis et limositatis*

417 3 *stronge*: *multus*. Cf. 417/36n. below

13 *to þe sight*: *uissibiliter*　cf. IJMNQTUW *insensibiliter*　K *uiolenter*　and the better R *sensibiliter*

20 *euel*: adds *et durissimus ad curandum*

34 *beþ many open holes*: *multa orificia inueniuntur et oriuntur*

36 *wide*: *multum*

419 15 *wyne*: adds *per os offeratur*　cf. N *offeratur*

32–3 *defouliþ* . . . *vnsemelich*: *defendant*

420 12 *skilfulliche*: *merito*

22 *þey were ifedde*: *alebantur*

28, 33 *kynde*: JKLPR *naturam*　cf. the better *materiam*

33 *redy*: *cautus*, translated *wise and ware* 436/11 and 437/5, *ware* 437/14; *caute* 367/25 is translated *warlich*. Cf. the treatment of *prudens* 410/19–20n. above

421 1–2 *Also* . . . *phisician*: *etiam nutrix uel medicus*

13 *an euel 'ful of greynes'**

26 *smale*: *liquide*

31 *wiþ*[2]: adds *prurigine*

422 27–8 *But* . . . *fury*: *serpigo de minus ignita*

423 3 *likynge and qualite*: *delectationem*, translated *likinge* at 393/7

10–11 *ful cresinge*: *complementum in fontibus siue*

11–13 *For . . . corrupt*: *nam corrupto humore nutrimentali de facili corrumpuntur membra que ex humoribus nutriuntur*
30 *hatte*: *hec proprie dicitur*

424 5 *þis euel*: *istam lepre speciam*
6 *place*: adds *et spoliari notabiliter consueuit*
28 *is*: *redditur*

425 12 *þat hatte allopucia*: *uero allopiciam*
20 *wiþ mony luys and wormes*: *squamositatem non modicam et pediculorum uermium multitudinem*
23 *oþir suche diseses þere beþ*: *huiusmodi*
28–9 *hit . . . rennynge*: *coagulatur*
35–6 *chapres, chines, and cliftis*: *scissuras*

426 7 *fleischly lygynge*: *accessu et coitu*
12 *of a leprous norse*: *mulieris leprose*   Z *nutricis leprose*
25 *if it be confermed*: *postquam perfecte confirmatur*
27 *of metis*: *nociuis*

427 3 *To hele oþir to hide*: *ad curationem*. A doublet of ambiguity, *curationem uel celationem*
8–9 *a . . . housbonde*: *ut patet in ceco*
10–11 *he*[2] *. . . clere*: *uisum recuperauit*
24 *smale*: adds *et mollibus*
36 *oynementis*: OR *unguentis*   cf. *apozimatibus*

428 5–6 *þat . . . toforehonde*: *superius nominatas*
20 *seiþ þere*: S *dicit ibidem*   cf. the better *dicit*
21–2 *of grete and longe*: *magnorum*
23, 24 *hooueþ, woneþ*: both translate *habitant*. *hooueþ* is perhaps a scribal creation
26 *is scharpere*: *deterius est et acutius*
29 *by cold tyme*: N *in frigido tempore*   cf. the better *in frigore et in frigido tempore*
32 *heuynesse*: *stupor*, which is not translated in 350/24, 25, 29, etc.

429 3 *kokatrice*: *reguli et basilici*
16 *dwelliþ*: T *moratur*   cf. the better *commoratur*
20 *depnes and closing*: *profunda clausio*
29 *girdinge of oþir brennynge*: *combustio*. A doublet of ambiguity, *circumuestio uel combustio*

430 6 *vltimo*: *ultimo*   cf. JLR *uel ultimo*   U *xviii*. BA probably wrote *penultimo*
18, 19 *wood*: *rabiosus, rabidum*. JT normally uses *wood* to translate *furiosus*, as at 348/12 and 430/34
22 *of þe bitinge*: *qui fuit infixum*
27 *colera*: N *colera*   cf. PRSW *calida*   and the better IJKLMOQTU *melancolia*

431 3–4 *and . . . also**
23 *herte*: adds *et epatis*

432 19 *and dreueleþ*: *et saliuam effluere fecerint*
24 *medicyne*: adds *primo*
28 *venym*: adds *et hoc tribus diebus*

433 1 *it is isaide*: I *Andromacus*   J *Andromancus*   O *Andronicus*   Q *Andromaticus*
W *Androniancus*   cf. the better KLMNRSTU *Andromanthus*. All MSS. add *dicit*
7 *venyme*: *uiolentiam ueneni*
9 *Galien*: *Constantinus*. The source is in fact Galen whom BA perhaps quoted in
the commentary of Constantinus; Z is most likely due to the confusion of an abbreviation
24–5 *citry vel tiriti*: *citri*. A doublet of ambiguity, *citri uel tiritri*, possibly present in
Z
37–**434**/1 *wormes* . . . *bloodsoukers*: *sanguissuge*
1 *and also cuppes and hornes*: *et uentosa*. Cf. 434/3–4 and notes to 367/27–8 and 373/
34 above
5 *garlik*: adds *et sale*
6 *And*: *cum predictis*
20 *laste*: R *vltimum*   cf. JO *utilimum*   Q *utilum*   W *summum*   and the better
vtilissimum
27 *þe asschen of hem*: *sub cinere*

435 11 *De medicina*: IKLMOT omit. The rubrics of this chapter and chapter 70 are
interchanged in NQU, as in all English MSS. Cf. S *de prudencia medici* and the
better JR *de officiis medicorum*
13 *good*: *prudens*. See 410/19–20n. above
24 *one* . . . *ȝouþe*: *etas puerilis*

436 19 *by hondlinge and gropinge*: *tactum*

437 3 *awelde*: *digerere*
6 *the state*: *statum pristinum*
20 *þan and þan*: *per interualla*

438 12 *þat sleeþ*: *mortificatiua*
17 *cureþ*: *primo curat*
27 *oþir þat smackeþ of aloe*: *alia aloata*   cf. the better IKNORS *alia* (IK om.)
alleata 'other compounds'. If Z read *aloata*, JT could have mistaken this to mean
'tasting or smelling of aloe'.

439 10 *beþ*: *latitant*
27 *swetnes*: *sua dulcedine*
29 *boystous*: *grossa*, translated *grete* at 409/1 and 412/31
32–3 *constreyneþ and stintiþ blood*: *restringunt specialiter sanguinem*

440 12 *mytigatiues, swaginge*: *mitigatiua*. JT perhaps intended *mytigatiues* 'swaginge'

BOOK VIII

441 5 accidentis] *fn.* A accident/tis
29 The] þe

442 1 licness   2 all   **443** 13 wiþout   **446** 20 worschip   **448** 10 last
457 3, 22 about
461 17 cold   **464** 28 aspect   **470** 12 long   **489** 34 bow   **493** 10 her
495 8 about   **496** 10 and[1]   **498** 9 ny3t   **501** 18 and **514** 25–6 certeyn
501 20 whateuer   **512** 29 byschinyng] *add final -e*

442 12 withoute] wiþoute
20 rounde   **461** 26 some   **464** 4, 5 stronge   **469** 5 grete   **480** 20 faire
488 25 noþinge   **496** 30 euene   **503** 21 a3enwarde] *delete final* -e

443 21 qualitee] qualitee[s]   *and fn.* ABDEFGHW qualitee   LS qualitatum
26 n. and] ⁊

444 9 *Genesis*] *Genesim and fn.* ABCFH genesis   ES Geñ   W Gen.   L gñ   S
Genes.
18 lowe noþir partykel,] lowe, noþir partykel
36 matiere of oon] *fn.* A of matiere o/on   E mater on

445 17 parties] partie *and fn.* A pties
2 n. pties] pties of erþe
16 n. A] AG   *add* LS digniores
28 n.[2] *increase space before* vertuos   ACF] ACDEF

446 5 wrecchidnes] *fn.* A wrecchidines
28 þarties] parties
1 n. F defini3tes] *delete*
4 n. of] of[2]
13, 14 n. *delete* 14 *and add new note* 14 he] ACFGH þey
14–17 n. ulstimum] ultimum *and insert after* not *within round brackets* 15 deceyueþ
and gyleþ] E *reverses* 16 playeþ] E lasteþ
23 n. ABFGH] ABEFGH

447 5 *aerium*] *aereum and fn.* A aerium
15 *etheros*] *ethereos and fn.* AEG etheros   L ethereos   S etheros
24 is] *read* [beþ] *and fn.* *ABCDEFGH is   W ben   *cf.* LS fixas
4 n. *add* E empereum
14 n. ABCDEFGH] ABDFGH *and add* C and þerfor þat
29 n. ABCFG im*per*eum H impereum] ABCH im*per*eum CF imperium DE
om.

448 1 ili*c*he] iliche *and delete fn.*
10 philosophrz] philosophres
33 mi3te] my3te

19n.[1] ABCDFGH one cause] ABCDH one cause   FG on cause   19n.[2]
ACF] AC

449 8 to] *add* [þe] *and fn.* A *om.*
18 noþeir] *fn.* A noþ'
29 i-ioyned] i-ioynede

450 16–17 more, as hit is seide toforehande. What] more. [For,] as hit is seide
toforehande, what *and fn.* For] ACFGHW *om.*   L quia   S et
19n. ACDEFGHW] ABCDEFGHW

452 9 meouynge] *m*eouynge *and fn.* A neouynge
16 pat] þat

453 33 inner] ner *and fn.* ABDEFGHW īner   *cf.* LS profundius

454 28n. co/contrey] cō/contrey

455 21 *quintum*] 5ᵐ
33 *metheorologicarum*] *metheorologicorum*

456 23 pe] þe

459 14 by þe signe] þe signe by

460 19 *Aristoteles*] *Aristotiles*

462 19 þridde gree] þr*e* gree[s] *and fn.* AF þridde gree   CGH þe þridde gre (C
degree)   LS gradibus tribus

463 22 befalle] bifalle
29 folewiþ] *fn.* A forlewiþ

464 9 þe[1]] the

466 11 þa[t] *read* þat *and delete fn.*
14 priuey] preuey

467 7 *Taurus*] *Taur*[*u*]*s and fn.* A taurs
10 sterris] sterres
30 Pollix] Pollux

468 16 þingis] þinges
31 *b*e] be *and delete fn.*

470 21 lite] liȝt

472 10 legges] leggis

473 1 prison] preson

474 13 a] an
34 þerfore] And þerfore

475 27–8 yuel. As . . . worchiþ, þey] yuel, as . . . worchiþ. þey

478 18 *natura*] *natur*[*i*]*s and fn.* A naturs
24 Beda] Bede. Also at 487/26, 497/9

479 2 and n. fullen[dip] *read* fullen[diþ]
16 isemed] ifeined
2n. fulfilliden] *add* CW fulfilliþ

480 13 þat is] þat is,
27 passen] pass*i*n[g] *and fn.* *ADFG passen   CHW passeþ (H *corrected from* passen)   LS discessus

481 19 teliers] telieres

482 10 warnyeth] warnyth
21 spicers] spiceres

484 2 Isidir] Ysidir

485 5 temperat] temporat

486 11 were²] *read* [ben] *and fn.* ACFGH were   W is   LS *lack phrase*

487 28 myddel] myddil

488 9 contraccioun] con*f*raccioun *and fn.* *ACDFGHW contraccioun   LS confraccione

489 20 hireself] hirself

490 2 rowndnesse] rowndenesse

491 8 her] hire

492 9 schadowe] schadewe

495 25 reuers] *read* þeues *and fn.* A reuers   C þeftis   LS predones
36 beþ] be *and fn.* AF beþ   CH ben   *cf.* LS sufficiant

496 35 mone] mo*n*e *and fn.* A mo/me   H *om.*   LS lune

498 4 Alphraganus] *fn.* A alpharag̃us
9 to²] *delete*

499 5 here] hire
19 semith] *fn.* A sem/mith
21 one] one [by] *and fn.* *ACDEFGHW *om.*   LS per

500 26 anotir] anothir
27 sercles] serclis

501 3 chaunginge²] changinge
21 tovs] to vs

502 8 vndirstondinge] *read* [line] vndirstonde *and fn.* *ACFGH vndir/stondinge D line vndirstondinge E line *cf.* LS linea quedam intellectualis

503 23 serclis] cerclis

504 19 *Orioun*] Iubiter *and delete fn.*

505 1 it²] *fn.* A it/it   34 Taurus] *Cancer and fn.* *ACDEDFGHW taurus
7 it] *h*i *and fn.* *ACDEFGH it   W they   *cf.* LS generant

506 24 Basilius] *fn.* A Basilianus
25 schulde be] *fn.* A schulde bemene ⁊ be

507 2 nounes] *fn.* A noū/nes
14 þat] þe *and fn.* A þat   DE *om.*   LS *lack phrase*
29 oninge] o*n*inge *and fn.* *ACDEFGH outinge   W ioynyng   LS coherenciam

508 4 imellid] imelled

13 come] come[þ] *and fn.* AFGH come   *cf.* LS relucentem

510 34 Calchidus] Calcidius

11n. ACDEFG] ACDEFGH

511 4 product] pro duct *and fn.* A ṗduct

18n. uppon] vppon

34–5 wiþ oᵽe[n] ... wiþ] *fn.* *ACDEFGH wiþoute ... wiþouten   *cf.* LS cum

... manifestacione cum multiplicione

513 17 li3t] ly3t

The English MSS. ACDFGH are complete, although D omits 443/17–5/2 and repeats 455/22–8/17 after 465/30. B begins imperfectly at 443/27 and ends imperfectly at 459/20. E lacks 473/18–90/29. De Worde's edition throughout Book VIIII is based on F. The Latin MSS. IJKLMNOQRSTUVWY are complete. P begins imperfectly at 444/35. X begins imperfectly at 481/9.

441 4 *of men*: de homine et eius partibus

33 *God*: adds *esse perpetuum*

442 32–3 *he puttiþ ... passide*: *cessit ... conuertit* 'passed ... he put'

443 14 *it ... of tyme*: *nondum fuerant tempora et temporum uicissitudines*

25–6 *þat ... fire*: *que modo per rarefaccionen manet forma ignis et est sub igne*

444 6 *For þe worlde haþ most nedeful*: JOT *summam enim necessariam habet mundus*   cf.
the better *summam enim et necessariam* ...

6 *in al itsilf*: *in suo toto* 'in its totality'

9–10 *possibilite ... schappe*: *passibilem ... speciem et formam*

11 *kynde*: LQV *naturam*   cf. the better *materiam* and 449/16n. below

21 *but ... pees*: *sed cum armonia est pars* (Y *et pace*) *summa*

22 *noble*: adds *secundum materiam* (MNRUY *naturam*   T *numerum*)

24–5 *þe more spiritual is þe matere*: (*illa pars mundi*) *que spiritualior est*

26 *takeþ, fongiþ*: Q *recipit*   cf. *reddit*. BA may have written *requirit*

445 19–20 *þan in þe neþere**

20 *at al*: *in universo* cf. 449/17n. below

23 *of charite*: JLMOPRTVW *caritatis*   cf. the better *claritatis*

32 *perlez*: *gemmarum*. Perhaps JT wrote *perrey*, cf. 851/2 *precious stone* for *gemma*

446 31 *is iseye in many maner wise*: *est multiplex*

447 18–19 *moost sotilnes and worchinge*: *subtilitatem et summam ... actualitatem*. Cf. 473/10–11n. below

22 *Beholde*: *intuere celum*, paraphrasing Job 35: 5

29–30 *on-maner-wise*: adds *et motum*

30–1 *as ... stone**

448 5 *bri3t, schinynge heuene**   7 *of ayres kynde**

10–11 *þe ouermest partye*: *conuexitate*, translated by *holou3nes and vttir roundenes* 452/6

12 *Exameron*: adds *primo*

30 *þe ... schipman sterre**

449 1 *þerof*: adds *superius et inferius*

5–7 *meoveþ . . . heed*: *oblique mouetur*

10–11 *Aristotel vndirstondiþ a certeyn lyne*: *uocat artistoteles quandam lineam intellectua-lem*. Cf. 457/22–3, 502/6–8

13 *and þat lyne he clepiþ axis**

16 *whanne*: JMPW *quando*   cf. the better *quoniam*

16 *kynde*: JLMNRTUVW *naturam*   cf. the better *materiam* and 444/11 n. above

17 *of alle*: *tocius scilicet uniuersi*

29 *to profite of lif of men þat abidiþ*: *ad utilitatem hominum propter permanenciam uite*

35 *hem*: *ea* 'those things'

35–6 *but þe roundenes bendiþ fro hemwarde**

450 12 *most*: *maxima*   cf. the better S *marina*

16–17 *as hit is seide toforehande**   21 *diuers*[1]*

17 *is more liȝt*: *superius est et* (IJLOTVY om.) *leuius*

23 *þere*: *idem*, i.e. Rabanus. Z *ibidem*

33 *nameliche in a point*: *saltem in puncto nullatenus*

36 *principle worchinge and doere*: *principium effectiuum*

451 14 *for þere is a middel point*: *cum sit centrum*

37–8 *and euen round**

452 7 *briȝtnes*: adds *dyaphanitatem siue transparenciam et perspicuitatem*

11–12 *temprith . . . noyse*: *acuta cum grauibus temperans*

16 *it is iseide þat it is ifounde*: *dicitur per se et sensibiliter inuenitur*

453 11 *by clere and sotile vertu of God*: *glaciali soliditate uirtute diuina* 'by their ice-like solidity through the power of God'

28 *clere*: adds *philosophantibus*

33 *more clergialliche and inner to þe ground*: *profundius*

454 19 *for hit is hard as cristalle, and for*: *non* (JLMNRT om.) *quia durum in summo dicitur sicut cristallus sed quia*

29 *for*[1]: PQRSTUY *quia* (JLMO *quod*   IKV *eo quod*)   cf. the better NW *quasi*

29 *it is al iclepid*: *sit dictum* cf. the better NPTUW *sic dictum*

455 6 *vttirmest*: *scilicet extremum* 'as being the extreme'

13 *in largenesse*: properly belongs to the following clause

27 *al þing þat brenneþ*: *omne inflammans et inflammabile*

34 *oon*: OVW *unum*   cf. the better *quintum*. JT may have written *oo vyſþe*, cf. DE *þe wyf*

456 11 *is ireuled*: MP *regitatur*   J *regicatur*   cf. the better *regiratur* 'spins'

29 *space of tymes*: *spaciis* 'spaces'

457 23–4 *be . . . anoþir þing*: *per mediam pilam spere*

28–9 *as . . . herre*: *sicut cardo ostii*

29–30 *croked inward*: *recurui scilicet circumflexi* 'turning upon themselves'

458 11 *armonye and acorde*: *stridor id est armonia*, cf. the better L *stridor et armonia*. At 478/33–4 *of chirkinge of noyse and armonye* renders *stridoris et armonie*

16 *meue*: adds *citissime*

25 *þe oþir*: *alius* 'another'

25–6 *þat . . . somer*'*   27–8 *and . . . schorte**

459 3 *of stentinge of þe sonne in winter** 4 *and daies wexiþ long** 25 *libro 3º**
21 *a souþ cercle*: *circulus meridianus* 'the meridian', cf. 489/3n., 497/26n. below

461 5–6 *passiþ no ferþer vpwarde*: *remocius non recedit*

464 8 *and þe norþerne hous*: *domus uero celi siue septemtrionis*
15 *þe fourþe*: K *scilicet leo et* (I *scilicet secundum leonem* QU *et* L *iii.* JMNOPRSTVWY om.). The *domus succedentes* are the second, fifth, eighth, and eleventh signs (Taurus, Leo, Scorpio, and Aquarius), cf. 463/27–30
19 *þe ferþe, þe v.*: *iiii. v* W *iiii. vi* cf. the better I *tercium*
22 *þe signe þat is iclepid þe sixte hous*: *viª domo uel signo*
27 *biholdiþ*: *dicuntur . . . aspicere*
29 *trinus*: *tercius* cf. DE *tercius aut trinus* and 465/8n. below

465 8 *tercius, and trinus also*: *tercius* cf. 464/29n. above
11 *þe nynthe*: QT *ixº.* cf. the better *xº.*
17–18 *enemite and imperfectioun*: *inimicicie et imperfecte* cf. the better IK *inimicicie perfecte*
34 *as it is seide*: T *sicut dictum* M *ut dictum est* cf. the better *sic dictum* antecedent to the next clause

466 2 *dayes of craft*: *dies artificiales*
4 *Mars*: adds *in xix. gradu eius est exaltacio solis*
9 *þe body and face croked*: *corpus curuum faciem obliquam*
19 *þe þridde*: *xxv.* (J *xx.* LO *xxvi.*)
29–30 *of þe triplicite he is þe secounde*: *de triplicitate est secunda* 'he is of the second triplicity'. Also at 469/19 and elsewhere

468 20, 21 *chaungiþ þe aier*: *mutatur aer*, as at 471/17. *chaungiþ þe aier* 472/18 translates *mutant aerem*

469 7 *of goode*: T *bonorum* cf. the better *honorum*
7 *And þis*: IJLTVY *et hoc* cf. the better *de hoc. and þis* 470/4 also translates *de hoc*, usually translated by *herof*, as at 470/26
8 *Ihelon*: Q *ihilo* cf. the better *abiron*
9 *þe nyntenthe*: O *xix.* cf. the better *xxx.*
34 *wiþ ham*: adds *de triplicitate est tercia*

470 10–11 *a balaunce, þat is**

471 3 *Draconis** 29 *gilful and wraþful**
12 *worschipe*: adds *ex magistratu*
30 *of quene*: O *regine* cf. the better *regni*
30 *of blisse*: *glorie*. JT takes 'glory' in the religious sense, cf. 510/17–18 *bodies þat ben blisful* for *corpora glorificata*

472 3 *Taurus*: cancrum cf. 505/34 and footnote
11 *glad and ioyful*: *gloriantem* 'boastful'
20–1 *and ȝeueþ hem a watirpotte*: *manibus eorum aquam infundens unde tenet urnam*
30 *þe fourþe*: *quarta* cf. the better U *tercia* and 462/4–5

473 5 *Orisoun*: *orison* (JO *ozizon*) cf. the better KQ *orion*
10–11 *þe priuey propirtees and vertues*: *proprietates et occultas uirtutes* cf. 447/18–19n. above

14 *schortliche*: adds *et pariter*

17–18 *conspect and si3t*: ILOTW *conspectus*   cf. the better *aspectus*

19 *diuers and wondirful*: *uarios et mirandos*, qualifying *conspectus*

21 *diuers: suas*

23 *errancia*: adds *certis ut dicit beda spaciis discreta ab inuicem et distincta que dicitur errancia*

474 5 *fiue and fourty*: *xlv.* (M *xv.*). BA wrote *lx.*, cf. 481/28

13–14 *on bisse lasse*: *bisse unius* (IK *bisemis*   W *bisenius*   P *semisse unius*) 'two-thirds of one', sc. *hore* 'hour'. Z *bisse minus*

19 *Miscalat*: properly in apposition to *philosophres*

25 *helpiþ*: *cooperantur* 'work with', cf. 504/24 *worchiþ wiþ þe sonne* for *soli cooperatur*

29 *Conable setting*: *aptacio* (L *aptaco*) 'repairing, restoring'

34 *Misael**: in apposition to *he*

475 9–10 *temporat, hoot*: *temperate calidi* 'moderately hot'

11 *drines*: adds *sol masculinus diurnus calorem et siccitatem operatur*

22 *nou3t . . . owne*: *quia non suis semper obsunt*

476 1 *spiritual lif*: *uitalem calorem et spiritum*

12 *Iupiter his vertue comeþ a3en*: *regnat iupiter iterum*, translating *uirtus Saturni tunc redit*

24 *Aries*: adds *et scorpius domus ueneris*, i.e. the houses of Mars are Aries and Scorpio, the houses of Venus Libra and Taurus

36–7 *þe signe þat hat**

477 22–3 *and first*: *et primus*   cf. the better IKO *inprimis*

478 14 *þe commentour*: *ptolomeus*

479 1 *perfectioun*: *immutacionis*   cf. 512/29 n. below

24 *yuel drye chines*: *ragadias id est fissuras*

25 *broun . . . scharpe*: *liuidi . . . asperi*

32 *he drawiþ out of his kyngdom*: *regnum abstrahit*   cf. the better Q *regnum abstrahitur* 'his kingdom is taken away'

35 *false*: *falsidicus*

36 *colour chaungiþ*: *mutat colorem*

480 21–2 *faire berde and round*: *barbamque rotundam*

481 8 *sterre*: adds *beniuole*

9 *firy*: *rutilans sicut ignis*

21 *chaungers*: *trapezete id est cambitores*

482 5–6 *þat . . . bri3t**   21 *and spiceres**

12 *ihid*: *absortus* 'swallowed up'

16 *only Venus socouriþ*: *soli succurrit*, i.e. Venus passes beneath the sun. Z *solis* qualifying the preceding *semitoniis*

34 *place*: *obsidis* (IK *assidis*), i.e. *absidis* 'circle'

483 2–4 *he . . . sonne*[2]: *in superiori parte sui circuli coniungitur cum uenere in inferiori uero conuenit cum sole* 'he is joined to Venus in the upper part of his circle but in the lower part he meets with the sun'

28 *semyth*: *uidetur*   cf. the better IK *dicitur*

28 *as Macrobius seiþ*: adds *secundum tholomeum autem* (IK om.).). Cf. 36–7 *Huc usque Ptholomeus*

32 *fortune*: *fortunium* 'good luck'

484 17 *and iliche swift**   18 *swifter or slower**   26 *þat is day and ny3t**
28 *oþir ei3te and fifty**
29 *tweye secoundes, oþir two and fifty*: NOPRVWX *duo secunda* (M *duo signa*)   KU *quinqueginta duo secunda* (IY *lii.*)

485 1–2 *of inwit and mynde and of resoun*: *mentis id est memoria* (S *memorie et*) *rationis*
7 *roundenes of cerclis*: *sperarum*
9 *made slily and wisly*: *ingeniauit*. BA probably wrote *igniuit* (as in Chalcidius)
11 *and he is mesure of al þat haþ lif*: *et* (OK *ut*) *numerus existeret omnium animancium*
18 *Dionysius*: adds *beatus*
22 *þe sonne**   38 *of worchinge**
22 *fediþ*: adds *custodit perficit et discernit unit et refouet*
24 *mynystriþ*: *uiuificat*   Z *ministrat*
26 *substaunce*: adds *seu essencia*
28 *þe foure*: *inferiora*
31–2 *withouten corrupcioun*: ILOT *incorruptibilem*   cf. the better *incorruptibilitatem*

486 3 *schinynge*: adds *et cetera nam uirtutem habet illuminatiuam*
11–12 *þat . . . welwid**   27 *of makynge of knowinge**
15–17 *And . . . moysture*: *ui sua attractiua quod semini et radici simile de illa humiditate attrahit*
27–8 *colours . . . schappis*: *colores et rerum species et figure*

487 6 *Aristotel*: *philosophus*
10 *for þe sonne comeþ to*: *usque ad*. Perhaps JT wrote *forto*, not *for*
18 *dayes*[2]: *ipsos dies*
22 *and þanne at vnderne**
24–5 *reed . . . erþe*: *ericeus id est rubeus secundus artricheus id est splendens tercius lampas id est ardens quartus philogeus id est amans terram*
32 *to comforte þe neþir þingis*: *inferiorum informatiuam*. Probably Z *confortatiuam*, as at 487/8, but cf. 453/2 *conformiþ* for *conformat*

488 10 *of þe body*: *obiecti corporis*, translated *of a body þat is aforn ham* 498/28, *þe body þat lettiþ li3t* 514/20, and 514/14 translating *corpus obiectum*
12 *þe science of**   38 *in quantite**
18 *Occean*: adds *ab ethiopibus cum aliis diis ad epulas inuitatus putauerunt enim antiqui calorem aquis occeani nutriri*
25 *þe sonne beme*: *uirtus solis*

489 3 *in poynt of þe souþ*: *in puncto meridiei* 'at high noon'. Cf. 459/21 n. above and 497/26 n. below
6–8 *for . . . sight*: *pre nimie enim claritatis intensione et excessu sicut eius quantitas sic et motus uelocitas subterfugit uisum nostrum*
13 *as it is seide*: IKPQUVY *ut dicitur*   cf. the better *ut dicit ambrosius*
14–15 *modir of alle humours, mynystre*: JLTW *mater tocius humoris ministra*   cf. the better *mater roris humoris ministra*

29 *and vpwarde**

490 1 *half ful*: *per medium secta* 'divided in the middle'
3 *is bischine atte fulle*: *ex toto est plena* 'is entirely full'
6 *is next to þe sonne*: *accenditur* 'is combust'. Cf. 491/25–6n., 497/3–5n.
13 *voyde*: i.e. of light, cf. *uacua . . . lumine repleta*
19 *mone*: adds *et eius decrementum est detrimentum ut dicit marcianus*
27 *Macrobius*: *marcianus macrobius*. Marcianus is the authority for the preceding statement, Macrobius for the following one
29 *þe mone*: *crescentis lune*

491 5, 12–13 *seuene . . .houres*: *xxviii*. (L *xxvii*.) *dierum, xxviii*. (LT *xxuii*.) *diebus*
25–6 *whanne þe mone chaungiþ*: *quando de nouo accenditur* 'when it is first combust', i.e. at the new moon. Cf. 490/6n., 497/3–5n.
27–8 *and . . . zodiacus**

492 5–7 *for . . . þerþe*: *quia non semper* (IJLMOPRTWXY add *est*) *in eadem linea que inter solem et terram dyametraliter est opposita solari corpori se opponit*
9–10 *makeþ . . . sonne*: *emittit sol umbram tumoris terre in lineam sibi oppositam*, i.e. the sun sends forth the shadow of the earth in a line perpendicular to its own diameter
21 *is reboundid*: *resultat* 'is produced'
28–9 *and of wedres**

493 2 *and of roundnesse of heuene**
12 *a goddes*: *dianam*   Z *deam*   Also at 916/1

494 5 *dredeful*: *terminabiles* (U *terrabiles*) 'determinable' Z *terribiles*
23 *made*: *dicitur composuisse*
34–5 *lesiþ . . . perfeccioun*: *perdit lumen suum et suam prodit* (JPTY *perdit*   X *percipit*) *deformitatem et defectibilitatem* '. . . betrays its ugliness and imperfection'

495 1 *a foule spleke and vnsemeliche*: *maculam et deformitatem*
4 *and*[1]: adds *minorem uersus celum obtinet claritatem et quanto plus proficit et crescit uersus terram*
10–11 *and somme a webbe opir an perle*: *siue orbum* (Y *morbum*) 'blind'
14–15 *passinge . . . eiȝen*[1]: *accessum* (JKLMOPQTUV *excessum*) *lunaris humiditatis*. A doublet of ambiguity, *accessum uel excessum*
22 *wyndis*: adds *preterea* (MNW om.), beginning the next sentence
28 *of þe puple*: O *in populo uel bello* (R *in bello*   IJLTVWX *in ipso*)   cf. the better *in x°*. with the next clause
35 *hem þat haþ þe fallinge euel*: *lunaticis et caducis*

496 12 *And*: X *et*   cf. the better *ut*
17 *in þree grees*: *gradibus totidem*
35–6 *in*[1] *. . . signe*: *in coniunccione debet fieri solis et lune quoad idem signum* 'in conjunction an eclipse of the sun and moon shall take place in respect of the same sign'

497 3–5 *chaungiþ . . . chaungiþ noȝt neiþer haþ coniunctioun alwey*: *accendatur . . . non semper accenditur* 'is combust'. Cf. 490/6n., 491/25–6n. above
10 *of kynges*: *regis*
12–13 *so bysette wiþ blasinge lemes*: *comatice* 'comet-like'

13–14 *it . . . meuable*: *permanent immobiles sicut* (NPY *siue*) *fixe* 'they remain immobile, like the fixed stars'
17–18 *also 'Wateling Strete'**
20 *seuen*: *viii.*
26 *by þe southe*: *ad meridiem* 'to the meridian', cf. 459/21 n., 489/3 n. above
36 *by . . . sterris*: *secundum opposicionem aliquarum stellarum corpora*   cf. the better INUX *secundum opinionem aliquorum stellarum corpora* 'according to the opinion of some the bodies of the stars'

498 6–7 *in fairnesse, clernesse*: *pulcrioris claritatis*
8 *sterris*: *stelle siue sydera*
15 *and bischine*: *illustrant omnia*   cf. the better Q *illustrantur*, translated *ben bischine* at 485/11
17 *Plato*: *platonicos*. Cf. 453/14–15
23 *in subiect*: *subiectiue* (LQ *substantiue*) 'in themselves'
31 *rounde*: *sperice et rotunde*

499 5–6 *and³ . . . opir*: *uniformiter*
8 *comynge and risinge*: JLNPTY *ortu et occursu* (V *cursu et occursu et ortu*), cf. the better *ortu et occasu* 'rising and setting'
14 *nygh*: *uicinius* (LP *uicinus*) 'more closely'
15 *þe seuene sterris*: *pliadibus*. Cf. 505/29
16 *þat is 'Watling Strete'**   19 *þan ellis**   24–5 *for² . . . lesse**
25 *For*: adds (not JLT) *ut*
25–6 *þe . . . heed*: *quanto sunt cenith capitis nostri magis uicine* 'the closer stars are to the zenith'
31 *A poynt*: *aliquid* 'something'

500 7–9 *weneþ . . . yȝe*: *putat . . . omnino uidere in alio scilicet in lumine uiso quod non est in altero sed potius in se ipso*
10 *as*: *idem* (S *item*   W *idem ut* O *prout idem*)
10 *toforehonde*: adds *de uisu*, i.e. Book VII. 19, but the phenomenon is not mentioned there
12 *tones and acord of musik*: *toni musici* (O adds *et*) *concentus* 'tones of musical harmony'
30 *þat þey metiþ*: *per quas transeunt*
35 *of vneuenesse*: *ex dispari altitudine*
36 *arisinge*: adds *uel ex eleuacione siue depressione climatum in quibus occumbere uidentur*

501 4 *and cuntrees**: cf. 515/2 n. below
10 *triplicite*: adds *ad triplicitatem*
17 *þat ben in heuen*: IJKLMQSTVW *que aplanes habent* 'which are fixed'
20 *ȝere*: adds *et cetera*
21 *For*: JLNPTW *quia* (Q *quod*), cf. the better *quando*, modifying the previous clause
27–9 *schineþ . . . schinyth*: *pollet* (W *pallet*   Y *apparet*) *et relucet . . . pollet* 'rules over'. BA's copy of Isidore XIII. 5. 5 may have had *pollendo* (as in line 29); cf. the better *poliendo* 'polishing'

502 5 *al*: *tocius*, qualifying *firmamenti*. Z *totus*
25–6 *and . . . Wayne'**   32–3 *þat . . . Wayne'**

35–6 *a signe þat hatte Vrsa*: *arcton id est ylicen* (T *elycon*   Q om.) *ursam*

503 9 *and istoppid**
19–20 *out of siȝt*: *ad ima* 'to the bottom'. The phrase is twice omitted in translation after *gooþ donwarde* in lines 21 and 22
27–8 *falliþ . . . Draco*: *draco ad modum fulminis* (ORTX *fluminis*) *elabitur*
34 *dymme*: IK *nubilosus*   cf. the better *nimbosus* 'stormy'. Z *umbrosus*
35 *hugenesse*: *inundacione*   Z *immensione*

504 6 *briȝtnesse*: *fulgoris sui pulcritudine*
7 *þilke þre signes*: *totam . . . illorum trium signorum superficiem*
19 *Iubiter his*: OR *iouis*   cf. the better *eius*. DE *orion* is presumably a scribal conjecture. Cf. 727/30n. below
30 *qualite*: adds *ut dicit marcianus*
33 *libro iii°**   36 *and ischad and iturned**

505 1 *as it were 'soukers'**   16 *for þey beoþ many**
11 *and*: *que* 'which', referring to *sterres*. Perhaps JT wrote *þat*
16–17 *and distinguid atwinne*: *ab inuicem tamen sunt distincte*
19 *is isene schine . . . þat*: *latere uidetur quia* 'seems to lurk . . . for' Z *que* for *quia*
23 *þilke seuene sterris**   26 *god**, *þe goddas**   29 *þe seuene sterris**

506 5–6 *laxatif medicyne*: *farmacie* 'drugs'
13 *schulde woose and passe out*: *euaporaret*
17–18 *ȝif . . . tyme*: *si (W si enim   IY nec   K et) calor aeris tunc* (NWX *cum*   R om.) *est* (U *sit*) *fortis*.   Z *si calor aeris non est fortis*
28 *substance*: *ypostasim id est substanciam*

507 2 *liȝt*: adds *siue irradiacio defluens a substancia lucis*. Cf. 512/1–2
3 *is i-oned*: IJLOTX *unitur*   cf. the better *innititur* 'is based'
9 *liȝt¹*: adds *naturaliter*
12 *but þerinne**   14 *wiþ þat wynde**
15–16 *þe aier meoveþ nouȝt sodeynliche*: *moueri subito non conuenit aeri*
26 *þe conteynynge*: *superficiem*, translated by *vttir partie(s)* in lines 27–8 and 36, cf. 442/7. Its translation here may be prompted by *conteyned* in the next clause

508 10 *priuey*: *diligentem* 'exact, precise'
15 *þe liȝt**
16 *while þey ben þere alle ifere*: *totis inconfuse* (R *confuse*) *inuicem contemperatis* 'although all are joined together without confusion'
17–18 *While . . . distinctioun**
22 *liȝt*: adds *et cetera*
31 *verrey*: *uere* (R *uera*) 'in truth'

509 3 *alle bodies wiþ soules*: *omne corpus animatum*
8 *chines, holes, and dennes*: *uisceribus* 'bowels'. Z *interioribus*
20 *þe sonne*: *solari corpori*
28 *formal*: *penitus formalis*
35 *in kynde*: S only *nature*

510 1, 2 *bicause of*: *ratione* 'with regard to'
3 *meuiþ to his owne forme*: *habet ita moueri ad locum sicut ad formam suam* 'has to move to a place as it were to its own form'

10 *in parties*: *in sua essentia*

11 *place*: *actu* 'actuality'. Cf. *in dede* 486/7, 509/31 for *ad actum*, *actu*. *Z situ*
18 *as . . . heuene**: cf. 471/30n. above

511 2 *gendriþ²*: *simul gignitur et generat* 'is simultaneously generated and generates'
3 *and liȝtneth forþ** 3–4 *þat is product**
5–7 *of heuene . . . worchiþ diuers effectis*: *colorum* (JLMNPTWX *celorum*) . . . *effectiua*
'producing colours'
6 *and clere liȝt*: *perspicui* 'transparent', with *a moist bodye*
10 *bringiþ in*: *tribuit et inducit*
21 *þe liknes of siȝt*: *uisibilem speciem* 'visible appearance'
29 *liȝt²*: adds *sine alterius nature commixtione*

512 1 *eueryche** 8–9 *and . . . reflexum**
11–12 *and¹ . . . fongiþ liȝt in hitself*: *quod non est omnino densum uel durum recipit lumen
in se*. An extended paraphrase
21 *eiȝen*: adds *occulis lippis et infirmis est lumen odiosum et molestie illatiuum*
27 *of alle bodyes*: *omnium subiectorum* 'of everything placed before it'
29 *perfeccioun*: *immutacionis* 'changing'. Cf. 479/1n. above
32 *as cristal is and ayer**: cf. 507/21–2
32–3 *into al suche a matiere*: *per eam irradians*

513 1–2 *þanne . . . worchinge*: *illic habet obscuriorem distributiuam apercionem* (KN
operacionem) 'there it has a fainter opening out and distribution'
2 *For*: *sicut enim* 'for just as'
3–4 *and¹ . . . wiþoute*: *quod totum* (PRW *et totum*, cf. the better U *ita cum*) *se effudit
extrinsecus apparet obscure* '(just as when it shines into thick matter it is imperfectly
received,) so when it shines out it seems dark'
13 *Beda*: N *beda* (JPQRST *ba* Y *b'a* W *þa* V *ralb*), cf. the better *basilius*
18 *but aslynte, and blenchiþ*: *sed obliquat motum suum*
20–1 *fro þe body of liȝt*: *a suo principio* 'from its source'. *body of liȝt* translates *corpore
luminoso* in lines 14 and 17 above
26 *a streiȝt beme*: *perpendicularis*
28 *opir aȝenwarde*: *et quandoque ad partem oppositam proici* 'and sometimes cast in
the opposite direction'

514 2–3 *Alwey . . . sodeinliche*: *ex subito semper motu radiorum et continuo*
6 *betiþ eueryche opir*: *mutuo conculcantur*. Perhaps JT wrote 'betiþ down'
18 *þat lettiþ liȝt**
20–1 *þe body þat lettiþ liȝt*: *corpore obiecto* (LMNOPQTV *subiecto* Y *obiecto uel
subiecto*) 'the body placed before it'. Cf. 515/14–15n. below
21–2 *as-a-schielde-wise . . . forþwarde*: *in acutum et in conum*
24 *þat is 'ischape as a schielde'**
28 *þe spere of þe erþe*: *tumorem spere* (IK *terre*). Cf. 492/9–10 *þe greetnes of þerþe* for
tumoris terre
31 *euene . . . sonne*: *opposita soli*

515 2 *and contraie**: cf. 501/4n. above
4–5 *barainnesse*: adds *et fecunditatis* (UY *infecunditatis*)

5–6 *and keleþ . . . hote*: *estuancium et itinerancium refrigeratiua*

7–8 *and smytiþ . . . horriblenesse*: *timoris et horroris multiplicis* (P *multis*   cf. the better IKX *malencolicis*) *incussiua*

10 *reste*: *inquiete*   cf. the better U *quieti*. Z *quiete*

14–15 *þe body þat makeþ it*: *obiecti corporis*. Cf. 514/20–1 n. above

BOOK IX

517 4 ysette] *fn.* AFGH ay sette   C euere set   W alwey set   LS inflammatur

518 30 tyme] tymes

519 27 comeþ] *fn.* A comeþ comeþ
28 heruest] *fn.* A herue/est
21 n. 21] 20

521 15 and] *delete and fn.* *ACDEFGHW and   *Invert commas round phrase*

522 14 also. And] also and

523 12 and] *read* and [is] *and fn.* *ACDFGHW and   E and isette   cf. LS distat
15 springinge] *add* [tyme] *and fn.* *ACDEFGHW *om.*   cf. LS tempus uernale
29 n. 29] 30

524 4 muche] moche
10 *commento*] *fn.* ACFHW cōmentor   LS commento
20 hidiþ] hiʒ[t]iþ *and fn.* ACFGHW hidiþ   LS renouat
24 greennesse] *fn.* ACFGHW greetnesse
16 n. 16] 17 *and add* CEG nedeli þe   D nedeliche a   H needly sich a   *cf.* LS necesse . . . est . . . abortire

525 18 eft] oft *and fn.* ABCFGHW eft   *cf.* LS generare et inducere consueuit
36 exalaciouns] *fn.* A exaltacioūs

526 4 moisture] moistuþ *and fn.* *ABCDEFGHW moisture   LS rigat
34 qualite] qualite[s] *and fn.* *ABCDEFGHW qualite   LS qualitatibus

527 8 and²] as *and fn.* *ABCDEFGHW and   LS ut
33 lastiþ] *fn.* A last/tiþ

528 2 coldnesse] colde *and delete fn.*
6 ben] *fn.* *ABCEFGHW is   D *om. sentence*   *cf.* LS adnichilantur
16 erþe] *read* e[i]r *and fn.* *ABCDEFGHW erþe   LS aeris

529 11 same] *add* [poynt] *and fn.* *ABCDEFGHW *om.*   LS punctum

531 28 is] *read* [for] *and fn.* ABCFGHW is   LS propter
28 and²] *delete and fn.* ABCFGHW and   LS *lack word*

532 20 þat tyme] *delete with preceding point and fn.* *ABCDEFGHW þat tyme   LS *lack phrase*

534 9 ackornis] ackorns
10–25 *fn.* DE *lack chapter*

535 11 calender] *fn.* A calend/der
27 *neomene*] *fn.* A neominie
30 departing] departin[g] *and fn.* ACFGH departid

536 2 lasse] laste *and fn.* ACFGHW lasse   LS finalis
15 ner] *fn.* ADEFGH neþir   W nerer of   *cf.* LS accessum solis et recessum
13 n. *add* LS enim

537 1 sendiþ] *read* s[ch]endiþ *and fn.* *ACDEFGHW sendiþ   LS diffundit
14 *b*e liʒtiþ] *a* liʒtiþ *and alter fn.*
18 iclepid and] *delete and fn.* ACFHW clepid and   *cf.* LS assimilatur
32 *diluculo*] *fn.* ACDEG diliclo
33 *diluculum*] *fn.* ACDEG diliculū
37 digestioun] *fn.* A digest/tioū

538 7 worlde] *fn.* A wo/orlde
9 many] *read* [iiii.] *and fn.* *ACDEFGHW many   LS iiii
24 sone] *read* sone[re] *and fn.* *ACG and sone   DEFGHW and som
LS facilius
6n. *add* LS quia tunc

539 11 and¹] a*s and fn.* *ACDEFGHW and   LS sicut
17 tor este] to reste
29 restid] *fn.* A rest/tid
33 of¹] *read* [and] *and fn.* ACFGHW of (A of/of)   *cf.* LS est *and delete existing footnote*

540 2 of¹] *read* [and] *and fn.* ACFGHW of   *cf.* LS est

541 22 feste] *r*este *and fn.* ACFGHW feste   LS quiete

544 11 wepenene] *fn.* ABCFGH wepene now   D wepen mowen   LS armis
27 fasting] *fn.* *ACDEGH *om.*   FW our   LS ieiunio
34 impugnaciouns] impugnaciounis
35 pryue] *fn.* A pry/yue
35 is²] *fn.* A is is

545 11 of²] *read* [and] *and fn.* ABCFGHW of   *cf.* LS est
29 in] *read* [an] in *and fn.* *ABCEFGH in   D *om. sentence*   LS et per
29 and] a *and fn.* *ABCEFGH and   D *om. sentence*   *cf.* LS ostendit

546 2 *passio*] *fn.* A passioū
10 þerof] þe roþ[er] *and fn.* *ABCDEFGHW þerof   LS agnum
21 See] see by a columpne of fyre þat wente byfore *and add to fn.* precedente columna ignis et nubis

547 2 figures] figure and [lyknes to] *and alter fn.* *to* AFG figures and   BH into
LS figura

548 11 priuylege] preuylege
20 seintis] *put square bracket after* ihalewid *and add to fn.* et merore quamuis sanctorum passiones
27 hatte emperour] haþ emper*e and fn.* *ABCDEFGHW hatte emperour   LS habebet imperium
28 writ, of] writ [and] *and fn.* *ABCDEFGHW writ of   *cf.* LS scripturarum
34 þe pascale candele iblessid] and þe pascale candele is ifette to be itend and þan arered and *and add to fn.* benedicitur et ad accendum paschalem cereum custoditur deinde cereus paschalis erigitur et
4n. *add cf.* LS unctionis
7n. *add* LS in

549 35 turnyþ] *read* turnyþ *and fn.* A turnyp
7n. *add* LS in qua

550 22 *heleden*] *read* he *h*[i3t]*ed and fn.* *ACDFGHW *heleden*   E *heled heled* LS *ornauerunt*

The English MSS. ACDEGH are complete. B begins imperfectly at 524/29. De Worde's edition is based throughout Book IX on F. The Latin MSS. IJLM NOPQRSTUVWXY are complete. K lacks 526/13 to the end of the book.

516 15 *and þat meovinge is incorruptible*: *ex incorporali* (I *incoruptibli*   KPR *corporali* O *in corrupibili*)

22 *round windid*: *spericus* and cf. 519/2–3. JT perhaps wrote *round windinge*

25–6 *þat trendiþ rounde aboute*: *circularis quandoque mutat locum. circularis* has been attracted to the preceding *partes* after the rest of the clause has been lost.

28 *for*: *aut enim*. JT probably wrote *or for*, cf. 519/32

517 27 *3if þow . . . clene*: *si vis helleborum ducere moue corpus.* Repeated at 947/20

30 *vttir roundenesse*: *circumferentia*, translated as *roundenesse* 516/28, 517/29, *vttirward roundenesse* 647/13. *vttir roundenes* translates *conuexitatem* 452/6, *superficies* 477/4–5

518 2 *meovable*: *mutabilium*, generally translated as *chaungeable*. Z *mobilium*

4 *and no mo*: JLMORV *non plura*   cf. the better *uel* (X *in*) *plura*

7–8 *passiþ wiþ . . . and biginneþ þerwiþ*: *incipit*

13 *whanne hit . . . lassen*: *quando incipit deficere incipit decrescere* (QS *crescere*). If Z lacked one *incipit* the emendation is unjustified

21 *and so . . . ny3te**

28 *apeireþ*: *inmutat*. Cf. 249/3n.

31 *temperat*: *moderato . . . et . . . temperato*

36 *contynued*: QS *continue*   cf. the better *contigue*

519 4–5 *þat is sixe houres**   15–16 *and þat 3ere is**

7 *as it were*: *quasi*   cf. X *eo quod quasi*   IKQS *quia quasi*

16 *first*: properly qualifies *place*

28 *wintir*: *uere*. Perhaps JT wrote *lent* unless Z read *ieme*. Cf. 127/12

32 *for²*: *uel quia*. JT probably wrote *or for*. Cf. 516/28

34 *aboue oure wonynge place*: *in nostro emispherio uel in inferiori*. Cf. 535/16

520 7–8 *for in eueryche . . . dayes**

19 *comeþ*: NPRTUX *emissarum*   cf. the better *omissarum*

23 *twies*: adds *in februario*

24 *bisse of momentis*: *bisse* (ORT *bis sex*) *momentis*   Z *bisse ex momentis*

25–6 *þritty ny3t*: Q *xxx noces*   cf. IJLMNRSUX *trigenta t'entes* (N *t'entos* X *t'ennos*)   KT *xxx trientibus*   O *tentes*   P *tricentos*

32 *same*: S *idem*   cf. the better *aliud* (MN *alium*)

521 2 *chaunge to chaunge*: *illuminatione ad illuminationem*   cf. a similar translation at 529/17–18. Z *mutatione ad mutationem*

12 *ouertake*: MSS. *þenne take*   cf. *consequatur.* The emendation is tentative cf. *consequimur* 'we getiþ' 544/20, *consequitur* 'comeþ' 693/16

22 *comounliche þe 3ere*: cf. *annus solaris communis.* JT perhaps wrote *þe comoun 3ere of þe sone*, cf. 520/13. *comounliche* renders *uulgariter* 547/16

23–4 *þe prime . . . and also þe age þerof*: *etatem*

30–2 *And in . . . on mone**
34 *embolismalis*: adds *ex illis xi diebus in quibus superat annus solaris lunarem*

522 1–2 *for þanne . . . dayes**   3 *sixe in al**   6 *þat makeþ . . . dayes**   8–9 *þat is . . . dayes**
     10, 11 *cicle*: IJLNPU *ciclus*   X *siclus* (i.e. the abbreviated form without the suspension bar through *l*) of the better *circulus*, regularly translated *cercle*. *O.E.D.* sub *cycle* mistakes JT's form here
     11 *of þe mone*: cf. *embolismalis* (JL *embolis*   S excised)   Z *lunaris*
     12–13 *in eueryche þerof . . . lunaciouns**
     23 *Also ouer al*: cf. *preter annum autem*. The ME. phrase, however emended, looks suspicious and may be due to a false expansion in Z, *preter omnem preter annum autem*. JT translates *preter hoc* 'and ȝit more' 540/13, *preter hec* 'oþir þise' 459/10

523 17 *eiȝtþe*: *xviii.* Perhaps JT wrote *eiȝteneþe*
     17, 19 *seuenthe*: *xvii.* Perhaps JT wrote *seuentenepe*
     21 *Iuyl*: *Iulii.* BA presumably wrote *Iunii*, but the error recurs in all Latin prints

524 6 *rootiþ*: JT perhaps wrote *rotieþ* 'rots', as at 527/8
     26 *tyme of*: adds *agriculture et laboris*
     36 *brediþ*: a paraphrase of *semen proiicientibus*, more literally translated at 530/13

525 31–2 *makeþ . . . holes*: *exasperat et indurat*
     37 *moisture and by vapoures*: *humiditatis euaporatio*

526 3 *fediþ*: adds *et satiat*
     4, 5 *he . . . he*: scribally confused pronouns, i.e. summer . . . herbs. JT probably wrote *a . . . he*, cf. *generat . . . arescant*
     20 *binymeþ*: *amputat et precidit* (OPT *prescindit*   SU *precindit*)

527 17 *cooldnesse*: A *coolnesse*, a genuine variant form but not, on the collated evidence, JT's form, cf. 528/2 and fn.
     25 *signe*: *prima parte*. JT perhaps wrote *firste parte of þe signe*
     26 *is ende of*: JT perhaps wrote *is þe ende of þe*, cf. *est finis descensionis*

528 22 *as þey doþ in somer**
     27–8 *tymes of wyntir*: *horis*
     30, 33 *sekenesse*: here and often elsewhere a plural form, cf. *passiones, infirmitates*

529 4 *þan þe meuynge of þe mone**
     12 *ii. partyes of an houre*: *bisse hore*. A period of six hours is meant, cf. lines 14–15
     16 *and viii. houres*: *xii. uero bisse spacium supplent unius hore integre ex quo patet quod luna circuit zodiacum a puncto ad punctum per xxvii. dies et vii.* (I *viii*   S *sex*   U *duas*) *horas*
     25 *a god ifeyned þat hiȝte**: the phrase recurs, with variation, at 529/35, 530/2–3, 541/30 and 31, 733/15

530 7–8 *and hondis**   17–19 *And þanne . . . Marcius**
     15 *Marche*: adds *tertius mensis*
     26 *gardinere*: *uinitor uel hortulanus*

532 4–5 *of stentynge of þe sonne*: *solsticialis*, translated *solsticial* at 534/15 unless this latter form has been anglicized by a ME. scribe from the Latin form preserved by JT. Cf. 458/25–6

17 *tyme*: adds *ex sole*

30 *spoiliþ*: A *spiliþ*, a genuine form but not JT's form here

533 14 *solempne*: *celebris et solemnis*, translated *solempne and holy* 549/4. *celebris* is translated *highe* at 542/5

21 *Also*: cf. DE *and*, where BA has *qui*. Z perhaps *itaque*

534 11 *is²*: cf. *est sic dictus*, translated as *haþ þat name* at 533/2 and 18 and 30. Z *est*

12 *reyny tyme, and Decembre*: *ab imbre marcii est* (R *qᵃ*) *decimus* (R *December*) *martius* (R om.) *quidem est mensis pluuiosus*

21 *growinge tyme*: *uer* JT probably wrote *springinge tyme*, his regular translation

23 *islawe*: adds *potissime et mactantur propter quod depingitur tanquam carnifex qui cum securi percurit et mactat procum suum*

24 *þise*: adds *xii*

33 *dayes*: cf. *diis . . . quorum nomina*

535 4 *to his disciplis**

6 *haþ þe name of Mars*: IJLMQRSUX *a marte*   cf. the better *marti*, i.e. they gave their name to Mars

15 *artificial*: adds *siue usualis*

16 *in oure siȝt*: *in nostro emisperio*   cf. 519/34

536 31 *schorter¹*: adds *continue* (I *cotidie*)

33 *trauaile*: adds *exercitio et labori*

537 12 *grete*: *precedente*   Z *excedente*

28 *seiþ*: adds *nimia autem serenitas in aurora cum radiis solaribus directis contra austrum signum est future tempestatis ut dicit idem Beda*

37 *i-endid*: *celebrate* cf. 542/10

538 11 *bemes*: adds *et propter radiorum spissitudinem et eorum confractionem*

539 7 *vapours, and fumosite*: *fumosi uapores que materia*

540 9 *in þe iii. quarter*: *in media nocte siue ipsius noctis in tempesto*

10 *wakiþ*: adds *et excubant*

11 *haueþ mynde and fyndiþ*: *inueniunt*. A doublet of ambiguity, *meminiunt uel inueniunt*

27 *gooþ aboute*: *euagari non cessant*

541 8 *Also**

12 *mete*: *cibis*. BA adds *templum orationis gratia plus quam in aliis diebus frequentabatur*

22 *feste*: emended to *reste* in *corrigenda*. Since JT wrote *in þe reste* here, the absence of a preposition in temporal phrases which include days or months (as at line 3) throughout the work may be scribal

542 3 *trompinge*: *clangore buccine*

10 *when alleluya is closid**

543 19 *weke of septuagesme*: *quinquagesimalis septimana*

32 *þat is Cene þursday**

545 1 *doynge*: *negocium*, translated *chaffaris* at line 22

7 *quykynge*: D *quekenyng*, cf. *reuiuificationis*. JT perhaps added *aȝen* or *eft*, cf. line 8

32 *reyne*: adds *pluuialis irrigationis tunc enim oriuntur yades et alie stelle imbrigere que sunt causa roris et pluuie* where *yades* is a relic of *Plyades*

546 25 *Also*: *et ideo*. JT perhaps wrote *an so*, cf. 558/8

547 8 *swetenesse*: *sinceritatis*   Z *suauitatis*
17 *floures*: adds *quod in illo die florentes* (ONPR *flores*   N before erasure   S *frondes*) *arborum et uirentes ramos in manibus gerimus*
20 *foot and steppis*: the phrase appears corrupt, cf. *uestigio*. JT perhaps wrote *footsteppis* as a genitive adverb, cf. *footdrye*
32 *sexpe*: IJLQT *vi^a*   cf. the better MNRSU *v^a*

548 17 *Fryday*: adds *et dicitur bona sexta feria*
25–6 *and eke*: here and at 549/23 and 28 and 550/33 probably a scribal intrusion

549 2 *nau3t ifounde*: *inconsueti*, generally translated *incouenable*. Z *non inuenti*
7 *foure*: IMNORU *in q^a duplici*   JQPS *q^{a}druplice*   L *druplici*   T *in qua*   cf. 542/27
24 *swerde*: *cingulo seu gladio*
31–2 *burgonyth and spraiep and springip*: *frondent*
33 *gardynes*: adds *nemorum*

550 1 *And Aristotel seip*: *ut sicit Aristoteles et etiam*. JT perhaps wrote *as Aristotel seip and also*
2 *swetere*: *purius et dulcius*
7 *of plente of herbis and of gras*: *satietatis tunc graminibus et herbis habundant loca omnia pascuosa*
21 *per of alle*: *de omnibus*. *per* (omitted by De Worde) is probably a scribal intrusion
23 *fruyt*: adds *arboris pulcherrime* (R *decoros et pulcherrimos*) *id est*

551 8–9 *holi watir*: *aqua benedicta ecclesiam*. JT perhaps wrote *pe chirche wip holi watir*

NOTE: this short and simple book was originally edited in a most unscholarly manner. When the enormity of error, due to an almost total failure to collate the English and Latin MSS., became apparent during First Proof, the General Editor remade the book within the constraints of the printed page, reserving to the *corrigenda* those corrections which could not be accommodated on proof.

BOOK X

553 9 seiþ] seiþ [þat mater fletiþ] *and fn.* *ABCDEFGHW *om.*   LS dicit . . . quod materia fluit

554 30–1 in dede and] *read* [it be in] dede *and fn.* ABFGW dede and   C in dede and   D be in dede and   H deede be   *cf.* LS nisi cum materie (S materia) actu sit coniuncta

555 22 matiere] matiere,
25 of] *delete and fn.* *ABCDEFGHW of   *cf.* LS spiritualis forma
26 soule] soule,

557 12 þey] he *and fn.* *ABCDEFGHW þey   *cf.* LS recipit

561 7 þerfore] *add* [fore] *and fn.* *ABCDEFGHW *om.*   LS quia
9 and¹] a *and fn.* *ABCDEFGHW and   *cf.* LS quia . . . calidior existit . . . inflamat
27n. LS] L naturam   S

563 27n. LS] L reignitur   S

565 5 for] *read* [þer]for *and fn.* *ABCDEFGHW for   LS unde

The English MSS. ACDEFGH complete. B ends imperfectly at 567/22. De Worde's edition based on F. The Latin MSS. IJLMNOPQRTUVWXY are complete. K lacks the whole book. S defective through excisions. Mrs. S. Clinton has edited the Anglo-Latin text (Northwestern Ph.D. 1981: D.A.I. 8225899).

552 16 *his: hoc*   cf. C *þis*
22 *where a þing is gendred: ubi est generans* 'where there is an engenderer'. Perhaps JT wrote *gendreþ*, as in line 20
24 *of þe persones in þe trinyte: in diuinis*   Z *iii. diuinis*   cf. 47/17
26 *of special: speciei* 'of a species'
30 *Also . . . fourme:* this sentence properly follows *nat by fourme* in line 27. BA adds *ut dicitur x methaphysice*
31 *matiere of naturelle þingis: materia phisicorum*   cf. I *in ph's*   RXY *iii° phisicorum* 'according to the third book of the *Physics*'
31–2 *matiere þat. . . quantyte: causa quantitatis continue in infinitum est materia* 'matter is the reason why quantity is infinitely continuous'

553 1 *in lengþe and brede and deepnesse: dimensiue* (MNQUW *dimensione*   R *dimensionem*   X *dimensionate*)
3–4 *for . . . for: uel quia . . . uel quia*. Perhaps JT wrote *or for . . . or for*
15 *comen: communis* 'common'
19 *hete: frigido*   cf. 373/4n. above
28–9 *of fourme: illius forme*
33 *suyth: relucent*. Perhaps JT wrote *schyneth*
36 *fourme oþir liʒt:* IJLNRTV forme aut lumen   cf. the better *forme autem lumen* Z *forma aut lumen*

554 9 *in philosophris*: *in philosophis*   cf. QSTX *in phisicis*. BA perhaps wrote *iii phisicorum*, as at 552/31. Cf. 644/30.

27 *we sueþ*: adds *male* (LOPVW *materiale*   MSTX *materiales*   N *materialiter*)

555 2–3 *þe perfeccioun of heuenly matiere*: *et perficientis celestem materiam* (JLMNRUV WY *naturam*) *substancia celi* 'and which perfects heavenly matter, the substance of heaven'

13 *in aungels*: *in intelligenciis*   cf. 60/2

22 *more noble*: *nobilior*   cf. the better Q *nobilis*

25 *actualite in dede*: JT perhaps intended *actualitate* 'in dede'

556 12 *Euene*: *autem*

20, 23–4 *in hete and cooldnes*: *in frigiditate* (N adds *et caliditate*) . . . *in frigiditate*

30 *vertue in worchinge*: *uirtutem operacionem*. JT perhaps wrote *an*, not *in*

30 *of þe body of heuene*: *ex uicinitate orbis siue celestis corporis*. JT perhaps wrote *of þe nerenes of þe spere or þe body of heuene*

31 *meuablenesse*: *mobilitatis*   cf. IOQRTY *nobilitatis*

557 1 *and substaunce**

7 *ferenesse*: *summam* (U om.) *elongacionem*

22 *to be aboue þe eire*: *super* (NW *semper*) *aerem sedere*   cf. OR *super ascendere*. BA perhaps wrote *semper ascendere*

22–3 *3if fyre is* . . . *iholden*: Q *detentus*   UX *detentum*   Y *detinetur et*   cf. IOR *descendens*   JLMNPSTVW *decenter*

27 *more excellent*: *longe excellencius*

558 2 *distyngynge*: *discretus distinguens*

2–3 *fedynge* . . . *donward*: *deorsum pascens et sursum mouens* 'feeding downward and moving upward'

8 *Also*: *vnde*. Perhaps JT wrote *An so*, cf. 546/25

9 *of comentoures*: *commentatoris* (T *comm*). Z *commentatorum*

19–20 *neþir, ouere*: perhaps JT wrote *ouere, neþir* or (in view of JLNOPRTUV *inferioribus* 19) *neþir, neþir*. Cf. 120/2, 165/33

23 *For*: properly introduces the clause beginning *as longe as* (cf. *quamdiu enim*); the clause *3if . . . endeles* modifies the previous sentence

25 *wurchiþ*: *crescit*. Perhaps JT wrote *cresiþ* (as at line 23) or *wexiþ* (as at 560/4)

29 *þat . . . inne**

559 4 *strong*: *foris* (JL *oris*) 'out'. Z *fortis*

35 *comen*: *communicatiuam* 'to make common', cf. 553/15

560 7 *amendiþ*: *emendat*, cf. JMNPQRSUXY *emundat* 'cleanses'

9 *humours*[2]: adds *et cibos crudos* 'and raw foods', the proper referent of *þerinne* and subject of *makeþ*

22 *for þe substaunce and distaunce of þat opir*: MU *quia inter unius substanciam et alterius sensibilis distancia penitus non sentitur* 'for between the substance of the one and the other no perceptible distance is felt at all'. All the other MSS. are variously corrupted

24 *fire is in his owne spere*: *ignis enim* (RWX add *carbo*) *est in sua spera*   cf. the better PQSUY *ignis enim lux est in sua spera*

31 *ispred*: *accensa* 'kindled'

561 4–5 *as it were . . . pere: et in conum*

7 *strongly*: adds *propter concursum radiorum in angulo acuto*

10 *he is colered: calorem* (M *colorem*) . . . *recipit*

11 *trowbly . . . dym and derke: turbida et rumosa turbidam et obscuram*   Z *turbida et obscuram*

21 *tendiþ þingis þat he towchiþ: incendit*   cf. the better *incedit* in Remigius (ed. Lutz, p. 79)

23 *Iuno: iunone* (N corrected to *ioue*)

31 *humours: humidioribus*   Z *humoribus*, or JT wrote *humid*

562 8 *pray*: adds *ut dicit idem*

17–18 *corneris and placis: loca angulosa*. Perhaps JT wrote *cornerid placis*; cf. 498/33 and *Polychronicon* I. 179, 305, where *cornered* translates *angulosus*

21–3 *plesiþ . . . heed: est sensui olfactus delectabilis et amicus cerebri namque est confortatiuus et spiritum cordis et capitis reparatiuus* 'pleases the sense of smell and is good for it, for it strengthens the brain and restores the spirits of heart and head'

38 *woodnesse*: adds *ut in freneticis et ebriosis obliuionem et desipienciam generat*

563 8 *þis*[1]: probably a scribal addition

11 *Gregory*: I *Basilius*   MNUXY *Rabanus* (JLTV *Ras*   OPRSW *Ra*   Q *ha*). Z perhaps *Ra'* which an ME. scribe falsely expanded

14 *cole*: adds *crepitando et scintillando* 'as it crackles and sparks'

29 *and þat bicause of: propter*   cf. the better INU *preter*

564 5 *soles . . . þat trediþ*: U *plantas concultantes*   cf. the better *plantas concultantis* 'the soles of whoever treads'

6 *hym þat trediþ þeron: tangentem*; perhaps JT wrote 'him þat toucheþ hit'

11 *for: ui enim ignea* 'for by the force of fire'

13–14 *for þe meuynge þerof is clere: motus eius cum clarissimus est*, cf. the better IMNSTUY *motus eius clarissimus est*

15 *grene wiþ bemes of liȝt: uiridis radiosus* (L *uidiosus*)   cf. the better MY *undique radiosus*

21 *þat puttiþ: impetuose* (N *inpenetrabilem*   P *in plentitudine*   R *impellendo*   W *impenetrabilem*   U inserted after omission). Z *impellentem* unless JT wrote *by putting* (cf. R)

22 *chaungiþ sumdel hit: parum alterat uel inmutat* 'changes it little'

28 *asken: cinis. asken* regularly translates *cinis*, and *asschyn* (*asschis*) translates *fauilla*

30 *smale*: adds *mollis* 'soft'

565 5 *wiȝte*: adds *ut dicit Gregorius*

6 *by rauyschinge of oþir þingis*: cf. *et rapitur impetu*. Z *raptu alieno*, or an ME. scribal error caused by *by rauyschinge* above

9 *falliþ and**

13 *clensinge: colatiuam* (ILPSTVW *collatiuam*) *siue mundificatiuam* 'straining or cleansing'

BOOK XI

567 15 and to] *read* [of] *and fn.* *ACEFGHW and to   *cf.* LS *spirituum*

569 35 fyre] *read* [hete of] fyre *and fn.* ABCFGH fyre   LS calorem ignis

571 11 n. intrare] introire

575 20 n. ariseþ] arisiþ

577 14 on] *an and fn.* *ABCDEFGHW on   LS et
    20 tisik] *add* [for] *and fn.* ABCEFGHW *om.*   LS quia

578 24 n. luce] luci

579 13 i-iunyed] i-ioyned *and fn.* A i iunyed   BCDGHW ioyned

582 33 n. aere] aeri

589 30 *men] me and fn.* ABCFGH men   E *om.*   *cf.* LS aspiciatur

590 32 Arystotelis] Arystotel

The English MSS. ACFGH are complete. B begins imperfectly at 567/36 and ends imperfectly at 592/2. D begins imperfectly at 570/3. E begins imperfectly at 568/8. In Book XI De Worde's edition is based on F. The Latin MSS IJLMNOPQR STUVWXY are complete. K lacks the whole book.

566 14 *picke and reyny*: *conspissatus pluuias* 'thickened (it makes) rains'. *Z conspissata pluuiosa*

567 3 *þat is*: adds *odoriferam*
    12 *humours*: *spiritus et humores*
    30 *iii⁰.*: *in*
    31 *in þe reynbowe*: *in assub et in iride.*
    34 *coolde*: *humidas*   cf. 177/2 n., 574/4 n.
    34–5 *of generacioun . . . hitself*: *ex generacione noui aeris secundum in se recipiente*. Perhaps JT omitted *secundum*, cf. the better M *sensum*, as untranslatable

568 3 *imaad by certeyne wurchinge**
    6 *he*: *Auicenna*. The mistake perhaps arose from confusing an abbreviation of the name with *a* 'he'
    18–19 *souþerne wynde . . . westerne wynd . . . esterne wynde*: *australis . . . orientalis . . . occidentalis*   cf. the better IMNRY *australi . . . orientali . . . occidentali* 'in the south (side air)' etc.
    22 *out of an hie place**: perhaps a scribal intrusion from the next line
    24 *eyry þingis*: I *aerea*   cf. the better *aera* and 573/18

569 11 *often . . . heruest*: *in fine estatis et ut sepius in autumpno*
    12 *þenne and clene*: *subtilior*. JT perhaps wrote *þennere and clenere* (or *clerere*)
    27 *ischape as a schielde*: *piramidalem*

570 24 *euerich þing*: *omnis aer*
    31 *thristiþ*: adds *aerem*
    35–6 *For 3if . . . estward*: *nam in aquilone brachium australe conflictum facit in orientem*

comouetur mare cf. the better IQS *nam cum aquilonare brachium et australe conflictum faciunt in oriente commouetur mare*

571 3 *Zephirus*: *fauonius siue zephirus*
6 *wynde*: adds *si uero in septentrione fit uentus qui uocatur boreas*
6 *see*: adds *dicunt*
21 *wynd is meved*: *uentus mobilis et motus*

572 7 *rentiþ*: cf. *euellat*. Perhaps JT wrote *rootiþ* (as in DE)

573 8 *and*[1]: *sicut*
14–15 *as . . . wynd**
18 *passynge betynge*: *transuerberacione* cf. LT *transsubstanciacione*
18 *eyry matere*: W *aerea* cf. the better *aera* and 568/24
19 *þat hatte Subsolanus, þe esterne wynde**
23–4 *þat is . . . wynde**: the emendation *est* (cf. l. 32) may be unjustified. I interpolates *northest* before *uulturnum*
27 *þe menynge . . . wyndes*[2]*

574 3 *pure and ek*: IJLV *parum et* Q *rarus et* cf. the better *et parum* Z *purus et*
4 *colde*: *calidum*. Cf. 567/34n. above
9 *stremes*: *flumina*. Perhaps JT wrote *ryuers* (as in DE)
14 *ouer*: *sub*. JT perhaps wrote *under*, as at 573/16, 574/34, 576/12
20 *This . . . west**
25 *west*: adds *et ad nos uenit antequam a solaribus radiis incalescat*
31 *coold*: *nimis . . . frigidus*

575 4 *The meninge . . . souþ**
16 *and makeþ heuynesse of witte*: I *et sensus grauitatem faciunt* cf. the better *sensus et grauitatem faciunt* 'of wit and make heaviness'
18 *men*[2]: DE *makeþ men* may be right, cf. *podagram et pruritum commouent* 'stirs up gout and itching'
24 *lyne þat hatte axis*: *axe*. Also at 576/25
25 *þe contrey þat hatte torrida zona*: *torridam zonam*
29 *oþirwhile he blowiþ þat*: *ipso flante* 'when he blows'
31 *streyt contray*: *nostram angustam*

576 12–13 *þe schipmannes sterre**
18 *alto*: *alto* cf. the better Q *artho* (i.e. *arcto*)
19 *þe meninge . . . norþ**

577 4 *purifieþ*: INSUY *purificant* cf. *putrificant*
13 *membres*: *alia membra*
17–18 *blosmes, flowres, and fruyt*: *flores et fructus teneros*
18 *smytiþ*: S *excutit* cf. the better *exurit*
19 *spolyeþ herbis and treen and grenes*: *herbarum et arborum uirorem spoliat atque tollit*
28 *nubibus*: DE *nube* may be right
32 *hayle*: *grandinem et cetera*
32 *is gendred*: *habet . . . generari* 'has to be engendered'

578 2 *þickenes*: adds *aeris*
6 *wyndes*: adds *a calore in concauitate uentris nubis intercluso*
12 *his*: JLTV *eiusdem* MNW *eius* cf. the better *cuius*

35 *diuers þingis*: properly, the object of *sendiþ*

579 1 *hire*: the antecedent is *cloude* 578/33 and *he* 578/35
8 *see*: *maris amaritudinem*

580 14–15 *in endeles* . . . *myrour*: *in stillicidiis infinitis tamquam in speculo relucens* 'shining in countless drops as in a mirror'
20 *bodyes*: *partes*. JT perhaps wrote *partyes*, or Z mistaken for *corpores* abbreviated
32–3 *þe more he is bifore and strecchiþ donwarde*: IJLOQTV *quanto contrahendo deprimitur*   cf. the better *quanto contrahendo comprimitur* 'the more it is drawn together and compressed'. Z *quanto contra est et deprimitur*

581 9–10 *a maner of broune coloure*: *lactatiuum* 'milky, cloudy, unclear', cf. the better IU *iacinctiuum* (described at 854/2, 976/28). *broune*, not among the colours treated in Book XIX, here perhaps means 'dark' as JT attempts to reconcile the conflicting demands of the word before him (whatever it was), the colours of the rainbow, the colours associated with air, and the fact that blue is pre-empted by water. Cf. 387/9 n.
12 *red*: *rubeus seu uinosus*   cf. P *rubeus*
19 *saiþ þat*: adds *multos alios habet colores inter quos distinguere sensui est difficile et ideo dicit philosophus*
24 *one partye*: NPRSW *parte*   cf. the better *pariete*
36 *þerof*: i.e. of the rainbow, cf. *per sui resolucionem*

583 1 [*not*] *iseye*: The emendation may be unjustified, cf. P. *uisibilis*   S *uisibiliter*. Cf. 417/13 n. above
8 *eyre*: MSS. *whiche*. The emendation may be unjustified if a^{em} (*aerem*) was misread as q^{em}
10 *strengþe*: *uim ardoris*. JT perhaps wrote *strengþe of þe brennynge*
11 *by wurchinge*: PRSWX *ad actum*   cf. the better *ad tactum*
13 *and in herbes**: perhaps a scribal intrusion from the next line
20 *bryngiþ forþ*: *impregnat*

584 13 *glose*: adds *Ieronymi*
14–15 *brucus . . . gras**   19–20 *Som . . . myldew**
30 *resolued*: adds *guttatim* 'drop by drop'

585 13 *reboundinge þerof*: adds *contra nubem*
17 *aʒeines*: NU *contra*   cf. the better *circa*
32 *aswagiþ and tempreþ strengþe of hete*: *caloris temperiem mitigat*. JT perhaps wrote *aswagiþ þe temperure of hete*

586 3 *derknesse*: *profunditatis* 'depth', i.e. in the context 'deep holes'
5 *seedes*: adds *et caloris naturalis in seminibus extinctiua*
7 *lettiþ þe work of worchers and of workmen*: *operacionum et operancium impeditatiua*. Z om. *et. workers and workmen* may mean 'craftsmen and laborers'
10 *hungir*: *sterilitatis et famis*   cf. 325/6 n. above
19 *more stronge*: *uelocior*   Z *forcior*
21–2 *þat þey beo þe raþer . . . sonner*: *ut cicius congelata submergantur*. JT makes explicit what the Latin implies, that *cicius* modifies both verbs
26 *briʒt*: adds *terre inebriatiua*
29 *xiiº.*: *xiiº* (P *ii*   U *xvi c. 72 de petra*   I om. phrase)   cf. the better NQS *iiiº*.

The reference is to Book XIII. 24 at 675/11–15, where the 'tokene' (*signum*) seems to be the line of verse

587 2 *hore froste*: ADEH *here furste*. The emendation may be unjustified, cf. O *prime* P *primo* alongside the better *pruine*
14 *strenge*: I *uigore*   cf. the better *rigore*
25 *for*: *enim*. BA probably wrote *autem*, since hail requires heat but not *swiþe stronge hete* as in summer

588 17 *dryeþ*: *arefacit*   cf. IORSTUY *rarefacit*
20 *matiere*: supplied by JT as the unexpressed subject (properly *substantia* or *nubes*) of *frangitur* 'is ibroke', unless he misread the following *in* as an abbreviated *materia*
24 *is igendrid*: Y *generatur*   cf. the better *congelatur*. But JT may have generalized his translation of *congelatur* to parallel the preceding clause

589 1 *inward to mores and rootes of herbis and sedes*: *ad interiora radicum et seminum*. JT perhaps wrote *innermore partes of rootes and sedes*
10 *and exaltaciouns*: *uel exalantes* 'either steaming'. JT perhaps wrote *and exalaciouns*, or Z *et exaltationes*
23–4 *þe whiche* ... *imolte*: *quam ante resolucionem frigiditatis sue coartacione in sua super-*
on the surface by the force of its coldness'. JT may have thought *in sua superficie* otiose; *makeþ* suggests Z *indurat*
28 *vppon þerþe*: R *terre*   cf. the better *superficiei terre*

590 1 *þat*: perhaps a scribal intrusion from *and þat* in line 2
6 *tofalle*: adds *in aquam pluuialem*
11 *þe lasse*: ABCFGHW *more*   LORV *nimis*   cf. the better *minus*
11 *derk*: adds *quando nebula a sole attracta totaliter sursum mouetur in naturam redit nubis et ideo future pluuie est significatiua* 'but when mist is drawn by the sun to move altogether upward, it becomes a cloud again and so bodes rain'
16 *vynes*: *florum et* ... *uinearum*

591 4 *tonitrus*: *tonitruus* (see fn.) may be better, cf. INQ *tonitruus* for the better *tonitrus*
8 *comeþ*: adds *repente*
12 *of men and of beestis**
14 *3if* ... *ibroke*: *complosa*   BDEFGH add *and þan iblowe* after *iblowe*
16 *oure**
27 *þerwiþ*: *sibi* 'into each other'
31 *cloude*: *nube aquosa*

592 1 *wiþoute rayne*: *cum coruscacione et fulmine sine pluuia*
7 *smytiþ*: adds *sepe*
9 *ofte and more euidenliche*: *et semper euidencius*   Z *et sepe euidencius*. BA apparently wrote *et frequencius*
22, 23 *schovynge*: i.e. 'showing', cf. *apparitio* and 594/10n. below

593 3–4 *And so for to speke*: *et secundum hoc*
9 *and*: ACFGHW om. The emendation, based on DE, may be unjustified, since RW om., but cf. the better *et* (O *a*)

12 *betynge . . . cloudes*: *collisione uentorum et attritu nubium*

12–13 *comeþ donward*: adds *ad modum iaculi* 'like a bolt'

15 *stones*: IR *lapidum*　cf. the better *lampadum*

26 *saiþ*: I adds *dicit plinius*　OS *et plinius*　QX *plius*　JLMUVW *phi*　NT *ph's*　P *ph'i*　R *ph'*　Y *et phi*. Perhaps JT wrote *saiþ. Plinius* (or *þe philosophir*) *saiþ*

594 4 *seiþ*: N *dicit*　cf. *dixit* and note to 8 below

5 *and is igendred**: the clause makes explicit that the sunbeams do not hide fire in clouds but rather turn into fire in the process of being hidden

8 *seiþ*: S *dicit*　I *d¹*　cf. *dixit* and note to 4 above

10 *worchinge and schovinge*: IJNOTV *aparicio*, LMQ *operacio*, cf. the better RSUWXY *apercio* (P *aspercio*) 'unfolding'. A doublet of ambiguity

28 *libro*: adds *ii*

595 5 *lyƷt wynde imeued*: P *aer leuis motus*　cf. the better *aer leuiter motus*

18–19 *in þat same book*: *in eodem libro*. JT perhaps wrote *in þis same book*

BOOK XII

597 20 eyr] ey *and fn.* A eyr

599 21 and n c*l*eyn] tey*m*

601 24 Also] *add* [f. 141vb]

604 20 sche] he *and fn.* ABCEFGH sche   *cf.* LS percutiunt
26 sche] he *and fn.* *ABCDEFGHW sche   *cf.* LS uolant
35 li3t] li3t[er] *and fn.* *ABCDEFGHW li3t   LS leuiori

606 11 clawes] *fn.* A chawes
17–18 Suche strengis ... wolues] *delete with preceding point and fn.* *ABC DEFGHW *add* Suche strengis imade of guttes of wolues
18–20 strengis ... harpe] *read* [hem[] *and fn.* *ABCDEFGHW strengis imade of guttis of schiepe 3if hit so be þat beþ so isette among hem as in fethele or in harpe LS eas

607 31 þat be] but he [be] *and alter fn. to* be] ABCDFG *om.*   *cf.* L nisi habeant   S si haberet

608 19 sche^{1,2}] he *and fn.* ABCEFGH sche   *cf.* LS impinguantur ... pigrescunt

611 19 narewre] narew3e

613 3 sche] he *and fn.* ABCEFGH sche   *cf.* LS eiiciunt

616 6 þei] *read* [for þei] *and add to fn.* ABDEFG om.   H þei   LS quia

619 10 heo] *add fn.* *ABCDEFGHW he   *cf.* LS nuncia

620 23 cleþith] clepith

626 6 sight,] *transfer commma to* sacrifise

627 19 lyght] lyght[er] *and fn.* *ABCDEFGHW lyght   LS leuiorem

632 14 As Constantinus seiþ,] *repunctuate to modify previous sentence*
26 ,also] also,

637 24 n. LS nati] *delete and add* LS *lack phrase*
30 aboute] abou[f. 150rb]te

638 12 seiþ and Aristotel] seiþ. And Aristotel:
27 highe] high*t and fn.* ABCFGHW highe   LS ornatum

645 8 *fine*] f

The English MSS. ACEFGH are complete. B lacks two discontinuous leaves (623/28–627/23, 631/3–638/17) and ends imperfectly at 642/14. D ends imperfectly at 640/24. De Worde's edition is based throughout Book XIII on F. British Library MS. Additional 45680 f. 48 gives a fragment of text (617/30–621/28) which belongs to the DE (rather than the ABCFGH) manuscript tradition: *Neuphilologische Mitteilungen* lxxviii (1977), 48–52. The Latin MSS. IJLMNOPQRSTVWY are complete. K (f. 121) begins imperfectly at 640/17. U lacks one leaf (609/24–614/14). X is wholly lacking

596 8 *pinges*: adds *creatoris*   cf. the better W *creaturis*   Z *creatoris*, which then affected translation of *dei* line 7

13 *speken*: JT's form was probably *spekeng*

16 *distinguyd*: *determinate et distincte*   cf. 597/19

22 *so*: *alis* 'by wings'

597 4 *meve*: adds *leuiter*

11 *vertue*[1]: *rationem*   cf. 1053/9

20 *eyr*: *oui testa* 'shell of the egg'

23 *linyacioun*: *augmentacione* (L *a. immitacione*   T *augmentricione*) *liniamentatione* (IP *lineamentacione*   JLO *lim*[ne]   T *lunacione*   Q *liniatione*) 'when the lineaments have developed'

24 *membres*: *singulorum . . . membrorum*

28 *þat comeþ out of on schelle, oftyn**

34 *and loue weddynge*: *coniugalis amoris*. Perhaps JT wrote *of* instead of *and*

598 3 *þat is. . . female*: JT's gloss on *sexum*, of which *sext* (here and elsewhere) may be a scribal form. Cf. 637/21–2, 306/14

6 *taken*: *sentitur*

7 *whanne*: adds *inquit*

13 *voys*: *uocibus* 'voices'. The ME. form may be plural, cf. 680/4

24 *manere of place to wonye inne*: *habitacula et . . . mansiones*, cf. 624/3–4

25 *colde*: *magis . . . frigide*   cf. 599/1

33 *rowynge*: adds *caudas etiam habent breues ne in natando* (L *paludo*) *caude madefacte pondere impedimentum sentiant*

33 *Also*: *autem* (ILOT om.)

599 6 *strongliche*: *fortius*

12 *primo*: MN *ii.*   cf. the better *i.*

12–13 *wildirnesse and desert place*: IJLOPSTVW *solicitudinem*   cf. the better *solitudinem* (N corrected)

20 *grounde*: adds *quedam uero e conuerso in terra aues capiunt*

26 *in þe eir*: *eleuata a terra in aere*

31 *syngen*: adds *maxime*

600 7 *leuen*: *declinant*

9 *stempnes*: *uices*   Z *uoces*

11–12 *þe crane . . . ny3te*: *uigil* (MO *grus uigil*)

29 *fruyt*: adds *ac herbis terre nascentibus*

31 *as leef on as oþir*: JT's gloss on *indifferenter*, of which *indifferentliche* may be a scribal anglicization

601 1–2 *to wiþdrawe eiþir to warne*: *denegare*. A doublet of ambiguity, *defugare uel denegare*

10 *and scharpe*: adds *sicut et collum longum*

12 *to hale, and to drawe and to rende*: *dilacerandum*. A doublet of ambiguity, *deducendum uel dilacerandum*

13 *þise propirtees*: *hoc . . . proprium*. JT probably wrote *þis propirtee*

24 *toutenned*: *continuatur*. JT probably wrote *conteyned*, cf. 600/10

28 *hennes and**

602 4 *ful busy*: *sollercie amplioris*
17 *þat takeþ heede*: IMNOQTU *uiuens* L *iuiunens* JPSW *minuens* Z *inuens*
20 *echydes*: the emendation, based on DE, is tentative, cf. MOY *achates* and T
achades, alongside JLNPQ *ethedes*, I *ethates*, U *echites*, SVW *echedes*
29 *fro*: MSS. *and out and fro*. The complex sentence (as emended) follows BA's
structure, but the emendation, cf. *de*, is tentative

603 4 *fleische*: adds *et multum neruositatis*
11–12 *wiþ*...*disparpled*: the awkward word-order is probably scribal, cf. *nec claritate solaris luminis disgregatur*
21 *And*: *si autem*
30 *place*: adds *ab omnimodo cursu aduersario*

604 1 *sielde, sielde*: *difficulter*
10 *byni: Kim* cf. ITU *kin* MN *kun* P leaves blank
13 *fediþ*: *cubant et nutriunt*. Z *cibant* for *cubant*
29 *briddes*: adds *in aliquo*
31 *iheight*: JT perhaps wrote *ihau3t*, cf. 607/23 *ihi3t*
34 *puttiþ*: *uomit*, a contextual translation

605 2 *haþ*: *patitur*
14 *and*[1]: *et sic*
14–15 *and my3t and strengþe*: *resumptis uiribus*. Perhaps a syntactical compression
by JT, but more likely scribal
18 *þider*: adds *post predam*
18 *biholdeþ*: *inspicere non desistit*

606 3 *fultur*: adds *unde*
3–4 *suche an egle**: cf. *suche tame hawkes* for *domestici* 608/27
5 *see*: adds *quando ascendunt ab aqua et si uiderit uulturem uenientem timebit unde fugit
ad aquam sed uultur qui est acuti uisus semper uolat circa locum*
10 *comeþ doun*: *solet descendere* cf. 621/8 n. below
28 *longe**

607 4 *he*: perhaps JT wrote *heo*, cf. *natura...recompensat*
7 *raptour and rauyschere*: *id est raptor*
8 *Boicius*: JLPT *boe'* Q *boi'* S *boici'* W *loc'* I *āborum* cf. the better
basilius
11 *And for*: *quia*. The clause properly modifies the previous sentence
16 *diuers**
17 *manere hawkes*: *aues* Z *accipitres* cf. 608/12
19–21 *þe briddis...iseide*: *inter hos hoc columba discernit sicut de aquila dictum est*
22 *is*: *est igitur*
24 *þerto*: adds *in agilitate et*
26 *and*: *et ascendit in tantum quod ab hominum aspectibus se subtrahit*

608 1–2 *colliries 'medicynes of y3en'*: *oculorum colliriis*. Also at 1031/12
9 *and*[2]: *et sic*
12 *And*: *enim*
12 *foules*: *accipitrum* Z *auium* cf. 607/17
27 *And so*: *autem* Z *unde*

27 *suche tame haukes*: *domestici uel domiti*   cf. 606/3–4
29 *in fayrenesse of 3outhe*: *in iuuentute et in decore*
30 *þat²*: *et sic*
32 *and doþ hem harme**

609 1 *þey²*: *et*. The clause properly modifies the next sentence
2 *And**
13 *meneþ*: adds *uero*
14–18 *alietus* ... *vnmy3ty*: the full quotation from the *Aurora*, Liber Leviticus
643–6, is

> Optinet exiguos alietus corpore uires
> Sunt (LT sicut) et aues minime preda cibusque suus
> Exprimit hic aliquem qui solos vexat egenos.

JT may have given the text in Latin and then translated it
17 *som men*: perhaps JT wrote *me* 'one', cf. *aliquem*
28 *honycombes*: adds *mirabili artificie* (not in Isidore XII. 8. 10)
28–9 *iwounden and iwrithen wiþ wax*: *textisque ceris*. The ablative absolute properly
belongs to the next clause

610 8 *to²**
19 *loueþ*: *sibi substituunt* ... *diligunt*
34–5 *concours and metynge of dewes*: *concursus*

611 7 *wiþ brennynge of wreche*: *ardore uindicte*
10 *geawis*: *sua fauces*
17 *bawmeþ*: MO *illiniunt*   cf. IQ *liniunt*   JS *illumunt*   L *illimiunt*   NP *alliniunt*   W *alliniunt*
18 *huyue*: *superficiem aluearis*
21 *kyng*: *reges*   cf. 716/2
23 *gadreþ*: *mutant*
27 *nedeful*: adds *sed colligit ex eo quo indiget*
29 *matere*: *propria materia*

612 8 *he*: perhaps JT wrote *heo*, cf. *apis* ... *constricta*
15 *attercoppes*: *aranea*. Perhaps JT's singular form was *attercops*
21 *hony¹*: adds *et laborant eiicere eas de aluearibus*
27 *goon*: *eat* ... *ad alias apes tunc ille pauce residue uadunt*
31–2 *drawiþ nou3t out of stiginge place*: *non retraxerint aculeum suum*. Perhaps a contextual translation

613 15 *moþir*: JT perhaps wrote *mo oþir*
23 *out*: adds *et contrahendo* unless JT wrote *drawynge in*
27 *kaliroyz*: JLNV *Kaliroiz*   M *Kaliroim*   O *caliroz*   P *Kaliron*   Q *kalibis*
S *kaliroz*   T *Kamin*   W *kalycoyz*
33 *Venus*: adds *neque ex diuersis generibus coeuntibus neque apibus per coitum*

614 8 *Seche þou*: adds *de melle in tractatu de liquoribus*
10 *Plinium*: IM *plinium*   JLNOQSTW *pli.*   P *alibz*   cf. the better *philosophus*. Similar confusion of abbreviation occurs at 554/9, 644/30
14 *slouþe*: *graui* ... *pigritia*
15 *and²*: *semper commorans*

15 *And*: *Deinde*   cf. 625/8

19 *day*: adds *et propter hoc capit monedula que est auis coruini oua bubonis et comedit ea de die*

22 *pulleþ*: *deplumant*. Perhaps JT wrote *pulleþ of*, cf. 600/5

24–5 *as*. . . *is nobut*: *sicut et bestiarum non est nisi*

33 *and³*: *euagatur et*

35 *and walles*: *parietum* 'of walls'

615 7–8 *conceyue wiþ cusse and loue*: *osculo amore concipiant*

616 11 *comyne, vsuel, and iknowe*: *vsuales et multum notas*

13 *And on caas*: *forte*, which perhaps modifies the previous sentence

20 *comynge*: adds *de longe*

27 *of¹*: *et sanat*

28 *also*: *ut eiiciant* 'to throw it out'

617 14 *heo*: the emendation may be unjustified, cf. *incipiunt*, in which case *sche* line 15 should be emended to *he*, cf. *amittunt*

618 14 *For*: *et ideo quia*. Perhaps JT wrote *And perfor for*   cf. 596/33

21 *cause*: *causas*   cf. 611/21 *kyng*

23–4 *perilous and poysoun*: *perniciosum*

24 *for*: *nam cum* 'for when'

25 *and**

619 2 *stork*: adds *uel ibis*

6 *puttiþ out*: *eicit et expullit* (LNO *expellit*)

620 8 *hem*: adds *nam eximia illis circa filios est pietas*

9 *longe*: adds *uice reciproca*

17–18 *takeþ*. . . *weyes*: *hominum curas agere insidiarum uias monstrare* 'announces the troubles of men, advises the ways of ambush'. JT has mistaken the syntax

29 *and is besy and gredy and contrarye*: *est enim auis improba*. . . *importuna*

621 8 *passiþ*: *solent recedere*   cf. 606/10 n. above

11 *and wiþ oþur signes ant tokenes*: *certisque indiciis*

25–6 *þe liknesse*. . . *feþeres*: *per pennarum nigredinem similitudinem proprii coloris*. Perhaps JT wrote *þe liknesse of here colour by þe blaknesse of here feþeres*

26 *þay*: perhaps JT wrote *a*, cf. *inspicit*

30 *þe fadir metis*: *prius escis*   Z *patris escis*

622 2 *axiþ and takeþ*: *querens*

7–8 *þe female sit*: *femine coruorum cubant*

8 *þe male bryngiþ hire*: *masculi deferunt eis*

16 *smale**

17 *hir wepene*: *armis*

19 *victor*: adds *uictoria forti*

21 *it is isayde þat*: JLNOSTV *prōnus*   M *Pat'nus*   P *Prū'*   W *patronus*   cf. the better *Petronius*. The quotation is repeated at 1348/7

25 *fetheres*: *plumis suis*

26 *white*: *totum album*. Perhaps JT wrote *al white*

29 *to make dyuers notes*: *et necesse est eluctantem uocem per et flexuosum inter uarias reddere modulationes*

623 2 *Ennucus*: JLQV *ennicus*   M *m'r*   N *mic'*   OR *ouidius*   P *eonuc'*   T *emuc'*
S *comitus*   W *comicus*   cf. the better IU *emilius* (as in Isidore XII. 7. 9)
   9–10 *drawiþ hire . . . as it were: quasi eam attrahit . . . colligando*
   20 *picke*: adds *cum* 'when'
   22 *Also: ideo*. JT probably wrote *an so*
   25 *cloos and hole and broode: latos et clausos*
   33 *puttiþ himself . . . and spareþ: se opponere et interponere* (M adds *se*)

624 9 *blood*: adds *ut dicit Isidorus*
   14 *bocchis, scabbis, and sores: et ulcera*
   15 *scabbid . . . sore-backed: equis etiam ulcerosis*
   18 *and: quia*
   28 *tendre: tenacitatis*   Z *teneritatis*
   31 *huydeþ hireself: se immergit et ibi se occultans*

625 2 *corrupt metis: fetidis et corruptis*
   4 *There . . . cicada: cicada*
   8 *eyre: spiritum aerem*
   8 *Also: Deinde*   cf. 614/15
   9 *he*: i.e. the grasshoppers, cf. *necantur*
   16 *And: unde*. JT probably wrote *an so*. Also at 628/22, 639/8
   24–5 *and brenneþ strongliche: quibus iam accensis*, which properly modifies the next sentence
   25 *brennynge**
   32 *rowinge and oores: remigia*, which JT has translated literally, cf. BA's sense of 'spines'

626 20–1 *crienge as hit were blamynge wiþ hir voys: quasi castigando et arguendo uoce*
   26 *high: suspenso uel eleuato*
   32 *comeþ*: adds *supra se*

627 10 *hit: consumunt*. JT probably wrote *he* 'they'
   12 *hoot and drie of: calide et sicce* 'of hot and dry'
   16 *betiþ himself: uerberat et se ipsum feriens*
   33 *weyes: plumas*   Z *uias*

628 3 *lyoun*: adds *timet et abhorret et maxime si fuerit albus*
   24 *v. pounde of watirwort: v. libris* (O *lagenis*) *aque*
   34 *lesiþ: cristam* (JLP *tristam*   N *pristinam*   O *Crestam*) *enim perdit audaciam deponit*

629 25 *alwey: semper*   cf. the better LPT *sepe*

630 25 *bereþ vpwarde: erigit atque leuat*
   26–7 *in diuers feþires and colour: in penna uaria in colore*. Perhaps JT wrote *in feþires diuers in colour*

631 2 *and²: quando*
   5–6 *litil affeccioun and takeþ litil hede: affectum pium et animum*   Z *parvum* for *pium*
   7 *office*: adds *inquit*
   12 *sechiþ: adquirat*
   14 *crienge: ab erundo*
   18 *And he seiþ**   32 *coold of**

632 16 *gnawinge*: *uriatum corrosiuus*
20 *and*: *ideo*. JT perhaps wrote *an so*

633 6 *brid*: *auicula* 'small bird'
6 *singeþ*: *est auis sonora et canora*
12 *habitator*: adds (not O) *et*
17 *þat worme**
31–2 *is ifattid*: *impinguantur locuste*. JT probably wrote *he ben ifattid*
34 *hungir*: *fame*   cf. the better IU *sanie*

634 3 *dede*: adds *et consopitur*
7 *and²*: *enim*. Perhaps JT wrote *for a*
8 *wederis*: adds *sub fluctibus*
31 *and³*: *nam*

635 1 *guttes*: LT *exta*   cf. the better *escam*
9 *briddes*: adds *sicut et vultur*
16 *and²*: *quia*
33 *As*: *Vnde* (P *ut*)

636 5 *helte*: *adhuc teneret*
7 *bill*: adds *et sic ipsius acumine*
17 *puttiþ*: *applicat et opponit*
22 *to moche**
24 *he*: i.e. 'the children'
31 *hoot*: *suum*

637 6 *infectiþ*: *inficit*. BA wrote *interficit* 'kills'
17 *leue*: i.e. 'live'
21–2 *sex and distinccioun of male and female*: *sexum*   cf. 291/5, 306/14
24–5 *beþ ihei3t and**
28 *bredinge*: adds *sicut alie aues*
31 *iflowe*: adds *et post fugam*

638 18–19 *as Aristotel seiþ**: the attribution *secundum Aristotelem* occurs at line 12
after *xx. 3ere*
29 *cercle*: *rote siue circuli* and adds *et per gyrum capitis circumponit*

639 16 *haþ*: *sustinet et incurrit*
25 *and*: *cui compaciens*

640 2 *dooþ*: adds *sed oua sua fouere negligit*
19 *Gregor*: *beatus* (T om.) *Gregor*
27 *is iseye*: *ascendit*

641 6 *Iob*: *beatum Iob*
15 *also vnliche and*: *longe dispariter*
22 *passiþ*: *petere consueuit*   cf. 651/22
22 *hye hilles*: *iuga montium*
24 *tyme*: *instantis temporis*

642 2 *clene¹*: *paucula*   Z *pura*
17–18 *betynge and bitinge*: *morsuum*. Perhaps JT wrote *of bitinge*

20 *fro a vulture þat is beȝonde þe see*: *existentes enim ultra mare sentiunt cadauea ex ista parte*

33 *And som men meneþ*: *hoc ei accidere . . . putatur*

643 1–2 *and þerfore . . . hunger**

8 *away*: adds *rostro*

12 *libro*: *idem libro*

14 *is*: *cum sit*. Perhaps JT wrote *heo is*

28 *serpent*: *serpentibus*

644 6 *so it is isayde**

8 *Capitulo*: *Idem liber*

12 *crienge*: adds (not N) *eius enim uox ululatum pretendit*

24 *ofte*: LMNPT *frequenti*   O *frequentissime*   K *fecenti*

25 *is coppide*: *cristis* (ISW *tristis*   MO *crestis*   P *testis*) . . . *exeuntibus galatea*

30 *phylosophres*: *ph'ici* (MNPSQ *ph'i*), i.e. the *Physici*. Cf. 554/9. But the reference is properly to the *Physiologus* (ed. Carmody, p. 109)

34 *clerely*: adds *sicut et ipsi*

645 2 *evetyde*: *tempore*

5–6 *boþe . . . and*: *non tam . . . quam*

BOOK XIII

647 18 kynde] *add comma*

34 watirs, as . . . seiþ. Thanne] watirs. As . . . seiþ, thanne

38 watres] wateres

649 4 fleeþ and fulueþ, and] *fi*leþ and fulneþ *and fn.* *ACEFGHW fleeþ and fulneþ and *cf.* LS deformitates

33 þerfore] þerfor

650 4 for] *add* [thre monthes it semeth troublous as it were tempred with powder] *and fn.* *ACDEFGH *om.* LS tribus mensibus uidetur puluereus ac si esset cum puluere mixtus

651–4 *delete* B *in fns. passim*

652 17 swyfteliche] swyftelich

655 20 is] *delete with preceding comma and fn.* *ABCDEFGHW and is *cf.* LS herbe aromatice (S *om.*) et (S *om.*) medicinales

23 oponyng] yonyng *and delete fn.*

656 23 Eufrates] Evfrates

35 hatt] hat

657 20 Libanis] Libani

26 *in historiis*] in *historiam*

26 glose] *glosam*

658 26–7 prisoniers] presoniers

33 e*f*te] *fn.* *ACDEFGHW este LS iterum

3 n. beste] best

13 n. þe*ᵃ*] þe²

30 n., 31 n. Thebar, theber] theber, thebar

659 3 *fine:* f

13 *limnin*] *limum*

660 6 Asfalticus] Affalticus

15 *fn.* *ACDEFGHW *om. rubric*

16 Asfalti] Affalti

29 *salinarum*] *fn.* A silinarum LS salinarum

30 Zozons] Zozoas

661 4 *fabulla*] *fabula*

30 watris] water

18 *fn.* *ACDEFGHW *om. rubric*

662 28 contynueliche] contynuelich

663 22 comeþ] come

23 most] moste

8 n. dificiunt] deficiunt

664 14 and¹] *read* [of] *and fn.* *ABCDEFGHW and *cf.* LS riparum

18 tredeþ] trediþ

665 7 And] *delete with preceding point and fn.* *ABCDEFGHW and   LS *om.*
  8 *terre*] *add point*
  8 *cimbolis*] *cimbalis*

666 18–20 as it is ... contre] in ebbyng and flowyng and is ireuled by the vertue
  þerof *and add to fn.* CFGH foloweþ þe kinde of þe mone as it is knowe for alwey
  when þe mone ariseþ in any tyme of þe daye oþer of þe niȝt þen þe see (C *adds*
  ariseþ oþer falliþ) in þat contraye and (F *om.* as it is ... mone)
  20n. *delete asterisk and* DE

667 9 yþrow] y*d*row *and fn.* ABCDFGHW yþrow   LS extrahi

668 14n. LS litus] L lutus   S litius

670 31 ymedlid] ymedled
  32 perileuse] perilouse

671 12 meveþ] meveth

672 31 comeþ] come

675 35 ben] *add* [grete] *and fn.* ABCEFGHW *om.*   LS magna

676 23 dwellen sumtyme] *reverse*

678 8 eirenne] eiroun

679 32 and Ysider. And] . And Ysider and

680 21 laste, as] laste. As   **684** 23 congour] congur

686 33 swoloweþ] swolo[we]þ *and fn.* A swoloþ
  33 whenne] when

The English MSS. AEFGH are complete. B begins imperfectly at 647/4, ends
imperfectly at 683/34, and lacks 650/28–654/32 and 658/22–662/28. C ends imperfectly at 685/5. D begins imperfectly at 649/29. De Worde's edition is based
throughout Book XIII on F, but cf. the *addendum* above at 650/4 where De Worde
uniquely corrects a scribal omission. British Library MS. Additional 45680 f. 49
gives a fragment of text (655/9–658/27) which belongs to the DE (rather than the
ABCFGH) manuscript tradition: *Neuphilologische Mitteilungen* lxxviii (1977), 52–6.
The Latin MSS. JKLMNOPQRSTUVW are complete. I lacks 670/29–677/12. X
and Y are wholly lacking. Collations for the English MSS. are given by P. P. Farley
(Ph.D. Fordham, 1974): *D.A.I.* 35.3676A..

646 5 *effectes and doynge*: *effectibus*. Also at 652/26, 669/10–11, 692/21
  25 *meuynge aboute*: *exhalationibus*   cf. 693/28–9n. below
  28 *leueynge*: i.e. leafing, cf. *uegetationem*
  29 *onynge of body and soule*: *animationem*

647 3 *and watir*: *aquea*. Perhaps JT wrote *watiry*
  5 *is and semeþ*: *apparet*
  17 *for*: *ideo quia*. Perhaps JT wrote *perfor for*
  18 *and*[1]: perhaps JT wrote *a*, cf. *representat*
  18 *his kynde*: *in se*   cf. *in hemself* line 24
  31 *And*: *aut*   cf. *Other* line 29

648 3 *And*: *quando* (KMN *que uero*)   Z *que*
  8 *v°.*: *v*   cf. the better P 6. The reference is to Book VI. 21

11 *stones . . . welles: petra . . . fonte*
13 *priue*: adds *et abditis*
19 *pilgrimes and strangers: peregrinis*
21 *of moste: maxime* 'greatly'. Perhaps JT wrote *moste of*
28 *to hete and drynesse**
36 *clerenesse*: adds *et transparencie*

649 3 *and other pinges: et resultant*
19 *hier*: adds *de facile*
25 *quekynge hem with vertue: uiuificatiuus*
28 *in poynte and state: simpliciter*
32 *And pere beep: et cetera secundum f.*
34 *sore eyen: oculorum uulnera*   Z *oculorum ulcera*

650 10 *he seip: dicunt*, i.e. not a reference to Isidore
12 *Garamantes*: adds *dicunt*
29 *for²*: adds *nimiam*

651 3 *is yshewed: se ostendit*
6 *nere: uicinior.* JT's form was perhaps *nerre*
20 *ystopped oper yturnede and ylette: intercipiatur*
20 *is: est igitur*
21–2 *euerlastynge . . . meuynge: quoad fluxum perhennitatem quoad situm profunditatem quoad motum circularitatem.* JT's rendering of *quoad* constructions are compressed throughout this chapter, e.g. 652/10–12; at 652/26 he translates *quoad* as *touchinge*, his usual form
22 *rennep: currere . . . consueuit* cf. 641/22
24–5 *manere of spryngynge: amaritudinis qualitatem*
34–5 *pe modir pat is pe see: matrice abysso*, translated *pe modir of watir* 664/24
35 *oute of welle heuedes: in sua principia*

652 2 *and also: et principium*
6–7 *pe si3t . . . perto: quoad aspectum specularem perspicuitatem* '(there needs to be known) the clarity of its mirror-like quality'. Z *speculatorem* for *specularem*
8–9 *pat bep perynne . . . ryuers: obiectarum in fluminis superficie representantur* '(things) which are reflected on the surface of a river are seen'
10–12 *pe substaunce . . . vertuouse: quoad fluminis substantiam mundiciam et puritatem quoad eius cursus decliuem et precipitatem uelocitatem quoad impetum sui maximam uirtuositatem* '(there needs to be known) the cleanness and purity of a river's substance, the fall and force and speed of its flow, the greatest force of its flowing'
18 *and²*: perhaps an ME. addition, but cf. K *enim*

653 19, 22 *And: enim.* Also at 668/28, 681/1
24, 25 *he*: sing. pronoun, cf. *perdere . . . consueuit, recipit*

654 2–3 *pat is . . . speche**
9 *eueryliche pat: omnis.* JT's usual form was *eueryche*
10 *brynkes, brerde and brymmes: riparum suarum*
12 *chanayle and brymmes: terminos aluei sui* 'banks of the channel'
18 *fordwyneth: torrexit id est arescit*

655 3–4 *þat is longe in vertue, faire, and grene*: *et suum uigorem et uirorem* (LORTU om.)
diutius retinent et reseruant
  13 *qualite*: *facie*
  17 *and somewhare streyte**
  27–8 *vpon the same worde*: *ibi* (LOP *ubi*). Cf. 653/1
  28 *þat**: probably scribal and falsely dependent upon the antecedent *seith*
  36 *x°.*: *xii*

656 8 *and þere*: *unde*. Perhaps JT wrote *and þerefor*
  27, 30 *place*: plural, cf. *locis*, *loca*
  29 *a*: *uno* 'one'

657 3 *þat is in his waie**
  6 *a litil*: *breuibus interuallis*
  7 *þens*: *deinde*   Z *inde*
  10 *The glose seith*: *ut dicit glosa*, modifying the previous sentence
  30 *ryght-byleued men*: *fidelium Iudaeorum*
  31 *for*[1]: *scilicet*
  32 *departeþ*: *aperuit*   cf. M *separauit*
  32 *in þe presence of Iosue**: the whole sentence is scribally distorted, cf. *qui coram
filiis Israel se aperuit et eius ad terram promissionis transitum prebens in arche domini et populi
presentia se diuisit*
  35 *of his lepre*: *lepram* 'the leper'

658 5 *yre þat felle þeron*: *ferrum*. A doublet of ambiguity, *ferrum uel serra*. Cf. 850/20
  6 *prophetes kynde*: *prophete. kynde* is perhaps an intrusion from line 4
  9 *of gostlich gendryng*: *regeneratiuam*
  20 *multiplicacoun . . . gras*: *multiplici genere herbararum et arborum ac fructum multipli-
cacione* 'with diverse kind of herbs and trees and with abundance of fruit'

659 22 *comen*:*subintrans et influens*

660 15 Here and at 661/18 the rubric is editorial, the latter perhaps unnecessary as
Lake Genesareth and the Sea of Tiberias are one

661 20 *þre score . . . fourty*: *lx . . . xl*
  31 *mare Tiberiadis**

662 6 *stondynge*: adds *et non mote*
  12 *ful fruytful*: *magis uirentes et fructifere*
  19 *þe autour*: N *auct'*   cf. the better *Auicen* (variously abbreviated)
  19 *ofte**
  26 *þe oþer partie*: *eminens liquor*

663 6–7 *bereth hem . . . noyse*: *litora se cum strepitu constringunt* 'shores straighten
themselves with noise'. The ME. clauses may be confused relics of an earlier
brymmes holdeþ hem streyte wiþ soun a noyse
  31 *swyfteliche*: *celerrime*

664 13 *And þen*: *quanto*   Z *quando*

665 8 *terre*: JT has mistaken *terre* 'of earth' as part of the title of Augustine, *De fide et
symbolo. terre et abyssi nomine* begins the next sentence
  15 *Also*: K *eciam*   cf. the better *unde*

21–2 *þat is depnesse of water* *

666 5 *he seith*: *dicit idem ibidem*
11 *For*: *seu quia*. Perhaps JT wrote *or for*, cf. 672/7 n. below
26 *watres*: adds *et est aquarum quies*
28–9 *þat oþer drye. And of þo vapours þat is*: *siccus subtilis et aquosus*

667 1 *is*: *sentitur*
3 *and thikke, and freisshe water*: *aqua dulci quia hec grossior illa uero* 'than fresh water because it is thicker, and that'
4 *tokenes*: *signum*. Probably JT wrote *token*, cf. *is*
8–9 *þat may be drawen oute and* *: perhaps a scribal anticipation of the next clause
14 *fresshenesse and* *
18 *as it is yknowe*: *quod patet*, introducing the next sentence
19–20 *þe see. . . himself*: *flumen ingrediens mare . . . ipsum mare*
30 *clere*: adds *Item Macrobius in libro Ciceronis*

668 7 *in brekynge and springynge*: *duas scilicet crescendo et duas in decrescendo*
23 *3itte* *

669 27 *by oþer þinges*: *per seipsum . . . tamen per alium*

670 8 *stormes*: *procellosum feruidum et tumultuosum*

671 4 *And*: *unde*. Perhaps JT wrote *and so*. Also at 676/14, 677/4
11 *þen whan*: *quando ergo*
15–16 *or bycause. . . see*: *aut ratione maris aut ratione aeris aut ratione nauis. Z uenti* for *nauis*
20 *ylette*: adds *de facili* cf. 680/33 n. below

672 7 *For*: *quoniam uel*. Perhaps JT wrote *or for*, cf. 666/11 n. above

673 2 *of myddil erþe*: *siue mediterraneum*. Perhaps JT wrote *or þe see of myddil erþe*
3 *wyndes*: *tendit*. JT's form was probably *wyndeþ*
8 *the first cost is yclepid sinus Hispanicus and*: *prime partis sinus qui in hispanis perfunditur . . . appellatur*
13 *the holy londe*: *terram* cf. the better KU *Cretam*

674 8 *is yfounde*: *excerpitur* Z *reperitur*
9 *þerwith oþer colours ben ymade diuerse*: *alii colores quibus pictura uariatur*
12–14 *smale stones . . . grounde*: *huiusmodi lapilli homo inuoluti cum inter arenulas sint attriti maris colorem retinent atque fundi*

675 5 *clere*: *clara et dyaphana*
27–8 *and turneth into spounge*: *quandoque in pumicem quandoque in*
33 *crepynge*: adds *eo quod natandi reptandi speciem habeant*
34 *þerof*: *unde*. Perhaps JT wrote *herof*, as at 678/5

676 1 *of*: *et*. Perhaps JT wrote *a*
18 *shappe*: *formam uariam*
21 *place*: adds *igitur*
21–2 *and in . . . abidynge* *
25–6 *he vseth . . . kynde*: *ambulandi in terris vsum et natandi in aquis officium retinent a natura* 'they have by kind the ability of walking on land and the power of swimming in water'

29 *vnresonable*: *improba*, usually translated 'unnatural, unclean, greedy'

677 1–2 *þis fisshe*: plural, cf. *hi*
10 *restreyne*: *sustentandum*
10 *kynde*: adds *fluidam*
15–16 *beste and swetteste*: *meliores uel dulciores*
16 *rennynge*: *currentibus*   cf. the better W *currentes* qualifying *þilke*
19 *in*[2]: *et in*. All these adverbial clauses modify *water* in line 16
20–1 *is gode, and þe whiche þat is sotil is beste*: *laudabiliores qui sunt subtiles et meliores sunt illi qui sunt pelagini*
23 *from*: *supra*
23, 33 *blastes, blestes*: *flatu*
35 *þat water*: *illarum aquarum*

678 13 *slyme and in wose*: *humido*   Z *limo*
22 *briddes*: *pullos* 'young', to which JT gives his normal translation
30 *3if*: *quia cum*. The addition of *And* in the next sentence partly restores the sense
37–**679** 1 *flicke and his make*: *par cum pari*   cf. *euenness and make* for *paritatem* 678/16. *O.E.D.* sub *fleck* sb.[2] records the phrase from 1529
15 *he telleþ*: *dicunt*, i.e. not a reference to Isidore
27 *shelle fysshe*: *quidam pisces in conchis degentes*
31 *voyde*: adds *semper*

680 2 *seith*: adds *libro vi. de quibus dicit Yisdorus*
4 *voys*: *uoces*. Cf. 598/13 n., 656/27 n. above
6 *stertelen*: *transuolant*
8 *And*: LP *et etiam*   cf. the better *est autem*
16 *And*: P *et*   cf. *etiam*
26 *stronge*: *fortiores*. Perhaps JT wrote *strenge*
29 *as . . . ytoþede**
30 *And*: *ut*
33 *anone*: adds *facile*. Cf. 671/20 n. above
34 *strengþe*: *alluuione*. A contextual translation

681 8–9 *and makeþ it strowte**
32 *Ysider*: *Isidorus*. But BA wrote *Iorath*
35 *anone**: also added at 682/1

682 7 *and so faren . . . watir*: *sicut nec aues*
20 *Ysider seith*: LK *dicit Ysidorus*   cf. the better *dicitur*
25 *litil**
26 *And*: *et*. BA wrote *ut*, modifying the previous sentence
30 *stondeþ*: *stare . . . uidetur*

683 11 *fysshe is*: *pisces sunt*. Probably JT wrote *fysshe ben*   cf. 677/1–2 n.
20 *sowrenesse*: *grossam neque aerem*, cf. BA's *grossam maciem*. Z *acetum* for *aerem*
30 *to þe stomak and also**: perhaps a scribal intrusion from the previous sentence

684 2–3 *in þis place**
8 *where he is disposed*: *dispositas*, qualifying *insidias*
11 *þe same is yseide*: *idem dicit* 'the same author says'

13 *it is ysaide*: *tradit Plinius*

685 3 *is voide*: *cauantur id est euacuantur*

7 *mariori perles*: *margarite*, translated *mariories* in line 9

8 *soulede þinges*: *animantium naturis*

11 *when in*: *in quibus* Z *quando in*

19 *And*: *et exinde*

27 *knowen noȝt*: *agnoscunt* cf. the better IK *cognoscunt*

NOTE: Mr Farley supplied most of the *corrigenda* and some brief notes collated with ILRUW, which the General Editor found useful in making this commentary.

BOOK XIV

690 30 hi3e] hi3[t]e *and fn.* ACFGH hi3e   *cf.* LS pro ornatu

691 34 norisshe] *fn.* *ACDEFGH norisshede   LS nutrix
36 bowrys] bo*rw*ys *and fn.* AF bowrys   DGH boures   E bowres   LS ciuitatibus

692 21 *a*n] *fn.* ACFGHW in   *cf.* LS effectum
33 of] *fn.* ADFG and   *cf.* LS siccitatis
33 drynesse] *add* [as he seith] *and fn.* ACFGHW *om.*   *cf.* LS ut dicit Beda

694 19 ben] *read* [is] *and fn.* ACFGHW ben   LS est
21 of kynde] *delete and fn.* ACFGHW *add* of kynde   *cf.* LS uentorum
18n. D] C *and add* D ys

696 17–18 for . . . Fruyte] for [for] . . . fruyte *and fn.* *17 for²] ACDEFGHW *om.*
cf. LS propter puritatem enim

699 12 rennynge and] *read* [g]renn*es* [fro] *and fn.* *ACDEFGHW rennynge and
LS uirore ex
22 gras] gr*es and fn.* ACFGH gras   D grete   LS pinguedines et adipes

700 3 *fine*] *f.* Also at 708/27
14–15 it is . . . hem] *read* [as] it is ysaide amonge hem [þe cheef is] *and fn.*
ACFGH it is ysaide amonge hem   *cf.* LS dicuntur esse viii. inter quos precipuus

701 26 and so] *read* so [þat] *and fn.* ACFGHW and so   LS ita quod
31 mounte²] *read* [þe lynage of] *and fn.* ACFGHW mounte   LS in tribu
34 hilles] hille *and fn.* ACFGHW hilles   LS montis

703 11–12 þise ben þe hilles] þis [ys] þe hille *and fn.* ACFGHW þise ben þe hilles
cf. LS mons

704 20 Gode] gode

710 1 fructuous] u[n]ctuosus *and fn.* *ADFGH fructuous   E fuctuous   W vnccioris   LS unctuosus

713 1 Loth. þer] Loth, þer
2 and] *in and fn.* ACFGHW and   LS in
3 *alter comma to point*

715 20 n. *xxxᵐ*] *xxxxᵐ*

717 16 drynesse] d*en*nes *and fn.* ACFGHW dryenesse   *cf.* LS peruuis speluncis
et antris plenus

718 6 bysprynge] byspryng[yng]e *and fn.* ACFGHW bysprynge   LS irrigacionem
34 filþe] *add* [f. 169ᵛᵇ]
35 þilke] þi*k*ke *and correct fn. number to* 35
36 myste] *add* [Also valeyes ben more derke and dymme with þykke derkenesse
þanne mounteynes] *and fn.* ACFGHW *om.*   LS et densioribus tenebris obscurantur

723 25 spryngynge] *l*yuynge *and fn.* *ACDEFGHW spryngynge   LS uiue

The English MSS. ACDEFGH are complete. B is wholly lacking. De Worde's edition is based throughout Book XIV on F. The Latin MSS. IJKLMNOPQR STUVW are complete. X is wholly lacking. Y begins imperfectly at 699/34.

689 11 *substaunce*: *eius substantiam*
    14–15 *and oþer suche* *
    15 *wherefore*: *uero*
    16 *roþeren and oþer bestes*: *bestias et iumenta et uegitabilia*. Z perhaps *alia* for *vegitabilia*, but cf. 825/12
    19–20 *Therefore here þerof*: *ideo de illis*
    24 *arewe*: *interscalariter per ordinem*
    27 *Also*: *itaque*. Cf. *unde* 'also' 690/27. Perhaps JT wrote *an so*
    28 *and hat terra in latyn* *

690 2 *helpeþ with fruyt*: *opem fert frugibus*
    4 *and*[2]: *quod enim*
    13 *himself*: adds *qualitate obscurum et ex se opacum*
    16 *bodies*: *omnium corporalium*
    17 *feete*: adds (not O) *quod* (IQS *eo quod*   KR *quia*)
    26 *fongeþ*: adds *ab ipso*
    30 *sterres*: *solas*   Z *stellas*
    35 *parties*: *singularum partium*

691 5 *or*: *quousque*. Perhaps JT wrote *forto*
    7 *and noble*: *nobiles et*
    9 *alle reuerence and worshepe*: *diuinis honoribus . . . uenerari et colere consueuit*
    12 *he*[1]: here and throughout the passage JT probably wrote *heo*, cf. line 31
    18 *danesca*: JPSV *danesca*   LW *danesta*   MN *uesta* (N earlier *dauesta*)   O *da/uesta*   R *honesta*   cf. the better IKUY *dea uesta* (as in Isidore VIII. 11. 16) and Q *deauesta*
    19 *And he seith þat*: *ut dicit idem*. Perhaps JT wrote *as a seiþ*

692 9 *þerefore*: *et ideo*. Also at 694/13
    10 *and mete*: JLS *metis* (L *metit*   S *uirtus*) *gracia*, cf. the better *uictus gracia* 'by way of food'
    21 *effect an doynge*: JT perhaps wrote *effectum 'doynge'*. Cf. 646/5 n. above
    32 *and þe parties þerof*: *resolutis partibus*
    34–5 *as substaunce þerof and*: *sicut substantia eius quelibet pars*

693 8–9 *of wyndes*: *uenti* 'of wind'
    9 *erthe*: adds *et est significacio super hoc quia non quiescit in terra donec scindatur terra et exit ventus audita uoce et cetera*
    10 *liȝtnynge*: *concursus*   Z *coruscatio*
    15 *a grete cite þat ȝitte*: *ciuitatem cuius impressio*
    16 *cometh*: *sequitur uel concomitatur*
    23 *noȝt*: adds *ad aerem*
    28–9 *owtlawed*: *exhalat*. Perhaps JT wrote *owtlaied* 'led out'   cf. 642/25 n.

694 29 *sotil*: adds *et depurat*
    32 *is hoge*: *ampliatur*

695 6 *souþe see*: *mari*

17 *fatteþ*: *mollificatur impinguatur*

22 *fote. þerfore*: R *pede erigens vnde*   cf. the better *pede reliquam terram tangens uel*

24 *þat*: AFGH *þan* may be the better reading, cf. *quidam dixerunt quod* which begins a new sentence

35 *grete reyne of water cometh holownesse*: *ex aque ductu accidit concauacio profunda* 'from a rain of water comes great hollowness'

696 2 *brekeþ þe lond in some place*: *quedam loca cauat quedam extollit*

4 *abide*: adds *et in quibusdam locis congessit*

6 *sadde*: IJLOTV *compacti*   cf. the better *solidi et compacti*

8 *of dennes*: *concaui et cauernosi* (K *concaui* only). Also at 701/27

11 *rennynge*: adds *et origo et principium fluuiorum ut dicit Aristoteles*

19 *valeyes*: adds *licet pauciores*

23–4 *and þereof . . . mounte Olympus*: *in altissimis tamen montibus ut in Olimpo* 'yet in the highest mountains as on Olympus'

30 *snowe is yfrore*: *congelantur et constringuntur*

35 *liʒtenynge*: *ictus fulminis et fulguris*

37 *of fyre and of lyʒtenynge*: *a crebris fulminum ignibus*. Perhaps JT wrote *of ofte fyres of lyʒtenynge*. BA had *ictubus* for *ignibus*

37 *grewe*: adds *ignis dicitur latine*. Cf. 698/9n., 711/22n. below

697 5 *or þe toppes*: perhaps a scribal addition due to the graphic ambiguity of the previous *coppis*. Cf. *cacumina*

5 *and wayten aboute**: also at 722/24–5, 723/34

33 *þat lefte*: *arche solute reliquias*. The phrase may be corrupted from *ylefte*, cf. 705/17 and 698/5 *lignorum reliquias* 'some of þe tymber'

698 9 *grewe*: adds *fulmen latine dicitur*. Cf. 696/37n. above, 711/22n.

15 *treen*: adds *fertiles et fecundi*

15–16 *of herbes . . . þinges*: *graminibus in herbis aromaticis pleni* 'full of grass in sweet-smelling herbs'

17 *ben þerinne*: *frequentare illorum montium cacumina sunt sueti*

22 *white snowe þat lieþ þeronne*: KLMQ *niuium candorem*   cf. the better *nimium candorem*

24 *þe citees*: probably a corruption of *Scythe* 'the Scythians' (as in Isidore XIV. 8. 2), cf. I *siche*   JLNOST *scire*   K *Scythe*   M *scithe*   P om.   QU *scite*   R *homines*

699 2 *praiers*: JLMORS *interpretacionis*   cf. the better *imprecationis*

2 *praiede*: LO *interpretabat*   IPS *imprecabant*   cf. the better *imprecabantur*

12 *of water*: *roris et aque*

13 *offred*: *immolari . . . et offeri*. Cf. 546/5 and 15 *immolabatur* for *i-offred*

20–1 *for als moche*: *pro tanto*

26 *whi*: RU *quando*   IK *quia*   cf. *quare*

700 3–4 *he put . . . Caleph*: *deleuit ex eo Calef* 'Caleb put out of it'

16–17 *and waste in þe myddel estwarde*: *in medio ad orientalem autem plaga deserta* 'in the middle waste to the eastern side'

31 *waters*: adds *et*

701 1 *It is seyde þat*: *qua flat Eurus uel Affricus*

9 *is place*: *sint loca* cf. 656/27n. above

34 *hilles*: *alios . . . montes*

702 2 *fruyteful, for welle stremes*: *riuulis fontium montem irrigancium fertilior*
10 *Adam seith*: *ut dicit adam*
19 *ii⁰.*: *vii* (JLMOQRS add *g* K *capitulo* P 7)
20 *Regum 1⁰*: adds *et ibidem conuersatus quia ab eo in eodem loco Saul in regem primitus est iniunctus ut patet i. ix et x a*
27 *mounteyns*: *montis*

703 13 *to þe children of Israel and to þe peple*: *populo Israelitico*, cf. DE *to þe pepyl* (E *children*) *of Israel*, probably JT's reading (as at 542/29, 549/12–13)
17 *in¹*: probably a scribal addition, cf. *mons*
28 *and fley*: *septima die de saura quando fugiebat*

704 2 *of lese*: *et refectionis est enim fertilissimus in frugibus in pascuis*
10 *it was*: *mons fuit*
21 *sixe: sex tribus*
24 *aftir*: adds *et frequentaretur*
34 *ouercome*: *corruit . . . Israel*

705 3 *ii⁰.*: *super* (IK om.) *ii*
14 *litil**: perhaps a scribal anticipation of line 20
16 *Iosue*: I *iosue* cf. the better *in libro Iosue*
18 *libro*: *in predicto libro*
21 *oute of*: *ab*. A *fro* may be right
24–5 *boþe . . . half²*: *siue fuerint ultra Iordanem siue citra*

706 2 *and seiþ þat**: BA begins a new sentence with *Samaria*
4 *hatte*: adds *ab Augusto*
4 *lieþ*: *similis*. Perhaps JT wrote *liche*
10 *ben*: *pascebantur*. Perhaps JT wrote *ben vedde*
15–16 *of Israel*: *israel* (K *illorum*), cf. the better PRSU *superius* (P *ri'* and S *s'rius* abbreviations show source of error)
26 *is*: *sunt*. Perhaps JT wrote *ben*, as in line 27
28 *wodes*: adds *ex maxime*
31 *slee*: *permiant ac occidant*
35–**707** 1 *and of . . . Carmelus**
3 *oþer*: *uterque*. BA probably wrote *inferiori*
16 *mounte*: adds *redolentie et*
18 *thus*: adds *conualescunt*
18 *hatte*: adds *a medicis nuncupatur*
21 *of¹*: adds *herbis habundant precipuis*
33–4 *as Salamon meneþ*: *iuxta Salamonis sententiam in canticis . . . ut dicitur*

708 15 *Lyban*: *Libani* 'of Lebanon'
20 *also*: adds *et Io*
26 *when Dauid hadde tolde him*: *pro numeratione quam fecit Dauid* Z *quando* for *quam*
35 *menynge*: adds *idcirco*
35 *for*: *quia ibi est*

709 6 *a litil by*: *a latere*
7 *And here*: *unde*. Perhaps JT wrote *and hereof*, cf. 675/34n. above
16 *þey*: JT probably wrote *a*, cf. *fuerat*
20 *wreche*: *iubente*, translated as *heste* 541/25
28 *venged*: *suscepit*. Probably JT wrote *vonge*

710 13 *byshynynge*: *illuminabatur*   Z *illuminabat*
17 *whan*: *quia*   Z *quando*   cf. 708/26n. above
17 *plente of oyle and matere of liȝte*: *lucis materiam olei sua abundancia* '(he gave) matter of light from the plenty of his oil'
18 *litel strete*: *uiculus* 'little village'. *viculus* is not recorded in this sense, but cf. *vicatim* 'from street to street'
25 *iiiᵒ. Regum ixᵒ.*: *ii. Regum R x*

711 2 *drowynge*: *attractionem*. JT's form was probably *drawynge*, cf. 696/9 and 12–13
9–10 *brenne . . . brennynge*: *ardentem et comburentem*. The expansion recurs at 713/16–17
22 *grewe*: adds *impetus dicitur latine*   cf. 696/37n., 698/9n. above
33 *harder*: adds *et compactiores*
34–**712** 1 *eendeles many*: JLT *innumerabiles*   IKMNQU *immeabiles*   O *immutabiles*   P *in nu'abiles*   R *in meabiles*   cf. the better *immobiles et immeabiles*. Cf. 51/29n. above

712 10–11 *þe lepynge of . . . cragges*: the whole clause (as emended) is a vigorous translation of *ad duriciam rupis undarum et procellarum impetus eliduntur*
26 *oute of*: JLPQR *deinde*   N *deindie*   IKT *de*   M *de in*   O *de inde*   U *de* (*inde* deleted)
27 *shippe*: *classes* (P *classis*   T *classe*)

713 7 *þei*: cf. *peccasset*. See 709/16n. above
12 *and seiþ þat**
14 *dorste*: *quia pastores ambulare minime presumebant*
34 *of forȝeuenesse*: *promissionis*   Z *propiciationis*   cf. *clementie* translated *forȝeuenesse* 714/8

714 11 *praiers*: *precibus Moysi et supplicationibus*
17 *citee*: *templum cum arce protereret ciuitatem*
22 *þe Iewerie land*: the emendation *land* (MS. *and*) may be unjusified. JT generally wrote *þe Iewerie*, and MS. *and* may be a scribal intrusion
29 *and ioyful*: *et locuplecationis maxime leticie et exultationis*
29 *parfyte, riȝtfulle*: *perfecte iusticie*. Perhaps JT wrote *parfytliche riȝtfulle*

715 11 *ofᵌ*: perhaps a scribal addition, cf. *deliciosus*
18 *plenteuous . . . corne*: *fertilissimi . . . tam frugibus quam fructibus ualde apti*
25 *xlviᵒ. vppon þat worde*: *super I'e xlvi ibi*   cf. 653/1, 655/27–8n.
29 *Now**
29 *cite*: *mons*

716 2 *kyng*: *reges*. Cf. 611/21n.
5 *Ierom*: *Iosephus* (R *I'o'*)
7 *agiltid*: *ad iracundiam prouocantes*
19 *myrthe*: IJLOTV *iocunditate*   cf. the better *rotunditate*

28 *foules*: adds (except R) *et canora suauitas*
30 *swetenesse*: adds *carnium*

717 1–2 *worshepful*: adds *qui ipsum sua frequencia honorauit*
5–6 *shewed himselfe blisful and chaungede his fygure passingliche*: *se transfigurare uoluit*
10 *picke*: *squalidus   Z solidus*
15 *laundes and leopes*: *consitus et saltuosus*
19–20 *for. . . Hec ille*****: the last two words may have been a note to a scribe which
has been incorporated into the text, cf. 739/19–21, 893/3 n.
35–6 *moost picke and grete*: *crassior et spissior*

718 1 *cleere*: *purior*. Perhaps JT wrote *clenere*, cf. line 2
5 *places*: adds *ut dicit Constantinus*
7 *stremes*: adds *super colles*
7 *sep*: perhaps a form of *suep*, cf. *diriuantur*
12 *so*: adds *patet quod*
24 *Houses*: adds *et edificia*
34 *longe*: *diutius*. Perhaps JT wrote *lenge* 'longer'
36 *myste*: adds *unde partes uallium plus quam montium profundantur ad centrum et celi
circumferencia amplius elongantur*

719 7 *and*[1]: *nec*. Perhaps JT wrote *and nouȝt*
32 *toures*: JLOTRUV *arcium*   cf. the better *arborum*

720 11 *eren*: A *erþe*. The emendation may be unjustified or JT may have written
eiþe   cf. *O.E.D.* earth *sb.*[2]
20 *cheseþ tofor alle oþer*: *in omnibus prouidetur*
24–5 *and hat. . . puruyaunce****

721 8 *breden*: adds *et augmentant*
23 *downes*: *colles*   cf. the better IKQ *calles*
24 *of brome, of firsone, and of shrubbes*: *miricis*

722 5 *clenynge*: *herens*. The ME. form is perhaps a form of *clengynge*, unless JT wrote
cleuynge 'cleaving, sticking'
7 *walkyn*: *euagantur*. Perhaps JT wrote *walkyn aboute*, as at 540/27
10 *nestes*: adds *et conuersantur*
15 *now*[1]*: tautologous and probably scribal
18 *noye*: adds *afflictionis tedii*
19 *auauntage*: *plurimum tamen optinet commodi*
22 *is*[1]: *est suffusum*
28 *and aspien*: perhaps a scribal repetition (D om.   E *and awaiteþ*), cf. *post suas
predas diligentius speculantur*

723 6 *þat*: perhaps a scribal interpolation. JKLMNOQTV begin a new sentence,
but cf. IKR *ut* (R *et*) *dicitur. . . leo*
14 *hunters*: adds *latendi gratia*
16 *nedeful*: *utiles sunt et necessarie*

724 4 *and so*: R *unde*   cf. the better *quidem*
8 *Damascenus*: JLMOTV *Adam   Q adam̄*   cf. the better *dam̄*
8 *nameliche*: *autem*

9 *ore*: MS. *oþer*   cf. *mineralibus. oþer* here suggests that JT wrote *or* for the conjunction which scribes have regularly altered to *oþer*

30 *crepynge wormes*: *reptilia et uermes*. Cf. 837/12

34 *þe egle and þe hauke*: *aquilas et accipitres*

725 5 *addres*: *colubri et serpentes*

10–14 So JLMOTUVW, but in IKNQR this paragraph properly begins Book XV

BOOK XV

730 11 south] *add* [and] *and fn.* *ABCDEFGHW *om.*   LS et

737 22 n. *add* et qualitatem calidi regionis

751 18 londe] *read* [i]londe *and fn.* *ACEFGW londe   H *om.*   LS insula

752 21 oþer] ouer *and alter fn.* E oþer   D *lacks folio*   ABCFGH *lack clause*   LS superiori

758 7 Geba] Greca *and delete fn.*

762 4 lesse] lefte *and delete fn.*

764 7 Gadis. In here langage] Gadis in here language.

777 26 as] ar *and fn.* *ABDEFGHW as   C for   LS antequam

784 14 Bytalassium] *bytalassium*

789 31 in þe eeste. þat] In þe eeste þat *with preceding point*

793 7 Egipt. As . . . þare, the] Egipt, as . . . þare. The

795 9 *f*eselen] *y*selen *and add to fn.* *DE feselen
16 saphire;] saphire,

798 35 *delete second comma*

802 22–5 lanndes . . . wonndres] laundes . . . woundres

803 20 Liuones] Amones *and delete fn.*

805 1 and n. camen] *delete*

807 19 Seres. Also] Seres also.

809 16 wit] wiþ *and delete fn.*

810 19 Dacia, Denmarche] Dacia 'Denmarche'

811 2 *merules*] merules

The English MSS. ACFGH are complete. B begins imperfectly at 727/22 and ends imperfectly at 796/19 and lacks 754/17–64/5, 782/20–87/6. D lacks 794/20–99/2 and ends imperfectly at 812/20. E begins imperfectly at 727/22. De Worde's edition is based throughout Book XV on F. The Latin MSS. IJKLMNOPQRSTUVWY are complete. X is wholly lacking. U adds other names of places in the upper and lower margins, presumably by a former owner.

726 4 *wyde**   15 *boþe**
10 *But onelyche*: sola quoque
11–12 *tweye parties*: partes scilicet Affrica et Europa
19 *Paralepomenos*: adds *i.*
20 *and*: Isidorus et
22 *Asia*: adds *itaque*
22 *hauendele*: media pars
30 *wille, herte, and þou3t*: affectibus mencium

727 5 *Also**　　17–18 *a tree . . . encense**　　20–1 *þat is . . . holy**
　　5 *come*: *inuentus est* (KNPR *fuit*)
　　9 *places²*: *terre mansiones*
　　13 *myddel cuntre of þe londe*: *indorum* (L *indeorum*　　P *iudeorum*　　U *midorum*) *fines
omnium in medio terre*
　　17 *Ysider*: adds *libro xv*
　　19 *smelle*: adds *propter quam sacram aromatum fragantiam*
　　25 *As*: *nam ut*
　　30 *douȝter of Iupiter*: OR *filia Iouis*　　JLV *filiocus* (T om.), cf. the better *filio Chus*
(IPW *thus*　　N *nun*　　S *rus*). Cf. 504/19 n. above
　　31 *strecching*: JL *coangusta*　　T *angusta*　　cf. the better *coangustata*

728 4 *þe story*: *historia*, i.e. Peter Comestor's *Historia scholastica*
　　9 *seith*: adds *et Plius et Orosius*
　　12 *shape*: adds *quoad nos*
　　16 *iiii¹⁰.*: *ii°*
　　21 *And**

729 2 *londe*: *stadio*
　　4 *þat*: *adeo ut*
　　16–17 *Denyses doctour of þat cite*: *ariopagita*
　　17–18 *makeþ . . . famous*: *commendat*
　　20 *of þe wyse doctour Athenes*: *Dionysii areopagita*. Perhaps JT wrote *of Denyse doctour
of Athenes*, cf. line 16
　　20 *and*: *prout*
　　24 *in oolde tyme*: *antiquitus*, which properly modifies *haþ þat name*

730 14 *xii°.*: *xv*
　　15 *fro*: *ad*　　Z *ab*
　　20 *wymmen londe**
　　24 *xi°.*: *ix*. Also at 731/17, 746/21, 748/9, 763/14
　　25 *þan*: adds *maritis suis in dolo interfectis*
　　29 *delede prayes*: *hostium spolia diripientes*

731 10 *marites*: cf. *housebondes* lines 6–7. Perhaps in both cases JT wrote *maritos*
'housebondes'
　　21 *Amozenes*: adds *dicit autem Isidorus*
　　28 *for euermore**

732 12–13 *þe hiȝe mounteyns . . . yclepyde**
　　13 *erþe*: adds *siue Adriaticum*
　　17 *And*: *unde*. Also at 745/20, 756/2, 767/31, 770/14, 812/9. Perhaps JT wrote *an
so*
　　22–3 *houndes rennyng on huntyng*: *captibus* (J *capsibus*　　L *capatibus*　　MOU *rapti-
bus*　　N om.　　R *reptu capitibus*) *et uenationibus* 'with hunting and the chase'. JT
perhaps read *cannibus currentibus* as a doublet of ambiguity
　　27 *and⁴*: *unde et sic*　　cf. 732/17 n. above
　　29 *oþer on see*: *ceteris piratis*

733 1 *Austria*: adds *bauaria*
　　3–4 *of Germania bycome Englys and here ofspringe and*: *a Saxonibus autem Germanicis*

angli processerunt quorum progenies et successio. Perhaps an ME. scribal confusion after omission

15 *here feyned god** cf. 529/25 n.

19–20 *and so þe ilande hatte Bretayn**: perhaps a scribal dittography

21 *kynges*: adds *potentissimi*

28 *name and nacioun: lingue . . . lingue et gentis sue memoriam reliquerunt* 'language . . . abandoned the memory of the language of their nation'

31 *seith: tamen dicit*

734 4 *of þe londe: terre* (QR om.), apparently a confused duplication of the antecedent *beda*

4–5 *in here face and in semblant: in puerorum uultibus*

6 *as: sed*

11–12 *And also þere ben . . . stones: fontes calidi et metallorum larga copia gagates lapis ibi plurimus et margarita*

14 *þere ben*[2]: *in insula reperiuntur*

24 *hec est cui libera lingua: cui libra mens et libera lingua.* The translation at lines 30–1, *free men of herte and with tonge*, suggests that *hec est cui* is due to an ME. scribe

735 7 *fayre ryuers, wodes: fluminibus irrigua syluis . . . decora.* Perhaps JT wrote *ryuers fayre wiþ wodes*

736 1 *syluer*: adds *referta.* Similar suppression of past participles and adjectives of location in the first sentence of chapters is general

2 *oyle*: adds *opulenta*

2 *noble*[2]: *nobilissimis*

3 *townes*: adds *premunita*

3 *fruyte*: adds *diuersi generis*

8 *heede*: adds *latine*

13–14 *boþe . . . ȝonde half*: *etiam transmarine*

31 *he*[1,2]: perhaps JT wrote *heo,* cf. *ditissima*

737 1 *is more bare ooneliche of treen: solis ardoribus* (NPR *arboribus*) . . . *exuritur*   Z *arboribus* for *ardoribus. bare* is perhaps a corruption of *ybrent* (later *baren*)

21–2 *semelyche of kynde, fayre of shappe: elegantis stature et pulchre forme.* The transference of adjectives is perhaps scribal, cf. 739/30

22 *here: calidi.* Perhaps JT wrote *hote*

31 *renneþ þer*: MSS. *closeth (þere). floweth þer* would be nearer the scribal forms, but JT translates *perfluit* consistently elsewhere: *þere rennen by* 738/6, *renneþ by* 739/28. *closen* 739/10 translates *includit* Z *perfunditur*, cf. 762/25

738 22 *ybatred: in artum coangustata*

739 1–2 *ybeelded . . . Thezephion: scilicet tesephon et fuerunt in edificate*

7–8 *pleyne parties þereof þat beren corne: huius partes que sunt plane pro pane iugis. Z pro parte frugis.* The error *pro pane* for *pone* 'at the back of' (as in Isidore XIV. 3. 30) may have occurred in BA's copy of Isidore

8–9 *ben byclyppede . . . Inde: que autem aduerse sunt indii fluuii* (K adds *fontibus*) *terminantur.* Z *montibus* for the intrusive *fontibus,* and perhaps omitted the following *ochus fluuius,* tentatively inserted in the ME. text

17 *itsilf*: adds *pene*

20–1 *De . . . mergyne*: the scribal (perhaps authorial) direction has survived the insertion of the next chapter *De Brabancia* in its proper place in all examined Latin MSS.

29 *tounes*: adds *habens* (LT *hominis*)

740 16 *noble bestes*: *iumentis et pecudibus*   cf. 800/9 n.

741 1 *in þat place*: *a tergo*
    6 *þe north norþe weste*: *circium*
    14 *þat woned þereinne*: *ipsam optinentibus*. Perhaps JT wrote *þat wanne hit*, cf. *acquisita* 'wanne' 733/23, *obtinebunt* 'wynne and holde' 745/29
    31–2 *to be exiled*: *confirmato animo elegit exilium*

742 1 *he fonde þe place*: *locum ubi ipsa recubuit adinuenit et ideo nomine bouis locum illum boeciam nominauit*
    11 *syde*: *plagam*   Z *partem*   cf. 743/7
    12 *aboute*: adds *undique*
    18–19 *hath plente . . . fruyt*: *in uineis habundans et annona*
    23 *Multa*: *Multa*, the scribal form of the better *Mulda*, the modern Moldau. The scribe of the common ancestor of ACFGH has translated the name as *many pinges*, cf. D *fulta*, E *vulta*. Cf. 754/19 n. below
    23–4 *rennen togedre to*: *preterfluit*. The ME. follows the confusion of *Multa*. Perhaps JT wrote *rennen þorgh* or *by*, cf. 738/6, 739/28
    28 *beers*: adds *apri* 'boars'. Cf. 743/21

743 13 *burou3tounes*: adds *Isidor ix*
    14 *Ytaile*: adds *eo quod*

744 16 *Babilonia*: adds *ut patet supra in litera b quere ibi de Babylonia*
    19 *Asia*: *tocius Asie*
    26 *But*: adds *ex toto periit quando a tiro et Dario* (i.e. Cyrus and Darius)
    33 *yseie ferre þennes*: *patens*

745 2 *places*: adds *eque* 'equally'
    10 *Ysider*: *Orosius*
    24 *venisoun*: *uenacionibus* 'hunting'. Cf. *O.E.D.* s.v. 3
    32 *kynggedomes*: adds *in locis sacratis*

746 17 *Galles and Cellices*: *gallis* (LOT *gallicis*) *celticis* (L *celiscis*   OT *celicis*) 'celtic Gauls'

747 1 *and*: *unde et*. Also at 809/26
    3–4 *Sometyme alle Ytalie*: *ex qua aliquando prouincia ytalie*
    8 *of wylde beestes*: KLOT *ferarum*   M *ferax*   P *fra*   R *fertilis*   cf. *felix* (as in Pliny III. v. 60)
    18 *eldest*: *antiquore*
    21 *chief cite*: *matrem . . . urbium*
    22 *Poule*: only K adds *natus*, the palmary reading
    23–4 *beste smellynge*: *optimus et in spiramine fragantissimus*

748 4 *chief*: *caput et metropolis*
    9 *me*: cf. *dicit*. KMTU add properly *ysidorus*
    12–14 The geographical directions are scribally confused, cf. *mari cyrico cingitur*:

ab occidente mari pamphilico, a septentrione Cicilio, a meridie syrie et phenicis palago circumdatur. JT normally translates such syntax without trouble, cf. 750/12–14, 20–2

15 *prouynce: pelago* 'sea'
20 *streccheþ: tractu porrecta.* Cf. 749/16–17
21 *of Grece: grecie,* modifying *septentrione*
26 *wrote lawe and**

749 3 *and also: gignit enim*
5 *venym: maioribus venenis*
23 *soupe:* adds (not P) *habent l. milia passuum a septentrione in meridiem*
24–5 *As Orosius . . . tweye hundred pasez: Orosius uero milia 200 Prima uero inter has insulas ut dicit Orosius.* The emendations, based on ME. readings, do not restore the original sense

750 6 *ben: dicitur nutrire*
8 *iii°.*: T *3* cf. the better *iiii*
24 *and²* . . . *theues: piraticum et enim ex ipsis plurimum deduerunt uitam*

751 6–7 *and of face . . . shappe: decore faciei generaliter et formose*
9 *mylde of herte, and plesynge: pia est et mente placida*
15 *he hath þat name Delos: nomen Delos insula est sortita*

752 6–7 *and is a coste of þe Grete See**
18 *Dennemark**: also at 810/19
23 *Grecia:* adds *finibus suis*
28 *men of**: the antecedent is *he,* i.e. Europe, in line 25
29 *Affers, men of Affrica: affros*

753 5 *makeþ: et efficiuntur*
6 *in face and in skynne: in exterioribus in cute scilicet et facie*
6 *and²: et ex repercussione*
17 *þat come of him and of his sone Iothan: per Iectan*
24 *depper: profundior uel altior*
25 *spicerie:* adds *ut bdellium*
27 *parcial: parciales,* an abbreviated form of *particulares* without the contraction stroke. Cf. *parcial* 767/19, *particuler* 756/10, and *O.E.D.* sub partial

754 2 *bloo mennes londe**   3 *and rosteþ and tosteþ ham**   13 *a beeste with many colours**
5 *continuel hete: iugis estus*
15 *crisopassus:* adds *ac topasius*
18 *is²: magis est*
19 *Numedia:* ABCFGH *in þe myddel*   cf. JLMNOQT *in media* and the better *Numedia.* JT read *in media,* which was then fortuitously corrected in DE and falsely translated elsewhere, cf. 742/23 n. above
21 *adusta: exusta*
22–3 *men þat hauen here feet aȝens our feet**

755 1 *ben: vigent*
1 *Some: nam quidam*
6–7 *more ferlyche grisbaytynge: potius*
8 *lawe:* adds *passim*

11 *þat*: *capita non habere sed*
11 *in þe breeste*: adds *insitos et infixos*
19 *as it is yseyde**
23 *sonne*: KN *sole*   cf. the better *sale*

756 9 *douȝter: filia*   cf. the better KS *filio*. Cf. 727/30n. above
22 *Nigris*: JLOQW *nigris*   cf. the better *Tigris*
23 *Nilus*: adds *qui Egyptum preterfluit*

757 3 *Deucalleoun*: adds *et pure*
17 *of serpentes*: *anguium et serpentum*

758 1 *þat hatte Eole*: *eolarum*
2 *hem*: perhaps a scribal intrusion, cf. *ab imperitis uisus est*
13–14 *grete ryuer þat hat Mogum*: *amnem mogum* (P *magnum*). A doublet of ambiguity, *mogum uel magnum*

759 4 *xvᵒ.*: adds *et Orosius hec francia glebam habet uberem arborum uinearum fructuum ac frugum fertilem fluuiorum ac fontium affluentia insignem quam duo flumina nobilissima perfundunt in extremis eius scilicet rhodanus et rhenus ut dicit Isidorus*
5–6 *an þerynne ben special manere stones*: properly *lapides et lapidicines* are the subject of the previous clause, cf. *quarrers*, and *singulares* qualifies *beldyngges*
7 *gipsus*: adds *siue uitro*
11 *boldes*: *parietes et edificia*. Perhaps JT wrote *beldes*
12 *worke*: adds *et plasmatum litum*
17–18 *and made it . . . Grekes**: perhaps expanded from the previous *greciam decorauit* 'hiȝte Grece', cf. the following sentence
25 *gode*: *gaudentes*, properly defining the previous *in pace*

760 6 *and most nyȝe al aboute with Scaldeleia*: *scilicet Scaldaleia undique irrigua et profusa* 'i.e. the Scheldt, everywhere watered and fertile'. Z *proxima* for *profusa*
22 *with ful axen*: *uilior*. Perhaps JT wrote *foul wiþ axen*, cf. 737/21–2n. above
25 *glebis Thebis*: PUVW *glebe*   (UW *glebis*, U deleted) *thebis*   cf. the better *Thebis*. A doublet of ambiguity, *glebis uel Thebis*

761 26 *free*: adds *extra gentem suam*
32 *reuleþ*: *ordinant et disponunt*

762 25 *renneþ*: *perfunditur*
25 *most noble*: *nobiles maximos* 'noble and very large'. Cf. 739/10

763 4–5 *name of þe oolde Galles*: *antiquo Gallorum nomine*
12–13 *gode and catalle*: *bonis*. Perhaps a doublet of ambiguity, *bonis uel bouibus*
22 *in on ȝere*: *auro*   Z *anno*

764 5 *welles*: OPW *fontibus*   cf. the better *faucibus*
7 *Gadis²*: adds *id est septam*
21–2 *fynder and maister of alle gode craftes*: *inuentrix omnium bonorum artium magistra* 'source of all good things, mistress of arts'
25 *londe*: adds *et domesticis quieta*
25–7 *And were wrooþ . . . myȝt*: *contra hostium iniurias intolerabilis nimium et infesta*

765 6 *þe name*: adds (not NW) *Getuli*
7 *hem*: *Grecos*

22 *feminine; and þey are yseide aliti, id est veloci*: the reading derives from multiple error. Isidore XIV. 6. 9 *femine aliti pernicitate* was corrupted in its last word to *pro uicinitate* (IKNP *pronicitate*), which JT perhaps translated *for ney3ebrowinge togedir*, cf. MSS. *for ny3e growinge togedir*. K adds *id est inclosi*, cf. JT's *id est veloci*; both corruptly derive from *hirsuto* in Isidore's next phrase, *hirsuto et aspero corpore*, the latter part of which survives as *sharpenes of body* line 23

    28 *He seith*: *unde dicit*

766 9–10 *moneye oþer merchaundys and chaffare*: *ceterarum*

    17 This chapter properly follows *De Italia* 774/24. Its transposition, due to a confusion of *Hiberia* 766/18 and *Iberia* 773/16, apparently occurred in the common ancestor of ABCFGH and was independently corrected in B and F

    24 *is*: *equalis*

767 3 *as it were a gurdelle*: *sicut zona*. Probably BA wrote *situ trigona* 'three-sided' (as in Orosius I.2.69)

768 3 *welles...metalle*: the adjectives *irrigua...amena...fecunda* are absorbed into the antecedent *most plente*

    4 *stone*: adds *scilicet iris*

    8 *þer*: *enim ibi*

    28–9 *is byspronge*: *aspera*   Z *irrigua*

    30 *addere*: adds (not N) *ibi auis rara*

770 33 *hi3e*: adds *nec exprimunt*

771 10 *men*: *saturi et ceteris homines*

    13–14 *in mosse... treen*: *frondium lanugine*

    22 *coppe*: *iugis*

    23 *many men*: *multas gentes*

    27 *plente*: *infecunditatem* (O *in fecunditatem*). Z *fecunditatem*

772 4 *in*: *in principio*. The reference is *Historia scholastica*, *sub* II Mach. 3: 11, which cites Josephus

    8 *also**   18 *þe Iuerye**   19 *Iacobes sone**

773 3 *of name*: *resurrectionis* (generally *rr°nis*   cf. O *in tronis*)   Z *nominis*

    8 *departeþ*: *diuidit et distinguit*

    12 *3if*: *sed si*

    21 *cuntrey*: *regio... magna*

    31–2 *grete mounteyns... mounteyns*: *alpium iugis*

774 2 *oþer*: adds *nobiles*

    4 *stoones*: adds *scilicet ligurium gagatem margaritas et*

    4 *bea, and*: *beam quoque*

    5 *briddes*: adds *singulares*

775 3 *or with a water**

    9 *ilondes*: *riparum*

    12 *Also*: adds *quandoque*

    15 *of moysture, of waters*: *aque vicine*. Perhaps JT wrote *of ney3bourynge waters*

    23–4 *þis... þan Scipio*: *cum* (JR *tum*) *fuerat... Scipio*

    24 *ost*: adds *romanorum*

    27 *Affrica*: *uera Affrica*

31 *partie*: adds *uero*

776 16 *glires*: adds *comestibiles*

20 *Sardina*: adds *freto contracta*

22–3 *and come aȝeyne in noble poynt* *: perhaps a scribal anticipation of lines 25–6

26–7 *what pasture þe bole hadde founde*: *incognita sibi pabula* (NP *pascua*)

29 *toolde*: adds *Ligures* (S *ligutes*)

33 *stoone*: adds *quem greci catotiten* (N *catonitem* in margin   R *gagatem*   U *baccen*
JLQS om.   W om. leaving blank), O adds *gagates* only. The stone is properly the
catochiten (as in Isidore XIV. 6. 41).

777 10 *in þat manere*: *sic ex promiscuo virginum* (I adds *et maritum*   J adds *non*) *concu-bitu inuenies*

19 *but*: adds *flumina*

29 *auguyres*: adds *mortuorum cadauera tumulo non tradebant* (R *ponevant*) *sed pocius*

778 3 *as he was worþi*: *pro uiatico* (R *macie*   PW *marito*)   Z *pro merito*

6 *graciouselych*: *feliciter*

7 *ybrent*: adds *sic ob graciam domini combustorum*

23–4 *Toforhonde*: IKM *antea*   cf. *aurea*

24 *and*: *que dum pre breuitate*

30 *Smyrnia*: adds *urbem*

31 *waters*: *pactelus et herinus*, properly the rivers Pactolus and Hermus (as in Isidore XIV. 3. 43). The forms in the Latin MSS. are variously corrupt

779 3 *seith*: adds *lib. xv* (I om.)

18 *Hericius*: IKQU *tercio*   JLORSTW *icio*   M *nico*   N *hinto*   P *inchio*

21 *Genesim*: adds *xi*

780 7 *lxxii°*.: cf. *xxii*   QRSU *xxxii*   N om. ref.   P *ll*   W *lxxii*

15 *haþ*: *traxisse . . . perhibetur*

16 *Cesaris*: adds *ciuitatis* (I om.)

17 *Boþe*: *utraque igitur*

19 *hulle mount*: *montem*. Perhaps JT wrote *huye mount*

23 *citee*: adds *Tingi metripolitana*

781 1 *ii°*: adds *in Mauritania* (S om. clause)

2 *Athlant*: adds *versus Occianum*

7 *þat*: IKT *illum*   cf. L *ille* and the better *eundem*

7 *is fuyre . . . syȝtes*: *mutari* (U *micare*) *crebris ignibus* (J om.)

8 *of lykynge melodie*: *egipanorum satyrorum et lasciuia*

11 *with here*: *tenui*   Z *crine*

18 *Macedonia*: adds *in exordio*

30 *firste* *

34 *norse*: *nutrix*   cf. BA's *vitrix* 'conqueror'

782 8 *messis 'rype corne'*: *Messium prouentu*

17 *hat*: i.e. *haþ*   cf. *possidet*

22 *in lengþe and in brede*: *tam in latum quam in longum*

783 2 *ryuers*: adds *irrigua*

3 *tounes*: adds *multorum populorum domina*

16–17 *myddel place*: *punctuali medio*

18 *dou3tren*: VW *filias*   cf. the better *filios*

19 *as beste and moste noble place*: *Medicullium*   Z *meliorem locum*

25 *and vertues*: *et uirtutis situm*, properly a phrase governing *lykynge aspect*

784 7 *corne*: adds *scilicet*

10 *fruytfull*: W *fertilitatis*   cf. the better *feritatis* (T *ferocitatis*)

14 *bytalassium*: the reference is Acts 27: 41

18 *They*: i.e. 'though', cf. *quamuis*

19 *straunge*: i.e. 'pagans', cf. *barbari*

21 *pey*: cf. *nauigauit*. JT probable wrote *a* 'he'

22 *scapede*: adds *in Sarmenta*

22–3 *and lepe out of pe fuyre**

785 13–15 *also pere ben . . . yhuntede*: *ibi etiam sunt fibri qui et castores dicuntur*

26 *Gallia, Fraunce*: *Galaciam*

32 *propere*: LT *propris*   KNOPV *proprie*   M om.   cf. the better *populis*

786 16 *fines*: *fines*   cf. the better I *circes*   K *syrtes*   M *sirthes*   U *sirtes* (i.e. *Syrtes*
as in Isidore XIV. 5. 9)

19–20 *wiþ many . . . places*: *in multis locis ubi autem syluestris est feras generat*

21 *it is hi3e*: *iugis est ardua*

26 *Ysider*: *Plinius lib. iii. c. v*

787 12 *gon alonde and gaderen**

15 *with hast*: *facile*   Z *festine*

22 *Ophir*: *de Iudea*

30 *xi°.*: IKNPUW *x*   JLMORST *x f*

788 3–5 *Braban . . . Bryttisshe see*: JT has mistaken the word-order and so the geo-
graphical directions, cf. *Brabancie contigua a meridie, vicina Frisie ab oriente, ab occasuin-
sule Britannice coniuncta*   cf. 748/12–14 n.

10 *dyuers bestes*: *armentis pecudibus et iumentis*

12 *with many manere of gode venisoun*: *utiles habens venationes*

15–16 *þe neþer**

25 *Orcades*: adds *insule*

30 *latyn*: adds *ex greco*

789 5 *ane eyre*: *aeris*. JT probably wrote *of eyre*

6–7 *þat fyndeþ water ynogh to þat place*: *totum nemus irrigat*

7 *stremes and*: *nascentia*. Perhaps JT wrote *stremynge*

22 *hi3e*: *editus, id est altus*

23 *mone*: adds *ubi etiam*

26–7 *of vnsey and seye creatures*: *uisibili et inuisibili creatura*. JT has misconstrued the
dative of reference

29 *lond and cuntrey*: *locus diuinus*

30–1 *and is yset . . . voluptee*: *dei manibus in Eden id est in deliciis et voluptate plantatus*

790 1–2 *ful of. . . þe celer*: *pulcritudinus uniuerse gaudii et exultationis promptuarium*. The
confusion is probably due to an ME. scribe, cf. line 20

2 *of sensible creature and*: *creature sensibilis*, properly qualifying *witte* and probably
confused by an ME. scribe

3 *God*: adds *et digna ei*

4 *beeste**
15 *capitulo*: adds *x*
32 *plente*: IUW *fecunditatem*   cf. the better *securitatem*
36 *vapours*: adds *humidorum*

791 5 *of Paradys*: *eius*
9 *corrupcoun*: IPM add *ut*   UW *sicut*
10 *þat*: *enim*
21 *corne*: adds *et oleo*
24 *afore*: *contra leuam*
30 *also*: adds *ex illo autem lacu uelut ex uno fonte procedunt illa Nilus dicitur*

792 2 *of Parchia*: *eius*
6–7 *han here owne names*: *finibus suis discrete*. Either Z *nominibus* or an ME. scribal distortion
8 *of þat londe*: *suo*
11 *Hircania*: adds *solum*
15 *adders þat ben ycleped aspides*: *aspides ibi et serpentes*. JT probably read *id est* for *et*
29 *takeþ þerefore a name of grewe*: *pro eo greco utitur* 'uses a Greek letter in its stead'

793 11–12 *to þe Iues*: *prosperitate Iudeorum*
18–19 *bult þat citee and Anthia also*: *qui Anthiochiam condidit fundauit*
24 *and hath þe name of þe same people, and*: *ab eodem populo*

794 2, 6 *moste, most*: i.e. 'moist'. Also at 746/9
12 *bereþ wele wyn*: *frugifera . . . et uinifera*, cf. 798/6–7, 799/29–30
18 *three*: the emendation may be unjustified, cf. IKNOR *duobus* (W om.) alongside JLPQSTU *tribus* (M *ascribus*)
18 *Danubius*: the emendation may be unjustified, cf. IMT *dño*   JRSW *duo*   K *Adrano*   Q *dauo*   OU *dano*
18–19 *the whiche ben noble ryuers*: presumably an ME. addition unless Z gave a corrupt form of the third river *ac Tacia* (omitted in all Anglo-Latin MSS.), i.e. the Tisza, alongside the rivers Danube and Save
24 *renneþ aboute . . . Histria*: *hystriam uocant terram quam iuxta Pannoniam circumfundit*
29 *and*: *nutrit etiam et*

795 4 *sometyme*: *olim*   cf. the better W *enim*
9 *for*: Q *enim*   cf. the better *autem*
32 *Greges*: JLTV *gregibus*   cf. the better *regibus* (U *regionibus*)

796 8 *Iucusa*: *icussa* (S *cum missa*). The palmary form *Aracusia* (as in Isidore XIV. 3. 9) may have been corrupt in BA's copy-text
11 *sonne*[1]: Q *solem*   cf. the better *ignem* (as in Isidore XIV. 3. 12)
29 *lefte*: adds *et cetera* (U om.)

797 7 *grew*: adds *ignis est latine*
8 *fyre*: *fulminibus*
12 *and tounes**   25 *Peytowe**
28 *writer of stories*: IKNOT *historiographus*   cf. JW *historiarum grassus*   L *hystorum grossus*   M *historia grassus*   SU *historio grasus*   Q *in histi Grastus*   R *istorum graccus*

33 *and now þat tounne hat Peyters**

798 10 *moost*. . . *in þe syde*: *circa partes maritimas*   Z *maximas* for *maritimas*
16 *men*: adds *quibus mixti sunt*
19 *hert*: *corporum*, variously abbreviated (RW *cor^m*). Z *cordum*
27–8 *Erodotus seith de regionibus et descripcione*: *dicit idem de regionum descriptione videlicet Erodotus*

799 6 *Flaundres*: adds *et recie finibus*
12 *þat hat Chanir also*: *que et cham* (N *Tham*   R *iam*   S *chin*   T *tam*   W *tham*) *zota* (R *zoca*   IK om. phrase)

800 2–3 *strange*. . . *gode feyþe*: *barbara distans*   cf. the better I *barbara distans a dacia*
9 *bestes*: *pecudum et armenta*   cf. 740/16, 809/8, 813/18
17 *Ryne*: adds *usque ad montium cacumina*
18 *plenteuous*: adds *tante enim pulchritudinis est et tam incredibilis fertilitatis*
28 *is moche oþer gode*: *oriuntur multa alia habet*

801 7 *xv°.*: *ix*
12 *kynge*: adds *romam a romulo urbem ampliante et muniente romani dicti sunt*
19 *reede*[1]: adds *romanorum actum probitates si quem imitationis*
23 *naciouns*: *gens*. Presumably JT wrote *nacioun*

802 3 *was*: *dicitur esse*
6 *capitulo*: *est autem rodus insula eadem que et cyprus ut dicit ysodorus libro xv in capitulo*
11 *acordeþ moste*: *maxime concordans* 'very large'
31 *as Isider seith libro xv°*: properly modifies the next sentence, its misplacement being due to a mixed alignment of the last and first words of adjoining chapters

803 5 *þe emperour**

804 14 *Sardus*: adds (not L) *hercole procreata*
20 *seuen score*: *mcxl*
30 *here fadres*: *patentibus campis* 'the fields being open'. Z *parentibus in armis*

805 1 *Denculus*: adds *danubio*
2 *of Occisies*: LJTV *ociseorum*   NOS *occisorum*   W *ocisorum* (cf. IKMU *processerunt*   Q *ociserunt*   R *deciseorum*   P *sicut bipedes*). Perhaps BA wrote *orti sunt* which is lacking in the source (Isidore IX. 2. 92–3)
3 *foote*: adds *et ideo sic sunt dicti*
10 *as glewe*: *et glutinosa*. Perhaps JT wrote *an glewy*
26 *brasse and metalle*: *eris substantiam*
29 *in*: I *in*   cf. the better *ex*
30 *mony stronge*: *fortissimas et munitas*. Perhaps JT wrote *most stronge*
30 *castelles, and tounes*: *fortia oppida et castra fortissima*

806 1 *þe ryuere Danubius*: *cenobium*
21–2 *ben acounted in Boemia*: *in coma* (JTV *oma*   NPQRSQ *roma*) *sunt accensi*

807 1 *Wandales*: adds *lingue sue populos habens coterminos*
15 *þe men ben yclepede*: *eosdem enim dicunt antiqui*
21 *nulle fere*: *uellere* (S *nulle*   U *uelleris*   W *nlle*) *seres*. (as in Isidore IX. 2. 40)

808 10 *Gallys*: adds *siue Galatis*
18 *Also**

21 *it*: i.e. the letter *z* (variously transcribed in mss., omitted by IRSW)

27 *Abrahames*: properly *Aram* (as in Isidore IX. 2. 4), the error was perhaps present in BA's copy of Isidore, *Aram nepotes Sem quattuor* being corrupted to *Abraham nepotis Sirus Ceture*

809 8 *roþeren, shepe, and geete*: *armentis et pecudibus*. Cf. 819/24. 822/6–7
24 *xv°.*: *xvi*
30 *lambrum*: *agnis*. The historic form is noteworthy, cf. *lambren* 208/14–15

810 11 *drynke*: *de illius putei aqua*
12 *bareyne*: *fertilitatis*   Z *sterilitatis*. Cf. 823/33 n., 891/18
17 *Occean*: adds *septentrionalem*
22 *and no men wone þerynne**
27 *desert*: *desertis et*
34 *alone þe sone of Archaia, as it were*: *filius Archaia ut platani folium*   cf. the better
IU *sinus . . . folium*   Z *filius . . . solum*

811 12 *caues*: adds *penetrabilis ventis*. The error *ventis* for *venis* perhaps occurred in BA's copy of Isidore XIV. 6. 32
16 *Scicanes*: *citanorum*, cf. the better I *tirannorum* (as in Isidore XIV. 6. 33)
20 *seinte Agas*: *agathe*, cf. the better U *acathe* (*Achate* in Isidore XIV. 6. 34)
22 *a wondir maner salt**

812 1 *þinge*: adds *cumulos enim harenarum ad se trahunt*
4 *perilous*: adds *illac ire et dicitur hec sirtis sunt autem tales sirtes periculum*
13 *þe*: *nam*
19–20 *more þanne Bretouns*: properly modifies the next clause

813 3 *nouȝt onelyche in tyme of Bretouns*: *nec etiam ipsi Britannico solo impar est*
18 *beestes wylde and tame*: *feris pecudibus et iumentis*
32 *wymmen of wymmens londe**

814 9 *tounes*: *pagos et populos*
12 *he*: *idem*   cf. the better W *ysidorus*
15 *in²*: IJLSQVW *in* (RU om.), cf. the better *cum*
30 *þat breden not þerynne*: *quos dum ipsa nesciat*

815 1 *foure score and fyue*: RSUW *lxxv*   cf. *lxxxv*
25–6 *And þe prynce . . . Tetrarcha**

816 17 *þat*: *in quorum aquarum illuuione*
22 *was made of stones*: *hominum genus de lapidibus reparasse*
27 *ilonde*: adds *vacuam culteribus*

817 8 *eft*: *iterum*, properly modifying the next clause

818 12 *londes*: adds *et multas nationes expellentes*
17–18 *mounteyns*: *difficilibus montium iugis et accessibus locorum valde altis*
19–20 *of ofte sacrifice . . . dede men*: *nam in illis partibus in mortuorum exequiis antiqui thura cremare et offerre . . . consueti erant*

819 24 *roþeren, shepe, and opere bestes*: *armentis et gregibus*. Cf. 809/8
25 *ymyned*: *inueniuntur*. Perhaps JT wrote *vonde* 'found'

820 10 *anoþere*: adds *in alia uero planiciem prouincie Tholosane*
22 *spedde . . . Venia*: *ad triumphum uenire festinans*

821 2–3 *In the cooste . . . þbylt*: in all Anglo-Latin MSS. this sentence follows *Adriaticum* 820/30

    7 *Alpina*: *alpina*   cf. the better IU *cisalpina*

    12 *chasteþ*: *reprimit et compescit*

    18 *I trowe* *

    20 *redynes*: adds *unitate ciuium et concordia*

822 4 *welles and ryuers* *

    6–7 *and oþer beestes smale and greete*: *pecudibus et iumentis*. Cf. 809/8, 819/22

823 21 *firste*: *remotioribus*. Perhaps JT wrote *ferreste* 'farthest'

    33 *bereþ wele corne*: ILS *fertilis*   cf. the better *sterilis*

824 3 *bredeþ*: *gignit . . . nutrit*

    13 *in þe verreye*: IJLUV *in uera*   cf. the better *minora* (R *minor*)

NOTE: Mr Greetham had completed a first draft of a commentary when the General Editor passed to him the direction of a forthcoming edition of Hoccleve's *Regiment* and undertook this commentary.

BOOK XVI

825 10 *to* tretyng] *fn.* *AEFGH contretyng   C for to speke
   11 and soule¹] *delete and fn.* *ACEFGHW *add* and soule   *cf.* LS vegitabilia
   28 substance] substaunce

829 18 manere of] ma*t*ere o*r and fn.* *ACEFGHW manere of   LS materia uel

837 6 bochches] bocches *and fn.* A boch/ches

846 12 another] anoþer

847 18 men in] menni[s] *and fn.* *ACDGH men in   E men in here   F of men
LS hominum

848 23 strechche] strecche *and fn.* A strech/che
   25 scarce] scarse

854 32 n. *increase space before* firste

855 10 wommannes] mannes *and fn.* *ACDEFGHW wommannes   LS hominis
   11 sche] he *and fn.* *ACDEFGHW sche   LS ipsum
   20 Kallirates] *fn.* A kalliartes

859 6 202ᵛᵃ] 202ᵛᵇ
   29 þe] *fn.* *ADEF þere   C sore   GH here   W the
   34 Anoþer] *fn.* ADG and oþer

862 15 *adjust line number*

863 8 togidres] togideres

866 8 n. substaunce] *add square bracket*

870 14 ventosite] ven[e]*n*osite *and fn.* *ABCDEFGHW ventosite   LS uenenositatis

871 25 beþ] beþ [yseye] *and fn.* ADFGHW *om.*   *cf.* LS reddit
   34 n. gleymyn/ge] glemyn/ge

872 17 lechcherous] *fn.* A lech/cherous

873 31 *libro*²] *fn.* A ho   DFG hoc   H hº   LS liº

876 15 and n. s*o*ft] s*we*t
   19 vnsauery] vnsauory

878 11 dep] deþ

881 3 that] þat
   5 wip] wiþ

The English MSS. ACEFGH are complete. B lacks the whole book except 867/2–
868/2 and 870/4–871/4. D lacks 825/1–830/14. De Worde's edition is based
throughout Book XVI on F. The Latin MSS. JLMNOPQRTUVWY are complete.
I lacks 831/33–838/30. K ends at 858/6. S is damaged until 826/7, X until 830/7.

825 12 oþer beestes: *iumenta*   cf. *aliis iumentis* 738/11
   20 *xvii.*: W *xvii*   cf. the better *xvi* (IN *xv*)

826 8 *Isider*: Io' cf. the better KMNO *Ierom'*

9 *He sette*: IKNPV *posuit* OQRS *posui* JLMTUWX *posu.*

16 *to smyte inwarde*: *repercussiuam*

18 *stoone*: adds *que ualet ad omnia supradicta*

21–3 *and also. . . yfounde*: U *inter harenulas* cf. *lapides etiam polliti et gemme preciose in marino littore inueniuntur* (L adds *lapides*) *inter harenulas* 'also polished stones and precious gems are found on the seashore among gravel'. The intrusive *lapides* in L recurred in Z.

24 *pere*: *in maris ostiis et littoribus*

26–7 *and stoppeth . . . see*: *et ex harenis sic accumulatis aque fluuiales ne mare subintrent aliquotiens retardantur* 'and because of the gravel thus accumulated the waters of the river do not run into the sea, being somewhat held back'

27 *Isider*, **827** 4 *Isider*: *I'o'* cf. the better KN *Ieron'*

4 *it is harde and moste perel*: IJLOTU *maxime est periculosum* cf. the better *maxime est difficile et periculosum*

26 *seip*: adds *argilla est frigiditate sua sanguinis restrictiua ut dicit constantinus*

30 *xv.*: MNQW *xv* cf. the better *xvi*

828 16 *crises*: *crises* cf. the better IKMNP *ophaz (S opiz)*

26 *nesshe*: *compactius* (IJ *compacius*)

829 4 *is*: *inuenitur*. Perhaps JT wrote *is yfounde*, but cf. 840/5 n., 841/25 n., and 848/25.

20 *comfortep*: ORUW *comfortat* JLMPRVX om. K *delet* N *meditur* T *confricat* cf. the better IQ *corrodit*

20 *venomes*: *maculas* 'blemishes'

28 *cleuep*: IMP *finditur* 'is split', cf. *funditur*

37 *oipery-ioynede perto*: *malleando incorporari*

830 13 *metalles*: *medicaminibus* (as in Isidore XVI. 20. 3)

29 *Richardus Ruphus*: JL .R. IT R KM *idem* cf. the better OPRSVW .D. and NQU *Dyas*, i.e. Diascorides

32 *citrine*: IKMOTUX *citrinum* (JLNPQRSVW om.)

831 6 *haue away pe skyn*: *excoriaret*. Perhaps JT wrote *hulle away*, cf. *strepip* at 858/31

11 *arguis*: *arguis* (R. om.), cf. the better KMN *argiron* and I *argirion* (as in Isidore XVI. 19. 9)

15 *brymstone*: adds *plus autem est ibi de aero et aqueo et argenti uiui quam sulphuris*

20 *Quiksiluer*: the rubric *De argento uiuo* occurs in NY only

32 *Richardus Ruphus*: KNOPRX *Ric'rufo* IQSU *a ricardo* JLMVW *ari.*

832 14 *of an henne*: MR *sepe* O *sepi/es ei* cf. the better *sepie* 'of a cuttlefish'

17 *mouth*: JLMSV *ere* cf. the better *ori*

28 *ydo pervnder*: TV *subposita* cf. the better *superposita* (as in Isidore XVI. 19. 2)

30 *noper coper**

32 *weight of two pounde*: JT's equivalent of *sextarium*

35 *matier*: JLO *materiam* cf. the better *naturam*

833 6 *colour*: JLRUV *calorem* cf. the better *colorem*

6 *white*: *solidum* (P adds *album* V adds *candidas*)

13 *markyng instrument*: JL *cauterium* cf. the better *cauterium*

23 *blood: sanguine*　cf. the better KMNPW *sanguine hircino* 'goat's blood'

834 7 *in þe left schuldre or**

9 *feendes* . . . *sleepe: incubos*

10 *sweuenes: uana sompnia*

17 *vertue of hete: uini colorem*　Z *uim caloris*

835 2 *fair schewyng:* LV *fecundum*　cf. the better *facundum*

17 *gemmis:* KNPRUV *gemmis*　cf. the better *gemmis nigris*

20 *Alabandina:* L *a lalabanda*　KO *Alabandina*　cf. the better *Alabanda* (as in Isidore XVI. 14. 6)

20 *colour:* JLV *calor*　cf. the better *color*

21 *more strong:* S *carior*　cf. the better *rarior* (as in Isidore XVI. 14. 6)

836 20, 21 *amarite, Amarites: amarite, Amarites*　cf. K *Amantos*, V *Amantes*　MNX *amantide, Amantides*　S *amatide, Amatides*. The stone is *amiantos* 'amianth' (as in Isidore XVI. 4. 19)

25 *xⁿ.:* NPQRSWX *xⁿ*　cf. the better *iiiiⁿ*

29 *place:* JLOPRSUV *locum*　cf. the better *lacum* 'lake'

837 12 *slepyng litergiks: sompnolentis et litargicis*

838 7 *Capitulo de calculo:* this reference, inherited from Z but independent of the citation of *Costantyn* quoted in Book VII. 55 (409/13–14 above), may be a relic of BA's reference to Isidore XVIII. 15 *de calculis*

11 *Isider:* JLTUV om.　cf. *ysid'*

22 *in handelyng: actu*. Z *tactu* (as in Isidore XVI. 3. 10)

26 *fyre:* adds *oleo uero extinguitur que solet ignis accendi* 'also it is extinguished by oil which usually is ignited by fire'

839 1 *ysode: ad modum pultis decocta* 'prepared as potage'

13 *parties:* adds *ut dicit isidorus et est idem quod plastrum quod in greco dicitur gypsum sed in teutonico spedecalo nuncupatur*

15 *precious:* L *presiosus*　cf. the better *preciosissimus*

15 *and schyneþ as fuyre: sic dictus quia ut* (U om.) *carbo est ignitus*　Z *et lucet ut ignis*

17 *and it semeþ as it were flame: adeo ut flammas ad oculos vibret*　Z *et flamma videt*

19 *xiiiⁿ.:* J *iii*.　IO om.　cf. the more common *xiii*. Perhaps BA wrote *xiiii* (as in Isidore)

20 *carbuncle: carbunculus*　cf. the better M *anr'x* (properly *anthrax*, as in Isidore XVI. 14. 1)

22 *pilke:* NOPQRSTW om.　cf. the better *antractatis*

30 *signes: signes*　cf. the better I *lichnus*　M *lignes* (properly *lychnis* as in Isidore XVI. 14. 4)

33 *of colour of reed silk: coccenei coloris seu ruboris*

840 5 *is yfounde:* the emendation may be unjustified. R om. *inuenitur*, and at 829/4, 841/25, 848/2 *inuenitur* is translated *is*

6 *and perfor: et ideo* (JNPRSVW om.)

10, 14 *crisopassus: Crisopassus*　cf. the better IMNS *Crisoprassus*. Identical forms, apart from the case ending, occur in the rubric

15 *prassius:* JLPVW *passio*　T *p'mo*　cf. the better *prassio*

841 6 *crisolentus*: JLV *crisoltistus*   IM *crisolectrus*   KQ *crisolectus*   T *crisolitus*
U om.   cf. the better NOPRSWX *crisolentus*
9 *xvᵒ*.: JMNRSTVW *xv*.   cf. the better *xvi*
25 *is*: *inuenitur*   cf. the better I *nec . . . inuenitur* (as in Isidore XVI. 13. 1). See
840/5 n. above
26 *And . . . longe*: *est ei* (MOUVX *ibi*) *glacies ideo reddit hanc speciem*, and the better
IK *duricia reddit hanc speciem* (as in Isidore XVI. 13. 1). NPW om. the whole phrase

842 1 *colde*: *calida*
9 *Exodo*: R *exe*   cf. the better *ecclesiastico*
12 *matere*: *materialiter*
18 *Gregor his resoun*: adds (not O) *et ecclesiastici*
25 *whanne it pondrep*: IJMOQRSTV *contonat* (L *contenat*   N om.), cf. the better
KPUWX *cum tonat*

843 24 *smellep*: *flagrat*   cf. the better MQX *fragrat*
30 *it is pat stoon*: *sacer hic lapis est* 'this stone is sacred'. Z om. *sacer*

844 8–9 *brymstone . . . brymstone*: LO *ex sulphure*   cf. the better *ex sulphure et argento*
uiuo sed hoc accidit quando plus est de sulphure
14 *conthium*: JLORTW *conthio*   V *co'chio*   S *co'uerthio*   KMNPX *corinthium*
IQU *corinthio*
37 *brennep*: *uritur* (IJKLOTVW *utitur*) *et crematur*

845 9 *more noble*: *efficacius*   cf. the better IJMU *defecatius* 'more purifying' (as in
Isidore XVI. 24. 1)
10 *And so*: *vnum quod ex pino* (JLV *primo*   M *pini*   P *praua*   TX *puro*) *arbore*
(JLV *ardore*) *fluit quod succum dicitur*. Z *unde*
14 *as . . . Plato*: *in pretio* (LQ *p't'ito*   P *p'ti*   R *Plateario*) *habetur* 'it is held
precious'
19 *Isidorus*: adds *libro xvi* (JKNQRSTX *xvᵒ*   IMR add *capitulo*)

846 3–4 *liche . . . galle*: *similis galle* 'like gall'
28 *yseide*: adds *frigide esse et sicce complexionis et*

847 8 *wip clerenesse*: IJKLNQSU *claretatē* alongside *claritatem*
13 *radium*: R *radium*   cf. the better *radiis*
27 *isⁱ*: U *fit*   cf. the better *efficitur* 'is made'

848 12, 13 *excolericos*: *excoliceros* (I *excoluceros uel exococalicus*   KM *excalliceros*   L
excolicetos), properly *exacolitus*
25 *it . . . scarse*: *magis durum uel minus inuenitur*
35 *to hard and itempered*: the emendation is tentative; perhaps JT wrote *to harded if
tempered*

849 3 *is in*: *accidit*
13 *suet*: *cerusa* 'white lead' (as in Isidore XVI. 21. 7). Z *cerula* 'wax'

850 12 *flux*: *dissinteriam etiam fluxum*
17 *makep it foule*: *maculam deformem post se relinquit*
20–1 *of a sawe or of fyle*: JLORSV *ferre*   cf. the better *serre*. A doublet of ambiguity, *ferre uel serre*
35 *xxiiiiᵒ*.: *xxviii* (as in Job 28: 6)

851 5 *dyuers*: *care* 'costly'. Perhaps JT wrote *dere*

852 1 *Gagas*: *gagante* (IU *gagate*), properly *Gagatis* (as in Isidore XVI. 4. 3)
12 *3elow*: adds *attritu digitorum calefactus*

853 16 *prassina*: OR *prassina*   cf. IU *pinasim*   JKLSTVWX *pimasim*   Q *pinnas*
uero (N om.), properly *pinasin* (as in Isidore XVI. 7. 8)

854 5 *dymme*: *obscurus uel obtusus*
13 *citrine . . . blew*: *granati citrini et ueneti* 'pale blue, citrine, and bright blue'
18 *malicolik*: JLOTV *multiplice*   R *multe*   cf. the better *melancholice*

855 5 *stoon*: adds *ut fertur*
8, 9 *kiena*: ORX *kyena*   S *yrene*   Q *kyena* and *Hiena*   cf. the better *hyena* (as
in Isidore XVI. 16. 28)
18 *schappis*: adds *et politur*
19, 20 *kallirate*: JT's forms of this word are uncertain, cf. AH *kallirate*   and A
kalliartes   H *Kallirates*   DE *caluate*   CG *kalbate* and *Kalbrates*   F *kalbrate* and
Kalbrate   and their relation to their Latin form *kabrate* (JLNTW *kabiate*   P
kabate) doubtful

856 5, 6, 11 *lapparia, lapparea*: *lipparia*
14–15 *in schellis and in schellefissh*: one noun is probably an ME. addition, cf. I
coculis   JLV *cocteis*   KOQ *cocleis*   T *cocceis* and M *choncheis*   NPR *conchis*
SWX *concheis*. The latter better reflect BA's *conchulis* (as in Isidore XVI. 10. 1)
18 *margaritis*: JLUV om.
22 *ayer of þe euentyde*: *senectus uel uespertinus aer*

857 22 *lapidario*: NTU *lapidario*   IM *lapidarium*   L *lapidum*   JOVWX *lapid'*

858 4 *feni*: JLORSTUV *feni*   W *f'ri*   X *fenim*   cf. the better *feniculi* and the
ME. variants CF *fenill*   E *fern*   H *fenn*
6 *here*: adds *attrahit enim fleuma et melancoliam*
7, 8 *melante, Melantes*: N *melante* and *Melan'te*   cf. the better *melanite*. Perhaps
JT wrote *melanite*, cf. D *melanice*
23 *ston*: Y *gemma*   cf. the better *gemma uel lapis*
28 *wiþ cotoun or vpon leper*: cf. *super cutim* (P *cortum*) 'on a whetstone'. A doublet of
ambiguity, *coccum uel cutem*

859 3 *boistous grene*: *spissioris . . . et grossioris . . . uiroris*
6–7 *and it . . . happes*: KLMNPVW om.
30 *doucheum*: OPRSX *doūcheum*   J *concheum*   LTVW *coutheum*   cf. the
better INQU *corintheum* (M *dorintheum*). BA adds *gutte amoniacee similum*
32 *of aspectu*: *ab aspectu* (LPQSX om. phrase, T *ab aptum*)
34 *nirundicum*: PX *nirundicum*   JLOT *niridicum*   QRSUW *virundicum*   V
uiriudicum   cf. the better IMN *Numidicum* (as in Isidore XVI. 5. 16)
35 *golde*: *croco* 'saffron'

860 6 *to grauynge*: *sculpitur et politur*
24 *lest heuy*: *minime ponderosum*   cf. the better *minime fuerit ponderosum* (as in
Isidore XVI. 2. 8)
26 *soure*: *acidum* (IJLTUV om.)

861 2 *Isider*: *constantinus*. Cf. 867/29

4 *orapondien*: LMOQRWX *orapondine*   N *orapondice*   P *opandine*   TU *poro-pondine*   SV *.p. oropondine*   I *Noserpora*   cf. the better J *crapondie*, properly *crapondine* 'toadstone'

8–9 *serpentes*... *wormes: reptilium*   cf. 133/3

14 *onyx*[1]: adds *ut dicit Ysidorus Greci enim unquem onicen dicunt*

31 *fuyry colour*: JLT *renus et ignis*   OPQR *genus ignis*   cf. the better *tenuior ignis* (as in Isidore XVI. 12. 3)

862 1 *þis: hunc lapidem*, but the gallicism *þis* 'this one' is possible

2 *Ynde*: adds *ut dicit Ysidorus*

7 *auaricia: auricia* (JOV *aurusia*   L *amnsia*   MX *aurisia*). JT perhaps wrote *aurisia* (as in DE)

13 *white*: NPQRSWX *alba*   cf. the better *aspera*

864 14 *and opere euele bestes**

26 *cracetas*: JLTV *tracetas*   OQS *traceras*   R *crateas*   cf. the better *crateras* 'a vessel for mixing wine' (as in Isidore XX. 5. 3)

865 7 *brenneþ*: LV *adducit*   cf. the better *adurit*

14 *ʒolow*: R *croceus*   cf. *roseus* and the better S *rubeus* (as in Marbod ch. 51). Cf. 965/11

866 22 *destroyeþ: albescit et destruit*

867 2 *is as: est*

5 *gendreþ*: adds *per exustionem siue resudationem*

5–7 *as tewly*... *bredeþ: et* (MNU *ut*) *minium stibum et huiusmodi*

8 *By vse: est autem utile plumbum secundum usum medicine*

9, 29 *Isider: Constantinus*   Cf. 861/2

9 *aʒeins: contra vsturam ignis et*

22 *colour*: JLMOPUVWX *calorem* (Q om.), cf. the better *colorem*

34 *þat beþ alyue*: NOPQRSWX *uiua*   cf. the better *infirma*

35 *oignement: inunctionis et malagmata*

868 10–11 *Also*... *beem: et resolutione etiam pulueris siue in athomis solis radius*. JT's expanded translation, perhaps distorted by scribal error, confuses the sense, i.e. it is the sunbeam that cannot be seen

20, 21 *quandros*: JLTUV *qvamdias*   I *quandiade* and *Qvandias*   QS *quandros* and *Qvamdros*   cf. the better *qvandros*

21 *grene*: IJLMQTUVW *uilis*   cf. the better *uiridis*

26 *armonicus: armenicus* 'Armenian'

27 *and*[2]: NPQRSX add *inuenitur in armenia*   cf. the better *sub rufo colorem habens et inuenitur in armenia*

27 *vertu: naturam*. Z *uim* as at 870/25, or *virtutem* as at 667/27

869 19 *ʒiueþ lyf to*: JLTV *cogitat*   U *corroborat*   cf. the better *uegetat*

24 *laxurium*: JLTV *larurium*   I *laurium*   cf. the better *laxurium*

870 10 *blowyng: tumoris et inflature*. Perhaps JT wrote *bolnynge*, see 405/14n. above

22 *I haue assayed: uidi*... *experiri* 'I have seen assayed'

26 *bocches*: adds *nam ut dicit Dias puluerizatus et lacti admixtus ulcera sanat*

26 *woundes: uulneribus*. If Z read *mulieribus* no emendation is needed

871 28 *Braduþ*: JT possibly wrote *Bradany*   cf. CGF *brandanth*   EGH *bradany*

D *brandany* and JLOTVW *bradiam*   N *bradiām*   PR *bradiani*   S *bradia*   and the better IMQU *bactriani* (as in Isidore XVI. 7. 1)

872 5 *may nou3t*: JLNOPSTVWX *possint*   R *vbi . . . possint*   cf. the better *ne . . . possint*

    11 *hap*: adds *tertio*

    13 *seip*: adds *et lapidarium*

    15 *emitriceum*: L *emitecheum*   J *emitrocheum*   T *emitrocleum*   cf. the better *emitricium* (PWX *emitritheum*) (as in Marbod ch. 7). Cf. 153/27n. above

873 3 *is wip*: *constat*. The idiom is a possible translation

    17 *spekke*: adds *que* (better *quasi*) *fulgore continens lune ymaginem illa autem candida macula in corpore*

874 8 *reed*: O *mineum*   cf. *mineum unde* (QRS *siue*   U om.) *vermilium* (N *uirmiculum*)

    19 *takep*: adds *ex vi ignea ipsius sulphuris*

    19 *whitenesse*: JLSTV *candorem*, better *calorem* (OPR *colorem*)

    22 *Coleys*: *coleys* and OR *calidus*, cf. the better M *eoleys* (as in Isidore XVI. 1. 9). The variant *calidus* is interesting in view of ACFGHW *hoote*, but the emendation is supported by DE

875 2 *certeyn siknesse*: LNP *mitiales morbos*   cf. the better *comitiales morbos* (as in Isidore XVI. 1. 10). The ME. adjective reflects JT's solution of a meaningless corruption in Z. Cf. 896/22n. below

    20 *wastyng*: adds *attrahendi*

876 2 *rokkes*: *rupes et montes*

    7 *argencium*: JLT *ager gentium*   OR *gentium*   cf. the better *agrigentium* (as in Isidore XVI. 2. 4) and 811/22

    10 *is²*: the emendation may be unnecessary since U uniquely omits *est*

    22 *dyuers bestes*: *pecudes et armenta* 'cows and cattle'. Cf. 809/8n. above

    35 *druyep*: *maiorem habet vim in disiccando*

877 7 *brede*: IJLMOQTUV *passis*   cf. the better *panis*

    23 *and . . . nebulis*: R *testam nebulis*   cf. the better *quam insulam tectam nebulis* 'when clouds covered the island'. The phrase properly belongs to the next sentence (as in Isidore XVI. 7. 9)

878 19 *Dyas*: *Platearius*

    24 *in lapidario*: U *in lapidario*   L. om.   cf. the better *Platearius*

    33 *vitrum*: adds *ut dicit Ysidorus*

879 5 *Bellus*: NOPQRSW *bellum* (JLTUV *telum*   I *uelum*), cf. the better *bellus* (as in Isidore XVI. 16. 1)

    19 *ybete*: adds *aliquando torno* (RSV *coruo*) *teritur* 'sometimes it is ground on the lathe'

    23 *osianus*: JLQTUV *osianus*   cf. the better *obsianus*

    26 *is wip fatty sight*: *crassiore visu* 'with a more fatty appearance'. The phrase properly qualifies *bright* in line 25

880 5 *brutil*: JLOTU om.   cf. the better *fragile*

15 *spirit*: LNOPT *ip'm*   JRSV *sapientes*   cf. the better *spiritum*
23, 24 *zyneth*: IMPQ *Zymeth*   cf. the better *Zymiech*
24 *is*[1]: *est idem quod lapis lazuli et est*

881 2 *as Dias seiþ* *

BOOK XVII

884 20 falleþ] fa*i*leþ *and fn.* *ACDEFGHW falleþ   LS subtrahitur

885 30 of² *add* [euenes and likenesse for] *and fn.* *ACDEFGHW *om.*   LS equalitas et similitudo quia

887 10 and] *delete and fn.* *ACDEFGHW and   LS *lack word*
10 seiþ] seiþ.
11 and Albu] a*s* Albu [seiþ] *and fn.* ACFGHW and Albu   DE *om. clause*   LS ut dicit Albu

889 3 þan anoþer¹] *delete and alter fn.*
5 alle] *read* [f. 209ᵛᵇ] alle
7 and²] .And [som] *and fn.* *ACDEFGHW *om.* LS quedam

897 21 *e*ntre] *fn.* *ACDEFGHW in þe tre   LS ingredi

902 1 oþre] o*tt*er *and fn.* *ACDEFGHW oþer   *cf.* LS extremitates

911 15 beþ] *fn.* ACFGH *om.*   *cf.* LS coniungitur

917 2 vyne wiþoute] vyne. Wiþoute
3 of bowes. For] *delete and fn.* *ABCDEFGHW of bowes for   LS *lack words*

923 3 *Canticum* and] *Canticum*. And

930 7 219ʳᵇ] 219ᵛᵇ

934 3-4 waste . . . þirle] waste; . . . þirle;
3 and¹] *delete and fn.* *ACDEFGHW and   LS *lack word*
5-6 helpiþ . . . aʒeins scabbes] helpiþ aʒeins . . . scabbes *and fn.* *ACDEFGHW helpiþ . . . aʒeins scabbes   cf. LS valere contra

936 12 and²] *fn.* *ACDEFGHW *om.*   LS et

937 15 cloues in] in closed *and delete fn.*

947 5 so*n*est] ferst *and delete fn.*

951 14 some] *s*uch *and fn.* *ACDEFGHW some   LS tales

953 26 and longe] andlonge

956 30 , þanne by strong hete] by strong hete, þanne *and fn.* *ACDEFGHW þanne by strong hete   LS ui caloris tunc

959 3 Ysdier] Ysider

960 22 seiþ þat] seiþ. *and fn.* *ABCDFGHW seiþ þat   E *om. clause*   *cf.* LS vbi dicit glosa

967 3 of²] *to and fn.* *ABCDEFGW of   H fro   LS ad

968 9 229ʳ] 229ʳᵃ
30 þat] a*n and fn.* *ABCDEFGHW þat   LS et

973 24 n. 24] 22

974 15 for] *read* [or] for *and fn.* *ABCDEFGHW for LS uel quia
15 [if] *and n.*] *delete*
21 bereþ] *add* [fruyt] *and fn.* *ABCDEFGHW *om.* LS fructifera
25 *delete 2nd comma*

975 25 candentem] *cadentem and fn.* ABCEFGHW candentem LS cadentem
35 Anticlaudyan] Claudyn *and delete fn.*

977 9–10 resoun. Isider seiþ þis] resoun, Isider seiþ. þis

979 22 mastik] *mastix*

982 6 heed] heed,

986 3 223] 233

988 30 and¹] *read* [for] a *and fn.* *ABCDEFGHW and *cf.* LS habet enim

995 24 yformed] yfeyned *and delete fn.*

997 27 Plius, also] Plius also,

1002 26 he] *delete and fn.* ABCFGHW he *cf.* LS conueniunt

1003 29 þrusching] þrushing

1005 13 and n laxing] laxen[g]

1008 27 ȝere] ere *and fn.* AFG ȝere D erþe LS spica

1010 16 fructuous] vnctuous *and fn.* ABCFGHW fructuous LS vnctuosior
26 seith whanne] seith. Whanne

1012 23 þat is,] ,þat is,

1013 7 mochil] *read* [so] mochil *and fn.* *ABCDEFGHW *om.* *cf.* LS tanta

1014 8 a vyne ... ygraffed²] *transpose clauses*
14–15 oþer oþer] *of* oþer *and alter fn.*

1018 13 worme ete] worme-ete

1019 13 flewme] flux *and fn.* *ABCDEFGHW flewme LS fluxum

1021 31 places] place *and fn.* *ABCDEFGHW places LS locus

1022 28 n. *transpose bracket*

1023 21 n. *add bracket*

1027 14 *add point after* loynes

1032 14 erþy] eiry *and fn.* *ABCDEFGHW erþy LS era
34 n. 34] 35

1033 17 water] mater *and fn.* *ABCDEFGHW water LS materiam

1035 29 oof] of *and fn.* A oof
30 and] *delete and fn.* ACFGH *om.* LS *lack word*
31 closeþ] cle[n]seþ *and fn.* *ABCDEFGHW closeþ LS purgat

1036 27 and²] *read* [wiþ] *and fn.* *ABCDEFGHW and *cf.* LS habentium

1037 9 iuys] *fn.* *ABCFGHW muste DE myste LS succus
10 fruyte] *fn.* A fruytz D froytes LS fructus
10 werissh] neissh *and fn.* *ABCEFGHW werissh D wors LS molli

29 hem] *fn.* *ABCDEFGW *om.* H of hem   *cf.* LS inuadentium

1039 10 membris] *add square brackets and space fn.*

1044 15–16 n. þn] þan

   28 speres] sp*ores and fn.* ABCFGHW speres   LS calcaria

1045 9 *first comma should be point*

1049 30 *adjust line number*

1050 14 purgynge] *add comma*

1052 1 difference] differente

   3 propreliche, and *sementinum*] propreliche *sementinum*, *and fn.* *ABC DEFGHW and   LS *lack word*

   35 and[1]] a *and fn.* *ABCDEFGHW and   *cf.* LS inualescit

1054 29 240] 249

1059 10 Roof trees] R*a*ftres *and fn.* ABFGHW roof trees   D rustres   LS ligna

1064 7–8 and n. sprayes [worþeþ . . . sprayes] *read* [ryndes worþeþ . . .] sprayes

   30 þynne] *add* [and] *and fn.* *ABCEFGHW *om.*   *cf.* LS tenuissimus laxatur

1065 5 n. *and] *7 and

1067 19 for to] forto [a] *and fn.* *ABCDEFGHW *om.*   *cf.* LS quousque perueniat

1068 31 n. have] haue

1069 7 and[1]] *read* [þat] *and fn.* *ABCDEFGHW and   *cf.* LS extensiones

1075 13 þis] þat þis *and delete colon and fn.*

1089 12 n.[2] 12] 14

   35 *add line number*

1090 18 þerof. Isaac seiþ] þerof, Isaac seiþ

The English MSS. ACFGH are complete. B begins imperfectly at 888/27, omits by textual lacuna 925/19–958/9 (the equivalent of one quire of 8 in double-columned folio), lacks 1042/28–1047/24, and ends imperfectly at 1084/10. D lacks 1063/4– 1067/12. E ends imperfectly at 1088/8. De Worde's edition of Book XVII is based on F. The Latin MSS. IJLMNOPQRSTUVWXY are complete. K is wholly lacking.

882 21 and torneþ into þe kynde of: in

   22 into: in arbustam id est

883 2 tree: adds *uel plante*. Also at 892/8, 893/12, 898/23

   3 ykutte: adds *nec delectat quando nutritur et cibatur nec uigilat*

   13 þe herte: *cor* (M om.), a partial repetition of *corrumpens*

   15 and[1]: ut

   24 duryng: adds *et ex radice animata* (MT *annuam*   P *müam*) *renouacionem*

   28 al þe hole: *ex suo toto*. Perhaps JT wrote *of þe hole*

   37 i°: i (OPX om.), a false expansion of *li* to *libro i*

884 1 torneþ alle into fedyng of þe tree: *totaliter a regimine nature dimittitur*

   3–6 Also . . . togidere: *item quedam habent nodos quia illis mediantibus partes successiue generate ad inuicem colligantur*, repeated in Z

14–15 *a tre takeþ soone fuyre and light*: *habet lignum siue truncum*. Perhaps JT wrote *haþ a spuyre and schaft*, a scribe then anticipating lines 15–16

16 *and²*: *vnde et*. Also at 922/1 and 4

17 *schaft: pars . . . fortior et solidior et substantialior*

23 *seiþ*: adds *Albu et*

23 *Ysider: Constantinus*. Also at 861/2, 867/29, 902/33, 903/3, 973/26

32 *pilere comunliche al rounde*: *figuram columpnalem . . . vtique*. Perhaps JT wrote *columnliche* or *columpnale* 'al rounde'

885 2 *beþ in þe stede of synewes*: *similes sunt neruis in corpore animalis*

4–5 *kynde partyes of office*: *determinate a natura*

7 *and²*: *scilicet* (V om.)

14 *quauy*: ACFGH *þynne* may be better, cf. *raram* 886/34. Similarly at 899/34

15 *leues*: adds *cicius*

21 *gleymy*: *piceus* (LO *pisceus*   T om.) *uiscosus*

23 *þis: ita*   cf. M *ista*. Perhaps JT wrote *þus*

28 *þat: hoc in quibusdam*

33, 34 *neisshenesse*: *raritas* 'thinness' in this context

35 *sadde*: adds *spissitudo autem accidit propter sufficientiam* (P *insufficientiam*) *caloris ad condensationem humoris et eius terminationem* (MP om. last phrase)

886 4 *mighty: sufficientem*   cf. the better MQS *insufficientem* (P om.)

6 *moiste**

10 *by helpe of þe roote*: *de radice immediate*   Z *de radice mediante*

27–9 *groweþ . . . herbes¹*: *quedam sunt domestice et ortenses quedam uero sunt syluestres*

36 *quantite*: *magnitudine et paruitate*

887 3 *kynde*: OPT *naturalis*   cf. *materialis*

888 3 *cornerede*: *angulosi id est figure angularis*

23 *þat makeþ digestioun*: *digerendum*, properly in apposition to *to make þe fruyt rype* line 21

28 *fatty*: adds *sed fluidi*

889 15 *eiþer to oþer*: *inter surculum et truncum cui inseritur*

22 *humour*: *humiditatem sibi exeuntem*

25 *nought*: adds *de facili . . . nec ex bono semine uel radice arbores male*

28 *appetyte*: adds *siue appetibilis uoluntatis*

890 14 *Also*: adds *ut dicit idem*

24 *þat: quod*, generally translated *þat þat* in such contexts

27 *and makeþ it good to ete**

891 18 *bareyn*: O *sterilis*   cf. the better *fertilis* and 810/12 n.

31 *to þe hete and to digestioun*: *digestioni caloris*. JT probably wrote *to þe digestioun of hete*

31–2 *in pyries, and in peres*: *pyris*. Perhaps JT wrote *pyris* 'peres', cf. 1020/2

892 20 *libro iiii°*: *in x*. (Q *4°*) *libro*

24 *more parfyt*: *forciorem*   Z *perfectiorem*

893 3 *And*: *similiter . . . ibidem*

3 *pomgarnate*: adds (not MOPQ) an apparent scribal direction, *sed hic ponitur pro arbore scilicet mala granata*

4 *þerwiþ*: adds *eo quod balaustie habundant in calore conueniente nature oliuarum*
10 *and¹*: *id est*
14 *þre vertues*: *tres uires*. Presumably BA wrote *iiii*
19 *of fuyre*: *et humido*
24–5 *by fuyre þat makeþ it**
35 *and þe water bereþ it vp by kynde*: *contra aque superficiem eleuantis*   Z *natura* for
contra

894 4 *faste*: adds *inferiora petunt et*
6–7 *of þe sonne**
13 *of itself*: *cum propria caliditate naturali*
23 *yrunne*: adds *decoquitur*
26 *is sad*: *per actionem caloris terminantis et dirigerentis*
33 *grenenesse*: I *uigorem*   cf. the better *rigorem*
35–6 *seelde hoote where hoot water renneþ*: *essentialiter frigidis et accidentaliter calidis*

895 3 *humour*: adds *inhibito* (L *in debito*   T *inbibito*)
6 *plaunt*: *talis plante*
27 *digestes*: JT probably wrote *digestioun* as at line 28, cf. *digestum . . . indigestum*
29–30 *a fyndeþ . . . torneþ*: *ex natura plante insite in stipite*. Perhaps JT wrote *fro þe
kynde of graffe þer comeþ good digestioun and*

896 2 *oþer**: perhaps JT wrote *þe*
3 *is*: *exit*   Z *est*
22 *certeyn*: *terminato* (L *termato*   O *nutritio*   X *teriato*). Z *determinato*, cf. 353/34

897 12 *it*: *uapor unctuosus*
13 *And*: *vnde*. Also at 908/21, 921/13, 934/5, 945/7, 946/20, 948/24, 949/2, 960/6,
1002/36, 1006/34, 1009/7, 1019/26⁴, 1052/32, 1081/5
20 *it comeþ vpward in þe stok*: *expellitur*

898 10 *forsayde*: adds *multos*
14 *men*: *sapientes*. Perhaps JT wrote *wise men*

899 3 *parfyt*: properly qualifies *accioun*
4 *infect*: *inperfecta*. Perhaps JT wrote *inperfect* or Z *infecta*
10 *meueþ in comune vertue of fuyre*: *ascendit in communi virtute ignea eleuantur*
13 *ben grete and lowe*: *in grossum . . . coarctantur*
21 *rypyng*: adds *dilatationem*

900 7 *the neþer ende is scharpe also, and*: *parte inferiori cauda etiam existente*, properly
modifying the next clause
28 *þere*: *dicit enim circa finem*
32–3 *suffreþ nought þe humour passe out in vapour, for**

901 7 *and somtyme*: *in modum*
10 *Albumus*: *Aluredus*
15 *and woode**
25 *humour*: adds *augmentato*

902 8 *þe commune springyng tyme*: *dies uernales*. Perhaps JT wrote *comyng of* for
commune
28 *Also trees beþ dyuers*: *etas tunc maxime consideranda est*
33, **903** 3 *Isider*: *Constantinus*. Also at 884/23 etc.

4 *þat for defaute of hard humour*: *attracto humori adhuc iucinum*
5 *as: si. . . mouebatur* (MP *moueatur*)
11 *water-bowes and superfluite*: *superfluis*
20 *beries*: JT has read *morā* (as scansion shows) as *mŏra* 'mulberries'
22 *18: xvii*

904 7 *ofte: sepe enim*
18 *awakeþ*: adds *caducos et*
27 *and*¹: *et ideo*
32 *and*: adds *de facile*

905 8–9 *and brenneþ wiþ light leye**
27 *broun reed*: *subnigri. . . et subrufi*

906 13 *is. . . amendid*: *immutatur* Z *adiuuatur*
19 *fruyt*: *succus* Z *fructus*

907 3 *it takeþ newe disposicioun and chaungeþ*: *innouatur*. A doublet of ambiguity,
innouatur uel immutatur
6 *more stynkynge and most bitter*: *fetidissimum. . . amarissimum*
8 *it is*: adds *de sua natura*
16 *kepeþ*: *corpus preseruat et. . . curat*
28 *and*³: adds *nodosa leuis*

908 14 *redissh*: *fului*
34 *herbe*: adds *cuius semen consimili nomine est uocatum cuius semen primo conuenit
medicine radix secundario sed tertio ipsa herba*

909 2–3 *to tempre hard matiere*: *diureticam*. Cf. 939/7–8, 1001/29
34–5 *distourbeþ*: adds (not L) *siccat*

910 16 *poune*: adds *enim*
19 *soore*: *morsum* Z *ulcerum*
26 *sauce*: *salce* cf. the better P *sale*

911 6–7 *þe menynge. . . more**
10 *of*²: *in granis suis natis in*
11–13 *Of þe cloue. . . seed*: *et ideo cepula alii posita in terram producet plantam similiter et
eius semen*
17 *nou3t*: properly modifies *seedeþ*, cf. *uero non* (JLOT om.) *coniungit grana sua*.
Perhaps JT wrote *oynoun makeþ seed nou3t. . . but atte foot*. Adds *nutrit ea et facit*
28 *cloue*: adds *carnosa*
28 *lilie*: adds *quod de tunica sua plantata in terra emittit plantam*
29 *vertu*: adds *sicut in carnosis partibus alliorum*

912 1–2 *þe stalk and þe spire . . . cloue*: *eius partes carnose quando plantatur emittunt
gramina sua et folia per medium carnis sue*
4 *ende*: *medio*
9 *somdel horissh*: *subalbidum*
9 *vertuous*: adds *quam primum*
12 *Dias*: *Platearius*
22 *colour*: adds *emulsum* cf. M *euulsum*

913 2 *Viaticus*: *Macro* (P *auic'*)

13 *16°*: T *xvi*   cf. the better *xvii*
14–15 *of þe see*: LPT *naris*   cf. *maris*
16–17 *And wiþstondeþ . . . clopes**
21–2 *þerof*: *a picis id est capitis*
22 *Hercules*: adds *enim*
24 *venym*: *insidias veneni*
29 *petrapium*: adds *vt dicit Isidorus* (P *idem*   IT om.)
30 *kynde*: adds *vt dicit dyas* (LO *ysid'*)
34 *if it is yleyde**: perhaps scribal repetition

914 6 *if me pisseþ ofte and lite**
10 *spleen*: adds *et epatis*
19 *euel*: adds *caducum*

915 18 *mooder*: adds *agni casti*
25 *þe goddas*: *dyane   Z dea*. Also at 916/1, 493/12
28 *superfluyte*: *sterilitatem* (P *subtilitatem*)
34 *þou3tes*: O *meditamentis*   cf. *medicamentis*

916 17 *combes*: O *uirgulis*   cf. the better *vngulis*
25 *balsamum*: adds *tantam vim habent vt*
26–7 *Plinius . . . Ysider*: *Ysidorus . . . Plinius*
29 *londes*: adds (not JLOT) *scilicet Iudee*

917 4 *þe tre*: *interiora ligni*
23 *a wasteþ*: *tantum consumit*

918 8 *not heuy**
23 *and þat is ycleped a maner gomme**

919 1 *vtter**   4–5 *It semeþ . . . nou3t**
19 *sight*: adds *cum virore continuo*
23 *Whan*: adds *vnde*
24 *worchynge*: *tactus   Z actu*

920 6 *spewynge*: adds *colericum*
20 *saluaticus and sacer*: JLOT *saluaticum*   cf. the better *sacrum* (X *saluaticum* in margin). A doublet of conflation

921 3 *super Ecclesiasticum**: perhaps an insertion by Trevisa, since Rabanus did not write a commentary on the Psalms although *psalterium* is found in all examined Latin MSS. except Q *c"c*. Alternatively, the reading may be a doublet of ambiguity
11 *doynge*: *efficacie   Z effectu*
12 *þe gomme*: *est gummosa in substantia*
18–20 *tree . . . þerinne*: *in ligno cedrino . . . virtus cedrina*
18–19 *anoynt wiþ his owne gomme*: properly qualifies *bodies*
21–2 *secundinas . . . wombe*: *secundinas*. Similar expansions at 925/6, 942/30, 946/12
24 *and*[1]: adds *vrinam mouet*
28 *gedria*: *agedia*   cf. P *agridia   QT agedria   I cedria*
29 *vertu*: *odorem et virtutem*
30 *xviii°*: *xvii*

922 2 *anoþer*: *altera*   cf. the better M *alta*
3 *conus*: adds *eo quod conum imitetur*

8 *smeche and smoke*: *rogum*

923 2 *And*: *item dicit*
24 *ix°*: *i o'* (an ambiguous graph), cf. the better M 24
34 *v° capitulo*: *in capitulo xxiiii* (i.e. Ecclesiasticus 24: 20)
36 *þe double*: *duplo . . . quam*

924 1 *xxi°*: xii   cf. P *21*
7 *þe litel**
10 *a stok of foure oþer sixe ynche greet*: *x uel f* (M *xi*) *digitorum*
12 *most fructuous in wynter*: *in semine sterilior*   cf. M *in ieme fertilior*
16 *by mesure*: *hasta*
20 *stok*: adds *quod est proximi radici*
28 *of certeyne names*: *nominatis*   cf. the better MX *uomitiuis* (I *uomitis*)

925 1 *an oignement for þe yhen**
5 *postemes*: *fleuma* (LQ *flegma*)
20 *tree*: *frutex*, translated *litel tree* 926/3
28 *bytyng scharp*: *pauci et acuti*   cf. *feruentis et acuti* at line 33

926 21 *hydeþ*: *palliat*
30 *wiþinne*: properly modifies *distyngued*

927 4 *guttes*: *intestinorum dolorem*, translated *ache of þe stomak* 930/22
7–8 *And so . . . cassia**
11 *and*: *et Percius et*
17 *or ykutte*: *scinditur et diuiditur* 'it splits and fragments'
34 *herte*: adds *quem Greci sincopim vocant*

928 6 *Strawe*: *canna stipule uel segetis*
21 *it hatte*: *idem est quod*
31 *wiþinne*: adds *quidam ex toto concaui qui ad fistulas faciendas sunt multum apti*

929 11 *oþerwise, and*: *in ore*
16 *xiiii°. capitulo xxiii°*: *xiii capitulo xxiiii* (M *xxiii*)
19 *herbe*: adds *siue frutex* (cf. 948/29) *spinosus expansus super terram*
35 *woundes*: *manibus*   cf. the better MX *auribus* (X corrected)
35 *festrid*: adds *Hucusque Platearius*

930 10–11 *indignacioun*: *indignacionem*   cf. the better P *indigestionem*. Also at 971/16
20 *colde*: *causa frigida*, cf. *colde yueles* lines 23–4. Also at 975/20, 1044/9
26 *wormes*: adds *aurium*
31 *it is seyd*: *dicit Isidorus*

931 1 *Dias*: *Plinium*
7 *salectum*: adds *a salice*
16 *male*: *mlis*   cf. the better IQT *multum* and X *mlt* (corrected)
22 *sautes*: *saltus*, elsewhere translated *fordes* or *laundes*. Perhaps JT retained the
Latin quotation here which a scribe then translated
27 *oon*: *vno* (IQM om.) *flore*
32–3 *By þese . . . smale**

932 22 *His menyng . . . pale**   32 *and yleyd ofte þerto**

31 *yhe*: *oculo*. BA wrote *oleo*, properly modifying *medlid*

933 7 *xvi*: *xvi* (Q *xi*)   cf. the better PW *xxi*
9 *melk*: *uino*
24–5 *as it were a maner wilde weþewynde**

934 10 *and*: *id est*
14 *iiii⁰*: adds *et Trenorum vltimo*
31 *beste*: *nobilior quam hortensis*
31 *medicynes*: adds *vomitiuis* (IQT *uomitis*)

935 6 *þat*: *quia*
12 *body*: *carnis*   Z *corporis*
19 *onyouns*: *lilium*
24 *multiplicacioun*: adds *et sue speciei conseruatiua*

936 2 *abatiþ*: adds *torsiones* (JLT *bormia*   O *tortura*   P *gorima*) *et*
26 *euelonge*: adds *magis quam rotundam*
29 *þerof*: adds *cum melle caliginem oculorum detergit succus eius*

937 10, 12 *as it were an houndes oynoun**   *as it were a see oynoun**
14 *Men*: *Salernitani* (I *ierosolitani*   L *solernitaileam*   T *icanicam*). Z gibberish
15 *cloues*: MSS. *closed*, cf. *sigillatim*. If Z *cingullatis* or similar formation on *cingo*,
the emendation is unjustified
22 *xvii⁰*: *xix capitulo xvii*
27 *destroyed*: adds *vnde*
32–3 *to kepe . . . he*: *quod libeat capita inueterari . . . capita*

938 6 *bocches*: adds *oris*
15 *swete**

939 7–8 *to schode hard matiere*: *diuretica* (LT *duretica*). Cf. 909/2–3, 1001/29
11 *matiere*: adds *infirmitatis . . . aliquantulum*
21 *iii⁰*: *iiii*
25 *postemes*: *clauis . . . id est apostematibus*
27 *ysode*: adds (not JLOT) *et trita*
32 *haþ*: adds *et fructum rotundum facit sicut cucumer vsualis*

940 3 *he helpeþ*: *matres* (LMT *uires*) *illis ex hac herba medicantur*
6 *yputte oute*: LT *exuti*   cf. the better *eruti*
33 *meridies*: *medidies que nunc meridies solet dici*

941 7 *tremelynge*: *timore*   cf. the better M *more*
26 *And*: adds *quia*. Perhaps JT wrote *And for . . . a hadde perfore*

942 3–4 *as it were . . . maistry**
20 *and*: adds *precipue*
24 *hoot*: *solida*   Z *calida*
26 *and³*: *vnde valet contra*

943 3 *Ysider*: *Plinius*
12 *body*: adds *hanc quidam pulegium martis vocant*
16 *dragoun*: adds *uel quia herbam ipsam vipere timent*
18 *yschape*: *apertum*

21–2 *womman wiþ greet seed*: *semine grosso*. A doublet of ambiguity, *femine uel semine grosso*

32 *and druyeþ þe nepere veynes*: *id est inferiores venas . . . et desiccat*. Probably an ME. scribal reversal

35 *beste*: *corpus*. Perhaps JT wrote *body*

944 4 *norisshyng*: *uel actione*   Z *nutrimento*
27 *Collirium . . . yhen**
32 *light and smeþe*: *nigrum et lene*   Z *lene*
34 *xvii°*: LP *xvii*   cf. the better *xii*
35 *tree*: adds *auro et ebori comparabilem*

945 2 *suche þinges*: *talia ligna*   Z *talia*
12 *xvii°*: *xvi*
17 *temple*: *sacris* 'rites'
35 *streynynge*: *stiptica et constrictiua*

946 4 *rypynge*: adds (not P) *attractiuam*
15 *in*: adds *multis*
18 *þe styntynge . . . lengest*: *solstitio estiuo*
20 *þis is þe roodewort**: also at 963/20

947 31 *seede*: *semine gaudet*
31–3 *And so . . . roote**
33 *leues*: adds *et rapta*
34 *humour*: adds *lacteum*

948 2 *herbe*: adds *alba* (IMT *aliquando*   P om.)
8 *and is ofte yclepid enula campana**: cf. the quotation in line 17
18–19 *þe menynge . . . sounde**
29 *weed*: *fructus siue herba*
31 *and¹*: adds *secundum Dyas et Plius*

949 1 *humours**
4 *colde*: *frigida siue alba* (P *calida*)
7 *strokes betyng*: *concussiones corporis*
22 *hawkes*: I *alelantis*   LO *allece*   cf. the better *athlete* (as in Isidore XVII. 7. 17)   Z *accipitres*
28 *libro vii°*: *libro xvii*

950 2 *scharpe*: *pirita et acuta*
8 *In*: *vnde . . . in*
30 *schadewe*: adds *et densitatem*
32 *and weder**
32 *tree*: *matris*, translated *olde tree* at line 34

951 1 *in scheldwise*: *ad modum pelte amonite*
5 *xv°*: LT *xvi*   cf. the better *xv*
19 *þan in þe souþ contray**
29 *ygendred*: adds *materie causa*
30 *scharp vpward*: *pineata folio*

952 3–4 *and . . . floures*: *nec ante flores conditos folia dimittit*
13 *a maner spray*: *fungis*

15 *spewynge also*: *vomitum ex defectu virtutis retentiue cohibent*
19 *And*: *ut*   cf. Q *sed*   M *sed ut*
19 *seiþ*: adds *et Plinius libro xvi*, which properly begins a new sentence
25–6 *þat semeþ . . . quantite**

953 8 *ycloue and ysette afyre*: *incinditur*. A doublet of ambiguity, *inciditur uel incinditur*
15 *and serueþ to potage**

954 6–7 *þe clene bene whan þe hole is aweye it*: *fabe* (LT *falx*   M *eius*) *medulla* 'the hull of the bean'. Cf. 972/12n. below
11 *templis*: adds *humores ad oculos reumatizantes compescit scissa*
19 *where þat groweþ in coddes**

955 7 *þe geniculatus and stalke*: *est eius culmus siue calamus geniculatus* 'its stalk or branch is jointed'
11 *intus, uel nitro*: *intus*. A doublet of ambiguity
34–5 *namely in som contray as in Tuscan**
35 *is colde*: *tantum est frigida*

956 5–6 *of þe grounde . . . of þe ground*: *soli siue terre qualitas*
8 *manere and tyme*: *qualitas*
19 *and . . . speche**
22 *xiii°*: *xvii*

957 1 *þrift*: *virorem*   Z *vigorem*
2 *and*: *quorum dente*
5 *ylost*: adds (not T) *et ideo cauendum summo opere ne talibus misceantur*
13 *corn*: adds *que dicitur rubigo quia spica corumpitur*
16 *s*: J *s*   M *m*   IT *l*   QX *c* (LO om. phrase), cf. the better P *t*, i.e. a reference to the chapter *De tritico* (cf. esp. 1060/6)

958 2–3 *as þe flour . . . wei3t*: *sicut et simila id est sine mola*
7 *piled, holed, and schelid wiþ betyng and pownyng*: *tunsi*. Perhaps a scribal expansion, repeating the previous phrase, of an earlier *betyn and powned*
15 *and som is ybake**
20 *maner brede*: perhaps JT wrote *manes body*, cf. *cor hominis confortant et corpus nutriunt*
34 *mylk*: adds *et mollificat locum*

959 2 *hatte*: *a feruore est dictum*
10 *and[1]*: *nam*
13 *rereþ*: adds *corruptiua*
15 *Epistolam*: adds *i. Corinth. v*
19 *oþer . . . eorþe*: *uel sic dicitur quia generatur a quadam fumositate grossa a terra resoluta et circa terre superficiem adherente*
27 *fenel*: *aniso et feniculo*
33 *cause*: *causa*   cf. the better PX *substantia*

960 18 *Dias*: *dias* (O *idem dyas*), cf. the better PX *idem*
32 *yuel*: adds *omnes autem ferularum murenis infestissima est nam eius lacte statim commoriuntur*
33 *Platearius*: *plius*

961 19 *and groweþ þe lasse*: *tanto minus crescit* 'the more it grows the less'. Unless Z lacked *tanto*, a scribal confusion between *þe more* 'radicem' and *þe more* 'tanto

962 3 *for*: *et ideo*
   3 *veynes*: adds *in eorum substantia*
   5 *folia*: adds *apud nos*
   6–7 *as it were 'yhen'*: *de virgulis et flagellis*
   9 *by scharpnesse þerof*: *et ex acumine suo penetrat ad exterius*
   32 *Floures*: adds *ut dicit Isidorus libro xviii* (IM *xvii*)

963 11 *humour*: adds *medulle arboris*
   20 *and is þe rodeworth**

964 2 *floures*: *stipite*
   5 *serene*: *serene*   cf. O *feruere*   P *ferene*   and the better M *fel terre* (as at 940/13)
   15–16 *and þerforþ . . . ychewed**   24–5 *of þe forseyde . . . roote**
   28 *þat*: *et*   Z *ut*

965 4 *grene*: adds *duri*
   11 *reed or 3olow*: *uel rubentem*
   15 *And þe more*: *tanto etiam sunt meliores et in substantia laxiores quanto*
   26 *seiþ*: adds *ut patet supra eodem*

966 7 *in*: MT *in*   cf. the better *aut in*
   8 *and*: *quia*
   13 *straw*: adds *ut dicit Plius*
   19 *a**
   33 *draweþ*: adds *ui caloris*

967 1 *roote*: adds *et ideo*, beginning a new sentence
   12 *þikke*: *nigro*   Z *pingue*, unless JT wrote *blakke*
   19 *ygreued*: adds *frigido aere*
   20 *sprayes*: adds *enim*
   29–30 *flies . . . wormes*: *brutis locustis et erucis*

968 6 *matiere is able*: *propter humiditatem* (LT om.) *materie*   Z *potest materia*
   18 *Plius and Ysaac and oþer auctours*: *et idem super librum vegetabilium commentator*
   21 *Constantinus*: *et cetera*
   33–4 *þe reule is þis**

969 4 *vertu*: adds *medicine*
   15 *sores*: *vulnerum*   Z *ulcerum*
   17 *hemsilf*: adds *ut dicit Plius*
   23 *ykuyt*: adds *in estate*
   28 *degree*: adds *ut dicit idem*

970 11 *aboue*: adds *ut cortices et huiusmodi*
   18 *matiere*: *feculentie*

971 4 *And beþ*: *eligendi autem sunt qui*
   16 *indignacioun*: *indignacionem* (variously abbreviated), cf. the better P *indigestionem* and 930/10–11
   22 *sprayes*: adds *graciles*

972 12, 16 *holes: folliculis* 'hulls', cf. *hulk* 978/8, *hulles* 985/33. JT's form was probably *hulles*

13 *in harde . . . schales: in substantia callosa*

20 *whete: triticum et spelta*   cf. 1061/14n. below

21 *barlich and spilt: grana ordei*

973 1 *with many sydes: uel multilaterem*

9 *Platearius:* adds *Aristoteles*

26 *Ysider: Constantinus.* Also at 884/23 etc.

974 2–4 *wiþ many bowes . . . schadowe: multe ramositatis et ratione foliorum vmbrositatis iocunde* (M *rotunde*)

10 *matiere and kynde: naturam* (generally abbreviated to *ñm*). A doublet of ambiguity, *materiam uel naturam*

10 *mysbilieued men**

23 *þanne:* adds *quasi*

27 *þerof:* adds *congruunt medicine qui*

975 13 *cleueþ: infigens*   Z *infingens*

17 *dymme: vmbroso . . . et non fumoso*

20 *colde: causa frigida.* Also at 930/20, 1034/11, 1044/9

25 *uitulam:* JLTV *uitulam*   O *uiculam*   X *mul'a* after caret, cf. the earlier *vuulam* (R *uuilam*) 'vulva'. Presumably JT interpreted *vitulam*, cf. *vitellum* 'yolk of egg', as a form of *vuvla*, and so left the clause untranslated in his normal manner of treating female sexual organs

32–5 *þese . . . vers**

976 1 *iiii°:* O has arabic *4*, very similar to L *x̊*, cf. MX *x f* and the better *x*

1–2 *and is . . . folweþ**   8–9 *So he is . . . þerof**   23–4 *and of his dede body**

13 *Also:* vnde etiam

22 *deed:* adds *in saltibus*

27 *is:* adds *itaque*

29 *and coccus of fuyr: siue ignis.* Perhaps JT wrote *or coccus or fuyr* (*coccus* 'scarlet-red berry' being a semantic addition) unless Z *coccus ignis*

30 *xii. oþer xiiii.: xii* (P *11*). A doublet of ambiguity

977 9 *mirilidium: miliridium*   cf. the better M *milimindrum* (as in Isidore XVII. 9. 41)

10 *Isider seiþ: quam inducit* (M adds *hucusque*   O adds *ut*   R *ut dicit*) *Ysidorus*

16, 17 *floure leues: folliculos,* generally translated *hulles* or *codware,* cf. 972/12n. above. Perhaps a doublet of ambiguity, *flores uel folia*

17 *better:* X *meliores*   cf. the better *molliores*

978 2 *In þat: vnde in hoc*

7 *Isider:* adds *libro xvii*

13 *fuayle:* adds *eius fructus valent ad cibum*

23 *oþer: uel . . . decoquantur*

25 *tem002 pereþ: generant,* generally translated *bredeþ*

27 *zuger oþer actata:* JT perhaps wrote *zacara* (as in D) *oþer actata.* I *zucarra* MO *zucara* X *zukaro* (over erasure) PR *accara* S *arcla* JLVW *actata* T *aceto.* A doublet of conflation

979 5 *victorie*: adds *laureati dicebantur*
6 *propretees*: *virtutes et . . . proprietates*
6 *dampnis*: M *daphnem* X *dapnem* cf. *dampnem*, called *daphiris* at 940/28
10 *tre*: adds *humilis* (O *ulmis*). O adds an extra chapter on *laurus*
24 *tow3*: *glutinosa*, generally translated *glemy*
30 *lentiscus*: *cini siue lentisci* cf. the better P *cum semine lentisci*
31 *clopes*: adds *munde* cf. the better M *inde*

980 3 *lentiscus*: M *lentiscus* cf. *cuius* (O om.)
10 *lilye*: adds *vt dicit Isidorus*
16 *bocchis and sores** 18 *matiere**
21 *purgeþ*: adds *vnde valet ad faciem* (T *contra*) *colorandam*
23 *sores**
27 *and*: *et ideo*. Also at 981/18, 1000/11
34 *potagre and knottes of þe feet*: *clauos pedum et nodos*

981 1 *sore**: perhaps a scribal anticipation of line 2, but cf. 980/23
10–11 *wiþ brerdes aboute as it were of a belle*: *in circuitu labris* (M *laboris* P om. X *labrum*), properly qualifying the next clause
12–13 *And is gracious to þe lilye*: *vnde nichil* (L *uel*) *lilio graciosus* (JLTV *grossius*) *est*. Z omitted *nichil*
14 *of worchinge*: X *operis* cf. the better *corporis*
24 *of þe roote*: *de tunicis suis siue de bullis cepulis scilicet radicis*
33, 35 *vertu*: *rationem*
35 *and oþere**

982 14 *six*: *vii*
15–16 *is wonderliche white*: *miro decore*. Perhaps JT wrote *is wonderliche hi3t*
29 *and dryere*: *ponticitatis respectu illius que domestica est quia*

983 7–8 *dedeþ þe feelyng*: *virtus vifiua . . . cuius causa est sensus animalis mortificatio*
13 *wiþoute tiliynge**
20 *ysopon oþer esapon*: *ysopon* (P *ysopam*), cf. I *esapon*. A doublet of conflation. Pliny XX. 59 has *caesapon*
21 *stancio*: I *staton* OP *stacio* cf. *steracon* and Pliny *ibid.* ἰσάτιν

984 11 *olde** 19–20 *for it is . . . dokkes**

985 2 *ydropped*: adds *in modica quantitate*
5 *gardyns*: adds *recentibus lappaciis similibus*
8 *þe menyng . . . herbes**
10 *fatte*: adds *subalbida*
11 *schort*: adds *et grossum*
17 *xx°*: adds *cap. x* (P *18* X *xx*)
18 *mete in dronkenesse*: *crapulam*
29 *legendo*: *eligendo*, which was presumably JT's form

986 11 *waterynge*: adds *ut* (TX *et ut*) *dicit Plinius*
18 *oþer of streme*: *immo ad perfectam decoctionem indigent aqua fontana siue fluuiali*
19 *ymade*: adds (not OP) *et succus* (M *suetus*)
23 *by medlyng of þinges*: *per corticis decoctionem et assacionem et per earum . . . appositionem*

33–4 *þe menyng... mouþ**

987 1 *tylle*: *lens uel lenticula*

12 *And*: *ut*, properly introducing the previous clause

988 1–9 *And... trauaile*: this vigorous translation, made more simple and concrete by vernacular terms, suggests a personal knowledge of spinning flax, cf. *et euulsi a suis capitellis semen continentibus carpinantur. deinde colligentes partes lini in fasciculos colligantur. et longo tempore in aqua maturantur. et extracti de aqua ad solem dessicantur et postea multis tunsionibus et carpinationibus a suis superfluis expurgantur et sic partes desicate* (MO *defecate*   P *defedate*) *in fila contorquentur. et per multiplicem decoctionem ad albedinem deducuntur non enim linum a suo virore terrestri potest spoliari et perfecto candore decorari nisi multocies contundatur et decoquatur et soli appositum aqua iterum et iterum aspergatur*

12 *xii°*: *ii*

13 *kynde*: *gracissime*

19 *inne*: adds *cortine ad ornandum*

22 *vnctuous*: *et vnctuosum*, properly following *drye*

31 *þynne*: adds *ratificatiuam maturatiuam* (M om.)

989 3 *of swetnesse*: *suauitate*, properly qualifying *lykynge*

5–6 *And... also*: *dicitur autem malum li ipsum pomum siue fructus sed hec malus dicitur ipsa arbor siue pomus*

22 *if*: *quia*

990 32 *in þe wombe*: P *ventris*   cf. the better *veteres*

991 5 *neisshe*: adds *iocunda*

7 *Ysaac*: I *bernardus*   JLO *beñ*   M *beda*   P *pli*   RW *bñ*   S *ueñ*   T *leu'*   X *yñ* (corrected)   Q *plius*

11 *fruyt*: adds *et virgula*

14 *yprowe oþer yleide*: *superiacta*. A doublet of ambiguity, *superiacta uel superiacita*

23 *lippes*: *faucium* 'throat', cf. 992/8

992 11 *a litel tre and*: *est dicta eo quod*

12 *and of adamant'*: *et adamantis*. BA wrote *et alibi*, linking two separate quotations

29 *woundes*: *vlcera et vulnera*

993 13 *aromaticum*: adds *artheatum* (I *atantum*   P *aricl'atum*   X *aroth'iram*)

25–6 *ben ykorue, ykutte, and yslitte*: *inciduntur*

31 *gelbatica*: JLSV *gelbonica*   OR *galbonica*   T *gelboita*   IM *gelbonitica*   X *gelbcuntica* (corrected)   W *gelbanitica*   P *galbanica*   Q *gelbanica*

32 *pracena*: X *pracena*   cf. the better *empracena* and I *Sambracena*   P *prudencia*

994 7–8 *and þat in... smelle*: properly modifies the next clause. Perhaps JT wrote *and in... smelle, a dissolueþ*

21 *atte beste**

28–9 *hole and sounde*: *in delitacione*   cf. O *inde linita*   P *in linita*   R *in delinita*

995 3 *þe sore keruynge*: *dolorem*

14 *wyne*: adds *dormire faciunt et*

23 *is¹*: *inuenitur*. Cf. 841/25 n. above

26 *xxx*: *xxx*   cf. RX *xix* (P om. reference)

29 *auctor*: *auctoritate* (generally abbreviated *aūcte*)

31 *Ysider*: *Constantinus*

996 12 *cercles*: *tres circulos*

13 *soone*: *ita*. Perhaps JT wrote *so*

24 *if þey ben yparched*: *est autem secundum dyas* (LO *dyasco*) *diureticum et assatum sedat ventris torsionem* (T om. chapter)

997 23 *tonge*: adds *asperam*

23 *and*: adds *assuefacta in cibo*

36 *gleymyng*: *viscositatis*, translated *glemynesse* 996/22

998 10 *iugilans*: *iugilandem*   cf. I *inglantem*   M *ioglandem*   P *vigilantem*

10 *name*: adds *quasi Iouis laudem* (M *glandem*)

32 *note*: adds *est domestica que*

35 *disposicioun*: adds *scilicet viridi*

999 1–2 *is . . . and harder*: *testam paulatim optinet corio extrinseco duriorem*

3 *is*[1]: adds *vnctuosum*

4 *skyn*: adds *velut quadam tunicula est vndique circumtecta*

12 *perfore*: *stomacho*

14 *Dias*: *Ysaac* (OPX *ysa*)

21 *bredeþ*: adds *adustiones*

23–4 *for so . . . ynough*: *bene eas digerunt et eis congrue nutriuntur*

1000 2 *euelong*: *pyramidalis et oblonga*

4 *cop*: adds *ad modum crucis tecta gnomaliter*

11 *groues*: *nemore siue sylva*

20 *water*: adds *et exteriores pellicule auferantur*

32 *3olow*: *terreus*

1001 1 *þynne*: *tenuissima*

3–4 *and semeþ rody in colour*: properly follows the next clause

7 *colde*: adds *enim*

14 *cirica*: LT *sirica*   cf. the better *Syriaca*

16–17 *smeþe . . . yles*: *leuis et fusca* (W adds *uel fulua*) *comosa et spica odoratissima ciprum similans*

29 *hard matiere*: *diuretica*   cf. 909/2–3, 939/7–8. Adds *ut dicit Platearius*

1002 6 *men*: adds *vnde*

15 *spray*[2]: adds *et molles*

33 *hoteþ*: adds *ut dicit idem Plinius*

1003 8 *vnkynde superfluite*: *quasdam tuberositates et adulterinos ramusculos circa ueros radices*

29 *gret*: *nimiam*   cf. NO *mutuam*

1004 7 *water*: N *aqua*   cf. the better *aqua calida*

7–8 *he kepiþ . . . aryse, and*: *uesicam reprimunt ibi* (LT *in*) *nascituram . . . enim*

13 *vertues*: *uires*. BA wrote *vites*

15 *drastes*: *sanies . . . siue fex*

28 *drastes, holes*: *amurca*, cf. line 16. A doublet of ambiguity, *amurca uel antra*

1005 18 *oyle-de-bay**

21 *puls-veynes*: *vene pulsatiles*. Perhaps JT wrote *veynes of þe puls*

31 *þanne*[2]: *tertio*

33 *and is moste*: *maxime quod* 'especially that which'

1006 6 *glasen*: adds (not MN) *uel uitreatis*
9–10 *water*[2] . . . *nouȝt*: *superficie uix*
11–12 *oyle drastes*: *siue fece*. Perhaps here and at line 18 JT wrote *oþer drastes*
13 *corrumpeþ*: adds *et immutat*
14 *fotles** 19 *þat is ybawmed þerwiþ**
25 *þe qualite þerof*: *uim . . . radicis*
33 *hony*: adds *ut dicit Dias*

1007 3 *putteþ of*: *reprimit*
4 *and*: *id est*
5 *aȝeins*: adds *alopeciam*
14–15, 16 *olus . . . plurelle*: *olera*
20–1 *in þe crop*: *in timis huius herbe quam*

1008 5 *deffyed*: adds *et sic efficiuntur magis sapida*
27–8 *þis corn . . . ordeum**
32 *it is yripe in þre monthes*: *uerno* (N *vno*) *tempore celeriter recolligitur*. JT's form of the past participle was probably *yrepe* 'reaped'

1009 4 *Ytalyans*: *alii ut Italici*
6 *most noble*: *mollissimum* Z *nobilissimum*
12 *manere*: adds *et farinam accuratissimam seu polentiam*
14 *clenseþ*: adds (not X) *et exicatiuam*
19 *mete and drynke*: *potus mundificans*. Perhaps JT wrote *medicinable drynke*

1010 1 *sauour*: adds *myrabolani uero saporis sunt horribilis et amari*
12 *crop and cop*: *superioribus*
26 *seith*: *idem* (JL *item*) *etiam dicit*

1011 1–2 *by confort . . . generacioun*: *ex uicinitate masculi quasi ex coitu*
6 *waste*: adds *salis siccitate*
12 *efte*: adds *ex se ipsa*
23 *and*[1]: adds *in superficie*
24 *þikke*: adds *et flexibilia*
29–30 *elate in grew and alates also*: *elate tamen* (X *elatetum*) *siue elates* (JLT *elatos*). *alates* is probably a scribal form of JT's *elates*

1012 2 *Ambrosius*: *Aristotiles* (I om. R om. clause), cf. the better M *Augustinus*
7 *dyuersliche*: adds *secundum diuersos situs*
10 *hete*: *ipsius* (J om.) *arboris* Z *caloris*
14–15 *palmes . . . þrifte*: *nullatenus conualescunt*

1013 2 *þat is*: *siue*. Perhaps JT wrote *oþer*
5 *stomak*: adds *tamen de stomacho de facili non recedunt vnde diutius ibi* (L *in*) *facientes moram*
11–12 *as it were*: *et* Z *quasi*
17 *And*: *enim*. Also at 1026/8, 1030/33, 1043/24, 1046/24[1]
25 *aȝeins*: adds *dysenteriam*
31 *pampinus*: adds *enim*
32–3 *of frostes . . . falleþ** 35 *and doon . . . rypyng**
35 *he*: *Ysidorus*

1014 1–2 *and draweþ strongly bycause . . . and draweth: quia . . . fortis est attractionis multum attrahit*. Probably JT wrote *a draweþ . . . a draweþ*
8 *ygraffed*[1]: *inseritur uiti inmarcio fiat insertio*
13 *But: sed quia*
27 *and þat as: secundum quod*
30 *smale crokes*: N *uimina* cf. the better *uimina siue vincula* (X *vinela*)

1015 3 *be*: adds *successiue*
6–7 *spredeþ . . . kynde*[1]: *degenerant*
14 *ysette*: JL *et incūso* T *immerso* cf. the better *infixo et immerso*
17 *multiplye newe vynes: renouationem terre*

1016 1 *crafte: propagationis artificium*
2 *and*[2]: *ut* (X om.)
3 *spray: palmes siue flagellum*
6 *norissheþ þe doughtres**
10 *vii°.: xvii*
13 *hoot yueles: causis calidis et humidis*
15 *bones: ossium aliorum*
16 *hele*: adds *et . . . mitigandi*
18 *þerof*: adds *in uino*
28 *Ytaly*: adds *iuxta eridanum flumen*
30 *rennynges and droppynges: fluxus noxios*
32 *hete*: adds *tumoris repressiuum*

1017 2 *colde passiouns and yueles: causis*
14–15 *And is þer ycleped pynus also. þis tree is: dicitur etiam ibidem pinus et dicitur*. MN properly omit *et dicitur*, giving the sense 'also the pine-tree is said there (to be)'
19 *mastes: optimi . . . mali*
21 *cometh nyh the fuyre: igni casu aliquo applicantur*
21 *fatnesse: pinguedinis et unctuositatis*. Cf. line 23
36 *bettre*: adds *nam*

1018 4–5 *þat is . . . rynde**
6 *Ysider seith: dicit*. The reference is properly to Pliny
20 *atte þe ende: in summo uero pyramidalis*
21 *more ful: fertilius* (M *cerulius*)
29–31 *beþ so ysette . . . cornelis: ad graciliorem locum et acutiorem*
33–4 *holdeþ faste and closeþ þe corneles: fortis adherentie et magne glutinitatis*

1019 32 *white colour and**: probably a scribal mistake (not expuncted) of the following *white clopes*

1020 20 *sethynge: elixationem et decoctionem* (X om.)
21 *ony: mellis*. JT's usual form is *hony*
29 *stomak*: adds *ante prandium uero sumpta constipant*
30 *passio*: adds *duram et incurabilem*

1021 2 *funges: fungos*. JT probably retained the Latin form, cf. 980/33, 1050/33. O.E.D. sub *frog* sb. 5 records a scribal corruption
13 *druye: acida* Z *sicca*
24 *and: quia*

1022 2 *Niphin*: JLW *nimphim*   X *iumphim*   N om.   S *phi*   cf. the better *Menphim*
    16 *beth as grete as*: *crescentia spissitudinem*
    20 *dyuers . . . houshold*: *uaria vtensilia*
    22–3 *papyre to wryte inne*: *carte* (L *corte*   T *corde*). Adds *hucusque Plinius*

1023 7 *opium oper opion*: *opium* (M *suopium*   U *obpium*   P om.   L om. clause) cf. I *opion*. A doublet of conflation
    9 *thus diuersite*: *hee species*. Perhaps JT wrote *þese diuersites*
    10 *purpur, reede*: *purpureos siue* (N om.) *roseos*
    17 *medicynes*: *multis antidotis et medicinis*
    17 *Dyas*: adds (not MT) *Macer*. N om. phrase

1024 3 *vertues*: adds *magnificas*
    20 *tree*: *arboris aut fruticis*. OT om. phrase
    22 *Diascorides*: *ut . . . Isidorus*
    23–4 *þat peper groweþ inne**   24 *of peper**

1025 3 *whyte*: *ponderis*. JT's form was probably *wyȝt*
    27 *hoot*: *acutum*
    32 *vertu*: *raritatem*   Z *virtutem*

1026 13 *rebate*: *extenuandi*. JT's form was probably *abate*
    18–19 *and is so . . . plurelle**   21–3 *This vers . . . plurelle**   24–6 *þis auctorite . . . gendre**
    28 *a litel knotte*: *nodum*. BA wrote *nondum* 'not yet' (cf. Pliny XIX. 108)
    29 *and take*: *quod . . . translatum est*
    30 *xviii⁰*: NX *xviii*   cf. the better *xvii*
    33 *smale skynnes*: *pelliculis siue tuniculis*

1027 1 *heed*[1]: adds *vt dicitur in libro vegetabilium*
    19 *of leek*: *solo*. Z *allei* unless JT wrote *alone*, later read as *alei* and so translated
    27 *and þat noun . . . cui**   28–9 *and dureth long tyme**
    32 *contray*: *nemoribus*

1028 1 *and so**: perhaps Z *et sic*, anticipating the adjacent *et sicci* 'and druye'
    9 *there*: *vnde*   Z *vbi*
    10 *in*[1]: adds *magnitudine*
    16 *nayl oper fuyre*: *vnguis*. A doublet of ambiguity, *vnguis uel ignis*
    16 *so*: *sicut* (generally written *sic̃*)   Z *sic*
    19–20 *þikke fumosite*: *fumos grossos ex glandibus resolutos*
    22 *hooles yschape as themelis*: *capsulis rotundissimis*
    24 *þat litil skyn*: *quadam pellicula circumdatam que*
    26 *sauour*: adds *maxime adhuc viridis*

1029 3 *capitulo*: MNO om. rest add *viii*
    4 *wiþ syve or with riddil**
    16 *wilde and groweþ in woodes*: *siluestris*
    18 *yschred and ypared and yclensed*: *purgata* (J *purgat* corrected   L *purga*   N *expurgata*). Perhaps a doublet of ambiguity, *purgata uel purata*
    33 *rose**

1030 1 *grene*: *viridi seu virente*

31 *of herbes**

1031 5 *yryped*: *maceratis*   Z *maturatis*
7 *causes*: *causis*, generally translated *evyls* in medical contexts, cf. 1017/2. The clause properly follows *oleum rosaceum* in lines 5–6
9 *and feuere agu*: *in acutis*, properly modifying *makeþ*
13 *away*: adds *pannum superfluum*

1032 21 *parties*: adds *rotundatur et sic*
29 *edraue and ecorporat*: *attrahitur et incorporatur*. The ME. prefix *e-* (instead of the regular *y-*) may be relics of JT's spellings
35 *norisshynge and corrupcioun**: probably a scribal intrusion, perhaps corrupted from an earlier *werisshe (water) and corrupte*

1033 10 *grounde*: *terre uisceribus*
19–20 *þat springeþ þat tyme**
25 *defyed*: *digeritur et dulcoratur*
26 *puryfyeþ*: MNQT *depurantis*   cf. the better *subtiliantis et depuratis*
28 *of þe vyne, of þe note tre*: *uitis*. JT probably wrote *or of* in a doublet of ambiguity, *uitis uel nucis*
30 *seeke*: adds *ēt non fructificant*

1034 13 *harde*: *redarguentem*. A contextual translation
24 *lampis*: adds *non tamen licitum fuit tale oleum apponere in lucernis*
24–5 *in þe temple of Ierusalem**

1035 2 *neisshe*: *mollia et lenia*
5 *ix°*: M *ix*   cf. the better *xx*
10 *other impressioun**: probably an ME. scribal dittography
15 *xiiii°*: *xxiiii*
20 *þat . . . wombe**
24–6 *þough . . . lucidus*: *in quibus aculeis lucidum dicitur*

1036 5 *cera lupoun*: *sera lupim* (O *pim*   NQTX *lupini*   P *phim*   T *seralu*). BA wrote *ferule pini* 'of fennel, of pine'
29 *sshurbbe*: adds *spinosa*

1037 1 *prikkes*: adds *subrubeos* (T *rubeos*)   L *seu rubeos*
4–5 *þis rubus . . . prikkes²*: *textus* (M *tectus*   O *totus*) *rubet aculeatus est*
11–12 *smalle dynes and valeys*: *ualliculis*. BA wrote *folliculis*

1038 17 *libro xx°. capitulo xxvii°.*: JLOT om.
24 *ywasted*: *desiccatur . . . et consumitur*
27 *tormentes and gnawynge*: *tormenta*. Cf. 400/19n. above

1039 23 *and oþre wormes**
32 *graueres, lymynours*: *sculptores* (T *scriptores*). Perhaps a doublet of ambiguity

1040 2–3 *aȝeins þe seruice of Venus*: *uenerem*, properly the object (cf. *lechery*) of *meteth of*
10 *xii°*: *xiiii*
14–15 *þanne in woode þat hatte saltus**: possibly an ME. dittography. Elsewhere (e.g. 727/21) *saltus* is translated *fordes* (unless this is a scribal error for *woodes*)
15 *beþ*: adds *pauciores sed*

30 *xvi°: xvii*

1041 5 *woodes*: adds *precipue montuosis*
6 *with bowes*: *uirore frondium*
10–12 *oftere . . . ofte: sepius . . . sepius.* JT probably wrote *oftere* twice
17 *knottes*: *nodi et signa*　cf. line 20
18 *in tokne and marke of þe hihe weye**
19 *ofte*: *aliquando*
27 *colde*: adds *consite*

1042 24 *pliaunt*: adds *cortice*
26 *handelynge*: adds *non nodosi*
33 *commune*: *aciduas*　Z *vsuales*

1043 3 *And*: *quoque*
14 *And*: *etiam*
31 *twyes*: *pluries*

1044 6 *oyle*: adds *et cataplasmata folia eius*
10 *stronge wyn helpeþ*: *vino fortissimo multum confert*
33 *ful wel nyh*: *multum aromatica fere* 'very sweet-smelling close at hand'

1045 9 *Ysaac*: *Isa* (M *Ysaac*　O *Ysi*). The reference is properly to Isidore IV. 12. 5
15 *þe sterre**
21–2 *and is fastned togidere and*: *cuius gutta profluens et coagulata* 'and the drop thereof both liquid and solid'
28 *calamenta*: *calamenta*. BA wrote *calamita*, as at 1046/7 where the form *calamenta* is found only in ME. MSS

1046 3–4 *ytorned . . . hond*: *malaxatur. ywent* is perhaps an error for *ywrouȝt*
13 *netes*: *tineam* 'worm'. JT's form was probably *nytes*, as at 971/28
29 *swete*: *subdulces*

1047 2 *and¹*: *quia* (L om.　O *eo quod*　T *ta*)
7–8 *groweþ . . . prikke**
14 *vnfastenesse and vnsadnesse*: *raritate*
20 *dartes*: *spiculi uel celi* (M *teli*)

1049 9 *closynge*: *munitionis*
9 *ymade*: adds *nam*
16 *frogges*: *vt rane*
17 *and is name . . . þat*: *serpens* (L *serps*) *cuius*
28 *aboute*: adds *enim*
29 *sceptum*: JLT *sceptum*　cf. the better *septum* (S *ceptum*)

1050 1 *stakes*: adds *per eam ex transuerso figuntur vt dicit Ysidorus secundum Hugacione uero sudes dicitur a sudo sudis siue a sudus sudi dum quod est mundus et purus*
19 *ix°*: JLO *exo* (T om.), cf. the better *xv*

1051 1 *conforteþ*: *purgat*
2 *appetite*: adds *et stomachum confortat*
11 *praysynge*: adds *et uirtutes*
16 *coddes*: *folliculis siue tecis*
28 *bestes*: adds *quod emittatur ad procreandum fetum*

1052 12 *lest*: *nec* (T *uel*). Z *ne*
22 *comaunded*: *precipiendum*, cf. the better N *preripiendum* and R *prerapiens*
26 *contrarye*: *contrarium* cf. the better OT *congruum*
30 *xx°*.: *xx* cf. the better QRX *xxiiii*

1053 4 *and²*: adds *ui caloris*, translated *by vertu of hete* line 10
9 *vertu*: *ratio*. Cf. 597/11 n. above
19 *somtyme foure-egged*: *quandoque triangula ut in spelta quandoque tetragona seu quad-rangula* (T first two words only)

1054 8 *byclippe*: adds *quia* (J om.) *stipula facit culmum quem stipat*
12 *þerwiþ¹*: adds *quidam loco straminis stipulam sibi sternunt*
17 *and wiþ wynd*: *et vento subdita* 'carried by wind', properly part of the previous clause
22 *mele*: *forme* Z *farine*

1055 22 *to þe crafte*: *in uallibus*
24 *xx°*.: *xix*
25 *of flex*: *a lini uel a canabi*
29 *bondes and knyttels and maches*: *ligamina* cf. O *lichini*. BA wrote *elychnia* 'wicks', cf. Isidore XIX. 19. 3 *lychnium*
31 *yseleen*: *cinerem*, generally translated *asken* (as at 565/8)

1056 2 *xx°*.: *xix*
4 *wiþ venym and poysoun*: *venenata ex cuius succo venena* (L *nonena* N om.) *toxica* (N om.) *exprimuntur*
31 *table*: *tabulata scilicet laquearia*. Cf. 1059/24

1057 1–2 *castyng . . . planynge*: *superfluorum resectionem*
17–18 *for lenyynge*: *incuruationem . . . patiantur*. Probably JT wrote *lenen*

1058 13 *and¹**: the next clause properly modifies the previous clause
28 *Ophir uel Effir*: *effir*, cf. the better ONSTU *offir*, I *Ophir*. A doublet of conflation. Cf. 786/22 n. above
31 *þe nayle of þe honde*: *vnguis*. Perhaps JT wrote *nayle or horne*

1059 2 *an herbe*: *olerum et herbarum*
5 *tendre*: *tenerior*. In Latin all adjectives in this sentence are comparative
7 *sprayes*: adds *et est utilior* (cf. the better X *melior*) *in medicina*
11 *þerof*: adds *ad modum coni uel pyramidis*
16 *þe laþþe*: *tegule autem dicuntur ligna quedam*

1060 22 *fast*: *densum*
32 *accidental*: *actualem*
36 *by druyenesse*: *colatiuum* '(is) filtering'. The translation recurs at 1061/14 *druyeþ*, 1091/12 *to druye and to clense*

1061 11–12 *scabbes . . . tetres*: *serpiginem et impetiginem*
14 *whete*: *tritici siue furfur*. Cf. 972/20 n. above
18 *is*: adds *cito*
34 *yscheled*: adds *et dicitur a tipeo quod est percutio qui percutitur in pila dum decorticatur*

1062 8 *many teeth and scharpe prikkes*: *dentes . . . acutissimos aculeos et dentatos*
13 *reede*: adds *sparsas* (O *asperas*)

1063 6 *capitulo glosa*: g (N *q^c* T om.). Perhaps an ME. scribal expansion. The reference is to the Gloss on Exodus 30: 7
  11 *of thimiama*: properly qualifies *confeccioun*
  22 *neysshed*: adds (not L) *masticatione in puluerem*

1064 2 *leues*: *cortice et folio*
  4 *somer*: adds *melius est que uero in estate*
  8 *faste*: adds *mundum odoriferum*
  19 *Saba*: *Saba*, cf. J *rabi*   L *raba*   T *fala*. The doublet is present in Latin

1065 9 *on coles*: *carbone*, properly in apposition to *whitnesse*
  11 *to poudre*: *in puluerem uel in micam*
  30 *wyne*: adds *tumoribus intestinorum subuenit si* (L om.) *cum uino bibatur*

1066 2 *and 3iueth lyen**
  7 *schadoweþ*: *immutans*... *et obumbrans*
  26 *bounden*: adds *et idcirco in uirga hos sustinent alligatos*
  27 *3erde*: adds *ut dicit Isidorus libro xvii*

1067 1 *stok or stalk*: *lignum*. An ME. doublet of ambiguity
  11 *defoule*: *aliqua uiolatione*
  16 *fongeþ*: adds *pariter*
  19 *norisshyng*: M *nutrimentum*   cf. the better *incrementum*
  31 *right*: adds *imo sepe facilius frangitur quam rectificetur*

1068 5 *3erde*: adds *dicitur que*
  9 *for it is filled*: *precissum* 'after having been cut'. Perhaps JT wrote *for-yfelled* 'cut down'. The chapter *de orto* is missing in all Latin mss. and prints
  11–12 *herber*... *virgultum*: *uirgultum uiridarium*. The reversal in ME. is perhaps scribal
  16 *it is ybounde*: *uincitur et ligatur*
  24 *þise*... *vynes**   27 *wiþ blastes of wedir**   30 *fro þe socoure**   31 *þey schulde haue socoure**
  30 *slaked*... *hurled*: *longius*... *dissipentur*
  33 *vynes*: adds *oblaqueatio oblaqueari*

1069 4–5 *superfluite*... *veyne*: *uirgam*... *superuacuam refecare cuius flagellum luxuriat*
  16 *to feede*... *vyne*: *uel* (L om.) *nutrire*
  18–19 *þe sonne*... *eyre*: *uue liberius aerem purum capiant*. Perhaps JT wrote *þe son-nere may þe grapes come to þe pure eyre*
  21 *By leues of þe vyne*: *quorum* (L *quo*) *subsidio*
  25 *by bowes*... *palmites*: *de palmite*
  27 *ben gadered to make of wyne*: *prescinduntur et recolliguntur*
  28 *xviii^o.*: *xviii*   cf. L *xii*   O *xvii*

1070 4 *Smale*: *graciles et tenues*. Cf. line 11
  16 *þe knottes*: *oculis siue gemmis*
  24 *gardyners*: *cultoribus aut circumfossoribus*
  35–6 *and grieueþ it. Also þe vyne hateþ raphanus and alle maner caule*: *ledit etiam uitem raphanus odit etiam caulem et omne olus*. Probably an ME. scribal confusion or JT's misreading

1071 3 *to vynes*: *uitium*, properly qualifying *kuttynges*

9 *to þe coppe of þat temple**: adds *antiquitus*

13 *springeþ . . . traylynge*: *circumduci possunt*

15 *and of opere hihe trees**   22 *medicines for yhen**

1072 6 *he seiþ, and*: *idem et*. BA wrote *dicit idem Plinius*

12 *The rynde of þe vyne*: properly in apposition to *druye vyne leues*

22 *xiiii°.*: *xiiii* (O *xiii*), cf. the better MX *xvii*

27 *neyþer bykitte . . . ypared*: *nec putatur*

1073 8 *bestes*: adds (not X) *Hucusque Plinius*

11 *spray*: *spuria*. Probably JT wrote *spuria* here as in line 25. *sprayes* translates
plante line 13

13 *vnkynde*: *degeneres . . . et innaturales*. Cf. line 20

15–16 *to norisshynge of hemself**

17 *perfore*: adds *citius*

19–20 *spray . . . vitulamina*: *plante* (X om.) *adulterine dicuntur spuria vitulamina*

1074 13 *and conforteþ þe touche þerwiþ**

15 *clowdes, myst, neyþer to moche reyn*: *tempus nubilosum*

27 *soure*: *stipticus et acetosus*

1075 29 *hyeþ for fere**

30 *vuiacie*: *uiciarie*   cf. J *uticizie*   L *uertuarie*   MQ *uuciarie*   N *verciare*   O
uuacie   P *uertiace*   R *uiracie*   T *uersiarie*. Isidore XVII. 5. 15 has *unciariae*, cf.
Pliny XIV. 42 *uncialis*

1076 4 *whyte*: O *albe*   N *mineo*   cf. the better *albe mineo*

5 *bere*: *facientes*   Z *ferentes*

7 *perfore*: *pro quarum depredatione*

8 *biccubite*: *bicubite*, cf. I *biculate*   M *biturice*   N *butulate*   OQ *bictulate*   Isidore XVII. 5. 22 has *biturica*, cf. Pliny XIV. 27 *biturigiaca*

10 *hete*: adds *et in terra macra non deficiunt huiusmodi*, the last is falsely joined to the
next sentence as *such and of suche kynde*

18 *dyuersitees*: *famose*. Z *forme*

24 *skynnes . . . moyste*: *carnis parui humoris et corticis* 'pith, with little juice and skin'

1077 5 *þe synewes . . . colde*: *neruos sua frigiditate* (MN *stipticitate*) *dentium et radices*

14–15 *þe stalke . . . ywounde*: *torquetur illud per quod vua dependet a vite*

20–2 *beþ ydo . . . so ydryed*: *postquam panis est extractus de clibano quando calor est* (JL
-em) *temperatus imponuntur ibidem racemi siccantur*

28–9 *þe menynge . . . sonne**

1078 28 *restoreþ*: adds *ac custodit*

30 *likkenesse and companye*: *familiaritatis consortium*   cf. the better OX *familiari-
tatem confortium*

36 *alle*: *tocius*   cf. the better X *citius*

1079 20 *contraries*: X *rerum contrariarum*   cf. the better *rerum*

22 *Also*: *sed*

35 *cytryn, and reede*: *glaucus* (X om.) *citrinus* (N om.) *et roseus siue rufus*

1080 5 *þan white wyn or blak**

5–6 *fro white or blakke . . . to white and blak*: *ab illis extremitatibus . . . illis*

17 *þat*: *quia*

22 *softe*: *aromaticum*, translated *of þe good odour* line 28. Perhaps JT wrote *swete*, as at 878/20

26 *and*[2]: *valde enim*

32 *troubly*: *obscuri et turbidi*, translated *trowbly and derk* 1081/5

1081 23 *vel viii⁰.* *: a doublet of ambiguity

23–4 *and drynkynge*: *ipso hausto*

34 *þe same*: JL *idem* cf. OX *ibidem* N om. and the better MT *item*. BA adds *mala autem que facit vinum intemperate immoderate sumptum*

1082 16 *madnesse*: *vim*

19–20 *and graunteþ*... *graunted* *

29 *and wrynge*: *quando scilicet de torculari primo est expressum*

1083 9 *brekeþ*: adds *mox*

11 *For*: *unde*. Perhaps JT wrote *þerfor*

15 *is so ytrode and ywronge and ypressed*: *eliquatur*

18 *rogelyng*: *rugitum*, generally translated *grollynge* and occasionally and doubtfully *crullynge*. The form here is also doubtful

19 *smoky*: *spumosum*, translated *fomy* 1091/5. Z *fumosum*

26, 27 *atte fulle* *

29–30 *þanne*... *kynde*: *et lucidum atque clarum laudabile est et amicum nature*. Probably JT wrote *and bright and cleere þanne it is good and freend to kynde*

1084 6 *and nouȝt ydronke* *

7 *þere*: *ideo*. Probably JT wrote *þerfor*

10 *druyenesse*: adds *et caliditate*

18 *gariofilatum*: *gariophilato* cf. JL *gasophilato* N *garofilato* T *garosophilato*

1085 9 *substaunce of*: *substantialiter*, properly in apposition to *naturaliter* (O *pluraliter*) 'kyndliche'

16 *as vynegre* *

21 *for vertu*: *habet enim vim viuacem*

1086 3 *þe slepyng yuel* *

7 *an egge*: *hebetes et stupidos*

10 *þe hierynge and þe weyes*: *uias auditus* 'ways of hearing'

13 *vynegre*: adds *per plures dies*

14 *bytynge*: *morsus serpentis cornuti qui dicitur cerustes similiter contra morsus* (as in Pliny VIII. 85, XI. 126)

25–6 *Thise*... *acinum* *

30 *is ykepte inne*: *occultatur et reponitur* (JLMT om.)

32 *þat þerinne comeþ and vessel of wyn*: *vina in doliis reposita*

1087 7–8 *þat is*... *Melos* *

9 *and*: *et eciam*

13 *concepcioun*: *partum*. Cf. 1089/30

22 *rewarded*: adds *pariter*

23 *and Plius*: X only and properly includes

25 *moyste*: *vliginosis et humidis*

26 *for vligo*... *erþe* *

30 *haþ*: *ex se mittit*

1088 19–20 *ouþer 'þe blynde nettel'**

   24 *aʒeins*: adds *ictericam* (JL *ultericiam*   O *utericiam*   T *ulterusam*)

   28 *wiþ salt and**: perhaps by eyeskip to line 26

1089 12 *whan he groweþ furst**

   13–14 *slyly . . . þerfro*: *ab eo cautius separetur*

   17 *whete*: adds *uel zizaniis parcatur* (JTX *pertura*   P *partis*   Q *perdatur*   R *procreetur*) *uel triticum sub zizanie specie* (LO last phrase only)

   27 *greuous*: adds *et occidit*

   34 *postemes*: adds *sileriticum* (L *cliroticum*   T *icliroticum*) *siue durum*

1090 14 *web*: *pannum siue telum*

   16 *iii*: *per duos uel tres*

   25 *somdel scharp in sauour*: *stipticum cum acumine modico*

1091 3 *after þe restynge*: *post facta residentia*

   9 *fuyre . . . sonne*: *solem*

   10 *and*: *et omnino* (PT *ideo*)

   24–5 *coldnesse and scharpnesse*: *acumen*   cf. T *accionem*

NOTE: Mr. V. E. Watts collated the manuscripts QT, I to p. 989, M to p. 996, and passed these collations to the General Editor who incorporated them in this commentary.

BOOK XVIII

1097 5] *delete last comma*
20 been, and] been. And

1100 21 and] *delete and fn.* *ABCDEFGHW and for   LS propter
23 and to] to *and fn.* ABCDEFGHW and to   LS ut

1111 15 neissh] neissh[eþ] *and fn.* *ABCDEFGHW neissh   LS soluit
22 of^1] or *and fn.* *ABCDEFGHW of   *cf.* LS membris

1113 26 gootes, and bukkes] goote bukkes *and fn.* *ABCDEFGHW gootes and bukkes   LS capri

1115 33 folk] *flo*k *and fn.* *ABCDEFGHW folk   LS gregis

1116 20 and is] is *and fn.* *ABCDEFGHW and is   LS est

1118 13 brawne] *bo*ne *and fn.* *ABCDEFGHW brawne   LS osse

1119 8 byteþ] *fyteþ and fn.* *ABCDEFGHW byteþ   LS pugnant
29 las] *add fn.* *ABCDEFGHW *om.*   LS minus
31 in] *on and fn.* *ABCDEFGHW in   *cf.* LS exponitur

1121 3 of þe lyddes] *add fn.* ABCFGHW *om.*   LS ciliorum

1129 11 addres^1 . . . serpentz] addres. And generalliche of alle addres and serpentz
31–2 erþe. As . . . seiþ,] erþe, as . . . seiþ.

1130 21–2 stede . . . maner] stede, as Ysidorus seiþ libro xii°. þe maner
32 vncloþeþ] vncloseþ *and delete fn.*

1132 22 þerafter] þer *and fn.* *ABCDEFGHW þerafter   LS in quo

1136 5 þrowynge] *kn*owynge *and fn.* *ABCDEFGHW þrowynge   *cf.* LS incredibilis

1138 36 spekked, and dyuerse] spekked and dyuerse,

1141 13 ykeþte] ykepte
19 .And] , and

1142 9 mosts wete] most swete

1143 3 be wake] bewake
12–13 And . . . Furst] and þe eldere worcheþ at home. And wiþ floures þat þay
bryngeþ, furst

1146 16–17 *Plinius libro*] *Plinius. Libro   Begin paragraph after point*

1148 14 and betynge of bacynes] *delete and fn.* *ABCDEFGHW and betynge of bacynes   LS *lack phrase*
17 huyes] huyues

1154 7–8 hyssynge and blast. He] hyssynge, and [wiþ] blast he *and fn.*
wiþ blast] ABCFGHW blast   DE breþinge   LS afflatu
15–16 toforehond. And aȝeins . . . Auicen, furst] toforehond aȝeins . . . Auicen.
Furst

1151 38 of] *add fn.* *ADEFGHW and   *cf.* LS neruorum

1157 33 n. 33] 32

1160   37 bestes *super*] bestes. *Super*
    15 n. add asterisk

1162 16 n. 16] 14
    34 tofore þre ȝeer and] and tofore þre ȝeer

1165 24 Jason] Iason

1166 21 *xli°*,] *xli°*.

1176 27 beste] beste,

1177 26 flotyng] fle tyng *and fn.* ACFGHW flotyng   LS liquidas

1179 32 *iii°*.] in *and fn.* *ACDEFGHW iii   LS in

1188 23 *fine*] *f*

1189 16 onl yue] onlyue
    22 n. carica] carice

1193 22 yseyd] ysey*e and fn.* ACFGHW yseyd   LS uidetur

1194 2 fyuere] fyueþe *and fn.* A fyuere

1201 2 n. meneþ DE meneþ] meueþ   DE and meueþ

1204 6 and²] *add* [scheleþ and] *and fn.* AEFGHW *om.*   LS decorticant

1212 39 *fn.* by þe] AGH whyche   LS unde

1214 33 spous] spous[hode] *and fn.* A spous   *cf.* LS adultere

1216 1 chasteþ] chaseþ *and delete fn.*

1218 11 n. *leontezones*] *leonzefones*

1220 22 n. *add cf.* LS ipsum insequentes
    32 *fn.* *And . . . hulle] ACDEFG *om.* LS unde difficilius capitur contra montem
quam contra uallem

1228 14 n. 14] 15 *and* 33 n. 33] 34

1230 11 large] large,

1239 19 fe st] fast *and delete fn.*
    27 ta ken] to ken *and fn.* AFGHW taken   LS signum

1246 28 fnesy] *v*nesy *and fn.* *ACDFGH fnesy   LS inquieta

1250 9 n. brederen] breder   22 n. *add at end . . .* producit
    32 vii°., sche] vii°. Sche

1251 4 n. A.A.] A A.

1254 27 *delete semi-colon*

1264 17 fo] of

The English MSS. ACDEFGH are complete. B begins imperfectly at 1076/6 and
ends imperfectly at 1152/4. De Worde's edition is based on F. MS. Ashmole 1397
f. 114ᵛ contains an extract from the end of Chapter 1 (1111/2-27 above) with these
variants: 2 þe] his   5 And] and so   and²] he   6 þey seen] he seieþ
7 wolues yhe] wolfes yen   þe] his   9 hem] hym   fallynge] *adds* euellius

10 a] *om.*   12 þe no   13 it] þat ryng   14 saiþ þat] so þat þe
16 onlyue] a live   beeþ] ben   of[1]] and   23 ysayde] seid   hierafter]
after   kyndes] kynde   and] and in   25 or] oþer   hidde] priuey
þe] no   26 and] or

The Latin MSS. IJMNOPQTUVWXY are complete. K is wholly lacking. R lacks
1072/36–73/15. S is damaged at beginning and end (i.e. before 1094/1, after 1264/
17). At 1164/34 I adds an example of canine fidelity; at 1142/4 U adds a passage
from Isidore XII. 8.

1093 34 *Auycenne*: NOPR only *Auicenna*. All add *libro i*

1094 15 *þat is aboute the herte*: *circumstans*

1096 13 *vertu*: adds *exceptis paucis beluis aquaticis et marinis et subdit quod omne animal
habens sanguinem nobilem quatuor mouetur instrumentis*
    31–3 *þe symple . . . þinges**

1098 36–7 *wiþ hornes wiþoute**
    38 *hors*: adds (not S) *et omne animal cornutum habet cornu uacuam preter ceruum et
unicornem*

1100 2 *Helyas*: *helias* (I *hesticius*   MN *hesias*), properly Ctesias (as in Pliny
VIII. 75)
    30 *longen*: adds *uel aliquid loco pulmonis*

1101 37 *drynke*: adds *est magna differencia*

1103 36 *and also Constantyn**

1105 27 *encresseþ*: adds *et pinguedines multiplicantur et ideo talium animalium corpora sunt
multa nutritiua*

1107 10 *lasse*[2]: *amplioris*
    31–2 *is fordruyed*: *minuuntur . . . et desiccantur*

1108 3 *fatnesse*: adds *humidum stomachum dissoluit deficiente contentiua et confortatiua et
expulsiua*

1109 20–1 *schepes fleissh in springyng tyme*: *pecorina in uere bouina in fine ueris*
    29 *moysture*: adds *illaudabilis*
    36 *druye bestes*: *siccorum et macrorum*

1110 36–7 *þat is anoynt with leouns dryt*: *qui linit corpus suum cum sepo renum leonis aut qui
iniungitur eius fimo*. The retention of *leonis* in translation suggests that JT compressed the meaning

1111 27 *dryt*: adds *sed hec ad presens dicta generaliter hic sufficiant*

1113 20 *coloures*: IMOR *colorum*   W *delorum*   cf. the better *telorum*
    24 *And bussheþ . . . ynough**

1114 1 *tyme*[2]: adds *dormiunt in latere altero*

1115 5 *vii°.*: *xii*
    26 *knees*: *anteriores poplices*

1116 24 *vii°.*: *xii*

1117 3 *body*: adds *pariter et roboris quam sit sonus et minoris caloris*

16–17 *haþ lasse kynde hete . . . hornes*: *minus est animosa propter quod etiam caret cornibus*

27 *seiþ*: adds *libro xii capitulo i*

1118 19 *of his teeþ*: *culmorum*. At line 39 *dentibus* is translated *teeþ and toskes*. Cf.
1193/21

1119 1 *toskes*: adds *aper uero ledit culmis sursum feriendo*
36 *drytte*: adds *desiccatus*

1120 7 *vii°.*: *xii*

1121 25 *and also*: *item si*
32 *olde*: adds *aut duo*

1125 7 *olde*: i.e. 'held', cf. *tenetur*

1126 4 *xiiii°.*: *xxiiii*

1127 5, 9 *vii°.*: *xii*
25 *quadragumen*: JLSTW *quadraguium*   M *quadragenum*   O *quadranguinum*
P *quadragnum*   R *quadranguium*   U *quoddam*. BA wrote *quedam anguium*

1128 2 *xvii°.*: *xlvii*   cf. D *xxvii*
16–17 *þat hatte terbenus and chelydros*: *et terrenus* (LMTW *terbenus*   O *repens*)
nomine chelidros 'and a land snake called *chelydros*

1129 32 *As Ysidorus seiþ*: *ut idem recitat Ysidorus*

1130 16 *kurteles*: adds *senectam deponere*
23 *philosopher*: *phisologus*

1131 4 *olde skynne*: *senectutem id est senectam pellem*

1132 2 *wery*: JLMNORSW *uerax*   cf. the better *uorax*
17 *streccheþ*: LST *striccius*   cf. the better *strictus*. Perhaps JT wrote *strei3t*, as at
1134/29

1133 32 *smale*: *strictum*

1135 5 *And hatte*: *scilicet*
5 *dispas*: IJOPRS *dispas*   cf. LNW *dipsas*   M *dipsa*   T *dispsas*   U *dipsa*
19 *by*: *in*. Perhaps JT wrote *in*

1136 22 *somtyme*: *quedam*   Z *quandoque*
35 *tyme*: *tempore*   cf. the better U *corpore*

1137 11–12 *righteþ and amendeþ þe þredes*: *per fila repit*

1138 12–14 *aboute þe goynge doun . . . sonne*: *contra occasum solis uel ortum econtra maxime
laborat*. An ME. expansion, perhaps by JT
22 *as*: *ac si*
33 *Aristotilis*: OT *Aristotelis*   M *in*. The other MSS. properly omit, the reference being to Pliny XI. 79 and this sentence dependent on the previous

1139 1 *and weueþ in dennes by itsilf*: *cauernas sibi texens*. Perhaps JT wrote *weueynge
dennes for itsilf*

1141 22 *as þe leoun*: O only omits, but the emendation may be unjustified

1142 6 *xii°.*: *xi*   cf. D *xi*

35–6 *þe floures beþ nyh yspended*: *flores uicini sunt consumpti*. Perhaps JT wrote *þe ny3 floures beþ yspended*

1143 3 *or²*: *ut*   Z *uel*
20 *werk*: *temporis*   cf. the better NPR *operis in temporalis*
26 *whanne þay beþ ycharged*: *et quando sunt honuste redeunt*
36–7 *abydeþ stille*: *strepunt*

1144 34 *and²*: adds *furtim*
37 *multiplied*: adds *et mella depauperantur econuerso quando uer est siccum deficiunt in prole et in melle multiplicantur*

1145 16 *gadereþ hony and makeþ here nest among corne*: ILORSU *que in messe mella faciunt*   cf. the better *que bis in mense mella faciunt* (as in Pliny XI. 59)
18–19 *þat stikeþ þere he smyteþ*: *uentri consertum* (IN *insertum*   S *consextum*   T *sexum*   U *contextum*)
30 *þanne þey bereþ mete togidres*: *nam cibos tunc conuehunt*, where *nam* is an error for the better *non*

1146 14 *sikenesse... sikenesse*: *mortis* (P *morbi*) *... morbi* (P *morti*). Z *morbis... morbi*
27 *but*: ILTU om. The emendation may be unjustified
35 *more*: adds *pigre* (I *pingues*   MNPT *pingre*)

1147 5 *defende*: adds *vis enim ignea est in aculeo et ideo cooperatur ualde*
7–8 *and brede... greuous*: *que faciunt aliis muscis paruis* (ILMNPSTUW *alias muscas paruas*) *tedium*
9 *fighteþ wiþ*: I *pungunt contra*   cf. the better *pugnunt*

1148 11 *heruest*: adds *et in uere*
31 *xiiii°*.: *xii*

1149 15–17 *of þe kynde... togideres*: *de natura boum in trimatu post trimatum autem nimis est sera sed ante prematura optime uero cum boue iuuencus imbuitur*, where BA wrote *domitura... minus est fera... cum domitura*
20 *þat*: adds *procaci animo motus*

1150 13 *drytte*: adds *cum aceto*
25 *Papias*: a misreading of an abbreviated *propter*

1151 4 *hem¹*: adds *cum uirga*

1153 6 *and*: adds *cum debilitatur pugnans*
27–8 *cocatrice... dedly*: *reguli autem sicut scorpiones arentia queque sectantes et postquam ad aquas peruenerint hydrophobos et limphaticos* (ILS *lyrefantes*   T *lire ephantes*) *faciunt*
32 *and Ethiops*: JT perhaps wrote *in Ethiope*, cf. *Hesperios ethiopes*

1154 2 *and in brede*: I *et magnitudine*   JLMOTW *magnitudine*   SUP om., cf. the better *magnitudinem*

1155 13 *stynkynge*: *fetida muscida*

1156 31 *xxx°*.: *xix*

1157 17 *schoon*: adds *et abluunt eis pedes*
31 *generacioun*: adds *femina trahit in utero per xii. menses et non coeunt ante triennium*

1158 1 *slough*: *momordit et occidit*
30 *yfounde*: adds *aut si inuenitur*

1159 17 *xxx°.*: *xix*

29 *beste*: adds *cuius corpusculum ita recipiat*

1160 15 *skynne*[1]: adds *simili corio*

21–2 *And haþ . . . herte*: *parum enim habet* (I adds *carnis*) *nisi in capite et radice caude ubi parum habet sanguinis similiter in corde*

1163 6 *armitum*: JMNOSTUVW *armitum* R *armutum* cf. the better *aruncum* (P *arantum*)

1164 8 *xxxiii°.*: *xxviii*

1166 16 *after þe oon and twentyþe day*: *non post xxi. diem nec ante vii.*

17 *ones*: adds *ix. die uidet quando gemini x. die et quando trini die xi. et ita quanto plures pariuntur*

35 *blynde*: adds *xiiii. diebus et quedam per tres menses et est quarta pars anni et filii istarum erunt ceci*

1167 6 *male*[2]: *leporarii masculi*

13 *xxiiii°.*: *xxviii* cf. DE *xxviii*

1168 5 *tyme*: adds *quam canes sed canes uenatici masculi . . . minus uiuunt*

27 *croked*: *longas*. Cf. line 22

1169 22 *bred*: *carnem* Z *panem*

27 *þough noþyng greue him*: *et inspici* (LT *insipidi* J *insipiti*) *a nullo pacientes*

34 *worme*: adds *qui grece dicitur licta*

1170 12 *alle oþre*: *omnes*

35 *serueþ*: adds *indifferenter*

1171 6 *away*: adds *se excutiendo*

34 *And noþing*: *quorum sanguine nichil*

36 *And*: adds *adhuc in presenti*

1172 5 *sight*: adds *ut supra dicit Aristoteles similiter quanto uberiori lacte nutriuntur tanto tardius in uidendo perficiuntur*

1173 33 *precious*: adds *pro qua uenatur*

1174 5 *pere*: *ibidem* cf. the better M *idem* (N om.)

1175 18–19 *þey . . . serpentes*: *spiritu narium eos extrahunt de cauernis et superata pernicie ueneni eorum pabulo reparantur*

24 *and bereþ doun þe eeren*: *submissis ruthe* 'when the ears are down (they hear) nothing'. Perhaps Trevisa wrote *and hereþ noþing whan he bereþ doun þe eeren*. The next clause properly belongs to the next sentence

33–4 *weyes . . . bestes*: *semitas tritas ab hominibus quam semitas feris*

36 *and*[2]: *interdum eciam*

1176 38 *but þe forhede passynge þe lasse tyndes*: *immo ante frontem preminent minoribus*

1178 8 *songe*: adds *et sequitur ipsum cantum*

34 *Dias*: *Dias Plinius*

1179 1 *sonde*: adds *solis cornibus sine cooperculo derelictis*

32 *iii°*: *in*. Perhaps JT wrote *in*

1180 17 *hoolefooted*: adds (not L) *sicut equus*

21 *hornes*: adds (not JM) *et vnguium*
30 *eyren*[1]: adds *in terra*

1181 27 *Plinius*: a false expansion of an abbreviated antecedent *ipsum*. BA is here still citing the *Phisiologus*

1182 11 *withinne*: *in parte inferiori*   Z *interiori*
31 *dar nou3t fighte*: *inbelle* (O om.) *et inbecille*
34 *Marcianus*: *marcianus*   cf. the better MNP *marcialis*

1183 16 *and twenty**: H three minims crossed and cancelled, DE *and tweyne*, AFG *and twenty*. Probably JT wrote *ii*, mistaking an abbreviated *enim* as a numeral

1184 21 *nought oonly in teep but also*: *non in dentibus sed*
22 *bope wip bytyng and with styngyng*: *uerbere plusquam ictu*. JT's form was probably *beytyng* 'beating', and its scribal misreading then induced the change of syntax and sense

1185 16 *Leuitici*: *Leuitici*   cf. the better MX *Ieremie*

1187 12–17 *Of schappe . . . sad*: *forma ut sit ualidum corpus et solidum et robori conueniens altitudo latus longum et substrictum maximi et rotundi clunes pectus late patens et totum corpus musculorum densitate nodosum pes siccus et ungula concaua solidatus*

1188 8 *wepep for here frendes and lordes*: *amicos* (cf. the better X *amissos*) *deflent dominos* (OR *pro dominis suis*)
19 *3eere*: adds *et generat a tercio anno usque ad xxx. annos*
34 *pat matiere fallep to pe roof of pe moup*: JLSTV *ad eius palatum*   cf. the better *quod cadit ei palatum*

1189 27 *loue*: adds *idem dicit Aristoteles libro vii.*

1190 15–16 *frikelich*: *libere*. Perhaps a genuine form, but cf. DE *freschelyche*, FGH *frely*, and 1190/17 *freliche*

1191 16 *bluwe to pe see . . . colour*: *uenetos aeri atque aque quia cerulei sunt coloris*   Z *mari aque* for *aeri atque*, cf. lines 5–6
21–2 *for many . . . Sathanas*: *quia* (L *qui*   cf. BA's *quem*) *plurimi specie sathane repleuerant*
36–7 *And gop yfeere in here manere goynge*: *gregatim incedunt motu quo ualent*. All examined Latin MSS. omit the final *salutant* (as in Isidore XII. 2. 16) and so destroy the sense

1192 7 *redynesse*: *probitas* (X *prohibitas*)
31–2 *and ledep . . . doynge*: *ducit agmen maximus natu* (JLSV *nam*   T lacks clause) *cogit et cooperatur etate proximus* 'the eldest leads the herd, the next in seniority helps'

1193 18 *tynels*: *bolizatus*. Perhaps an error for *tyndes* 'tines', as at 1176/33
30 *vii°.*: *v*

1194 7 *vi°.*: *vii.*
24–5 *litera f, it folwep pat*: *f*
35 *pat his complexioun*: *hoc propter suam complexionem que*

1195 17 *ywounded*: adds *nam fessos et uulneratos in medio sui recipiunt*

1197 2 *aloude*: IJLOSUV *ambe*   cf. the better *alte*
21 *hete*: adds *ut dicit Constantinus*

23 *i⁰.*: *l*

25 *viciapoli*: JLSVW *uiciapolos*   IU *noctilucos*   MOR *noctilupos*   P *uesptinam*. BA wrote *nyctalopas* (as in Pliny VIII. 86)

1198 11 *xxii⁰.*: *xii*   cf. DE *xii*

1200 10 *ambitice*: *arabitice* (M *Archaphacite*   N lacks clause) 15 *sinodopes*: IJLOSVWX *sinodopes*   cf. the better *sinopedes* (PR *synapes*)

1201 8 *v⁰.*: *xv*

1202 6 *xii⁰.*: *xi*

1203 34 *i⁰.*: *iii*

1204 20 *profytable*: adds *sed hee condunt*

1207 11 *hors*: adds *et uiuos homines discerpunt ut dicit Isidorus libro xii. Adeo autem infestat equum* 24 *seip*: adds *libro xii*

1208 1 *xlᵐ.*: *xiᵐ* (I *lx*   LO om.   SW *xl*   U *i.v*) 10 *hinniendo*: ORU *hinniendo*   cf. the better *innuendo* 29 *is*: IORSUW add *petulum* (cf. the better *petulcum*) *et*

1209 19 *viii⁰.*: *xviii* 34 *cancres*: adds *et alios morbos ulcerosos*

1210 38 *grete men*: JLOVW *magni*   cf. the better *magi* (R *magistri*) translated *wicches* 1211/2. See 1264/17

1211 13 *closed*: *claudit*. Perhaps JT wrote *closep*

1212 17 *xx⁰.*: *xix*

1214 11 *tayle*: adds *animos eorum*

1215 25 *Ysidorus*: *Plinius* 27 *pey*: cf. *latitat*. Probably JT wrote *a* 'he'

1216 1 *him*[1]: adds *et eum non tetigerit* 38 *he*: *Dyas*

1219 19 *leoun*: adds *et leoni masculo mirabiliter est exosus* 21 *outgoynge*: adds *unum* (L *donum*) *per quod intrat*

1220 37 *seip*: IJLORSTUVW *uidet*   cf. the better *vitet* in the clause *et ideo ut in fugiendo uitet casum* 'and therefore in order to avoid a fall in fleeing'

1221 5 *For*: *nam in alpibus sunt quidam et in siluis habitant* 18 *encressynge*: *excrementa*   Z *incrementa*

1222 11 *moup*: adds *cum quibus uiam querit*

1223 28 *hunte*: adds *bestias propter etatem et quia eorum culmi iam sunt debilitati et uiuunt multo tempore et eius senectus deprehenditur in dentibus quia constringuntur in senectute*

1225 6 *xv⁰.*: *xii* 18–19 *is forbode*: JLSUVW *iubetur*   O *inbuitur*   R *inibetur*   cf. the better *medetur*. The clause is otherwise correct, *mulus calcitratus potu uini medetur* (cf. Pliny VIII. 59) 22 *mare*: *asina*   Z *equa*, as in line 13

1227 2 *3ere*: adds *et per dimidium uigilant*
   23 *locidas and ilqwyde*: JLOQVW *locidas*   R *licida*   S *locidalus*   U *locidamie*
cf. the better *ictides* (as in Isidore XII. 3. 3). A doublet of conflation, *locidas uel
ilcides*, an initial barred *l* being read as *lo* by one scribe and as *il* by another

1229 13 *is*[1]: *mouetur*
   35 *candele*: adds *et maxime circa posteriora*
   38 *anoþer litel oon*: IJLSTUVW *onige*   cf. the better *musce*. Perhaps a contextual
guess at a non-existent word

1230 26 *enuyous*: *uiuidus*. Z *inuidus*
   27–8 *where his femel is he goþ aboute and styeþ*: *ubi eius femina euagatur ascendet*. Probably JT wrote *where his femel goþ aboute, a styeþ*

1231 2 *ix*°.: *xxxiv*
   7 *for*: adds *ad umbilico et sursum figuram habet hominis et ab eodem inferius*
   10 *might*: adds *satis inter prodigiosas posuisse gentes et ponit in eodem capitulo exemplum
de multis monstris*
   13 *oþre*: *alii*, i.e. Isidore XI. 3. 37 quoted verbatim
   16 *he*: JLORSTUVW *idem*   cf. the better *Isidorus*. See line 13
   25 *li*°. *i*°.: IJLORTVW *li. primum*   cf. the better *li* (i.e. the numeral, not the
abbreviation of *libro*). See 1232/18n. below

1232 18 *iii*°.: IJLOSTUVW *iii*   cf. the better *liii*. See 1231/25n. above
   18 *sompniferis*: IJLORSTUVW *sompniferis*, cf. the better *semiferis* (as in Pliny
VIII. 79) and *pigrasti* for *pygargi* line 26
   21 *ilices*: JLRSTUVW *ilices*   cf. the better *ibices*

1233 9 *as Seneca meneþ*: *secundum senecam* (S *senectam*). BA wrote *senectutem* (as in
Bede)
   12 *y-eued*: adds *hic bidens huius bidentis dicitur ut dicit Beda*
   30 *conceyuen*: *inpinguantur*   Z *inpregnantur*
   34 *night*: *motus*   Z *noctis*. The next phrase *by ferre wayes* depends on *motus*

1235 22 *more white splekkes*: *maculas albiores*. The ME. translation is ambiguous, cf.
whiter

1236 32 *iii*°.: *ii*
   34 *here boundes*: *ternos ut ferunt* (IOSUW *sunt*) *dodrantes*
   35 *mounteyns*: adds (not I) *compositis*. BA wrote *oppositis* (as in Pliny VII. 2)

1237 25 *ytoþed*: adds *ut tradit nigidius*
   35 *þerto*: adds *de uespere*

1238 1 *fumosite*: adds *per calorem uernalem resolutis ab humoribus in hyeme et in ipsorum
corporibus aggregatis et ideo tunc suauius dormiunt et diucius propter resolutos mulcebres
fumos*
   15 *gendreþ*: adds *prius*
   37 *of*[1]: *et*. JT probably wrote *a* 'and'

1239 14–15 *greueþ ... bytyng*: *pedum motu quam morsu ledit cutem* 'grieves the skin
(more) with creeping of the feet than with biting'
   25 *aisshen*: adds *id est sub nigri*
   29 *waisshynge*: adds *capitis*

1240 26 *figge tre*: adds *ut dicit Constantinus*

1242 15 *buphone*: the proper reference is to chapter 17 *de botrace* which describes *bufones* 'taddes' at 1155/10

1243 14 *Ysidorus*: *Plinius*
16 *his song is crikynge*: *tantus ei est rigor*   Z *cantus* for *tantus*

1244 29 *eschiewen*: *necant*   Z *uitant*   cf. DE *schone*   FG *schenen*   H *schonen* BC lacking
31 *glas*: IU *uitrum*   cf. the better *nitrum*
32–3 *and þe galle*. . . *weseles*: *et fel stellionis tritum in aqua mustelas dicitur congregare*. The false syntax of the ME. is presumably due to mistranslation
35 *clouefoted wiþ fyngres departed*: *habens pedes latos et digitos scissos*

1246 22 *clyma*: *clunam*   Z *climam*
26 *myldenesse*: *feritatis*   Z *suauitatis*, unless an ME. scribe miscopied *wyldenesse*

1247 8 *beres of Inde*: *Indi Orsei* 'the Orsaean Indians' (as in Pliny VIII. 31). Z *Indi ursi*
22 *Aristotel*: adds *libro ii*

1248 3 *s*: *g*
36 *pogo*: *poio*

1249 4 *greueþ*: *cautos*. . . *ledunt*
8 *it is yseyde*: *dicit uersus*
23 *double*: properly qualifies *stynges*, cf. *per colores geminos habent quidam aculeos*
36 *but*: LW *sed*   cf. the better *si* (as in Pliny XI. 21)

1250 18 *eorþe*: adds *rostro*

1251 19 *ful*: *fetosis* 'prolific'. Perhaps JT intended 'foul' and wrote *ful heery* after Z *setosis*

1252 7 *xi°*.: *xix*
14 *groweþ*: adds *rictum*
17 *he hunteþ alle wilde bestes*: *feras omnes uenantur* 'all hunt wild beasts'
26 *þiȝen*: *armas*. But if Z *auras*, the emendation of MS. *eeren* is unjustified
26 *Aristotilis*: IR *Aristotelis*   cf. the better *Auicenna*

1254 23 *hec*: *hic*
28 *gleymy and synowy*: LSU *uiciosus*   ORW *uiscosus*   cf. the better *numerosus*. A doublet of ambiguity, *uiscosus uel neruosus*

1255 6 *whelpes*: *omnes catulos*
33 *þat leueþ*: S *derelinquit* (I *dereliquit*)   cf. the better *derelicto*

1259 10 *soukeþ anone*: *matris uberibus statim reficitur et lactatur*
13 *forhede*: adds *sicut et equo*
34 *lond*: adds *more pecudum*

1260 8 *floweþ*: *recedente*. Perhaps JT wrote *floweþ bak*
8 *wilde*: LSW *feram*   cf. the better *somniferam*
10 *viii°. capitulo vii°*.: *ix capitulo xii*
14 *Auicen*: IRSW *Auicenna*   cf. the better *aiunt*
22 *pre dayes*: ILORSW *in triduum*   cf. the better *interdum*

1261 9 *vanyssheþ*: *crescere*   Z *uanescere*

10 *almerye*: LS *alueo* cf. the better *aluo* 'belly'

15 *vii.*: *bis* (O *hiis*) *septenis*

1262 7 *secounde*: adds *et si tercius eum statim leserit dimittit primum et secundum et mox contra tercium insurgit*

 20 *slegge*: adds *cum reste* (L *recte* S *nocte*)

 21 *anhongred*: adds *et mel extrahere cupiens*

 23 *despitouseliche*: *quasi pede*

 29 *in þat wyse*: *propter stulticia*

1263 6 *libro*: adds *x. capitulo*

 19 *takeþ*: *replet* Z *rapit*

 34 *leste*: adds *nimis expectando plenam formacionem*

1264 9–10 *doþ schrewed tornes*: *syluas petit*. Perhaps JT wrote *seweþ treen*

 17 *grete men*: *magnorum*. See 1210/28. The palmary reading is *magi*, as at line 20 *wichches*

 32 *ver*: adds *et ideo forsan uermes a uerno exitu nomen sumunt*

1265 21 *seiþ*: adds *et Plinius*

 30 *xxiiii.*: *xxiii*

1266 10 *xi°.*: *x*

1267 8 *serpent*: adds *maxime uenenositatis*

 31 *some men knoweþ þat and*: *quod percipientes scire* cf. the palmary *Scite* 'Scythians' (as in Pliny XXIX. 69)

BOOK XIX

1268 8 our] oure
9n. *delete* W

1269 16 is] *add* [y3eue] *and fn.* ACFGHW *om.*   *cf.* LS fit iudicium
18 *Perspectif*] *fn.* A p'spectif
30 vnderstondynge] vndurstondynge
36 elementis] elementz. Also at 1388/29, 1391/24, 1392/30

1270 27n. A] AD

1271 7 of] at *and delete fn.*
15n. LSA] LS

1272 25 heardere] hardere
26 druye] d*y*me *and fn.* *ACDEFGHW druye   LS obscuram

1273 8 ferrer] *u*erre*y and fn.* AG ferrer   LS uera
22 And] *add* [þogh] *and fn.* *ACDEFGHW *om.*   LS licet
24 dymme. 3it] dymme, 3it
31 þat is] *delete and fn.* *ACDEFGHW þat is   LS *lack words*

1274 3 þ*o*y] þey
3–4 yliche . . . poynt,] yliche, . . . poynt
18 alweye] alwey
19 alwey] *delete and fn.* ACFGHW alwey   LS *lack word*
22 *remove brackets*
3, 4n. baþe] boþe

1275 7 myddle] myddel

1276 24 Some] Some [men] *and fn.* AFG some   *cf.* LS ponunt

1277 1 ydo] *read* y[f. 306ʳᵇ]do

1278 14 sight] sight[y] *and fn.* ACFGHW sight   LS perspicui

1279 5 a*s*] and *and delete fn.*
16 of¹] o*r and fn.* *ACDEFGHW of   *cf.* LS formam
33 *delete commas*
33 þikke] þikke,

1281 4 blood] blood and *and delete fn.*
9n. suppositus)] *read*) suppositus

1282 10 For] Or *and fn.* *ACDEFGHW for   LS aut
14 colde, and] colde. And

1283 7 yuel] for yuel
15 contynaunce] contyn[u]aunce *and fn.* ACFGHW contynaunce   LS continuitatem

1284 5 of] *add* [medlyng of] *and fn.* *ACDEFGHW *om.*   LS ex mixtione
27 dew. þerfore] *read* [hor frost]. *and fn.* *ACDEFGHW þerfore   LS pruina
32 skome] *f*ome *and fn.* ACFGH skome   D lome   LS spuma

34 vaporable. Bestes] vaporable, bestes
36 toschedeþ] to schede *and fn.* *ACDEFGHW toschedeþ   *cf.* LS disgrega-
tiuam

1285 14 it is] *delete and adjust fn.*
5 n. alboribus] albo*rum*
5 n. palloribus lyuoribus and . . . flauoribus] pallo*rum* lyuo*rum* . . . flauo*rum*

1286 5 þerfor] þerof *and delete fn.*
13 colour] coloure
21 men, and] men. And
22 þat] a*n and fn.* *ACDFGHW þat   *cf.* LS estuantis
22 and[1]] *delete and fn.* ACFGHW and   LS *lack word*
24 parties. And] parties, and

1287 8 rednesse] redenesse
22 o*f*[2]] *fn.* ACFGHW and   *cf.* LS caloris
30 yueles] *add* [as] *and fn.* AFGHW *om.*   C *for*   LS ut
13 n. *delete* C
22 n. *reverse bracket*

1288 2 iuned to] inne *and delete fn.*
16 sighty] *add* [and] *and fn.* ACFGW *om.*   LS et
18 right] *read* [swiþe] *and fn.* ACFGHW right   D whyte   LS multum

1289 10 is] ,and is *and delete fn.*

1290 5 *t*hanne] whanne *and delete fn.*
5 and[1]] a *and fn.* *ACFGHW and   DE *om.*   *cf.* LS repercutitur
20, 29 *delete 3rd comma*

1291 21 wanne] *add* vryne *and delete fn.*
22 pe] þe
33 flesish] fleissh

1292 33 n. incorporal *for* incorporal'] incorporal' *for* incorporat

1293 5 þat brenneþ] a*n* [y]bren*t and fn.* *ACDEFGHW þat brenneþ   LS et
exustis

1294 11 Cirenensis] Cirenencis
13 n. *om*] *om.*
30 is . . . and] *read* [and] is . . . is *and fn.* *ACDEFGHW is . . . and   LS et

1295 14 and makeþ] *read* [for to] make *and fn.* A and makeþ   *cf.* LS ut

1296 12 yrekened of hem. Be] yrekened. Of hem be

1297 34 of] a*n and fn.* *ACDEFGHW of   LS et

1298 5 nouȝt] *add* [so] *and fn.* *ACDEFGHW *om.*   LS ita
6 *delete 1st comma*
36 him] *delete and fn.* ACFGHW him   LS *lack word*

1299 5 hete worchyng. And] worchyng [of hete þat] *and alter fn.* of hete þat
*ACDEFGHW and   *cf.* LS a calore . . . resoluente
7 brayne. And] brayne, a*s and fn.* *ACDEFGHW and   LS sicut
15 *delete comma*

18 inwitte] witte *and fn.* *ACDEFGHW inwitte   LS sensum
25 þey be] *read* [is] *and fn.* ACFGHW þey be   D *om.*   LS efficitur
34 schoneþ] soner *and fn.* *ACFGHW schoneþ   D sowneþ   E *om. phrase*   *cf.*
LS primo ... quam
   15 n. pey] þey

1300 3 passeþ] p*e*rseþ *and fn.* *ACDEFGHW passeþ   LS penetrat
   14 *De*] *fn.* AFGH *I*tem de
   34 þat] þanne þat *and alter fn.*
   34 partia*l*] particular *and delete fn.*

1301 19 i*f*] is *and delete fn.*
   20 chaungeþ] *read* [and] chaungeþ *and fn.* A *om.*
   21 þerinne bitwene] þerinne. Bitwene
   22 as²] *delete and fn.* *AEFGHW as   D is   C for   LS et
   22 ,and] *delete and fn.* ADEFGHW and   LS *lack word*

1302 33 the] *read* [to] the *and fn.* ACDFGHW the   *cf.* LS sensibus
   35 Also] *add* [al] *and fn.* *ACDEFGHW *om.*   LS omne
   36 foule, for] foule. [þer]for *and fn.* ACFGHW for   D fer   LS ideo

1304 1 For] *read* [þer]for *and fn.* *ACDEFGHW for   LS et ideo
   34 passyng. For] passyng, for

1305 7 sourisch, suche sauour] sourisch sauour, suche *and fn.* ADFGH suche
sauour (H *corrected*)   C sauour   *cf.* LS ponticem qualis

1306 33 grollyng] gro*l*lyng *and add to fn.* CE *om.*

1307 26 and¹] *delete and fn.* ACFGHW and   *cf.* LS spiritis vitalis
   14 n. AF] ADF

1308 6 it] *read* [þey] *and fn.* *ACDEFGH it   *cf.* LS obturant
   13 himself] h*e*mself *and fn.* AFG himself   LS sibi
   16 and n. or] *read* [nedes] *and alter fn.* LS oportet quod uel

1309 9 swiþe[r[] *read* swiþe *and fn.* *ACDEFGHW swete   *cf.* LS inuiscant
   9 *delete 1st and 2nd commas*
   20 hete, and] hete. And
   28 þinges] þe*y and fn.* *ACDEFGHW þinges   *cf.* LS sunt
   15 n. þ] th

1310 7 *delete comma*
   12 n. *delete* * *and* E

1311 5-6 n. 5-6] *5- 6 is
   8-9 n. *delete cf.*
   14 n. *delete* W *and insert* W *and after* of

1312 14 row3 ... frotynge] sme*r*tinge and *f*rotynge *and fn.* *AEFGH smeþinge
and softynge   C smoþe and softe   LS sunt exasperatiua

1313 6 entreþ] *add* [depe] *and fn.* ACFGH *om.*   LS profunde

1316 3 insipido] nono [*et insipido*] *and alter fn.*
   5 Priuatif] *add* [þing] *and fn.* A *om.*   *cf.* LS priuatiue
   12 mene. And] mene and

25 þat,] ,þat
19n. delete * *and* CE

1317 17 som]so*ur and fn.* *ACEFGHW som   LS oxizacra
23n. simplex] *add* absolute

1318 14 alime] al*u*me *and fn.* AEFGH alime   C aluñe   *cf.* LS aluminosa
29 *delete 1st comma*

1319 27n. *add* (F *corrected*)
30n. uel] *add* mundificandum

1320 14 hony combe] honycombe
17 of[1]] *delete and fn.* ACFGH of   LS *lack word*
30 *delete comma*
36 gold] golde

1321 14 crollynge] *g*rollynge *and fn.* *ACEFGHW crollynge   LS rugitus
21 streccheþ] stan*ccheþ and fn.* *AEFGHW streccheþ   C *om.*   LS stringit

1322 18 pigmentaries] *pigmentarius and fn.* AGHW pigmentaries   CE pigmen-
tariis   LS pigmentarius
25 *violaceus] fn.* A violacēs

1323 4–5n. A] ACH *and* CFGH] FG
15 taperes] *add* [for wexe taperes were y-offred at *ceremoniis* of temples] *and fn.*
*ACEFGHW *om.*   LS quia in templorum ceremoniis cerei offeruntur

1324 4 mache] macche
7 norissheþ þe . . . *and* complement] norissheþ. þe . . . complement
7 and[2]] *delete and fn.* *ACEFGHW and   LS *lack word*

1326 6 þynne,] þynne;
16 *delete 2nd comma*
33 wiþoute, and] and wiþoute *and fn.* *ACEFGHW wiþoute and   LS et
exterius

1327 30 ofte] *e*fte *and fn.* ACFGHW ofte   LS secundo
35 drawe . . . out of] drawe out . . . of *and fn.* ACFGHW drawe . . . of   *cf.* LS
sanguinis

1328 4 into] *delete and fn.* ACFGH into   W in   *cf.* LS exuperat

1329 16 And] *add* [for] *and fn.* *ACDEFGHW *om.*   LS quia
17 mete, . . . spray. Here] mete . . . spray, here
28 þerfore] *add* [more] *and fn.* *ACDEFGHW *om.*   LS magis

1330 21 laxith] laxeth

1334 5 harde] hard
9 þey] *read* [yt] *and fn.* *ACDEFGH þey   *cf.* LS inuentum
26, **1335** 5 *fine] f.*
28n. ysmedled] ys medled

1336 18 neische] *u*est *and fn.* *ACDEFGHW neische   LS obtusa
24 moystures] moysture *and fn.* ACFGHW moystures   LS humiditatis
28 vertues] *fn.* ACFGHW vertues   LS virtus
11n. AF] A

1137 18 þat²] *delete and fn.* ACFGHW þat   *cf.* LS hoc fit eo quod

1338 26 kepeþ] *add* [and] *ACDEFGHW *om.*   LS et

1339 2 and¹] *delete and fn.* *ACDEFGHW and   *cf.* LS diuisum
9 to] into
40 *add line number*

1340 2 is] *delete and fn.* *ACEFGHW is   *cf.* LS decisum
4 and¹] *delete and fn.* *ACEFGHW and   LS *lack word*
10 be] be[n] *and fn.* ACEFG be   *cf.* LS fuerint
25 n. AF] A

1341 18 of] *add* [oþir] *and fn.* ACFGHW *om.*   LS aliarum
23 sperhauk] sperhaukis

1342 8 hete] *add* [þat] *and alter fn.*
9 þanne hardeþ] *read* [haþ more hardenes] þanne hap *and alter fn.*
12 6°, þat] 6°. þat
23 here] bare *and fn.* ACFH bare   W folkys   LS nuda

1343 7 a. And] And a *and fn.* AFGHW a and   LS et cubat
7 *Libro*] *read* [Also] *libro and fn.* ACFG *om.*   LS Item
18 of²] *delete and fn.* A of

1344 2–3 webbe . . . kynde] webbe for diuersite of kynde. [And þe kynde] *and fn.*
ACFGHW *om.*   LS et nature
6 *transfer comma from* colde *to* moiste
8 þerof and þe] of *and fn.* *ACFGHW þerof and þe   *cf.* LS pulli
24 beþ] *read* [and] *and fn.* *ACFGHW beþ   LS et
24 and²] *delete and fn.* *ACFGHW and   *cf.* LS sunt
26 helþ] helþe

1345 3 *delete 2nd and 3rd commas*
6 fuyr] fuyre
8 for] *add* [for] *and fn.* *ACFGHW *om.*   LS cum
9 and] a *and fn.* *ACFGHW and   *cf.* LS permittit
26–7 vndigeste and menge. And] vndigeste. And mene and *and fn.* *ACFGHW
menge   *cf.* LS mollia tamen et
35 In 3olkes,] And in 3olkes *and alter fn.*

1346 9 podagre,] podagre;
15 *delete 2nd comma*
24–5 he² . . . and] an . . . a *and fn.* *ACFGHW he . . . and   *cf.* LS quando aspicit

1347 3 3it anone,] 3it, anone

1349 22 *griffis*] *grifis*

1352 12 *delete comma*

1353 11 n. *add* E *om.*
14 n. *add* E cultus   L *lacks rubric*   S vulturum
29 n. *delete* CE

1354 4 noumbre] *add* [we] *and fn.* *ACEFGHW *om.*   *cf.* LS instruimur
22 *delete comma*

26 conteyneþ] conteyne *and fn.* *ACEFGHW conteyneþ　LS continere
9n. *delete* F

1358 26 somme, þat] somme. þat

1359 28–9 compouned, and] compouned *and fn.* *ACFGHW *add* and　*cf.* LS
representat
30–1 and endynge] *delete and fn.* *ACFGHW and endynge　LS *lack words*
9n. *add* F *expuncted*　W euen *for* euene

1361 8 foure] ferre *and fn.* *ACFGHW foure　LS longe
35 by] *add* [f. 327va]

1362 5 som] som,
7 uncompouned] compouned *and delete fn.*

1363 28 and n by] in

1364 9 þre] þre-
30 letter] lettre
34 And] *fn.* *ACFGHW and ferþe and　LS et

1365 9 by þre] *delete and fn.* *ACFGHW by þre　LS *lack words*
16 and[1]] he *and fn.* *ACFGHW he　*cf.* LS oriuntur
23 dyuisioun] dymensioun *and delete fn.*
24–5 fyfty . . . party. And] fyfty, . . . party and
22n. pars] par

1368 25 depenesse] þikkenesse *and delete fn.*

1369 28 eyþer] eyþer,

1370 33 oþere] *read* [of] oþere *and fn.* A oþere　CFGH þerof　LS ab alia
31n. FW] CFW

1372 2 some] somme
6 conteyneþ] conceyueþ *and delete fn.*

1373 33n. *delete* C *and add* C sarcios
33n.[2] *add* (H *corrected*)

1374 25 sextaris] sextari[u]s *and fn.* AFGW sextaris　C sextaries　LS sextariorum

1375 7 water . . . wynde;] water; . . . wynde
8 and[1]] he *and fn.* *ACFGHW and　*cf.* LS exceduntur

1376 24 gru] gru,

1377 18 likke þe] likkeþe
19 aboueforþ] aboue forþ
35 barell] barelle
14n. *delete* C *and add* C þing

1378 7 brere] brer[d]e *and fn.* A brere　LS orificium
35 þer] þe *and fn.* *ACFGH þer　LS *lack word*

1379 19 water, and quencheþ and] water and quencheþ. And
19 þe] *add* [altars wiþ þe] *and fn.* *ACFGHW *om.*　LS cum eisdem . . . aras
26 a] o

1380 15 *delete comma*

25, 30, 35 *adjust line numbers*
26 made] *mete and fn.* *ACFGHW made LS mensurauerunt
29 n. *add* *

1381 3 made] *mete and fn.* *ACFGHW made LS mensurantis
31 þer [þei] innecomeþ] þerin *he* comeþ *and alter fn.*

1382 26 *biuium* is. *Ambitus* is] *biuium. Ambitus* is *and alter fn.* *ACFGHW is ambitus
30 tredynge] tre[n]dynge *and fn.* A tredynge
34 lefen byneþe] *leu*eþe *and fn.* *AFGHW byneþe C lefen byneþen LS relinqunt

1383 17–18 and . . . [t]oward] *read* [and . . .] toward
19 n. *read* 20

1384 21 lentilles] tilles *and delete fn.*
28 and] *add* [denarius] *and fn.* *ACFGHW *om. cf.* LS denarii pondus
29 Is] *read* [and] is *and fn.* *ACFGHW is LS autem est
30 ten] for ten
35 þe²] *delete and fn.* A adds þe

1385 3, 4 solid] *solidus*

1386 25 smytyng, 32 moche] *add comma*

1388 7 longe] alonge *and delete fn.*
17 yhe₃de] yherde *and delete fn.*

1389 7 n. *delete* * *and* H

1390 13 *ystola*] *read* y[s] *stola* *ACFGHW ystola LS stolia
30 ellerne tre,] ellerne, tre

1391 12 nakires] nakirers
23 some] somme
14 n. *delete* C *and add* C haþ
23–4 and **1392** 30 instrumentis] instrumentz
3 beþ] *add* [and] *and fn.* *ACFGHW *om.*
16 *fn.* dyuerse] A dy'u'se
17 somme] som me[n] *and fn.* A somme
26 and n. An] *read* A[l]s

1393 6 *tintinabilo*] tintinabulo *and fn.* A tintinabil'
15 all] alle
17 *dyatesseron*] dyapente *and delete fn.*

1394 3 *delete 1st comma*
5 in] *a*n *and fn.* *ACFGHW in *cf.* LS iiii
33 n. dyuersly] dyu'sly

1395 22 *delete 1st comma*
29 symple] *add* [werk] *and fn.* AF *om.* LS simplicia
33 do] do and *and delete fn.*

1396 2 *delete 2nd comma*
9 Feuerer] Feuerere
5 n. *add* *

The English MSS. ACFGH are complete. B is wholly lacking. D ends imperfectly at 1310/9. E lacks 1342/23–1350/22 and ends imperfectly at 1355/3. De Worde's edition of Book XIX is based on F. The Latin MSS. IJLNOPQRSTUVWX are complete. K is wholly lacking. M lacks 1342/33–1390/21 after f. 279ᵛ. Y lacks 1375/4–1385/25.

1268 20 *scheweþ*: O *ostendit*   cf. the better *dicit*
26 *chaungeþ*: *motiuus*   Z *mutiuus*
28–9 *ymedled in a body*: *in corpore mixto*. Perhaps JT wrote here and at line 31 *yn a medled body*
29–30 *chaungynge and dede of perfeccioun*: *actum immutationis*. A doublet of ambiguity, *immutationis uel inimitationis*

1269 9 *chaungyng and likenes*: *immutatione*. Perhaps a doublet of ambiguity, *immutatione uel immitatione*, but cf. 1277/27–8, 1297/2–3
22 *in þe yhe sight*: *in visum nisi per lucem*   cf. DE *in þe bylyȝte*. Perhaps JT wrote *in þe sight but by liȝte*, but cf. 1277/26 *to þe yhe and to þe sight* for *visui*
25 *matiere*: IQ *materiam*   cf. the better *naturam*
36 *foure*: properly qualifies *elementis* (as in E)

1270 12 *ayre*: adds *deficiens ab humiditate erea*
15 *matiere*: S *materiam*   cf. the better *naturam*
15 *ayre*: adds (not S) *si autem est grossum tunc est alteratum*
16 *of eorþe*: XY only *terre*

1271 2 *matiere* ... *þanne*: *magis* ... *siccum quod* (LNPQRY *quam*)   Z *materia* ... *quam*
13 *It*: *calor agens*
28 *and of oþre þinges**   30 *gadereþ moyste matiere togideres**
31 *to fonge*: *natum* ... *esse*
36 *and openynge*: properly in apposition to *to fonge* line 34

1272 16 *worchinge*: adds *extra*
17–18 *nouȝt* ... *ymade*: *non effectiue neque formaliter*
27 *þerinne*: adds *et calidi maius fuerit dominium*
28–**1273** 2 *hete* ... *druyenesse*: *frigiditas* ... *frigidi*
9 *matiere*: adds *perspicui*
15 *white eye*: *albumen*. Perhaps JT wrote *white of eye*
24 *proprete*: adds *de humido*
28 *þynne*: adds *quia eius operatio specialis est subtiliare materiam in quam agit*
28 *druye oþer stabulich ypight*: I *fixa*   cf. the better *sicca* (X adds *uel fixa*). A doublet of ambiguity, *sicca uel fixa*
35 *Quando*: *quando*   cf. the better V *quomodo*
36 *hete*: adds *et frigidi*

1274 2 *and makeþ it faste and þikke**   5–6 *þat is nouþer white ne blake**
11 *matiere*: adds *per dominium*
14 *to fonge*: *respectu*   Z *receptu*
31–2 *And in som* ... *worcheþ, for*: *in sicco autem non inquantum huiusmodi respectu uero agentes saltem vno modo est humidum obedientis sibi quam*

1275 7–8 *euene þe myddel colour . . . blake: extremis.* Similar expansions at lines 13–14, 23
  15 *colours: medii colores*
  16 *ymade: diuisam*
  30 *alwey: simpliciter*   Z *semper*

1276 1 *et quot sunt:* V *et quot sunt*   cf. *quot sint*
  3 *cytrine: puniceum id est citrinum*
  16 *corrupcioun . . . tornyng: corruptione*
  22 *apposicione: opinione*   cf. DE *disporcicione*
  25 *is in clene and clere matiere: est lux incorporata* (IMT *in corpore*) *perspicuo*
  31 *in a litel plae oþer in a poynt: in puncto*
  30, 32 *nouþer moche** *and moche** *and grete light**: E lacks these tautologies
  33 *merour: speculi superficiem*

1277 3 *clere:* adds (not X) *nam albedo est color ex luce multa et clara in puro perspicuo generatus*
  3 *Albumaser:* MV *Albumasar*   I *id'*   P *abu°*   Y *albedo*   cf. *al*
  4–5 *and nou3t ful clere but somdel dymme: obscuro*
  6 *þis: iste sermo*
  7 *clerenes:* adds *et albedinem habitum siue formam*
  9 *blake:* adds *similiter septem erunt proximi nigredini a nigredine versus albedinem procedentes donec fiat occursus alicuius septem colorum quibus ab albedine ad nigredinem descenditur*
  20 *myddel:* adds *in idem*
  23 *hereof:* adds *breuiter*
  31–2 *þat hilde Pictagoras his lore**   35–**1278** 6 *A sighty body . . . wiþoute**
  8 *viii°: vii*
  10 *appulles greynes: pomi grano*   cf. BA's *pomogranato*
  15 *sensato:* adds *vii*
  16 *clere body: corpore perspicuo non terminato ut ere presencia luminis facit actu lucidum absencia uero tenebrosum sic in corpore*
  17–18 *so þat somwhat of light schyne þerinne**
  28 *matiere:* adds *uel assumunt*   cf. BA's *nihil assumunt*
  29 *b: b* (IPTV om.)

1279 5 *space and place . . . þe yhe: medio.* Cf. 1269/12
  5 *as:* V *ac*   QUX *et*   cf. the better *ut*
  6 *by¹:* adds *subitam*
  7 *8:* M *viii. g*   OQU *g*   IJLST *iiii*   N *ix*
  12 *d: d* (IOPVX om.)
  24 *g:* ONPUVY *8*   Q *4*   cf. the better *g*
  31 *ofte**

1280 5 *is tokne: indicat dominium*
  18–20 *And . . . light: vnde sicut . . . sic lux*

1281 1 *inward fro þe partyes: ad interiora.* Perhaps JT wrote *to þe innermore partyes*
  10 *infirmite:* VX *infirmitatis*   cf. *informitatis*

1282 10 *inner þynges*: *aut ab exterioribus ab interioribus*
13 *of*: *per*   cf. CFGHW *bi*
13 *humours*: adds (not I) *aliquando per frigidum nam contingit humores calidos*
14 *and*: *etiam frigidas uel infrigidates calefieri* (PQRY om. these five words) *et secundum hoc solet in cute color variari nam quando*
17 *in þe skynne*: *color*. Perhaps JT wrote *colour in þe skynne*, cf. lines 7, 8–9, 12
17 *passiouns*: adds *interioribus* (JLNSTVW *exterioribus*)
29 *fleisshe*: adds *et denigratur et sic adustus a cuius denigrate sanguinis diffusione inter cutem et carnem*
32 *moder*: *consimili matre*   cf. E *blak modre*

1283 15 *streyte*: *solidis*   cf. I *sol'*   OU *solius*   QX *solucionis*   T *solis*

1284 11 *yseyde*: adds *supra*
33 *For*: *et ideo quia*. Perhaps JT wrote *þerfor for*
36 *if*: *et ideo si*
37 *makeþ*: *corrumpit visum et facit*

1285 10 *matiere is*: *materias*. Perhaps JT wrote *matieres beþ*
22 *clerenesse*: *puritatem*   cf. I *paucitatem*   PX *paruitatem*
32 *destruyed*: *destruitur uel destitur* (PTX om.) *in calore eleuante materiam*

1286 1 *moche*: *magis*. Perhaps JT wrote *mo*
7 *worcheþ and makeþ*: *tactus . . . fit*   Z *actus . . . fit*
19 *blood*: *calor*
26 *as he seiþ*: *iuxta illud*   cf. DE *as þe verse seyeþ*   G *as he seiþ versus*
28–9 *þis vers . . . louyre**
34 *is*: MS *restat*   cf. *resultat*

1287 4 *makeþ hem þynne*: IOVY *rarificantem*   cf. *rectificantem* (NPQR om.)
9 *worse*: *minus*. Perhaps JT wrote *þe lesse*
14 *colour*: *color*   cf. the better IORVY *calor* (V corrected)
22 *colour*: adds *in materia subtiliori ac magis perspicua radicatur magis rutilat et apparet secundum uero quod materia est terrestris ac grossa minus claret talis autem color*

1288 10 *moche*: *superabundantia*. Perhaps JT wrote *to moche*
18 *bright*: I *lucidus*   cf. *uiridis*
22 *See*: adds *ab illa infectione*
24 *smal*: *subtilissime*
24 *gleyre*: M *glarea*   cf. *clari*. Both words mean 'white of egg'
28 *wiþ a certeyn herbe*: *succo herbe cuiusdam*. Perhaps JT wrote *wiþ þe iuse of a certeyn herbe*

1289 1 *faste*: *uehementissime*
2 *þat*: *quod inde uix poterit post deleri quod*
4 *þerof abyde*: V *sui derelinquat*   cf. *post inueniet*
11 *as*: *unde*   Z *ut*. Also at 1292/15
31 *vndygest*: adds *vt dicit Auicenna*
34 *but*: *in materia*   Z *uero*

1290 7 *librum*: adds (not N) *Aristotelis*
9–10 *malencoly*: adds *colera enim cum sit rubea transit in melancholicam*

34 *maistry*: adds *glaucus uel pallidus aut citrinus si autem preabundauerint ignee partis cum ereis erit color*

36–**1291** 1 *mich might þe colour be*: *posset quidem fieri color*. Perhaps JT wrote *euerich colour might be*

8 *for likynge and for sight*: *propter uisum*. A doublet of ambiguity, *usum uel uisum*

8 *hunters*: adds *semper*

11 *Gregorius*: JT probably retained the MS. abbreviation *g* (C *gg'*   DE *g'*   F *greg'*), cf. IMNT *g'g'* alongside *G* and UV *Gal'*

18–19 *And perfore*: *quia* (V *quare*)

24 *beþ*: adds (not JS) *tibi*

26 *malo**: perhaps added to distinguish this chapter from the previous

30 *al*: *colorem omnino et*

33 *fleissh*: adds *ut patet in fustigatis in quibus humor intercutaneus*

1292 1 *tofore*: *supra*   cf. the better MNPTV *super*

2 *Ysaac*: adds *ibi*

18 *blauio*: *indico*

20 *brightnesse*: JLOQUVWY *nitore*   cf. the better *uirore*

24 *azure*: *asurio*   cf. BA's *lasurio*

31 *sensato*: adds *idem dicit Aristotelis* (V *idem in*) *libro xix*

1293 13 *blak*: *nigrior*

19 *þe ylond**

21 *xliiii°.*: *xviii*

21 *rede*: *prima rubra*

22 *þe tweyne*: *has*   Z *duas*

23 *rede*: *colori*   Z *rubori*

26 *pigmento**: DEG om.

1294 3 *Auicen seiþ*: *auic' enim dicunt*, cf. the better MX *aiunt enim* (as in Isidore XIX. 17. 8)

4–5 *For . . . oliphauntes*: *dum implicant elephantes*

7 *coloureþ*: adds *terram*

8 *dyeþ*: adds *solum* (V *terram*)

16 *of golde**: *indicat*   (cf. the better *indicum*, as in Isidore XIX. 17. 10), which JT reads here, is taken as one of two synonymous verbs

17 *metalles*, 25 *sandix*: adds *ut dicit Isidorus*

28 *most pure*: *purius*

33 *þere . . . yfounde*: *vnde* (IM *vbi*) *venit et sandaracha*   Z *vbi . . . inuenitur*

1295 13 *coles*: *redas*   cf. the better RUVWY *tedas*   Z *prunas*

24 *Isider*: *idem* (P *y'*   Q *idem y'*)

31 *Cerusa hatte also þe flour of leed**: adds *quare supra de plumbo*, i.e. Book XVI. 80 which concludes with these words

1296 6 *beþ most and next byschyne*: *illuminat proprius et illustrat*

10 *boþe²**

13 *xxv°.*: N *xxv*   cf. the better *xxxv*

13 *xxxiii^m.*: adds *et Isidorus libro xviii et xix*

14 *cloþe*: adds (not Y) *libro xix*

18 *fugata*: *fugata*   cf. BA's *figura*

21 *to make*: P *fingere*   cf. *augere*. Perhaps JT wrote *to waxe*
23 *suche a feyned beste**
27 *So*: adds *paulatim*
29 *liknesses*: *vmbras*
31 *holdeþ*: adds *adhuc*

1297 18 *prenteþ his liknesse in*: *se incorporat et in suam similitudinem ipsum alterat et informat*
24 *ben proporcionate to*: *proportionem complexionalem habent et armoniacam cum*
28 *fordoþ*: *prescindit*, generally translated *forkutteþ*

1298 22–3 *Oon manere*: *enim*   Z *unus*

1299 33 *fro . . . perceyued**

1300 3 *of smellynge*: *animatum*   Z *aromaticum*
24 *þat is a bytyng oynement**

1301 6 *spiritual þing*: *spiritu animali* (RT om.), generally translated *þe spirit of feelyng*, which JT perhaps wrote here
14 *wiþoute*: adds *gustui* (NPQRY om.) *substantialiter*

1302 4–5 *Botraces . . . frogges**: supplied from Book XVIII. 17 (p. 1154 above)
10 *stynche*: adds *inficit et*
28 *fisshe*: *eorum substantia*   cf. 1299/12–13

1304 3 *whanne*: NPRY *quando*   cf. the better *quia*
26 *to colde and**

1305 10 *rose*: adds *et in coctanis maturis*
17 *sauour**
23 *in*: *in tali*

1306 8 *lyme*: *nocumentum*   Z *instrumentum*
17, 24 *pores*: adds *venarum*
29 *blood*: adds *et ille sanguis multum nutrit*
30–1 *bredeþ . . . in þe body*: *generat . . . et inducit*   Z *in dicto*, i.e. in the blood, for *inducit*
34 *echeþ*: *concitat uel augmentat*

1307 3 *body*: adds *facilius*
11 *a*: *vnus bonus*
14 *ben*: *recipiuntur*
28 *membres*: adds *spiritualibus*
30 *For*: adds *maior est ex calore dulcis resolutio quam*
31 *wasteþ of*: *humidi . . . saltem consumptio*

1308 15 *oute*: adds *cum vrina*
18 *vryne*: *humore*   Z *vrina*

1309 15 *water*: *maiorem aquositatem*
15 *matiere*: *naturam*
16 *þan doþ . . . grece*: *vt patet in axungia que minus nutrit ignem quam ouina*

1310 1 *byndeþ*: adds *magis*

12 *substaunce*: adds *vnde salsus sapor habet fieri ex moderato dominio caliditatis et siccitatis mediocri*, of which *perfore* and MS. *hoote* in line 12 are perhaps relics

18 *moisture*: adds *et relaxant et sic mollificant item substancie mollis sunt induratiua nam sua caliditate et siccitate superfluam humiditatem consumunt*

19 *pinges*: adds *sunt depuratiua et per consequens conseruatiua nam*

34 *salt*: *multum salsa*

1311 5–6 *destroyed*: *adnichilatur*. The MS. addition *in no wise*, emended here, is perhaps a relic of an associated adverb (e.g. *holiche*) or *in al wise*

10 *xvº.*: *xv*   cf. the better M *xvi*

21 *ayre*: *eree* 'airy'. The form is probably adjectival, cf. CE *eiry*

27–8 *þe partyng and delyng*: *continuitatis solutionem*, translated *dissolucioun and departynge* line 29

30 *in þe tonge*: *in lingua*, properly modifying the previous sentence

1312 9 *dissolued*: P *dissolutos*   cf. the better *resolutos*

12 *fleume*: adds *et ideo colerica et amara eis aduersantur quia colera phlegmati contrariatur*

17–18 *depe in þe þing*: *in profundum acumine et calore suo*

33–4 *grete . . . grete*: *maximo . . . maxima*

1313 4 *suche þinges*: *acuta*   cf. C *sharpe*. Perhaps JT wrote *suche sharpe þinges*, but the phrase is a formula and cf. 1314/6

6 *wiþinne*: adds *et ideo dissoluunt et incidunt*

9 *bycause . . . strenger*: *fit ratione vacui appetitis*   Z *robore* for *ratione*

12 *litel*: adds *preterea subtilis sunt substantia et ideo de facili consumuntur et a membris cito dilabuntur*

20 *sauour*: *completionem*

22 *water*: adds *et terre mediocre et ex mediocri dominio aque*

29 *þerof*: NOPQR only *ita*. Perhaps JT wrote *þerfor*

1314 6, 15 *suche þinges*: *acetosa, ponticum*. Perhaps JT wrote *suche soure þinges* but cf. 1313/4n. above

17–18 *In . . . ben*: *ad ponticum saporem perficiendum . . . conueniunt*

31 *sauour*: *humore*   Z *odore*

36 *of*[1]: adds *melancholia*

1315 15–16 *if þey ben leyde to dueliche wiþoute*: *exterius autem apposita*   Z *debitum* for *autem*

19 *is also a sourissh sauour, and**   22–3 *þe oþer sourish sauour þat hatte**

35 *stipticus*: adds *et stipticitas remissa ponticitas*

1316 8 *þat þey ben*: *eius*. Perhaps JT wrote *þat þer beþ*

23 *strong*: VXY *fortem* (X corrected)   cf. the better *forciorem*

31 *auctours*: *et aliorum auctorum medicine*

1317 12 *strengþe*: *natura*   Z *ui*

15 *bodyes*: Q *corporibus* (corrected)   UV *liquoribus uel corporibus*   cf. *liquoribus*

26 *symple*[1]: adds (not LNOR) *simplices etiam dicuntur*

36 *pthisane*: adds *et huiusmodi*

1318 1 *comeþ*: adds *sponte*

2 *lacrimis*: Y *lacrimis*   OR *lacrima*   cf. the better *lacrimus*

3 *of þe sonne*: VX only *solis* (X added)

3 *clensed . . . and yfastned*: V *mundatur et inuiscatur*　Y *inuiscatur*　cf. the better *mundatur*

5 *oyle*: adds *sicera*. Perhaps JT wrote *syther*, misread as *syche* 'such' and omitted

10 *ydryed*: adds *postea*

14 *opere*: adds *de quibus arte uel natura fit sal nitrum alumen et huiusmodi*

18 *acounted and ygendred*: *dicuntur . . . generari*

20 *ymelked*: *emunguntur*　Z *mulguntur*

27–8 *to þe ayre*: V *eri*　cf. the better *erei* (as in Isidore XX. 2. 36, quoting *Georgics* II. 1)

34 *ȝonge*: adds *et perfectis*

35 *and colde, with wyne*: *qui parua vita laborant et frigore . . . cum vino veteri*

1319 5 *boþe of fuyre*: *tam terre quam ignis*

10 *body*: adds *et humorum putridorum expulsiuum*

15–16 *and wiþoute medlynge of oþer sauour**

1320 4 *laxeþ*: *uero stipticum est*　Z *diureticum est*

4 *and³*: adds *est . . . occultatiuum* 'conceals'

6 *þe more*: *humorum magis*

21 *ypurged*: *depuratum*. Perhaps JT wrote *ypured*, but cf. 1083/29

22 *beste*: adds *fauum mellis petit et requirit maxime*

25–6 *brekeþ . . . honycombes*: *fauis extrahendis* (NRY *distrahens*　P *distruens*) . . . *in arbores altas* (V om.) *scandit*　Z *extrahens* for *extrahendis*

1321 9 *macianes*: emendation of MS. *mananes* may be unjustified, cf. R *mananorum* VW *marianorum*　O *manatorum*　alongside the better *macianorum* 'crab-apples'

29 *yhilde*: adds (not NOV) *et reperfunduntur*

30 *ofte helde*: *renouatur*. Perhaps JT wrote *efte helde*

1322 6 *Of þe whiche spicery*: *nam in pila species aromatice aguntur quibus*

17 *hony*: *et herbarum*

17 *makeþ it flete aboue*: *supernatando vsque ad oxymellis superficiem secum ducit*

21 *matiere*: adds *mundificationem*

29–30 *medled wiþ þe drastes of wexe*: *corrumpit autem ipsum mel . . . quando nimis diu cum cere fecibus admiscetur*

1323 21 *wex*: adds *simplici vel colorati*

24 *bookes*: adds *inuolutos*

25 *soukeþ*: JLNOSTVW *suggat*　cf. the better *fugat*

27–8 *cleueþ . . . rouȝ*: *humidis et humefactis cedit siccis uero et asperis inherescit*

34–5 *Hec . . . igneus Subdicta*: *Hic . . . ignis Subducta* (as in Isidore XX. 10. 3)

35 *luxum*: JLOSW *luxum*　cf. the better *lux sum*

1324 1 *þe menyng foleweþ**: JT's translation here is lost

6 *taper*: adds *totius*

7 *norissheþ*: *est luminis nutrimentum*

11 *þerof*: *eius pyramidalis*　Z *eius*

16 *of bestes**: perhaps JT wrote *or brestes*

1325 10–11 *haþ humour white as mylk*: (*habent humorem lacteum*) . . . *cuius lacte*. Perhaps JT added *of whyche*

29 *and moche**

31–2 *If þe norice . . . greueþ*: *si fuerit lactans corporis fertilis tunc nocet multitudo lactis*

36 *and oþer: aut*. Perhaps JT wrote *or oþer* 'or in the second manner'

1326 5 *þe substaunce of whey is wattry*: *substantia aquosa et serosa acuta est*

8 *is scharp, and: et acuta*, modifying *substaunce*

13 *of þe mylk of camels: si fuerit ex animalibus calide complexionis ut ex camelis*

35 *ete þe melk hoot: calidum esse* 'it should be hot'. *Z edere* for *esse*

1327 10–11 *wiþouten eny heuy smelle: abhorrore et grauitate remotum*

15 *saltnesse*: adds *nec acedine*

18 *temperat*: adds *ideo et muliebre lac maxime est temperatum*

25 *helpeþ*: adds *potissime*

1328 21 *to moyste: ad calefaciendum et humectandum*

34 *by watry hete: calore tamen suo Z calore aquoso*

1329 33 *wombe*: adds (not IJNOSTU) *et neruorum remollitiuum*

1330 5 *colour: calore Z colore*

6 *exciteþ: apertiuum et . . . prouocatiuum*

17 *humours: aquei humores*

28 *slidre: lubricorum* cf. the better NOTU *lumbricorum* 'of worms'

32 *exciteth: rugitus et ventositatis excitatiuum . . . effectiuum*

1331 1 *þese humours: has*

25 *rypeþ*: adds *proprie*

25 *tempreþ: humorum dissolutiuum*

33 *astonyed: indignatos* cf. BA's *induratos*

1332 8 *creme: flos lactis siue superenatans pinguedo*

22 *wel*[1]: *bene et munde*

25 *moisture: eius potentialis humiditas*

32 *acordeþ*: adds *tamen nichilominus*

34 *seiþ*: adds *libro xx*

1333 12 *þre**

13 *chese*: adds *omnis*. Also at 1334/9

18 *þe more esyere*: the double comparative is not typical of JT

26 *salt*: adds *nimis* (JLOPVWXY *minus*) *uero salsus stomachi fit morsiuus*

32 *it is not but þikke and faste: subtilitatem exit* 'drives away the thinness'

33 *ymade*: adds *ita*. Perhaps JT wrote *ymade so sotile*

35 *many: duobus Z diuersis*

1334 1 *in þe secounde manere: secundo* cf. the better MOPR *stomacho*

8 *bely*: the emendation of MS. *body* is tentative, cf. *ventrem* which JT usually translated *wombe*. Perhaps Z *corporem*

12 *y-yȝed: vnctus* 'rich', cf. MV *vnctuosus* P *vnicus* QX *ininctus* and the better Y *vinctus. y-yȝed* is perhaps *yhiȝt* corrupted unless JT wrote *þyȝed* 'tied' for *vinctus*

14–15 *chese . . . olde: qui autem porosus est minus est malus quando est recens* (IPQV adds *quam*) *cum nimis est vetus Z nimis* for *minus*

26 *f*: MOQR *f* WXY *fi* rest omit

28 *moysture: butyrositate* I *vnctuositate Z humiditate*

29 *malice*: *vim*   Z *malum*

35–6 *in many cases*: *in multis etiam* (V *enim*) *aliis*   Z *in multis causis*

1335 10 *melk*: *lacte ficuum quando lac*

10 *ydo*: V *ponitur*   Y *reponatur*   cf. *cicius*

24 *wasteþ*: NT *sumitur*   cf. the better *finitur* (Y *fantur*)

1336 14 *ryndes*: *mediano* (IJL *melano*   NT *meiano*   V *medio*) *cortice*

15 *sprede*: adds (not N) *cutem*

35 *of openynge*: INPTX *aperitiua* (X altered)   cf. the better *asperitiua*

1337 1 *outward*: *in conum* (NLNST *bonum*   P *coctum*   V *nonum*) 'to a point'

10 *ygendred*: *derelicte* 'imprinted in matter'

14 *þat*[1]: adds (not PQRVY) *uel*, antecedent of *opere* line 19

21 *aier*: *interiora* (IPQRVX *interstitia*) *eris*

27 *þerinne*: adds *vt dicit commentator*

1338 15 *hete*[1]: adds *superabundante calore alieno*

20 *þat*: *omne*. Probably JT wrote *al þat*

23 *to be ouercome*: OPXY *vinci*   cf. *vniri*

31 *Also a*: *omne autem*

1339 7 *þikke*: adds *ex substantia autem subtili aquea uel erea*

21 *nyȝ*: *magis uicina*. Perhaps JT wrote *nerre*

27 *and bestis**: perhaps a scribal intrusion from the next phrase

35–6 *in rounde bestes . . . as*: *in animalibus anulosi corporis ut in*. Perhaps *in* is scribally transposed from an earlier *as in*

1340 4–5 *and beþ . . . oua*: *coagulatur et transformatur ex quibus per operationem diuersa animantia procreantur et talia corpuscula oua sunt dicta eo quod sunt munda*   Z *umida* for *munda*

6 *Som*: *nam*. Perhaps JT wrote *for*

7 *som*[1]: *humidum quid*

9 *oluan*: *oua* (IMQ *oa*   Y *o.a.*)

9 *doth perto þis lettre l*: *litera* (IQX *v litera*   M *ii. litera*) *allata* (JLNST *albata*). Perhaps JT wrote *doth perfro þis lettre v*

11 *tredynge or worchinge*: *concubitu*. A doublet of ambiguity, *concubitu uel cum actu*

15 *parties*: *uitri fragmenta*   Z *inter* for *uitri*

15–16 *þat somme men meneþ**: adds *igitur*

19 *eiren*: *oua tam volucrem quem piscium et serpentium*

26 *seiþ*: adds *in libro suo*

28–9 *in seuene dayes*: *vii. diebus*, properly modifying *makeþ*

31 *kynde*: *natura rerum*

31–2 *to brynge forþ foules of kynde*: *eius fetibus educandis exhibente obsequium*. Perhaps JT wrote *foles* 'young', mistaking the antecedent of *eius* as *kynde*, cf. the better *alicioune*

33 *in Exameron*: properly qualifies *Basilius*

1341 4 *monþes*: adds *tropicorum*

6–7 *at oon bredynge**: adds *et quandoque multa ouat multociens ut columbe*

12 *broode*: adds *oua sua nec cubat super ea sed calore solis complentur et animantur in arenis et quedam oua fouentur*

13 *hey*: *altissimis*
14 *foules*: JLNOST *auium*   cf. the better *oua auium*
29 *and perof*. . . *briddes*: *complentur*
37 *panne²*: adds *paulatim*
38 *peraboute*: *in extremo*

1342 3 *For*: *unde*. Probably JT wrote *perfor*
3 *parfiteliche*: *perfectissime*
12 *vel 6º*: V only adds *uel vi* in a doublet of ambiguity
16 *þolke*: *citrinum*, generally translated *ʒelowe* (as at 1341/37), cf. *uitellum*, generally translated *þolke* (as at 1343/2). But the identity of meaning makes emendation hazardous, cf. *þolke* for *uitelli uel citrini* 1344/4 and for *citrinum²* 1344/4
20 *wynter*: adds *quia*
20 *openeþ*: *funduntur*   Z *finduntur*
25 *smallere and lasse þan oþre olde hennes eyren*: *minoris corporis et uniuersaliter si gallina non cubauerint super oua sua*
30–1 *bareyne*. . . *briddes*: *non pullificatiua sed sunt sterilia quemadmodum oua uentri*

1343 1 *tretise*: adds (not I) *de auibus*
2 *tweye²*: *gemellos*. Perhaps JT wrote *tweyne* 'twin'
3 *litel*: adds *et subtili*
6–7 *Huc*. . . *6º*: in all Latin MSS. this properly follows the next sentence
7 *a**: perhaps from an earlier *a a* 'and he'
8 *harde*: *dure*, cf. JLNSPT *due*
13 *somdel*: SUW *parum* (R *purum*)   cf. the better *paruum*
16 *briddes*: adds *parui corporis*
38 *tyme¹*: *diebus*
38 *and generacioun*: *creationis*

1344 1 *matiere*: adds *et sustentatio*
2 *y-ioyned by a litel webbe*: *disiuncta* (NT *iuncta*) *sunt quadam tela*
7–8 *it is þe matiere þerof and*: *sustentatio pulli est ex quo quod*
16, 33 *smale*: *iunioribus*   Z *minoribus*
18–19 *þan þe þolke*: *uitellorum comparationem quod testatur earum aquea saporositas et ideo in odore sunt uitellis grauiores*
22 *and¹*: *et faciliora*
23 *dyuers*: adds *secundum diuersitatem animalium ex quibus generantur*
30–1 *nouʒt ytrede wiþ*: *carent*   Z *coeunt*

1345 4 *in emeres oþir in hote axen*: O *cinere*   cf. *iure* (P *iuce*   R *cute*)
10 *yrosted*: *posita*   Z *assata*
13 *hoote fuyre*: *calore ignis*
14 *moisture*: adds *substantiali*
16 *þe schelles wiþoute beþ harde and holdeþ inne*: *grossiciei et fumositati repugnant cortices exterius*
23 *las*: *minus*. If Z read *nimis*, the emendation is unjustified
25 *digest*: adds *bene*
32 *soone*: *magis*   Z *mox*

1346 3 *restoreþ*: *resumptiua et deperditorum restauratiua*
5 *Also*: V *item*   cf. I *et*   R *autem*   omitted by all others

19 *a venemous frogge þat hatte rubeta*: *ab alio uenenoso ut a rubeta*. *Z a rano* for *ab alio* abbreviated, causing *rubeta* 'toad' to be left untranslated. Cf. 1038/2

    21–2 *coketrice*: *basilisci siue reguli*

    23 *al þe venyme*: *omne uiuum*, properly the object of *doþ* in line 21. *Z omne venenum*

    26 *Ysaac* . . . *Ysaac 41°*: *tangere Ysaac 41* (I *xiiii*   QRY *xlix*   U *lix*   W *xl*)

    32 *won*: adds *aspersa*

1347 1 *anoon*: adds *et suis additamentis interioribus*

    2 *endeles*: *multe et innumerabiles*, generally translated *endeles many*

    4 *weuy*: *telas retexere . . . ita*

    5 *beste*: *opusculo*

    11 *5°*: *xv*

    12 *and*: *et ideo*. Also at 1352/7

    22 *beþ yleyde*: *cubantur* 'are hatched'. *Z ouantur*

1348 2 *seiþ*: adds *libro vi*

    14 *sitteþ þeron on broode*: *fouentur in terra*   cf. *cubat super ea* line 22

    15 *18°*: VX *xviiii*   cf. the better *viii*

    24 *in oon 3ere**

    28 *rounde and ful many*: *multa sicut et aliorum serpentum valde rotunda*

    28 *wanne*: INOT *liuida*   cf. the better *humida*

1349 1 *for*: *sed*

    4 *grete*: *uirulenta*   Z *ingenta*

    6 *wiþ dyuers colour*: *uaria*, translated *spekked* at 1350/28, 1351/2

    13 *body*: adds *paulatim*

    15 *yschadde*: adds *de suo nido*

    16 *þe*: *suos*   cf. De Worde *theyr*

    17 *beres*: IV *ursi*   cf. JS *non*   LNRUWY *nisi*   O *nisibus*   P *inuicem*   T *ubi* QX om.

1350 3 *eiren*: adds (not I) *ut dicit Aristotelis*

    5 *som 3eere*: *aliquando*   Z *aliquo anno*

    13 *male*: adds *ut dicit Aristoteles*

    17 *þerof*: *aliquando*

    28–9 *somdel white*: *alba*   Z *albida* or *subalba*

1351 2 *and eek**   21–2 *beþ yhaught and**

    16 *and*: *si*   cf. EH *if*. The usage *and* 'if' is probably scribal

    27 *eiren*: adds *corrumpuntur uel casu aliquo admittuntur*

    28 *makeþ* . . . *arise*: V *inflatiua*   cf. *inflamatiua*

1352 6 *ofte**   15 *ful wikked**

    14 *rinatrix*: ultimately a misreading of *et natrix* (Lucan IX. 720)

    17 *more hereof*: perhaps corrupted from *Isidori* (as in E)

    28 *And whanne*: IPTV *sed cum* (V *autem*)   cf. the better *si tamen*

1353 5 *stikkes*: adds *dura*

    13 *30°*: *xxx* (Q corrected)   cf. RV *xix*

    17 *heuy*: *ingrati*   Z *graui*

    21 *eiren²*: *ouationis*, cf. E *syringe*. Perhaps JT wrote *leyynge*

1354 3 *and tymes*: *temporum*. Probably JT wrote *of tymes*

8 *bestes... men þat: homines... animalibus qui... adhuc*

14 *nombre: cognitione numeri*

15–16 *by ofte takyng of oon: ex vnitatibus*

16 *nombres:* adds *non proles siue numerus*

19 *roote of þe manye: radix... siue mater.* Probably JT wrote *roote or þe moder*

22 *For: nam cum*

25 *and¹: et illam retinere et*

1355 7 *oon: quia vnum*

12 *vnderstonde: utique intelligitur de vnitate prima et simplici*

15 *parfite¹: perfecta* cf. the better IVX *imperfecta* (V corrected)

17 *vnite:* adds *ut dicit Aristoteles v physicorum capitulo iiii quia perfectum sufficit ad esse vnum*

24 *þerto:* adds *vnum simplex dicitur in quo non cadit multitudo nec actu nec potentia ut punctus et vnitas*

26 *tree: lectus* (O *corpus lectus* R *corpus* Y *letrus*). Z *lignum*

29 *and hors**   30 *and oþer white þinges**

29 *sortes: sortes.* BA intended *Socrates,* of which *Sortes* may be a form. Also at 1356/2

34–5 *accidente oþer subiecte... substaunce and subiecte: accidente... subiecto.* Doublets of ambiguity

1356 8 *5 maner wise: ix modos*

9 *For:* adds *vnitas naturalis gratuita et est super vtrunque constituta vnitas autem naturalis est in quadruplici differentia quedam est*

15 *of dyuers kyndes: naturarum differentium conuenientium*

21 *body:* PRW *corpus* cf. *cor* (Q altered)

22 *likynge: uotiua* 'willing, longing'. Perhaps JT wrote *wilcinge*

22 *almighty**   23 *wiþ al his might**

24 *sone: uerbo* cf. 56/28. Perhaps JT wrote *sonde*

25–6 *of þe secounde persone in trinite: persone diuine*

26 *By þat... oon**   27–8 *in þre... God**   29 *wiþoute piere**

34 *nombre:* adds *sed forma sunt vnum quorum ultima perfectio est vna et totalis*

34–6 *And þilke... bestes: vnum genere quorum forma predicamenti vna*

1357 4 *sownes:* adds *et cetera*

4 *10:* adds (not PQR) *libro* (S *xl'*)

6 *is: est expressiua*

8 *metaphysice:* adds *capitulo iii*

10 *heed:* adds *tanquam motor sed tanquam forma et finis et actus vltimus*

11 *þat may be chaunged: omnino et cetera*

1358 1 *of þe fader and of þe sone: a patre per filium*

6 *yseide:* adds (not U) *libro*

7, 15 The rubrics are found in JNTV and (the second only) in S

12 *in vertues and: tam in virtute quam*

18 *and: et... ideo*

21–2 *þe fyue 3okke... wittes: v. iuga boum ementibus* (L *erantibus*) *comparantur quia in v.... voluptatibus adhuc detinentur* Z *euntibus* for *ementibus,* with loss of *adhuc detinentur*

25 *euene parties: partibus*   Z *paribus partibus*. Cf. 1361/29–30
28 *byneþe: nisi in*. Perhaps JT wrote *but in þe nombre*
29 *þerfore:* adds *libro i* (I *v*)

1359 5 *moste verray:* JLV *verissime*   R *veracissime*   cf. the better *beatissime*
    8 *or: scilicet*   Z *uel* or an ME. scribal intrusion
    11 *3ifte of grace: graciam* (IVWX add *hic in via*, Q adds *hic*)   Z *gracie dona*
    17 *euene: inequalia*   cf. Q *equalia*,   T *sequalia*
    19 *fader:* adds *luminum*, cf. the better Q *mei* 'my'
    29 *and*:* probably a scribal intrusion
    33 *þerto:* adds *uel replicatione* (L *explecacione*, NTU *repeticione*)

1360 3–5 *And ten . . . forþ: articulus continet x. et reliquos denarios*
    8 *ten: decies.* Perhaps JT wrote *ten sithes*, cf. 1361/1
    11–12 *Nombres . . . euene: recipit autem numerus quantitatem et aceruus ex vnitatibus profusus multiplicem diuisionem numerorum alius par* 'And number takes quantity, and the mass gathered from single numbers takes multiple division. Of numbers some are even'
    16 *in þre: iii* (S *in*). A doublet of ambiguity, *in uel iii*
    18–19 *som is vnpar:* IR *alius pariter inpar*, cf. the better *alius pariter impar alius est impariter par*
    20 *alway anoon to: quousque ad*   Z *quoque usque ad*
    21 *foure and sixty . . . two and þritty: lxiiii . . . xxxii*   cf. JLPQRSVWXY *xliiii . . . xxii*
    36–**1361** 1 *and comeþ . . . nombres**
    9 *nombre: plurimi*   Z *numeri*
    12 *itslf: partibus suis computatis*
    16 *þerof:* adds *perfectus numerus qui suis partibus adimpletur*
    17 *parties:* adds *scilicet sextam tertiam et dimidiam*
    17–18 *sixte party þerof is oon: sex sunt vnum* 'the six parts are one'
    20 *foure score and sixtene: quadringenti nonaginta et vi.* Perhaps JT wrote *foure hundred and foure score and sixtene*
    21 *and twenty**
    25 *ordre:* adds *ut dicit idem*
    26 *be: sunt multi et*
    29 *euene: aliam*   Z *parem*
    33–4 *But . . . nombre**   36–**1362** 1 *of multiplicacioun of oþer numbres**
    7 *uncompouned:* WX *compositus*   cf. the better *incompositus*. The emendation may be unjustified in the *corrigenda*
    10 *fiftene:* NQTU *xv*   cf. JLORSVY *xxv* (P *et 5*   Q corrected   W *xi xxv* X *24*)
    13 *and wiþ comparisoun: aut ad alium per se est numerus qui sine relatione aliqua dicitur*
    21 *ben þe more and þe lasse: ad inuicem inequalitatem demonstrant*
    24–5 *somwhat ouer . . . þre: eius alias partes duas*
    27 *foure . . . foure: quinarium . . . eo.* Perhaps JT wrote *fyue . . . fyue*
    30 *siþes:* adds *multipliciter*
    32 *And: econtra*

1363 1 *conteyneþ: est dum fortior continet in se*
    6 *subsuperparciens: superparciens*

14 *foure: aliis*. Perhaps JT wrote *ouer*, cf. lines 4, 5

15 *more: inferiori* cf. Q *superiori* and Isidore III. 6. 10 *fortiori*

18 *superparticularis: subparticularis*

20 *as: et* Z *ut* or perhaps JT wrote *an*

21 *oon ouer: unitatem que nouenarii est pars vna*

23–5 *Also . . . perof, as eiȝte . . . perof*: in the Latin MSS. these clauses are properly transposed

25–6 *conteynep . . . perof: ad vii*

32 *secundum Ysidorum*: properly modifies the next sentence

35–6 *A numbre conteyned: continens uero numerus est qui coniunctis monadibus continetur*. Perhaps JT wrote *a contynuel numbre is a numbre conteyned*

1364 5–6 *is ywrite . . . brede*[2]: *est ita qui non solum in longitudine sed in latitudine continetur*

8–9 *in lengpe and in brede: in plano pede id est in superficie*. Perhaps JT wrote *in pleyne foote*, as at 1364/2 and 5

10–12 PRU omit the figures, T inserts standard scribal space-fillers, other Latin MSS. have various figures, those of JLVY being closest to JT's forms (very similar in all ME. MSS.)

11 *wise*: adds *et tetragonus dicitur*. Similar omissions of *tetragonus* at line 35 and 1370/16, 1371/20

14–15 *and efte . . . wise: et in se conuertitur*

15 *and makep a spere al rounde**: probably anticipates line 17

20 *symple*[2]: *simpliciter*

25 *menynge: mysteria*, generally translated *derke menynge*, cf. 1374/34

25 *inspired: inspirate* (JLNSTUVY om.) cf. the better PX *aspirare*

33 *ouper pridde: vbi primi secundi et vltimi siue tertii ratio non habetur*

1365 1 *consonanciis and acordes: consonanciis*. Perhaps JT wrote *consonanciis 'acordes'*

6–7 *pe ensample . . . noumbre: rationis numeralis fuit exemplaritas in animo conditoris* 'the concept of numerical reasoning was in the mind of the creator'

7 *by: sub*

13 *hemself*: adds *et proportionem ex aliis quam ex seipsis*

23 *dymensioun: dimensione* (V adds *uel duisione*) cf. the better IS *diuisione* (OPR *dione* Y om.). Cf. 1367/22n. below

25 *pys diuisioun: in li* (LN *li°*) cf. the better IOPQUX *l* '50' Z *ille*

26 *it is diuidid: non enim diuisum est nisi semel*

32–3 *in contynual quantite: secundum magnitudinem* Z *semper* or perhaps JT wrote *in cause of*

1366 24 *pou makest: generabis* (NOQRST suspend inflexion) cf. the better PX *generabit* (W *generatur*)

28 *oon*[3]: V *uniario* Q *vnitati* cf. *binario*

1367 12 *general: analogicum*

21 *in lengpe . . . distancia**

28 *dymmensioun: dimensio* cf. the better NOPST *diuisio*. Cf. 1365/23n.

33 *gretnesse*: adds *per iudicium rationis sicut irrationales quarum mensure*. If Z eye-skipped, the emendation of MS. *irracional* is wrong

35–**1368** 1 *and is . . . depe**

1 *many*: IPQRUX *plures* (rest om.)

4 *lynes þat comeþ fro þe roundnesse þerof**   5 *And þe cercle is**

6–15 P omits the figures. Of the various figures in other Latin MSS. those of J are closest to JT's figures

7 *Diategramon*: O *dyategramon*, cf. IJLNPSUV *dyatratecongramon* and other forms more distant in other MSS. of *diatetragrammaton*

8 *Ortogonium*: adds *id est* (T *et*)

8 *figure*: adds *id est triangulus et habet angulum rectum*

9 *strei3t, ordeyned vnder þe solid*: *recta subter in solidum constituta* 'straight underneath, constructed in solid'

14–16 *scharp . . . streight*: *angustum . . . acutum*

15 *yschape*: adds *in modum ignis*

23 *Spissitudo*: adds *habet trinam dimensionem scilicet*

30 *seuenty*: adds *media uero* (PQRX add *scilicet*) *viii. et ix. multiplicata tantum faciunt*

34 *moste clene*: *remotissima*   cf. *most ferre* line 35. Z *mundissima* or JT's form was *ver*, mistead as *ter* 'clean' and then modernized

34 *wiþinne*: adds *motui aptissima et reuolutioni congrua*

36 *figures*: adds *omnes figuras et figurabilia ambiens omnia potestatiue*

1369 3 *of non*: IQ *non . . . aliquo*   cf. the better *non . . . alio*

5 P omits the figure. Of the other MSS. those of JLNT are closest to JT's figures

8–9 *and . . . sterres*: *et motum Sic planetarum orbes in se circulariter reflectuntur Sic siderum*. Z's loss of *in se circulariter reflectuntur* interrupts the sequence of the *Sic* clauses

21–2 *of þe same lengþe, ysperimetarum id est equales ambitus habentium*

1370 15 *solid, long*: *solidum habens longitudinem altitudinem*

20–31 PY omit the figures. Of those in other MSS. JNO at 20 and JNVW at 22 are identical to JT's figures, and JLVX at 31 are closest

33 *principles*: *principiis*   Z *principlis*   Also at 1371/1

1371 4 *of oon, þat makeþ foure ydo to þre*: *ex vno qui potestate trigonus est generatur* 'is created by one which by its power is a trigon'

5 *oon*: adds *que mater est omnium numerorum*

7 *xiº . . . . xiiiiº*: *ii* (R *xii*) *. . . xviii* (LOP *viii*   W *xxviii*)

21, 25 The figures, inserted for clarity, are lacking in all ME. and examined Latin MSS.

23 *piramis*: adds *sic etiam supra basim hexagonum potest* (JS om. these six words) *surgere pyramidalis figura sex continens triangulos manifeste et sic de aliis ipsa etiam figura trianguli poterit pyramidalis esse basis*

38 *anngels*: i.e. angles. Perhaps the scribe intended *aungels*

1372 12 *materia vel natura*: *materia* (Q *natura*). A doublet of ambiguity

15 *beþ y-ooned*: OR *vniuntur*   cf. the better *finiuntur*

19 *soule²*: adds *vegetabilem sic quadrangulus animam*

24, 25 *concupiscibill, irascibill*: both forms in AF have barred -*ll* (G -*ibel*). Perhaps JT preserved the Latin forms in -*ibilis*, as in CH

29 The rubric, inserted for clarity, is lacking in all ME. and examined Latin MSS.

30 *xiiº*: *xvi*

32 *of space and of place*: *spacii localis*. Also at 1380/20–1

1373 7 *makeþ*: dicitur
   9 *Concula*: ILOPQRV *concula*, cf. the better *cotula* (cf. *cotyla* in Isidore XVI. 26. 5)
  10 *cote*: JLOQUVW *cote* (as in Isidore loc. cit.), cf. I *toto*   NSTX *coce*   P *cocte*
R *chote*   Y *conce*
  13 *and is*: est autem sextarius
  14 *euer*: assumpcio, cf. the better IQUW *assumptus*. *Z semper* unless JT wrote *euen*
  30 *informe*: adds *angelos*
  32 *oonliche*: *solum*   cf. OT *celum*
  35 *of þe water**: cf. *of þe londe* for *terre* at line 36

1374 16 *cours*: *chorus*. Probably JT wrote *chorus*, as at line 28
  27 *þre or foure*: iiii (V adds *uel tria*). A doublet of ambiguity

1375 2 *appreued*: adds *an esset purum uel corruptum vas autem vbi probabatur et acceptabatur*
  9–10 *þe kynde*... *ymade of*: suo genere
  13 *vessel*: QRUWX add *repositorium*, the rest *depositorium*
  13 *mesure oonliche*: mensura tantum   cf. the better I *mensuratium*
  18 *hondeles*: siue auribus   Z *siue armis*. Alternatively *hondeles* is 'handles', JT's gloss for *ansis*, and Z *ansis siue auribus*
  18 *Bacus*: ILNOTVWX *bacus*   cf. the better *batus* 'bath'
  19 *Bachi is a mesure*: bachia est mensura bachi
  30 *figes*: *vuis* (JS *uini*, LNV *uinis*) *et ficubus* 'grapes and figs'
  33 *chaffe*: adds *nam grana que sunt parua transeunt per foramina paleis in cribro remanentibus ac lapillis*
  34 *cistella*: cistula et cistella

1376 1–2 *ymarked wiþ euydent signe*: signis euidentioribus (cf. *eminentioribus* in Isidore XX. 4. 7)
  10 *distinccioun*: distincio (cf. *distichon* in Isidore loc. cit.)
  11 *Siue*: OVT perhaps *siue*, cf. the better *sum* (as *ibid.*)
  21 *þerfore*: de quo. Perhaps JT wrote *þerof*, but cf. 1373/16–17
  22 *drynke*: poculi 'cup' in this context, cf. 1379/1
  28 *parchemyn*: adds *uel breuitellus*... *ut religiosi viderentur*

1377 11 *prestes*: adds *ut dicit glossa super iiii. libro regum*
  12 *vessel*: adds *usibus deputatum*. A similar addition at 1378/14
  14 *frute*: adds *cartallum est consimile vasculum ex virgis albis et flexis artificialiter preparatum*
  17 *and light**: perhaps a relic of *ad nutriendum flammam* omitted after *oyle* at the end of the sentence
  18 *euerich*: omne vasculum
  22 *horne*: cornu lucido (JLNOSTV *liuido*)
  24–5 *wiþ light þerinne**
  26 *þerof*: vnde. Perhaps JT wrote *þerfor*
  27 *mouere*: mouere, cf. the better I *uomuere* (as in Isidore XX. 10. 2)
  30–1 *licinius*... *also*: licinius autem qui et lucinus... ut dicit idem. Probably JT wrote *licinius and lucinus also, as he seiþ*
  35 *of þe wyne*: et virtus ipsius vini. Adds *vnde si lagena fuerit corrupta vinum fit corruptum*

1378 9 *luderes*: JLVW *luderes*   cf. IQRU *luteres*   N *Luceres*   O *licces*   P *landeres*   S *ludens*   T *Lucerens*

17 *perinne*: adds *nisi* (JLOPS *ut*) *ab eis cicius* (JLNOST om.) *extrahantur*

23 *so*: adds *primitus*

25 *such a belle**

30 *And*: *vnde et*

32 *yliche*: adds *id est paribus absidis*

1379 4 *lede*: *ferreum*

8 *ofte**

9 *metal*: adds *nunc de ebore*

11 *electuaries*: adds *odoribus*

13 *ysaued*: adds *ut dicit p* (I *pap*   P *y'*   R *plat*   U *pli*)

19 *wiþ*: *talibus*

23 *golde*: *uitreum*   Z *aureum*

23, 32 *hondes   lepir*: adds *ut dicit Isidorus*.

30–1 *3erdes of a schrob þat is**

31 *Scortella*: JLOPST *Scortici*   I *Sportica*   R *Scortin*   cf. the better *Scortia* (as in Isidore XX. 7. 1)

36 *saler*: adds *id est vas aptum sali*

1380 3 *sens*: adds *ignis incendio resolutus*

5 *beþ ycheyned togideres*: *tribus cathenulis pariter continentur*

8 *and clene**

8 *abydeþ*: *occultatur*. Perhaps JT wrote *hydeþ* or Z *occubatur*

13 *water*: adds *effundendis comuniter*

15 *3iueþ*: *infundit*

16 *Phisolagia*: O *phisalogie*   R *phisologie*   cf. the better *philolagie*. The reference is to Martianus Capella, *De nuptiis Philologie et Mercurii*

18 *mesure*: adds *secundum diuersas mensurandi capacitates*

25 *oughte*: JLNORSTUV *omnino*   cf. the better *animo*. Perhaps the emendation of MS. *weighte* should be *owhiht* 'aught, anything'

27 *prouynce*[1]: *partes in prouincias*   cf. the better IY *in partes et partes in prouincias*

36 *elleuene . . . ten*: SUW *xi* (QRY *duos*   JLNPV *xxi*   T *pedes*   X *xx*) . . . IOQW *xxx* (JLNPSTU *xx*)

1381 7 *side*: adds *actus quadratas vndique finitur pedibus cxx*

8 *actum*: *autem actum* (cf. *autem* in Isidore XV. 5. 2)

11 *tyme*: adds *ut dicit idem*

21 *signes*: *signes* (cf. *schoenos*   va. *signes* in Isidore XV. 16. 1)

23 *myle*: adds *mille passibus terminatur quia*

28 *it*: *cxxv pedum spacium*

36 *Lucanus*: QVW *lucanus*   cf. the better *Lucretius* (LNSV *lucernus*   O *bucanus*   P *leucrecius*   T *laternus*   X *lucianus*)

38 *wiþoute obstacle*: misplaced from the end of the sentence, *sine obstaculo et offensa* 1382/1–2

1382 2 *he*: *idem Lucretius*   Z *idem*

5 *way*: adds *ab aggere id est coaceruatione*

6 *histories*: *historici* (PX *historia*). Perhaps JT wrote *historiens*

6 *Talis*: *qualis*

7 *deprehensus*: *deprensus* (as in *Aeneid* V. 273).

9 *passe*: adds *et ideo appellamus iter*

10 *passe*: adds *ut quo uelis peruenias*

10 *semis*: I *semis*   OPQUW *semitu*   R *semi itu*   cf. *semita* (*semiitu* in Isidore XV. 16. 9)

16 *benthinge*: i.e. a form of *bendynge* in line 15. But perhaps the emendation of MS. *benchinge* here should be *blenchinge*

17 *wey*: adds *publice et priuate*

28 *y-ordeyned* . . . *place*: *derelictus* (X *delictus*) *ad circumeundi facilitatem* (IPQRX *facultatem*)   Z *delectus* . . . *facultatem*

30 *whele*: adds *tanti* (IN *canti*   PQU *carri*   OR om.   cf. the better X *curri*) *sic dicta ab orbiculari figura rote* (Isidore XV. 16. 13 has *carri*)

31 *slider*: R *limosum*   cf. the better *cliuosum*

34 *tokne*: adds *odoris*

36 *perfore*: *caude* (L *tanta*) *sua* 'with his tail'. Z *tanta causa*

1383 5 *wei3tes*: adds *etiam*

12 *sotile*: *simplici* . . . *et subtili*

13 *moeuep*: adds *suo pondere*

25 *chief*: *maxima* . . . *et potissima*

1384 3 *is²*: adds *aliquando*

7 *trucina*: *trutina* . . . *secundum Isidorum*

7 *of double wei3tes*: *gemina ponderum* 'double of weights'

8 *hundred and talentus*: both plural forms, cf. *centenaria et talenta*

9 *And smale balaunces*: *sicut momentanea*. Perhaps JT wrote *as momentana* '*smale balaunces*'

11–12 *a þyng þat bereþ it vp in þe myddil*: *vno in medio stylo*

14 *hongeth*: *correspondent*. Z *pendent*

16–18 *þe hongels . . . filium*: *filium medium* . . . *examen* 'the middle thread is called *examen*' (as in Isidore XVI. 25. 5). *hongels* (va. *hangels*), not otherwise recorded, may be a form of *thong* or *angle*

27 *dragma*: the error for *gramma* 'the weight of two *oboli*' may have occurred in BA's copy of Isidore XVI. 25. 11

29–30 *weyeþ pre pans* . . . *ten pans*: *denarii pondus argenti tribus constat scrupulis id est xviii siliquis denarius autem est dictus quasi pro x nummis reputatur*. The translation of both *scrupulis* and *nummis* as *pans* 'pence' produces the contradiction, cf. lines 34–6

32–3 *cleped* . . . *totum*: *integrum solidum dicebat atque totum* 'called something unblemished and whole *solidum*'

37 *twies sixe vnces*: the extant error for *his sex vncia* was already present in BA's copy of Isidore XVI. 25. 14

1385 9 *vnce*: *vncie*, a corrupt variant of *assis* (cf. Pliny *quadrans* . . . *a tribus vnciis*), already present in BA's copy of Isidore XVI. 25. 17

9 *quadrans*: *dodrans*   cf. the better R *codrans* (as in Isidore XVI. 25. 17)

13 *dragmes*: adds *vnde*

14 *oonep*: *uinciat* (JLSV *uunciat*   ORU *vnciat*) (as in Isidore XVI. 25. 19), Z *vniat*

20 *leberata*: *libera* (as in Isidore XVI. 25. 20)
22 *Coma*: *prima*, cf. the better I *mina* (as in Isidore XVI. 25. 21)
28 *Plius*: *Plautus* (as in Isidore XVI. 25. 22)

1386 4–5 *to knowe mistik menynge*: *mysteriis*
7 *iii°*: *iii* (PR *xi*   W *xiii*)
13 *conforte*: *consolatio*   cf. the better IQRX *modulacio* (OP *modulo*)
15 *abateþ... mankynde*: *exercitos... animos*
22 *sounes*: adds *secundum arsim et thesim*
30 *Voice comeþ to oon acorde*: *et dicitur harmonia ab 'ad' et 'monos' id est unum quia ad unam concordiam tendunt in cantibus omnes uoces*
33 *if*: *vbi*
33 *suche*: *talis diuersitas contra*
36–7 *temperate modulacioun*: *modulationis temperamentum*

1387 1 *hiȝe vois*: *uoces acutiores et grauiores*
5 *discording*: adds *et deformis*
22 *gronynge*: IPQRU *clamores*   cf. *clangores*. Cf. *gronynge* for *gemitus* at line 26; *trompeng* 1386/11 and *noice* 1388/33 for *clangor*
25 *sonnere*: *citius et facilius*
27 *wreyste*: *plectro*, as at 206/10. *O.E.D.* s.v. sb. 5 states that it is a mistranslation, but see 1392/4
31 *wordes*: adds *lingue organo... enim*
36 *and is yknowe*: *exterius se extendit* (PQUVXW *ostendit*). Perhaps JT wrote *a is yknowe*

1388 4 *voice*: *uoces siue tonos*
7 *beþ lowde and draweþ longe*: *longius protahuntur*
9 *also þe harde voys is grym and grisliche**
11 *wiþ grete slegges*: *ferrum durum*
14 *pliaunt*: adds *atque leuis*
17 *eeren*: adds *fortis ne trepidet aut deficiat*
18 *and to comforte þe hertes to take heede þerto*: *sed potius ut aures demulceat et audientium animos blandiendo ad se allicit*. Perhaps JT wrote *eres* for *hertes*
22 *sownes*: adds *et*, essential to distinguish *quantitate* and *qualitate*
31 The rubric, found in JNS only, was probably lacking in Z

1389 19 *is yrewled vpward*: *regitur erigitur*
21–2 *to arraye... smyte togidres*: *bella committantur*
25 *parua*: properly qualifies *trompe*
28 *somtyme*: *pariter*

1390 2 *first*: *penitus*   I *primitus*
3 *noyse*: *cantus*. Perhaps JT wrote *notes*, as at 1391/5 and 21
5 *reed*: adds *quia a quibusdam calamis antiquitus fiebat*
18 *foules*: adds *dum canendo earum simulat et fingit uoces*
22 *he*: adds *prius* (INT *primus*)
25 *þe same*: JLMNSTV *idem*   cf. the better *ideo*

1391 3 *beþ*: a syncopated form of *beteþ*, as in CFGH

15 *a tabour or . . . a symphony: symphonie.* A doublet of ambiguity, *tympanie uel symphonie*

22 *toricha*: MRX *toricha*   cf. *corica* (IL *dorica*   V *corita*   P *thorica*)

24 *and had þat name cithara**

26–7 *þe strynges . . . dyuers: cordarum etiam multiplicatus est et commutatum genus*

30–1 *And beþ as þe nexte strynge þerto: discrimina autem dicta ideo quia nulla corda uicine corde similem sonum reddit*

31 *And: ideo*

1392 4 *the wreyste: instrumentum quo temperantur corde et tenduntur.* H's unique addition, *þat men wresten with pynnes and strynges of þe harpe*, may be authorial

12 *clepeþ: habent.* Perhaps JT wrote *habbuþ*, which was reduced to *haþ* or *hat* and then modernized as *clepeþ*

19 *chanell: suos meatus*

21 *ystreyned: extenti.* Perhaps JT wrote *ystrei3t*, as at 1391/14

1393 2 *lumina*: MOQRSWX *lumina*   cf. the better *limina*

8–9 *vasis in v: vasis in litera n* (cf. *nola* at 1378/24–8) occurs in all examined Latin MSS. but all except T give the *litera* as *n* (or *u*)

17 *dyatesseron: diatessaron consonanciam vi. uero ad ix. et viii. et xii. comparati reddunt sesqualteram proportionem et diapente*

18 *sixe*: IPQU *vi.*   cf. *vii.*

21 *sownes*: adds *omnium enim sonorum est paruissimus*

21 *bitwen*: adds *consonantiarum*

29 *nombres*: adds *ut patet . . . enim*

32–3 *þe soune and þe acorde in diapason: sonus in diapason symphonia* 'sound in the accord diapason'

34 *comeþ: colligitur uel componitur*

35–**1394** 1 *And he . . . hatte: quam diapente symphoniam vocant hemiola mediante coniungitur qui in numeris epogdonus id est supra viii. dicitur*

1 *þere*: adds *sesquitertia proportio in arithmetica dicitur diatesseron in musica et que hemiola id est*

3 *lasse: minorem notulam duplo*

5 *þerof: minoris*

5 *al in þe fourþe del: iiii*, i.e. the less number and a quarter. Perhaps JT wrote *on an* for *al in*

7 *wise*: adds *unde sesquitertius est qui minori comparatus habet eum semel et eius tertiam partem uerbi gratia si iiii. compares tribus*

10 *ei3tene . . . sixtene: xix* (I *xviii*   MQT *xvi*) *. . . xv*

13 *oþer half: totalem . . . et eius medietatem*

14 *tweyne*: adds (except QR) *scilicet unitatem sic vi continet in se iiii*

19 *musik*: adds *nam arithmeticis geometricis et musicis*

23 *in*: adds *arithmethicorum*

30 *abateþ*: adds *malitiosos*

1395 6 *opere²: ista et alia*

9 *we haueþ . . . yplaunted: interseruimus*   Z *intersevimus*

16 *redy: exquisitis* 'choice'

21 *ysewed*: adds *simpliciter*

1396 2 *me*: adds *pauperem*

7–13 *Endeles...fourty**

14–21 This list of *auctours*, probably added at Paris *c.* 1275, includes these writers not cited by BA: *Alquinus, Anselmus, Ciprianus, Haymo, Elipitrus, Pamphilius, Patricius, Robertus Lincolniensis, Symon Corniensis, Stephanus*

15 *Amantinus*: *adamantius* (JSY *adamantinus*)

16 *Eusicius*: *Esicius* (I om.   J *Eficius*   N *Cicius*   O *Essitus*   T *Cusin*   W *elisius*), perhaps Isichius, b. of Jerusalem

16–17 *Crisostomus. Damasius Damascenus*: behind the partial repetition, found in all Anglo-Latin MSS. (PQR lack third word) lie the separate identities of *Iohannes Crisostamus* and *Iohannes Damascenus*

20 *Sener*: *Seneca* (variously abbreviated, P *senon'*). Perhaps (with the preceding *Petrus*) *Petrus Comestor* or Petrus Lombardus, author of *Sententiae*

22–**1397** 2 This list of *philosophos* includes these writers not cited by BA: *Ipartus* (i.e. Hipparchaus), *Orbasius* (i.e. Oribasius), *Litus Liber* (i.e. Titus Livius), *Williemus Conches*. The last is cited as 'Bede' in some contexts

26 *Epinus*: JLSUX *Epitinus* (INT om.)   OQR *Epicinus*   cf. the better P *Epicurius*

29 *Scinus*: JL *Scinus*   O *Orinus*   P *kipeius*   Q *Omerus*   S *Seynus*   Y *Minus* cf. the better RUVX *Ninus* (perhaps Ninus Delphicus)

31 *Permenides*: JLNSTV om. U adds later, the rest include

31 *minor*: O *Minor*   PVX *iunior*   the rest ambiguous. Perhaps JT wrote *iunior*

32 *sanus*: *sanus* (R *solus* corrected to *Salus*), presumably a reference to the pseudo-Pythagorean *Liber romanorum*, a book of cures

34 *Litus Liber*: this corruption of *Titus Liuius* occurs in all Anglo-Latin MSS. except Y *Titus Libeus*

34 *Boecius*: *boecius*, an error due to the false expansion of the antecedent *Liber* (va. *Libeus*) as *li.* and *be'* (as in V *lit' li. boe'*) and subsequent false expansion of *be'*

SELECT GLOSSARY

The categories of inclusion of words in this selective glossary are:

(*a*) words now archaic or extinct
(*b*) words which survive without their primary fourteenth-century meaning
(*c*) words which have radically changed their form since 1398
(*d*) neologisms and nonce-words and phrases.

These categories exclude Latin words printed in italic in the text (including those treated as English words in the *M.E.D.*) and compounds formed with the suffix -*wise* and with *to* before a noun with enclitic -*warde*. The glossary comprehends the *corrigenda* and *addenda* printed in the Textual Commentary for each book.

To avoid a multiplicity of forms which the slightly differing spelling habits of the three scribes of the printed manuscript would otherwise produce in each entry, round brackets are used: thus **pom(m)egarnat(e)** implies the occurrence of four forms, **pommegarnat, pommegarnate, pomegarnat, pomegarnate**. Also, forms showing these minor orthographic variations are not recorded:

(*a*) *i/y* in forms with ME. long and short *i*
(*b*) addition or omission of final -*e*
(*c*) *o/u* in forms with ME. short *u*
(*d*) *e/i* and *e/y* in both stressed and unstressed environments (e.g. *resiþ/ risiþ*)
(*e*) single or double letters in forms with ME. long vowels (e.g. *breed/brede, beete/bete, moon/mone, oon/one, maad/made*)
(*f*) *ou/ow* in forms with ME. long *u*
(*g*) *ei/ey/ai/ay* and *eu/ew/u* and *ou/ow* and *au/aw* where they represent ME. diphthongs
(*h*) *ȝ/gh/h* and *d/t/th/þ* and *s/c* and *c/k* and *cc/ct* and *ou/ow/ouȝ/owȝ* and *if/iue* when they represent ME. consonants and alternate in free variation

Alphabetic order follows normal practice: ȝ follows *g*, vocalic *y* is treated as *i*, vocalic *v* is placed with *u* and consonantal *u* with *v*, þ is placed with *th*. The initial *i-/y-* prefix of the past particle is ignored.

The headword is generally the most common form, and cross-references are given to minority spellings listed alphabetically (except for a grouping of words with initial *v-* for etymological *f-* and *w-* at the start of the letter *V*). In exceptional cases of potential confusion (e.g. *hulle* 'hill', *hawel* 'hail' alongside *hille*, *hayle*) the headword is the less common form.

In each entry grammatically variant forms follow the headword. Wherever

possible, the headword of a noun is listed in the singular; of adjective and
adverb in the positive form; of verb in the infinitive or in an equivalent present
tense uninflected form. Variant mutated plural forms of nouns are recorded,
but variant plural forms in -*en* alongside -*s* are not. Verbs listed in infinitive or
present forms only either have weak forms throughout their conjugation or do
not occur in the past tense. Strong verbs are recorded in full, including any
variant weak forms. Verbs and their derivative verbal nouns are generally
listed together; exceptionally, verbal nouns with meanings developed beyond
their verbal roots are listed separately.

Grammatical notation is that of the *O.E.D.* Definition is limited to Trevisa's
usage in this text, followed, where necessary, by phrases incorporating the
headword which have specialized meanings. Page and line reference are to
those of the first occurrence of the word, irrespective of form or sense. A
dagger marks words not recorded in *O.E.D.*

Etymologies are given within square brackets for those words which lack a
clearly identifiable modern English form, and follow the standard notations of
linguistic origins. Neologisms and fere-neologisms, generally dependant on
the Latin text of Bartholomaeus, are referred to Latin forms only, as are new
senses imposed on ME. words by the translator.

Diacritical notations are as follows:

(*a*) long vowels of OE. and Latin are indicated by a macron, and of ON. by
an acute accent

(*b*) OE. historically short vowels which probably lengthened in late OE. are
indicated by an acute accent

(*c*) OE. historically long vowels which probably shortened in late OE. are
indicated by a macron and a mora

(*d*) for the OE. grapheme *g*, the voiced stop and the second element of the
diagraphs *cg* and *ng* are indicated by *g*; front glide by *ġ*; voiced velar
spirant by *ȝ*

(*e*) for the OE. grapheme *c*, the affricate is indicated by *ċ*; the unvoiced
stop and the second element of the digraph *sc* by *c*.

As with the listing of forms after the headword, round brackets indicate
alternative forms of etymologies; e.g. (*ġe*)*wær* implies both *wær* and *ġewær* as
possible etymons.

Where the etymon exists only in compounds, the etymological stem of the
ME. simplex is preceded or followed by a hyphen. Compounds first formed in
ME. have their separate etymons joined by a plus sign. Where the word and its
etymon are different parts of speech, *from* before the etymon indicates that
ME. word is formed by a regular derivational process.

Uncertain etymologies are marked by *cf.* or, as an indication of greater
uncertainty, by question mark. Hypotheses and reconstructions are marked by
asterisk. Glosses for etymons are given for words of uncertain ancestry and for

words which derive from earlier compounds. Variant forms of a single etymon are separated by comma; *and* separates different etymons.

The glossary originally prepared for this edition listed all textual senses and all etymons for each cited word and gave many more forms and cross-references. Its reduction is due to the cost of things.

A glossary for Trevisa's translation of Aegidius Romanus, *De regimine principum* (Bodleian Library MS. Digby 233) is given by K. C. Conroy (Univ. of Washington, Ph.D. 1964) and of Trevisa's translation of the *Gospel of Nicodemus* by H. C. Kim (Univ. of Washington, Ph.D. 1963).

a *pron.* he, she, it 52/34
a *prep.* in, on 101/3
a, see **an**
abate *v.* to diminish, lessen 390/18
†abatinge *sb.* declination, loss of influence 478/32
abedde *adv.* in bed 410/9
abestone *sb.* mineral which, once set on fire, was reputed to be unquenchable 835/7 [OF. *abeston* and ML. *a(s)bestos*]
abhominacioun *sb.* a loathsome act or object 352/11
abide v. (abode, abood, abidde *pa.*; **abiden** *pa. p.*), **abidinge** *sb.* to wait, remain, last 61/5 (*v.*), 61/18 (*sb.*)
abigge *v.* pay for 365/24 [OE *ābycgan*]
abilliche *adv.* effectively 269/25
able, abil *a.* capable, strong, agile 66/19 [OF. *able*, last two senses calques on L. *habilis*]
ablenes(se)*sb.* ability 454/15
ablete *sb.* power, fitness 485/37 [OF. *ableté*; cf. **hability**]
ableþ *v. pa. p.* endowed with capacity (to perform an act) 827/9
abnegacioun *sb.* denial 47/5
†abolynge *v. pres. p.* needing a bull 1257/24
†aboue forþ *adv.* out from above 396/9
†a-bow-wise *adv.* in the manner of a bow 489/34
abraydynge *sb.* erasing 1289/5
abrood, on brood *adv.*[1] abroad, spread out 124/22
abrood, on brood *adv.*[2] on its brood, hatching eggs 227/19 [OE. *on brōde*]
absence, absens, abcence *sb.* absence 131/29
absteyne *v.* to refrain from 354/30
abstinence *sb.* privation 290/6

abstinteþ *v. pres. 3sg.* avoids, refrains from 357/26 [byform of **absteyne**; form perhaps infl. by derivatives of OE. *styntan* with parallel senses]
abstract *pa. p., a.* (of nouns) not referring to palpable objects 47/26
abstractif *a.* (of nouns) abstract, not referring to palpable objects 48/13 [L. *abstractīvus*]
abstractlich *adv.* in the abstract, absolutely, in itself 47/21
accesse, see **axesse**
accherne *sb.* (**accornes, ackornis, accerns** *pl.*) acorn, nut, mast 534/9 [OE. *æcern*, with forms infl. by OE. *corn* 'grain' and folk-etymology *āc-corn* 'oak-grain']
accident *sb.* a non-essential quality of an object (opposed to 'substance'), a pathological state dependent on a preceding disease, something fortuitous 42/37
accidental *a.* non-essential 176/9
accidentallich *adv.* by 'accident', as a result of non-essential qualities 886/25
accompt, see **acompt**
accreesiþ *v. pres. 3sg.* grows 560/2
ache, age, ake *sb.* ache 166/17
†achilde *adv.* in birth, in bearing a child 592/6
acolde *a.* chilled, cold 357/17
acompt *v. pres. pl.* regard, consider (as of a certain status) 635/33
acord *sb.* good will, harmony (musically and generally) 93/22
†acordeþ *v. pres. pl.* draw together, collect 1142/8 [? from OF. *corde* 'woven rope']
acordinge (to) *pres. p., a.* agreeing, corresponding to 60/11

acordith *v. pres. 3sg.* agrees, corresponds 59/7

acountiþ *v. pres. 3sg.* counts, regards 218/11

†**acroswise** *adv.* at right angles, as the beams of a cross 109/26

act *sb.* deed, active principle 128/35

actual *a.* real, effective, active 511/25

actualite *sb.* efficacy, effective power 485/38

actualnesse *sb.* efficacy, effectiveness 510/8–9

acu, acute, see **agu**

adamas, adamans, adamand, adama(u)nt *sb.* diamond, loadstone, magnet 474/26

adder, addre, eddre, naddre, nedder *sb.* snake or serpent 87/2

adduccioun *sb.* prompting, persuasion (to an action) 69/8 [L. *adductio*]

adiectiue *a.* adjectival; *noun adiectiue,* an adjective 47/24

admynystret *v. pres. 3sg.* provides, gives 136/13

admixecioun *sb.* mixture, mingling 45/3

adoun *adv.* downward, to a lower position; *setten adoun,* overthrow 495/29

adreint, adraynt *v. pa. p.* drowned, immersed 106/10 [OE. *ādrenćan*]

†**adulled** *v. pa. p.* numbed 100/27

aerliche *a.* air-like, made of the element air 87/6

afalle *v. pa. p.* fallen, dropped 1030/14

afered *v. pa. p.* afraid 83/33

aferre *adv.* far, far off 183/22

affeccioun, effeccioun *sb.* emotional or volitional faculty of the soul, emotion, feeling, love, one of the four Stoic 'affects' 57/27

affect *sb.* capacity for feeling emotion or desire, the will, emotion, feeling, desire 61/6

affect(-), see **effect(-)**

affinite, afynyte *sb.* kinship, association, connection 408/24

†**afforsinge, afoorsinge** *sb.* exertion, endeavour 65/8

affraye *v.* (**afraied** *pa. p., a.*) to frighten 83/33

afire, afu(y)re, ofire *adv.* on fire 141/25

afyve *adv.* in five parts 783/18

†**afoystid, afuysted** *v. pa. p., a.* infected, stale, musty 101/37 [obscure; cf. OF. *fust* 'cask'?]

afore, aforne, aforen, afoure *adv. prep.* before, in front (of) 109/31

aforehonde *adv.* before, formerly, earlier 209/10

†**aforsyd** *v. pa. p.* seasoned 1321/22 [cf. OF. *farsir*]

afray *sb.* fear 392/9 [OF. *effrei*]

aftir *a.* second, later 82/6

aftir *prep.* after, following 79/22

†**aftirschipe** *sb.* stern 173/20

afuyre, see **afire; afuysted,** see **afoysted; age,** see **ache; agewe,** see **agu**

agiltiþ *v. pres. 3sg.* (**agilte** *pa.* once) offends, wrongs 310/33

ago *v. pa. p.* past, gone 528/6

agreue(d) *v. pa. p.* troubled, injured 118/17

agrise *v. pa. p.* frightened 431/3 [OE. *āgrīsan,* strong 1]

agu, agewe, agw(e), acu, acute *sb., a.* acute fever, a fever characterized by periodic eruptions, a disease accompanied by such a fever 194/16

†**aȝeinturnynge** *sb.* return, turning back 332/33

aȝen, aȝenne, aȝein, aȝe(e) *adv.* opposite, back, again 55/35

†**aȝencomynge** *sb.* return 308/36

aȝens, aȝenes, aȝenst *adv. prep.* opposite, towards 46/23

aȝensmytynge *sb.* bending (of a beam) backward, reverberation or reflection, a double image 183/13

aȝenward *adv.* on the contrary 51/7

†**ahiȝtiþ** *v. pres. 3sg.* adorns 196/9 [OE. *ā-* + obscure; cf. OE. *hyht* 'hope, joy']

ayery, eyry *a.* airlike, composed of the element air, having the nature of air 235/28

ayren, see **ey**

aisshe *sb.* the ash tree 951/25

aisshen, see **asschen**

aisshene *a.* from the ash tree 951/37

aiþir, aieþir, see **eiþir; ake,** see **ache**

akelid *v. pa. p.* cooled, chilled 618/26 [OE. *ācēlan*]

alayeþ *v. pres. 3sg.* allays 843/18

alblastes, alblastres *sb. pl.* crossbows, arbelasts 1125/16

alday *adv.* everyday, always 65/18

†**aleye, alie** *adv.* on fire 570/5 [OE. *on līġe*; cf. **leye**]

aliche *a.* like 272/7

alicioune *sb.* kingfisher 1340/23

aliene *a. sb.* foreign(er), remote from, free from 64/34

aliȝte *v. pa. p.* descended 643/20

alym, alime, alum *sb.* alum, potash 836/24

alkonemye *sb.* alchemy 1154/23 [ML. *alconomia*]

†**allectorie** *sb.* a precious stone found in a capon's gizzard 836/12

allegged *v. pa. p.* cited in support of an idea 1396/14

alles *sb. pl.* spines, prickles 274/5 [OE. *eġl, eġle* 'awn, (barley-)beard, claw'; cf. **eyle**]

alloren, see **elleren; alloweþ,** see **aloweþ**

almerye *sb.* storing-place, the stomach 1261/10

almounde, alma(u)nd, amounde *sb.* the almond tree or its nuts 367/22

aloe, aloes *sb.* the aloe tree, its juice, the herb aloes 118/16

alon *a.* alone, solitary, unique 44/15

alonde *adv.* on land, ashore 787/12

alonly(che) *adv.* merely, exclusively 116/28

aloweþ, alloweþ *v. pres. 3sg.* commends 316/25

als *adv.* also 115/18

als(e) *conj.* as 130/4

alteratifes *a., sb. pl.* (medicines) causing or aiding changes in bodily quality 367/9

alum, see **alym**

alwey *adv.* always 62/16

amende *v.* to improve 101/24

amendement *sb.* improvement 567/11

amenyte *sb.* pleasantness 654/32

amys *adv.* wrongly 832/5

among *adv.* here and there 220/27

†**amongwhiles** *adv.* at intervals 340/23

amorwe *adv.* in the morning 61/24

amounde, see **almounde**

ampte, empte *sb.* ant 354/10

an, and(e), ant, a *conj.* and, if 40/9

anete, annete *sb.* dill 960/26

anfelde *sb.* anvil 828/32

angiltwaches *sb. pl.* earthworms, angleworms 1265/8 [OE. *angeltwicce*]

angle, angule *sb.* angle, figure formed by two lines which meet, one of the sectors of the zodiac (see next) 463/23

anguler *a.* pertaining to an angle; *housis anguler,* the four sectors of the zodiac located at the cardinal points of the compass and believed to be locations of greatest planetary influence 463/23

angwissche, angwisse, anguysse *sb.* anxiety, pain 216/14

anhangid *v. pa. p.* hanged 107/6

anhongred *v. pa. p., a.* starved 304/27–8

any, see **eny**

animat *a.* living, pertaining to the activities of the animal spirit or virtue (motion and sensation) 335/15

anyntised *v. pa. p.* enfeebled, destroyed 189/20 [OF. *anientiss*-, stem of *anientir*]

anneys, anise *sb.* anice 367/33

annete, see **anete**

anoynte *v.* (**anoynt** *pa. p.*) to anoint 56/25

anoyntinge *sb.* smearing with a liquid 58/2

anon, anoun *adv.* at once; *anon as,* as soon as 94/21

anon to *prep. conj.* so far as, as long as, until, up to 86/6

anothir, anouþer *pron.* another, the second 45/4

apayed *v. pa. p.* satisfied 316/18

apassid *v. pa. p.* past, passed away 582/10

apeire *v.,* **apeiringe** *sb.* to damage, injure, grow worse 101/26 (*v.*), 72/20 (*sb.*)

appetite *sb.* natural urge (of an organism or material); *vertu of appetite,* the urge inherent in organs which draws proper nutriment, one of the Galenic faculties 97/9

appil *sb.* the apple-tree, any variety of fruit; *applis of cedre,* citrons; *pyne-apple,* pinecone; *pyn-appil tree,* pine; *apples of palmes,* palm hearts 300/26

applicacioun *sb.* material contact, an influence resulting from such contact 336/25

ap(p)lieþ *v. pres. 3sg.* attaches, fits closely 212/1

apposicioun, see **opposicioun**

apprehencioun *sb.* perception, learning 183/4

apprehendiþ *v. pres. 3sg.*, **apprehen-dinge** *sb.* learns, comprehends 59/28 (*v.*), 98/8–9 (*sb.*)

apprehensiue *a.* capable of perceiving or comprehending 96/4

appreued *v. pa. p.* tested 1375/2

ap(p)roprid, aproprete *v. pa. p.* acquired possession of, devoted to; *ben approprid* (*to*), to be an attribute of, be characterized by, be proper to 53/28

apropriacioun *sb.* annexation, application (of a word) 1051/29

apt *a.* suitable 117/22

aquikeþ *v. pres. 3sg.* revives, recovers 636/28 [OE. *ācwician*]

ar, see **ere**

aray *sb.* order, condition, equipment 65/28

araye *v.* to arrange, equip 65/16

arayne *sb.* spider 1321/3 [OF. *araigne*]

arayseþ, see **areseþ**

archier, archere *sb.* archer 471/18

areche *v.* to reach, be able 199/18

areyned *v. pa. p.* rebuked, examined, charged 314/2

arere, arrere *v.* to lift, raise 76/30

areringe *sb.* raising, swelling, the astrological ascendant 233/3

areseþ, ariseþ, arayseþ *v. pres. 3sg.* falls upon, rushes upon, attacks 111/2 [OE. *ārǣsan*]

aright *adv.* in a proper manner, in a straight line 626/20

†aripe *v.* to bring (an abscess) to maturity, to cause to come to a head 988/29

arise *v.* (**aros, aroos** *pa.*; **arise** *pa. p.*) to arise (in its various senses) 392/7

ariseþ, see **areseþ**

armonye, armenye *sb.* singing, music-making, concord, orderly arrangement of parts 93/22

arowe, arewe, areu, on rowe *adv.* in order 121/15

arowe, arwe, arewe *sb.* arrow 471/18

arsmetrik *sb.* the science of measurement and calculation 1354/10

arst, see **ere**

arterie, artarie *sb.* blood vessel (esp. of the Galenic arterial system), tube for bearing liquid or air, the windpipe 122/9

article *sb.* a particular item or event, a moment, a critical moment 88/29

artificial *a.* man-made; *artificial day*, the day as it appears to man, daylight 520/3

arwe, see **arowe**

ascape *v.* to escape, avoid 489/8

ascendent *sb.* the degree of the ecliptic rising above the horizon at any given moment 464/31

†aschame *sb.* in *adv. phrase for aschame*, on account of shame or embarrassment 630/33

†aschildewise *adv.* in a form describing a triangular (shield-shaped) solid, in the form of a pyramid or cone 110/24

†y-ased *v. pa. p.* baited (of a fishhook) 1265/10 [cf. OE. *ǣs* 'carrion' and Middle Dutch *asen* 'to bait']

†asidehalf *adv.* on one side, aside, alongside 237/20

†asidewarde *adv.* sideways, horizontally 142/36

†askabbe *a.* crusted over 424/26

askes, see **asschen**

askeþ, axiþ *v. pres. pl.*, **axinge** *sb.* ask, demand 75/9 (*v.*), 1204/38 (*sb.*)

aslonte, aslynte, aslunt *adv.* at an angle, in a curve, from the side, deviously 449/37

asmyes *sb. pl.* diseases in which difficulty of breathing forms an outstanding symptom 374/16

aspe *sb.* the aspen tree 1054/30

aspect *sb.* the relative position of one planet to another, the effect of such a position, heavenly influence on worldly affairs, faculty of perception, gaze, consideration 95/26

aspergy *sb.* asparagus 433/26

aspye *sb.* scouting, spying 712/21

aspye, espie(n) *v.*, **aspiynge** *sb.* to observe stealthily, discover 87/25 (*v.*), 703/14 (*sb.*)

aspiracioun *sb.* the continuous breathing which changes a stop to a spirant, the orthographic *h* written after a stop to indicate this spirantic quality 1065/33

aspyreþ *v. pres. pl.* seek to reach, approach 66/15

assay *sb.* testing, evidence 86/2

assaye *v.*, **assaynge** *sb.* to test, ascertain, attempt 43/7 (*v.*), 945/31 (*sb.*)

assaiers *sb. pl.* experimentalists, investigators 252/7

assayle *v.*, **assailinge** *sb.* to attack, assault, harass, afflict 78/14 (*v.*), 84/19 (*sb.*)

asschen, aisshen, askes, axen, exen *sb. pl.* ashes 133/6

assent *sb.* agreement, consent, sentiment 67/2

assigneþ *v. pres. 3sg.* assigns, designs 145/28

assimilatiue *a.* having the power to convert nutrients into organic materials 97/18

asta(a)te *sb.* state 77/16

asterte *v.* to escape 326/30

astint *v. pa. p.* stopped, brought to an end 356/9

astonyed *v. pa. p., a.* stupified, perplexed 113/17

astreiʒt *v. pa. p.* stretched out 502/9

†atast *sb.* taste 149/20

atentiþ *v. pres. 3sg.* starts to burn 905/8 [OE. *ǎténdan*]

aþre *adv.* in three parts 98/27

aþurst, aþriste *a.* thirsty 244/30

atones, see **o**

†atopwise *adv.* in a form which describes a triangular (top-shaped) solid, in the form of a pyramid or cone 110/11

atrament *sb.* a black colouring material made of soot, used in producing ink and dark pigments 1295/17 [L. *ātrāmentum*]

atte, at *prep.* at (the); *at al(le)*, in all ways, in all respects; *atte beste*, in the best way, most effectively; *atte fulle*, completely 46/34

atthomus, attomos *sb.* the smallest indivisible part of a thing; esp. the smallest unit of time (1/2256oth of an hour) 93/26

attircoppe, attrecop *sb.* spider 92/2 [*ǎtor-coppe*]

attractiue *a.* drawing, having power to draw in nutriment 138/5

atweye, atweyne *adv.* in two 98/16

atwynes *adv.* in pairs 1175/36

atwynne *adv.* in two 49/1

atwynneþ *v. pres. 3sg.* leaves 1113/35

atwo *adv.* in two 726/14

†aucipiters *sb. pl.* hawks 608/27 [ML. *aucipiter*, var. of L. *accipiter*]

auctour, autour *sb.* authority, writer 110/7

auguyres *sb. pl.* divinations 777/29

auripigment *sb.* a bright yellow salt of arsenic 830/12

autentik *a.* reliable 43/5

auter *sb.* (**autiers** *pl.* once) an altar 245/27

avaunsinge *v. pres. p.* advancing, enhancing 53/14

avauntage *sb.* advantage 1070/1

auellane *sb. a.* hazelnut 432/32

auence *sb.* an herb 845/29

auenture *v.* to venture, hazard 40/18

auyse *v.* to consider, ponder; *auyse him*, reflect on, notice 200/31

auysement *sb.* consideration, thought 60/9

avoydaunce *sb.* voiding, expulsion 438/31

avoyded *v. pa. p.* expelled, voided 393/28

awaite *sb.* ambush, watchfulness 210/9

awayte *v.* to lie in wait (for), watch (for) 722/27

awakeþ *v. pres. 3sg.* (**awook** *pa.*; **awaked** *pa. p.*) awakens, wakes up 127/36

aweyward *adv.* to the side 1129/36

awelde *v.* to control, govern 437/3

aworke *adv.* to work 93/24

awreke *v.* to avenge 1170/4

ax-, see **ask-, assch-**

axesse, accesse, axes *sb.* onset of a disease, fit or attack, return of a periodic fever, such a periodic fever 354/32 [OF. *aces*]

axstre, see **extre**

azure *sb.* lapis lazuli 1292/24

bacbitinge *sb.* slander 473/1

bacyn, basyne *sb.* flat dish or pan, gong 364/24

bayes *sb. pl.* the berries of the laurel tree (or of *mirtus*), used in medicinal recipes (incl. *oile de baye*) 941/20

ibake *v. pa. p.* baked, roasted 419/21

balaunce *sb.* scale, scales of justice 68/9

baleyne, balene *sb.* whale 685/32

balyis, see **belies**

balkes *sb. pl.* beams 1057/6 [OE. *balca* 'ridge'; senses infl. by cognate ON. *balkr*]

ballockes *sb. pl.* testicles 261/13

bameþ, bamynge, see **bawmeþ**
bane *sb.* destroyer, poison 323/34
banyour *sb.* standard-bearer 1125/30
bar *sb.* pole, bolt 87/1
barayne, bareyne *a.* sterile 532/33
barai(n)nes(se) *sb.* sterility 478/22
bareliche, see **barlich; bark(-),** see **berkeþ**
barlich, bareliche, barly *sb.* barley, the grain or the plant 972/21
barnacle, bernacle *sb.* bit for a horse 1124/22 [OF. *bernicle*]
barnische *v.* to grow, become large or strong 292/4
barwes *sb. pl.* domesticated boars, esp. gelds 1237/19
basis *sb.* the base of a geometrical figure 1371/21
basnettis *sb. pl.* small cap-shaped helmets, worn usually under visored warhelmets 945/21 [OF. *bacinet*]
bastarde *sb.* a mongrel, a wild shoot; *a.* mixed, hybrid, wild 1070/17
bataylynge *sb.* a notched design, indentation, an ornamental dovetailing of boards to make a larger flat wood surface 1056/33
batail(l)e, batel *sb.* battle (incl. spiritual struggle) 65/22
bateþ *v. pres. 3sg.* abates 670/3
baþinges *sb. pl.* baths (prescribed as medical cures) 402/7
ybatred *v. pa. p., a.* constricted 738/22
bausines *sb. pl.* badgers 262/12 [OF. *baussan*]
bawdeþ *v. pres. 3sg.* dirties 1237/13
bawme *sb.* balm 713/1
bawmeþ, bameþ *v. pres. 3sg.,* **bawmynge, bamynge** *sb.* treats with a lotion or ointment, smears 305/5 (*v.*), 347/33 (*sb.*)
be-, see also **bi-; be,** see **buth; beckes,** see **bekkes**
beclippe, biclippe *v.,* **biclippinge** *sb.* to surround, enclose 48/32 (*v.*), 298/12 (*sb.*)
becloþid *v. pa. p., a.* covered (as with clothes), having the form or appearance of 443/25
become, bycome *v.* (**bicam** *pa.*; **bycom(e)** *pa. p.*) to become, attain (a state) 85/1
bedes *sb. pl.* prayers 67/11

bee *sb.* (**been, bees, beon** *pl.*) bee 271/2
behotiþ *v. pres. 3sg.* (**behote** *pa. p.*) promises, pledges 87/31 [OE. *behātan,* strong 7]
behuydeþ *v. pres. pl.* conceal, shelter 1215/27
bekkes, beckes *sb. pl.* signals 598/13
bekkyng *sb.* signalling 1208/10
belde, bilde *v.* (**ybelde, ybeldyde, beelde, bildid, ybilt, (i)bulde(de)** *pa. and pa. p.*), **beldyngges** *sb. pl.* to dwell, live, construct 297/16 (*v.*), 759/5 (*sb.*)
belies, balyis *sb. pl.* bellows 105/5
bellican, pellican *sb.* pelican 223/27
beme *sb.* light ray, gleam 41/13
bemy, beme *a.* bright, radiant 451/7
bemynge *sb.* emission of light, shining 508/27
bende *sb.* band, bond 165/28
bende, biende, binde- *v.* (**ibende** *pa. p.*), **bendinge, benthinge** *sb.* to bend, be flexible 85/15 (*v.*), 267/8 (*sb.*)
benefice, benefys *sb.* favor, kindness; useful action, property, or state 121/21
benygne *a.* gracious 740/2
beraft *v. pa. p.* deprived 242/15
bere *sb.* barley 1008/28
bere *v.* (**bare, bere** *pa.*; **ibore** *pa. p.*) to bear, carry, beget, be born 51/2
berere, beryere *sb.* one who bears 220/8
berkeþ, barkeþ *v. pres. pl.* (**barke** *pa.*), **berkinge, barkinge** *sb.* bark like a dog 430/24 (*v.*), 167/21 (*sb.*)
berne *sb.* barn 67/19
berþene, see **burþon**
besi, busy *a.* busy 71/31
besynes, busines *sb.* activity, task 55/29
besomes *sb. pl.* brooms 1055/1
bestissche *a.* bestial 90/15–16
bete, beete *sb.* a beet 889/20
ibete, beteþ, see **betiþ, bite; beþ,** see **betiþ, buth**
beþenke *v.* (**byþought** *pa. p.*) to consider, ponder 63/21
betiþ *v. pres. 3sg.*[1] (**beþ** *pres. pl.*) once; **bete** *pa.*; **ibete** *pa. p.*) beats 120/14
betiþ *v. pres. 3sg.*[2] assuages 578/29
betokeneth *v. pres. pl.* signify 48/4
†**beueringe** *sb.* trembling, shivering 385/25 [from OE. *bifian* 'tremble, shake']
bewake *v. pres. subj.* awaken 1143/3
bi-, see also **be-; bi, by,** see **buth**
bide *v. pres. pl.* remain, live 573/28

bidewed(e) *v. pa. p.* moistened with dew 695/17

byes *sb. pl.* rings, esp. large bracelets or collars 1177/16 [OE. *bēaʒ*]

bygge *v.* (**byeþ** *pres. 3sg.*; **biggeþ** *pres. pl.*; **(i)bouʒt(e)** *pa.* and *pa. p.*) to buy, purchase 93/11

biggers, bigers *sb. pl.* buyers 547/24

bigrowe *v. pa. p.* grown over 781/11

biheste, beheste *sb.* promise; *þe lond of byheste*, the Promised Land 310/29

†bihiʒte *v. pa. p.* adorned, honoured 748/23 [OE. *be-* + obscure; cf. **hiʒt**]

byhindeforþ *adv.* from behind forward 219/1

biholde *v.* to look at, gaze on, observe, look after 66/22

†bykitte *v. pa. p.* pruned 1072/27

ibyknowe *v. pa. p.* recognized 1364/21

bilad *v. pa. p.* handled, treated, dealt with 313/27

byles *sb. pl.* boils 853/25

†bileþ *v. pres. 3sg.* pecks, jabs 639/20

biliþ, see **boile**

bille *sb.* a pruning hook, a pick, or hoe 1047/34

bilt, see **belde**; **bimynges**, see **biumynge**

bynde *v.* (**bynt** *pres. 3sg.* occ.; **ibounde** *pa. p.*) to bind 181/22

byndinge *sb.* binding, pressure, ligament, freezing 166/12

bindiþ, see **bende**; **byneme**, see **bynyme**

byneþeforþ *adv.* from the lower part 396/7

bynyme, byneme *v.* (**bynome** *pa. p.*) to take away, deprive of sensation, paralyse 106/2 [OE. *beniman*, strong 4]

byreyned *v. pa. p.* rained on 695/17

birþe, see **burþe**; **birþon**, see **burþon**

bischadewe *v. pres. pl.* shadow 187/33

byschedinge *v. pres. p.* moistening, drenching 439/27

byschine, beschyne *v.* (**bischine, byshene, bys(c)hynede** *pa. p.*), **bischinynge** *sb.* to shine upon, enlighten 44/8 (*v.*), 68/29 (*sb.*)

†byschrudde *v. pa. p.* trimmed, pruned 1072/27 [OE. *be-* + *scrȳdan*; cf. **schrudde**]

bisekeþ *v. pres. 3sg.* looks for, searches for 87/25

bysemeþ *v. pres. 3sg.* befits 302/1

bisette *v.* to surround 500/3

bisext *sb.* the extra day in a leap year, formed by grouping the extra six hours of the three previous and the current year 520/18

bysmere *sb.* scorn, contempt 699/3 [OE. *bismer*]

bysmokeþ *v. pres. 3sg.* fills with smoke (as part of a medical treatment), fumigates 1111/18

bysountes *sb. pl.* bisons, wisents 776/15

bispringe *v.* (**byspronge** *pa. p.*), **byspringynge** *sb.* to sprinkle 531/18 (*v.*) 580/4 (*sb.*)

bitakeþ *v. pres. pl.* (**bitake** *pa. p.*) give up, entrust, assign 84/28

bitauʒt *v. pa. p.* given up 174/11

bite *v.* (**bet-** occ. *pres.*; **bote** *pa.*; **ybyte, ibete** *pa. p.*), **bitinge** *sb.* to bite 257/8 (*v.*), 106/22 (*sb.*)

bytyme *adv.* soon 1320/35

bytrauayleþ *v. pres. 3sg.* works to produce 1206/20

bytrendeþ *v. pres. 3sg.* surrounds 689/32 [OE. *betréndan* 'to roll']

bytwene(ne) *prep.* between 60/28

biumynge *sb.* (**bimynges** *pl.* once) trumpetings 1143/3 [from OE. *bȳmian*]

bywycched *v. pa. p.* enchanted 778/9

bladder, bladdre, bleddir, bleddre *sb.* bag in an animal's body (esp. the urinary bladder), blister, boil, pustule 224/14

blakeþ *v. pres. 3sg.* makes black 1293/4

blamere *sb.* accuser 86/29

blames *sb. pl.* censures 86/30

†blasenes *sb.* brilliance 1290/27

blast, blest- *sb.* gust, (puff of) breath, spirit, (breath of) flame 105/12

blaunche *v.* to blanch 1000/19

ybleight *v. pa. p.* bleached 988/6 [OE. *blǣcan*, pa.p. *blǣht*]

bleynes, blaynes *sb. pl.* sores, blisters, pustules, boils 201/34

blemscheþ *v. pres. 3sg.* (**yblemysshed** *pa. p.*) impairs 263/27

blenchith, blenschiþ *v. pres. 3sg.*, **blenchinge** *sb.* moves, turns aside 109/19 (*v.*), 66/23 (*sb.*) [cf. OE. *blencan* 'deceive' and ON. *blekkja*, earlier *blenkja* 'delude']

blendeþ *v. pres. 3sg.* (**yblende** *pa. p.*) blinds 862/5 [OE. *bléndan*]

†blensith *v. pres. 3sg.* conceals, disguises 438/5

blered *pa. p., a.* bleary 343/35

blerey3ed *a.* bleary-eyed 361/15

blernes, blereynes, blerey3ens *sb.* blurring of vision, an eye disease 329/8

blestes, see **blast**; **blew**, see **blowiþ**

blewe, bluwe, blu(e), blw(e) *sb.* blue 581/10

blewissh *a.* bluish 1191/16

blynde *a.* blind, dim, dark; (of sound) dull 271/6

blisse, blesse *v.*, **blissynge** *sb.* to bless (*pa. p., a.* fortunate) 41/29 (*v.*), 703/8 (*sb.*)

blomen *sb. pl.* Ethiopians 127/18 [ON. *blár* + OE. *mann*]

blones *sb.* lividness 199/28

bloo *a.* dark, livid 157/9

bloodlese *sb.* blood-letting 360/32 [OE. *blōd-lǣs(wu)*]

blos(s)om(e), blosme *sb.* flower, blossom 141/11

bloumeþ *v. pres. 3sg.* blooms 931/26

yblowe, blowyng, see **blowiþ, blowwe**

blower *sb.* blowing device, bellows 235/23

blowiþ *v. pres. 3sg.* (**iblowe, blowen, blew** *pa. p.*), **blowinge** *sb.* blows, breathes, smelts or founds, inflates 236/15 (*v.*), 404/24 (*sb.*)

blowwe, blouwe- *v.* (**yblowe** *pa. p.*), **blowyng** *sb.* to blossom, flower 900/12 (*v.*), 987/27 (*sb.*)

†bobelynge *sb.* rumble 594/11

bocc(h)e *sb.* boil, ulcer, sore 142/18

bocchinge *sb.* formation of ulcers or boils 376/5

bode *v. pres. pl.* (**bode** *pa.* once), **bodinge** *sb.* indicate 183/1 (*v.*), 337/10 (*sb.*)

†bodines *sb.* form as a body or corporate entity, distinct substance 507/29

boffinge, see **buffeþ**

boile *v.* (**biliþ** *pres. 3sg.* once), **bo(y)lynge** *sb.* to boil 71/21 (*v.*), 121/32 (*sb.*)

boysters, see **bosters**

boistous *a.* crude, rude 108/8

boistousnes *sb.* earthy nature, coarseness 325/16

bokeler *sb.* small round shield 260/4

boldes *sb. pl.* buildings 759/11 [OE. *bóld*]

bole *sb.* bull 212/21

bolericchesses *sb. pl.* bulrushes 754/34

bolysme *sb.* insatiable or perpetual hunger 1169/3 [L. *bolismus*]

bolkinge *sb.* belching, belch 205/5

bolle, bulle *sb.* bowl, bubble, ball 404/12

bollers *sb. pl.* drunkards 410/9

bollinge, bolnynge, boylynge *v. pres. p. sb.* swelling, protruding 390/3

bomme *sb.* anus 401/10

bonch-, see **bunch-**

bonche *sb.* (**bunchis** *pl.* once) swelling, hump 412/23

bonchy *a.* swollen, humped 424/26

bonde *a. sb.* a tenant or serf 305/19

bonde, see **bound, bounde**

bone *sb.* request 55/5

boos *sb.* boss 260/3

bo(o)te *sb.* boat 491/20

borage *sb.* the herb borage 829/13

borg-, see **buriowneþ**; **borgiþ, borgynge**, see **burgen**

borieth *v. pres. 3sg.* bores, pierces 832/37

bost *sb.* boasting 86/12

bosters, boysters *sb. pl.*[1] boasters 695/2

†bosters *sb. pl.*[2] men coarse or heavy 116/12

bote, see **bite, boote**

botel *sb.* flask 379/20

boteler *sb.* servant in charge of drinks 472/20

†botractes *sb. pl.* venomous frogs 1092/34 [ML. *botrax*]

bouchere *sb.* butcher 1213/35

boue, see **bowe**

bougyng *sb.* swelling, protuberance 248/25

** youkid** *v. pa. p.* bucked, cleansed and bleached by soaking in lye 988/7

bound, bonde *sb.* boundary marker, limit 53/7

bounde, bonde *sb.* material for tying, dominating or uniting force 101/16

bourde *sb.* board, table 308/31

bourg-, see **buriowneþ**; **bourgiþ, bourgynge**, see **burgen**

bow(e), bou3, boue, bowgh, bowh *sb.* bough, any branching anatomical structure (esp. dividing nerves and veins) 98/19

boweþ *v. pres. pl.* bend, curve 55/5

bowges *sb. pl.* swellings, humps 248/19

†**bowinges** *sb. pl.* boughs, branches 97/13
bowrys *sb. pl.* towns, houses 691/36 [OE. *būr*; sense perhaps infl. by blending with OE. *burʒ*, or perhaps scribal for *borwys*]
ibrad, see **brede**
bragge *sb.* arrogance 86/12
ybrayed, breyed *v. pa. p.* pressed, pushed 988/5
brayn(e) *sb.* brain, marrow 98/15
brake *v.,* **brakynge** *sb.* to vomit 1130/26 (*v.*), 997/10 (*sb.*)
brakynges *sb. pl.* crushings and poundings of flax to prepare fibre for thread 1055/24
bran(ne) *sb.* the husk of wheat 142/29
brasen(e) *a.* made of brass or a similar metal 638/8
braunchis *sb. pl.* branches, any branching parts (esp. breathing tubes or gills of fish) 236/17
brawn(e), brawen *sb.* muscle tissue, the fleshy or muscular part of a member, a muscular string or fibre, nerve or sinew 99/35
breche *sb.* breach, fracture, injury 411/21
bredcorn *sb.* grain for making bread 954/20
brede *v.* (**ibred, ibrad** *pa. p.*) to breed 145/13 [OE. *brēdan,* pa. *brēdde*; *a*-forms from analogy with *sprad* and *schad*, with etymological *a* from OE. *ǣ*]
breder, see **brother**
breede, brede *sb.* width, breadth, area; *on brede,* crosswise, across 91/33
breideþ *v. pres. pl.* move suddenly, resist 162/8
breyed, see **ybrayed**
breke *v.* (**breyk-** common *pres.*; **brak** *pa.*; **ibroke** *pa. p.*) to break, fall, ebb 109/23
bremmes, see **brymme; bremstone,** see **brimstone**
brend(e), brande *pa. p. a.* burned, baked 153/28
brenne *v.* (**brent** *pa.*; **brende, ibrent** *pa. p.*), **brennynge** *sb.* to burn 66/6 (*v.*), 68/10 (*sb.*)
brennynge *pres. p., a.* burning 64/13
brerd, brere *sb.* (**breerdes** *pl.* once) edge 198/32 [OE. *brērd*]
bresynge, see **bruse**
brestepitte *sb.* bottom of the breast, the stomach 920/7

brestplate *sb.* breastplate, the sternum or front of the chest 106/18
breth *sb.* breathing, smell 94/18
briddes *sb. pl.* birds, newly-born brood of any animal 612/24
brigges *sb. pl.* strifes 861/22 [OF. *brigue*]
brigges, see **brugges**
briggeþ *v. pres. pl.* break 1195/11 [app. OE. *brecan,* strong 4; cf. *bricð* pres. 3sg.]
brymme *sb.* (**bremmis** *pl.* once) seashore, river bank 137/19
brim-, brem-ston *sb.* sulphur 132/8
brynstonynesse *sb.* a sulphurish state (characteristic of over-dried humours) 381/24
bristle, see **brustle**
brok(k)e, brocke *sb.* badger 262/12
brome *sb.* the plant broom 721/24
brood, brode *sb.* offspring, the young of animals, unborn young; *on brode,* see **abrood** 167/8
bro(o)de *a.* (**braddere** *comp.*) broad 110/1
brose, see **bruse**
broþ *sb.* broth 285/4
brother *sb.* (**breder, breþiren** *pl.*) brother 467/30
brotil, brutil *a.* fragile, brittle (both physically and morally) 281/24
broun, brown *a.* dark, brown 136/21
brugges, brigges *sb. pl.* bridges 864/13
bruse, brose *v.,* **brusinge, bresynge** *sb.* to shatter, crush 198/1 (*v.*), 204/31 (*sb.*)
brustle, brustel, bristle *sb.* bristle 624/30
buffeþ *v. pres. 3sg.,* **boffinge** *sb.* stammers, stutters 207/26 (*v.*), 71/3 (*sb.*) [OF. *bofer, bufer*]
bugle *sb.* buffalo, wild ox, aurochs 218/5
bulde, see **belde; bulle,** see **bolle**
bulted *v. pa. p.* sifted, winnowed 957/30 [OF. *buleter*]
bunchynge *pres. p., a. sb.* bulging, swollen (place) 219/2
bunchis, see **bonch**
bundelles *sb. pl.* piles, bales, rafts 663/28
†**burd** *sb.* (**burdones** *sb. pl.*) mule 1122/22 [L. *burdo*]
burgen (borg-, bourg-) *v.,* **burgynge, bourgynge, borgynge** *sb.* to grow, sprout 264/8 (*v.*), 892/23 (*sb.*)
burgeon-, burgon-, see **buriowneþ; burghtownes,** see **burouʒtounes**

buriel(e)s, buriel *sb.* tomb 468/18
buriouns, burgones *sb. pl.* sprouts, shoots, vegetable growth, swellings 136/8
buriowneþ, bo(u)rgoneþ *v. pres. pl.*, **burg(e)onyng, borg(e)onyng, burionynge** *sb.* grow, bud 504/14 (*v.*), 526/18 (*sb.*)
burouȝ-, burgh-tounes *sb. pl.* towns 743/13
burþe, birþe *sb.* birth 46/9
burþon, birþon, berþene *sb.* weight, bearing of a child, giving birth 214/12
burtilnes *sb.* weakness 672/8
busshe *v.*, **busschinge** *sb.* to push, attack 178/4 (*v.*), 415/12 (*sb.*)
but (if) *conj.* unless, except 41/19
buth, beþ, ben *v. pres. pl.* (be, by, bi *v.*; **is** *pres. 3sg.*; **was, were(n)** *pa.*; **ibe** *pa. p.*), **beynge** *sb.* be 40/4 (*v.*), 42/7 (*sb.*)

caase *sb.* box, container 165/1
calament(e), calamynte *sb.* an aromatic herb 367/33
calculynge *sb.* computation, counting 483/16
call(e) *sb.* net, membrane; *wondir calle*, the 'rete mirabilis', a confluence of blood vessels between the menenges 167/2
calstok, see **caulstok**
calue *v.*, **caluynge** *sb.* to calve 942/35 (*v.*), 1176/4 (*sb.*)
camayle, see **camelle**
camamille *sb.* camomile 356/11
cambmok *sb.* the cammock, a thorny shrub 1034/31
camelion, cameleon *sb.* chameleon, giraffe 754/13 [L. *chamaeleon* for first sense; ML. *cameleo* for second]
camel(le), camayle, cameyle *sb.* camel 218/9
campernole *sb.* small bell 1393/7
camphora *sb.* camphor 877/10
cancre (k-) *sb.* spreading sore, cancer 116/15
ycancred *v. pa. p.* become cancerous 1164/14
cancry *a.* cancerous 417/22
candele *sb.* candle, wick 1377/30
cane, canne *sb.* a cane-like plant, a reed 619/10

canel(e) *sb.* cinnamon, the tree from whose bark cinnamon is made 700/27
caniculer *a.* pertaining to Sirius (the Dog Star); *caniculer dayes*, dogdays, late summer 506/20
capitoile *sb.* citadel 802/3
†**capriole** *sb.* wild goat 1162/18 [ML. *capreola*]
carbuncle, see **char-**
cardiac *a.* pertaining to the heart; *cardiac passioun*, palpitation of the heart 930/10
cardiacle, cardeakle *a., sb.* (pertaining to) palpitation of the heart, (characterized by) heartburn; *cardiacle passioun*, a disease associated with these symptoms 241/7
cardinal *a.* chief, principal (of the four signs of the zodiac at the solstices and equinoxes, of the winds which blow from the four primary points of the compass) 461/1
carduis *sb.* (**carduies** *pl.*) thistle 931/32 [L. *carduus*]
careyne, carrayne, carien- *sb.* corpse 116/33
ycarfled *v. pa. p.* carded 988/5 [? cf. ON. *krafla* 'to paw']
cariage *sb.* means of transport, vehicle, burden 123/6
carien-, see **careyne**
caroles *sb. pl.* round-dances, songs accompanying such dances, songs 300/23
cas (cause once**)** *sb.* event, chance; (*vp*)*on cas*, perhaps 41/7
caste *v.*, **castyng** *sb.* to throw, throw off, intend, think 262/4 (*v.*), 850/7 (*sb.*)
casteyn(e), see **chesteynes**
castelles *sb. pl.* camp (*pl.* to translate L. *castra*), strongholds 709/26
castis *sb. pl.* throws, stratagems, forms 89/27
castor *sb.* the beaver, the drug castor prepared from the glands of the beaver 262/12
casualle, causalle *a.* accidental 142/9
catel(le), catalle *sb.* possessions 101/18
caudroun *sb.* cauldron 929/6
caule *sb.* kale 433/24
cauleworte *sb.* cabbage 1008/6–7
caulstok, calstok *sb.* cabbage-stalk 895/28
cause *sb.* cause, one of the Aristotelian

four causes, affair, side in a controversy, legal action, case of illness 41/28

cautel *sb.* caution, precaution 388/6

†cecerys *sb. pl.* chick-peas 973/2 [L. *cicer*]; see also **chicchis**

celar, celer *sb.* storeroom, cellar 256/4

celydoyne, celidony *sb.* the celandine, swallow-wort 644/7

celle, selle *sb.* cell 98/28

cene, sene *sb.* the Last Supper; *Cene þursday* (*þors-*), Maundy Thursday 543/32 [OF. *cene*]

†cense *v.* to excite 298/32

cense, see **sense**

centuries, centories *sb. pl.* a Roman political division; a Roman measure of land 531/35

centuriones *sb. pl.* commanders 318/18–9

cercle, cerclye *sb.* a circle; *cercle of þe yer*, the passage of a year's time 83/22

cerclewise *adv.* in the shape of a circle or a part of its arc 580/31

cered *v. pa. p.* waxed 1323/26 [L. *cērātus*, *pa. p.* of *cērāre* 'to suffuse with wax']

certeyne, serteyn *a., sb.* definite; *in certeyne*, truly, surely 186/34

certifieþ *v. pres. 3sg.* affirms 257/20

ceruse *sb.* 'flower of lead', a compound of white lead used in drugs and ointments, a pigment made of white lead or tin 1121/22

ces(s)eþ, sesiþ *v. pres. 3sg.*, **cessinge** *sb.* stops 71/18 (*v.*), 61/15 (*sb.*)

chace *v.* to drive from a place 1171/5

ichad, see **schede**

chaffar *v. imp.*, **chaffaringe** *sb.* buy and sell 315/13 (*v.*), 483/32 (*sb.*)

chaffare *sb.* buying and selling 535/32

chafynge, see **ichaufed**; **chayn-**, see **cheyne**

chalenge *sb.* false accusation 319/31

chalengeþ *v. pres. 3sg.* makes a claim to 182/22

chammeþ *v. pres. pl.* bite, chomp on 906/5

champiouns *sb. pl.* warriors, athletes 324/38

chape *sb.* a metal plate or inlay, metal trimming 1023/25

chapmen *sb. pl.* merchants 704/11

†chapres *sb. pl.* chaps, fissures in the skin 425/35

charbuncles *sb. pl.* (**carbuncle** *sg.* once) carbuncles 769/31

chare *sb.* chariot 123/5

†charemen *sb.* charioteers 691/28

charge *sb.* burden, weight, obligation 62/4

charge *v.* to load, burden 265/19

Charleman-, Cherlemaynes-wayne *sb.* the constellation Ursa Major 502/26

chastye *v.* (*-i-*less forms frequent), **chastynge** *sb.* to discipline, correct; *sb.* also taming 77/34 (*v.*), 816/15 (*sb.*)

ichaufed *v. pa. p.*, **chaufyng** *sb.* (**chafynge** once) warmed 348/11 (*v.*), 946/30 (*sb.*)

chaunch-, see **chaunge**

chaundeler *sb.* candlestick 331/4

chaunge *v.* (**chaunchiþ** and **chongeþ** once each), **chaunginge** *sb.* to change; *day of chaunginge*, the day of crisis in a periodic fever 44/17 (*v.*), 120/21 (*sb.*)

chaungers *sb. pl.* moneychangers 481/21

ch(e)yne *sb.* chain, bond, row, anklejoint 269/7

cheyne (chayn-) *v.*, **cheynynge, chaynynge** *sb.* to join 214/29 (*v.*), 222/26 (*sb.*)

che(y)nes, see **chyne**; **cheke**, see **chick**

cheke, cheoke *sb.* (**chikes** *pl.* once) cheek, jaw 195/2

cheketeeþ *sb. pl.* molars, back teeth 203/28

chepinge *sb.* trade 472/14

chere *sb.* face 195/25

cherid *a.* disposed, having a certain manner; *heuycherid*, sad 89/3

cherischliche *adv.* lovingly 307/18

cherles, chorles *sb. pl.* bondmen, peasants 910/14

cherliche *adv.* lovingly 627/23

chese, see **shese**

chese *v.* (**chese** *pa.*, **ichose** *pa. p.*) to choose 61/16

chesefat *sb.* a sieve-like container for straining curds from milk 1333/1

cheselle *sb.* a pebble 838/1

chesteynes *sb. pl.* (**casteyn, kastayne** *sg.*) the chestnut tree, its nut, the colour chestnut 737/16

cheteringe, see **chitereþ**

chewe, chiewe, chu- *v.*, **chiewinge** *sb.* to chew 64/17 (*v.*), 84/13 (*sb.*)

chicchis *sb. pl.* chickpeas 986/1; see also **cecerys**

chick, cheke, chicoun, chikene, chik(k)en *sb.* chick, young of any bird 167/5

chief, che(e)f *a. sb.* most important or principal (part) 316/22

chieueþ *v. pres. 3sg.* thrives, buds 882/19

chiewe, see **chewe**

chymeneye, chimene *sb.* furnace or fireplace, vent for fumes (incl. humours) 170/28

chyne *sb.* (**chynnes, chenes, cheynes** *pl.*) gap, crack, cleft 138/14 [OE. *čine*]

chyneþ *v. pres. 3sg.* splits, cracks open 894/24 [OE. *činan*, strong 1]

chipperynges *sb. pl.* cracks 1036/1 [frequentative from OE. *-čippian*, cf. *forčippian* 'cut off']

chirkeþ *v. pres. 3sg.*, **chirkinge** *sb.* creaks, crackles; *sb.* roaring 845/18 (*v.*), 478/33 (*sb.*) [primarily OE. *čircian* 'roar', but with infl. of OE. *čearcian* 'creak']

chirtynge *sb.* twittering, chirping 524/21 [obscure, perhaps a scribal form of **chitrynge**]

chitereþ *v. pres. pl.*, **chiterynge, cheteringe** *sb.* twitter, chirp 212/11 (*v.*), 212/13 (*sb.*)

chiþes *sb. pl.* sprouts, stamens 981/12 [OE. *čīð*]

†chitoneþ *v. pres. pl.* give birth 1227/25

chittes *sb. pl.* whelps, young of any animal 1227/18

chiual(e)rie *sb.* knighthood, warfare (incl. spiritual battle against sin) 544/4

ychoked *v. pa. p.* suffocated 1013/23

chongiþ, see **chaunge; chorles,** see **cherles**

chose *a. sb.* the best 1327/8

chose *sb.* thing; *priue(y) chose*, the pudendum 846/8

ichose, see **chese**

chowgh, chow3he, chowhe *sb.* chough 600/32

cyates *sb. pl.* measures of liquid or weight, orig. the size of a ladle used in serving wine 960/29 [L. *cyatus*]

cicada *sb.* cicada, locust 1151/31

cicile *sb.* a little leek 1026/28 [L. *sectile*]; see also **secels**

cylens, see **scilens**

cipre, cipris *sb.* the henna shrub (also of the mastic tree), the ointment made from henna 916/20 [L. *cypros*]

cipres(se) *sb.* the cypress tree 708/13

circumcided *v. pa. p.* circumcised 546/8–9

circumstaunce *sb.* situation, details relevant to an event 143/12

cirurgye *sb.* surgery 363/2

cite, si3t *sb.* site, place 182/21

citrine *a. sb.* yellowish, yellow-red 159/9

citrulles *sb. pl.* watermelons 1316/14 [L. *citrullus*]

cyuel, ciuyle *a.* civil; *ciuyle profit*, the public good 742/2

clammy *a.* sticky, slimy 905/6

clarefye, clarifye *v.* to purify, make clear or bright 860/29

clariouns *sb. pl.* trumpets 542/3

clausure *sb.* enclosure 1049/30 [L. *clausūra*]

cle, claw, clow- *sb.* claw, hoof 228/6

clechyng, see **cliche**

†cleylonde *sb.* clayey soil 1064/23

†clemy *a.* sticky, slimy 353/15

clemyd, iclemeþ *v. pa. p.* stuck together, glued together 360/16 [OE. *clǣman* 'smear']

clene, cleyn *a.* clean 57/28

clene *adv.* fully, purely 825/7

clennes *sb.* purity 301/34

clense, clanse *v.* to cleanse, purge 386/4

clepe *v.*, **clepinge** *sb.* to call, shout, name 40/6 (*v.*), 55/35 (*sb.*)

clere *adv.* clearly 94/15

clerete *sb.*[1] clarity 70/15

clerete, clarette *sb.*[2] light-red wine with clarified honey and spices 1321/26

clergialliche *adv.* learnedly 453/33

clernesse *sb.* clearness 482/12

cleue, clief(fe), clifte, cliue, clife *sb.* cliff, headland, shore, bank 137/19

cleue *v.* (**cleueden** *pa.*, **cleuen** *pa. p.*) to stick, last 134/11

cleveth *v. pres. 3sg.* (**icloue, iclofe** *pa. p.*) splits, cuts 228/4

clewe *sb.* wad or ball of yarn, a ball 822/30

cliche *v.* (**icli3t** *pa. p.*), **clicchinge, clechynge** *sb.* to clench 227/25 (*v.*), 272/22 (*sb.*) [OE. *clyčean*]

clief(fe), see **cleue; clyfes,** see **cleue, clifte**

clift(e) *sb.* (**clyfes** *pl.* once) cleft, crack 138/15

clifte, see **cleue; icli3t,** see **cliche**

clyme, clime *sb.* a climatic zone on the

earth, the celestial region above it, a region or country, a measurement of land (3,600 sq. ft.) 515/2

yclynge, iclonge *v. pa. p.*, **clyngyng** *sb.* stuck together 138/28 (*v.*), 896/32 (*sb.*)

clynkery (k-) *a.* rough, hard, divided into rough sections as a brick pavement 525/31 [MDu. *clinker* 'paving brick']

clippith *v. pres. 3sg.* encircles 65/1

clips, eclips *sb.* eclipse 491/24

iclipsid *v. pa. p.* eclipsed 491/36

clistire, clisterye *sb.* clyster, enema, instrument for administering an enema 351/29

†**clites** *sb. pl.* the heads of small flowers (with reference to the prickly ones found on the burdock) 984/7 [obscure; perhaps a shortening of a compound such as *clite-bur* 'burdock'; cf. **clote**]

clyue(s), see **cleue**; **iclofe**, see **cleveth**; **icloffote, cloffotid**, see **clouefooted**

clogge *sb.* wood used as a hobble 1247/29

cloggeþ *v. pres. 3sg.* clogs 1150/35

cloistres *sb. pl.* walled enclosures 63/16

iclonge, see **yclynge**

cloos *pa. p., a.* closed, undivided 256/6

clo(o)þ *sb.* cloth, clothes (*pl.*), membrane 64/36

clos *sb.* stronghold, dwelling 1172/28

close *v.* (**cloþ** *pres. 3sg.* once), **closynge** *sb.* to close, join (the edges of a wound), fold up, enclose 102/12 (*v.*), 105/28 (*sb.*)

clot, clotte *sb.* lump, clod of earth 660/35

clote, clotte *sb.* the burdock 984/6

cloþinge *sb.* clothes, clothing, membrane 64/27

cloutis *sb. pl.* pieces of cloth, sheets 304/29

cloue *sb.* (**cloues, clowes** *pl.*) a clove, a root or tuber 911/9

icloue, see **cleveth**

clouefooted, clouefeet, clouefooteþ, clouenfoot, cloffotid, icloffote *a.* cloven-footed 226/18–19

clowes *sb. pl.* the spice cloves 970/32

clowis, see **cle, cloue**

cluddes *sb. pl.* clots of blood 150/8

clustre, cloustre *sb.* bunch, constellation, ball, compact mass 850/25

iclustred *v. pa. p.* gathered in a cluster 253/10

cocle, cocel, cokil *sb.* cockle or darnel, tares 957/9

cod, codde *sb.* seed-pod, shell, husk, scrotum 411/6

codware *sb.* peas or beans 953/15

cofer *sb.* coffer; *þe cofer of þe herte*, the pericardium 99/18

cognicoun *sb.* apprehension, knowledge 69/9

coyne *sb.* die, imprint stamped on a coin with a die, coin 294/10

cokadrille *sb.* crocodile 197/27

cokatrice, coketrys, cocatrice *sb.* the basilisk 429/3

cokil, see **cocle**

cokkes *sb. pl.* small conical piles of hay, shocks, haycocks 961/25

colera, colora *sb.* choler, yellow bile (one of the four humours), any form of bile (esp. *blak colera*, melancholia), excessive bile as a cause of disease 107/3

colery *sb.* eye-medicine or ointment 257/12 [L. *collȳrium*]

colerik *a.* characterized by excessive choler or yellow bile, having a choleric temperament 143/11

coliphonie *sb.* a resin, pine resin precipitated in the distillation of turpentine 969/28 [L. *colophōnia* (*rēsĭna*)]

collacioun *sb.* comparison, act of correlating diverse materials, logical reasoning 61/31

colosus *sb.* a gigantic statue, the Colossus of Rhodes 802/4

colour *sb.* colour, pigment 42/37

comaundeþ *v. pres. 3sg.* commands, rules 318/11

com(b)e *sb.* comb, the part of the hand between wrist and fingers, the metacarpal bones 223/1

combewise *adv.* with the shape of a comb, with closely-placed teeth 1100/4

combred *v. pa. p.* troubled, impeded 109/7

combustioun *sb.* the 'burning up' (of influence) of the moon by its near conjunction with the sun, obscuring of the moon by its proximity to the sun 494/12

come *v.* (**com(e)** *pa.* and *pa. p.*; **camen** *pa.* once) to come, approach, extend 44/7

†**comelinge** *sb.* numbness, stiffness 351/3 [cf. OF. *combler* 'load, heap']

comentour *sb.* learned commentator on a text 153/15

comfortabilly *adv.* pleasantly 482/7

comfortatif, confortatif *a., sb.* invigorating, stimulating; a food or drug with these properties 361/4

comforte, co(u)nforte *v.* (**ycomfort** *pa. p.* once) to encourage, support; *þe vertu of comforte*, a physiological force invigorating and reviving various organs 82/23

†**comycial** *a.* epileptic 1217/7 [L. (*morbus*) *comitiālis*]

comyn *sb.* cumin, the plant or its seed 362/36

†**comyn(e)** *sb.* a plant with husked, grain-like seeds, perhaps belonging to genus *Nigella* 956/13 [ML. *cyminum* (*ethiopicum*)]

comynte, communete, comountee *sb.* commonwealth, common people 602/17

commynycable *a.* communicating, passing water into other streams 665/26

commyxioun *sb.* the process of mixing together 88/15

communete, see **comynte**

communeþ, comyneþ, commoneþ *v. pres. pl.* distribute, share, impart 132/18

comoun *sb.* community, the people 44/28

comountees, see **comynte**

compaciens *sb.* sympathy, joint suffering 166/13

compact *v. pa. p., a.* compacted, firm 131/27

compactioun, compaccioun *sb.* joining, construction 75/12

compaynye *sb.* company, fellowship, society, association, conjunction 245/13

companyeþ *v. pres. 3sg.* couples with, has intercourse with 619/22

†**comparisiþ** *v. pres. 3sg.* compares, likens 297/5

comparisoun *sb.* pairing, comparison 91/10

compassioun *sb.* suffering, sympathy, pity 82/25

compendiousliche *adv.* concisely 516/6

compendiousnesse *sb.* brevity 549/1

competent *a.* sufficient 1109/14

compiled, compile *v. pa. p.* compiled 41/7

complement *sb.* something necessary to complete an action, completion, fulfilment 239/35

complet(e) *v. pa. p.* completed 81/25

complexional *a.* induced by the (humoural) composition of a substance, induced by the constitution of a substance 1038/23

complexioun, compleccioun *sb.* constitution of a substance (resulting from blending of the four qualities), nature of a substance, nature of an organ (resulting from blending of the four humours), nature of a person or animal, structure of an organ 116/7

composicioun *sb.* formation, workmanship 239/29

compot *sb.* calculation or computation of the calendar, the art of calculating 1354/7

compotistes *sb. pl.* authorities on the calendar 521/15

compouned, compowned, componed *v. pa. p.*, **compownynge** *sb.* mixed, complex 51/28 (*v.*), 485/32 (*sb.*)

comprehendiþ *v. pres. 3sg.* includes, unites, consists (of), understands 92/30

compressinge *sb.* pressing together, constriction 216/24

comunalte *sb.* people of a country, nation 719/14

comun(e), comoun, comyn *a.* common, usual, popular, universal; *in comune*, jointly, generally; *comoun wit*, the general faculty of sensation (as opposed to individual senses) 42/6

comunicacioun *sb.* communion, fellowship 69/8–9

comunycatif *a.* allowing passage or traversing, diffusive 506/35

conable, see **couenable**

concaues *sb. pl.* shallow vessels, vessels with hollow interiors 832/27

conceyue, see **conseyue**

†**concile** *sb.* a plant, perhaps lungwort or hellebore 845/29 [ML. *concilium*]

concilid *v. pa. p.* (**counseiliþ** *pres. 3sg.* once) reconciled 498/15

concours *sb.* running together, confluence 229/7–8

concret *a.* (of nouns) designating a substance, rather than a quality 48/4

†**concretiues** *a. sb. pl.* (nouns) designat-

ing a substance, rather than a quality 51/8

concupiscible *a.* pertaining to desire or that part of the soul controlling volition 95/33

concurant *a.* occurring or operating together 143/12

condicioun *sb.* situation, nature 79/35

condites *sb. pl.* channels or pipes to convey liquids, blood-vessels of the body 260/30

conerers, see **corner**

confeccioun, confexioun *sb.* something prepared from a mixture of ingredients, esp. a medicine 482/21

confecte *v. pa. p.* blended, mixed 860/28

conferme *v.* (**conformed** *pa. p.* occ.) to make like something else, assimilate 77/5

confessours *sb. pl.* saints canonized for their perseverance in the faith, rather than for martyrdom 1359/15

confexioun, see **confeccioun**; **conform-,** see **conferme**

confusion *sb.* shame, disorder 45/3

congeled *v. pa. p.* frozen, made solid 240/31

congelynge *sb.* fat 1141/26

conger *a.* correct, logical 60/20 [a nonce-formation, probably representing **congre,** OF. *congru*]

congour *sb.* (**congres** *pl.* once) conger eel 684/23

coniectiþ *v. pres. pl.* suppose 614/26

conyng(e) *sb.* rabbit 1102/9

coniunccioun *sb.* joining or uniting, esp. the joining of planets in the same or adjacent signs of the zodiac 464/1

coniunct, coniuned *v. pa. p.* (of the planets) in conjunction, in near proximity 467/21

coniurisouns *sb. pl.* charms, magic spells 1135/30

conneccioun *sb.* union 57/14

conoun *sb.* cone, point or apex of a cone 922/2 [L. *cōnus,* acc. *cōnon*]

conseyue, conceyue *v.,* **conseyuinge** *sb.* to conceive, beget, imagine; *vertu of conseyuynge,* the rational soul 136/24 (*v.*), 303/26 (*sb.*)

conseruacioun *sb.* preservation 454/13

conseruatyue *a., sb.* preservative 1319/30

consideracioun *sb.* manner, aspect 291/11

considred *v. pa. p.* determined 182/19

consonancye *sb.* harmony (esp. the music of the spheres or a musical note), a fixed relationship between things 478/36

consonant *sb.* musical note, melody 1392/7

conspect *sb.* (of the stars) aspect 473/17

constipiþ *v. pres. 3sg.* crams together, constipates 329/18

constitute *v. pa. p.* established, made up 81/25

constreyne, constreigne *v.,* **constreinynge** *sb.* to compel, oppress, thicken (a bodily fluid), contract 123/27 (*v.*), 135/12 (*sb.*)

consume *v.* (**consumpt** *pa. p.*) to consume, destroy, make feeble 140/14

consummacioun *sb.* mystic perfection 69/30–1

consumpt, see **consume**

consumptifes *a., sb. pl.* medicines which destroy or eliminate morbid substances, corrosives 361/3

†consumptiþ *v. pres. pl.* are increasingly feeble 1292/4–5 [L. *consumptus, pa. p.* of *consummere*]

contagioun *sb.* a contagious disease, plague 63/4–5

contagious *a.* causing corruption, contaminating 1186/1

contary, see **contray**

conteyne *v.* (**conteign-** frequent; **content, conteyned** *pa. p.*), **conteinynge, conteignynge** *sb.* to enclose, surround, contain, have as a part or subdivision; *sb.* contents, capacity for holding; *pa. p.* restrained, comprised of parts or units; *conteyned numbre,* one visualized as composed of the sum of various units 42/4 (*v.*), 96/30 (*sb.*)

contemplacioun *sb.* sight, religious meditation, musing 69/11–12

content, see **conteyne**

contynaunce, contynence *sb.* restraint, abstemiousness, contents 1283/15

continual, -el *a.* continuous, incessant, unremitting; *continual feuer,* a chronic infection, one not characterized by intermittent periodic eruptions 109/8

contynuauns, contynuaunce *sb.* persistence, continued pursuit or occurrence, continuousness of a surface, restriction 219/28

continue *v.* to persist, be joined, be connected, join 111/16

contract *v. pa. p., a.* shrunk, paralysed 120/5

contray, contrary, contary *a., sb.* contrary (in its various senses) 106/13

contrarious *a.* opposed, contrary to 137/12

contrariousnesse *sb.* opposition, conflict (of the elemental qualities), variation 444/4

contrey, contre, cuntre(y), kontre *sb.* land 67/13

conueniens *sb.* similarity, resemblance, propriety 67/34

conuenyent *a.* suitable, appropriate 108/24

conuersacioun *sb.* conduct, company, mating 598/22

conuersioun *sb.* transformation, change, turning toward God 52/16

coote *sb.* coot, any diving bird of similar type 598/28

copious *a.* plentiful 62/14

coppe (k-) *sb.* the top, the highest point 114/17

cop(pe)web(be) *sb.* cobweb 1070/34

coppewise *adv.* forming a point, in a pointed manner 887/32

coppide *v. pa. p.* pointed, crested 644/25

copwebbe, see **coppewebbe**

coriours *sb. pl.* tanners 1113/18

corkles *sb. pl.* twists 1126/1 [obscure]

corne *sb.* grain, cereal 694/25

cornemuse *sb.* hornpipe, a bagpipe-like instrument 331/1 [OF. *cornemuse*]

corner(e) *sb.* (**conerers** *pl.* once) corner 96/21

cornerid *v. pa. p.* having an angular shape 96/25

corny *a.* granular 257/36

corowne *sb.* crown 184/33

corpolentnes *sb.* corporeality 455/11

corporal *a.* bodily, material 554/36

icorporat, see **incorporith, corepeþ**

coreþ *v. pres. 3sg.* (**corporate, i-, e-corporate** *pa. p.*) incorporates 138/18

corpulent *a.* material, fleshy 488/1

ycorrayed *v. pa. p.* curried, combed 1190/13

corrumpe *v. pres. subj.* (**corrumpt, corrupt, corrump** *pa. p., a.*) destroy, corrupt 55/35

coruen, see **kerue**

cosynage *sb.* kinship 676/1

cosines *sb. pl.* kinsmen 467/35

coste, cooste- *sb.*[1] shore, coast, gulf or sea, limit, edge 673/8

coste *sb.*[2] costus root 912/23

costlew *a.* costly 309/4

costrel *sb.* a small keg (esp. for storing wine) 1377/34 [L. *costrellum*]

cotidiane, quotidiane *a., sb.* characterized by daily recurring eruptions, a fever of this sort 386/14

couche *sb.* couch, bed 1166/20

counforte, see **comforte**

counsailinge *v. pres. p.* advising 89/5

counseile *sb.* counsel, secret, wisdom 55/19

counseiliþ, see **conciled**

counterfeteþ *v. pres. pl.* imitate, emulate 1246/10

icountid *v. pa. p.* considered 445/17

cours *sb.* running, motion, flow or current (of water and humours), planetary orbit 114/23

court *sb.* an enclosed yard 1172/28

couþe, see **cunne**

coueiten *v. pres. pl.* desire 85/17

coueitise *sb.* desire, avarice 213/36

couenabilnesse *sb.* fittingness, opportuneness 324/25

couenable, couenabil, conable *a.* suitable, apt 75/7 [OF. *covenable*]

couenabliche, couenabley *adv.* appropriately, suitably 41/26

couenant *sb.* mutual agreement 316/22

couer-, see **keuereþ**

couert *sb.* shelter, lair 1215/29

cow, cowhe, koue *sb.* (**kyne, keen, kuyn** *pl.*) cow 212/20

coward *a.* timid 627/22

crabbe *sb.* crab, the constellation Cancer 417/8

crabbes *sb. pl.* crab-apples, wild apples 1317/18

cracche *v.,* **cracching** *sb.* to scratch, scrape, paw 149/25 (*v.*), 345/3 (*sb.*)

crackes *sb. pl.* crashes, splitting sounds 594/11

craft *sb.* skill, art 41/12

crafty *a.* skilful, clever 130/14

craftilich *adv.* skilfully 56/18

crakkeþ *v. pres. 3sg.* crackles, makes a sputtering sound 876/6

crampey *a.* spasmodic, subject to spasms or contractions 394/36

†**crasynges** *sb. pl.* cracks, holes 1019/19

creatures *sb. pl.* created beings, things created 44/18

creym *sb.* chrism 709/32

crepe *v.* (**ycrope** *pa. p.*) to crawl, spread, climb; *crepyng bestes*, reptiles 269/31

cresinge *sb.* increase 135/5

cresith *v. pres. 3sg.* increases 86/21

†**cressynge** *sb.* hissing, cracking 874/6 [obscure, perhaps a scribal form of **crikynge**]

cribbe *sb.* stall for cattle 1111/1

crie *v.*, **cryenge** *sb.* to cry out or yell, sing (of birds) 212/11 (*v.*), 212/13 (*sb.*)

criket *sb.* the salamander 1127/26

crikynge *sb.* croaking 1243/16 [cf. OE. *crǣcettan*, *crǣcettan*]

crympeþ *v. pres. pl.* crimp, become twisted or drawn up 1101/16

crioures *sb. sg. poss.* crier, herald 1389/13

crisma, crisme *sb.* holy oil 56/20

crisp, crips *a.* curly, curly-haired, rippled, wrinkled 64/2

crispy *a.* curly 196/36

crodd-, see **cruddy**

croys, croyce *sb.* cross 40/4

croisinge *v. pres. p.* intersecting 457/17

croke *v.* (**croked** *pa. p., a.*), **crokynge** *sb.* to bend, curve 120/4 (*v.*), 1057/24 (*sb.*)

crokes, see **crowkis**

crokkers *sb. pl.* potters 827/9

†**crolled** *v. pa. p., a.* curled, twisted 196/33

crollynge, see **crullyng**

cropouns *sb. pl.* crupper 1187/15

crop(pe) *sb.* the crop of a bird, sprouts or blossoms, tip or top of a plant 255/34

crouste, croste *sb.* crust, scab 362/12

crowkis, crokes *sb. pl.* buds, shoots, tendrils of a plant 1014/4 [cf. OE. *gecrōcod pa. p.* and ON. *krókr*]

crowstinge *sb.* crust, formation of a crust 416/10

cruddes *sb. pl.* curds, clumps 916/21

cruddy *a.* not solid, full of clumps or curds 261/19

cruddy (crodd-) *v.*, **cruddynge, crod-**

dynge *sb.* to coagulate, congeal, curdle 240/30 (*v.*), 235/5 (*sb.*)

crullyng, crollynge *sb.* rumbling (of the bowels), a growling noise 968/31

crusschinge *sb.* crackling, crashing 564/7

cubite *sb.* a measure of length (about eighteen inches, from elbow to fingertip), the lower arm, one of the bones of the (lower) arm (*nepir cubite*, app. ulna and radius; *ouer cubite*, app. humerus) 220/6

cuype *sb.* (**kuyppes, cupes** *pl.* once each) basket 1022/7 [OE. *cȳpa*]

cultre, culture *sb.* plowshare 692/12

culuer, coluer *sb.* dove 57/31 [OE. *culfer*]

cunne, conne, kanne *v.* (**can** *pres. 3sg.*, **couþe** *pa.*) to know, know how, understand, be able, can 63/14

cuntre(y), see **contrey**; **cupes**, see **cuype**

curacioun *sb.* cure 709/34

cure *sb.* duty, care 1390/24

curious *a.* careful 315/15

curiousliche *adv.* carefully 316/26

curlewe *sb.* quail 323/35

currour *sb.* courier 483/24

cusse *sb.* kiss 615/8

cusse, see **kissiþ**; **curtil-**, see **kurtel**

custome, costume *sb.* custom, customary payment, tax 89/8

dayisch, dayes *a.* pertaining to day (of signs of the zodiac which are hot in quality) 461/16

damacene, damacien *sb.* a damson plum 1021/7

damage *sb.* injury, harm 292/35

dampnacioun *sb.* condemnation (for a crime) 610/31

ydampned *v. pa. p.* condemned 89/18

dar, dere *v. pres. 3sg.* (**dorste, durste** *pa.*) dares 365/32

dart *sb.* spear, javelin 593/8

dawinge *sb.* dawn 536/37

dawnes *sb. pl.* down, fuzz 931/24

deceite, deseite, deceipte *sb.* deception, ambush 473/1

declaracioun *sb.* explanation, indication 62/29

decoccioun *sb.* medicine produced by boiling 881/1

dede *sb.* deed 49/18
dede, dedy *v.* to kill 135/32
dedeborn *a.* stillborn 524/10
dededoinge *sb.* performance of deeds 49/8–9
dedeyneþ *v. pres. 3sg.* contemns, scorns, refuses 608/20
dedliche, dedeliche *a.* mortal 64/30
defaced, defasid *v. pa. p., a.* disfigured 224/6
defactif *a.* defective 140/17
defamed *v. pa. p.* accused 312/29
defaute *sb.* lack, defect 102/27
defautiþ *v. pres. 3sg.* is lacking, is defective 144/20
defecte *v. pa. p., a.* disfigured, debilitated 224/6
defence, diffens *sb.* fighting for protection, shelter, prohibition, commandment not to do something 82/13–14
defende *v.* to fight to protect, shelter, prohibit 190/23
defete *a.* disfigured, changed in appearance 140/18 [OF. *deffet, pa. p.* of *desfaire*]
defye, diffye *v.*, **defyenge, diffyynge** *sb.* to digest, cause to suppurate 104/26 (*v.*), 135/14 (*sb.*) [AN. **defiier*, derived from L. *defæcāre*]
defoileþ *v. pres. 3sg.* dirties, pollutes 825/19
defoul *sb.* injury, pollution 63/4
defouliþ *v. pres. 3sg.*, **defoulinge** *sb.* injures, defaces, pollutes 57/18 (*v.*), 62/27 (*sb.*)
degedres, see **togedre(s)**
degre *sb.* stage of development, rank, condition, measure of intensity of a drug or nutrient 78/12
deye *sb.* dairymaid 1333/6
deye, dye *v.* (**dei3eþ** *pres. pl.* once) to die, fade away 40/15 [ON. *deyja*]
dele *sb.* part, piece 141/7
dele *v.* to separate, distribute 52/35
delicatliche *adv.* daintily, fastidiously 306/9
†deliciouste *sb.* deliciousness 331/5
deliueraunce *sb.* escape, rescue 147/12
delyuere, delyure *v.* to rescue, give birth to 348/27
delphyn, dolphyn *sb.* dolphin 236/13
deluers *sb. pl.* ditchdiggers 723/1

deluynge *sb.*, **ydolue** *v. pa. p.* dug 650/22 (*v.*), 339/9 (*sb.*)
demayn *sb.* demesne 720/19
deme *v.* to judge, sentence 68/30
demynge *sb.* judgement 60/31
denye, denuyeþ, denyueþ *v. pres. pl.*, **denyuynge, dinyuynge** *sb.* deny 990/15 (*v.*), 48/27 (*sb.*)
den(ne) *sb.* cave, lair, cavity (esp. in a bodily organ, as the cerebral ventricles), pore 122/12
denny *a.* hollow 237/31
denominaciouns *sb. pl.* names, acts of naming 63/34
†dented *v. pa. p.* barbed, pointed 1245/31
dentynge *sb.* indenting, cutting a slot or mortise in 1057/1
denuyeþ, see **denye**
deole, dool *sb.* sorrow, grief 161/34
departe, deperte *v.* (occ. -tie-forms), **departinge** *sb.* to separate, break up 44/32 (*v.*) 451/22–3 (*sb.*)
depe *adv.* far down, below the surface 182/26
depe, see **doep**
dependaunt *a.* dependent 100/10
depnes(se) *sb.* deepness, depth(s), deep places, sinking 218/16
deputat *v. pa. p.* assigned, established 119/22
dere, see **dar**
deryen *v. pres. pl.* harm 834/9 [OE. *derian*]
derk(e), dirk(e), durk(e) *a.* dark, obscure 41/23
derkeþ *v. pres. 3sg.* (**idirked** *pa. p.* once) dims, obscures 257/31
derkliche *adv.* darkly, mysteriously 41/11
derknes, dirknesse *sb.* darkness, mystery 44/9
derstes, see **drastes; des-,** see also **disdesceyuable** *a.* deceptive 438/34
descreue, descriue, see **discreue; deseite,** see **deceite**
desert(e) *a.*, *sb.* barren, desolate, wasteland 721/12
deserueþ *v. pres. pl.* deserve 83/2
desgiseþ *v. pres. 3sg.* alters his appearance 337/21
despensacioun *sb.* ordering, management, Providence 318/8
despise *v.* to look down on, resist 293/17
desseuered *v. pa. p.* separate(d) 1207/1

destemperat *a.* not temperate, not having or forming a balance of elemental qualities or humours, unhealthy 282/5

destigne, see **distingwe; destru-, destruy-,** see **distroye**

determinate *pa. p., a.* definite 647/7

determyne *v.* to define, limit (by defining), treat (a subject) 51/22

deþeburþe *sb.* abortion, miscarriage, stillbirth 303/28–9

dette *sb.* one's due, one's duty 314/7

†detty *a.* indebted 759/23

deuoided *v. pa. p.* evacuated, cleared out 378/30

deuoute *a.* devout 309/11

dewe, dwe, þewe *a.* due, appropriate 68/6

dewy *a.* dewlike, misty 580/14

dewinge *sb.* falling of dew, dew 537/5

dewte *sb.* duty, homage, one's duty 314/7

dichis *sb. pl.* trenches, ditches, pits (for trapping a wild animal), holes 540/27

difference *sb.* difference 42/31

diffy-, see **defye**

diffineþ *v. pres. 3sg.* defines, describes 91/13

diffinicioun *sb.* statement concerning the distinctive nature of a thing, opinion 91/19

digest *v. pa. p., a.* digested, purged 294/27

digestes *sb. pl.* digestion 895/27

diggeþ *v. pres. 3sg.,* **dyggyng** *sb.* digs, excavates 805/25 (*v.*), 996/13 (*sb.*)

dignacioun *sb.* anger 1006/4

dignyte *sb.* worth, nobility, high rank, the position of a planet in which its influence is increased 56/24

dikkinge *sb.* excavating, penetrating 371/10

dimencioun *sb.* dimension of measurement (incl. time), division, part 192/14

dyminitif, diminutif *a., sb.* a diminutive noun, a number the sum of the perfect divisors of which is less than the number itself 195/9

dynes *sb. pl.* valleys 1037/12

dinyuynge, see **denye**

dynte *sb.* blow, stroke with a weapon 730/27

dyrige *sb.* dirge 915/8

disauauntage *sb.* detriment, harm 605/12

discharge *v.* to unload, unburden 151/1–2

discipline *sb.* ordered conduct, learning 90/13

discolour *sb.* discoloration 132/7

discoloureþ *v. pres. 3sg.* changes the colour of, makes pale 135/22

discontenuaunce *sb.* interruption 511/34

discontinued *v. pa. p.* broken, interrupted 423/6

discontinuel *a.* discontinuous, (of fevers) characterized by intermittent eruptions 385/16

disconuenient *a.* unsuitable, unfit 532/19

discordiþ *v. pres. pl.* differ, disagree, do not exhibit harmony 60/17–18

discrecioun *sb.* discriminating ability 71/5

discreet *a., adv.* separate(ly), distinct(ly) 78/30

discreue, descreue, descriue *v.* (**discryed** *pa. p.* once) to describe 47/6

discure *v.* to discover 336/10

disese *v.* to trouble, disturb 88/21

disherited *v. pa. p.* disinherited 311/15

disordeyneþ *v. pres. pl.* bring into disorder 404/10–11

disordynauns *sb.* disorder (in an organ), medical disorder 247/12

disparpliþ (-parb-, -perb-) *v. pres. 3sg.* scatters, dispels, distracts 109/8 [OF. *desparpillier*]

dispensith *v. pres. 3sg.* deals out 63/21–2

disperbliþ, see **disparpliþ**

dispite, despite *sb.* contempt, disdain 62/11

dispitous *a.* contemptuous, haughty 306/9

dispitouslich *adv.* contemptuously, haughtily 657/6

disposicioun *sb.* arrangement 42/4

disposith *v. pres. 3sg.* arranges, directs 74/31

†dispred *v. pa. p.* scattered widely, broken up 565/12

disputesoun *sb.* formal debate 351/24

disputid *v. pa. p.* debated, discussed 126/8

dissencioun *sb.* descent, lowering in position 527/26

dissolucioun *sb.* disintegration, separation into parts 117/19

dissolutifes *a.*, *sb. pl.* medicines producing dissolution and causing morbid conditions to dissipate 361/3

dissolue *v.* to dissolve, separate, waste 100/32

distans, distaunce *sb.* strife, distinguishability 52/10

dystemperaunce *sb.* humoural or qualitative imbalance, excess of one humour or quality, inclement weather 246/35

distign-, see **distingwe**

distinccioun (des-) *sb.* definition, distinctive nature 97/19

distinctith *v. pres. pl.* (**distinct** *pa. p.*) distinguish, examine 65/13

distingwe, destigne *v.* (**distigned, distingued, distingt** *pa. p.*), **distinguinge** *sb.* to divide, separate, distinguish; *pa. p.*, *a.* diverse, characterized, marked 42/3 (*v.*), 487/15–16 (*sb.*)

distract *v. pa. p.* distracted, diverted 539/28

distribucioun *sb.* division, dispersion 513/1

distr(o)ye, destroye, destru(y)e *v.* to destroy 114/13

disturbelaunce, disturbleaunce *sb.* strife, discomposure 362/26

disturbliþ *v. pres. 3sg.* hinders, troubles 237/22

dyte *sb.* poem 791/22

diuersed *v. pa. p.* varied in colour 848/13

diuersite *sb.* variety, kind 163/18

dyueþ, duyueþ *v. pres. 3sg.* sinks, penetrates 416/30

dyuyne, deuyne- *v.* to divine, state 755/17

diuynour *sb.* augur 614/15

doelful *a.* sorrowful 1165/30

doep, depe, deep *a.* deep, profound 44/8

dokkes *sb. pl.* various broad-leafed plants, esp. the burdock 984/20

ydolue, see **deluynge**

dombe, dom, doumbe *a.* mute 207/19

dome *sb.* judgement, justice; *þe dome*, Last Judgement 65/5

domesmen *sb. pl.* judges 770/18

dompiþ *v. pres. 3sg.*, **dompinge** *sb.* plunges downward, dives 623/4 (*v.*), 634/6 (*sb.*)

ydonged, see **ydunged**

doo *v.* (**dede, dide** *pa.*; **ido(on)** *pa. p.*),

doinge *sb.* to do, cause, put, add to, place; *sb.* deed, act(ion) 55/7 (*v.*), 65/15 (*sb.*)

dool, see **deole**

doppeþ *v. pres. 3sg.* dives, plunges 634/8 [cf. OE. *-doppa sb.* and *doppettan*]

dory, dorrey *a.*, *sb.* gold in colour, golden, reddish yellow 229/13 [OF. *doré*, *pa. p.* of *dorer* 'gild']

dorrock *sb.* the bilge (properly, of a ship) 263/34 [OE. *ðurruc*]

dorste, see **dar**

doten *v. pres. pl.* behave foolishly 292/28

doufes, dowfes *sb. pl.* doves 600/29

douȝtir, douter *sb.* daughter 304/2

doumbe, see **dombe**

doumbiþ *v. pres. pl.* become quiet, become still 162/14

douncomynge *sb.* descent 583/3

doune, downe *sb.* hill, upland 703/23

doungoynge *sb.* descent, setting 473/17

doute *a.* doubtful, dubious 851/8

doutiþ *v. pres. 3sg.* dreads, is afraid 365/9

doutous *a.* fearful, terrifying, dangerous 1382/21

ydowede *v. pa. p.* endowed with 764/22

†dowers, dowweres *sb. pl.* burrows, caves 722/24 [OF. *douvre*]

dowfes, see **doufes**; **downe**, see **doune**; **dowweres**, see **dowers**; **dracon**, see **dragoun**

draffe *sb.* refuse, waste or worthless portion (left after running olives through an oilpress) 1004/24

dragantes *sb. pl.* gums used in binding medicines 1336/18 [L. *dragantum*]

dragme *sb.* a dram, one-eighth of an ounce 858/4

drago(u)n, dracon *sb.* dragon; *heued* and *taill of the dragoun*, the two portions of the moon's orbit viewed with respect to the zodiac, the ascending and descending portions of the orbit respectively; *dragouns blood*, a vermillion dye 208/31

draye *sb.* a sledge, a flat board used for dragging or hauling 1173/16

drane *sb.* drone 1206/17

drapeers *sb. pl.* cloth-merchants 1287/7

drastes, drestes, derstes *sb. pl.* dregs, faeces 131/6 [OE. *dærst*, *dræst*; ME senses occur only in pl. in OE.]

drasty *a.* dreg-like, poor in colour or quality 906/33

drau3t, draught *sb.* drawing or pulling movement, line, swig of a liquid 670/30
drawe *v.* (**drowe, drou3** *pa.*; **drawe, ydrawd, edraue** *pa. p.*) to draw, stretch, attract 47/28
drede *v.* (**dredde** *pa.*; **idradde** *pa. p.*) to fear 54/3
ydreyned *v. pa. p.* (**dryneþ** *pres. pl.* once, **ydreynt** *pa. p.* once), **dr(e)ynynge** *sb.* strained, filtered 256/36 (*v.*), 669/17 (*sb.*)
dreynes, see **dreynes(se); ydreynte**, see **ydreyned, drenchiþ**
drenches *sb. pl.* drinks, medicinal potions 364/20
drenchinge *sb.* immersion, a drench 101/17
drenchiþ *v. pres. 3sg.* (**ydre(y)nte** *pa. p.*) drowns 101/14
drestes, see **drastes; ydreue**, see **dryue**
dreueleþ, dryueleþ *v. pres. 3sg.*, **dreue-lynge** *sb.* dribbles 432/19 (*v.*), 430/31 (*sb.*)
drie *v.* to endure 219/31 [OE. *drēo3an*, strong 2]
drifte *sb.* impulse, impetus 905/22
drynes(se), dreynes, druy(e)nes *sb.* dryness, esp. the elemental quality 129/25
dringe, dringke, see **drinke; dryneþ, drynynge**, see **ydreyned**
drinke, dringe, dringke *sb.* drink 105/21
drinke *v.* (**drank** *pa.*; **ydronke(n)** *pa. p.*), **drinkinge** *sb.* to drink 84/7 (*v.*), 144/31 (*sb.*)
drit, dritte *sb.* excrement 250/12
drytty *a.* characterized by faeces, muddy 408/1
dryue *v.* (**drof** *pa.*; **ydriue, ydreue** *pa. p.*) to drive 196/16
dryueleþ, see **dreueleþ; droghþe**, see **drou3te**
dromedes *sb. pl.* dromedaries 1183/11 [ML. *dromedus*]
dronkelew *a.* habitually drunk 171/31
dronkelewnesse *sb.* drunkenness 420/4
dronkeschipe *sb.* drunkenness 843/24
dropmele, see **droppingemele**
droppe *v.*, **droppinge** *sb.* to drop, drip, give birth to 148/8 (*v.*), 116/9–10 (*sb.*)
dropping(e)mele, dropmele *adv.* drop by drop 409/8
drou3, see **drawe**

drou3te, droghþe *sb.* dryness, esp. the elemental quality 137/8
droukes *sb. pl.* medicinal preparations, drugs 918/16 [OF. *drogue*]
drowe, see **drawe; drowen, droweþ**, see **þrowe; drueneþ**, see **druye**
druye, drye, dreye *a.* dry 103/29
druye, drye *v.* (**drueneþ** *pres. 3sg.* once), **dryenge, druynge** *sb.* to dry 137/15 (*v.*), 142/2 (*sb.*)
drunkenhede *sb.* drunkenness 1082/24
ydrust, see **þriste; duyueþ**, see **dyueþ**
duk(e) *sb.* leader, duke 67/22
dulle *v.* to dull, weaken 227/23
ydunged, ydonged *v. pa. p.*, **dungynge** *sb.* manured 890/9 (*v.*), 1069/15 (*sb.*)
durable *a.* lasting, permanent 340/24
dure *v.* to last, endure 79/28
duringe *sb.* continuation, space of time 61/29
durste, see **dar; dwe**, see **dewe**

ebbe *sb.* the ebb tide; *grounde ebbe*, low tide 490/15
eche, icche *v.* (**ekeþ** *pres. 3sg.* once), **echinge, icchinge** *sb.* to increase 122/10 (*v.*) 150/5 (*sb.*)
echynge, see **icche; ecorporate**, see **corporeþ; eddre**, see **adder; edraue**, see **drawe**
e(e)lden *v. pres. pl.* grow old, decline 518/36
eer, see **here; eere**, see **erre**
i-eered *v. pa. p.* (of grain) come into ear 584/11
eet, see **ete; effeccioun**, see **affeccioun**
effect, affect *sb.* performance of an act, act, a property regarded as the result of an act, celestial influence 42/8
effectiue, affectif *a.* efficacious; also used to designate one of Aristotle's four causes, that one bringing a material into a certain state 117/8
effectualliche *adv.* effectively 273/15
effectuel *a.* powerful in effect, efficacious 685/14
efficient *a.* designating one of Aristotle's four causes, that force which brings about an effect or action 108/24
effimeroun *sb.* fish with extremely short lifespan 679/4
effluence *sb.* pouring out, flowing forth 652/33

eft *adv.* again, afterwards; *eft and eft*, again and again 67/10 [OE. *eft*]

eftsones *adv.* soon, immediately 136/18

egge *sb.* edge; *makeþ þe teeþ an egge*, numbs the teeth; *eggetool*, a bladed implement 205/15

ey *sb.* (**eyr** *sg.* once; **eiren, ayren** *pl.*) egg; *wynde eiren*, malformed or shell-less eggs 130/32

eye, see **iȝe**

eyeschelle *sb.* eggshell 349/14

eiȝe, eihe, see **iȝe**

eiȝt(e)þe *num.* eighth 42/24

eyle *sb.* (**yles** *pl.* once) the awn (of grain), the small spikes near the top of the ear or the top of a flower 955/20 [OE. *egl(e)*; cf. **alles**]

eysel *sb.* vinegar 369/21 [OF. *aisil*]

eiþir, aiþir, aieþir *pron., a., adv.* each (of two), one or the other, or 44/20

ekeþ, see **eche**

elde *sb.* old age 64/16

elde(r) *a. comp.* older 213/2

eldiþ, see **eelden**

elebor, ellibore *sb.* hellebore 947/24

electis *sb. pl.* choices, elections 84/32

electuary, eleccuarie, elettuary *sb.* a medical recipe based on a syrup 350/21

element *sb.* one of the four basic material substances (earth, air, fire, water) 42/16

†**element** *a.* pertaining to an element; always occurs in phrases *element qualitee* (one of the four basic qualities, hot, cold, wet, or dry), *element propirte*, or *element forme* 132/15–16

elementliche *a.* physical, taking its nature from the four elements 554/37

elenge *a.* tedious, unpleasant 188/27

elengenesse *sb.* sadness, melancholy 188/17

elleren, alloren, ellern(e) *sb.* the elder tree 948/29

elles *adv.* otherwise, else, other 48/23

embolismal *a.* intercalated (to align the Hebrew lunar calendar with the solar calendar) 521/28

embolisme *sb.* insertion of additional days or months into the calendar 522/8

emerys *sb. pl.* embers, ashes 565/3

emeroides, emerodes, emeraudes *sb. pl.* haemorrhoids 327/32

emygrayne *sb.* a severe headache 146/11

emnyte, see **enemite**

empere *sb.* dominion, power 471/30

empte, see **ampte**

y-emptyde, y-empted *v. pa. p.* emptied 665/25

emunctories *sb. pl.* bodily organs or structures for removing waste from other organs 134/19 [ML. *emunctōrium* 'a means of cleansing']

en-, see also **in-**

enarmeþ *v. pres. pl.* arm 1038/12

encennya *sb.* the ceremony of dedication 551/2 [L. *encænia*]

encensed *v. pa. p.* censed 1063/12

encres(s)e, encrece, encresce *v.*, **encres(s)ynge** *sb.* to increase 86/14 (*v.*), 292/14 (*sb.*)

endeles *a.* eternal, limitless; *to* and *in endeles*, on to infinity, *ad infinitum* 51/26

endeles *adv.* immeasurably 443/9

endlonge *prep.* from end to end (of), lengthwise along 1167/20

enemite, emnyte *sb.* hostility, danger 161/22

enfourme, see **informeth**

engendrid (in-) *v. pa. p.* begotten, developed 104/8

engleymed *v. pa. p.* made slimy, clogged 398/14 [OF. *en-* + obscure; cf. **gleymy**]

enhaunsid *v. pa. p.* raised in position, (of a planet) raised to a position of greater influence 462/8

eny, any, ony *a.* any 45/17

enke, ynke *sb.* ink 929/4

enleuene *num.* eleven 521/22

enleuenthe *a.* eleventh 42/28

ensample *sb.* example 176/28

entente *sb.* intent 71/29

enterclos, see **interclose**

entrynge *sb.* beginning, entry, way 572/27

enuye *sb.* envy; *haþ enuye to*, is hostile towards 340/2

eorþe, see **erþe**

epatike *a.* afflicted with a disease of the liver 908/28

epilency *sb.* epilepsy 354/1

epilentik *a., sb.* afflicted by epilepsy, an epileptic person 175/8

epythime *sb.* the flower of thyme (properly a parasitic plant which grows on thyme) 1062/34

equite *sb.* even-handedness, impartiality 53/14

ere, ar, or *adv., conj.* (**erst, arst** *super.*) before, early 182/28

ere, erye *v.* (**herid** *pa. p.* once), **eryenge** *sb.* to plough 66/19 (*v.*), 916/30 (*sb.*) [OE. *erian*]

†**erebowys** *sb. pl.* the temples, the bones of the side of the head 278/4

er(e)liche *a., adv.* early, in the morning 330/19

eren *sb. pl.* harrows, rakes 720/11

eres, see **ers, here**

erre, eere *v.*, **errynge** *sb.* to wander, fail in operation 246/31 (*v.*), 721/22 (*sb.*)

ers, eres *sb.* the buttocks 407/28

erþe, eorþe *sb.*[1] earth, the earth, the element earth 42/32

erþe *sb.*[2] the act or process of ploughing; *dayes erþe*, the *jugerum*, a measure of land area, the amount which can be ploughed in a day by a single team 916/30 [OE. *éarð, ýrð*]

erþeliche *a.* resembling the element earth 119/23

erþeschakynge *sb.* earthquake 456/12

erþeteliers *sb. pl.* farmers, those who live by tilling the soil 481/19

erþy, eorþy *a.* resembling earth, having the properties of the element earth 108/9

erthynesse, eorþynesse *sb.* a substance or property partaking of qualities of the element earth 1020/21

eschetour *sb.* collector, official who oversees property reverting to a lord owing to absence of an heir and who collects the revenues of such property 1376/31

eschiewen *v. pres. pl.* refrain from, avoid 1244/29

esement *sb.* comfort, support 281/34

esy, eesy, ese *a.* easy, comfortable, kind, calm 109/6

esy *v.*, **esynge** *sb.* to comfort or relieve, make easier 166/22 (*v.*), 537/31 (*sb.*)

esiliche *adv.* (**esilokere** *comp.*) easily 173/22

essencia *sb.* (**essencies** *pl.*) substance, the true being of an object (as opposed to the accidental qualities) 46/30

†**essenciabliche** *adv.* essentially, as an essence 103/8

essencial, essensial *a.* pertaining to the essence of a thing, to the real being rather than accidental qualities 47/14

essencialliche *adv.* in its essence, by its nature, actually 556/25

estern, estir *sb., a.* Easter Sunday 542/11

estimacioun *sb.* evaluation 99/15

estimatiue *a.* capable of judgement; *vertu estimatiue*, the mental faculty 'estimation', a quasi-rational sense 98/31

ete, hete *v.* (**eet, ete** *pa.*; **i-ete, yȝete** *pa. p.*) to eat 84/10

ethe *a.* easy, simple 324/16 [OE. *éaðe*]

eþeliche *adv.* (**eþeloker** *comp.* once) easily, readily 200/16

†**eþenes** *sb.* ease, facility 272/30

ethik, etik, ethice *sb.* hectic fever, one who suffers from such a fever 140/13

eþilicher *a. comp.* easier 209/28

ethymologye *sb.* (of a word) the original form and meaning 873/23

euyen *v. pres. pl.*, **euenge** *sb.* to lamb, kid 1115/10 (*v.*), 1234/6 (*sb.*)

euaporacioun *sb.* turning into a gas, gas 57/33

eue, euen *sb.* evening, the eve of a festival 482/3

euel, see **yuel**

eueleþ (yuel-) *v. pres. 3sg.*, **euelinge** *sb.* fills, fills up 106/10 (*v.*), 106/8 (*sb.*) [OE. *gefyllan*]

euelith *v. pres. pl.* turn bad, injure 613/32

euelong, euenlong *a.* oblong, elongated 109/10

euen(e) *a.* level, even (number) 46/2

euene *adv.* smoothly, evenly 181/34

euenes(se) *sb.* smoothness, regularity, the even nature (of a number), uniformity, moderation; *þe lyne of þe euenes of day and nyȝt*, the equator 53/14

euenyng *v. pres. p.* making equal or exactly the same 477/16

euenliche *adv.* equally, exactly, uniformly, solely 454/20

euentyde, see **evetyde**

eueriche *pron.* every one, any one 45/6

euerlastingnes *sb.* eternity 452/29

†**euerlastith (-lest-)** *v. pres. pl.* are eternal 75/25

i-euesed *v. pa. p.* (of the hair) cut, trimmed 288/32 [OE. *efesian*]

euesinge *sb.* the eaves of a roof (the edge

euesinge (*cont.*) where thatch is cut off), hair-cutting 288/32

euete, ewte *sb.* newt, lizard 256/24

evetyde, euentyde *sb.* evening, dusk 645/2

euidens *sb.* proof, authority 47/8

euydent *a.* plainly visible 1376/1

euiden(t)liche *adv.* plainly 592/9

euorye *sb.* ivory 769/29

ew *sb.* the yew tree 1056/4

ewe(n), owen *sb.* ewe 1112/28

ewte, see **euete**

exaccouns *sb. pl.* demands for payments of fees, fees or taxes so collected 319/27

exactours *sb. pl.* officials who extort payments 319/28

exalacioun, exsolacioun, ex(h)altacioun *sb.* breathing, emission of breath, vapour 106/27

exaltacioun *sb.* the position in the zodiac where a planet exercises its greatest influence, esp. the point of highest elevation of the sun 461/26

excellent *a.* surpassing, supreme, noble 100/26

excercitacioun *sb.* exercise, esp. spiritual exercise or discipline 1110/24

excite *v.*, **excitinge** *sb.* to urge, incite, call up 65/27 (*v.*), 299/28 (*sb.*)

excludid *v. pa. p.* shut out, eliminated through medicinal aids 1164/17

exemplare *sb.* the model of the universe (in the mind of God), the Platonic Idea of the universe 1394/32

exen, see **asschen; exhaltacioun,** see **exalacioun**

exilynge *sb.* exile 446/4

experiment *sb.* proof, a proven medical remedy 354/36

expone *v.* to express, explain 54/26 [L. *expōnere*]

expositour *sb.* a lecturer on Scripture or a work of exegesis 943/1

expouneþ *v. pres. 3sg.*, **expounynge** *sb.* declares, explains 443/6 (*v.*), 305/31 (*sb.*)

expresliche *adv.* explicitly 126/6

expresse *adv.* clearly 60/1

expulsiue *a.* putting out; *vertu expulsiue*, a Galenic faculty, dealing with elimination of wastes 97/15

exsolacioun, see **exalacioun**

extendiþ *v. pres. 3sg.* stretches, spreads 510/4

extre, axstre *sb.* axle 266/32

fablis *sb. pl.* legends 479/11

facounde *sb.* eloquence, elegant speech 133/27 [OF. *faconde* and L. *fācundia*]

fadiþ *v. pres. 3sg.* fades, ebbs 251/19

†fagynge *v. pres. p.* infectious 1212/35 [obscure]

fayl(l)e *v.* to lack, fail 55/35

faint *a.* weak 185/20

faintes *sb. pl.* faintness 446/7

fakettis *sb. pl.* bundles (of wood or kindling) 1047/35

falewiþ *v. pres. 3sg.* withers 237/2

falle *v.* (**fil, fille, fel** *pa.*; **ifalle** *pa.p.*) to fall; *þe fallynge yuel*, epilepsy 85/19

fame *sb.* rumour 1237/1

famuler *a.* intimately associated, well-known 344/26

fangiþ, see **fonge**

fantasie *sb.* the faculty closely associated with *vis imaginativa*, a figment or apparition 101/18

fantasmes *sb. pl.* delusions (esp. of the senses), imaginary apparitions 334/31

fantastik *a.* pertaining to fantasy 107/19

fare *v.* (**ferde** *pa.*) to go, behave, happen (usually impersonal **it fariþ**) 40/17

farweþ *v. pres. 3sg.*, **far(o)wynge** *sb.* farrows 235/11 (*v.*), 1238/19 (*sb.*)

faste, fest *a.*, *adv.* firm(ly) stable, secure(ly), solid(ly) 271/19

fastene (festn-, fastn-) *v.*, **festenyng** *sb.* to make firm, join 138/32 (*v.*), 837/5 (*sb.*)

fastnesse *sb.* stability, firmness 131/2

fat, fatte *a.* fat, full of grease, thick, fertile 150/27

fatnes(se) *sb.* fat, corpulence, greasiness, fertility 133/26

fatty *a.* full of grease, greasy, cohesive, thick, fertile 424/28

fattiþ *v. pres. 3sg.* grows fat, fattens, fertilizes 251/20

fau(u)coun, faucown *sb.* falcon 562/8

faute *sb.* lack, fault 354/36

fawneþ *v. pres. 3sg.*, **fawnnynge** *sb.* (of animals) shows delight, wags the tail, shows fondness 1115/28 (*v.*), 633/5 (*sb.*)

feble *v.* to grow weak 79/28

fechches, see **vecchis**

fede, vede *v.* (**ifed(de), feedede** *pa. p.*), **fedinge** *sb.* to feed 74/18 (*v.*), 74/17 (*sb.*)

feer(-), see **fer(-); feere,** see **ifere**

fegge, figge, fige *sb.* the figtree, fig 432/33

fey, fei, fay *sb.* faith; *maken fey,* to pledge one's word 72/27

feyneþ, feigneþ *v. pres. 3sg.,* **feinynge, feignynge** *sb.* makes, creates, invents (esp. a fiction) 64/21 (*v.*), 505/28 (*sb.*)

ifeyntid *v. pa. p.* become feeble 526/1

feires *sb. pl.* fairs 472/14

fel *a.* shrewd, clever 1224/11

fel *sb.* (**uelles** *pl.* once) skin, pelt, husk (of fruit) 224/19

felawshepe, felaschipe, feleschipe *sb.* fellowship 641/18

fele *a.* many 118/34 [OE. *fela*]

fele (fiel-) *v.* (**feled** *pa., pa. p.*), **felynge** *sb.* to feel; *vertu of felynge,* the force or faculty animating the nervous system 53/12 (*v.*), 95/8 (*sb.*)

fel(l)awe *sb.* companion 56/21

felleþ, see **fulle**

ifellid, yfelde, yfulde *v. pa. p.* hewed down, knocked or struck down 902/32

felnes *sb.* fierceness, cruelty 282/33

felþe, see **fulþe**

female, femel(e), femelle *a. sb.* female 126/14

femyne *a.* feminine (gender) 47/19

fen, fenne, ven *sb.* mud 102/2

fend *sb.* devil, demon 65/8

fendiþ *v. pres. 3sg.* defends, protects 196/10

fenge, see **fonge; fenymous,** see **venymous**

fenix *sb.* the Phoenix, the date palm (so called because of its long life) 625/15

fenny *a.* muddy 528/8

fentyngez, see **ventynge**

fer, feer, ferre, varre, feire *adv.* (**ferre** *comp.,* **firrest** *super.*) far 60/34

ferde, see **fare**

†ferd(e)ful *a.* fearful 89/3

fere *v.* to frighten 537/10

fere, see **ifere**

†ferenes *sb.* fearfulness 87/33

feretinge, see **frete**

ferforth *adv.* far; *as ferforth as,* in so far as, as much as, to the degree that; *so ferforth þat,* to such an extent that 77/24

ferlyche *a.* terrifying 755/6

fernesse, feernes, vernes *sb.* distance (between two objects), remoteness 110/2

ferre, see **fer; ferrey,** see **verrey**

ferst, first, furst, þurst *sb.* thirst 378/3

ferþe, ferþere, furþere, forþer *a.* farther, forward, front, first 116/22

ferþe, firþe, furþ(e), fourþe *a.* fourth 42/15

feruent *a.* burning, feverish 70/29

feruentliche *adv.* intensely, unpleasantly 193/15

feruor, feruour *sb.* ardor 156/24

fest *sb.* feast (of the Church), festival 213/34

fest, see **faste; fest(e)n-,** see **fastene**

festir, festre *sb.* sore, ulcer, fistula 417/26

fethele, fithel-, fedele *sb.* a stringed instrument played with a bow, a fiddle or violin 329/33

ifette *v. pa. p.* fetched, brought 548/34

feuerowse *a.* fever-like, of the nature of fever, affected by fever 990/25

fewe *a., sb.* a small number, a little 227/28

†fibres *sb. pl.* beavers 1210/27 [L. *fiber*]

ficchiþ, see **fiȝte; fieleþ,** see **fele; fier,** see **fure; fiere,** see **ifere; fiery,** see **fury**

fyfte, fyfþe *num.* fifth 42/20

fiftiþe *num.* fiftieth 543/12

figuracioun *sb.* shape, outline 578/14

figuratif *a.* metaphorical or figural (language) 41/24

figure *sb.* form, image, symbol, biblical type 41/12

fiȝte *v.* (**fitt-, feiȝt-, ficch-** occ.; **faught** *pa.*), **fiȝtinge, fitinge** *sb.* to fight 67/21 (*v.*), 67/23 (*sb.*)

†fiȝttes *sb. pl.* pelts, fitches 204/3 [OE. *feht*]

fikel *a.* treacherous, dangerous 1382/31

fikeleþ *v. pres. 3sg.* (of animals) wags the tail, deceives through flattery 1170/7

fikelinge *sb.* flattery 365/36

fil, see **falle**

fyle *sb.* file; *þe fyle of hete,* a troublesome condition or tribulation brought on by excess heat 130/8

fylyng *sb.* filing, particles rubbed away through filing 829/8

fille, see **falle; filosophir, -phre, -fir,** see **philosophir**

filte *sb.* felt, woollen or hair cloth 1303/23

fynaliche *adv.* in the end, firmly 340/23

fynde *v.* (**fint** *pres. 3sg.* once; **fond(e)** *pa.*; **ifounde** *pa. p.*) to find, maintain 45/3

fynder *sb.* inventor, originator 764/21

fynge, see **fonge**

finger, fengir *sb.* finger 55/16

fint, see **fynde; fire,** see **fure**

fyren *a.* flaming, fiery 789/9

fyret *sb.* ferret 1228/21

firhoot, fuyrehoot *a.* red-hot 560/19

firmament *sb.* the heavens 448/9

firrest, see **fer**

firsone *sb. pl.* gorse, thorns, or brambles 721/24 [OE. *fyrs*]

first(e), see **ferst, furst; firþe,** see **ferþe**

fisik, see **physik; fithelis,** see **fethele; fitinge, fittiþ,** see **fiȝte**

flaket *sb.* flask, bottle 405/25 [ONF. *flasquet*]

flappiþ *v. pres. 3sg.*, **flappynge** *sb.* beats, strikes, claps the hands 619/9 (*v.*), 624/12 (*sb.*)

flatereþ *v. pres. 3sg.* (usually with complement **wiþ**) beguiles, fawns on 172/27

flecche *v.* to waver, turn aside, cease 51/28 [OF. *flechir*]

flee *v.*[1] (**fle(e)þ, flye** *pres. pl.*; **fleigh, fliȝen** *pa.*) to fly, move swiftly; *fleinge sterre,* shooting star 66/2

fle(e) *v.*[2] (**fleeþ** *pres. occ.*; **fleigh, fliȝe** *pa.*; **iflowe** *pa. p.*) to flee 55/2

flegge *a.* fit to fly, feathered; *flegge ripe,* fully fledged 607/10

fleischli(che) *a.* made of flesh, carnal, physical 64/28

fleissch *sb.* flesh, muscular tissue, meat 54/30

fleisschy *a.* made of flesh or muscle 124/13

flemyd *v. pa. p., a.* outlawed 717/17 [OE. *flieman*]

flete, fleote *v.*, **fle(o)tynge** *sb.* to float, flow; *fle(o)tynge a.,* liquid 133/21 (*v.*), 86/26 (*sb.*)

flewmatik *a.* phlegmatic, the temperament characterized or caused by excess phlegm 143/11

flewme, fleume, fleuma *sb.* phlegm (one of the four humours) 104/21

flex *sb.* flax 653/13

flicke *sb.* the masculine member of a pair; only in phrase *flicke and his make* 678/37

flye, see **flee; fliȝe(n),** see **flee**

fliȝt *sb.* flight; *fliȝt ripe,* ready to fly 59/14

flittinge *a.* moving, changing 51/28

flocke *sb.* flock, herd 678/37

flood *sb.* river, high tide 490/15

florischiþ *v. pres. pl.* burgeon (of flowers and hair), thrive, adorn 531/24–5

flour *sb.* blossom or flower, the best or choicest part (e.g. butter as *þe flour of mylk,* or as term for wheat meal after winnowing), a powder (as *flour of lede,* precipitated white lead) 445/30

flow *v.*, **flowinge** *sb.* to run, flow 174/29 (*v.*), 265/1 (*sb.*)

iflowe, see **flee**

flowes *sb. pl.* waves, high tide 659/12

flume *sb.* river 663/19 [OF. *flum*]

flusshynge *sb.* commotion, sudden movement 1101/6

fluuial *a.* of or from a river 1329/4 [L. *fluviālis*]

flux, flix(e) *sb.* flowing of humours or fluids in the body; esp. pathological states typified by movement of fluids, e.g. *þe flux of þe wombe,* diarrhea 145/23

†fnatted *v. pa. p.* (of noses) flattened, snubbed 1246/6 [cf. OE. *fnæstian* 'breathe hard']

fnese *v.*, **fnesinge** *sb.* to sneeze 932/28 (*v.*), 351/30 (*sb.*) [OE. *fnēosan*]

†fnesy *a.* restless, snorting or whistling 1246/28

foisned *v. pa. p.* nourished, supplied (abundantly) 290/22

foysoun *sb.* plenty, vigour 484/10

foysted *v. pa. p., a.* stale, musty 1083/33 [from OF. *fust* 'cask'; cf. **afoysted**]

folde *sb.* a pen, enclosure for animals 852/36

folde *v.* (**foldid, ifolde** *pa. p.*), **foldynge** *sb.* to fold 218/20 (*v.*), 253/7 (*sb.*)

fole *v.* (**ifole** *pa. p.*), **folynge** *sb.* to foal 562/7 (*v.*), 562/6 (*sb.*)

fol(e)we (volow-) *v.* to follow 55/25

folwinge, fullinge *sb.* baptism 136/15 [OE. *fulwian* 'consecrate completely (to a god)']

fome *sb.* saliva, froth 149/1

yfomed *v. pa. p.* foamed at the mouth 352/34

fomentz *sb. pl.* ointments or lotions applied warm to the skin 346/22

fonde *v.*, **fondynge, foundynge** *sb.* to test, try, seek 71/3 (*v.*), 676/7 (*sb.*) [OE. *fándian*; some coalescence in senses with OE. *fúndian*]

fonde, see **fynde**

fonge, vonge, fange- *v.* (**fenge, fynge, veng, fongede** *pa.*; **ifonge, iuonge, fongede** *pa. p.*), **fonginge** *sb.* to take, receive 52/33 (*v.*), 69/4 (*sb.*) [OE. *fōn*, strong 7; forms based on pa.p. *fángen*]

fongers *sb. pl.* receivers 73/32

fool *a.* foolish, ignorant 1046/27

foole, foule *sb.* fool 317/4

for *adv.* forward 1124/35

forbarred *v. pa. p.* hindered, obstructed, blocked 284/16

forbedith *v. pres. 3sg.* (**forbode(n), forbede** *pa. p.*) forbids, hinders (of a bodily function) 55/19

forbere *v.* (**forbore** *pa. p.*) to spare, respect 310/34

yforbysshed *v. pa. p.* polished, rubbed 849/12

forbode, see **forbedith**; **forbore,** see **forbere**; **forcutte,** see **forkutte**

fordes *sb. pl.* forest paths 727/21

fordoþ *v. pres. 3sg.* destroys, vitiates 1297/28

fordrye, fordruye *v.* to dry up, wither 255/26

fordwyneth *v. pres. 3sg.* dwindles, dries up 654/18

fore, veer, vore *sb.* track, footprints, furrow 66/18 [OE. *fōr*]

for(e)hed(e), for(e)heued *sb.* forehead 188/15

†**forekitters** *sb. pl.* front teeth 202/17 [OE. *fore-* + from *cyttan*, a calque on L. *præcisor*]

foreschipe *sb.* front of a ship, prow 173/19

forete(e)þ *sb. pl.* the front teeth 203/27

forew, see **forow**

forgendreþ *v. pres. 3sg.* ignores, neglects 312/21 [OE. *for-* + OF. *gendrer*]

forgiþ *v. pres. 3sg.* heats (to moltenness) 131/31

forȝemeþ *v. pres. 3sg.* neglects 312/21 [OE. *forȝieman*]

forȝete *v.* and *pa. p.*, **forȝetinge** *sb.* to forget 55/28 (*v.*), 61/32 (*sb.*)

forȝeteful *a.* forgetful 136/31

forȝeter *sb.* one who forgets, a forgiving being 616/32

forȝetilnesses *sb. pl.* forgetfulnesses, neglects 1082/3

forȝeue *v.* (**forȝaf** *pa*, **forȝeue** *pa. p.*) to forgive 55/28

forȝeuenesse *sb.* forgiveness 543/11

forkerueþ *v. pres. 3sg.* cuts to pieces, dissolves 436/25

forkutte *v.* (**forkutte, -cutte** *pa. p.*) to cut off, cut up 199/5–6

forlanges, forlonges *sb. pl.* (**furlong** *sg.* once) furlong, square furlongs (about ten acres), a footrace (of a furlong's length) 543/4

forleft *v. pa. p., a.* deserted, desolate 931/20

forleued, forlyued *v. pa. p., a.* decrepit, having outlived one's strength 224/6 [OE. *for-* + *libban, lifian*]

forlonde *sb.* headland 765/20

formal *a.* pertaining to the substance or essence of a thing (as opposed to the material of which it is made), having the power to confer properties of a species; *cause formal,* one of the four Aristotelian principles of causation, the principle by which material is directed to exhibit the properties innate in a thing 263/2

forme *a.* front, first 277/16

forme, fourme *sb.* form, archetype, essence (opposed to matter), formative principle 42/13

yformed *v. pa. p.* shaped 995/24

formefadres *sb. pl.* ancestors, forefathers (the Patriarchs of *Genesis*) 773/1

formere, fourmere *a.* front, first, preceding 90/5

formest *a., super.* frontmost, farthest forward, first 98/28

forneys *sb.* oven, furnace 1047/36

forow, forew, forough *sb.* furrow, the track left by a plough, a trail or track (esp. a rutlike one) 589/15

forsake *v.* (**forsook** *pa.*, **forsake** *pa. p.*) to repudiate, reject 71/23

forscorchet *v. pa. p.* burned up 795/6

forseþ *v. pres. 3sg.* compels; *forseþ him*, strives, does his utmost 298/17

forsinge *sb.* exertion, pressure 396/34

forþbringenge *sb.* production, generation 451/16–17

forþbringere *sb.* one who nourishes or fosters 446/2–3

†forþirled *v. pa. p.* thoroughly pierced 1090/17 [OE. *for-* + *ðyrlian*]

forþriȝt *a., adv.* straight (on), direct(ly), precise(ly), 477/26 (*a.*), 109/19 (*adv.*)

forthwarde *adv.* in front, forward, afterward 222/30

forto *conj.* (**fortil** once) until 61/24

fortunat *a.* favourable, beneficent, propitious (of astral influence) 494/5

†forwasshe *v. pa. p.* washed away, dissolved 711/33

forwery *a.* very tired, exhausted 162/6

forwerieth *v. pres. 3sg.*, **forwerynge** *sb.* wears away, erodes 695/29 (*v.*), 1215/13 (*sb.*)

fot, foote *sb.* (**fet, feet(e), fiet(e)** *pl.*) foot 55/21

foule, see **foole**

ifounde *v. pa. p.* established, based 98/25

foundement, fundement, fundament *sb.* base, foundation 120/34

foundynge, see **fonde**

fourme, see **forme; fourþe,** see **ferþe**

fownes *sb. pl.* fawns 1098/24

frayel *sb.* basket, esp. one to hold fruit 1377/13 [OF. *fraiel*]

frayes *sb. pl.* frights, fears; *night frayes,* nightmares 841/2

frainsshe, frenssh, frensche *a.* French 81/29

fre *a.* free, at liberty, noble 59/21

fredom *sb.* freedom, nobility 69/18

freehertede *pa. p. a.* generous, benevolent 769/9

freel *a.* fragile, changeable, susceptible to moral collapse 281/24

ifreyned *v. pa. p.* asked 214/11 [OE. *freȝnan, friȝnan,* strong 3]

freisch(e) *a., adv.* fresh; *freissch and freisch,* afresh, anew 362/20

freisshlappe *sb.* dewlap, fold of skin hanging from an ox's throat 1148/28 [obscure + OE. *læppa* 'lobe']

frenesye, franesie, frenasye, frannesy *sb.* madness, rabies 153/35

frenetik, frentik *a., sb.* suffering from frenzy 123/12

frensche, frenssh, see **frainsshe**

†frenschipeþ *v. pres. 3sg.* accompanies,

goes in company with, grows beside 1039/28

fresiþ *v. pres. 3sg.* (**ifrore** *pa. p.*) freezes, congeals 151/35

frestoone *sb.* a finely grained and easily cut stone, here of an arsenic ore (and not limestone) 830/24

frete *v.* (**ifrete** *pa. p.*), **f(e)retyng** *sb.* to chew, gnaw, gnash (one's teeth), corrode 86/17 (*v.*), 114/31 (*sb.*)

freþe *v.* to enclose 1049/27 [from OE. *fyrhðe, gefyrhð*]

frikelich *adv.* eagerly, willingly 1190/15–16 [OF. *frique* + OE. *-lice*]

frithes *sb. pl.* enclosures 1048/9 [OE. *fyrhðe, gefyrhð*]

frogge *sb.* frog, an abscess or boil in the tongue (cf. modern 'frog in the throat') 207/19

fromward, froward *adv.* away, onward, from; *prep.* opposite to, contrary to 73/8

front *sb.* the forehead, the face 369/21

ifrore, see **fresiþ; froteþ** 680/37, see **wrooteþ**

froteþ *v. pres. 3sg.*, **frotinge** *sb.* rubs, (of fish) breeds by rubbing together, digs or grubs (in the ground) 298/30 (*v.*), 276/22 (*sb.*) [OF. *froter*]

froward *a.* contrary, obstinate 313/4

fructuous(e) *a.* fruitful 648/31

fruyt(e), frute, froyte *sb.* crops, fruit 53/14

fuayle, fuelle *sb.* fuel 788/13

fuyle, see **uile; fuyre,** see **fure; fuyrehoot,** see **firhoot; yfulde,** see **ifellid; fulend-,** see **fullendiþ**

fulfille *v.*, **fulfilling** *sb.* fulfill, fill up, complement, remedy 51/33 (*v.*), 53/17 (*sb.*)

fulle *sb.* fullness 46/35

fulle, felle- *v.*, **fullynge** *sb.* to fill 52/30 (*v.*), 957/26 (*sb.*)

ful(l)endiþ *v. pres. 3sg.* completes, accomplishes 441/3

fullinge, see **folwinge**

fulþe, filþe, felþe *sb.* filth 63/3

fultur, see **vulture**

fumetere *sb.* fumitory 1315/2

fumosyte *sb.* vapour, smoke, exhalation arising from humours 116/17 [OF. *fumosité,* senses from L. *fumus*]

fumous *a.* smoky, vapourlike 115/36

fundament, fundement, see **founde-ment**

funges *sb. pl.* mushrooms 998/12 [L. *fungus*]

funte *sb.* font; **funte halewinge,** consecration of a baptismal font 548/36

fure, vure, fire, fier, fyire, fuyre, vuyre *sb.* fire, the element fire; *afire, ofire, on fire,* on fire; *þe holy fuyre,* the disease erysipelas 57/33

fury, vury, firy, fiery *a.* fiery 64/36

furst, first(e) *num.* first; *firste burþis,* first-born offspring 40/7

furst, see **ferst; furþ(e),** see **ferþe; furþere,** see **ferþe**

furþermore *adv.* still further, more, moreover 161/9

gaderers *sb. pl.* gatherers, collectors 1376/32

gadre, gedre *v.,* **gadringe, gedringe** *sb.* to gather, conclude, contract 44/10 (*v.*), 145/14 (*sb.*)

galle *sb.*[1] the gall-bladder, bile (one of the four humours), something bitter as bile 157/31

galle *sb.*[2] oak gall 846/4

galpiþ *v. pres. 3sg.* gapes 432/19 [cf. Middle Dutch *galpen* 'yelp']

gameful *a.* playful, humorous 1231/9

games *sb. pl.* entertainments 40/11

gangelinge, see **iangle**

gargarismes *sb. pl.* gargles 358/11

garlek(e), garleek *sb.* garlic 909/27

garneres *sb. pl.* granaries 1059/30

garse *v.,* **garsinge** *sb.* to cut to draw out a fluid, let blood, scarify 346/11 (*v.*), 354/37 (*sb.*) [OF. *garser*]

gastnes *sb.* a terrifying thing, a threatening action 87/33

gat(e), see **gete; geawis,** see **geowis**

gedy *a.* dizzy 999/21

gedines, gidinesse *sb.* dizziness 352/2

gedre(-), see **gadre; geete,** see **goot; gelded,** see **gilded**

geliþ *v. pres. 3sg.* congeals 983/10

gemetry *sb.* geometry 1367/18

gencian *sb.* gentian (used in medical recipes) 433/29

gendir *sb.* genus, class, grammatical gender 45/13

†gendrable *a.* capable of being generated or developed 553/20–1

gendre *v.,* **gendringe** *sb.* to bring forth, mate, *sb.* procreation, production; *gendringe stones,* testicles 45/8 (*v.*), 93/2 (*sb.*)

gendrure *sb.* development 1339/29

generacioun *sb.* procreation, production, development, origin 103/18

†generallich *a.* comprehensive, pertaining to all situations 876/27

generatif *a.* reproductive (organs), procreative (power) 97/25

†genetras, genytrace, genytras *sb.* (*pl.*) the testicles, the male sexual organs; *bagge of þe genytrace,* the scrotum 409/19 [OF. *geniteres, genitres* pl.]

gentil *a.* noble (by birth) 318/19

gentilnes *sb.* nobility (esp. of birth) 233/17

geowis, geawis, gewes (also **iaw-, iow-**) *sb. pl.* the jaws 55/6

gerfaucoun *sb.* a large falcon, esp. one used for hunting herons 1349/6

gesse *v. pres. pl.* estimate 463/21

gesses *sb. pl.* straps of leather fastened around the legs of a hawk (and attached to a leash in order to control the bird) 608/25

gete *sb.* jet, yellow jet or amber 768/6

gete *v.* (**gat(e)** *pa.;* **igete** *pa. p.*), **getinge** *sb.* to get, beget 44/21 (*v.*), 271/13 (*sb.*)

gewes, see **geowis; gidinesse,** see **gedines**

gildene *a.* made of gold 497/28

gildid, gelded *v. pa. p.,* **geldyng** *sb.* gelded 196/20 (*v.*), 978/9 (*sb.*)

gileful(le) *a.* deceitful, fraudulent 87/33

gyleþ, guyleþ *v. pres. 3sg.* deceives 446/15

giltid *v. pa.* sinned 710/28

gynne *sb.* scheme, machine, snare 307/5

gynnynge *sb.,* **gonne** *v. pa.* began 1389/5 (*v.*), 477/27 (*sb.*)

igird, gurde *v. pa. p.,* **girdinge, gurdynge** *sb.* struck, cut, severed 273/35 (*v.*), 429/29 (*sb.*)

gisarne *sb.* gizzard, entrails 256/3

giste *sb.* beam, joist 1057/6

gith *sb.* a plant with husked seeds used as a spice, a form of coriander 973/7 [L. *gith*]

glaas *sb.* ice 823/21

glade *sb.* setting; *goþ to glade,* (of the sun) sets 785/19 [cf. ON. *sólarglaðan*] gladeþ, gladdeþ v. pres. 3sg. (glad pa. p. once), gladinge sb. gladdens 214/8 (v.), 58/2 (sb.)

glasen a. made of glass 832/36

glasy a. glass-like; glasy humour, the vitreous humour in the eye 178/17

glasiere sb. glassmaker 879/18

glebe sb. soil, earth 716/23

gleyme sb. a slimy substance, phlegm or mucus 1030/35

gleyme v. (gle(y)mynge pres. p., a.), gleymynge sb. be sticky, stop up 409/15 (v.), 57/18 (sb.) [obscure; cf. ON. kleima 'daub']

gleymy, glemy a. sticky, thick 207/21

gleymynesse sb. stickiness, thickness 160/20

gleymyngnesse sb. stickiness 1012/27 [from gleyme v. + OE. -nes]

gleymous a. sticky, thick 409/10

gleyre sb. egg-white, albumen (used in the preparation of various paints) 1288/24 [OF. glaire]

glewe, glu(w), glwe sb. glue or some similar substance for sticking things together, pitch or tar, various natural gums or resins; glewe of parties, the natural moisture which binds together parts of the body 272/19

gleweþ v. pres. 3sg. glues or sticks together, seals (the edges of a wound), constipates, caulks 399/7

glewy, gluy a. sticky, glue-like, pitch-like 273/16

glide sb. kite, vulture 249/10 [OE. glida]

†glymysschyng a. glimmering, shining, glistening 834/15

glires sb. pl. dormice 776/16 [L. glis]

glysnynge a., sb. shining, glittering, gleaming (with sweat) 74/12

gloreþ v. pres. pl. shine, gleam, glisten 660/1 [cf. Middle Dutch gloren, ON. glóra]

glose, gloos sb. explanatory commentary on a text, usually the standard 12c. Gloss of the Bible 172/24

glotoun a. greedy, voracious 1170/13

glotounliche adv. greedily 1170/14

glu(-), gluw(e), glwe, see glewe(-)

gnawe v. (ignawe pa. p.), gnawinge sb. to gnaw; gnawe þe tonge, bite one's tongue in indignation 257/14 (v.), 158/9 (sb.)

ygnoddid v. pa. p. rubbed with the hands 988/5 [OE. gnuddian]

go, goo v. (3ede, went pa.; goone pa. p.) to go, walk, move 67/10

gobet, gobat sb. piece, mass of flesh, part or segment 115/9

gobetmele, gobettismele adv. piece by piece, bit by bit, in chunks 403/10

goddes(se), goddas sb. female deity, goddess 493/7

goinge sb. walking, journeying, motion, stretching; goinge wiþ childe, pregnancy 55/22

goldy a. golden (in colour) 840/11

gonne, see gynnynge

goodliche, godeliche a. excellent, noble, courteous 478/28

goorde-, see gorde; goost(-), see gost(-)

goot sb. (gothes poss. once; geete, goote pl.) goat 167/7

gorde, goorde-, gourde sb. cucumber, gourd plant 400/17

gorels sb. pl. gluttons, fat or paunchy people 358/8 [OF. gorel]

gost, goost sb. spirit or soul, a spirit, the spirit of God 41/11

gostliche, goostliche, goostly a., adv. spiritual(ly), holy 67/16

goter sb. channel or water conduit, trough for carrying waste, sewer, drain 154/15

gothes, see goot; goukkou, see kockowes

goule a. yellow, pale 601/35 [ON. gulr]

gourde, see gorde

goute, gute, gowte sb. gout, arthritis, a disease caused by dripping of fluids into joints, the drops of liquid producing such a disease 223/35

gouernaunce sb. rule, influence, self-control, medical regimen 90/25

gouernour sb. ruler, helmsman or pilot 169/3

gowte, see goute

gowty a. afflicted by gout 1034/21

gowtissh a. afflicted by gout 907/18

graffe sb. graft, twig, shoot 275/30

graffe v., graffinge sb. to graft, to make a graft 275/30 (v.), 545/30 (sb.)

graiel sb. the Gradual 542/26 [AN. grayel]

grayne, see greyne; grayþ-, see greythe

granates sb. pl. pomegranates 890/12

granulus *a.* granular 257/36
grapy, grapi *a.* grape-like, grape-coloured, dark or black 178/22
graunt *sb.* consent; *dedes of graunt*, legal documents conferring a right 308/26
graue *v.* (**ygraue, grauen** *pa. p.*), **grauyng** *sb.* to carve, engrave 840/1 (*v.*), 840/1 (*sb.*)
grauel, grauelle *sb.* sand, pebbles, a kidney stone 114/29
grauelie *a.* sandy 653/16
grauelouse *a.* sandy 668/18
grauer(e)s *sb. pl.* carvers, sculptors, engravers 833/23
graues *sb. pl.* tombs 614/15
grebicches *sb. pl.* female greyhounds 1166/33 [OE. *grīg-húnd* with substitution of OE. *bicce* for the second element]
grece, gres(e) *sb.* fat, tallow, lard 274/8
grece, see **grewe**
grediliche *adv.* importunately, eagerly 1242/11
grediþ *v. pres. 3sg.*, **gredinge** *sb.* cries out, shrieks, croaks 600/8 (*v.*), 620/21 (*sb.*)
gree *sb.* degree, stair, step, rank 69/22
greef, see **greue; grees,** see **grewe**
grehoundes *sb. pl.* greyhounds 1166/28
greyne, grayne *sb.* grain 66/21
greythe, grayþe- *v.*, **greiþinge** *sb.* to prepare, cook 329/24 (*v.*), 321/8 (*sb.*) [ON. *greiða*]
grene *a., sb.* the colour green, denoting crudeness, unripeness, youth, newness, freshness 158/17
greneflyes *sb. pl.* aphids or similar plant-eating insects 956/36–7
grenne, grene, gryne *sb.* snare, net (for capturing game) 213/26 [OE. *grin*, *grȳn*]
grenneþ, grynneþ *v. pres. pl.* grimace, growl 953/18
grete *sb.* ancestors 1380/26 [calque on L. *maior*]
gretter *sb.* one who greets 225/20
greue, greef *sb.* trouble, injury, pain 108/30
greue, grieue- *v.*, **greuynge, grieuynge** *sb.* to injure, afflict 76/14 (*v.*), 311/14 (*sb.*)
grew(e), griew, grev, gru *sb., a.* (**grece(s), gruys, grees** *pl.*) Greek, an inhabitant of Greece 56/22

grieue-, see **greue; griew,** see **grewe**
grillinge *sb.* trembling 385/21 [from OE. *grillan*]
gryne, see **grenne; grynneþ,** see **grenneþ**
grynteþ *v. pres. 3sg.* growls, roars 1218/28 [cf. OE. *grymetian*]
gripe, see **grippe**
gripe *sb.* (**grypes, griphes, griffouns** *pl.*) the griffin, the vulture 630/12
grip(p)e *sb.* hole, hollow dug in the earth 1015/23 [OE. *grȳpe*]
grisbaiteþ *v. pres. 3sg.*, **grisbaitinge, grisbattinge** *sb.* gnashes the teeth, chatters with the teeth, speaks uncouthly 1218/29 (*v.*), 348/34 (*sb.*) [OE. *gristbātian*]
gris(e)liche, gresilyche *a.* horrible, incurable 66/13
grisines, grysenesse, grysnes *sb.* horror 392/10
gristly *a.* gristly 115/14
grollynge, grullinge *sb.* growling, roaring, gurgling noise in the intestines 244/31 [echoic]
grontyn, see **grunteþ**
grope *v.*, **gropinge** *sb.* to feel, touch 118/24 (*v.*), 108/9 (*sb.*)
grotes *sb. pl.* pieces, motes, specks 93/27
ground(e), growne *sb.* bottom, base, earth; *grounde ebbe*, low tide 120/33
gru, see **grewe**
grucche *v.*, **grucchinge** *sb.* to complain, murmur 102/28 (*v.*), 670/12 (*sb.*)
grullinge, see **grollynge**
grunteþ (gront-) *v. pres. 3sg.* grunts, growls, roars 1215/18
grustil, grustle *sb.* cartilage, gristle; *grustil bon*, structure made of cartilage 228/27
guyleþ, see **gyleþ**
igurd, igird *v. pa. p.* encircled, girdled 65/1
gurde, gurdynge, see **igird; gute,** see **goute**

ȝaneth *v. pres. pl.* (**ȝenynge** *pres. p.*) yawn, gape 430/31
ȝate *sb.* way 231/18
ȝaue, see **ȝeue; ȝe,** see **iȝe; ȝede,** see **go**
ȝelde *v.* to yield, give 1003/25
ȝelk(e), ȝolk(e) *sb.* the yolk 167/1

ȝelowhe, ȝelewhe, ȝolowȝ, ȝoloȝ *a.*, *sb.* yellow, the yellow of an egg 112/13

ȝende *a.* the farther 775/31

ȝenynge, see ȝaneth

ȝeotinge *v. pres. p.* (yȝote *pa. p.*) pouring, shedding 66/34 [OE. *ġēotan*, strong 2]

ȝerde *sb.* rod, the penis 65/4

†ȝerdy *a.* stick-shaped 418/13

ȝeue *v.* (ȝiu-, ȝif also *pres.*; ȝaf, yaf, ȝaue *pa.*; yȝoue, yȝiue, iȝeue, ȝouen *pa. p.*) to give 41/11 (*v.*), 74/3 (*sb.*)

ȝeueles *sb. pl.* rakes or forks for turning earth, dung, or hay 961/23 [OE. *ġeafel*]

ȝif, if *conj.* if 50/1

ȝif, see ȝeue

ȝifte *sb.* gift 44/7

ȝit, ȝet, ȝitte *conj.* yet, still, besides 46/35

ȝiu-, see ȝeue; ȝolk(e), see ȝelke

ȝollynge *sb.* howling 1165/31 [imitative]

ȝolo(w)ȝ, see ȝelowhe

ȝolowhe-red *sb.*, *a.* citrin-colour(ed), the shade of some pathological phenomena 195/33

ȝonde *a.* (yonder *comp.*) far, distant 786/21

ȝone *demon. a.* that one, the one over there, the farther one 705/25

ȝonglyng *sb.* young one, youth, offspring 126/32

yonyng *sb.* yawning, opening 655/23

yȝote, see ȝeotinge; yȝoue, see ȝeue

ȝox(e) *sb.* hiccough, cough, belch 909/7 [OE. *ġeocsa*, *ġesca*]

ȝoxynge *sb.* hiccoughing, belching 245/2

h-, initially added to otherwise transparent forms beginning with a vowel, e.g. hendeles 52/40 for endeles

ha, see he, heo; habbeþ, see han

habergeouns *sb. pl.* shirts of mail 796/28

habilite *sb.* potential, capacity, proficiency, suitableness; *in good habilite*, favourably 49/7

habitacioun *sb.* dwelling place 65/12

habundauns *sb.* superfluity, plenty 265/2

hacche *v.* (iheight, ihaught *pa. p.*) to hatch 604/31

hayffare, heyfer *sb.* heifer; *reed hayffare* in allusion to Numbers 19 550/28

hayle, see hawel

hakker *sb.* a chopping tool 1047/34

hale *v.*, halinge *sb.* to pull, stretch, strain, tear 229/30 (*v.*), 397/25 (*sb.*)

halewe, halowe- *v. pres. pl.*, halwinge, halewinge, halowinge *sb.* to bless 70/24 (*v.*), 57/13 (*sb.*)

halowin *sb. pl.* the saints, the blessed 511/18

halpe, see helpe

halt *a.* lame 561/22

halten *v. pres. pl.* limp, are lame 270/17

ha(l)uendel *sb.* half, a half part 359/4

ham, see he

†hameroun *sb.* a part of a ship, app. the bilge 263/34 [obscure]

han, haue, hauy *v.* (haþ, haaþ *pres. 3sg.*; habbeþ, haueþ, han *pres. pl.*; had(de), ihad *pa.*, *pa. p.*) to have 40/21

hap, happe *sb.* luck, chance; *in hap*, perhaps 116/18

happe *v.* to happen 105/36

happiliche, hapliche *adv.* possibly, accidentally 147/27

†haragiousnes *sb.* severity 77/1 [cf. OF. *aragier* 'to become enraged']

harde *v.*, hardynge *sb.* to harden 139/4 (*v.*), 827/19 (*sb.*)

harden, see hurdes

hardy *a.* bold, rash, pagan 133/28

hardines *sb.* bravery, rashness, rigidity 86/10

harnet *sb.* hornet 1206/18

hastyf *a.* quick, rash 1144/8

(i)hat-, see hete, hoteþ; hateþ, see hiȝt; haþ, see han

hatte, hat *v. pres. 3sg.* (hitiþ *pres. 3sg.* once; heet *pa.*) is called 56/25

ihaught, see hacche

haukers *sb. pl.* those who hunt with hawks, falconers 1041/25

haunche, hanche *sb.* the haunch 412/37

hauntiþ *v. pres. 3sg.*, hauntinge *sb.* frequents, busies himself, becomes aroused; *ihauntid*, inhabited 87/16 (*v.*), 87/18 (*sb.*)

hauendel, see haluendel

hauene *sb.* harbour 672/11

hauenles *a.* lacking harbours 774/29

hawel, hayle *sb.* hail 327/12

he, hi, hy, hiȝ, ha *pron.* (here, hire, hiere *poss.*; ham, hem(e) *obj.*) they 46/13

yhecchelid *v. pa. p.*, hechelynges *sb. pl.* combed flax 988/6 (*v.*), 1055/24 (*sb.*)

hedid *v. pa. p.* beheaded 311/33
hedlynge, heedlynge, hedlynges *adv.* headlong 684/15
heedstrong(e) *a.* obstinate, impetuous 313/4
heelde, see **holde; heelful,** see **heleful; heer,** see **here; heet,** see **hatte, hotiþ yheʒde** *v. pa. p.* (of the voice) raised 1388/17 [OE. *hēan* 'praise', with forms infl. by *hēah a.*]
heyfer, see **hayffare; iheight,** see **hacche**
heysaule *sb.* hedge-stake 1049/31 [OE. *heǧe-sǎhl* (for *-sāʒol*)]
yheld, see **huldiþ; helde,** see **holde heldiþ** *v. pres. pl.* (**hilde** *v.*; **hielde** *pres. subj.*; **helde, yhelte, ihilde, ihulid** *pa. p.*) pour out, spill 66/34 [OE. *híeldan*]
hele *sb.* health, happiness 93/12
hele, see **helye; ihelid,** see **huldiþ; helede,** see **holde**
heleful, heelful *a.* wholesome 208/26
†**hel(e)fulliche** *adv.* healthily 390/22
heleþ *v. pres. 3sg.* heals 53/20
hely(e), hele *v.* (**hil-** also), **hel(y)inge, hil(y)inge** *sb.* to cover, clothe 161/26 (*v.*), 112/27 (*sb.*) [OE. *helan,* strong 4, and *helian*]
heliere, see **hiliere**
helpe *v.* (**halpe** *pa.*; **holpe, yhulpe** *pa. p.*) to help 63/22
yhelte, see **heldiþ**
helþe *sb.* health, happiness (granted by heaven) 153/8
hemmes *sb. pl.* edges 672/23
heng, see **hongiþ; hender,** see **hind**
hengelis *sb. pl.* parts of the lungs, perhaps lobe- or hinge-shaped structures 236/26 [cf. Middle Dutch *hengel* 'hinge']
heo, ha (sche, scheo more usual) *pron.* she 172/29
hepe *sb.* (**hupes** *pl.*) heap 654/26
herberweþ, herboroweþ *v. pres. 3sg.* entertains, shelters 174/27
herborewe *sb.* shelter 666/20
herde, hu(y)rde, hierde, heorde, hyrde *sb.* shepherd, watchman 56/5
herden, see **hurdes**
here, heer, e(e)r *sb.* hair 64/2
yhered *v. pa. p.* covered with hair 1152/32
hery *a.* hairy 159/11
herie, hire *v.* to praise 52/9 [OE. *herian*]

herisshe *a.* hair-like, made of hair 771/14
heritage *sb.* inheritance, succession 301/17
herkeniþ *v. imper.* listen 319/12
hernyous *a.* afflicted with hernia 411/32
herre *sb.* door-hinge, esp. the socket in which the spindle is inserted 457/29 [OE. *heor(r)*]
hert(e) *sb.* the male red deer 152/1
herte, hurte, hirte *v.* to hurt 82/19
yherted *v. pa. p.* encouraged 1095/29
herto *adv.* for this reason, in addition 252/31
heruest, haruest *sb.* autumn 127/7
heste *sb.* command 61/23
hete, see **ete**
hete *v.* (**ihat(te), ihette** *pa. p.*) to heat, grow hot 237/28
heue *v.* (**ihoue** *pa. p.*), **heuyng** *sb.* to lift, raise 64/35 (*v.*), 899/15 (*sb.*)
heued, hed, heed, hid *sb.* head, source, principal 64/4
†**heuycherid** *pa. p., a.* sad 89/3
heuyliche *adv.* heavily 112/17
heuynesse *sb.* weight (incl. descriptions of extremes of sensation, e.g. *heuynesse of uoys*) 114/22
ihewe, hewen *v. pa. p.*, **hewynge** *sb.* cut, hewn 274/4 (*v.*), 1057/1 (*sb.*)
hi, hy, hiʒ, see **he; hid,** see **heued**
hide, see **huyde; hidiþ,** see **huyde; hierde,** see **herde; highe,** see **hiʒt; hiʒt,** see **hotiþ; hyheþ,** see **hyʒeþ; (i)hilde,** see **heldiþ; hil-,** see **helye**
hidel(i)s, hidles *sb.* hiding place, hollow place (in a stalk of grain) 350/14
hider *a.* near(er) 824/16
hiderwarde *adv.* in this direction 826/25
hielde, see **heldiþ, holde**
hyenes *sb. pl.* hyenas 1210/26
hieþ, see **hyʒeþ**
hiew(e), hewe *sb.* hue 120/37
hiʒe, hye *a.* (**hy(ʒ)er** *comp.,* **hi(ʒ)est** *super.*) high 41/29
hiʒe *sb.* height, altitude 790/9
hyʒehertede *a.* proud 764/25
hyʒeþ, hyheþ, hieþ *v. pres. 3sg.* hastens 177/15
hiʒt *v.* (**hateþ, hyteþ** *pres. 3sg.* once each; **ihiʒt, highe** *pa. p.*), **hiʒtinge** *sb.* to adorn, distinguish 56/24 (*v.*), 76/1 (*sb.*) [obscure; cf. OE. *hyht* 'hope, joy'; *hyhtan* 'hope, rejoice']

†**hiȝtnes, hiȝtynesse** *sb.* adornment 196/7

†**hil(i)ere, heliere** *sb.* covering 184/14 [OE. *helian* + *-ere*]

hind *a.* (**hender** *comp.* once) back, rear 351/15

hyn(n)de *sb.* the hind 942/34

hindemest, -most *a.* rearmost 122/33

†**hynderward** *adv.* backward, from the rear 676/13

hyng, see **hongiþ; hier(-), hir(-),** see **hur(-)**

hirchoun, yrchoun *sb.* hedgehog 724/34

hyrde, see **herde; hire,** see **herie; hirte,** see **herte; hispiles,** see **ispile**

hit *pron.* it 46/22

hitiþ, see **hatte, hiȝt**

hyue, huyue *sb.* (**huyes** *pl.* once) beehive 1142/18

hocke, hokke *sb.* the mallow 383/27

hoeple, see **hupel; hoge,** see **houge**

hoystis *sb. pl.* sacrifices, offerings 542/5 [OF. (*h*)*oiste*]

hokke, see **hocke**

holde *v.* (**heelde, huld, hielde, helede, helte, hilde** *pa.*; **iholde, ihelde** *pa. p.*), **holdinge** *sb.* to hold; *þe vertu of holdinge,* one of the Galenic faculties, retention 45/11 (*v.*), 104/24 (*sb.*)

hole, hool *a.* whole, sound 53/20

hole *sb.* (**holis, hulles, huoles** *pl.*) husk, a weight (L. *siliqua,* 1/18 dram) 954/5

holefotid *a.* with an undivided foot, web-footed 227/28

holeliche *adv.* completely, fully 52/34

holfullich *adv.* beneficially, with healthy results 434/14

iholid *v. pa. p.* hulled 958/6

holly, holy *a.* full of holes 235/20

hologh(-), see **holowȝ(-)**

holowȝ, holouȝ, holow, hologh *a.* hollow, curved; *þe holowȝ veyne,* the vena concava 98/15

holowȝy, holouȝysch *a.* having cavities, porous 237/31

holowȝnes, hologhnes *sb.* hollowness, concave surface 115/20

holpe, see **helpe**

holsomeliche *adv.* healthfully 1171/36-7

homeliche *a.* familiar 221/1

homeliche *adv.* simply, plainly 309/21

hondeworke *sb.* handiwork, things made by hand 790/5

honest *a.* honourable 61/22

honeste *sb.* reputation, virtue 302/3

hongels *sb.* a suspension device, the support for the point of a balance 1384/16

hongiþ, hangiþ *v. pres. 3sg.* (**hyng, heng** *pa.*; **ihonge, yhonged** *pa. p.*) hangs 79/5

honysokes *sb. pl.* honeysuckle plants or flowers 755/23

hoof, see **houe**

hook *sb.* sickle, scythe 1047/34

hool, see **hole**

hoopis *sb. pl.* hoops 1042/15

hoore, hore *sb.* filth, slime 114/28 [OE. *horh, horu*]

hoores *sb. pl.* whores 1248/12

ho(o)reþ *v. pres. 3sg.* becomes hoary 177/18

hoos, hose *a.* hoarse 140/19

hoosnesse *sb.* hoarseness 145/22

hooueþ, houeþ *v. pres. pl.,* **houynge, howuyng** *sb.* hover, lie protectingly over young, linger, live (in a place) 428/23 (*v.*), 478/4 (*sb.*)

†**thoppen** *sb. pl.* the seedpods of flax 987/34 [OE. *ȝehopp*]

hore *a.* hoar, grey 177/16

hore, see **hoore**

hor(e)nes *sb.* hoariness, grey hair 177/17

horeþ, see **hooreþ**

hory *a.* dirty, filthy, soiled 142/25

†**thory** *sb.* dirt 142/32

horisch, horissh *a.* pale, somewhat white 487/28

horne *sb.* horn, vessel shaped like a horn, incl. a cup used in blood-letting 167/9

ihorned *v. pa. p.,* **horninge** *sb.* had blood drawn with a cupping horn, venusected 421/18 (*v.*), 373/34 (*sb.*)

(h)orrible *a.* dreadful 198/11

†**thorsinge** *sb.* a rumbling or crashing noise 114/17

hose, see **hoos**

hosen *sb. pl.* husks of an ear of grain, chaff 1054/9 [OE. *hosu*]

hote, hoot *a.* (**hat-** occ. in *comp., super.*) hot 70/28

hoteþ *v. pres. 3sg.* heats 329/19

hotiþ *v. pres. 3sg.* (**heet, hiȝt** *pa.*; **ihote** *pa. p.*) commands, prohibits, promises 63/19

houge, huge, hoge *a.* huge 89/24

hougelich, hugelich *adv.* greatly 553/12
hound *sb.* dog 99/13
houndissch *a.* dog-like, canine (of teeth) 202/21-2
houre *sb.* an hour 217/6
housbonde *sb.* husbandman, steward 245/14
housbondry *sb.* cultivation 957/6
hous(e) *sb.* house, the place in the Zodiac where the influence of a planet is enhanced 208/8
houe, hoof *sb.* hoof 271/23
ihoue, see **heue**; **houeþ, houynge, howuyng,** see **hooueþ**
hucche, whiche *sb.* chest 913/2
huddis *sb. pl.* husks, hulls 928/12
huyde, hide *sb.* skin 424/30
huyde, hude, hide *v.* (**ihid, ihud** *pa. p.*) to hide 41/11
huyr-, see **hureþ**; **huyrde,** see **herde**; **huyue, huyes,** see **hyue**; **huld,** see **holde**
huldiþ *v. pres. 3sg.* (**iheled, yheld** *pa. p.* occ.), **huldinge** *sb.* flays, peels, gnaws 145/23 (*v.*), 287/16 (*sb.*) [OE. *hyldan*]
ihulid, see **heldiþ**
hulk(e) *sb.* husk, hull 978/8 [OE. *hulc*]
hulle, hille *sb.* hill 138/4
hulles, see **hole**; **yhulpe,** see **helpe**
humour *sb.* liquid, one of the four basic fluids which form organisms (blood, bile, phlegm, melancholia), fluid portions of the eye (incl. *þe cristalline humour*, the lens; *þe glasi humour*, the vitreous humour) 42/18
hundred, hondrid *sb.* one hundred, a hundredweight 474/7
huoles, see **hole**
hupel, heple, hoeple *sb.* pile (esp. of hay or grain) 131/11 [OE. *hypel*]
hupes, see **hepe**
†**thuplyng** *sb.* heaping together 1374/30
hurde, see **herde**
hurdes, hurdenne, harden, herden *sb. pl.* the hards of flax or hemp, that portion which is carded out, coarse fabric made thereof 130/20 [OE. *heorde*]
hureþ, hereþ, hireþ *v. pres. 3sg.*, **heringe, hu(y)ringe, hierynge** *sb.* hears, obeys 108/14 (*v.*), 55/3 (*sb.*)
hurliþ *v. pres. pl.*, **hurlinge** *sb.* rush at, collide, destroy (by tossing about, as by the wind) 415/14 (*v.*), 397/21 (*sb.*)

†**thurride** *v. pa.* buzzed, made a humming or buzzing sound 624/13
hurstes *sb. pl.* hillocks, sand bars 827/5 [OE. *hyrst*]
hurtlynge *sb.* knocking, collision 594/22

iacincte *sb.* the gem hyacinth 840/20
†**iacinctinysche** *a.* coloured like hyacinth, bluish or purple 1003/23
iangelers *sb. pl.* chatterers, boasters 177/9-10
iangle *v. pres. pl.* (**gangelinge** *pres. p., a.* once), **iangelinge** *sb.* chatter, twitter 301/33 (*v.*), 351/24 (*sb.*)
iape *v. pres. pl.* deceive, behave foolishly, laugh, have sexual intercourse 263/19
iapes *sb. pl.* frauds, illusions 840/27
iaundes, see **iawndis**; **iawe,** see **geowis**
iawndis, iaundes *sb.* jaundice 406/20
icche *v.*, **ycching, echynge, hechinge** *sb.* to itch, rub 160/11 (*v.*), 114/31 (*sb.*)
icche, icchinge, see **eche**
Iche, I, Y *pron.* (**my, myne** *poss.*; **me** *obj.*) I 40/5
ydea *sb.* the exemplar, the Platonic Idea 93/22
ydel *a.* empty, useless; *an ydel*, uselessly, to no purpose 129/30
ydromancy *sb.* divination based on studying water 870/33 [L. *hydromantia*]
ydropesie *sb.* dropsy 590/3
ye, see **iȝe**
ientrie *sb.* noble rank, nobility of bearing or manners 318/16
ierarchies *sb. pl.* ranks in a sacred order, esp. the three divisions of angels, the angels 41/17
ifalle *v.* to fall down 437/16
ifere (also *phr.* **in fe(e)re, in fiere**) *adv.* together, in company, simultaneously 49/1
iȝe, yȝe, eiȝe, eihe, ye, ȝe, ey *sb.* (**-en** *pl.* invariable) the eye 54/36
y-yȝed, see **yhiȝt**
yles, see **eyle**
iliche, ilike, ilick *a., adv.* like, equal(ly); *euer yliche*, always 64/22
illuminacioun *sb.* knowledge of God (intuited by angels) 68/19
illumineþ *v. pres. pl.* enlighten spiritually 69/34
ymage *sb.* figure, likeness, resemblance, expression 50/20

imaginacioun *sb.* creative memory, illusion, dream, reflection of light from a surface 92/19

ymaginatif *a.*, *sb.* (and *phr.* **vertu ymaginatif**) ability to create images, the front cell of the brain where this power resides 99/12

ymagineþ *v. pres. 3sg.* forms an image of 107/22

†**immutatiue** *a.* having the power to effect change 97/18

impartibil *a.* not capable of division, indivisible 52/22

impressioun, imprecioun *sb.* imprinting, force or influence, a change or effect produced by such influence (esp. astral), atmospheric phenomena, a mental image or sensation 102/24

impugnaciouns *sb. pl.* spiritual attacks, temptations 544/34

in-, see **en-**

incastinge *sb.* throwing in, interjection 215/9

incessable *adv.* incessantly 71/10

inclynacioun *sb.* natural disposition (as shaped by the position of the planets), a tendency to perform an act 340/27

inclosinge *sb.* shutting up 366/33

incomynge, see **innecomeþ**

incomprehensibil *a.* limitless, unbounded 52/36

incongrue *a.* illogical, not correct 60/18

inconuenient *sb.* inconsistency, fallacy 510/22

†**incorpiþ** *v. pres. 3sg.* mixes, joins to 104/25 [L. *incorporāre*]

incorporacioun *sb.* joining together or combining with other substances 511/5-6

incorporith *v. pres. 3sg.* (**in-, encorporat, icorporat** *pa. p., a.*) joins with, blends 135/17

incorruptiblenes *sb.* incorruptibility 452/2

indifferentliche *adv.* indiscriminately, equally 178/32-3

indigest *a.* undigested, crude, immature 253/23

indignacioun *sb.* wrath, irritation of the stomach 107/9

indrawinge *sb.* inhalation, act of pulling inward 105/16

induccioun *sb.* a stage in the development of an angel, part of a hierarchy of stages by which it comes to direct perception of divine bliss 69/9

†**infames** *a.* of ill-repute, scorned 1357/21

infectif, infectiue *a.* infectious 967/21

infectioun *sb.* infection 101/36

infectiþ *v. pres. 3sg.* (**infect** *pa. p., a.*) infects, pollutes, stains 86/30

inflaumeþ *v. pres. 3sg.* sets on fire 70/15

inflexible *a.* rigid, steadfast 71/26

influens *sb.* power, the influence of the stars, the flowing of a fluid 61/1

informacioun *sb.* teaching, nature, construction 41/23

informatiue *a.* formative, shaping; *informatiue vertue*, *vertu informatiue*, the power inherent in souled matter contributing to the development of an embryo into its proper form 97/18

informe *a.* without form, (of prime matter) not endowed with 'form' 1373/30

informeth *v. pres. 3sg.* (**enfourme** *v.*) instructs, forms, develops, gives Aristotelian 'form' to (a material), creates 81/16

ingenerable *a.* incapable of being produced by another substance 443/29

inhabitable *a.* uninhabitable 810/21-2

†**ynkitters** *sb. pl.* foreteeth 202/16 [OE. *in-* + **cyttan*; a calque on L. *incisor*]

†**inmaterialliche** *a.* not made of matter, spiritual 52/28-9

inmest *adv., a., sb.* inmost, deepest 53/27

ynmoderat *a.* excessive 217/8

innecomeþ *v. pres. pl.*, **incomynge** *sb.* enter 1381/31 (*v.*), 578/9 (*sb.*)

inner *adv.* more deeply 453/33

innermest *a.* furthest in, interior 146/13

innermore *adv.* further inside, later on 68/14

inneste *a. super.* inmost 1079/18

innocentes *sb. pl.* harmless persons 317/25

innumerabil *a.* beyond counting 51/29

inordinat *pa. p., a.* excessive, irregular (of biological functions and regimen) 128/29

inow(з), inoзe, anow *adv.* enough, plenty, sufficient(ly) 111/33

inparfite *a.* imperfect 459/18

inpassibil, impassible *a.* incapable of suffering or harm 51/28
inpetuous *a.* rash, violent 159/10
inprentiþ *v. pres. 3sg.* fixes, imprints 121/1
inproporcionat *a.* disproportionate 364/28
inpugne *v.* to attack, tempt 87/35
inquire, enquere *v.* to seek out, try to find 453/32
inquisicioun *sb.* inquiry 436/17
inseparable *a.* incapable of being disjointed or disassociated 262/27–8
inspiracioun *sb.* divine communication, giving of divine power 55/7
instrumental *a.* used of one of the four Aristotelian principles of causation, the material cause: that material thing which serves as the physical means to a goal 117/10–11
insuperable *a.* invincible 836/10
intellect *sb.* understanding 92/20
intellectual *a.* perceived by understanding, imaginary, theoretical 59/20
intelligibil *a.* comprehended by intellect 59/26
interclos(e), enterclos *sb.* partition, dividing wall, husk or membrane within a seed pod 972/22 [OF. *entreclos*]
inwarde *sb.* the inner part, the spiritual nature of a being 71/30
inwit *sb.* intellect, soul 60/5
ioyneþ *v. pres. 3sg.* (**iune** *v.*; **ion-, iun-, iuyn-, iuny**-forms occur) joins, closes a wound, is in astrological conjunction with 52/22
ioynt pee *adv. phr.* with the feet together 270/22 [OF. *piés joins*]
iointure *sb.* union of like objects 75/6
ioneþ, see **ioyneþ**; **iouys**, see **ius**; **iowes**, see **geowis**
yppotami *sb. pl.* hippopotami 756/31
irascibil *a.* a level or part of the soul: that irrational nature which includes courage and passion (but not appetite) 96/1
yre, yrne *sb.* iron 154/8
irenware *sb.* articles made of iron 848/34
irnen *a.* made of iron 761/23
ysele(e)n *sb. pl.* embers, ashes, cinders 795/9 [OE. *ysl(e)*]
isope *sb.* hyssop 832/21
ispile, hispile- *sb.* hedgehog 433/27 [OE. *iles*, gen. of *il* 'hedgehog' + *pil* 'spike']

issueþ *v. pres. pl.* flow out 916/18
iubile *sb.* Jubilee, the year of remission at the end of a fifty-year cycle 1389/9
iugeres *sb. pl.* a Roman measurement of land ploughed by a team of oxen in one day, slightly less than an acre 1381/15 [L. *jugerum*]
iune, see **ioyneþ**
ius, iuys, iouys *sb.* juice, bodily fluid, broth 208/11
yuel, euel *sb.* evil; *þe kynges yuel*, scrofula; *þe slepyng yuel*, lethargy 63/24
yueled, see **eueleþ**; **iware, ywarre**, see **ware**

kalende *sb.* the first day of the month, the Hebrew new moon or new year, calendar 506/21
kancre, see **cancre**; **kanne**, see **cunne**; **kastayne**, see **chesteynes**; **keen**, see **cow**
kele *v.* (**kil-** once), **kelinge** *sb.* to cool, make cold 107/2 (*v.*), 57/32 (*sb.*) [OE. *cēlan*]
kembiþ *v. pres. 3sg.*, **kempyng** *sb.* combs, cards 301/26 (*v.*), 1239/29 (*sb.*)
kende(-), see **kynde(-)**
keole, kele *sb.* keel 230/21
kepe *v.* (**kep(p)e** *pa.* occ.; **ykeppe** *pa. p.* once), **kepinge** *sb.* to care about, take care to, attend or take heed, desire, hold, prevent 122/11 (*v.*), 82/16 (*sb.*)
kerf(e) *sb.* cut 1070/7 [OE. *cyrf*]
kernelle, cornelle, curnelle *sb.* seed, pit of a fruit, gland 276/9
kernelly *a.* glandular, full of glands 281/31
kertil, see **kurtel**
kerue *v.* (**ikorue, coruen** *pa. p.*) to cut, perform surgery on 151/9
keruers *sb. pl.* foreteeth 202/24
keruynge *sb.* cutting, surgical incision, burning sensation 120/13
keuereþ, kouereþ, couereþ *v. pres. pl.*, **keuerenge, coueringe** *sb.* cover 186/17 (*v.*), 215/30 (*sb.*)
kybes *sb. pl.* chilblains in the heel 1227/14
kydeneiren *sb. pl.* kidneys, loins 230/23
kykeþ *v. pres. 3sg.* kicks, is stubborn 301/26
kileþ, see **kele**
kynde, kende *a., adv.* natural(ly), innate(ly), pure 94/24

kynde, kende *sb.* nature, sort, character, species, what is natural, Nature 41/8
kyndeliche, kendeliche *a.* natural 41/31
kyndeliche *adv.* naturally, according to the nature of a thing, innately 92/13
kynrede *sb.* lineage, kinsmen 467/23
kissiþ *v. pres. 3sg.* **(cusse** *v.*) kisses 200/22
kiþeþ, kuyþeþ *v. pres. 3sg.* shows, demonstrates 930/35 [OE. *cȳðan*]
kitte, kuytte *v.*, **kittynge, kuyttynge** *sb.* to cut 206/25 (*v.*), 279/2 (*sb.*)
knappe *sb.* a knot or protuberance on the stem of a plant, a bud 922/27 [OE. *cnæpp*]
knaue *sb.* a boy 264/16
ykned(d)e *v. pa. p.*, **knedynge** *sb.* kneaded 958/26 (*v.*), 1046/1 (*sb.*)
knycches, knucches *sb. pl.* bundles or bunches (of plants) 988/1 [OE. *ġecnyċċ* 'bond']
†kny3tene *a.* military 1382/6
knyttels *sb. pl.* strings, bands for tying things together 988/18
knyttiþ, knettiþ *v. pres. 3sg.* (**iknit** *pa. p.*, **ykynytte** once) fastens, makes a knot, joins, hinders by fastening 305/7
yknokked *v. pa. p.* pounded, beaten (a process in producing thread from flax) 988/4
knot *sb.* knot, coil, bond, joint 219/4
knotty *a.* having knobs 214/25
knowleche *sb.* knowledge 47/8
knowleche *v.* to find out, admit 314/10
knucches, see **knycches**
kockowes *sb. pl.* **(goukkou** *sg.* once) cuckoos 634/28
kode *sb.* cud 684/13
konne-, see **cunne**
konneþ *v. pres. pl.* proclaim, teach, reveal 81/23 [OE. *kennan*]
konnynge, kunnynge *sb.* knowledge 53/16
kontre, see **contrey; koppis,** see **coppe; ikorue,** see **kerue; kouereþ,** see **keuereþ; kuyn, koue,** see **cow; kuyppes,** see **cuype; kuyþeþ,** see **kiþeþ; kuytte,** see **kitte**
kurtel, curtel, kertil *sb.* coat or cloak, the skin of a snake, coating or membrane in the body (esp. the tunics of the eye, the meninges, the layered walls of blood vessels, the eardrum) 111/8

ylaced *v. pa. p.* fastened or joined together (of timbers in a building) 1059/23
laces *sb. pl.* ornamental beams in a ceiling, crossbeams used to tie rafters together 1059/23
lackeþ *v. pres. 3sg.* (freq. impersonal *it lackeþ him*) is absent or deficient, fails 54/18
ylad(d)e *v. pa. p.* loaded 652/16
†lagenes *sb. pl.* small wine-barrels 1378/1 [L. *lagēna*]
laghweþ, la3heþ, see **lau3e; lay,** see **ligge**
laye, ley *sb.* lake, pond 327/13 [OE. *la3u* and OF. *lai*]
layeþ *v. pres. 3sg.* eases, subdues 833/14
lake *sb.* stream, conduit 279/7
lambe, lombe *sb.* (**lambren, lambrum** *pl.*) lamb 208/14
langage, longage *sb.* language, tongue 179/19
lanternes *sb. pl.* lanterns 331/4
lapidarie *sb.* a treatise on gems 842/25
lapwynke, lapewynke, see **lepwink**
large *a.* generous, ample, abundant, great, broad 73/15
largeliche *adv.* liberally, widely, loosely 74/7
largenesse *sb.* generosity, liberality, extent 213/36
las, lasse, les *a., sb., adv.* less, lesser, fewer, smaller 72/23
lassen *v.* to grow less 518/13
laste *a., sb.* last, final (esp. of the end of the world, *þe laste tyme*), concluding, furthest, most remote (heaven), most extreme or best 69/3
laste, see **leste; late,** see **lete; lateþ,** see **lotye**
laþþe *sb.* lath 1059/15
latoun, latone, latyn *sb.* alloy of copper, tin, and other metals 66/7 [OF. *laton*]
lau3e *v. pres. pl.* (**laghw-, la3h-, lau3h-**), **lau3enge** *sb.* laugh 161/33 (*v.*), 250/20 (*sb.*)
laumprays *sb. pl.* lampreys 1134/11
laundes, landes *sb. pl.* glades 717/15 [OF. *lande*]
laury, laurir *sb.* the laurel tree, the bay tree 932/30
laue *v.*, **lauyng** *sb.* to wash 260/15 (*v.*), 864/5 (*sb.*)

lax *a.* loose 1261/17
laxacioun *sb.* the act of loosening constipated bowels 506/17
laxatif *a., sb.* causing loosening (of the bowels), able to purge, a drug with these properties 333/4
laxe *v.*, **laxynge** *sb.* to loosen, purge 326/33 (*v.*), 1333/9 (*sb.*)
leche *sb.* physician, name for the ring finger 67/14
lede *v.* (**ilad(de)** *pa. p.*), **ledinge** *sb.* to draw, lead, instruct, carry 41/20 (*v.*), 41/18 (*sb.*)
leded *v. pa. p.* weighted with lead 924/5
ledy, leedy *sb.* lead-coloured, dull 479/35
le(e)disch *a.* lead-coloured, dull 425/31
leef, lief, leffe *a., adv.* (**leuer** *comp.*, **leuest** *super.*) dear, precious, pleasant; *comp.* preferable, preferably 86/13
leeful, see **liefful; leep**, see **lepe; leesard**, see **lusard; leese**, see **lese**
lef *sb.* (**leues** *pl.*) leaf, leaf-shaped object, esp. a lobe of the lung or a fold of tissue in the throat 211/21
lege *sb.* league 738/20
legge, laye *v.* (**lei-, legg-** *pres.*; (**i)leyde** *pa., pa. p.*), **legginge** *sb.* to lay 135/18 (*v.*), 615/23 (*sb.*)
leye *a.* fallow 719/19 [OE *lǣge*]
leye, lye, liȝe, leyȝe *sb.* fire, flame 66/5 [OE. *līg, lēg*; cf. **aleye**]
leyghtons, leightouns *sb. pl.* gardens, esp. herb-gardens 662/11 [OE. *lēahtūn*]
leykinge, see **lykeþ; leyse**, see **lese**
leke *sb.* leek 427/6
lemes *sb. pl.* flames, light beams 497/9 [OE. *lēoma*]
lemes, see **lymes**
lemynge *v. pres. p., sb.* blazing, flaming 460/15 (*v.*), 488/8 (*sb.*)
lendes *sb. pl.* loins, occ. as a figure of lechery 64/26 [OE. *lendenu* pl.]
lengere *a., adv., comp.* longer, taller 104/5
lengþiþ *v. pres. 3sg.* grows longer, extends 505/5
lente, lentene *sb.* spring, Lent 461/9
leopes *sb. pl.* woodlands 717/15 [OE. *hlīep(e)*]
leoun, lioun *sb.* lion, the constellation Leo, ant-lion 66/13
lepe *v.* (**leep, lepe** *pa.*), **lepinge** *sb.* to

leap; *sb.* throbbing, beating 71/21 (*v.*), 205/1 (*sb.*)
lepre, lepra *sb.* leprosy 161/4
lepres *a.* leprous 188/4
lepwink, lap(e)winke *sb.* the hoopoe 362/7
lere *a.* empty 139/28 [OE. *ȝelǣr*, **lǣre*]
lerned *v. pa.* was instructed, learned, taught 40/8
lernes *sb.* emptiness 106/9
les, see **las; lesard**, see **lusard**
lese, leese, leyse, lesue, lesse *sb.* pasture 539/13 [OE. *lǣs*]
lese *v.*, **lesinge** *sb.* to lose 71/27 (*v.*), 73/7 (*sb.*)
lesinges *sb. pl.* lies 302/29 [OE. *lēasung*]
lesingmongere *sb.* liar 470/23
lessiþ *v. pres. 3sg.* decreases 131/8
leste, laste *v.* to last 79/28
lesue, see **lese**
lete, late *v.* (**ilete, laten** *pa. p.*) to let, leave; *lete blood*, remove blood from, bleed 147/2
lethy *a.* flexible 300/22 [OE. *liðiȝ*]
let(te) *sb.* obstacle 83/21
lette *v.* (**ilet, iletted** *pa. p.*) to hinder, stop 53/7
letter *sb.* a graph, an epistle 40/9
lettrure *sb.* writing 222/1 [OF. *lettrëure*]
letwary *sb.* (**letuariis** *pl.* once) a medicine 944/12
leuke, lewke, luke *a.* lukewarm 367/11
leue *v.* (**liu-** occ.) to stop, remain, leave 93/6
leueþ *v. pres. pl.* grow leaves 528/4
lewed *a.* uneducated 45/3
lewere *sb.* cheek 195/11 [OE. *hlēor*]
liche *a., adv.* alike, similar(ly), equal(ly), suited to, identical (to) 46/2
licpot *sb.* the index finger 225/20
lief(f)ul, leeful *a.* permissible, allowable 643/3
life *sb.* life; *on lyue*, alive; *þe spirit of lif*, the vital spirit, responsible for conserving and regulating an organism's supply of heat 41/34
lifliche, lifly *a.* lively, vital 111/34
liflichenesse, lyuelynes *sb.* vigour, vitality 111/35
lyflode, lyuelode *sb.* food and drink, conduct 691/17 [OE. *līf-lād*]
lyftsomes *adv.* leftward 280/17
ligge, legge *v.* (**li-, liȝ-, ligg-** *pres.*; **lay**

ligge, legge (*cont.*)

 pa.; **ilaye, ileye** *pa. p.*), **lygynge** *sb.* to lie down, lie 172/28 (*v.*), 426/7 (*sb.*)

li(g)nage *sb.* lineage, tribe of Jews 318/17

liȝt *a.* light, swift, cheerful 66/5

liȝtiþ *v. pa. p.* reduced 537/14

liȝtliche *adv.* (**liȝtloker** *comp.*) easily, swiftly, soon 110/16

liȝtnes *sb.* lightness, swiftness, ease 159/5

liȝtneth *v. pres. 3sg.* burns 511/3

lykeþ *v. pres. 3sg.*, **leykinge** *sb.* leaks 148/8 (*v.*), 148/12 (*sb.*)

likynge *a.* pleasurable 89/6

likinge *sb.* pleasure 55/9

likingliche *adv.* pleasantly 299/30

liknes(se) *sb.* shape, similarity, image 41/11

likneþ *v. pres. 3sg.* (**ilikned** *pa. p.*, *a.*) makes similar, makes like, resembles 111/26

lymemele *adv.* limb from limb, limb by limb 1219/4

lymes, lemes *sb. pl.* limbs 89/23

lymynours *sb. pl.* illuminators 1039/32

line, ligne *sb.* a line; *by line*, in a linear fashion 53/6

lineacioun, linyacioun *sb.* outline or shape (of a part of the body) 63/31

lyneal *a.* having magnitude in one direction only; *lyneal nombre*, the first power of a number (as opposed to its square or cube) 1364/1

lyned *v. pa. p.* trimmed of the seed heads (a step in producing thread from flax) 988/1 [from OF. *ligne*]

lynen *v. pres. pl.* copulate with (of animals) 1165/13 [OF. *ligner*]

lyn(e)seed, lynneseed *sb.* linseed 973/19

lynx *sb.* (**lynces** *pl.*) the lynx 810/26

liquour, licour *sb.* a liquid (incl. fluids produced by animate bodies) 101/36

lyse, see **lous**

lissiþ *v. pres. 3sg.* assuages 284/26 [from OE. *lis* sb.]

list *sb.* the sense of hearing 366/10 [OE. *hlyst*]

lyste *sb.* a narrow strip of fabric for edging or binding 299/24 [OE. *līste*]

litargye *sb.* lethargy, an abscess producing this disease 183/10

lite, luyte *a.* little, few 143/15

litelwhat, see **litwhat**

literal *a.* pertaining to letters 199/26

ylitered *v. pa. p.* provided with fodder or straw to sleep on 1190/12

litergiks *sb. pl.* sufferers from lethargy 837/12

litil *a.* little, small, few; *litil and litil*, little by little, gradually 117/3

†litwhat, litelwhat *sb.* a little bit; *a lit(el)what*, somewhat, to some degree 150/16

lyue, leue *v.*, **lyuinge, leu(e)ynge** *sb.* to live; *þe vertu of leuynge*, the vital spirit, situated in the heart and controlling the organism's heat 55/34 (*v.*), 76/11 (*sb.*)

†lockinge *sb.* looseness, movement (of teeth) 198/18 [obscure; cf. OE. *lūcan*, strong 2, 'pluck out'; but forms may be scribal responses to a derivative of L. *laxāre*]

lodesman *sb.* navigator 1237/35 [cf. OE. *lādmann*]

loggis, lugges *sb. pl.* staves 938/32

loynes *sb. pl.* loins 254/17

loke *v.* to look 172/18

lokers *sb. pl.* watchers 1280/25

lombe, see **lambe**

longeflyes *sb. pl.* locusts 211/33

longe(n), lungen, longoun *sb.* (*sg.* and *pl.*, also **longes** *pl.*) the lung(s) 105/7

†longhaldes *sb. pl.* hobbles 1150/34 [OE. *lāng* + *ġehāld*]

longith *v. pres. 3sg.* (freq. impersonal *it longeþ to/on*) befits, belongs 41/18

loos *sb.* praise, fame 213/18 [OF. *los*]

loos(e), see **lowse**

lopsters, lobsters *sb. pl.* lobsters 1339/37

lordliche *adv.* powerfully 1075/2

lore *sb.* knowledge 90/13

lost *sb.* loss 97/14

loþ *a.* hateful, reluctant 635/17

loþeles *a.* innocent 1116/5

loty(e) *v.* (**lateþ** *pres. pl.* once) to hide, lie concealed 228/12 [OE. **lotian*, cf. *lūtian*]

lotte *sb.* share, heritage 702/15

lous, lows *sb.* (**luys, lyse** *pl.*) louse 425/20

louteþ *v. pres. pl.* bend, bow 192/2 [OE. *lūtan*, strong 2]

loueliche *a.* lovable 853/8

†louy *a.* given to amorous activities 133/28

louy(e)re *sb.* lover 482/20

loweþ *v. pres. 3sg.*[1], **lowynge** *sb.* lowers
1173/17 (*v.*), 527/26 (*sb.*)
loweþ *v. pres. 3sg.*[2], **lowynge** *sb.* lows
1152/17 (*v.*), 1241/28 (*sb.*)
lowse, loos(e) *a.* loose 100/10
lowsy *a.* prone to breeding lice 1224/33
lucyes *sb. pl.* pike-fish 1099/27 [late L.
lūcius]
lugges, see **loggis**; **luys**, see **lous**; **luyte**,
see **lite**; **luke**, see **leuke**
lullinges *sb. pl.* lullabies 299/32
†**lumineþ** *v. pres. 3sg.* illuminates 70/7
lunacioun *sb.* a lunar month 521/15
lunatik *a.* insane 175/7
lungen, see **longen**
lupines *sb. pl.* the seed of the lupine
plant, used as fodder 986/3
lurkeþ, lorkeþ *v. pres. pl.*, **lurkynge** *sb.*
hide, lie hidden 1131/26 (*v.*), 87/2 (*sb.*)
lusard, lusardis, lysard, le(e)sard *sb.* a
lizard or similar reptile 1127/17
lustles *a.* listless 157/7
†**lustlikinge** *sb.* pursuit of pleasure 292/
32

mac(c)he *sb.* candlewick 1055/29
†**macianes** *sb. pl.* crab-apples 1321/9
[ML. *matianus*]
madden *v. pres. pl.* are mad, behave
foolishly 292/32
magnas, magnes *sb.* magnet 833/25
maydenhode *sb.* celibacy 610/10
maymed *v. pa. p.* mutilated 212/27
mayny, see **meyne**
mayster *a., sb.* learned man; *a.* principal
380/2
ymaystred *v. pa. p.* seasoned, sharpened,
made brighter (of the preparation of
dyes) 1289/16
maistrie *sb.* control, domination, authority; *dedes of maistrie*, martial acts 81/10
make *sb.* mate 625/19
malardes *sb. pl.* wild ducks 598/28
†**malencolif** *a.* dominated by black bile
161/19
mali(n)-, see **melan-, melen-, melin-**
malis *sb.* malice 60/31
malschaue, malschragge *sb.* (mel-
once) caterpillar 191/8 [OE. *mæl-
sceafa*; the *-schragge* forms substitute
ME. *shraggen* 'lop, trim, prune' for
shaven]

malwes, malues *sb. pl.* mallow plants
440/9
mametes, see **mawmetes**
manasse, manace *sb.* threat, danger
714/1
manasseþ *v. pres. 3sg.* threatens 147/4
mandragora *sb.* mandrake 1196/24
maner *sb.* type of, behaviour, common
practice, moderation 47/9
manerliche *a.* seemly, modest 309/16
manhede *sb.* human form 56/27
many, see **mony**
manyfoolde *a.* many, (of the stomach)
having many folds 243/32
manliche, manly *a.* masculine 261/27
manna *sb.* resins that exude from plants
584/6
mansiouns *sb. pl.* stages of a journey
(esp. the resting places chosen by the
Israelites in the exodus), dwelling
places 709/23
manslauþe *sb.* manslaughter 1082/24
marche *sb.* boundary, border-district
716/20
mareys, marys, maryes, mares *sb.* (*sg.*
and *pl.*) *a.* marsh, swamp, lake; *a.*
boggy, swamp-like 327/13
mares, see **mareys**; **mareu3**, see
marou3
margarite, mergarite *sb.* pearl, oyster
378/32
mary, see **marou3**; **maryes, marys**, see
mareys; **mark**, see **merk**
mariori *sb.* pearl 685/7
marites *sb. pl.* husbands 731/10 [L.
maritus]
markeþ *v. pres. 3sg.* (**ymarked, imerked**
pa. p.) sets bounds, bounds, marks,
notices; *pres. p., a.* cauterizing 184/
33
marmusettes *sb. pl.* monkeys of some
variety 1110/23
**marou3, marogh, mareu3, marwe,
mary** *sb.* (**marou3, marwes** *pl.*)
marrow, pith 99/34
martiloges *sb. pl.* martyrologies 529/8
mased *v. pa. p., a.* confused, insane 123/12
masy, massy *a.* solid, heavy, unshaped
or without distinct form 220/23
mast(e) *sb.* acorns or other nuts used as
food for swine 534/8
mastik *sb.* mastic 367/20
matere, matiere, materie *sb.* physical

matere, matiere, materie (*cont.*)
matter, the physical substance (*v.* the form or essence), affair, subject 131/32

material *a.* consisting of matter, physical, pertaining to one of the four Aristotelian causes (that physical material which produces a result) 41/17

materie, matiere, see **matere**

materles *a.* immaterial, without physical substance 95/18

maþes *sb. pl.* maggots 1264/37 [OE. *maða*]

matrimoyne *sb.* marriage 1071/17

matto(c)k *sb.* pick, pickaxe 692/12

maturatiues, mataratifes *sb. pl.* drugs which produce pus 361/5

maunde, maundement *sb.* the Last Supper, the bishop's washing the feet of the poor performed as commemoration of that event 548/12

mawe *sb.* the stomach or a digestive organ in a lower animal fulfilling the same function (e.g. a bird's gizzard) 256/3

mawinge, see **ymowe**

mawmetes, mametes *sb. pl.* (**maument, mavmet** *sg.*) idols, gods 710/28

me *pron.* one, someone, people 41/30

meche, moche, miche, mouche *a., sb.* much, great, large 59/31

meddelid, see **medle**

mede *sb.* gift, reward 53/13

medecinable *a.* medicinal 435/30

medeful *a.* deserving reward, efficacious 293/7

medes *sb. pl.* meadows 531/24

medle, meddel- *v.*, **medlynge** *sb.* to mix together, have sex with, contain 115/29 (*v.*), 52/32 (*sb.*)

meer, see **mere**; **meyn-,** see **mene**

meinals *sb. pl.* members of a household, servants 329/31

meyne, mayny, menie *sb.* household 74/22

meked *v. pa.* humbled 314/27

melancolie, melancolia, melen-, malin- *sb.* black bile (one of the four humours), any of the normal or pathological species of this humour, the mental disorder caused by excessive black bile 147/33

mele *sb.* meal, flour 983/19

melencolik (male-, mali-) *a.* consisting of or dominated by black bile, caused by black bile, having a 'complexion' dominated by black bile 162/18

melincolie *a.* consisting or or producing black bile, having a 'complexion' dominated by black bile 161/26

melyne *sb.* a white colour or pigment 1087/7 [from L. *melīnus* a.]

melke, milke, melche *sb.* milk, sap, the milt of fish 204/22

ymelked, ymylked *v. pa. p.* milked 1325/36

melky, mylky, melkich *a.* milk-like 258/12

melle *v.*, **mellinge** *sb.* to mix 180/27 (*v.*), 52/23 (*sb.*) [OF. *meller*; cf. **medle**]

†melsche *a.* sandy, loose 1010/19 [? cf. OE. *melsc, milisc*]

melschragges, see **malschaue**

melte, mylte *sb.* the spleen 250/18

melte *v.* (**mylteþ** *pres. 3sg.* once; **imolte, ymulten, ymelte** *pa. p.*) to melt 130/28

imembred *v. pa. p., a.* having members, made up of parts 181/24

mendement *sb.* aid, improvement 295/18

mene *a.* in a middle state, mixed in character (cf. *mene noun, mene nombre*), moderate, mediating between 47/25

mene, moene-, meyne- *v.*, **menynge** *sb.* to mean 41/18 (*v.*), 41/10 (*sb.*)

ymened, ymynid *v. pa. p.* mined 696/16

meneliche *a.* moderate 588/14

meneliche *adv.* moderately 113/23

menesse *sb.* moderateness of size or character, intermediate state 194/4

menge *v. pa. p.*, **menginge** *sb.* mixed 1345/26 (*v.*), 52/32 (*sb.*)

meny, see **mony**; **menie,** see **meyne**

menstrual *sb.* menstruation 1023/33

mente, mynt(e) *sb.* spearmint 393/22

merchaundis, merchauntis *sb. pl.* merchants 483/17

merche *sb.* celery, wild celery 913/20

merciable *a.* merciful 49/8

mere, meer *sb.*[1] boundary, limit 53/7 [OE. (*ge*)*mǣre*]

mere *sb.*[2] mare 562/6

mereþ, mireþ *v. pres. 3sg.* confines 137/27

mergarite, see **margarite**

mergyne *sb.* margin 739/21

merk, mark *sb.* boundary 53/7

imerked(e), see **markeþ**

mermayde(n) *sb.* mermaid 1203/2
merour, mirour *sb.* mirror 62/23
meschief *sb.* misfortune, distress, trouble 55/25
mesel *a.*, *sb.* leper 106/18
meselrye *sb.* leprosy 423/9
mespiles *sb. pl.* medlar trees 1030/16 [L. *mespilus*]
message *sb.* message, the act of message-bearing 81/14
messager, messagier *sb.* messenger 280/25
messe *sb.* the mass 544/33
messelyng *sb.* brass or a variety thereof 830/10 [OE. *mæsling*]
messes *sb. pl.* courses or dishes of food 329/31
mest *a. super.* most 313/2
mesurable *a.* moderate, proper 143/15–16
mesure, mesoure *sb.* calculation, instrument to determine quantity, standard, moderation; *ouer mesure*, excessively, extremely 44/16
mesurith *v. pres. 3sg.* measures, governs 51/31
met *sb.* measurement 44/16
mete *a.* proper 340/36
mete *sb.* food, a meal 57/19
mete *v.* (**imette** *pa. p.*), **metynge** *sb.* to measure 51/31 (*v.*), 1367/19 (*sb.*)
†meteschipe *sb.* preparation for eating or feasting 329/23
methe *sb.* mead 1321/12
metycyne, medicine *sb.* a medical preparation or treatment, the theory or study of healing 140/6
metiþ *v. pres. 3sg.* dreams 99/8 [OE. *mætan*]
meuablenesse *sb.* mobility 226/1
meue, meoue, moue, meeue-, meui- *v.*, **meuynge, meouynge, mouynge** *sb.* to move; *þe spirit of meuynge*, the faculty responsible for voluntary motion envisioned as part of the overall nervous system (the spirit of feeling or the animal spirit) 55/37 (*v.*), 57/27 (*sb.*)
mevere, meouar, mouare *sb.* a mover, one who sets something in motion 91/23
mewis, mwes *sb. pl.* cages for hawks 608/28

mychinge *v. pres. p.*, *a.* lurking 309/6 [OF. *muchier*]
myddel *a.*, *sb.* mid, intervening, intermediate 53/3
myddilerþe *sb.* the earth, this world 673/2
mydwintir day *sb.* Christmas 520/12
myȝt(e)liche *adv.* strongly 818/17
mylie, myle *sb.* millet 421/14
milk-, see **melk-**; **mylte**, see **melte**; **mylteþ**, see **melte**
mynde *sb.* the faculty memory, remembrance, mention 42/21
myngiþ *v. pres. 3sg.* reminds 582/9 [OE. *myndgian*]
minished *v. pa. p.* diminished 167/14
mynystir *sb.* agent, high officer 133/7
ministracioun *sb.* service 59/6–7
mynystreþ *v. pres. 3sg.* helps, furnishes 97/17
myrabolanes *sb. pl.* the astringent plum-like fruit of several Asiatic trees 902/11
mirdrommel, myrdromble, moreþrumbil *sb.* the bittern 635/28 [ON. *mýrr* and OE. *mōr* substituted for first element of OE. *rāra-dumbla*]
mireþ, see **mereþ**; **mirour**, see **merour**; **mir(r)y**, see **mury**
myrþe, merþe, murþe *sb.* pleasure, delight 300/25
mysbyleue *sb.* superstitious or erroneous belief 823/3
mysbil(i)eued *a.* pagan 657/30
myscroked *a.* deformed 304/32
mysdoynge *v. pres. p.*, *a.* doing wrong 479/21
mysgoynge *sb.* going astray 721/21
†myspassiþ *v. pres. 3sg.* fails 346/26
mystakeþ *v. pres. 3sg.* mistakes, errs 329/13
misterie *sb.* riddle, secret or hidden thing 1353/30
mistik *a.* symbolic 41/23
mystorned *v. pa. p.* turned in the wrong direction, turned about 852/21
†mystringe *sb.* dimness of eyesight 388/22 [frequentative based on OE. *mist*]
mysuse, mycevse *sb.* mis-statement, misapplication 90/21
myter, mytre *sb.* head-dress worn by the biblical high priest 977/31
mytigatiues *sb. pl.* medicinal preparations to alleviate pain 440/12

myxcioun, mixioun *sb.* mixture 52/16
mna *sb.* a unit of weight or denomination of money (uses based on Luke 19: 24) 315/12 [L. *mina*, oblique forms sometimes *mna-*]
mo, moo *a.* more (in quantity) 120/23
†mochedel *sb.* a great part 166/18
mochil *a., adv.* much, great 1008/14
mociens *sb. pl.* motions 70/29
moderatour *sb.* ruler, director 485/3
modies *sb. pl.* a Roman grain measure, corresponding to a peck or bushel 1374/30 [L. *modius*]
modir *sb.* (*poss.* uninflected) mother, the uterus; *þe harde modir*, *þe milde modir*, the two meningeal coverings of the brain (the *dura mater* and *pia mater*) 94/21
moen-, see **mene**; **moeue,** see **meue**; **moyle,** see **muyle**
moyste *v.*, **moistinge** *sb.* to moisten 141/34 (*v.*), 531/15–16 (*sb.*)
moisty *a.* moist 974/7
molde *sb.* the top of the head 177/34 [OE. *mólda*]
mole *sb.* discoloured spot, blemish 361/25
moment *sb.* a measure of time, $\frac{1}{40}$ of an hour 529/21
mone *sb.* lament 1145/31
moneþ *sb.* month 127/25
mony, many, meny *a.* many 54/28
more *sb.* root, root-system of a plant 111/14 [OE. *more* 'carrot']
more *a. comp.* greater, larger (of extent and degree, as well as quantity), additional (similarly **moste**, greatest) 127/30
mored(e) *v. pa. p.* rooted 205/31
moreyn *sb., a.* plague 147/19
mores, mooris, mures *sb. pl.* marshes, moors 416/28
moreþrumbil, see **mirdrommel**
morische *a.* marshy, soft 1243/9
morsellis *sb. pl.* small meals, single dishes 1056/15
morteres *sb. pl.* bowls filled with oil and having wicks so as to serve as candles 1034/24 [OF. *mortier*]
morwe, morowe *sb.* morning 679/29
morwe(n)tyde *sb.* the morning 354/33
mot, mote, mut *v. pres. pl.* (**moste** *pres. 3sg.* and *pa.*) may, be compelled to, must 61/11

moþir 613/15, for **mo oþir**, see **mo**; **moþþe,** see **mowþes**; **mouche,** see **meche**; **mouȝtes,** see **mowþes**; **moun,** see **mow**
mous, mows *sb.* (**my(y)s, myes, muys** *pl.*) mouse, mole 645/5
mow, mowe, mowen, mown, moun *v. pres. pl.* (**may** *pres. 3sg.*, **miȝte** *pa.*) may, have power or permission to, be able to 41/19
ymowe *v. pa. p.*, **mawinge** *sb.* mown 961/1 (*v.*), 532/8 (*sb.*)
mowes *sb. pl.* grimaces 301/24
mowȝtes, see **mowþes**
mowly *a.* mouldy 1245/29
mowþes, mouȝtes, mowȝtes *sb. pl.* (**moþþe** *sg.* once) moths, moth larvae 344/28
muyle, moyle, mule *sb.* mule 249/11
multiplie *v.* to increase 185/25
multitude *sb.* a great number (of) 94/9
mures, see **mores**
mury, meri, mir(r)y *a.* merry, joyful 301/37
must *sb.* grape-juice in its process of fermentation into wine 148/36 [OE. *must*, from L. *mustum* (*vinum*) 'new wine']
mut, see **mot; mwes,** see **mewis**

naciouns *sb. pl.* nations, gentiles, pagans 94/18
naddre, see **adder; naȝt,** see **nouȝt**
naissche, neissche, nessche, nasche, naisse *a.* soft, tender (of physical consistency) 107/29 [OE. *hnesce*]
naisschiþ, neisschiþ, nesschiþ *v. pres. 3sg.*, **neisschinge** *sb.* becomes soft, makes soft 130/6 (*v.*), 142/24 (*sb.*)
naisschnes, neisschnes, naschnes *sb.* softness 125/1
nakires *sb. pl.* kettle-drums 1391/12 [OF. *nacre*]
namecouþe *a.* famous 917/34
nameliche, nemeliche *adv.* especially 142/27
nasch-, see **naissch-; natheles,** see **neþeles**
naturalle *a.* found in nature, having basis in the nature of things; *naturalle daye*, twenty-four hours (*v.* an artificial day) 534/31
naueye *sb.* ships, a fleet 733/14

ne *conj.* nor, not, neither 113/1
necligense *sb.* carelessness 435/15
necligent *a.* careless 191/19
nedder, see **adder**
nedeful, nudeful *a.* necessary 84/5
nedefulliche *adv.* necessarily 331/5
nedeliche *adv.* necessarily 121/21
nedis, nedus, nudes *adv.* necessarily 111/3
nediþ, nudiþ *v. pres. 3sg.* (usually impersonal) is necessary 59/27
neer, see **ner; neighiþ,** see **nyheþ; nei3, neyh,** see **ni3**
nei3bere *sb.* neighbour 77/21
neyinge *sb.* neigh 1189/6
ne(i)ssch-, see **na(i)ssch-; nemeliche,** see **nameliche**
nempneþ *v. pres. 3sg.* (**ynemened** *pa. p.* once) names 42/7 [OE. *nemnan*]
nepe *sb.* turnip 1050/26
ner, neer, nerre *adv.* (*comp.*) near(er) 70/14
nest(e)leþ *v. pres. 3sg.* makes a nest 643/6
netes, see **nytes**
neþeles, noþeles, natheles *adv.* nevertheless 63/23
neþemest, neþirmest *a. super.* lowest 81/22
neþir *a.* lower, under 69/7
neþir *conj.* neither, nor, and not 273/13
neþirmest, see **neþemest**
neuelyng *adv.* prone 1200/12 [OE. *neowol, nifol* + *-ling(a)*]
nevewe *sb.* nephew 543/25
newe, nou *a.* new 150/26
next, neste *adv. super., a.* nearest, right beside 70/25
nycete *sb.* folly 1046/26
nygromaneceres *sb. pl.* wizards, prophets 245/27
ni3, ny3e, n(e)yh, ny3ghe, nei3, ny *adv. prep.* nigh, nearly, near to (temporally and spatially) 53/21
ny3tcrowe *sb.* the owl 539/11
ny3tisch *a.* pertaining to night (of zodiacal signs) 461/17
nyheþ, neighiþ, nei3eþ, nei3gheþ, ny3heþ *v. pres. 3s.* (**ny3he** *pres. subj.*) draws near 134/25
nyhnes, ny3enes, ny3ghnesse *sb.* nearness 245/13
nyse *a.* foolish 292/29
nyseliche *adv.* foolishly 617/5

nytes, netes *sb. pl.* young lice 345/29
nobbes *sb. pl.* knots 1055/29 [obscure]
noblete, nobulte *sb.* nobility 318/16
nobly *a.* knotty 1055/26
nobut *adv.* only, merely 614/25 [OE. *nā* + *būtan*]
nocional *a.* pertaining to a concept or idea; *noun nocional*, a noun expressing a conceptual attribute of an essence 47/16
nocioun *sb.* idea, definition of a thing as it exists in its essence 46/13
noye *sb.* annoyance 73/10
noye *v.,* **noyenge** *sb.* to trouble 78/6 (*v.*), 539/19 (*sb.*)
noyeful *a.* harmful 158/14
noyefulnesse *sb.* harmfulness 481/8
noyous *a.* troublesome 562/23
noiþer, see **noþir**
nokkes *sb. pl.* nocks 1149/33
nolle *sb.* the back of the head, the nape of the neck 167/22 [OE. *hnoll*]
nolled *v. pa. p.* having a head (of a certain type) 1231/5
none *a.* no, not one, not a single 53/33
nonis *sb. pl.* the ninth day before the Ides of any month, usually the fifth of the month, in the Roman calender 506/21
noote, see **note; inorchid,** see **norische**
norisch, norice, nors(e), norsch *sb.* nurse 259/16
norische *v.* (**norrisse** *pres. 3sg.* once; **inorchid** *pa. p.*), **norschinge, nurschinge** *sb.* to feed 200/34 (*v.*), 96/22 (*sb.*)
norture, see **nurtur**
noseþirl, -þurl, -þrill, -trelle *sb.* nostril 55/10
not, see **wite**
note, noote *sb.* nut 432/32
notemuge, -mig(g)e *sb.* nutmeg 888/35
notes *sb. pl.* marks or signs used as symbols of a condition or quality (orig. of a musical sound) 54/31
noþeles, see **neþeles**
noþerwhere *adv.* nowhere 1260/34–5
noþir, noiþer *conj.* neither, nor 45/1
notifieth *v. pres. pl.* denote 46/13
nou3t, no3t, nau3t, na3t, nout *sb., adv.* nothing, not at all, not 43/4
nouthir *conj.* neither 48/29
nouelte *sb.* newness 619/12

nowches *sb. pl.* precious stones, large pearls 871/17 [OF. *nouche*]

nude(-), see **nede(-)**

nurtur, norture *sb.* food 198/6

nutritiue, nutratif *a.* nourishing; *þe vertu nutritiue*, the power instinct in living beings which controls sustinence 97/28

o, of *prep.* of, off of, out of 40/4

o, oo, oon *sb., a., adv.* one, a, single, alone; *oon and oon*, one at a time, singly; *atones*, all at once; *þe ton*, that one 40/18

obiect *v. pa. p., a.* placed before, exposed (to the senses), presented to perception 121/3

obiecte *sb.* a thing perceived or sensed 108/12

oblegiþ *v. pres. 3sg.* binds by an oath, contracts 308/1

obstinat, obstanat *a.* stubborn 85/13–14

occasioun *sb.* opportunity, chance juncture of circumstances; *by occasioun*, by chance, incidentally 167/14

occupie *v.* to take possession of, take up space, pass one's time, give one's attention to 225/2

oder, see **oþir**

offalle *sb.* dregs 829/19

offendiþ *v. pres. 3sg.* wrongs 263/24

of(fe)putting *sb., pres. p., a.* expulsion 104/27 (*sb.*), 97/15 (*a.*)

offys, office *sb.* duty, function 48/11

oft(e) *adv.* often 166/34

oygnoun, oynoun, onyo(u)n *sb.* onion; *houndes oynoun*, sea onion 158/20

oyn(g)ement, oynguement *sb.* ointment 219/30

oyntynge *sb.* anointing 1378/12

oiþer, see **oþir**

oldeþ, holdeþ *v. pres. 3sg.* grows old 642/31

olyaster *sb.* the wild olive 1002/13 [L. *oleaster*]

olympias *sb.* the period of four years from one Olympic games to the next 522/26

olyphaunt, elepha(u)nt *sb.* elephant 219/31

onde *sb.* breath 105/12 [ON. *andi*]

one, oone *v., onynge* *sb.* to unite 41/33 (*v.*), 42/12 (*sb.*)

ones *adv.* once 47/34

ony, see **eny; onyoun,** see **oygnoun**

onliche, only *a.* only, alone, mere, unique 46/29–30

onslepe *adv.* asleep 487/12

†**ontredinge** *sb.* walking upon, being walked on 271/24

oof *sb.* the woof 1139/28

oost, hoost *sb.* host (*oostis of heuen*) 54/4

ooter, see **vttir; open, opun,** see **vppon**

opposed *v. pa. p.* confronted with a question, questioned 1370/4–5

op(p)osicioun, apposicioun *sb.* the position of two planets when they appear from earth exactly 180° apart 463/33

optacioun *sb.* choice, good will 53/12

or, see **ere**

orcheȝard, orchard *sb.* enclosed area for growing plants, garden, orchard 330/21

ordeyneþ, ordeigneþ *v. pres. 3sg., ordeignynge* *sb.* puts in order 41/5 (*v.*), 877/23 (*sb.*)

†**ordinalliche** *adv.* in order 77/20

ordinat *a.* regular, moderate 64/3

ordinatliche *adv.* properly, moderately 113/10

ordinaunce *sb.* arrangement, rule 214/1

ordoure *sb.* filth 417/21

origanum *sb.* marjoram 367/34

orisoun, orizonte *sb.* horizon 83/16

orpede *a.* valiant 737/21 [OE. *orped*]

orpidnesse *sb.* valour 549/23

orribilenes *sb.* feeling of horror 118/17

ospringe, ofspringe *sb.* progeny 311/14

ostrugge, ostrigge, ostrich(e) *sb.* ostrich 700/28

ote *sb.* oats 916/5

oþ, oþ þe *prep.* of, of the 110/18

oþir, oþr, oder, oiþer *a., pron.* the second, one of the two, the remaining 40/9

oþir, ouþir *conj.* or 40/13

†**oþirdeele** *sb.* the other part 193/32

oþirwhile, oþirwhiles *adv.* at times, sometimes; *oþirwhile … oþirwhile*, at one time … at another time 46/14

oþr, see **oþir; ott(e)-,** see **vt-; oughne,** see **owe**

ouȝt, oughte *sb.* anything 179/6

out, ouȝt *adv.* out 44/9

outake, outtaken, ouȝttake *prep.* except 73/13

outakeþ *v. pres. 3sg.* excludes 203/21

outcast *sb.* refuse 1029/2

outcastinge *sb.* expulsion 510/31

outcomynge *sb.* a coming out, issuing forth 298/19

outdrawinge *sb.* drawing out, sucking forth 493/22–3

outemest *a. super.* outermost 110/13

outgoinge *sb.* passage outward 134/7

ouþir, see **oþir**

outlawed, owtlawed *v. pa. p.*, **outlawinge** *sb.* driven out; *sb.* an abscess causing the tongue to protrude from the mouth 693/28–9 (*v.*), 207/16 (*sb.*)

outpassed *v. pa. p.*, **outpassinge** *sb.* passed outward 1302/13 (*v.*), 335/17 (*sb.*)

outputtynge *sb.* expulsion; *þe vertu of outputtynge*, expulsion, one of the Galenic 'faculties' 104/27

outrage *sb.* intemperance 313/19

outrageous *a.* immoderate 76/11

outrageþ *v. pres. 3sg.* passes due bounds 1074/17

outschedynge *sb.* pouring forth 578/33

outsendinge *sb.* sending forth 499/4

outspringinge *sb.* casting out 432/1

outstremynge *sb.* streaming out or forth 512/1–2

†**outþurstinge** *sb.* forcing out 347/23

ouemest, see **ouermeste**

ouer *a.* upper, higher, superior 69/6

ouercastinge *sb.* throwing across 510/31

ouerchafid, ouerchaufid *v. pa. p.* overheated 382/16

ouerchargede *v. pa. p.* overloaded 724/14

ouercomeþ *v. pres. 3sg.* (**ouercom(e)** *pa., pa. p.*) conquers 82/28

ouerdruyeþ *v. pres. 3sg.* grows too dry 1074/19

ouerflowe *v.* to flood 826/32

ouergilt *v. pa. p.* covered with gilding or gold 832/30

ouerlepe *v.* to leap over 680/7

ouermeste, ouemest *a. super.* highest, uppermost 83/26–7

ouerpasse *v.* to remain undiscussed, be omitted 147/19

ouerpassinge *sb.* excess 701/23

†**ouerpulleþ** *v. pres. 3sg.* throws down, casts down, destroys 654/22

ouersemyng *sb.* outward appearance 1277/32–3

ouersette *v.*, **ouersettinge** *sb.* to oppress, disrupt or destroy (esp. of a bodily function) 76/34 (*v.*), 76/30 (*sb.*)

ouersode *v. pa. p.* cooked too long 148/27

ouertaketh *v. pres. 3sg.* catches up to, gets hold of 671/14

ouerthwarte *adv.* straight across, crosswise 1070/8

ouertornede *v. pa. p.*, **ouertornyng** *sb.* upset, disordered 1169/17 (*v.*), 858/30 (*sb.*)

ouerwaxiþ *v. pres. 3sg.* grows (too) great 382/12

owe, owen, oughne *a.* one's own, one's 52/30

owiþ *v. pres. 3sg.* owns 468/4

owen, see **ewen, owe; owt-**, see **out-**

oximelle *sb.* a medicinal potion composed of vinegar and honey 325/25

†**oxizakara** *sb.* a medicinal potion composed of vinegar and sugar 325/25 [ML. *oxyzacara*]

paas, pace *sb.* a step, the space of a step, gait, way of walking 638/25

pacient *a.* enduring, passive 306/22

pagyn *sb.* page 739/21 [L. *pāgina*]

pay(e)nymes *sb. pl.* pagans 733/34

payeþ *v. pres. 3sg.* pleases, remunerates, returns 579/31

paynture, see **peinture**

pale *a.* pale, grey or ashen, lacking colour 196/4

pallisch *a.* somewhat pale 1285/9

pame, palm(e) *sb.* palm 376/24

pament, pauement *sb.* paved surface 551/9

pampynacioun *sb.* pruning or trimming of vines 1069/17 [L. *pampinātio*]

pan(y)er *sb.* a large basket 514/19

pans *sb.* (*pl.*) pennies, pennyweights (about $\frac{1}{240}$ of a pound) 1384/29

panter(e), pantiere *sb.* leopard 627/8

papeiay, see **popyniay**

papyre *sb.* papyrus 1022/22

pappis *sb. pl.* the breasts, breast-shaped structures, esp. *þe pappis* (usually *tetis*) *of þe nose*, the olfactory bulbs 115/10

parafrenesye *sb.* a diseased state characterized by delirium, differing from frenzy in being caused, not by lesion of the brain itself, but by fervid exhalations of other organs 348/27

paralitik *a.* paralysed 359/7

parcelles *sb. pl.* component parts 244/19
parchemeners *sb. pl.* parchment-makers 1113/18
parchemyn(e) *sb.* parchment 357/31
parcheþ *v. pres. pl.* (**perch**-forms common), **parchyng** *sb.* roast, toast 932/27 (*v.*), 1024/31 (*sb.*)
parcial *a.* incomplete, component 753/27
pard(e), perde *sb.* leopard, panther 700/24
ypared *v. pa. p.*, **parynge** *sb.* trimmed 530/28 (*v.*), 545/23 (*sb.*)
parfite *a.* perfect 52/7
parfitiþ *v. pres. 3sg.* completes 484/32
parfitlich *adv.* completely 61/2
pargetteþ, see **pergette**; **parisch**, see **persche**
parte(y)neþ *v. pres. 3sg.*, **perteynynge** *sb.* belongs, is connected, refers to, regards; *sb.* partaking, sharing 523/15 (*v.*), 513/5 (*sb.*)
partener *sb.* sharer 52/5
partibil *a.* divisible 52/20
participacioun *sb.* partaking of 69/2
particle, partykel *sb.* a small piece 444/18
particulare *a.* partial or individual, specific; *þe particulare wit*, that psychic faculty which receives and contains sensory impressions, opposed to the 'common wit' 98/11
partie *sb.* separate part, part 42/20
partyemele *adv.* piecemeal 122/26
partiþ *v. pres. pl.*, **partinge** *sb.* separate, share out, leave 82/2 (*v.*), 95/5 (*sb.*)
partitiue *a.* referring to only a part; *partitiue noune adiectiue*, an adjective denoting only a portion of a collective whole 49/27
partrich(e) *sb.* the partridge 598/2
pask *sb.* the Passover 546/4
pasnepe *sb.* the parsnip 1034/5
passe *v.*, **passinge** *sb.*, **passinge** *a., adv.* to go, pass; *sb.* surplus, excess; *a., adv.* surpassing(ly), excessive(ly), very 51/35 (*v.*), 189/9 (*sb.*), 118/16 (*a.*)
passibilite *sb.* capacity to suffer, capacity to be influenced by externals 62/3
passible *a.* liable to suffer 101/27
passingliche *adv.* immensely 706/30
passioun *sb.* suffering, disease, perturbation (e.g. *passioun of þe aier*) 42/28
passiue, passif *a.* able to suffer 140/25

past(e) *sb.* bread dough 959/2
pasture *sb.* feeding, grazing 218/8
paten *sb.* a shallow dish or plate 832/27
patent *a.* open; *lettres patent*, open letters from a sovereign 1323/19
pauement, see **pament**; **pecoc**, see **pokok**
peyneþ *v. pres. pl.* hurt 360/17
peyntiþ *v. pres. pl.* (**ipeint** *pa. p.*) paint 63/32
peinture, paynture *sb.* a painting 349/9
peys *sb.* weight 83/7 [ONF. and AN. *peis*]
pe(y)sible *a.* peaceful 309/13
peisibleliche *adv.* in a peaceful or quiet manner 759/22
peleþ, pilieþ *v. pres. 3sg.* pillages, peels 319/9
penars *sb. pl.* pen-holders or -cases, small boxes to hold writing materials 65/19 [ML. *pennārium*]
ypenned *v. pa. p.* provided with feathers 1245/11
pennes *sb. pl.* feathers 576/6
pepyn, pypyn *sb.* the pip of a fruit 1078/2
perceyue, parceyue, perseue- *v.* to perceive 53/11
percely, persile, petrosili *sb.* parsley 367/21
perch-, see **parcheþ**
perched *v. pa. p.* propped or supported with a rod 1068/19
perches *sb. pl.* a rod or stick, a prop for a vine, a rod used in measuring fields, a land measure (of various lengths, none corresponding to the modern 'rod') 1042/12
percussifes *sb. pl.* drugs which drive out excess humours 361/7
perde, see **parde**; **pere**, see **piere**
perfeccioun *sb.* completion 56/7
pergette *v.* (**par**-form once) to plaster 839/7 [OF. *pargeter*]
perisch(-), see **persche**
iperischid, ipersid *v. pa. p.* killed 303/22
perle *sb.* cataract 495/11
perliche *a.* as a peer, equal to 1095/27
permutacioun *sb.* change from one position to another 501/10
perrey(e) *sb.* gems 787/33 [OF. *pierrie*]
persch *a.* pliant 1042/19
persche, perisch, parisch *sb.* a pliant twig, a withy or hoop 1066/13 [OF. *perche*]

persche, perse, perische *v.*, **perschinge, pirsynge, perischinge** *sb.* to pierce 52/26 (*v.*), 106/5 (*sb.*)

persed, see **iperischid**; **perseueþ**, see **perceyue**; **persile**, see **percely**

personal *a.* personal; *noun or substantiue personal*, a noun referring to one of the three persons of the Trinity 47/15

perspectiue *sb.* (usually as part of a title, *auctour of Perspectiue*, *science of Perspectiue*, to refer to Alhazen and his *Optics*) optics, the science of vision or sight 110/8

perteynynge, see **parteyneþ**

pesen, pisen(ne) *sb. pl.* pea(s), small round seed-like objects, granules, esp. the roe or spawn of fish, nodes or corrupt grains in flesh 426/19

pestilence, pestilens *sb.* plague; *pestilence euele*, a grave injury 116/6

pestilencial *a.* noxious 322/7

pestilente *a.* poisonous 89/10

petrosili, see **percely**

pewlynge *v. pres. p.* making a whining sound, piping plaintively (of the kite) 635/13

philosophie, filosophie *sb.* wisdom and its pursuit, the knowledge of things and their causes 514/13

philosophre, filosophre *sb.* wise man, one interested in knowledge (incl. science) 41/9

phisiciaun, fisician, ficician *sb.* student of natural science, doctor or physician 122/8

physik, fisik *sb.* the science of medicine 153/31

pyany *sb.* the peony 355/3

picche *v.* (**picce-** occ.; **piȝt** *pa.*, *pa. p.*), **picchinge, pucchinge** *sb.* to pierce, root; *sb.* usually twinge, piercing sensation; *pa. p., a.* set, stable 61/6 (*v.*), 198/5 (*sb.*)

ypicched *v. pa. p.* covered with pitch 1376/35

†**pyches** *sb. pl.* traps to capture fish or crabs 1101/8 [obscure]

piere, pere *sb.* peer, equal 69/4

pyes *sb. pl.* magpies 600/33

pigmentary *sb.* a maker of spiced drinks, a confection maker 1322/6 [L. *pigmentārius*]

pigmentis *sb. pl.* spiced drinks with a wine base 1307/14

piked *a.* pointed 231/10

piken *v. pres. pl.* pierce, probe 225/26

pikes *sb. pl.* picks or pickaxes, spines, prickles, spikes 1181/16

ypiled, pilieþ, see **peleþ**

pilednes *sb.* baldness 345/18

ipinchid *v. pa. p.* compressed, crinkled, curled 288/12

pyneappil *sb.* pine-cone 561/6

†**pyney** *a.* (of a sediment in urine) pine-cone shaped, having that shape which approximates human form (to allow prognostication of the state of human members) 257/25 [L. *pīneus*]

†**pynopyns** *sb. pl.* cone-like growths 939/34 [obscure]

pyntyl *sb.* penis 261/8 [OE. *pintel*]

pipe *sb.* flute, tube; *pipe wey*, a hollow passage 211/10

pypyn, see **pepyn**

pypynge *v. pres. p.* chirping 645/6

piram *sb.* pyramid, pyramid-shape, the cone-like body of light rays extending from the object seen to the eye 111/4

piramydale *a.* pyramid-shaped, triangular 1371/16

pyramis *sb.* pyramid, pyramid-shape, the cone-like body of light rays extending from the object seen to the eye 109/35

pyrye *sb.* pear-tree, wild pear-tree 889/17

pirre *sb.* asthma 106/20 [obscure]

pirsynge, see **persche**; **pisen(ne)**, see **pesen**

pistelle, pistile- *sb.* letter, one of the New Testament epistles 802/15

pistule, see **puscule**

piþ(þe), pitthe *sb.* the spongy tissue in the stems and branches of plants, the 'marrow' of the plant which bears nutriments 583/19 [OE. *piða*]

pitte, see **putte**

playnes *sb.* flatness, evenness 227/10

plane, playne- *v.*, **planyng** *sb.* to make smooth 864/20 (*v.*), 1057/2 (*sb.*)

planteyne, see **plaunteyne**; **planty**, see **plaunt**

plaster, plastre, plaistre *sb.* a medicinal plaster, a cloth with salve used as a medicament, building plaster, gypsum 839/11

plaunt, planty *v.* to plant 86/24

plaunte *sb.* plant or shrub 42/35
plaunteyne, planteyne *sb.* the plantain 947/16
plechyng *sb.* intertwining (bent down boughs) to form a fence-like structure, a process undertaken to thicken plant growth 1042/28 [OF. **plechier, plessier*]
†**plectorik** *a.* characterized by plethora, having an excess of humours 347/17 [ML. *plectoricus*, var. of *plethoricus*]
plee *sb.* legal action, presentation of a legal suit in court 836/14
plein, playn *a.* flat 169/22
pleyneþ *v. pres. 3sg.*, **pleynynge** *sb.* laments 316/30 (*v.*), 635/13 (*sb.*)
ipleited *v. pa. p.* braided, intertwined 289/3
plenteuous *a.* plenteous 53/13
plentevousliche *adv.* abundantly 526/11–12
plenteuousnes(se) *sb.* bounty 445/28
plesaunce *sb.* joy, courtesy 1248/37
pleters *sb. pl.* lawyers, those who plead in courts 481/21
pliaunt, pliaunde *a.* supple 199/5
pliauntenesse *sb.* flexibility 1042/23
pliȝtiþ *v. pres. 3sg.* pledges; *pliȝtiþ his treuthe*, betroths himself, promises marriage 308/2
ploddes, pluddes *sb. pl.* pools, puddles 721/26 [obscure; cf. Irish *plod*]
plomptynge *sb.* plunging, diving, sinking (into water) 634/20 [cf. Middle Dutch *plompen*]
pluddes, see **ploddes**
plumby *v.*, **plumynge** *sb.* to swell, grow fat or light 1271/33 (*v.*), 895/12 (*sb.*) [obscure]
plumy, plummy *a.* porous, loose in texture 899/34
plumines *sb.* porousness 898/23
plumyng, see **plumby**; **plummy**, see **plumy**
pluralite *sb.* plurality 45/2
pockes *sb. pl.* a number of diseases characterized by pustules on the skin, esp. smallpox 420/16
podagre, see **potagre**
poeple, pup(e)le *sb.* people 319/27
pohenne *sb.* female peafowl 638/14
point, punct *sb.* dot, spot or speck, measure of time (fifteen minutes), state, condition; *in good* or *noble point*, in the

proper condition, in order; *in point to*, on the verge of, ready to 105/22
poyntelles *sb. pl.* styluses, instruments for writing in wax tablets 1323/23
pokok, pekok, pecoc *sb.* peacock 638/10
pole, see **poole**
polipody *sb.* ferns 628/23 [L. *polypodium*]
polit *v. pa. p.* polished 837/16
pollute *v. pa. p.* soiled 984/1
pom(m)egarnat(e), pomegarnade, poungarnet, pomegranate *sb.* pomegranate 371/19
po(o)le *sb.* pole, the point in the heavens about which the stars appear to revolve, the point where the extension of the earth's axis meets the visible heavens 457/3
po(o)re, poure *sb.* pore, small hole for the evacuation of waste fluids, a separation between constituent parts of a material substance, channel, duct 100/33
popyniay (-geay), papeiay *sb.* parrot 223/27
populer *sb.* the poplar tree 950/21
porcioun *sb.* share 187/1
porosite *sb.* porous consistency 136/3
porouse *a.* full of pores 206/14
porred *v. pa. p.*, **porrynge** *sb.* stopped up 1055/22 (*v.*), 1055/21 (*sb.*) [Middle Dutch *porren*]
portynans *sb.* related organs, inner organs, appendages 328/27 [AN. *apurtenance*]
pose *sb.* cold, cough, catarrh 1291/23 [OE. *(ge)pos*]
positif *a.* (*adv.*) having actual existence, present, explicit(ly), actual(ly) 47/4
possessioun *sb.* position, opinion 152/35
postil *sb.* apostle, missionary 79/6
postume, posteme, postome *sb.* inflammation, abscess 116/13
potacary, see **potagre**
potage *sb.* soup, stew 792/18
†**potagewere, potagewhere** *sb.* an ingredient for a soup or stew 954/19 [OF. *potage* + OE. *waru*]
potagre, podagre, potacary *sb., a.* gout, gouty 301/3
pouder *sb.* dust, a powder (esp. one used as a medicament or a spice) 114/29
pouge *sb.* bag, bag-like weir 684/14 [OE. *pohha*]

poune, powne- *v. imper.* pound 298/28

poungarnet, see **pommegarnate**

poure, poore *a.* poor 135/25

poure, see **poore; poursue-,** see **pursue; pouus, powuce,** see **puls**

pouert(e) *sb.* poverty 480/35

powne-, see **poune; pray,** see **preyes**

praye *v.* to pray 40/14

praunsen, praunceþ *v. pres. pl.* bound or spring about 301/26

preent, see **prente**

preyes *sb. pl.* (**pray** *sg.*) booty, prey 233/15

preyseþ *v. pres. pl.,* **preisinge** *sb.* praise 54/13 (*v.*), 64/13 (*sb.*)

prelacye *sb.* the office or authority associated with a bishopric, authority 76/5

premis *sb.* a logical premise or proposition, one of the first two members of a syllogism 60/15

prente, preent, printe *sb.* impression, (mental or sensory) image 122/32

prente *v.* (**printe-** occ.; **iprent, prented** *pa. p.*), **prentinge** *sb.* to impress 133/10 (*v.*), 120/26 (*sb.*)

prerogatyf *sb.* special privilege 773/2–3

preseruatiues *a. pl.* (drugs) designed to maintain health and protect against (relapse into) disease 437/6–7

pressour *sb.* press 1315/6

prest *a.* ready 220/14 [OF. *prest*]

pretert *a.* past, previous 518/16

ipreued, iproeued *v. pa. p.* tried, tested 87/20

pricke, prikke *sb.* puncture, sharp object, spine, needle, incentive, goad 62/7

pricke *v.,* **prickinge, pricchinge** *sb.* to pierce, incite 82/16 (*v.*), 159/20 (*sb.*)

prikettis *sb. pl.* candles, tapers, spikes on which to stick candles 331/2 [ML. *prikettus*]

prikke, see **pricke**

prime *sb.* the beginning of a period or cycle, the first appearance of the new moon 521/23

primordial *a.* original, primitive 442/22

principal *sb.* chief, commander, spring, chief part, primary form or quality 56/9

principal(i)te *sb.* chief rank, sovereignty, regions or provinces 602/9

principate *sb.* the office or dignity of a prince, supremacy, primacy, order or host (of angels) 42/2

prys, pris(e) *sb.* reward or trophy, victory; *tellen pris,* to account of value, value; *han* or *beren þe pris,* to be pre-eminent 57/5

prise *a.* excellent 707/21

prisoun *sb.* imprisonment, prison 88/3

priuacioun *sb.* absence of an attribute, a negative quality 515/21

priuatiue *a.* (*adv.*) pertaining to the loss or removal of something, to the absence of a quality, negative(ly) 47/5

priue, priuey, preue(y) *a.* secret 56/9

ipriuelegid *v. pa. p.* honoured 535/1

priueliche *adv.* secretly 170/31

priueþ *v. pres. pl.* deprive 363/31

priuylege, -lage *sb.* a special gift or benefit 56/24

priuite, preuyte, priuete *sb.* secret, mystery 64/12

proces(se) *sb.* a series of actions, course or drift of an argument, narration; *maken processe,* to give a full narrative 343/6

processioun *sb.* a body of persons marching in a ceremonial manner, the act of issuing from a source, emanation (of the Holy Spirit) 1358/1

procre *v.* to procure, produce 315/8

product *v. pa. p.* produced 511/4

profitables *sb. pl.* beneficial or useful qualities 652/26–7

profitiþ *v. pres. 3sg.* advances, improves, is of value 68/30

propirliche *adv.* strictly, literally fittingly 54/34

proporcionat, proporciened *a.* proportioned 169/11

propre *a.* one's own, belonging to one particularly, strict, real, fine 67/34

propriþ *v. pres. 3sg.* is appropriate to, takes possession of, applies specially to 46/17

proses *sb. pl.* sung pieces of rhythmical prose or of verse in the mass, sequences 1388/28

prouision *sb.* foresight 65/10

pthisane, see **thisane; pucchinge,** see **picche**

pule *sb.* pillow 251/27

puls, pouus, powuce *sb.* the pulse 121/29

pulsatif *a.*, *sb.* having a pulse, arterial; (*þe*) *pulsatif* (*veyne*), the pulmonary artery 280/8

pulsif *a.* pertaining to the pulse, having a pulse 121/28

pultiþ *v. pres. 3sg.* (**ypult** *pa. p.*), **pultinge** *sb.* thrusts, pushes 867/17 (*v.*), 205/1 (*sb.*) [OE. **pyltan*]

punct, see **point**

punyschiþ *v. pres. 3sg.*, **punischinge** *sb.* punishes 311/15 (*v.*), 310/31 (*sb.*)

purchas *sb.* property, gains 310/17–18

pure *a.* unmixed, mere, very 47/33

pured *v. pa. p., a.* purified 104/24

pureliche *adv.* simply, merely 48/22

purgacioun *sb.* cleansing, spiritual cleansing 69/30

purgatif *a.* laxative 352/16

purge *v.* to cleanse 69/27

purpur, purpre *sb.* purple cloth or clothing, purple 685/18

purpurede *v. pa. p.* clothed in purple, coloured purple 1191/17–18

pursike *a.* short-winded, asthmatic 106/21 [AN. *porsif*, with substitution of OE. *sēoc*]

pursue, pursewe *v.* (**pour-** occ.) to pursue, attack 70/34

purtrayng *sb.* drawing 844/20

purueya(u)nce, purueaunce, puruyaunce *sb.* foresight, preparation 493/37

purueyeþ *v. pres. 3sg.* provides for 51/33

puruyour *sb.* steward, supplier of necessities 245/14

puscule, pistule *sb.* pustule 420/7

put, see **putte, putteþ**

putfalle *sb.* pitfall 1195/21

putte, pitte, put *sb.* pit, hole, well 416/32

putteþ, put *v. pres. 3sg.* (**iput** *pa. p.*), **puttynge** *sb.* pushes, thrusts, places; *iput to*, added 57/23 (*v.*), 61/29 (*sb.*)

†**quabby,** see **quauy**

quadrant *sb.* a quarter of a day 519/4

quadrate *a.* square, rectangular or rectilinear 1358/9

quayliþ *v. pres. 3sg.* curdles, coagulates 141/1

quake *v.* to tremble, shake; *pres. p., a.* (of the pulse) undifferentiated, not clearly spaced 128/1

quakynge *a.* loud, croaking 591/26

qualyte *sb.* attribute, property, esp.

element qualite, *qualite of elementis*, one of the four basic properties composing all material bodies (heat, cold, wetness, dryness) 42/16

quantite *sb.* size 97/30

quappinge *sb.* throbbing, beating 413/16 [imitative]

quarelles *sb. pl.* crossbow bolts 943/13

quar(r)er *sb.* (**quarres** *sb. pl.* once) quarry 689/13

quarteyn, quartan, quarten *a., sb.* (of a fever) having a recurrent access every fourth (i.e. third) day, such a recurrent fever 323/36

quatreble *a.* quadruple, having four parts 246/2

quatrebled *v. pa. p.* quadruple, fourfold 1126/7

quauy, quabby, qwauy *a.* soft, flabby, shaking 157/9

quauynge *v. pres. p., a.* shaking, trembling, soft 195/32 [from OE. **cwafian*]

queere *sb.* the choir of a church 1063/13

que(y)nche *v.* (**queynte, quenchede** *pa. p.*) to quench 67/7

quekynge, see **quyke**

quidite *sb.* essence, the 'substance' of a thing 47/22

quyk *a.* living; *quyk iren*, lodestone, magnet; *quyk siluer*, mercury 131/20

quyke *v.*, **quickinge, quekynge** *sb.* to revivify, give life to 186/28 (*v.*), 227/12 (*sb.*)

quynancyes *sb. pl.* diseases of the throat, infections of the tonsils 373/14

quynyble *a.* fivefold, having five parts 246/2

iquyt *v. pa. p.* set free 546/33

quiterous *a.* suppurating 1023/32

quyttir *sb.* pus 191/4 [? OF. *quiture* 'cooking']

quittri, quyttery *a.* containing pus 374/22

quyuer(e) *a.* active 487/35

quotidiane, see **cotidiane; qwauy,** see **quauy**

qwyrites *sb. pl.* Roman citizens 1389/31 [L. *quirītes*; perhaps Latin, as at 801/13]

rabette *sb.* a (young) rabbit 1221/11

rabissch, rabbisch *a.* unruly, rash 86/10

radical *a.* pertaining to the root, vital, primary 262/23

ragged *a.* having a broken surface, full of sharp edges 724/7

ray *sb.* cockle, darnel 1089/6

raieþ *v. pres. 3sg.* arranges, gets for 320/5

raylynge *sb.* the training of vines on supports 1042/5

irake(d), (y)reke *v. pa. p.* raked 564/2

ramaious *a.* wild 608/19 [OF. *ramageous*]

ranke *a.* luxuriant, fertile 697/16

rape *sb.* a turnip, cole-seed 1034/6 [L. *rāpa*]

raphane *sb.* (**raphynes** *pl.*) a radish 1005/10 [L. *raphanus*]

raptour *sb.* a bird of prey 607/7

rarefieþ *v. pres. pl.* make thin by stretching, expand 106/26

(y)rased *v. pa. p.* cut or scraped away 1070/18

rateleþ *v. pres. pl.*, **ratelinge** *sb.* stutter, make a rattling sound 207/32 (*v.*), 208/1 (*sb.*)

rateliþ *v. pres. 3sg.* closes, heals 944/14 [? cf. OF. *reddalle* sb. 'pole']

raþer *a. adv. comp.* earlier, prior, more quickly, previous(ly) 66/16

rauȝ, see **rawe**

raueyn, rauen *sb., a.* (the act of) seizing or eating prey; *raueyn beest, raue(y)n brid, brid of raueyn*, beast of prey, bird of prey 226/21

rauenynge *sb.* seizing prey, plundering 1228/33

rauenour, rauynour *sb.* destroyer, one who lives by prey 1102/16

raueþ *v. pres. 3sg.*, **ravinge** *sb.* is mad or insane, makes wild or furious noises 397/22 (*v.*), 230/2 (*sb.*)

rauysche, rauisshe *v.*, **rauyschinge** *sb.* to seize, drag, raise, transport (esp. in mystical rapture or contemplation); *rauyschinge brid*, bird of prey 64/35 (*v.*), 473/33 (*sb.*)

rauyschere *sb.* one who seizes prey 607/7

rawe, rauȝ *a.* raw 116/8

rawnesse *sb.* rawness 210/3

real, see **rialle**

realte *sb.* royalty, royal power 56/25

rebate *v.* to reduce, diminish 1026/13

rebel *a.* rebellious 65/9

rebelnes *sb.* insubordination 311/11

reboundiþ *v. pres. 3sg.*, **reboundynge** *sb.* springs back, reflects, dissipates 109/15 (*v.*), 185/24 (*sb.*)

recche, rekke *v. pres. 1sg.* (**rouȝte** *pa.*) take care or heed 620/33

recchinge *sb.* stretching, expansion 411/7

recheles *a.* heedless 191/19

rechelesnesse *sb.* heedlessness 198/15

reclayme *sb.* the act of recalling a hawk 608/20

recordacioun *sb.* memory 173/17–18

recouer(e) *sb.* recovery, deliverance, means or hope of deliverance 88/3

recoueringe, see **rekeuere**

recto(u)r *sb.* ruler, governor 611/33

redact *v. pa. p.* reduced to (a certain state) 1355/16

reddeþ *v. pres. 3sg.* clears away 1116/35

rede *sb.*¹ counsel, advice 40/24

rede, reed, reeod *sb.*² reed, stick, rod, measuring-rod 65/13

rede *v.* (**irad(de), iredde** *pa. p.*) to read 44/12

redels *sb. pl.* riddles 41/10

redy *a.*¹ wise, prudent 156/17

redy *a.*² full of reeds 634/12

redilich *adv.* wisely, prudently 337/24

redynes(se) *sb.* wisdom, prudence 346/32

reduct *v. pa. p.* brought back, drawn back, brought to a certain state 56/1

refeccioun *sb.* spiritual refreshment 547/6

referred *v. pa. p.* assigned, attributed 46/16

reflexioun *sb.* reflection of light beams, a reflected image 102/21

reformacioun *sb.* restoration, correction of defects 55/36

refreyneþ *v. pres. 3sg.* restrains 57/16

refreiss(c)hiþ, refresseþ *v. pres. 3sg.* refreshes 341/6

rehersith *v. pres. 3sg.* relates 87/3

reyne, reynes *sb.*¹ (usually *pl.*) kidney(s), loins 165/3 [OF. *reins* pl.]

reyne, rayne, rene *sb.*² rain 133/10

reise, reisinge, see **rese**; **reysyn**, see **resyne**; **reissche**, see **risshe**; **reyuers**, see **reuers**; **yreke**, see **iraked**

irekened *v. pa. p.* enumerated, counted 67/31

rekeuere *v.*, **rekeuerynge, recoueringe** *sb.* to recover 427/11 (*v.*), 194/32 (*sb.*)

rekke, see **recche**

relaxe *v.* to loosen 916/7

relif, relief, releef *sb.* remnant, ruins (of a dwelling) 329/35 [OF. *relief*]

remeþ *v. pres. 3sg.* stretches, distends 397/12 [OE. *ā-ræmian*]

remeved *v. pa. p.* (**remeweþ** *pres. pl.* once), **remeuynge** *sb.* moved from a place 45/4 (*v.*), 120/18 (*sb.*)

remynge *a.* sticky, thick, ropy, forming filaments 211/2 [obscure, perhaps formed on *rewme*]

remys, remous, remuys, see **reremous**

remissioun *sb.* lessening of force, decrease of quality 322/11

rende *v.* (**reendiþ** *pres. 3sg.* once; **irent** *pa. p.*) to tear, tear apart 172/29

renewe *v.* (also **renue-, reniu-, reniw-**) to renew 132/20

renne, ruyne *v.* (occ. **rynn-, renni-** *pres.*; **ironne, irunne, iren(n)e** *pa. p.*), **rennynge** *sb.* to run; *sb.* (rarely) flux 138/20 (*v.*), 149/17 (*sb.*)

irent, rentiþ, see **rende**

rente *sb.* income 472/14

renueþ, see **renewe**

reparailiþ *v. pres. 3sg.* repairs 356/10

repareþ *v. pres. pl.* repair 144/33

yrepen, see **rype**

repercussiue *a., sb.* (drugs) driving away excess humours or fluids, mitigating excess humours 361/2

replecioun, replexioun *sb.* fullness 116/8

replete *a.* filled up, filled full 347/17

†repliteþ *v. pres. 3sg.*, **replitynge** *sb.* fills, crams 284/28 (*v.*), 106/8 (*sb.*) [from prec. or OF. *repletir*]

repreuable *a.* blameworthy, deserving censure 68/27

repreueþ, reproueþ *v. pres. 3sg.* rejects, condemns, finds fault 570/22

rere *a.* not fully cooked, soft 1345/27

rere *v.* to lift up 72/10

reremous, remous *sb.* (-**mys, -muys, -mues** *pl.*) bat 109/2 [OE. *hrēre-mūs*]

resceytes, see **resseite**

rese, reese *sb.* onslaught, tide, rashness, anger; *reses of yhen,* ?rushing of humours to the eye, infections caused by such humoral movement 65/8

rese, rees *v.* (occ. **ris-, reis-**forms), **reisinge, rysenge** *sb.* to rush toward or upon, charge, rage; *pres. p., a.* uncontrolled 78/13 (*v.*), 711/21 (*sb.*)

†reseuered *v. pa. p.* separated, made discrete or unique 448/17

residens *sb.* deposit, sediment, esp. the sedimentary layers of urine 160/24

resyne, reysyn, rosyn *sb.* a gum or oil formed in a plant 704/3

resolucioun *sb.* separation or reduction of a thing into component parts, dissolution or dispersion (esp. of humours) 117/23

resolved *v. pa. p.* dissolved, broken into component parts, weakened 115/20

resonable *a.* rational, esp. *þe resonable soule,* man's mind, capable of abstract thought 42/11

resoun *sb.* statement, explanation of an event, the power of thought 52/9

respect, respite *sb.* relation, reference; *hauen respect to,* to be connected with, relate to, be in relation to, pertain to 49/6

resseite, resceyte- *sb.* recipe, receptacle, reservoir, refuge 246/15

reste *v.* (**reste** *pa.*), **restinge** *sb.* to rest 128/1 (*v.*), 125/22 (*sb.*)

restoratif *a. sb.* (drugs) restoring or renewing strength 378/26

restrei(g)ne *v.* to restrain 78/8

restrictorye *sb.* a drug having binding properties, which stops the flow of fluids 360/35

resumptif *a., sb.* restorative, (a drug) aiding the renewal of bodily fluids 373/9

retentif *a.* holding, preserving, esp. *þe retentif vertu,* one of the Galenic 'faculties', that power resident in organs to hold and preserve food until digested 104/31

reþer, roþer *sb.* ox, cattle 192/4 [OE. *hrīðer, hrȳðer*]

reule, rule, rewel- *v.*, **reul(e)inge, rulinge, rewelynge** *sb.* to rule 40/26 (*v.*), 91/30 (*sb.*)

reue *v.* (**irefte** *pa. p.*), **reuynge** *sb.* to plunder, deprive of 252/16 (*v.*), 750/24 (*sb.*)

reuel-, see **riueles, riueleþ**

reuelacioun *sb.* divine communication to man 337/24

reuerens *sb.* respect, deference 251/27

reuers, reyuers *sb. pl.* robbers 317/28

reueþ *v. pres. 3sg.* pierces 161/1

rewe, ru *sb.*[1] rue 368/27

rewe *sb.*[2] row, line, series; *in* or *on rewe*, in order, successively, in a line 186/25

reweleþ, rewelynge, see **reule**

reweliche *a.* sad, rueful 1178/21

rewmatik *a.* characterized by similarity to rheum, watery, mucus-like 140/4

rewme, reume *sb.* excess fluid in the body, a cold 116/10

rial(le), real *a.* royal 607/2

yribbed *v. pa. p.,* †**rybbynges** *sb. pl.* (of flax fibres) had the particles of core removed 988/5 (*v.*), 1055/25 (*sb.*)

riches(se) *sb.* wealth, plenty 471/30

riddil *sb.* a sieve 1029/4 [OE. *hriddel*]

ryde *v.* (**ryd** *pa. p.*) to ride 472/35

rigge, regge, rugge *sb.* back, spine 229/2

riggebon *sb.* backbone 99/34

†**ryght-byleued** *a.* having the true faith 657/30

righte *v.* to straighten, adjust 304/29

riȝt *a.* straight, correct, the right (side) 55/17

riȝtful *a.* righteous, just 49/9

riȝtfullich *adv.* justly, equitably 68/30

riȝtliche *adv.* justly, properly 80/11

riȝtlicheþ *v. pres. pl.* rule 165/32 [OE. *rihtlǽcan*]

riȝtsoms *adv.* to the right 280/17

riȝtwisnesse *sb.* righteousness, rectitude, virtue 51/29–30

rinde *sb.* the bark of a tree, the outer crust or skin 103/34

†**rynglynge** *sb.* ringing, tingling 912/27

rynneþ, see **renne**

rynocerota *sb.* rhinoceros, unicorn 700/23

ripe *v.* (**yripe, yrypid** *pa. p.*), **rypynge** *sb.* to become ripe 132/35 (*v.*), 1336/6 (*sb.*)

rype, irepe(n) *v. pa. p.,* **rypinge** *sb.* reaped 550/4 (*v.*), 550/3 (*sb.*)

ripemen *sb. pl.* reapers 43/3

rys *sb.* twigs, small branches 241/25 [OE. *hris*]

rise *v.* (**roos** *pa.*), **risinge** *sb.* to rise 334/8 (*v.*), 391/33 (*sb.*)

riseþ, rysenges, see **rese**

risshe, reisshe, russhe *sb.* the rush 931/1

ryuede *v. pa.* came to land 879/6

riueles, reueles *sb. pl.* wrinkles 279/30

riueleþ, reueleþ *v. pres. 3sg.,* **ryuelinge,**

reu(e)lynge *sb.* wrinkles 112/20 (*v.*), 189/18 (*sb.*) [cf. OE. *rifelede* and *rifelung*]

riuer *sb.* river, riverbank 138/21

†**triueþ, reueþ** *v. pres. 3sg.* (**iryue, ireue** *pa. p.*), **riuynge** *sb.* draws together 103/9 (*v.*), 105/4 (*sb.*) [cf. OE. *gerifian* 'to wrinkle' and **riueleþ**]

†**ryuyly** *a.* wrinkled, shrivelled by heat 1024/27

roche, rooche- *sb.* rock, cliff 603/29

rockinge, see **rokken; rodeworth,** see **roodewort**

rogglynge, rogelyng, rugulyng *sb.* rumbling, growling 592/13 [obscure; perhaps based on ML. *rugere*]

roylynge *sb., v. pres. p.* roaming, straying, wandering about 1169/15 (*v.*), 541/16 (*sb.*)

roines, roinen *sb. pl.* scabs, scurf, scales, pustules 287/14 [OF. *roigne*]

roineþ *v. pres. 3sg.* bellows, emits a cry 1178/12 [OF. **rognir*]

†**rokeinge** *sb.* spitting, vomiting 157/10 [obscure]

rokken *v. pres. pl.,* **rockinge** *sb.* swing, sway 205/10 (*v.*), 198/18 (*sb.*)

ironne, see **renne**

roo *sb.* roe-deer 698/17

roode *sb.* cross; *holy roode day*, Holy Cross Day, 14 September 520/11

roodewort, rodeworth *sb.* the marigold 946/20

roodid, see **rotye**

roote *sb.* root, base, source, primary word or form (in a language) 101/7

rooty-, rootid, see **rotye**

rooting *sb.* taking root 897/30

roppis *sb. pl.* guts 927/4

rosers *sb. pl.* rose-bushes 1044/22

roset *a.* made of the essence of roses 1031/3

rosyn, see **resyn**

roste *v.* (**irost, irostid** *pa. p.*) roasted 130/30

roþer(-), see **reþer**

roþir *sb.* rudder 623/27

rotye, rooty- *v.* (**rootid, roodid, rote** *pa. p.*) to rot 131/13

rotyngenesse *sb.* rottenness 322/32

rouȝte, see **recche**

roundnesse *sb.* rotundity, circumference, compass, a round object; *first,*

roundnesse (*cont.*)
secounde, þridde roundnesse, the junctures of the various membranes and coatings of the eye to make orb-shaped bodies 133/19

rounyng *sb.* murmuring, muttering 592/11

roust, roustyn *sb.* rust, a disease of grain 154/9

rousteþ *v. pres. 3sg.* rusts 833/15

rousty *a.* rusty 158/26

routhe, see **rowȝe; rowe**, see **arowe**

rowfoted *a.* having feathers on the feet 616/33

rowȝe, rowh *a.* (**routhe** once) rough, with a broken surface 104/2

rowȝnesse, rowenesse, rownys *sb.* roughness 139/7

rowtes *sb. pl.* troops, bands 621/4

ru, see **rewe**

yruddid *v. pa. p.* rubbed (to remove impurities) 988/5 [obscure]

rugge, see **rigge; rugulyng**, see **rogglynge**

ruye *sb.* rye 958/32

ruynyn, ruynnynge, ruennynge *sb.* curdled milk, rennet, a similar curdled substance 355/5 [from ON. *renna* and OE. *iernan*; cf. **renne, vrneþ**]

irunne, see **renne**

runtiþ *v. pres. 3sg.* reproves, berates 311/8 [obscure]

russhene *a.* made of rushes 1022/1

saaf, see **safe**

sacions *sb. pl.* cultivated areas 1373/33 [L. *satio*]

sacrilege *sb.* violation of any fundamental religious obligation, ? heathen superstition 835/10

sacringe *sb.* consecretation 548/15

sad(de), saide *a., adv.* firm, solemn, solid, dense, heavy, stable 66/10

saddeþ *v. pres. 3sg.* (**sadde** *pa. p.*) makes solid or firm, solidifies 104/12

†sadfast *a.* dense, massive 131/26

sadliche *adv.* firmly, solidly 919/28

sadnesse *sb.* solidity, denseness 75/12

safe, saue, saaf, sauf *a.* safe; *in saue warde*, safely, in safe keeping 64/26

saffro(u)n, safroun, saffran, saffrin *sb.* the crocus, the spice saffron, the colour bright yellow 628/23

safliche *adv.* securely 64/24

saide, see **sadde**

salamandra *sb.* the salamander 1265/22

salere, salar *sb.* salt-cellar 329/30

salt *a.* salty 118/11

saltnesse *sb.* saltiness 1310/35–1311/1

saluweþ *v. pres. pl.* greet 1195/4

sangwine *a.* sanguine, bloody, esp. *sangwine complexioun*, the disposition or character in which blood dominates over the other humours; the colour blood-red 150/29

sarchinge, see **serchith**

sardonyes *sb. pl.* onyx 727/26

sarmentes *sb. pl.* twigs, loose pieces of wood 1295/30 [L. *sarmentum*]

satires *sb. pl.* satyrs 737/4

sauf, see **safe**

sauge *sb.* the herb sage 359/29

†sautes *sb. pl.* woodlands, narrow passes 931/22 [OF. *saut, deriv. of L. *saltus*]

sautry, sawtry sb. a stringed instrument, a dulcimer 1391/12

sauacioun *sb.* salvation 53/20

ysauered(e) *a.* tasting 662/4

sauery *a.* pleasant to the taste 159/19

sauoures *sb. pl.* scents, tastes 42/37

sauournesse, sauorynesse *sb.* agreeable taste 549/34

sawd-, see **sowde**

sawe *sb.* saying 81/8

†sawewise *adv.* like the teeth of a saw 1171/21

sawynge *a.* like the teeth of a saw, close-set 1171/20

sawtes *sb. pl.* assaults 1119/16

sawtry, see **sautry; scabbe**, see **schabbe**

scald-hoot *a.* boiling 970/10

scallidnes *sb.* scabbiness (esp. of the head) 345/18

scande *v.* to scan 975/34

scape, skape, schape *v.*, **scapinge** *sb.* to escape 43/2 (*v.*), 540/33 (*sb.*)

scars, scaars *a.* scanty, greedy 289/14

scarste, skarste *sb.* scarcity 124/25

schabbe, scabbe, skabbe *sb.* scabies, scab 323/9

ischad, see **schede**

schadewe, schadue *sb.* shadow, reflection 316/16

schadewe *a.* shady 538/21

schadewiþ *v. pres. 3sg.* casts a shadow (of) 257/31

schaft *sb.* stem, trunk 882/23

schaylinge *a.* walking crookedly 468/25 [obscure]

ischake *v. pa. p.* shaken 595/5

schal, see **schulen**

schale, shale *sb.* shell, husk, scale 256/19

schalen, see **yscheled**

schame *v. pres. subj.* feel shame, be(come) ashamed 82/31

schamefast *a.* modest 133/30

schamefastnes *sb.* modesty 183/7

schameliche *a.* shameful 75/14

schap *sb.* form, appearance 54/31

schape *v.* (**schape** *pa. p.*) to shape 62/28

schape, see **scape**

schare *sb.*[1] the groin, the pubic area 300/20 [OE. *scearu*]

s(c)hare *sb.*[2] plough 692/12

scharpe *a.* sharp, ardent 70/29

scharpe *v.* (**ischarpe** *pa. p.*), **scharpinge** *sb.* to sharpen, make (the intellect) more acute, deepen (a colour) 228/33 (*v.*), 1288/33 (*sb.*)

scharpiþ, see **scrape**; **schart,** see **schort**

schaue *v.* (**ischaue** *pa. p.*), **schauynge** *sb.* to scrape, cut hair close 349/7 (*v.*), 402/27 (*sb.*)

sche, scheo, see **heo**

schede *v.* (**ischad, ichad, isched** *pa. p.*), **schedinge** *sb.* to divide, part (the hair), disperse, diffuse, cast off 52/13 (*v.*), 52/17 (*sb.*)

schelde, see **schilde**

yscheled, yschilded *v. pa. p.* (**schalen** *pres. pl.* once) shelled 958/6

scheltroms *sb. pl.* troops, warriors drawn up for battle 1193/6 [OE. *scieldtruma*]

schende *v.* (**ischent, ischende** *pa. p.*) to destroy, scold 114/27 [OE. *scéndan*]

yschened, see **schyne**

schere *sb.* a pair of shears, large scissors 917/17

schere *v.* (**ischore, yshore** *pa. p.*) to shear 188/8

schere(-), see **schire(-)**

scheren *sb.* dung 1353/11 [OE. *scearn*]

scherneboddes *sb. pl.* dung-beetles 610/3 [OE. *scearn-budda*]

s(c)hete *v.* (**yschote** *pa. p.*), **schetyng** *sb.* to shoot with a bow 181/33 (*v.*), 988/18 (*sb.*)

scheters *sb. pl.* archers 181/33

schetis *sb. pl.* pieces of linen 304/29

schettiþ, schittiþ *v. pres. pl.* (**ischet, ischit** *pa. p.*) shut 100/34

scheueþ, see **schowve**

schewe *v.*, **schewinge** *sb.* to show 41/13 (*v.*), 62/26 (*sb.*)

schewere, showre *sb.* mirror 109/16

schilde, schelde *sb.* shield, shield-shaped object (esp. the pyramid of beams extending from the object seen to the eye) 110/25

†schildewyse *adv.* in the shape of a shield, with the shape of a cone 185/14

yschiled, see **yscheled**

schille *a.* resonant, sonorous 1388/1 [OE. *scielle*, cf. *scyl*]

schyne *v.* (**schone** *pa.*; **yschined, yschened** *pa. p.*), **schyninge** *sb.* to shine 56/6 (*v.*), 56/6 (*sb.*)

schinere *sb.* shining object 485/3

schip(pe)breche *sb.* shipwreck 540/33

schire, schere *a.* pure, clean, thin; *Schir(e) þursday*, Maundy Thursday 547/27 [OE. *scír* and ON. *skærr*]

schyrnesse, scherenesse *sb.* thinness, porosity 1383/22

schitt(-), see **schettiþ**

schit(t)e *v.*, **schittinge** *sb.* to defecate 404/12 (*v.*), 412/12 (*sb.*)

†schiuynge *sb.* shoot, sprig, sprout, the first sprout of a plant branching off the seed 141/9 [obscure; cf. OE. *scife* 'slice, splinter, thread']

schode *v.* (**yschoded** *pa. p.*) to divide, separate 939/7 [OE. *sceádan*; cf. **schede**]

scholde, see **schulen**; **schone,** see **schyne; ischore,** see **schere**

schorf *sb.* a skin disease, characterized by flakes and scaling 345/17

s(c)hort, schart *a.* short 157/15

ischortid *v. pa. p.* shortened 216/35

yschote, see **schete; schou-,** see **schowv-**

schoures *sb. pl.* showers 969/6

schowve *v.* (**schow-, schou-, scheu-, shouu-** *pres.*; **ischoue** *pa. p.*), **schowvinge, schowinge, schouynge, schowfynge, shuffynge** *sb.* to push, thrust violently 570/21 (*v.*), 570/25 (*sb.*)

schowviþ, schoueþ *v. pres. 3sg.*, **scho-vynge** *sb.* shows 572/1 (*v.*), 592/22 (*sb.*)

ischredde, yschrud(de) *v. pa. p.*, **schredynge, sshredynge, schrud-dyng, schroudinge** *sb.* pruned, cut up into strips; *sb.* prunings, clippings 530/28 (*v.*), 545/23 (*sb.*) [OE. *scrēadian* and ?*scrȳdan; cf. **byschrudde**]

schrewid *a.* evil, dangerous 224/15

schrewidnes *sb.* evil 87/1

schrichynge *sb.* shrieking 644/12

schryne *sb.* box, coffer; *schryne of þe herte*, the pericardium 239/5

schrinke, scrinke, schrenke- *v.* (**i-schronke** *pa. p.*), **schrinkinge, schrenkynge, schrunkynge** *sb.* to shrink 132/27 (*v.*), 223/31 (*sb.*)

schrobbe, see **schrubbe; schroudinge,** see **ischredde**

schrub(be), schrobbe, sshurbbe, sshrubbe, scrub(be) *sb.* a shrub 916/11

schrud-, see **ischredde; schrunkynge,** see **schrinke**

(i)schuft *v. pa. p.*, **schuftynge** *sb.* pushed 513/27 (*v.*), 416/19 (*sb.*)

schul(en) *v. pres. pl.* (**schal** *pres. sg.*; **sc(h)ulde, scholde, sshulde** *pa.*) shall, should, ought, is obliged to 40/17

scilens, silence, cylens *sb.* silence 263/14

sciluiren, syluerene *a.* made of silver 638/7

scyoun *sb.* shoot, twig, slip 1015/14

sclat(te) *sb.* a slate 980/2

sclyme, slyme *sb.* mud, ooze 327/22

scoymous, see **squaymous**

scordioun *sb.* a wild plant which smells like garlic 910/8 [L. *scordion*]

scot *sb.* reckoning, payment for food or entertainment 331/16

scotyles *sb. pl.* large wicker-work baskets 1042/27

†**scowed** *v. pa. p.* spotted, cloudy 1229/4 [obscure; ? cf. OE. *scu(w)a*]

scrape *v.* (**scharpiþ** *pres. 3sg.* once) to scrape, scratch 628/5

scrinke, see **schrinke**

scripturis *sb. pl.* the Bible, writing or composition 47/6

scrupil, scrupul- *sb.* a small unit of weight, esp. used in the preparation of drugs, $\frac{1}{24}$ ounce 832/34

sculde, see **schulen**

†**secels** *sb. pl.* stocks, stems suitable for transplanting 889/10 [L. *sectile*]; see also **cicile**

seche, seke, suche *v.* to seek 87/24

seche, see **swiche; sechinge,** see **sichinges**

secundary *a.* (*adv.*) less important(ly), derived from or based upon something more important 48/27

secundines *sb. pl.* (**secoundyne** *sg.* once) placentas, afterbirths 925/6 [late L. *secundinæ*]

sed-, see **seþe**

sedere *sb.* a sower 533/28

see, se, isee, ise *v.* (**seiþ, seþ, su(w)eþ** *pres.*; **sey** *occ. pres. pl.*; **sey3e, seigh, si3e, sigh, sawe** *pa.*; **iseye, iseen, iseyne** *pa. p.*), **se(e)ynge** *sb.* to see 41/20 (*v.*), 109/31 (*sb.*)

seecalf *sb.* seal, sea-lion 1259/34

seediþ *v. pres. 3sg.*, **seedynge** *sb.* produces seeds; *þe vertu of seedynge*, the power to produce seeds 908/8 (*v.*), 883/7 (*sb.*)

seehoundes *sb. pl.* dog-fish 676/28

seek, seke, sieke, sike, siche *a.* sick 124/9

iseen, see **see**

seer *sb.* one who sees, one who experiences divine revelations 73/28

seesele *sb.* seal, sea-lion 1243/29

seeswyne *sb.* porpoise 680/36

seete, see **sete**

seetheues *sb. pl.* pirates 750/24

seewolfes *sb. pl.* some type of voracious ocean fish, perhaps the sea bass or the wolffish 676/28

sege *sb.* seat, member which serves as a container for some quality or substance 343/23 [OF. *sege*]

segge *sb.* sedge 882/25

seie, (i)seyne, seiþ, see **sigge, see; sey(e)de,** see **sigge; seigh, sey3e,** see **see**

seintuary *sb.* the Temple of the Jews 1385/32

seke, see **seche, seek**

sekelewe *a.* sickly 523/28

sekenesse *sb.* illness 464/24

selde, seldene, sield(ene) *adv.* seldom 124/31

isele *v. pa. p.* sealed 408/6

sely *a.* innocent, harmless 1190/24
selle *v.* (**selde** *pa.* once; **isolde, isoold** *pa. p.*) to sell 305/22
selle, see **celle**
yselt *v. pa. p.* salted, preserved with salt 929/31
selue *a.* the same, the very (thing) 1111/26
semblant, semelant *sb.* face, demeanour 200/11 [OF. *semblant, pres. p.* of *sembler* 'resemble']
seme *v.* to befit, suit, beseem, appear 56/12
semelant, see **semblant**
semynal *a.* pertaining to semen, pertaining to generation, generative 262/22
seminatyf *a.* having power to produce or generate offspring 1039/25
†**semisouneþ** *v. pres. 3sg.* speaks low 304/20
semple, see **simple**; **sene,** see **cene**; **seneuy,** see **senuey**; **senewe,** see **sinewe**
sens *sb.* incense 1380/3
sense *v.* to cense 1063/15
sensibil *a.* endowed with sensation; *soule* or *vertu sensible, sensible spirit*, psychic faculties concerned with sensation (and secondarily, motion) 98/8
sentence *sb.* opinion, view 153/1
senuey, synvey, seneuy *sb.* the mustard plant 932/13 [OF. *senevé, senevei*]
seoue, see **syve**
septuagesme *sb.* the seventy days before Easter 542/33
sepulture *sb.* burial 1124/27
sequences *sb. pl.* prose or verse compositions sung during the mass 1388/28
sequestre *v.* to separate 64/30
serchith *v. pres. 3sg.*, **sarchinge, serchinge** *sb.* searches 57/27 (*v.*), 57/15 (*sb.*)
seruage *sb.* servitude 305/16
seruyce *sb.* allegiance, duty 251/27
sesiþ, see **cesseþ**
sesouneþ *v. pres. 3sg.* renders digestible 201/2
sete, seete *sb.* seat, organ in which a quality or faculty resides, organ or specific part; *seete of þe heed*, the temples or cheek-bones; *seete of þe herte*, the bone or gristle within the hearts of some ungulates 168/30

seþ, seþþe, siþ *conj.* since, because, after, from the time that 45/4
seþ, see **see**
seþe *v.* (**suþ-, sith-, sed-** occ.; **isode, isothen** *pa. p.*), **seþinge, suthinge, sedyng** *sb.* to boil, cook 104/26 (*v.*), 121/33 (*sb.*)
sette *v.* (**isette, iset** *pa. p.*; **sitteþ** *pres. 3sg.* once), **settinge** *sb.* to set, plant, establish 53/15 (*v.*), 94/15 (*sb.*)
seurtee, see **surete**
seuereþ *v. pres. 3sg.* cuts apart, separates, allots; *pa. p., a.* distinct 120/35
sewe, swe-, sue- *v.*[1] (**seþ** *pres. pl.* once) to follow, flow, conform to, be consonant with 141/13
sewe, sowe- *v.*[2], **sewinge** *sb.* to sew, stitch, join 1049/32 (*v.*), 339/11 (*sb.*)
sewe, see **sowe**
sewet, suet *sb.* fat 849/13
sewyng *sb.* spasm, cramp, trembling 432/14 [? OE. *swegan* 'move']
sexe *num.* six 529/20
sext *sb.* sex 597/36
sexteþe *num.* sixteenth 467/10
sexþe, see **sixte**
sexty *num.* sixty 460/28
sextules *sb. pl.* Roman units of weight, apparently 1/12 ounce (*uncia*) 1385/2
shale, see **schale**; **share,** see **schare**; **yshaue,** see **schaue**
shese, chese *sb.* cheese 362/20
shete, see **schete**
sholde *a.* shallow 812/3 [OE. *scáld, scéald*]
yshore, see **schere**; **short,** see **schort**; **shouu-,** see **schowve**; **showre,** see **schewere**; **shuff-,** see **schowve**
sibnes *sb.* kinship 467/23 [cf. OE. *gesibnes*]
siche, see **seek, swiche**
sichinges, sikynges *sb. pl.* (**seching** *sg.* once) sighs 343/34
siclis *sb. pl.* shekels 708/24
syde *sb.* side; *on syde*, aside, to the side 228/11
sidlong *adv.* sideways, toward the side 222/28
sieke, see **seek**; **sieldene,** see **selde**; **syfe,** see **syve**
sigge, seye, seyne *v.* (**seiþ** *pres. 3sg.*; **seyn** *pres. pl.*; **sey(e)de** *pa. p.*) to say, speak 41/21

sigh, si3e, see **see**; **si3t,** see **cite**; **siht, sih3t,** see **si3t**; **sike,** see **seek**
sighty *a.* visible, conspicuous 1269/6
signeþ *v. pres. 3sg.* [1] assigns 111/19
sygniþ *v. pres. 3sg.* [2] blesses (with sign of the cross), marks 551/10
si3t, siþ, siht, sih3t *sb.* sight, vision, revelation 87/27
si3tliche *adv.* visibly 508/34
siker *a.* safe, certain, sure, reliable, firm 57/23 [OE. *sicor*]
sikerliche, sekerly *adv., a.* with certainty, safely 188/21
sikernes *sb.* sense of security, confidence, freedom from (feelings of) danger 334/15
sikynges, see **sichinges**; **silence,** see **scilens**
isilid *v. pa. p.* sewed shut, sewed up (of a hawk's eyes, as part of the process of training for falconry) 608/22 [OF. *ciller*]
sillers *sb. pl.* sellers 547/25
syluerene, see **sciluiren**
simphone, symphony *sb.* a musical instrument, esp. a drum 330/33
simple, semple *a.* simple, unmixed 47/9
simplete *sb.* simplicity, the state of being of a non-composite nature 42/12
simplicite *sb.* simplicity, the state of being of a non-composite nature, the act of perceiving without admixture 52/22
synagoge *sb.* the assembly of the Jews, esp. in its exegetical sense: the unregenerate type of the Church 309/9
syndir *sb.* refuse, slag 560/7
sinewe, synowe, sinwe, senewe *sb.* sinew, any stringy white cord-like structure in the body (incl. nerves as well as tendons) 98/6
sinewy, synewe, synuy *a.* full of sinews or nerves, supplied with sinews or nerves 198/4
singuler *a., sb.* single (one of a group), individual, unique, eminent; *sb.* individual, the singular number in grammar 59/25
singulerite *sb.* solitude, solitariness 330/9
singulerliche *adv.* singly, individually, especially 82/16
sinke *v.* (**sonken** *pa. p.*) to sink 660/6
synowe, see **sinewe**; **synvey,** see

senuey; synuy, see **sinewy; sinwe,** see **sinewe**
sirupe, syrop, sirip *sb.* a thick, sweet liquid, a medical potion based on sugar 325/25
siþ, see **seþ, si3t; sith-,** see **seþe**
sithe *sb.* (*adv.*) time; *sithe(s)* (between numerals), times, multiplied by 297/8 [OE. *sið*]
sither *sb.* cider or another alcoholic fruit drink 1317/17
syve, syfe, seoue *sb.* sieve, strainer 958/25
sixte, sexþe, sixe *num.* sixth 42/22
skabbe, see **schabbe**
skalle *sb.* a disease of the scalp, characterized by scabs or scales 344/27
skape, see **scape; skars,** see **scars; skarste,** see **scarste; skeymous,** see **squaymous; yskemede,** see **skymmeþ; skepet,** see **skipet; skibett,** see **skipet**
skyles *sb. pl.* causes, reasons 282/1
skilfulliche *adv.* reasonably, with good cause, naturally 420/12
skym *sb.* scum, froth or impurities on the surface of a liquid mixture 929/7
skymmeþ *v. pres. 3sg.* (**yskemede** *pa. p.* once) forms foam or scum (on the surface of a liquid), removes or clears away such foam 675/18
skym(m)ours, skumors *sb. pl.* searovers, pirates 785/25 [aphetic form of OF. *escumeor*]
skipet, skepet, skibett *sb.* box, small chest, the capacity of an organ to hold or contain something 99/18 [obscure]
sklendre *a.* slender 159/10
skolkynge *sb.* skulking 87/32
islayn, see **slee**
slake, slack *a.* unenergetic, relaxed, weak, moderate 140/11
slake, slack *v.*, **slakinge** *sb.* to decrease in force, lessen, restrain, moderate, relax 73/7 (*v.*), 124/32 (*sb.*)
slakenes *sb.* abating, lack of vigour 388/2
slakliche *adv.* slowly, without vigour 246/26
slaw, see **slowe; islawe,** see **slee**
slede *sb.* a drag used to carry heavy goods, a sledge 1173/16
slee *v.* (**slough, slowe, slou3, slew** *pa.*;

islawe, islowe, islayn *pa. p.*) to kill 132/9

sleer *sb.* killer 1136/5

slegge *sb.* a heavy hammer or its head, sledgehammer 1262/20

sleigh, see **sligh; sleliche,** see **slily**

sleighte, slyþe, sleyþe *sb.* trickery, wisdom, prudence, cleverness 684/4

slepeful, slepful *a.* sleepy 175/14

slepingenes *sb.* sleepiness 349/21

sleuþe, slouthe *sb.* slowness, sloth 125/29

slewþeþ *v. pres. 3sg.* (impersonal) it does not waste time, it does not constitute a neglect of other duties 1245/20

sliden *v. pres. pl.* (**islyde** *pa. p.*), **slidinge** *sb.* slide, pass, pass away, slip (and fall), err 86/4 (*v.*), 85/10 (*sb.*)

slider *a.* slippery, smooth 197/5 [OE. *slidor*]

slidery *a.* slippery 637/2

slideringe, see **slydreþ**

slidirnesse *sb.* slipperiness, smoothness 402/22

slydreþ *v. pres. 3sg.*, **slideringe** *sb.* makes slippery 1330/20 (*v.*), 224/32 (*sb.*)

sligh, slyghe, sleigh, sly3e, sly *a.* clever, ingenious, wise, wily 631/19

slily, sleliche, slilyche *adv.* cleverly, skilfully, wisely, secretly 257/13

slipernesse *sb.* slipperiness 402/22

slipir *a.* slippery 339/21

slipiþ *v. pres. 3sg.* slips, passes, slides, makes pass 142/26

sliþe, see **sleighte**

slobery *a.* slimy, dirty 1170/37

slobir-, sloburnes, see **slombirnes**

slogard *sb.* slothful person 189/7

slombirnes, slomburnes, sloburnes, slobirnes *sb.* sloth 351/8

slombry *a.* sleepy 1286/21

sloon *sb. pl.* wild plums 1338/4

slough, slou3, islowe, see **slee; slouthe,** see **sleuþe**

slow(e), slaw, slowh, slow3(e) *a.* slow 124/29

slowliche, slouliche *adv.* (**slowloker** *comp.*) slowly 134/3

smak *sb.* taste 150/7

smakeþ *v. pres. 3sg.* tastes 327/22

smale *a.* little, small, slender, narrow, limited, fine or rarified 98/6

smalenes *sb.* slimness, smallness 481/13

smaleþ *v. pres. 3sg.* makes small 1065/29

smaragde *sb.* emerald 837/15 [L. *smaragdus*]

smeche *sb.* smoke 922/8 [OE. *smēc, smīc*]

smel(le), smyl(le) *sb.* smell, the sense of smell 115/6

smelle, smylle *v.*, **smellinge, smyllinge** *sb.* to smell 108/15 (*v.*), 98/12 (*sb.*)

smere *sb.* fat, grease, tallow 151/14

smere, smery *v.* to anoint, smear 219/30

ysmert *v. pa. p.*, **smertinge** *sb.* pained 276/10 (*v.*), 153/11 (*sb.*)

ismete, see **smite**

smeþe *a.* smooth 104/3

smeþie *v.* to smoothe 104/2

smite *v.* (**smith-** occ.; **smit** *pres. 3sg.* once; **ismyte, ismete** *pa. p.*), **smitinge** *sb.* to strike, vibrate, attack suddenly (with a disease or morbid fluid), attack, drive, discomfit, perturb 83/37 (*v.*), 105/35 (*sb.*)

smyt(t)eþ *v. pres. 3sg.* (**ismytted** *pa. p.*), **smittinge** *sb.* pollutes, infects; *sb.* blemish 173/10 (*v.*), 62/27 (*sb.*) [OE. *smittian*]

smoke, smook(e) *sb.* smoke, fume, vapour 115/29

ysmoked *v. pa. p.*, **smokinge** *sb.* emitted smoke, fumigated, exposed to smoke 973/23 (*v.*), 204/35 (*sb.*)

smoky, smoke *a.* smoky 108/7

snacchiþ *v. pres. 3sg.* bites at 1171/7

snayl(e) *sb.* snail, turtle, tortoise 1096/33

snarliþ *v. pres. pl.* ensnare, overcome 89/1

sneuelardes *sb. pl.* snivellers 194/22

sneuely *a.* full of mucus 922/19

snewiþ *v. pres. 3sg.* snows 579/2

snytinge *a.* pertaining to the wiping away of mucus 170/34 [from OE. *snȳtan*]

snytinges *sb. pl.* wipings of the nose, removals of mucus, mucus 209/29

snyuel *sb.* mucus 157/10

snoffe *sb.* candlewick 562/5

sobre *a.* temperate, moderate 57/16

soche, see **swiche**

isocied *v. pa. p.* associated, joined 67/3 [OF. *socier*]

socour *sb.* aid, shelter 60/9

socoure, sokere-, soukere- *v.* to help 55/20

isode, see **seþe**

sodeyn *a.* immediate (and unexpected), prompt 61/21

sodeynliche *adv.* immediately, without warning 61/23

soffreþ, soffringe, see **suffre**

softe *adv.* softly, gently 299/30

soget, subiecte, subiet *a.* dependent, subordinate 62/10

soget, suget, subiecte *sb.* a subordinate, the substance from which something is made, the substance or essence of a thing 62/5

isoke, sokynge, see **souke; ysokerede**, see **socoure**

solas *sb.* comfort, pleasure 392/25

sole *a.* unique, unrivalled 1356/28

solempne *a.* famous, renowned 759/17

soler *sb.* an upper room in a house, one exposed to sunlight 1057/4 [AN. *soler*]

solid *a.* solid (figure at geometry), having three dimensions; *solid nombre*, a cube 1364/1

solid *sb.* a Roman weight (and coin of that weight), ⅙ ounce (*uncia*) 1384/23

solouȝe, solow *sb.* plough 719/11 [OE. *sulh*]

solsticial *a.* coming at the time of the solstice 534/15

solucioun *sb.* termination, crisis (of a fever) 385/15

solueþ *v. pres. 3sg.* breaks, loosens 880/34

som, somme, sum(me) *pron., a.* one of a group, a certain one, some; *som and som*, *som aftir som*, little by little, gradually 46/30

somdel *adv.* somewhat 47/8

somewhidir *adv.* in some direction 109/19

isommed *v. pa. p.* briefly summarized 43/1-2

somwhat *sb.* some thing, some part 101/20-1

son-, see **soun, sowne**

sonde, soonde *sb.* sand, gravel, a beach 825/27

sondes *sb. pl.* messengers, messages 308/12

sone *adv.* immediately, soon 153/31

song *v. pa.* sang 1248/9

sonken, see **sinke; soonde**, see **sonde**

sore *adv.* sorely 118/17

soþ *a.* true, real, proper 49/33

soþely *adv.* truly 123/5

isothen, see **seþe**

soþnesse *sb.* truth 46/1

sotil, subtil(e) *a.* (**sotillicher** *comp.*) approaching immateriality, of rarefied consistency, penetrating, delicate, slender, fine, minute, sensitive, discriminating, acute 57/31

sotileþ *v. pres. 3sg.*, **sotylyng** *sb.* makes thin or rarefied or less gross 1052/34 (*v.*), 1284/23 (*sb.*)

sotilnes *sb.* acuity 86/1

†**soudynes** *sb.* close juncture of parts, solidity 860/6 [OF. *souder* + OE. *-iȝ* + *-nes*]

souke *sb.* milk to suck 1176/9

souke, sowke- *v.* (**ysoke** *pa. p.*), **so(u)kynge, sowkyng** *sb.* to suck 151/22 (*v.*), 1103/7 (*sb.*)

soukereþ, see **socoure**

soukers *sb. pl.* suckers 505/1

soule *sb.* the soul or spirit, a psychic faculty or function associated with the spirit (or a part of it), e.g. *resonable soule*, reason, rational power 42/11

souled *v. pa. p., a.* endowed with a soul 139/33

soules, see **sowilis**

soun, sowne, son *sb.* sound, noise 108/6

sound-, see **sowne**

soundeþ *v. pres. 3sg.* makes sound or whole 1120/2

soupliþ *v. pres. 3sg.* softens 142/6

souredowe *sb.* leaven, yeast 547/7-8

sourissh, sowrissh *a.* sour 912/7

sourisshnesse *sb.* sourness 1314/36

souereynes *sb. pl.* superiors, authorities, rulers 1292/11

sowde, sawde- *v.*, **sowdinge** *sb.* to unite, join together (edges of a wound), fasten, close, heal; *pres. p., a.* used of drug types which promote healing of lesions 376/19 (*v.*), 837/5 (*sb.*) [OF. *souder, sauder*]

sowe *v.* (**sewe** *pa.*; **(y)sowe, ysewed** *pa. p.*) to sow 88/15

sowelis, see **sowilis; sowen**, see **sewe** *v.*²

sowilis, sowelis, soules *sb. pl.* sharpened stakes 1050/1 [OE. *sāȝol*]

sownd-, see **sowne; sowne**, see **soun**

sowne, soune-, sounde-, sownde-, sone- *v.* to make or produce a sound, to be heard as a sound, signify, imply, suggest or encourage 47/14

sowters *sb. pl.* shoemakers 1237/17 [OE. *sütere*, from L. *sütor*]

†spalange *sb. pl.* venomous spiders 749/5 [ML. *spalangio*, *-gia*]

spanne *sb.* a unit of linear measure, the width of the hand and extended fingers 924/9

spannels *sb. pl.* hobbles 1150/35 [from OE. *spannan*]

spanneþ *v. pres. 3sg.* grasps, seizes, fastens 1184/26

sparcle *sb.* spark 564/9

spare *v.* to abstain (from), refrain (from) 40/19

sparkeleþ *v. pres. 3sg.*, **spark(e)lynge** *sb.* sparks, crackles, glitters 564/29 (*v.*), 564/14 (*sb.*)

sparliuour *sb.* muscle, esp. the muscle of the calf 100/1 [OE. *spær-līra* 'calf-muscle', with substitution of OE. *lifer*]

sparpliþ *v. pres. 3sg.* (**sparp(o)led**, **sperp(e)led**, **sparpilled** *pa. p.*) disperses, scatters 539/28 [apheotic form of OF. *esparpeillier*]

ispatte, see **spete**; **spattil**, see **spotil**

special *a., sb.* excellent, particular; *in special*, specially, particularly 42/6

specialich *adv.* particularly 140/28

spede *v.* (**ispedde** *pa. p.*), **spedinge** *sb.* to succeed, accomplish, aid, hasten 40/6 (*v.*), 573/31 (*sb.*)

sped(e)ful *a.* profitable, successful, helpful, expedient, speedy 215/12

spedefulliche *adv.* speedily, effectively 156/28

speke, **speyke** *v.* (**spak**, **speke** *pa.*; **ispoke(n)** *pa. p.*) to speak 41/30

spence *sb.* storage place (for food), buttery, pantry 256/4 [apheotic form of OF. *despense*]

ispend, **ispendid** *v. pa. p.* spent 147/7

spere *sb.* sphere, ball 53/3

speredib, see **sprede**

spereþ *v. pres. pl.* close up 243/2 [Middle Dutch *sperren*]

sperhauk, **sparhauk** *sb.* sparrow-hawk 218/13

spermatik *a.* derived from sperm or from the generative organs 382/23

sperpel-, see **sparpliþ**

sperstone *sb.* gypsum, plaster 839/9

spete, **spitte** *v.* (**ispatte** *pa. p.*), **spetinge** *sb.* to spit 209/31 (*v.*), 210/11 (*sb.*)

spewe, **spue-** *v.*, **spewinge**, **spuinge**, **spevinge** *sb.* to vomit, spit 346/5 (*v.*), 159/21 (*sb.*)

spicerie *sb.* spices 482/21

spicers *sb. pl.* spice-sellers, druggists 482/21

spilliþ *v. pres. pl.* (**ispilt**, **ispiled** *pa. p.*) destroy, slay, injure, ruin, spoil 207/34

spilt *sb.* a wheat-like grain 972/21

spindil *sb.* bar or rod with grooves to make a screw 190/32

spynne *v.* (**ysponne** *pa. p.*) to spin (thread) 1055/27

spiracioun *sb.* act of breathing, divine act of creation 50/15

spiracle *sb.* breath, spirit 92/22

spire *sb.* stalk or stem of a plant 912/1

spire *v.* to sprout 937/37

spire, see **spyþer**

spireth *v. pres. 3sg.* breathes into, gives life to 45/31

spirit *sb.* spirit, soul, the vital principle of a being, any faculty or power concerned with vital function, incorporeal being 54/10

spiritualte *sb.* spiritual or incorporeal quality 59/25

spyþer, **spyþur**, **spire** *sb.* spider 1132/6

spitously *adv.* contemptuously, cruelly 1118/2

spitte, see **spete**

sple(c)k, **splikke** *sb.* spot, speck 492/21 [obscure; cf. Middle Dutch *gesplect*]

splecky *a.* spotted 487/26

†splecliche *a.* spotted 209/1

splekked *v. pa. p.* speckled 1187/27

splenetikes *sb. pl.* sufferers from diseases of the spleen 257/11

†splenked *v. pa. p.* spotted 1229/4 [obscure]

splikke, see **spleck**

splintis *sb. pl.* thin strips of wood, splinters of wood, chips 588/21

splyntres *sb. pl.* splinters, slivers of wood, strips of wood 907/30

spoyle *v.* (**spolyeþ** *pres. 3sg.* once), **spoylinge** *sb.* to despoil, harry (Hell), deprive 88/10 (*v.*), 548/25 (*sb.*)

spones, **spoones** *sb. pl.* thin pieces of wood 169/21

spongy *a.* porous, full of holes 206/13

spongious, spoungeous *a.* porous 368/14

ysponne, see **spynne; spoones,** see **spones; sporneþ,** see **spurneþ**

spotil, spottil, spattil *sb.* saliva, spit 200/25

spousailes *sb. pl.* nuptials 308/26

spousebreche *sb.* adultery 1195/16

spousebreker *sb.* adulterer 857/32

spousebrekyng *sb.* adultery 1082/24–5

spousehode *sb.* wedlock, matrimony, the bonds of marriage 309/9

spousiþ *v. pres. 3sg.* marries 93/10

spouteþ *v. pres. 3sg.* squirts forth 1004/33

spraye *sb.* twig or shoot of a tree, branch, branch-like structure (e.g. *sprayes of þe galle*, bile ducts) 97/13

spraieþ *v. pres. 3sg.* sprouts new growth, springs forth 549/32

sprancle *sb.* spark, sparkle 93/25 [cf. Middle Dutch *spranke* and Frisian *sprankel*]

spranclith, sprangleþ *v. pres. 3sg.*, **sprankelinge** *sb.* jumps about, sparkles, sparks, crackles 424/21 (*v.*), 499/10 (*sb.*)

sprawle, spraule- *v.* to move about (convulsively), toss about, spread out 296/23

sprede *v.* (**spered-** once, **isprad** *pa. p.*) to spread 41/8

isprenged, see **springe**

spring(e) *sb.* source or well of a stream, springtime, shoot or sprout of a tree, rise, rising of the sea at certain times 648/12

springe *v.* (**ispringed, isprenged, ispronge, isprunge** *pa. p.*), **springynge** *sb.* to spring, issue, sprout, proceed from, sprinkle, scatter, ooze, exude; *springing time*, spring 98/6 (*v.*), 119/6 (*sb.*)

springes *sb. pl.* snares to capture birds 716/32

ispronge, isprunge, see **springe; spu-,** see **spewe**

spurche *sb.* spurge, the shrub 915/16

yspurged *v. pa. p.* cleansed or purified, esp. by expelling impurities through fermentation 1083/29 [OF. *espurgier*]

spurneþ, sporneþ *v. pres. 3sg.* stumbles 365/11

squaymous, scoymous, skeymous *a.* squeamish 257/16

squekeþ *v. pres. 3sg.* squeaks 304/25

squyna(n)cye, sqynacy *sb.* quinsy, tonsilitis, a disease of the throat 216/24

squyntelokere *sb.* squinter 182/15

squirte *sb.* diarrhoea, a flux 299/12

ssh-, see **sch-**

staat *sb.* rank, status, condition 77/15

stablement *sb.* foundation, support 1142/29

stablenge *v. pres. p.* strengthening 57/22

stadial *a.* pertaining to the linear *stadium* (about ⅛ mile) 1381/11

stale *a.* (of wine) having stood until clear 1083/29

stalword, stalworth *a.* stalwart, brave, valiant 750/23

stanche, see **staunche**

stappe, steppe *v.*, **stappynge** *sb.* to step, go, advance 269/25 (*v.*), 1052/19 (*sb.*)

stappes, steppes *sb. pl.* steps 210/10

starte, see **sterte**

starteleþ, sterteleþ *v. pres. 3sg.*, **startelynges** *sb. pl.* moves swiftly, leaps, capers 680/6 (*v.*), 1178/17 (*sb.*)

stature *sb.* height (in a standing position), upright portion, build or bodily shape 694/30

sta(u)nche *v.*, **staunching** *sb.* to stop the flow (of a fluid), close (a wound) 327/31 (*v.*), 838/18 (*sb.*)

stede *sb.* place, point; *in* (*þe*) *stede of*, in place of, instead of 48/32

†**stedeful** *a.* firmly placed 692/21

ysteynt, see **stynte; steke-,** see **styke**

steliþ *v. pres. 3sg.* (**istole** *pa. p.*) steals 471/31

stem(p)nes *sb. pl.* (and *sg.* once) times, periods of time, turns; *kepen* or *chaungen stemnes*, to take turns 57/23 [OE. *stemn*; cf. **steuines**]

stenching, see **styncheþ**

ystened *v. pa. p.* pelted or struck with stones 1223/22

stenge, see **stonges; stenk-,** see **stynke; stent-,** see **stynte**

stepe *a.* steep, high, protruding or projecting (eyes) 112/32

steppe(-), see **stappe, stappes; ster-,** see **sturieþ**

sterne *a.* fierce, brave 734/26

sterre *sb.* star, planet; *schipman(nes) sterre*, Polaris, the north star; *þe seuene sterres*, the planets, the Pleiades 121/7

sterte, starte *v.*, **startyng** *sb.* to leap, jump, caper 876/8 (*v.*), 1208/18 (*sb.*)

sterteleþ, see **starteleþ**

steuines *sb. pl.* times, occasions; *by steuines*, at intervals, in turn 370/4 [OE. *stefn*; cf. **stempnes**]

stewinge, stu(w)ynge *sb.*, **istuwed** *v. pa. p.* bathed in hot water, suffused with a vapour from some boiling drug 389/9 (*v.*), 356/9–10 (*sb.*)

stieresman *sb.* helmsman 1082/18

stifles *sb. pl.* asthma or a similar disease 106/20

stigeþ, see **styke**

sti3e, stye *v.* to climb 41/16 [OE. *stīgan*, strong 1]

styke, steke *v.* (**stig**-forms occ.) to pierce, prick, stab, fix, press 113/32

stik(e)liche *adv.* directly, steadfastly 66/22

stile *sb.* stylus, pen 90/7

stynche, stenche *sb.* stink 135/11

styncheþ *v. pres. pl.*, †**stenching** *sb.* stink 1304/3 (*v.*), 829/19 (*sb.*)

stynge, see **stonges**

stinge *v.* (**istonge** *pa. p.*, **stynkynge** *pres. p.* once) to sting, bite 428/27

stynke, stenke- *v.* (**stynggynge** *pres. p.* once), **stinkinge** *sb.* to stink 115/16 (*v.*), 135/9 (*sb.*)

stynkyng, see **stinge**

stynte, stente- *v.* (**stint, stent, ysteynt** *pa. p.*), **styntynge, stentinge** *sb.* to stop 356/10 (*v.*), 290/1 (*sb.*)

styues, stiwes *sb. pl.* heated rooms used for baths, hot baths 106/25

stody, see **studie**; **stoffe, stoffinge**, see **stuffe**

stok, stokke, stock(e) *sb.* trunk, stem, stalk 103/33

stokes *sb. pl.* stabs, goadings 213/24 [? cf. OF. *estoquier*]

stole, stoole *sb.* a long robe 549/8

istole, see **steliþ**

stonde *v.* (**stonde, standen** *pa. p.*) to stand 68/3

stone, stoon *sb.* stone, rock, mineral, gem, testicle; *þe stoon, stoon of þe reynes* or *bladdre*, kidney stone 42/34

ston(e)y *v.*, **ston(e)yinge, stonynge** *sb.* to stun; *sb.* also amazement, madness 858/15 (*v.*), 348/6 (*sb.*)

istonge, see **stinge**

stonges *sb. pl.* (**stynge, stenge** *sg.*) stings (of insects) 610/26 [OE. *steng*]

stony *a.* stone-like, hard; *þe stony boon*, the hard portion of the temporal bone which protects the inner ear 190/28

storax *sb.* a sweet-smelling gum or resin 993/19 [L. *storax*]

store, stoor *sb.* supply, abundance 1094/12

stored *v. pa.* furnished, supplied 744/21

stoute *a.* proud, arrogant 305/36

stoutnes *sb.* pride, arrogance 184/19

stowiþ *v. pres. pl.* place, bring to a certain position 81/18

stowpinge *sb.* stooping 481/15

stracchinge, see **strecche**; **straches**, see **strake**

stray *v. pres. pl.* roam 765/11

strai3t, istreited *v. pa. p.* narrowed, contracted 226/13

strai3t, see **strecche**; **straite**, see **streite**

strake *sb.* (**strakes, straches** *pl.*) stripe or streak of colour on a surface, a strip of land, a swath or furrow 827/31 [cf. OE. *strica*]

straked *v. pa. p.* lined, streaked 835/15

strangeinge *sb.* alienation; *strangeinge of mynde*, irrationality, delirium 159/25–6

stranger, see **strengere**

strangle-, strongely *v.*, **stranglinge** *sb.* to choke, suffocate 237/6 (*v.*), 373/13 (*sb.*)

strate, see **streite**

stra(u)nge, strang *a.* foreign, alien, external, barbarous, pagan 74/24

strecche, streicche, stricche- *v.* (**strei3t** *pa.*; **istrei3t, istreiht, strai3t, streit** *pa. p.*), **strecchinge, stracchinge** *sb.* to stretch, reach out, draw out or enlarge 91/32 (*v.*), 212/7 (*sb.*)

istrei3t(e), see **strecche, streit(e-)**

streyneþ, streigneþ *v. pres. 3sg.*, **streynynge** *sb.* clasps, compresses, restrains, stretches or makes taut 115/18 (*v.*), 284/27 (*sb.*)

streit, see **strecche**

streit(e), straite, (i)strei3te *a., adv.*[1] straight, direct(ly) 109/13 (*a.*), 66/22 (*adv.*)

streit(e), strei3te, stra(y)te *a., adv.*[2]

streit(e), strei3te, stra(y)te (*cont.*)
tight(ly), narrow(ly), constricted, small,
constrained, strict(ly), rigorous(ly) 116/
11 (*a.*), 311/6 (*adv.*)

istreited, see **strai3t**

streitnes, strei3tnesse *sb.* narrowness,
tightness 124/4

**strenge, streng þe, strenk þe, stren þe,
strengh, strenhe** *sb.*[1] strength, power,
fortitude 71/14

streng(e) *sb.*[2] cord, rope, cord-shaped
structure (incl. ligaments, tendons,
veins, nerves) 197/31

strenge, see **stronge**; **stren(g)he**, see
strenge[1]

strengere (**stranger** once), **strengest** *a.*,
comp. and *super.* stronger, strongest
108/30 (*comp.*), 116/31 (*super.*)

strenge þ, strenk þe, stren þe, see
strenge

strepe þ, strype þ *v. pres. 3sg.*, **strep-
pinge, stripinge** *sb.* unclothes,
removes, flays; *sb.* tearing of the skin,
flaying 424/1 (*v.*), 276/8 (*sb.*)

strete *sb.* road, highway; *Wat(e)ling
Strete*, the Milky Way 497/18

stripelinge *sb.* youth 291/30

strype þ, striping, see **strepe þ**

striue *v.* (**ystriue** *pa. p.*) to strive,
contend with, rival 146/23

stronde *sb.* sea-coast 887/17

strong(e), strenge *a.* powerful, requir-
ing strength, healthy or active, difficult
(to perform), solid, intense, full 53/33

strongely, see **strangle**

strowte *v.* to bulge 271/1 [OE. *strūtian*]

strucioun *sb.* ostrich 640/4 [ML. *strucio*]

stubbis *sb. pl.* stubble, short pieces of flax
564/17

studie, stody *sb.* study, sympathy or
friendship, perplexity or anxiousness,
thought, concern (for a subject) 61/7

studientis *sb. pl.* those addicted to a
study 483/14

studinge *sb.* studying, anxiousness 381/5

stuffe, stuffy, stoffe *v.*, **stoffinge** *sb.* to
stifle, suffocate 99/29 (*v.*), 144/14 (*sb.*)

stuynge, see **stewinge**

stur(i)e þ, steri þ *v. pres. 3sg.*, **steringe** *sb.*
moves, arouses, impels, encourages
213/13 (*v.*), 271/14 (*sb.*)

sturnes *sb.* severity 193/36

istuwed, stuwinge, see **stewinge**

subarbes *sb. pl.* areas immediately
adjacent to a town 702/6

subiecte, subiet, see **soget**

substancial *a., sb.* essential, pertaining to
essence, principal; *sb. pl.* essential
parts, pieces which make up the whole;
moisture substancial, fluids inherent in
and nurturing a body 56/9

substanciallich *adv.* in substance, in its
nature 244/24

substaunce *sb.* essence, essential nature,
the essential being to which phenomena (accidents) are superadded,
material, material part, possessions,
wealth 41/4

subtil(e), see **sotil**

subtiliacioun *sb.* act of making a substance subtile (esp. turning a liquid into
a gas), reduction, rarefaction, evapora-
tion 147/12

subtilite, subtilte *sb.* fineness, acuteness
(of perception), skill 60/7

suche, see **seche, swiche**

sucre, sug(u)re, suger, zuger *sb.* sugar
978/27

sudewid *v. pa. p.* conquered, subdued
317/32

suerte, see **surete**; **sue þ**, see **see, sewe**

suffisaunce *sb.* sufficiency, sufficient
quantity 1275/19

suffisa(u)nt, suffisoun *a.* sufficient,
able, capable 53/34

suffisauntlich *adv.* sufficiently 1318/15

suffrauns *sb.* suffering, tolerance 75/22

suffre, soffre- *v.*, **suffringe, soffringe**
sb. to undergo, permit 86/5 (*v.*), 309/15
(*sb.*)

suffusioun *sb.* the pouring of a humour
over a part of the body; *suffusioun of
yhen*, cataract 935/36

su(y)tours *sb. pl.* followers 453/15

superficial *a.* pertaining to a plane
surface, two-dimensional; *numbre superficial*, a number composed of two prime
numbers 1364/1

superflue *a., sb.* excessive, unnecessary;
sb. excess; *superflue nombre*, a number
'immoderate' or 'inordinate' in its
composition, a prime number 138/9

superfluite *sb.* excess (esp. of bodily
fluid) 128/11

supplement *sb.* an extra supply, an aid
500/23

supplie *v.* to fill up, make whole, compensate (for the loss or absence of something else) 250/19

supposicioun *sb.* hypothesis, assumption 54/22

surete, suerte, seurtee *sb.* safety, security, confidence, certainty, bond or pledge, covenant 53/18

suspecte *a., sb.* suspicious, regarded with distrust; *hauen suspecte*, to be suspicious of 334/2

suspicion, suspeccioun *sb.* suspicion, expectation (of some baleful event to come), apprehension 161/24

suspiries *sb. pl.* breaths, respirations 275/25 [L. *suspīrium*]

susteyn(e), sustiene-, sustene- *v.* to foster, keep in life, hold up 217/16

suster *sb.* sister 1188/5

sustinaunce *sb.* upholding, support 269/14

sute *sb.* pursuit 1166/5

suþ-, see **seþe**; **sutours**, see **suytours**; **suweþ**, see **see**

swage *v.* to assuage 116/3

swaliþ, see **ysweled**; **swalwe**, see **swolowe**

swathed *v. pa. p.* wrapped up, bandaged 260/16

ysweled *v. pa. p.* (**swaliþ** *pres. 3sg.* perhaps better **sweliþ**) singed, turned dark 593/34 [OE. *swǣlan*]

swelle *v.* (**swolle** *pa. p.*), **swellinge, swillinge** *sb.* to swell, distend, form a tumour or morbid growth 125/14 (*v.*), 207/1 (*sb.*)

swelwe-, see **swolowe**

swengede *v. pa.* flung, dashed 784/23 [OE. *swengan*]

swepe *v.* (**yswope** *pa. p.*), **swepynge** *sb.* to sweep away 1054/28 (*v.*), 1054/26 (*sb.*)

swete *v.*, **swetinge** *sb.* to sweat 150/3 (*v.*), 364/18 (*sb.*)

sweþ, see **sewe**

sweuen *sb.* dream, sleeping vision 157/16 [OE. *swefn*]

sweuenynge *sb.* dream 336/19

swiche, suche, soche, seche, siche *a., pron.* such 45/7

swillinge, see **swelle**

swiper(e) *a.* nimble, quick 631/22 [OE. (*ge*)*swipor*]

swithe *adv.* strongly, greatly, excessively, very, rapidly 135/31 [OE. *swīðe*]

swolle, see **swelle**

swol(o)we, swalwe *sb.* whirlpool, eddy 663/10

swolowe, swolewe, swelwe- *v.* to swallow 209/28

swoneþ, swonynge, see **swowneþ**

swo(o)te *sb.* sweat, sweating (esp. as a means of excreting or purging the body of excess fluids) 151/4

yswope, see **swepe**

swo(w)neþ *v. pres. 3sg.*, **swo(w)nynge, swowenynge** *sb.* faints 106/1 (*v.*), 348/19 (*sb.*)

taber, see **tabour**

table *sb.* table, tablet (incl. tablets given to Moses at Sinai; *þe firste* and *secounde table*, those commandments pertaining to God and those pertaining to neighbour, respectively, each visualized as occupying one of the tablets) 102/23

tabour, taber *sb.* drum 113/22

tacchis *sb. pl.* moral blemishes, bad habits or vices, habits, traits, or characteristics 301/10 [OF. *tache*]

tadde *sb.* toad 768/24

tad(de)stoles *sb. pl.* mushrooms, toadstools 841/28

take *v.* (**itake** *pa. p.*) take, perceive, construe, commit 41/24

tale *sb.* narrative, account, enumeration or sum 297/1

talent *sb.* an ancient weight, the monetary sum associated with that weight of silver, desire, appetite 312/34

taliages *sb. pl.* forced taxes or levies 319/28 [OF. *taillage*]

talouȝ *sb.* fat, suet 285/10

ytamed, see **temede**

tapet *sb.* a piece of cloth used as a carpet or cover, carpet, cover or cushion 281/34 [OE. *tæppet*, from L. *tapētum*]

tarie *v.* to delay, impede, hinder, slow 220/33

tartar *sb.* tartar, produced by fermentation of grape juice 878/26

teamed, see **temede**

teere *a.* best in quality 1054/19 [Middle Dutch *teer*]

yteyed(e) *v. pa. p.* bound 949/26

teynde *v.* to enclose, hedge, or fence in 1049/27 [OE. *tȳnan*]

teynteth *v. pres. 3sg.* dyes, colours 1037/9

telle *v.* (**tolde** *pa., pa. p.*) to account, list, narrate, count, esteem or value 45/25

temede, teamed, tamed *v. pa.* made tame 731/18

temperad, see **temperat**

temperament *sb.* mixture or combination, esp. a due or moderate mixture; spec. the proportions of the four qualities or the four humours within the body 104/20

temperat, temperad *v. pa. p., a.* moderate 88/15

temperatines *sb.* moderateness, moderation 453/18

temperatliche *adv.* moderately 118/35–6

temperure *sb.* moderate condition, good condition (of weather or of a humour) 156/26

temporat *v. pres. pl.* moderate 519/24

tempre *v.* to moderate (esp. by mixture), tune 106/7

tenclinge, see **tinglen**

tende, tiende *v.*[1], **tendinge** *sb.* to light, excite 70/15 (*v.*), 135/5 (*sb.*) [OE. *-tendan* and *tending sb.*]

tende *v.*[2] to stretch 984/31 [L. *tendere*]

tendreþ *v. pres. 3sg.* softens 1105/26

teno(u)r *sb.* continuation, duration, course, movement, pitch (of a voice) 291/10

tercian *a., sb.* (of a fever) characterized by recurring accesses every second day, such a recurrent fever 386/14

terme *sb.* boundary, end, space of time, condition, expression 53/1

termyneþ *v. pres. 3sg.* bounds, defines 1270/2

ternaries *sb. pl.* groups of three 81/26

tesike, see **tisik**

tetrarcha *sb.* the ruler of one of the four divisions of a province, esp. one of the four rulers of Roman Syria 815/26

tetres, teteres *sb. pl.* a skin disease characterized by pustules 831/3 [OE. *teter*]

tewly *a.* a deep red colour 867/5 [obscure; perhaps from the place-name *Tolouse*]

þacch *sb.* straw 1054/11

þaccheþ, thakken *v. pres. pl.* thatch 928/25

þagh, see **þo3**; **þaym, þayre,** see **þey**; **thakken,** see **þaccheþ**; **þankynge,** see **þonkede**

þan(ne) *adv.* then; *þan and þan*, occasionally 40/8

þare, see **þer**; **þaugh,** see **þo3**; **þedir,** see **þidir**; **þe(e)fliche,** see **þeuelich**

þey *pron.* (**þayre, here** *poss.*; **þe(y)m, þa(y)m, hem, ham** *obj.*) they 46/14

þei3, þey, þey3e, þei *conj.* though, even though, even if 41/18

themelis *sb. pl.* thimbles 1028/22

þenke, see **þinke**; **þen(ne),** see **þinne**

þennes *adv.* from that place 460/13

þennesse *sb.* lack of density, fluidity or rarity, sparseness 566/17

þeofliche, see **þeueliche**

þer, þere, þare *adv., conj.* there, where 42/1

†þeraforn *adv.* before in order, in front 462/13

þera3en *adv.* against that 102/28

þereouer *adv.* over that, commanding that 815/23

þeretil *adv.* thereto, to that 831/5

þeretofore *adv.* before that, first in position 465/26

þerf *a.* unleavened, esp. *þerf bred*, the matzoh of the Exodus 546/7 [OE. *ðeorf*]

þerle, see **þurle**

þernyhe *adv.* near that thing 1062/29

þes, see **þis**

þeuelich, þe(e)fliche, þeofliche, þiefliche *adv.* in the manner of a thief 312/22

theuysche *a.* furtive, thief-like 1207/33

þewe *sb.* servant, bondman 305/17 [OE. *ðēow*]

þewe, see **dewe**

þewis *sb. pl.* customs, manners, virtues 316/24

þicke, þilke *a., sb.* thick, dense, (of time) coming frequently, (of the voice) husky; *sb.* the thick or dense part, sediment in a liquid (*þe þicke of vrine*) 125/23

þicke, see **þilke**

þickeþ *v. pres. 3sg.*, **þikinge** *sb.* thickens 133/14 (*v.*), 443/26 (*sb.*)

þiderward *adv.* over there, towards that place 826/26

þidir, þedir *adv.* to or towards (that place) 201/12

þiefliche, see þeuelich

þyȝe, þiȝh, þihe, þigh, þye *sb.* thigh 64/27

þilke, þicke, þulke *a.*, *demon. pron.* this, that, these, those, the same 87/9

þilke, see þicke

þing *sb. sg.* and *pl.* (also þinges) thing(s), creature(s), motive, cause, matter 40/22

þinke, þenke *v.* to think 467/2

þinne, þen(ne) *a.* thin, (of time) occurring at infrequent intervals 125/23

þynneþ *v. pres. 3sg.*, þynnynge *sb.* makes thin or slender 1065/29 (*v.*), 1284/23 (*sb.*)

þirle, see þurle; þirst-, see þriste

þis, this, þise, þes *demon. a.* (þise, þis, þuse *pl.*) this, these 40/23

thisane, pthisane *sb.* barley-water 1009/22

thisik, see tisik

þo *adv.* then 115/21 [OE. *ðā*]

þo, þoo *demon. a., pron. pl.* those 262/4

þoȝ, þogh, þagh, þaugh, þouȝ *adv. conj.* though 115/14

þonkede *v. pa.*, þonkynge, þankynge *sb.* thanked, praised 546/24 (*v.*), 1369/19 (*sb.*)

þorghoute *prep.* completely through 686/19

þorle-, see þurle

thowþistil *sb.* sow-thistle, a herb used in medicinal preparations 432/27 [OE. *ðū-ðistel*]

þraissh-, see þreisshe

thral, þralle *sb.*, *a.* thrall; *a.* servile, performing only with expectation of profit 76/25

þraldom, þraldame *sb.* servitude 59/31

þrastinge *sb.* pressing, squeezing 394/5 [OE. *ðrǣstan*]

þre, see þri

þreisshe *v.* (yþressche *pa. p.*), threisshynge, þrossching, þraisshynge *sb.* to thresh grain 532/29 (*v.*), 1059/28 (*sb.*)

þrell-, see þurle; þressch-, see þreisshe; þrest-, see þriste; þrewe, see þrowe

þri, þre, thre *num.* three 44/18

þridde *num.* third 42/11

þries *adv.* three times, on three occasions 125/27

þrift *sb.* growth, the growing portion 168/27

þriftiliche *adv.* properly, in a seemly manner 80/11

þrill-, see þurle

þringeþ *v. pres. pl.* press, oppress 229/25 [OE. *ðringan*, strong 3]

þriste, þruste, þreste-, þirste-, þurste- *v.* (yþriste, ydrust, yþrested *pa. p.*), þurstinge, þrustinge, þruschinge, þristynge, þrestyng *sb.* to thrust, press, compress, pierce 134/17 (*v.*), 134/18 (*sb.*)

þritteþ *num.* thirtieth 709/23

þritty *num.* thirty 460/27

þrossching, see þreisshe

þrowe, drowe-, trowe- *v.* (þrewe *pa.*, iþrowe *pa. p.*), to throw, cast, vomit 71/22

þrowynge, see trowe

þrowis *sb. pl.* spasms or pangs (esp. of childbirth), pains 298/20

þruschinge, þruste-, see þriste

þrusteþ *v. pres. 3sg.* thirsts 406/12

þulke, see þilke

þurgh, þuroȝ *prep.* through 52/23

þurle, þirle, þerle, þorle-, þrelle-, þrille- *v.*, þurlinge *sb.* to pierce, bore 104/1 (*v.*), 106/5 (*sb.*) [OE. *ðyrlian*]

þuroȝ, see þurgh; þurst(-), see þriste, ferst

þurstel (þurstlis *pl.*) *sb.* thrush 599/30

þurstlewe *a.* thirsty 1185/18

þuse, see þis

þwart, twhart, twart, thuart *adv.* crosswise, across; þwartouer, across 181/28

iþwite, thwiten *v. pa. p.*, thwytynge *sb.* cut, shorn, parted 274/5 (*v.*), 1376/18 (*sb.*) [OE. *ðwītan*, strong 1]

tiellen, see tyles; tiende, see tende

tygris *sb.* (tygris, tygres *pl.*) tiger 656/17

tikelynge *sb.* tingle, irritation 191/7

tyles, tiellen *sb. pl.* tiles 702/9

tiliere *sb.* husbandman, farmer 813/2

tille *sb.* lentil 986/4

tylle *v.* (frequent forms with -i-), til(i)ynge, tyllynge *sb.* to cultivate, plough (land) 310/17 (*v.*), 531/8 (*sb.*)

tilleþ *v. pres. 3sg.* reaches 767/7 [OE. -*tillan*]

tillynge *sb.* attracting 1148/15 [from OE. *-tyllan*]

tilþe *sb.* husbandry 720/3 [OE. *tilð(e)*]

tymbir, tymbre *sb.* a musical instrument, a drum or some similar stretched skin 113/22 [OF. *timbre*]

tyme *sb.* thyme 1062/33

tymeliche *adv.* early, quickly 903/16–17

tynde *sb.* tine of a deer 1176/33

tinglen *v. pres. pl.*, **tyng(e)lynge, tynkelinge, tenclinge** *sb.* have ringing in the ears, ring, (thus, of any bodily part) sting, tingle, vibrate 432/20 (*v.*), 191/11 (*sb.*)

tynkynge *sb.* sinking 1148/15 [echoic]

ytynned *v. pa. p.* coated with tin 844/36

tippynge *sb.* a piece which forms a tip (here, horn used for the nock of an arrow) 1149/32

tirandise *sb.* tyranny 62/12

tirandliche *adv.* tyrannically 78/13

†**tyrannres** *sb. pl.* lawlessness, violence, outrages 821/12

tiriacle, see **triacle**

tisik, tesike, thisik, tphisike *sb., a.* a disease of the lung, tuberculosis; *a.* (one) suffering from this disease 106/6

ytiþed *v. pa. p.* paid as a tithe 1065/5

tythinge *sb.* tithes 544/22

titles *sb. pl.* chapter headings, parts of a book 43/6

tixte, text(e) *sb.* text, the specific language of a passage (as opposed to its gloss or explanation), a specific passage (within Holy Scripture) 318/4

to, too *sb.* (**toon, tone** *pl.*) toe 269/8

to, see **tweye**

tobrekeþ *v. pres. 3sg.* (**tobrake** *pa.,* **tobroke** *pa. p.*) shatters, destroys, fractures 591/11

toche *sb.* feeling, the sense of touch, point of contact 186/1

tocleueþ *v. pres. 3sg.* splits apart 593/33

†**toconiuncte** *v. pa. p., a.* joined together 499/18

todeleþ *v. pres. 3sg.,* †**todelinge** *sb.* divides, separates (into constituent elements), destroys 130/34 (*v.*), 194/26 (*sb.*)

†**todestroied** *v. pa. p.* completely destroyed 402/6

todrawiþ *v. pres. pl.* pull apart 171/27

tofalle *v.* to fall apart, collapse, be destroyed 87/7

tofore, toforne *prep., adv.* before, earlier 56/33

toforehonde, tofehonde *adv.* beforehand 126/31

togedre(s), togidre(s), tokedres, degedres *adv.* together, in a mass or company, in unity 44/26

tohaleþ *v. pres. pl.* rend, pull apart, distend 171/27

toisshes, see **tossches; tokedres,** see **togedres**

tok(e)ne *v.* to show, denote, typify 47/11

tolleþ *v. pres. 3sg.* entices, decoys (animals in a hunt) 856/10 [OE. **tollian*]

ton, see **o**

tonnes *sb. pl.* casks, barrels (esp. for storing wine) 878/27

too, see **to; toole,** see **towle**

torpartid *v. pa. p.* divided, separated 324/35

topwise *adv.* in the shape of a top, as a pyramid, describing a conical solid 185/14

tordes *sb. pl.* turds 761/26

torendeþ, torenteþ *v. pres. 3sg.* (**torent(e)** *pa. p.*) tears to or in pieces 656/5

torenes *sb. pl.* torrents 778/23

torment, see **turnement**

torpid *a.* lazy, dull 327/6

toschede *v.* (**toschad, tosched** *pa. p.*) to diffuse, disperse 111/25

toschift, toschuft *v. pa. p.* separated, scattered 41/8

tosmyteth *v. pres. 3sg.* repels, causes to abate 1023/33

tossches, toisshes, tuskes *sb. pl.* (**tusk** *sg.* once) tusks, overgrown teeth 271/1

tosteþ *v. pres. 3sg.* heats, parches, browns (with or over a flame) 754/3

toswelleþ *v. pres. 3sg.* (**toswolle** *pa. p.*) swells 305/36

ytoþed *v. pa. p., a.* having projections like teeth, indented, jagged 680/9

touchith *v. pres. 3sg.* touches or feels, handles, treats or mentions (in writing), concerns or pertains 64/33

towailes *sb. pl.* towels 329/26

towarde *adv.,* **to . . . -warde** (with interposed *sb.* or *pron.*) *prep.* toward 73/9

towghe(y), tow3, towh *a.* cohesive, sticking closely together, not easily separated 827/8

towht *a.* taut 591/14

towle, toole *sb.* tool, weapon 65/10

townes *sb. pl.* settlements 468/17

townesse *sb.* viscousness, adhesive qualities 671/3

tphisike, see **tisik**

trace, traace, trase *sb.* path, footprint, track 741/32

tracte *sb.* an anthem consisting of scriptural verses, sung as part of the mass from Septuagesima Sunday until Easter 544/34

trad, see **trede**

ytrayled *v. pa. p.*, **traylynge** *sb.* (of vines) supported with stakes 938/32 (*v.*), 917/2 (*sb.*)

traytourlyche *adv.* treacherously 730/24

trampeþ *v. pres. 3sg.* stamps 1189/9

translatede *v. pa.* removed, translated (from one place to another) 801/25

transubstanciacioun *sb.* the act of changing into another form or being 548/15

transumpt *v. pa. p., a.* transferred, used in a figurative sense (of epithets for deity and angels) 54/25

transumptiue *a.* (*sb.*) figurative (expression), metaphorical, metaphor 54/29

trase, see **trace**

ytrased *v. pa. p.* drawn 1296/25

trauaile, traueile *sb.* labour, hardship, suffering 44/10

trauaile *v.*, **trauaylynge** *sb.* to torment, vex, labour, exert (oneself), work up (to a state) 72/11 (*v.*), 852/18 (*sb.*)

traueilous, trauaylous *a.* toilsome, painful 210/25

tre *sb.* tree, piece of wood, beam 109/10

treble *a.* threefold, triple 246/2

ytrebled *v. pa. p.* provided with three, made three times as many 1126/7

trede *v.* (**trad** *pa.*, **ytrodde** *pa. p.*), **tredynge** *sb.* to step on, walk, (of birds) copulate 598/8 (*v.*), 598/5 (*sb.*)

treen *a.* wooden 1006/6

treetis, see **tretys**

tremblith *v. pres. pl.*, **trembelyng, tremelynge** *sb.* tremble 80/20 (*v.*), 941/7 (*sb.*)

trendiþ *v. pres. 3sg.*, **trendynge** *sb.*

revolves 516/24 (*v.*), 516/9 (*sb.*) [OE. *trendan*]

tresorie, tresour *sb.* treasury, treasure-chest 98/33

trespas *sb.* sin, the Fall 75/10

trespas(s) *v. pres. subj.* sin 82/34

tretys, treetis *sb.* a written account, negotiation, discussion 100/5

treuthe *sb.* troth, fidelity 308/2

trewis, trewes *sb.* truce, armistice 320/5

treworme *sb.* some variety of wood-gnawing worm, a moth 920/32

triacle, tiriacle *sb.* a medicament, a salve or potion composed of many ingredients 419/14

tribunes *sb. pl.* heads of tribes (of Israel), officers 318/18

try(h)umphis *sb. pl.* Roman festival entries of victorious commanders, conquests or victories 820/22

triplicite *sb.* a grouping of three signs of the Zodiac (each separated from the others by 120°) 461/26

trist *sb.* trust 200/21

tristy, trusty *a.* deserving of trust 315/5

tristily *adv.* with confidence, assuredly, boldly 365/28

triumphes, see **tryhumphis; trobly,** see **troubly; ytrodde,** see **trede**

trolles *sb. pl.* trowels 65/9

trompe, trumpe *sb.* trumpet 65/26

trompinge, trumpinge, trompeng *sb.* the blowing of a trumpet 542/3

trompour *sb.* trumpeter 1389/17

trones *sb. pl.* thrones, Thrones (the third of the nine orders of angels) 68/13

tronglynge *sb.* ringing in the ears 573/9 [obscure, perhaps echoic]

troubly, trobly, trouble, trubily *a.* turbid, stormy 159/31

troublynge *sb.* agitation 581/26

trowe *v.* (**ytrowe, ytrowed** *pa. p.*), **trowynge, þrowynge** *sb.* to believe, think 41/24 (*v.*), 941/2 (*sb.*)

trowis *sb. pl.* conduits 1018/8

trowiþ, see **þrowe; trubily,** see **troubly**

trugged *v. pa. p.* deceived 1122/5 [cf. OE. *trucian*]

trumpe(-), see **trompe(-); trust-,** see **trist-**

tunycles *sb. pl.* membranes enclosing an organ, esp. the 'tunics' of the eye 179/27

tuo, see **tweye**

turbacioun *sb.* agitation, perturbation, disturbance 471/16

turkeys *sb.* Asian turquoise 878/14

turnement, turment, torment *sb.* pain, a catapult or similar instrument to propel missiles by torsion 314/5

turtil, turtur *sb.* turtle-dove 212/16

turtuse *sb.* tortoise, turtle 1131/32

twart, see **þwart**

tweye, tweyne, to, tuo, two *num.* two 46/21

twentiþe *num.* twentieth 217/5

twhart, see **þwart**

twies *adv.* twice, two times 125/27

twynyng *sb.* twisting (strands) together to make a heavier filament 1042/21

twynne *v.* to separate, be distant 459/9

twiseled *v. pa. p.* forked, split, separated (into branches) 219/13 [from OE. *twisla*]

twist *sb.* junction, fork, place where a body divides or branches, the groin (the main juncture of the body) 200/3

twistid *v. pa. p.* divided, branched 209/3

vddery *a.* soft, spongy 233/33

i-uyneþ *v. pres. 3sg.* (**i-uned** *pa. p.*) unites, joins 844/34

vnacordinge *a.* not in accord 532/20

vnavisid *a.* rash 313/17

vnbinde *v.* (**vnbounde** *pa. p.*), **vnbyndynge** *sb.* to untie, set free or release (from) 437/23 (*v.*), 440/8 (*sb.*)

vnbuxom *a.* disobedient 305/34

vnccioun *sb.* rubbing (as with oil), an unguent or ointment 929/19

vnce, vunce- *sb.* any of a variety of measures representing $\frac{1}{12}$ of some larger unit: an ounce ($\frac{1}{12}$ pound), a measure of length ($\frac{1}{12}$ yard, three inches), a measure of time ($\frac{1}{12}$ 'moment', $7\frac{1}{2}$ seconds) 529/22

vnchancheabil *a.* immutable 79/18

vnches *sb. pl.* inches 1380/31

vnclene *a.* impure, not chaste, unfit to eat (with reference to Jewish law) 64/9

vnclennes, vnklennes *sb.* lack of purity, filthiness 70/2

vnclose *v. pres. subj.* become open 981/22

vncomplete *a.* imperfect 1102/31

vncouenable *a.* unsuitable, useless, or harmful 104/23

vncruddeþ *v. pres. 3sg.* loses its curds, stops coagulating 1329/15

vnctuosite *sb.* greasiness 284/24

vnctuous *a.* greasy, fat, slimy 275/8

vncurable *a.* without remedy 518/6

vndefied *v. pa. p.* undigested 128/22

vnderne *sb.* midday 487/22 [OE. *undern*]

vnder(ne)tide *sb.* afternoon 487/22

vndersette *v.*, **vndirsettyngis** *sb. pl.* to support, prop up, strengthen 1057/24 (*v.*), 269/24 (*sb.*)

vnderwrotynge *sb.* breaking up or digging (soil) 1250/17–18

vndewe, vnþewe *a.* improper, unsuitable 85/18

vndigeste *a.* undigested 888/28

vndircrepynge *sb.* penetrating or undermining 664/9–10

vndirfonge *v.* to receive 665/19

vndirholynge *sb.* undermining, undercutting 664/9

†**vndirmeletyme** *sb.* afternoon 428/27 [OE. *undernmǽl* + *tīma*]

vndirstonde *v.* (**vndirstonde** *pa. p.*) to understand; *pa. p., a.* imaginary 41/22

vndistinct *a.* indistinct 212/17

vndo *v. pa. p.* destroyed, ruined, unaccomplished 87/7

i-uned, see **i-uyneþ**

vneuen(e) *a.* unequal, not corresponding, not level or smooth 139/5–6

vneue(n)nes *sb.* difference, distinction, lack of smoothness 139/7

vnfastenesse *sb.* lack of firmness or stability 1047/14

vnfelingnes *sb.* numbness 359/9

†**vnhauynge** *sb.* absence, lack 1332/35

vnhele, vnhile- *v.,* **vnhelinge, vnhilinge** *sb.* to uncover 124/10 (*v.*), 221/26 (*sb.*)

vnhiȝtiþ *v. pres. 3sg.* (**vnhiȝted, vnhiȝt** *pa. p.*) deprives of beauty 362/11

vnhiȝtnesse *sb.* lack of beauty 345/24

vnhile-, see **vnhele**

vnhonest *a.* ugly, uncomely, lewd 261/7

vnhoneste *sb.* lack of virtue, unseemly behaviour 941/29

vnhourne *a.* unpleasant to look at 193/32 [OE. *unórne*]

vnicorne *sb.* rhinoceros 700/24

vniones *sb. pl.* pearls of great size 769/32 [L. *ūnio*]

vnkinde, vnkende *a.* unnatural, lacking in natural virtue, degenerate 144/35

vnkyndeliche *a.* unnatural; *vnkyndeliche*

þinges, non-organic forms of behaviour affecting the health of organisms 144/29

vnknowe *v. pa. p.* unknown 93/17

vnkonnynge *a.* ignorant, unlearned 192/26

vnkonnynge *sb.* ignorance, heedlessness 67/18

vnladeþ *v. pres. 3sg.* unloads 1173/18

vnleeful *a.* impermissible, illicit 620/18

vnliche *a.* dissimilar 69/4

vnlikynge *sb., a.* displeasure, dissatisfaction; *a.* unpleasant, not agreeable 240/8

vnliknes *sb.* dissimilarity 76/35

vnmanliche *a.* dishonourable, degrading, discourteous 768/29

vnmesurable *a.* immoderate, inordinate 247/13

vnmesured *v. pa. p., a.* immense, utterly powerful 558/22

vnmeuable *a.* immovable, immobile 448/28

vnmight *sb.* weakness 888/25

vnneþe, vneþes, vnnes *adv.* scarcely, with difficulty 47/1 [OE. *unēaðe* + adverbial genitive *-es*]

vnobedient *a.* not obedient 125/4

vnordinat *a.* excessive 213/12

vnparfite *a.* imperfect 459/18

vnpeisible *a.* turbulent, restless 674/26

vnperceptible *a.* imperceptible 518/22

vnproporcionatnes *sb.* lack of proportion (to), immoderate size (with respect to) 363/33

vnredy *a.* rash 672/13

vnredily *adv.* unadvisedly, without caution 947/6

vnriȝt *sb.* wrongdoing, injustice 768/32

vnsad *a.* unstable, not firm, soft 298/25

vnsadnesse *sb.* lack of solidity or firmness 1047/14

vnsauer(y)nesse *sb.* insipidness, tastelessness 372/34

vnsauoury *a.* tasteless, insipid 156/5

vnschaplyche *a.* without shape 296/18

vnseye *v. pa. p., a.* unseen, invisible, incorporeal 41/19

vnsemelickenesse *sb.* lack of fairness or beauty 692/29

vnseneliche *adv.* invisibly 508/33

vnshapnesse *sb.* lack of shape or form 665/17–18

vnsiker *a.* unsafe, uncertain or insecure 724/19

vnskilful *a.* unreasonable, lacking rational power 96/19

vnsmeþenes *sb.* roughness, unevenness (of surface) 139/7–8

vnsmittid *v. pa. p.* unsoiled, undefiled 63/5

vnsode *v. pa. p.* uncooked, undigested 1330/11

vnstabilliche *a.* unstable 468/7

vnstedfast *a.* unstable, not firm, changeable 79/23

vnsuffisaunt *a.* insufficient 885/26

vntemperate *a.* intemperate 1308/28

vnþewe, see **vndewe**

vntilied(e) *v. pa. p.* uncultivated 719/22

vntyme *sb.* unseasonableness, the wrong or unsuitable time 963/22

†**vnvsynge** *a.* unaccustomed 755/31

vnware, vnwarr *a.* incautious, ignorant, foolish 192/15

vnwareliche *adv.* incautiously, unexpectedly, in ignorance 600/14

vnweeued *v. pa. p., a.* exposed, disclosed, open or transparent 70/32 [OE. *un-* + *wefan*]

vnwemmed *a.* unblemished 57/17 [OE. *unwemmed*]

vnwetinge, vnwitynge *pres. p., a., adv.* unconscious(ly), unaware 410/9

vnwilful *a.* involuntary 362/23

vnwreyen (vnwrie-, vnwrye-) *v. pres. pl.* reveal, tell 301/22 [OE. *unwrēon*]

vpholderes *sb. pl.* supports 269/24

vplondisch *a.* rustic 433/14

vppermore *adv.* higher, further up 67/10

vppon, open, opun, apon *a.* open, manifest 170/33

vpriȝt *a.* in a vertical position, erect, supine, prone 172/18

vreyn(e), vryne *sb.* urine 157/14

vrnnyng *sb.* running, going 339/9

vsage *sb.* habit, custom 176/29

vse *v. pres. pl.* (**vsed, vse** *pa. p.*) follow or pursue (as a habit), practise, put into operation, employ, be accustomed (to) 64/17

vtmest, vttemest, ottemest *a.* farthest out, outermost, last 100/26

vttir, otter, ooter *a.* (**vttrest, vttirmest, ottermest** *super.*) outer, exterior,

vttir, otter, ooter (*cont.*) external 65/6 [OE. *ûtera comp.*, formed on *ût* adv.]

vtward *adv.* outward, toward the edges 142/11 [OE. *ûtanweard*]

Initial **v-** in some words occurs in free variation with **f-** and **w-**. Thus a number of words may be referred to other entries: **varre** 1085/14, see **fer**; **vedeþ** 174/32 and **vedynge** 631/18, see **fede**; **veer** 84/30, see **fore**; **veirnes** 1030/26 is a form of 'fairness'; **yueled** 106/10, see **eueleþ** (for **ifilleþ**); **uelles** 344/9, see **fel**; **ven** 863/4, see **fen**; **vongeþ** 901/28, **venge** 99/7, **venged** 709/28, see **fonge**; **(in) vere** 500/34, see **ifere**; **vernes** 568/6, see **fernesse**; **uest** 222/13 is a form of 'fist'; **vyf** 963/34 is a form of 'five'; **uyle** 137/10, see **fyle**; **vingre** 416/31 is a form of 'finger'; **vluynge** 109/3, see **flee** ('fly'); **volle** 51/36 is a form of 'full'; **voloweþ** 116/31, see **folewe**; **uome** 1025/2 and **vomy** 209/15 are forms of 'foam(y)'; **vondeþ** 367/4, see **fonde**; **voode** 651/31 is a form of 'food'; **vo(o)re** 116/31, see **fore**; **vu(y)re** 560/18, see **fire**. Forms having **v-** for etymological **w-**: **veyes** 238/24, see **wey**; **verst** 1084/5 is a form of 'worst'; **vise** 343/15 is a form of 'wise' ('manner'); **vlach(-)** 349/7, see **wlach(-)**; **vrestis** 413/36, see **wrest**

vayne *a., sb.* useless, worthless; *in vayne*, uselessly 1113/26

valewe *sb.* standard (for monetary exchange) 315/13

van(y)schiþ *v. pres. 3sg.* disappears, dissipates, escapes 106/6

vanite, venite *sb.* play, pursuits or conduct without value 77/7

vanne *sb.* winnowing basket 1380/6 [OE. *fann*, from L. *vannus*]

vanne *v.* to winnow 1380/6

vanschiþ, see **vanyschiþ**

vaporacioun *sb.* vaporizing 670/1

vaporatyf *a.* capable of being converted into a vapour 827/20

vapores *a.* like a vapour 827/24

vapourable *a.* capable of being turned into a vapour 577/34

varieþ *v. pres. pl.* undergo change of condition, cause to change, induce change in 127/22

vecchis, fechches *sb. pl.* the bean-like fruit of the vetch 971/29

veer, see **ver**

uegatatiue *a.* (of a 'level' of the soul) having the function or power to stimulate growth 102/30

veileþ *v. pres. pl.*, **veilinge, weilinge** *sb.* hide 41/14 (*v.*), 41/15 (*sb.*)

veyne *sb.* vein, artery, similar channel for transportation of fluids or powers about the body, a lode of ore 98/6

venial *a.* (of sin) capable of remission, pardonable, not grave 63/5

venym(e) *sb.* venom 152/5

ivenymede *v. pa. p.* poisoned 429/25–6

venym(o)us, fenymous *a.* poisonous, secreting venom, malignant 86/35

venisoun *sb.* flesh of an animal hunted, any beast of the chase (esp. deer) 745/24

venite, see **vanite**

vented *v. pa. p.*, **ventynge** *sb.* (**fentyngez** *pl.* once) provided with an outlet for vapour (of casks in which fermentation goes on), discharged 1083/10 (*v.*), 275/25 (*sb.*)

vent(u)osite *sb.* wind, esp. a pathological state of gaseousness within an organ (incl. pressure within the ear), flatulence or gas 115/1 [OF. *ventosité*]

ventuouse *a.* windy, producing flatulence or vapour 1081/2–3 [L. *ventuosus*]

ver, veer *sb.* the fir tree 904/24

verdegres *sb.* copper acetate, a green rust produced by pouring vinegar on copper (used as a medicament) 1295/31

verified *v. pa. p.* confirmed 72/28–9

verlich, see **verreyliche**

vermyloun *sb.* mercury sulphide, used as a pigment because of its scarlet colour 674/9

verrey, verray, ferrey *a.* real, true, proper 44/15

verreyliche, verlich *adv.* truly, properly 69/36

vertual *a.* effective, capable of performing in accord with inherent powers 1276/31

vertualliche *adv.* in essence, in effect (but not in specific forms) 442/24

vertu(e), vertwe *sb.* power or strength

(incl. planetary influence), a power or faculty necessary for biological function (cf. modifying nouns and adjectives), moral conduct, a specific moral quality, valour; *by vertu of*, by the power of, as a result of, because of 42/12

vertuesnes *sb.* power or virtue inherent in an object 452/31

viages *sb. pl.* voyages, journeys 1237/5

vials, see **viole**

vice *sb.* immorality or immoral habits, fault, defect 65/2

vicious *a.* harmful, at variance with a commendable norm 341/6

vile, fuyle *a.* base or low, depraved or degraded, repulsive, unpleasant, destructive in its baseness (of animals and plants) 311/29

vyllich *a.* repulsive in appearance 563/19

vylonye, vylenye *sb.* indignity, degradation 560/1

vynour(e)s *sb. pl.* vine-growers or -tenders 1070/32

viole *sb.* (**vials** *pl.* once) vial, small container for liquids 879/32

violence *sb.* physical force, ardour, fervour 71/15

visage *sb.* the face 91/1

visible *a.* capable of seeing, causing vision 111/20

yvisyted *v. pa. p.* come (to a place) to determine its condition 1073/31

vitailles *sb. pl.* food, provisions 653/3

voydaunce, voydauns *sb.* excretion, evacuation, emptying out 259/25

voide *a.* empty, vacant, unfilled 125/12

voide *v.* to empty, evacuate, clean out, leave (a place), avoid, abstain from 53/17

voydenes *sb.* emptiness 106/9

volatile *sb.* (once as *pl.*) bird, fowl, flying creature (incl. insects) 192/10

volupte *sb.* delight, pleasure, lust 245/24

yvouted *v. pa. p.* vaulted 1146/24

vowtes *sb. pl.* vaults 759/11

vu-, see **v-**

vultur(e), vultour, fultur *sb.* the vulture 116/33

†**wachel, whachelle** *a.* alert, vigilant 834/20 [OE. *wacol*]

wagge *v.*, **wagginge** *sb.* to shake, sway, rock 205/10 (*v.*), 198/18 (*sb.*)

ywaie, see **weye**

wayne *sb.* wagon, cart; *Charlemeynes wayne*, the constellation *Ursa Major* 502/31

waissche *v.* (**wasce-** *pres.* once; **wissche, wesche** *pa.* once each; **wa(i)ssche** *pa. p.*), **waisschinge** *sb.* to wash, cleanse, bathe 134/32 (*v.*), 361/17 (*sb.*)

waistynge, see **waste**

wait *sb.* watch, watchman, scout; *setten a wait*, to prepare an ambush, to lurk in order to attack 178/13

wayte *v.*, **waitinge** *sb.* to watch in ambush, spy upon, prepare to attack, keep watch, guard 162/24 (*v.*), 511/8 (*sb.*)

wake *v.* to stay up at night, keep watch or guard (at night), awake, arouse, provoke or stimulate 87/16

wakemen *sb. pl.* watchmen, guards 67/16

wakere *sb.* watchman 626/25

walkers *sb. pl.* fullers 874/29

walmeþ, see **welmeþ**; **walowiþ,** see **walwe, welwiþ**

walwe, walowe- *v.*, **wal(o)wynge** *sb.* to roll about, surge, heave 656/3 (*v.*), 662/24 (*sb.*)

wan, wanne *a.* dark, livid, pallid 227/14

wan, see **whanne**

wanhope *sb.* despair 65/26

wany *v.*, **wanynge, wonynge** *sb.* to decrease 149/22 (*v.*), 175/5 (*sb.*)

iwanied, see **iwenyed**; **wanne,** see **wynne**

wannes, wonnes *sb.* livid colour, pallor 381/12

warde *sb.* guardianship, keeping watch, regard or care 82/13

warde *v.* to care for, protect, restrain 186/25

wardeyne *sb.* guardian, keeper, overseer 67/16

wardropis *sb. pl.* privies 832/26

ware, iware, warre *a.* aware, wary, prudent 99/10

ware *v. imper.* be careful, take heed, guard against 375/21

wark, see **werke**

warly, warliche *adv.* cautiously, prudently 78/6

warme *v. pa. p.* warmed 946/1

warmood, warmot, see **wormoot**

warne, warnye- *v.*, **warnynge** *sb.* to

warne, warnye- (*cont.*)
notify, announce, forbode 80/36 (*v.*),
76/28 (*sb.*)
warne, see **werneþ**
warnesse *sb.* care 1089/14–15
warre, see **ware**
iwarred *a.* knotty, having knots 272/21
[from OE. *wearr*]
wasceþ, wassche, see **waissche**
waste *v.* (**wast** *pa. p.* occ.), **wa(i)stynge**
sb. to lay waste, dissolve or evaporate,
digest; *sb.* waste, empty place 84/9 (*v.*),
72/20 (*sb.*)
wastour *sb.* extravagant spender 472/11
Wateling Strete *sb.* the Milky Way 497/
18–19
waterbowes, watrybowes *sb. pl.* under-
growth, boughs overshadowed by other
growth 903/11
waterhors *sb. pl.* hippopotami 676/27
waterwolues *sb. pl.* pike 1099/27
watircrowis *sb. pl.* quail 249/8
watirwort *sb.* a plant, water starwort or
maidenhair 628/24
watre, watry *v.* to water, become moist
1284/37
watringe, watiringe *sb.* wetting with
water 204/32
ywatte, see **wete**
wawe *sb.* wave 546/22 [OE. *waȝu]
wawynges *sb. pl.* tossings 683/4 [from
OE. *waȝian*]
waxe, see **wexe**
webbe *sb.* cobweb, tissue, membrane,
cataract 92/3
weddinge *sb.* marriage, pledging or
plighting 63/28
wedes *sb. pl.* garments 174/15
wedir *sb.* weather, wind, storm 459/34
weederes *sb. pl.* weed-pullers 931/31
wefte *sb.* a web, something woven 1137/1
[OE. *weft(a)*]
wey *sb.* way, path, movement or going,
pilgrimage, the pilgrimage of earthly
life 46/34
weybrede, weybrode *sb.* the plantain
1023/19 [OE. *weȝ-brāde, -brǣde*]
weye *v.* (**iweye, ywaie** *pa. p.*), **weyynge**
sb. to weigh, weight, oppress, depress
65/14 (*v.*), 193/22 (*sb.*)
weiȝte, weihte, see **wiȝt**
weike *a.* weak 146/4 [ON. *veikr*]
weyle *sb.* happiness, prosperity 53/17

weilinge, see **veileþ**; **weison,** see
woosen; weite, see **wiȝt**
wel, wele *a., adv.* well, quite, very, much,
plenty, fully, completely 108/19
weldes *v. pres. 3sg.*, **weldinge** *sb.* rules,
controls 40/22 (*v.*), 149/24 (*sb.*)
weles, see **wheole; welewiþ,** see **welwiþ**
welkene *v.* to wither, wilt, fade 587/7 [cf.
Middle Dutch *welken*]
welle *sb.* spring, source 51/29
wellen *v. pres. pl.* pour out 702/2
welmeþ, walmeþ *v. pres. 3sg.* boils, wells
up 71/21 [from OE. *wælm, wielm sb.*]
welnyh *adv.* very nearly, almost all 113/
29
welowiþ, see **welwiþ**
welþe *sb.* prosperity, well-being 85/18
welwiþ, welewiþ, welowiþ, walowiþ
wolewiþ *v. pres. 3sg.* withers, fades,
wastes away 251/19 [OE. *wealwian*]
wem, wemme *sb.* blemish, injury 51/35
[OE. *wem*]
wemles *a.* immaculate 506/38
iwemmed *v. pa. p.* spotted, stained 492/
26
wen, see **whanne**
wenche *sb.* maid 301/32
wend(e) *v.* (**wyndeþ** *pres. 3sg.* occ.,
ywent *pa. p.*), **wendinge** *sb.* to turn,
pass, turn over, depart, take one's way
106/35 (*v.*), 339/29 (*sb.*)
wene *v.* to think, believe, expect 161/21
iwenyed, iwanied *v. pa. p.* weaned 300/
13
wennys *sb. pl.* lumps, warts, spots 363/2
went, see **go**
wepen *v. pres. pl.* (**wepe** *pa.*) weep 82/24
wepen *sb.* (**wepenene, wepen(e),**
wepoun *pl.*) weapon 65/21
wery *a.* weary; *for wery*, on account of
fatigue 162/6
werieth *v. pres. 3sg.*, **weryng** *sb.* wears,
wears away 695/29 (*v.*), 988/16 (*sb.*)
werischnesse *sb.* a bad taste, lack of taste
386/19
weriss(c)he *a.* tasteless, thin or delicate
156/4 [obscure]
werke, worke, wark *sb.* work, deed, act,
labour 41/6
wermode, wermoot, see **wormoot**
werneþ, warneþ, worneþ *v. pres. 3sg.*
denies, forbids, prevents, hinders 100/
29

werp, see **worp; weryoures,** see **werri-oures**

werre *sb.* war 65/22

werreye, werry, werre- *v.* to make war on, destroy by warfare 65/7

werrioures, werreours, werriowres, weryoures *sb. pl.* warriors 716/3

wertes *sb. pl.* warts 946/23

wesche, see **waissche**

wete *v.* (**wette, iwett, ywatte** *pa. p.*) to wet 131/11

ywethe *v. pa. p.*, **weþyng, wythyng** *sb.* wound, twisted (as a hoop), joined together 1047/23 (*v.*), 1041/31 (*sb.*) [from OE. *wiðð̄e* and *wiðig sb.*]

weþer *sb.* ram, the constellation Aries 458/24

weþewynde *sb.* a climbing plant, such as ivy or bindweed 933/25

wetinge, see **wite**

weue, weuy *v.* (**iweue, ywoue, iwe(e)ued** *pa. p.*), **weuyng** *sb.* to weave, (of a spider) spin a web, wrap or bind, cover, veil 72/34 (*v.*), 1041/31 (*sb.*)

wex(e), waxe *sb.* wax 169/20

wexe, waxe *v.* (**wax** *pa.*; **iwoxe** *pa. p.*), **wexinge** *sb.* to grow, become more potent, turn (into) 64/15 (*v.*), 93/2 (*sb.*)

wh-, occasionally alternates with **h-** and **w-,** as in **who, ho, wo; whachelle,** see **wachel**

whan(ne), wan, wen *adv., conj.* when 48/28

whapping *sb.* thrashing about, striking, pushing 230/1

whare, see **where; whele,** see **wheole**

whelke *sb.* pimple, blemish 201/34

whelpe *sb.* the young of various carnivores 216/19

whelpe *v.*, **whelpynge** *sb.* to whelp 1103/16 (*v.*), 1217/34–5 (*sb.*)

wheole, whiele, whele, wele *sb.* wheel 67/4

where, whar(e) *adv., conj.* where, there 63/21

whestone *sb.* whetstone 838/9

whetemele *sb.* wheat flour 993/1

wheþir, where *conj.* whether 47/1

wheþir *pron.* which (of the two) 326/1

whette *v.* (**ywhette** *pa. p.*), **whettynge** *sb.* to sharpen 838/9 (*v.*), 838/15 (*sb.*)

whiche, woche, whoche, whilke, whice *pron.* which 53/3

whiche, see **hucche**

whidirward *adv.* which way, which direction, towards the place that, towards which 143/3

whiele, see **wheole; whiʒt,** see **white**

while, whiles *conj.* while, during the time that 50/21

whilyes, see **wiles²**

whilispiþ *v. pres. 3sg.* lisps, speaks like a child, speaks falteringly, slowly, or indistinctly 304/20

whirlebones *sb. pl.* the round heads of bones which turn in socket-like joints 220/28–9 [cf. OE. *hweorf-bān*; ON. *hvirfla* substituted for the first element]

whirliwynde, whirlyngewynde *sb.* whirlwind 579/31

white, whiʒt *a.* (**whitter** *comp.* occ.) white, pale, shining, light, bright; *white blood*, menstrual blood 66/25

whitelyme *v.* to cover with plaster, whitewash 839/7

whiteþ *v. pres. 3sg.* makes white 179/24

whitissche *a.* somewhat white, almost white 178/16

whitly *adv.* with a white colour, brightly 482/7

whitliche *a.* pale, light or white in complexion 157/9

wicchis *sb. pl.* wizards 88/19

wyche, see **hucche**

wifinge *sb.* marriage 63/28

wiʒt, weiʒte, weihte, weite *sb.* weight, heaviness 83/7

wyʒt(e) *a.* valiant, strong and courageous, active 763/10 [ON. *vígt, n.* of *vígr*]

wyʒtnes *sb.* bravery, vigour 763/9

wike *sb.* wick 884/16

wildeman *sb.* savage, hairy humanoid living in the wild 1199/24

wyles *sb. pl.¹* deceits, ruses, stratagems 1128/33

wiles, whilyes *sb. pl.²* baskets, basket-like woven fishtraps 1011/24 [OE. *wiliga, wilige*]

wilful *a.* desirous, avid, voluntary 61/21

wilfulliche *adv.* readily, voluntarily, deliberately 85/3

wilfulnesse *sb.* eagerness, inclination 1187/12

wille *sb.* desire, wish 43/4

wynde v. (**winded, ywounde** pa. p.), **windynge, wendynge-** sb. to wind, twist, move circuitously 67/4 (v.), 114/11 (sb.)

wyndronk(en) v. pa. p., a. intoxicated 1082/11-12

wyne-egre sb. vinegar 370/17

wyneȝerdes sb. pl. vineyards 737/26

wynne v. (**wanne** pa., **(y)wonne** pa. p.), **wynnynge** sb. to win, obtain by military victory, acquire 53/13 (v.), 482/26 (sb.)

wirche, wirkinge, see **worche**

wisp sb. a bunch of hay, a twisted wreath, a ring of some twisted material 113/16

wissche, see **waissche**

wissiþ v. pres. 3sg. makes known, shows, gives information about 620/17 [OE. wissian]

wit, see **witt**

wite v. (**woot** pres. 3sg., **not** neg.; **woten, witeþ** pres. pl.), **witinge, wetinge** sb. to know, be aware of 83/18 (v.), 91/6 (sb.)

wiþ, see **witt**

wiþdrawith v. pres. 3sg. retains, draws back, removes, distracts, goes away 60/31 (v.), 45/17 (sb.)

wiþholde v., **wiþholdinge** sb. to retain, keep back, hold, sustain or hold up; vertue of wiþholdinge, one of the Galenic faculties, the power of retention, of holding in and absorbing nutriment 169/24 (v.), 97/12 (sb.)

withy(e) sb. the willow tree, the flexible limbs of the willow, a hoop or bond made of these or similar boughs 348/3

wythyng, see **ywethe**

wiþout(en) prep. outside of, except, without 61/31

withschadewid v. pa. p. darkened 511/20

withseyde v. pa. p., **wiþsigginge** sb. contradicted, denied, resisted; sb. murmuring, grudging 813/28 (v.), 61/20 (sb.)

wiþstonde v. (**withstonde** pa. p.), **wiþstondinge** sb. to withstand 141/26 (v.), 61/19 (sb.)

witneseþ v. pres. 3sg. betokens, furnishes evidence of 213/14

witnesse sb. evidence, token, reference to (a fact or thing) 48/11

witsonwoke sb. the week of Pentecost 520/9-10

wit(t), wiþ sb. intellect, reason, knowledge, sense or faculty of sensory perception (þe fyue wittes, bodiliche wit), mental ability, prudence 41/16

witty a. clever, capable 300/23

wittiliche adv. wisely, cleverly 294/13

wlaissh a. lukewarm 1335/29 [OE. wlacu, wlæc]

wlasshe-hoot, wlache-hoot a. lukewarm 937/33

†**wlatfulnesse** sb. loathing, distaste, nausea 392/19 [OE. wlætta + -ful + -nes]

wlatyng, wlattyng- sb. nausea; wlattynges of þe see, seasickness 913/14 [OE. wlātung]

wlatyngnesse sb. nausea 1006/12

†**wlatisshnesse** sb. nausea 1083/22-3

†**wlatnesse** sb. nausea 303/20

†**wlatsomnesse (-sum-)** sb. nausea 159/21

wlonk a. flourishing, lush 138/11 [OE. wlanc]

wodewoses sb. pl. wildmen, satyrs 737/4 [OE. wuduwāsa]

woys, see **woos**

wole, wil(l) v. pres. 3sg. (**wolt** pres. 2sg., **wolde** pa.) wishes, wants, intends, has the power to, will 40/25

wolewiþ, see **welwiþ**

wolkin sb. the visible celestial sphere, the sky 83/20

wolle sb. wool, fleece 358/5

†**wol(l)ecrafte** sb. the manufacture of cloth from raw wool 750/6

wombe sb. belly, stomach, intestines, uterus, any hollow cavity in the body, the gut (as representing man's carnal desires); wombe ioye, desire for food, gluttony 55/24

wommannisch, wommenische a. woman-like, female 187/28

wondir a. astonishing, monstrous, marvellous 89/23

wondirful, wundirful a. marvellous, causing astonishment, monstrous 162/18

wondirliche adv. marvellously, astonishingly, monstrously 61/3

wondre v. marvel (at), admire 116/36

wone, wonye v. (**iwoned, iwont, iwunt** pa. p.), **wonynge** sb. to dwell, continue (in a state), be accustomed (to perform an action), be used (to) 81/29 (*v.*), 168/31 (*sb.*)

wonynge, see **wany; ywonne,** see **wynne; wonnes,** see **wannes; iwont,** see **wone**

wonte, woonte- *sb.* mole 645/9 [OE. *wánd*]

wood *a.* raging, mad 55/26 [OE. *wōd*]

woodliche *adv.* as if insane, furiously 1078/21

woodnes *sb.* madness 87/21-2

wo(o)ke *sb.* week 414/30

woos, woys *sb.* slime, juice, chyle or partially digested food, sap 244/20 [OE. *wōs*]

wo(o)se, wosy *v.*, **woosinge** *sb.* to ooze, exude, pass out through pores 139/11 (*v.*), 273/10 (*sb.*)

wo(o)sen, woose, woosus, wosons, weison *sb.* (*sg.* and *pl.*) the trachea or windpipe, an artery or vein, any tube or way in the body which bears fluid or air; *wosen lidde, lidde of þe woosun,* the uvula or epiglottis 98/24 [OE. *wāsend*]

worche, werche, wirche, wurche, wurke- *v.* (**wrouȝt** *pa.*; **iwrouȝt, wrowȝt, iworked** *pa. p.*), **worchinge, werchinge, wors(c)hinge, wirchinge, wirking(e), wurchinge** *sb.* to work, perform, create, cause, exercise, twist, soften, make pliable; *pres p., a.* active; *þe vertu of worchinge,* the immutative virtue, which directs the actual physical development of an embryo 55/16 (*v.*), 42/13 (*sb.*)

worchere *sb.* worker, maker 130/14

wor(l)dliche *a.* worldly, mundane, temporal 75/20

worm *sb.* serpent, worm, crawling beast; *hed worm,* louse, nit 106/23

wormeliche *a.* worm-like 191/8

worm-ete *a.* worm-eaten 966/11

wormo(o)t, wormo(o)de, wermode, warmood, warmot *sb.* the absinth plant, the drug derived from its leaves, wormwood 367/22 [OE. *wermōd*]; the **wor-** forms show infl. of OE. *wyrm*]

worneþ, see **werneþ**

worp, werp *sb.* warp 1139/21

worschinge, see **worche**

worshepeliche *adv.* honourably 799/16

worschipe *sb.* honour, renown 44/12

worschipe *v.* invest with honour, adorn 198/9

wortes *sb. pl.* plants or herbs used as food 985/9

worth *a.* valuable, worthy 76/5

worþe *v.* become, come to be, change (into), attain (to) 141/25

worthi *a.* good, honourable 46/24

wose(-), see **woose, woosen**

wosȝy *a.* muddy 655/24

woten, see **wite; ywoue,** see **weue; ywounde,** see **wynde**

wowiþ *v. pres. pl.* court, woo 598/12

iwoxe, see **wexe**

wrak *sb.* shipwreck, wreckage 784/20

wralle, wrolle- *v.*, **wrallyngis** *sb. pl.* to wind, twist, bend 113/16 (*v.*), 1066/6 (*sb.*) [obscure]

wralles *sb. pl.* twists, coils 1125/6

wrast(-), see **wrest(-)**

wrastliþ *v. pres. 3sg.*, **wrastlinge** *sb.* wrestles 483/19 (*v.*), 483/18 (*sb.*)

wraþþe, see **wreþþe**

wrawide *a.* angry, malicious 87/2 [? cf. OE. *wrāȝ* 'angry']

wrecche *a.* miserable, wretched 309/2

wreche *sb.* vengeance, retribution 55/27 [OE. *wræc*]

wrecheful *a.* vengeful 1147/34

†**wreching** *sb.* driving out, forcing out, casting out (of a place) 224/27 [cf. OE. *wrecan,* strong 5]

wreyste, see **wrest**[1]

wreke *v.* (**wreke** *pa. p.*) to vent one's anger (on someone), avenge, strike (someone) in retribution 1118/6

wrenchinge *sb.*, **iwreint** *v. pa. p.* twisted or turned (violently) 211/20 (*v.*), 223/34 (*sb.*)

wrenchis *sb. pl.* tricks, cunning devices 314/13

wrest, wreyste, wrast *sb.*[1] a tool to tune stringed instruments, a pick for playing such instruments 201/19

wrest, vrest *sb.*[2] wrist, joint, esp. the instep of the foot 413/36

wrestinge, wrastinge *sb.*, **wrast** *v. pa.* twisted, turned, wrenched 1125/29 (*v.*), 233/34 (*sb.*)

ywreþe, see **iwrithen**

wreþþe, wraþþe *sb.* wrath 107/9

wryng(e) *sb.* press, wringer for extracting

wryng(e) (*cont.*)
     liquid from fruit, wine- or oil-press
     1004/30

wringe *v.* (**iwronge** *pa. p.*), **wrynginge**
     sb. to press, twist, squeeze 134/29 (*v.*),
     216/26 (*sb.*)

write *v.* (**writen, iwrite** *pa. p.*) to write
     54/11

iwrithen, ywreþe *v. pa. p.* twisted,
     coiled, intertwined 609/29

wrolleþ, see **wralle; iwronge,** see
wringe

wrooteþ, froteþ *v. pres. pl.* turn over with
     the snout, dig up for food 224/25

wrooþ *a.* angry 55/26

wrotte *sb.* snout 681/2

(i)wrouȝt, wrowȝt, see **worche;**
wundir(-), see **wondir(-); iwunt,** see
wone; wurche(-), wurke(-), see
worche

zuger, zugre, see **sucre**

INDEX OF AUTHORITIES

This index lists and identifies the authorities cited by Bartholomaeus as they appear in the printed English text. Titles of books are listed after their authors where both are cited. An asterisk before a name indicates that the authority is cited as second hand, and in such cases the origin of the citation is given within round brackets after the modern identification. Where Bartholomaeus cites an authority both directly and at second hand, the latter is marked by an asterisk before the page number. Many other authorities are also probably cited at second hand, in particular Christian commentators (e.g. most of Ambrose and much of Augustine) incorporated in the Gloss and the *Sententiae* of Peter Lombard, and single citations of author or book. The word 'properly' before an identification indicates a scribal error in Trevisa's Latin copy-text. Arabic numerals refer to pages, Roman numerals to books, free-standing numerals within round brackets to Isidore, *Etymologiae*. In titles of books, forms are generally cited in the Latin case of their first occurrence, and not in other inflected forms, and variations of *i/y* and final *-e* are not recorded.

Achylaus, see **Archelaus**

*Adam, the *Adamantius super Iosue* of Origen (Gloss, Joshua 19: 1–2) 701, 702

Affrigus, see **Alfredus**

*Agrippa, Marcus Agrippa, general under Augustus (Pliny IV. 105) 787

Alanus, Alain de Lille (d. 1202) 626, 976

——, **Anticlaudyan, Anticlaudyn,** the *Anticlaudianus* 975

Albu, Albumus, see **Alfredus**

Albumasar, Albumaser, Albumazar (d. 886) 467–73, 476, 478, 484, 493, 495, 505, 515, 540, 545, 555, 583, 1277, 1279

——, **de iudiciis astrorum,** the *Introductorium iudiciorum astrorum* (trans. Scot) 509

——, **de motibus astrorum,** unidentified perhaps part of the *Introductorium* 466

——, **de motubus planetarum,** the *De elementis* of Mashallah 491

Albumasar, properly Alfraganus (q.v.) 499

Alexander, Alexandere, Alexandre, Alisaundre, Alexander of Hales O.F.M. (d. 1245) 447, 453, 454, 455, 486, 487, 791

Alexander Nequam, Alexander Neckham (d. 1217) 985, 1061, 1077

Alfraganus, Alfragoranus, Alphraganus, al-Farghani (d. after 861) 457, 478, 498

Alfredus, Affrigus, Albu, Albumus,

Alle, Aluredus, Alfred of Sareshel (d. c. 1200) 884, 886, 887–93, 895–7, 899, 901, 919, 989, 1014, 1032, 1053, 1282

Algazel, Alagazel, al-Ghazzali (d. 1111) 500, 510, 592, 1284

——, **phisice,** the *Metaphysica* 592

Algazel, properly Alfredus (q.v.) 1355

Alisaundir, Alexandre, Alexander of Tralles (d. 605) 162, 391

Alisaundre, see **Alexander**

Alisaundre story, see under **story**

Alle, Aluredus, see **Alfredus**

Ambros, Ambrose, Ambrosius, St. Ambrose (d. 397) 83, 88, 114, 116, 263, 310, 318, 511, 582, 601, 607, 610, 611, 617, 619, 622, 623–7, 637, 666, 675, 683, 791, 863, 864, 943, 991, 1012, 1340

——, **super Mattheum 17,** an unlocated comment on an unidentified verse of Matthew 991

——, **super Lucam,** the *Expositio evangelii secundum Lucam* 83, 84, 88

——, **Exameron,** the *Hexaemeron* 114, 116, 484, 489, 600, 601, 603, 610, 619, 620, 621, 625, 626, 631, 675, 680, 682, 685, 1340

Ambrosius, properly Augustinus (q.v.) 1012

Anathomia, the *Anatomi Nicolai* (early 12c.) 264

*Anaxagoras, Anaxagoras of Clazomenae (d. 428 BC) (*Meteora* II. 7; I. 8. *De plantis*) 455, 456, 460, 594, 882, 1158

super Iohannitium, see Iohannecius
and comentor super Iohannicio

Theophil, Theopilos Protospathatios (*fl.*
early 7c.) 258, 1285; see also Philaretus
*Theophrastus, Teophrastus, Theo-
phrastus the Peripatetic (Pliny VIII.
128) 1261, 1262
þe tretys of beestes wondirliche
yshape, *De Prop. Rerum* XVIII. 48, 771
Trimegistus, Trymegistus, see
Hermes
*Tullius, Cicero (d. 43 BC) (XI. 1. 67) 222;
see also Cithero

*Varro, Farro, Pharo, Pharro, Varro (d.
27 BC) 254 and 275 (both XI. 1. 97), 719
(XV. 13. 6), 757 (XIV. 6. 36), 764, 800,
803, 954 (Pliny XVIII. 19), 969 (XVIII. 9.
55)
—, de laudibis Grecorum, a lost work
764
*Varro, Varro Atacinus (*fl.* 1c. BC) (XVII.
7. 58) 908

*Virgile, Virgilie, Virgilius, (d. 19 BC)
654 (XIII. 21. 1), 903 (XVII. 7. 23), 943
(XVII. 9. 29), 944 (Pliny XII. 17), 955
(Pliny XVIII. 157), 956 (XVII. 2. 6), 992
(XVII. 7. 50), 1044 (not found), 1062
(XVII. 9. 12), 1089 (XVII. 9. 106), 1206
(XII. 8. 3), 1318 (XX. 2. 36), 1382 (XV.
16. 7)
*Virgil, properly Lucan (d. 65) (XIV. 8. 9,
XVII. 7. 36) 710, 944

þe wise man, Ecclesiasticus 37: 32–4, 146

Yprocras, see Ipocras
Ysaac, see Isaac
Yseder, Ysider, Ysidorus, Ysidre,
Ysidire, Ysoder, Ysodorus, see
Isider

*Zenon, Zeno of Elea (*fl.* 462 BC)
(Macrobius I. 14) 93
*Zorcastes, Zoroaster (*fl.* 7c. BC)
(Marbod XX) 843

A note on the authorities: G. Sarton, *Introduction to the History of Science*, ii (1931) and supple-
ments in *Isis*; G. Lacombe, *Aristoteles latinus* (1939, 1955) and the report in *Medium
Aevum* xlii (1973), 147–52; and the source material in the theses and publications noted
in individual headnotes in the Textual Commentary, offer much useful information.

Bartholomaeus' basic sources are the Vulgate Bible and the Gloss standardized by
Gilbert de la Porrée and Peter the Lombard. J.-P. Migne, *Patrologia . . . Series Latina*
contains editions of all biblical commentators before 1200 used by him. The *Corpus
Christianorum Series Latina* contains editions of Augustine, Bede, Beleth, Jerome (vols.
14, 38, 41A, 50–50A, 73A, 75, 76). The *Corpus Scriptorum Ecclesiasticorum Latinorum* contains
editions of Ambrose, Augustine, Boethius, Orosius (vols. 5, 28, 32, 67). Individual
editions of theological works used by Bartholomaeus are Alain de Lille, *Anticlaudianus*
(ed. R. Bossuet, 1955); Alexander of Hales, *Summa Theologica* (ed. Quarracchi brothers,
1951–7); Isidore, *Etymologiae* (ed. W. M. Lindsay, 1911); John Damascene, *De Fide
Orthodoxa* (ed. E. M. Buytaert, 1955); Peter Lombard, *Sententiae* (ed. Quarracchi
brothers 1971); Peter of Riga, *Aurora* (ed. P. E. Beicher, 1965); Remigius of Auxerre,
Commentum in Marcianum Capellum (ed. C. E. Lutz, 1962).

The *Loeb Classical Library* contains editions of Aristotle, Boethius, Pliny, Solinus.
Editions of other post-classical works used by Bartholomaeus are Macrobius, *Com-
mentarium in somnium Scipionis* (ed. J. Willis, 1963); *Physiologus latinus* (ed. F. J. Carmody,
1939); Marbod, *De lapidibus* (ed. J. M. Riddle, 1977).

Beiträge zur Geschichte der Philosophie des Mittelalters contains work by Alfred of
Sareshel, al-Kindi, Avicebron, Gundissalinus (vols. 1. 2–4, 2, 23).

Pantegny. Omnia opera Ysaac (Lyon, 1515) and *Constantini Africani opera* (Basel, 1536)
contain the work of Isaac and Constantinus. Other medical works used by
Bartholomaeus are found in *Articella* (Venice, 1483); Avicenna, *Liber canonis* (Venice,
1503); Johannes Platearius, *Practica* (Venice, 1503); Matthaeus Platearius, *Circa instans*
(Venice, 1503); Alhazen, *Perspectiva* (Basel, 1572). Modern editions of Giles de Corbeil

are edited by V. Rose (1907) and L. Choulant (1826). The Latin translation of Dioscorides, *De materia medica* used by Bartholomaeus is found in *Dyascorides* (Colle in Toscana, 1478).

The Latin versions of Aristotle used by Bartholomaeus remain in manuscript; e.g. at Oxford the collection *De animalibus* in Merton College MS. 278, *De caelo et mundo* in MS. Canonici Lat. 287, *Meteorologica* in MS. Selden supra 24 (book I is edited by P. L. Schoonheim, *Aristoteles' Meteorologie im arabischer und lateinischer Übersetzung*, 1978), *De sensu et sensibili* in C.C.C.O. MS. 113. William of Moerbeke's version of *De generatione animalium* (ed. H. J. Drossaart Lulofs, *Aristoteles latinus* XVII. 2. v, 1966) incorporates verbatim much of Scot's translation used by Bartholomaeus, as does Albertus, *De animalibus* (ed. H. Stadtler in *Beiträge* 15–16).

The anonymous *De causis* is edited by A. Pattin (1966). al-Ghazzali, *Metaphysica* is edited by J. T. Muckle (1933).

Fuller bibliographical details for many of Bartholomaeus' sources are given in *Robert Grosseteste. Hexaëmeron*, ed. R. C. Dales and S. Gieben (1982), pp. 351–6, and for the general background of medieval thought in *The Cambridge History of Later Medieval Philosophy*, ed. N. Kretzman *et al.* (1982), pp. 893–977. See further C. Wenin ed., *L'Homme et son univers au moyen âge*, Philosophies Médiévaux 26 (1986), and R. L. Benson and G. Constable, *Renaissance and Renewal in the Twelfth Century* (1982).

A further volume on Bartholomaeus (d. 1272) and his encyclopaedia (written *c.* 1245), detailing the sources of each chapter, is now almost completed.

INDEX OF PERSONS

This index lists the names of persons who are not authorities cited in the text. Biblical names are identified by their forms in the Authorized Version, and classical names by the forms preferred by the *Oxford Classical Dictionary* (2nd edn., 1970). Except in cases of multiple occurrence and familiar names, Bartholomaeus' sources for his citations of names are given within round brackets, where free-standing numerals refer to Isidore, *Etymologiae*.

Ydapsis, Hydaspes, king of the Medes (XIII. 21. 12) 658

Ydeyes Dactilis, Idae dactyli 'the fingers of Ida', i.e. thethree wizards of Ida of Crete (XIV. 6. 16) 748

Ysis, Isis, queen of Egypt (III. 22. 12) 1392

Ysmael, Hismael, Ishmael, son of Abraham and Hagar (Gen. 16: 11) 745, 784

Ytalus, see Italus

Zeb, Zeeb, prince of Midian (Judges 7: 25) 702

AFTERWORD

At the end of a long and uphill journey it is my pleasant duty to thank those who made the completion of this edition possible: my colleagues who marched the whole way without losing heart or sight of the end, the librarians and all who gave their time and scholarship, the officers and advisers of the Clarendon Press, and the staff of Joshua Associates Limited who set a much-marked and troublesome typescript.

M. C. S.

1 June 1987